$7.00

T D R

Fuchs and Dolan on Porn • Theatre of the Deaf
Montano, Sprinkle, and Vera at Camp • Frank Moore
Holly Hughes' *Dress Suits to Hire* • Theatre Rhinoceros

Published by MIT Press New York University/Tisch School of the Arts

TDR

The Drama Review *a journal of performance studies*

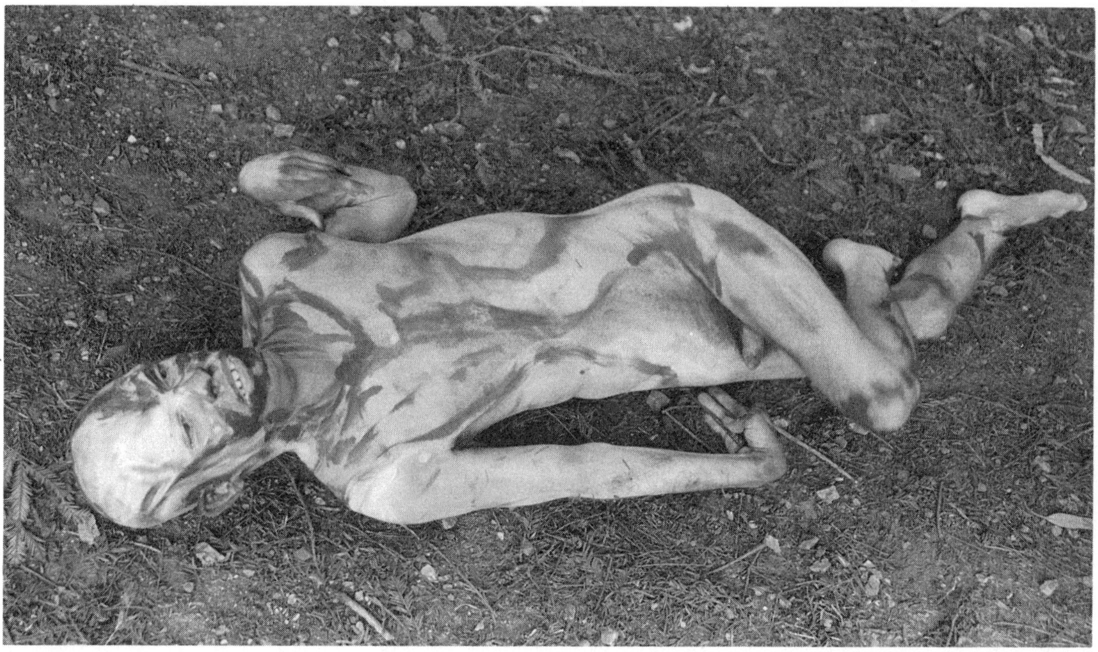

Frank Moore as Fiesto, *July 1986, in Berkeley California. See Moore's EROPLAY manifesto in this issue. (Photo by D. Moore)*

Front Cover: *A page from the scrapbook "Our Week at Sister Rosita's Summer Saint Camp" (with photo by Jennifer Bilek). See the article and interview by Linda Montano and the scrapbook by Veronica Vera and Annie Sprinkle in this issue.*

Back Cover: *Lois Weaver (left) and Peggy Shaw in* Dress Suits to Hire *at P.S. 122 in New York City, May 1987. See the script by Holly Hughes, the analysis by Kate Davy, and the Hughes interview by Rebecca Schneider in this issue. (Photo by Dona Ann McAdams)*

TDR

TDR Comment: 4
Race Free, Gender Free, Body-Type Free, Age Free Casting

Letters, Reports, Etc.

Terpischore in Combat Boots 13
letters from Sally Banes and Susan Manning

Théâtre du Soleil Shines Its Light on the Holy Land 17
a letter from Paul Golub

On getting the Message 19
a letter from Gerry Large

Of Time and Mime: A Polylog on Festivity 19
FRANK MANNING

Latin America and Beyond 29
IAN WATSON

(Birth) Announcements 30

In Memory: Jacques Chwat (1935–1988) 32

Staging the Obscene Body 33
ELINOR FUCHS

Desire Cloaked in a Trenchcoat 59
JILL DOLAN

Theatre By and For the Deaf 68
HILARY U. COHEN

Theatre Rhinoceros: A Gay Company 79
ERIK L. MACDONALD

Summer Saint Camp 1987: 94
With Annie Sprinkle and Veronica Vera
LINDA MONTANO

Our Week at Sister Rosita's Summer Saint Camp 104
Story by VERONICA VERA
Scrapbook by ANNIE SPRINKLE

EROPLAY 120
FRANK MOORE

Dress Suits to Hire 132
HOLLY HUGHES, PEGGY SHAW, and LOIS WEAVER

Reading Past the Heterosexual Imperative: *Dress Suits to Hire* 153
KATE DAVY

Holly Hughes: Polymorphous Perversity and the Lesbian Scientist 171
An interview by REBECCA SCHNEIDER

Volume 33, Number 1 (T121), Spring 1989

The Drama Review *(ISSN 0012 5962) is published quarterly (Spring, Summer, Fall, Winter) by The MIT Press, 55 Hayward St., Cambridge, MA 02142, and London, England, for the Tisch School of the Arts, New York University. Editorial correspondence:* The Drama Review, *NYU, 721 Broadway, 6th fl., New York, NY 10003. Subscription and business correspondence:* The Drama Review, *Journals Dept., The MIT Press, 55 Hayward Street, Cambridge, MA 02142. Subscriptions: $17.00 per year for students; $23.00 per year for individuals; $52.00 per year for institutions. Subscribers outside the U.S. and Canada add $9.00 for surface mail, $17.00 for airmail. Current single copies, $7.00; back copies, $13.00. Back volume rates available. Circulation Dept.: 617-253-2889.* *Second class postage paid at Boston, MA and additional mailing offices. Postmaster: Send address changes to* The Drama Review, *55 Hayward Street, Cambridge, MA 02142. For advertising information please contact the Advertising Manager, MIT Press Journals (see business correspondence; telephone: 617-253-2866). This publication is made possible, in part, with public funds from the New York State Council on the Arts and the National Endowment for the Arts.*

TDR Comment

Race Free, Gender Free, Body-Type Free, Age Free Casting

> *Suppose that there were a fine acting company made up of white actors and black actors and Hispanic actors and Asian-American actors; women and men; young actors, older, and old; deaf actors and the hearing; actors with other special characteristics. And suppose that one assigned roles freely, without prediction from history or from one's old habits of thought. What if one took non-traditional casting as far as one could?*
>
> —*Zelda Fichandler,* American Theatre, *May 1988:20*

> *[R]edefining the conditions of vision, as well as the modes of representing, cannot be predicated on a single, undivided identity of performer and audience (whether as "lesbians" or "women" or "people of color" or any other single category constructed in opposition to its dominant other, "heterosexual women," "men," "whites," and so forth).*
>
> —*Teresa de Lauretis,* Theatre Journal, *May 1988:171*

As far as one could? Redefining the conditions of vision?

Herschel Walker dancing the Sylph? Helen Hayes as Juliet? Meryl Streep as Willie Loman? Robert de Niro as Blanche du Bois?

If body type, age, race, and gender are set aside what then would the criteria be for playing a character or dancing a role? Is training plus insight into a role sufficient? If so, should we assemble "mixed" casts where the gender, race, age, and body type of the performers are, as it were, not perceived? Or should we make productions where some kind of social and/or aesthetic comment, framed by the world of the artwork, is expressed by means of the casting? These two approaches are very different.

At present, American theatre and dance (and those of many other cultures as well) have two kinds of performing arts in regard to gender, race, age, and body type. In mainstream theatres and dance companies a nominal "open casting" policy is enunciated—but practice actually conforms to prevailing social values. In America these remain profoundly racist and sexist. Discrimination against the old and preference for certain body types are also prevalent. So casts on or off Broadway, in regional theatres, and among our dance companies are mostly white. Roles are not only race-bound but gender-bound, which in theatre means that most of the best roles go to men and in dance it means that certain kinds of movements are assigned to women and other kinds of movements to men (see Daly 1987).

The second kind of casting and company-making is particularist. Groups are formed according to gender or race or social class or disability or ideology or age. Theatres are gay, lesbian, black, Chicano, deaf, poor,

Marxist, Jewish, AIDS, Asian, native American, antinuclear . . . and so on. Some companies are both mainstream and particularist, such as the Dance Theatre of Harlem or the Negro Ensemble Company.

Concerning particularist groups, let me enunciate my strong support of them both in principle and in practice. At several points in my life I have been active in particularist groups advocating civil rights and opposing the Vietnam war. Even when I disagree with what this or that group advocates or represents, I recognize how healthy it is for the society at large and for the participants in particularist groups to robustly exercise an always-to-be-defended freedom of expression. Particularism is the way specific associations of people form and express their collective experiences and opinions. Points of view that otherwise would get lost in the dominant discourse find visibility. Often enough, today's particularist opinion becomes tomorrow's mainstream.

But this Comment is about neither the mainstream nor particularism. It is about two other kinds of race free, gender free, body-type free, age free casting that might exist: (1) mixed (or "blind") casting and (2) intercultural casting.

Many acting classes—needing to exercise all the students enrolled regardless of race, gender, etc.—employ the mixed cast technique. Peter Brook's *The Mahabharata* used people drawn from 18 countries, giving the production an intentionally intercultural tone. Why aren't the classroom etudes carried over into publicly performed professional productions? Why aren't there many more works like Brook's?

Casting against gender, race, body type, and age has a history in European and American theatre and dance. Remember Orson Welles' black *Macbeth,* Sarah Bernhardt's Hamlet, or for that matter, Debby Holmes' Lear in my 1981 *Richard's Lear* or the Lee Breuer/Mabou Mines *Lear*?[1] Often, casting against type is the stock-in-trade of parody and travesty—witness the many plays Charles Ludlam wrote, directed, and starred in or the all-male Trocadero Ballet. Sometimes the intention is political—as when women play males at WOW Cafe or when Chicano farm laborers play white bosses at the Teatro Campesino. Furthermore, certain roles are increasingly being accepted as race, gender, and to a degree, body-type free—so we see on stage (even more in films and on TV) a smattering of black and women doctors, lawyers, police, business execs, and teachers; a detective in a wheelchair; a deaf heroine or two. But these examples are exceptions to the rule. The American theatre reserves the majority of its best roles for white males—not because these are the best performers available (sometimes they are, sometimes they aren't) but because the characters to be represented are white males. As for dance, youthful, slim body types prevail, and most companies are predominantly white. When non-white performers are "integrated" into mainstream companies and media they either need to perform stereotypes of their presumed racial type or adopt the performative idiom of the mainstream leaving behind ethnic, racial, or regional dialects of speech and movement.

Clearly, American audiences are not color or gender blind anymore than they are body-type or age blind. Our theatres and dance companies reflect the values and attitudes of their audiences. Gender, race, age, and body type each signal specific sociopolitical meanings. The categories themselves are definable only within specific contexts. That is, what constitutes a "black" or a "white" person is not some fixed objectively measurable entity, but a shifting set of circumstances that have emerged in America over the centuries and are continuing to change. Similarly, what constitutes a "woman" or a "man," an "old person" or a "young person," a "thin person," "normal person," or "fat person" (to use three of many possible body types) are all determined by flexible and changing criteria responsive to various social circumstances. Nor are the definitions in use objective indices—they are powerful determinants of social privilege (and despisement). It is impossible for spectators to see performers cast "against the text" (a narrative text, a body text) without wondering what such casting means.

But to understand the problems brought up by nontraditional casting, one must probe a little deeper into why it is that "traditional" casting, that is, casting according to type, is preferred in Western dance and theatre.

It is preferred because the baseline, the normative expectation concerning theatre and dance, is naturalistic. This term, like the others just discussed, is not objectively determinable. It refers to a socioaesthetic tradition dominant in Western arts since the Renaissance, that posits daily experience as the basis for reality. Attempts to destabilize this faith in daily experience—movements like surrealism and abstract expressionism in the arts or trance and speaking in tongues in religion—have only been minimally successful. The realities proposed by various artistic avant-gardes and the charismatic churches are not wholly taken seriously by mainstream people who continue to measure "what's real" by the yardstick of "common sense." Even scientific propositions regarding entities like "strange attractors" or "quarks" are not understood by many people—and are accepted as real only when these abstruse ideas, often enunciable only as mathematical equations, have been translated into "practical results" (bombs or energy sources, for example).

In terms of performance, the naturalistic bias trains spectators to desire a neat fit of who the performer is to what the performer represents. Sylphs are female, young, slim, and graceful—"light, dainty, and airy beings" (according to my Random House dictionary)—and no Herschel Walker type can dance them. Or if someone like Walker were to dance the Sylph, the performance could only be received as parody or travesty.

My object in this writing is to stake a claim for opening a much wider gap—a possibly playful and subversive space—between representers and represented. Staking such a claim means calling for the development of performing arts whose codes of representation are overt and therefore susceptible to critical analysis through practice, training, performance, and scholarship. And where such codes exist—as in ballet and modern dance—these established systems of representation might allow for a radical flexibility in terms of body type, age, gender, and race that is not in play at present (except as parody and travesty).

A stringent requirement of a close fit between the representers and represented is not always demanded, even in Western arts. Novelists are not required to be like their characters. Storytellers are likewise free to speak for and as characters as diverse as they can imagine. The emergence of critical and theoretical writings that move back and forth between extremely personal assertions and wide-ranging, abstract constructions is becoming more acceptable. But the stage—always, it seems, the most reactionary of the arts, possibly because its existence requires a concrete physical place of public assembly—enforces its own especially binding naturalistic rigor: any wide gap between performer and character must be "justified." Or if a gap does exist—as when an actor like Robert de Niro "stretches" to play widely diverse roles or when an older dancer like Margot Fonteyn continues to perform "young roles" even though she is not age suited to them—audiences marvel at such performers' abilities to mask the gap, to "become" who or what they are representing. Little delight is taken in the double and separate awareness of role and performer.

But it is more delightful to see the gap than to mask it. Brecht's *Verfremdung* (making the familiar appear strange and the strange appear familiar[2])—where the audience enjoys, and learns from, the dialectical tension between player and played—is rarely used in American theatre and dance. Verfremdung is a technique for opening a space between role and performer into which spectators may enter, admiring the performer while, say, critically evaluating the actions of the character. Brecht himself wanted to use Verfremdung as an educational tool, a means of communicating ideas, even propaganda. But the technique can have many uses (see Diamond 1988). It need not reduce audiences to single reactive units; it may encourage diverse, individual responses. At present, when Verfremdung is used, it usually takes the form of comedy or social comment (as Brecht himself often used it). In American dance and theatre, given as they are to sentimentality as well as naturalism, evoking responses of tears or sheer wonder by means of artistic distance is nearly unheard of.

Not so in kabuki. How clearly I remember Nakamura Utaemon VI's 1982 performance of Hanjo in *Sumidagawa:*

> Hanjo is an old woman searching for her son who was kidnapped by slave traders. Utaemon is elegant in her/his perfectly placed gestures of grief and madness; her disheveled hair is messy in a precise way with a few black wisps straggling across her white-as-paper face. Her bony fingers play the empty air as if it were full of harp strings. Hanjo meets a compassionate boatman who tells her of a sick child who was nursed by villagers until he died, his mother's name on his lips. In that instant, both Hanjo and the boatman know the boy was her son. Utaemon strikes a silent pose of grief, and lets escape a thin, shrill cry. More than Helene Weigel's silent scream for her dead son Swiss Cheese, less than Melina Mercouri's roars for Medea's murdered children. Utaemon's pose and cry are both male (the actor) and female (the mother). He/she is resplendent and pitiful in silk brocade and nearly voiceless despair. Yet, and this is the art of kabuki, such "unnaturalness" evokes in us responses of genuine emotion (Martin and Schechner 1982:40).

This scene works because the code of representation which enunciates "Hanjo" is very overtly separable from the skills of Utaemon VI. The role of Hanjo in kabuki is analogous to what Lee Breuer says about Hamlet: "There is no Hamlet. Hamlet is the sum of the known meaningful interpretations of the role in the context of their time, place, politics and aesthetics" (1988:22). And more. Hanjo is also the very particular conventions and techniques of kabuki. Utaemon VI can interpret the role (as any Western actor can interpret Hamlet); he can, additionally, interpret the kabuki code, specifically the portion of the code that articulates the *onnagata* tradition where men perform roles representing women. What most Western theatre still lacks is a clear sense of the abstract qualities of a role—underlining the fact (pointed out by Breuer) that a role does not equal a person but is rather a summation of the role's own historical eruption, placement, and continued development.

Let me here insert a qualifying note lest I be nailed for idealizing Asian genres. In regard to celebrating the distance between performers and roles, genres such as kabuki, kathakali, and jingju (Beijing opera) can be learned from. But these forms have their own problems relating to gender stereotypes, male privilege, and reactionary narratives.

In Western theatre there are no codes of performative behavior distinctly separable from the codes of behavior prevalent in everyday life. Actor training is under the aegis of the Stanislavski system which is based on the construction of a psychology of everyday life. Even when actors wear masks, portray fantasy characters, or perform dadaist or surrealist pieces, the baseline is ordinary life, which may then be denied, rejected, or mocked. An exception to this tendency is puppetry where the puppeteer stands in relation to the puppets as storyteller to story. But puppetry in America is still a deprivileged genre—even acknowledging the recuperative work of Peter Schumann and Theodora Skipitares, among others.

Another exception is the work of auteurs such as Tadeusz Kantor, Martha Clarke, Robert Wilson, and Richard Foreman who make performance texts the way painters paint or novelists write. But these auteurs privatize their approaches, and are apparently inimical to establishing schools to teach their methods of making performance texts. Their works form "styles" rather than codes of performative behavior that can be transmitted through time.

However, in Western classical and modern dance there are codes of performative behavior as rigorous as any found in Asia. Codes of "performative behavior" rather than codes of "representation" because the naturalistic paradigm still imposes what ages and body types are "allowed" on dance stages. For every Fonteyn there are dozens of other capable dancers who are forced to retire when they no longer "look" right; and in dance there is little gender switching even though there are many women strong enough to lift men and many men capable of dancing so-called female roles with appropriate "lightness." As far as refiguring dance roles originally conceived for sylphs (female or male) for heavy, bulky bodies, this would appear to be anathema—even though the dancers of the late 20th century are skinnier and lighter than those of earlier epochs. When prevalent strictures on body types are rejected, as in the 1970s work of such groups as Grand Union, or in contact improvisation, the tendency is to make the movement ordinary or "pedestrian"—a strong affirmation of the naturalistic.

One of the marvelous and startling things about Pina Bausch's Wuppertal Dance Theatre is the way their balletic training intersects Bausch's casting. Bausch's company consists of people who are more varied in body type, age, and style of physical expression than any other ballet or modern dance company I've seen. Bausch's choreography—often embodying gender tensions and violence expressed through irony and satire—frequently includes such actions as women lifting men and cross dressing.

Kazuo Ohno[3] is an old Japanese dancer in a woman's dress eliciting from an elite audience at New York's Asia Society in 1988 an admiration untinged by parody or travesty. Would this audience as easily bestow such unsnickering praise on an American dancer doing the same thing? Or on an old woman in men's clothing? I remember that in 1985 in Toronto when I first saw Ohno dance, I laughed at his gnarled movements, his blatant display of emotions, his weird mixing of Japanese and Western styles, his persona. I granted him his art, but located it as travesty. In 1988 I watched him differently, seeing this time more clearly Ohno's struggle against decrepitude written in the lyrical movements of his 82-year-old body. Instead of masking his years and celebrating the agile beauty of youth, as an aging onnagata might do, Ohno concentrated on being an old man in a kind of drag that referred to but did not attempt to imitate a woman.

Ohno's dances emit a special resonance not so different from certain moments in Bausch's *Carnations* where men put on dresses not to "become" women but to expose the gender tricks of orthodox dance. Women in men's clothing, common enough on the streets, where there is little or no deception, are less frequent on mainstream stages where males are allowed to dress down as women but women are not allowed to dress up as men. Such appearances are saved for lesbian stages like WOW Cafe. But theatre and dance, as body-based art forms, ought to be where cross dressing that ranges from the nondeceptive to totally convincing transformations should be systematically practiced, explored, and critiqued.

Performances such as Ohno's and Bausch's are not just about gender-busting or drag. They sidestep the usual canons of beauty (of the kind Martha Clarke drenches her spectators in) and go "against nature." That is, Ohno and Bausch are not offering representations that celebrate the socially idealized body (as advertising and the Olympic Games do). For Ohno and Bausch the body is an opaque instrument, the actions undertaken have their own logic, and the works as wholes are coded utterances whose meanings are not readily apparent. In other words, these artists do not collapse performer, techniques of performance, and performance text into a "unified production." Rather they tease out both the contradictions and congruencies among these "presences," creating thereby an extremely thick theatricality.

But what would it mean for a big-boned heavy-set person to dance the Sylph? Or for a woman to play Willy Loman not as "Wanda Loman" (as Fichandler suggests) but as a woman manipulating the stage codes for "man." That is, for women, blacks, Hispanics, Asians, native Americans, fat people, or "senior citizens"—to name categories whose gender, race, body type, or age are currently "visible"—to be cast with as little regard for these categories as is given today to the ethnicity of American men performers who have northern European foreparents? Or to put it another way, sometimes the race, gender, body type, and age of performers are extremely important and should be taken into account in the development of a choreography, a mise-en-scène, or a company. At other times, race, age, gender, and body type can be effectively represented by someone who is not of the particular kind being performed (as when an Englishman plays Othello, a Japanese woman dances the bride in Martha Graham's *Appalachian Spring,* Fonteyn dances a young role, or when Debby Holmes, both young and female, plays King Lear in *Richard's Lear*). And sometimes, these categories are, or should be, irrelevant.

Thus I am arguing for a dance and theatre where several different kinds of responses are possible: times when perceiving the race, gender, etc., of performers matters; times when spectators perceive the categories but it doesn't matter; and times when it should not even be perceived—not because of disguise (like in *Le Cage aux Folles*) but because spectators have been trained to be race, gender, age, and body-type "blind."

It is extremely difficult even to spell out this kind of situation because it is so unlike what currently goes on in America. It is hard to imagine flexibility with regard to these categories which are felt to be either "naturally" or "historically" fixed. Some Americans are barely able to slip in and out of certain kinds of Euro-American ethnicities—being very "Irish" or "Polish" or "Italian" on some days for some occasions (a parade, a picnic, a religious celebration) and very "just like everyone else" (which means behaving like white Americans whose ancestors came from northwest Europe) on other days. Furthermore, led by the Black Freedom Movement originating in the 1950s, many Americans have just recently come through a hard-fought period of winning the right to assert various "roots," rejecting the "melting pot" idea of a homogenized society. This right to be different, and to proudly and publicly express these differences, is the source of many particularist movements.

What I am arguing for is not the melting pot, which would be regressive, reimposing mainstream mid-American values, but an extreme flexibility that allows for situation-specific decisions regarding when to use, when to ignore, and when not to see race, gender, age, and body type.

Can spectators (and producers, directors, performers, choreographers) be trained to be responsive to these categories in some cases and not in others (as in sports where there is an effort toward race blindness)? How long would it take for differences in race, age, gender, and body type to "not be seen"? And why would such a state of intentional socioaesthetic blindness be a good idea?

First, it would mean some kinds of dance and theatre were in the process of developing codified systems of representation strong enough to exist independently of the particular individuals manipulating these systems. Second, it would give individual performers the chance to play roles that today are off limits to them by virtue not of their skills but because of their gender, race, age, or body type. Third, it would encourage spectators to see, savor, and critically examine the interacting performance texts that comprise a whole performance rather than insisting on a simple-minded identification of performer with role. Fourth, performers and spectators alike would be more able to see gender, race, age, and body type not as "biological destinies" but as flexible, historically conditioned categories.

In Minneapolis the Mixed Blood Theatre Company has for years followed a color-blind casting policy. We need many more companies like Mixed Blood—in fact, color-blind casting should be the rule now in mainstream dance and theatre. But color-blind casting is not enough. It is time to break the chains binding the performing arts to a narrow vision of human possibility. We need to see on our theatre and dance stages women and men dancing and acting in roles previously reserved for one gender or the other; old people playing a variety of parts; and a full-fleshed parade of body types. Sometimes we ought to see the body's opacity: the color of the skin, the lines on the face, the muscles' elasticity or lack thereof—all the textures of class, age, weight, ethnicity, race, gender. But sometimes a performative code is so mastered that the body is rendered transparent, almost nonexistent. A spectator sees through the body to the mastery of the code. Then life on stage becomes what Zeami said in the 15th century about his father, Kanami: "His *shin-no-hana* [profound skill] survived until he became old without leaving him, like an old leafless tree which still blossoms" (1968:24).

The "nature/nurture" or "biologically determined/socially constructed" debate is a classically irresolvable conflict. Categories of race, gender, body type, and age are in fact social categories constructed from the interpretations of "biological data"—but the biological data themselves are always changing in terms of social constructions and interpretations. Seemingly "objective" or fixed data are not only open to revision as new data are presented (the scientific method) but are interpretable in many different ways according to specific sociohistorical circumstances. Thus, when I lived in the deep South in the late 1950s through mid '60s, "race"—as it pertained to black/white distinctions—was variously interpreted as being determined by "blood" (ancestry) and/or "skin color" (direct visual observation). These determinants were put forward (by racists especially) as objectively verifiable. But sometimes they contradicted each other—

persons with "black blood" looked "white" while others looked "black" but were considered "white." A lot depended on who was doing the determining and for what purposes. At present, people speak of "male" and "female" hormones. But I foresee a time when sex-gland related blood chemistry is referred to as "gender hormones" measurable not according to a rigidly dimorphic scale but along a continuum. I suggest that race and gender are not atypical examples—that many if not all "scientific data" are in fact negotiations among what is observed, what is believed, and what is desired. From Heisenberg to the new historicists, the rationalist solidity of "objective data" has been undermined. Observation, belief, and desire all interact with and affect one another.

In the context of today's historical circumstances, race is entirely a social not biological category, while age (if considered simply as the measurement of elapsed time since birth) appears to be an "objective" category. But the social consequences of this "objective measurement"—jobs, retirement, assumptions concerning sexual activity, what's good to look at—deobjectify age, merging it with the category of body type. Gender—today's hot potato—appears to be both a social and biological category. The messy problem is a little more tractable when seen in historical and processual perspective. Interpretations (what is fancily called "hermeneutics") are always changing in response to sometimes open and sometimes hidden agendas. At this moment in American and perhaps world history, race and gender are at the center of a number of political as well as social, economic, and aesthetic conflicts. But hold on, age and body type are climbing through the ropes to enter the arena.

—*Richard Schechner*[4]

Notes

1. According to a story in the *New York Times,* during the summer of 1988 members of Mabou Mines under Breuer's direction were working on a *King Lear* that "transposes Shakespeare's tragedy to 1950s Georgia, reverses characters' sex, mixes their racial backgrounds and gives them Southern accents. Lear becomes a mean-spirited and narrow-minded blue-collar matriarch, and Gloucester is a rural black woman presiding over a household not of knights but of dogs. The Fool is played as a mincing transvestite with a candy-cane phallus dangling around his neck, and Oswald turns into a Caribbean-accented prostitute in hot pants" (Yarrow 1988:C15). *Lear,* which will have been produced by the time this comes to print, is not Breuer's first transgression of race, gender, or genre boundaries. His *Gospel at Colonus* was a rendition of Sophocles' *Oedipus at Colonus* as a black gospel sing/church service.
2. It is well known that Brecht found in the 1935 performance in Moscow of Mei Lanfang, a master of jingju (Beijing Opera), a precise embodiment of what Brecht had been groping toward for several years. In 1936 Brecht wrote about Mei's performance in "Alienation Effects [*Verfremdungseffekte*] in Chinese Acting" (1964:91–99). This was Brecht's first writing about the V-effect. Brecht scholar John Fuegi explains Verfremdung: "Brecht marveled at the fact that this male actor [Mei], performing in a Western dinner jacket, created extremely powerful women's parts. The term Verfremdung, once adopted by Brecht, would lead to endless confusion particularly when translated into English as 'alienation' or into French as 'distanciation.' What Brecht himself originally had in mind, wholly consistent with his Russian source [the formalist Victor Schklovski], was something richly and provocatively ambivalent. [. . .] The paradoxical trick is to disrupt the viewer's normal or run of the mill perception by introducing elements that will suddenly cause the viewer to see familiar objects in a strange way and to see strange objects in a familiar way" (1987:82–83).
3. See writings by and about Ohno and the genre he dances, butoh, in TDR 30, no. 2 (T110):107–170.

4. This Comment was developed and written in collaboration with the TDR New York editorial staff. Rebecca Schneider's close readings and criticisms were particularly helpful.

References

Brecht, Bertolt
1964 *Brecht on Theatre*. New York: Hill and Wang.

Breuer, Lee
1988 "How Tall Was Coriolanus?" *American Theatre* 5, no. 2 (May): 22.

Daly, Ann
1987 "The Balanchine Woman: Of Hummingbirds and Channel Swimmers." *TDR* 31, no. 1 (T113):8–21.

Diamond, Elin
1988 "Brechtian Theory/Feminist Theory." *TDR* 32, no. 1 (T117):82–94.

Fichandler, Zelda
1988 "Casting for a Different Truth." *American Theatre* 5, no. 2 (May):18–23.

Fuegi, John
1987 *Bertolt Brecht: Chaos, According to Plan*. Cambridge: Cambridge University Press.

de Lauretis, Teresa
1988 "Sexual Indifference and Lesbian Representation." *Theatre Journal* 40 (no. 2):155–77.

Martin, Carol, and Richard Schechner
1982 "Grand Kabuki: Japan's Classical Theatre at the Met." *Alive* 1 (no. 2):40–41.

Yarrow, Andrew K.
1988 "Mabou Mines Offering Open House at Retreat." *New York Times*, 27 July: C15.

Zeami
1968 *Kadensho*. Kyoto: Sumiya-Shinobe Scholarship, Doshisha University.

Attention Student Scholars! Win $500! Publish in TDR!

We want to get younger people involved in TDR—and through TDR in performance scholarship. To advance this, we are happy to announce the TDR STUDENT ESSAY CONTEST. The first prize is $500 and there are two $250 second prizes. Essays can deal with *any aspect of performance*, any genre, any culture, any approach. We want to see what the best younger minds are thinking. Deadline for submitting your essay is 15 December 1989. Winners will be announced in Spring 1990. The winning essay will be published in TDR soon thereafter. If possible, keep your submission to 25 pages, though there is no official limit: let the subject and your treatment of it determine the length of your essay.

Please mark clearly that you are submitting your essay to the TDR Student Essay Contest. To show that you are a student include a xerox of your student ID. NYU students not eligible.

—*The Editors*

Letters, Reports, Etc.

Terpsichore in Combat Boots

Ed. Note: In our last issue we published Susan Manning's "Modernist Dogma and Post-modern Rhetoric" (32, no. 4 [T120]), an analysis of Sally Banes' Terpsichore in Sneakers *(1987). Banes' response to Manning's article follows, along with Manning's reply.*

Sally Banes:

Susan Manning's ambition in attempting to rethink dance history is admirable. Dance history always needs young scholars who ask questions and enter into debates. But let us hope that future attempts will be more coherent.

To keep this reply brief I will dispense with a detailed account of various quotations taken out of context and of numerous historical and critical inaccuracies. (To cite only one procedural instance, Manning repeatedly refers to a "rewritten" or "revised" introduction to the 1987 edition of *Terpsichore in Sneakers*; but as any reader can immediately tell—especially since it is spelled out in the 1987 preface—the 1980 introduction stands intact, and there is, in addition, an entirely new introduction added to contextualize the 1980 text. More substantive mistakes, in terms of Manning's understanding of dance history, include her assertion that ballet became less pictorial in the early 20th century, and her apparent ignorance that Martha Graham's dances are expressive, not abstract—no matter what John Martin says; and that both early Soviet ballet and early '60s avant-garde dances, to name only two historical moments, mixed techniques from different dance traditions. But the informed reader will easily recognize such errors.)

Instead, I want to focus on the misdirection of the entire project Manning has attempted to outline.

Terpsichore in Sneakers is the historical account of a movement that once called itself postmodern and whose practitioners still use that title. There is no theoretical issue at stake here. It is simply a matter of historical fact that certain people choose to speak of themselves in this way and that they claim to belong to a specific tradition. *Terpsichore in Sneakers* offers the account of this movement. As such it is not partisan; "postmodern" is not an evaluative term, it is descriptive. It is not a term I made up. I used it because it was already in currency to categorize the group I wrote about.

Altogether, however, Manning's own project is rather obscure. She wants to use the terms modernist and postmodernist ahistorically or transhistorically as categories of essential modes or types of dance. This, she seems to think, will enable us to sort through dance history—cultural and historical contexts notwithstanding—and neatly slot people and works into one category or the other. No respect is paid to what choreographers might have been up to, or thought they might have been up to. If some vague critical description accords with a decontextualized version of modernism (e.g., movement for its own sake) then Manning terms it modernist even if it is not, in fact, fully reflexive in a way that really only made sense (i.e., had the appropriate conceptual foundations) after WWII in America. But this is not only anachronistic; it also makes dance-historical discourse self-destruct. To erase the content of already existing terms, only to impose different, arbitrary, and stipulated meanings, is myth-making, not history.

Manning's two rules for determining what counts as modernist (and hence, what counts negatively to define postmodernism) are woefully inadequate and misinformed. Recall that the first rule is "reflexive rationalization of movement." Since she never really explains what she means by "the rationalization of movement," Manning has not shown that the system of the 19th-century ballet vocabulary lacks its own logic for achieving specific goals—for instance, the turnout that allows for rapid lateral movement and increased theatrical legibility. This vocabulary is no more or less rationalized, in the literal sense, than any 20th-century vocabulary. Nor does she specify which 20th-century systems she thinks are especially rational. Furthermore, Manning does not seem to understand the concept of reflexivity in art. Interest in movement designs for their own sake is different from being reflexive in the sense relevant to modernism. Reflexivity requires something more—namely, that the formal elements so foregrounded be seen as revealing essential characteristics of the medium. Historically, this required an added semantic dimension—that the work not merely be itself but that it be about being the kind of thing it is. Something from the internal structure of the work or from its context is necessary to establish that this sort of reflexivity is operative. That is, though Manning's categories would have us count Graham, for instance, as a modernist, Graham's choreography is not reflexive and therefore not relevant to a discussion of modernism as it emerged in the dance world under the influence of the Greenbergian gallery aesthetic.

Manning's second rule for modernism is the "dual practice of modern dance and 20th-century ballet." But since, despite her mention of class and nationality, she doesn't seem aware that ballet was not the only form of theatrical dance practiced in the 19th century—or that ballet and modern dance are not the only two forms of 20th-century theatrical dance—the result is that a wide variety of dance activity, the constant history of crossovers between "high" and "low" culture and among genres (for example, George Balanchine's work for the Ziegfield Follies, Fred Astaire's film choreography, or Hanya Holm's many musicals), and almost all of black dance simply disappear from Manning's "history" of dance. Alarming, too, is the simplistic assertion that all-female companies lend dance feminist content. Margaret Thatcher is a woman; but she is not a feminist, nor is Britain a feminist state.

Terpsichore in Sneakers used "post-modern" as a term of historical style that was keyed to the movement that used it. Manning wants to erect modernism and postmodernism as essentialized/ahistorical styles and then rewrite dance history in terms of these reductivist categories. In her view, postmodernism would include Kurt Jooss, Kasian Goleizovsky, and James Waring. She also seems to think that Merce Cunningham's interest in ballet (his "newly polished," hence postmodern, dances) is something recent (perhaps she has only recently noticed it). This reductivist, anachronistic approach is unlikely to tell us anything about dance history. It is more likely to tell us about Manning's desires.

One of those desires seems to be to reduce dance—a complex, contradictory, changeable portion of the art world, embroiled not only in its own tensions, but also those resulting from its engagement with the other arts—to a field that is pleasantly and predictably consistent, clear, uncomplicated, and autonomous; to an imaginary field, that is, that has nothing to do with the reality of its institutions and practices. Manning seems to think that postmodernism is an idea one can abstractly construct and then go to find anywhere and at any time, rather than a tendency that emerges from a historically evolving artistic practice (and from the rhetoric of that practice) which, like human practices, is rooted in its own time, place, and culture. She doesn't seem to want actually to *do* history, but rather, to impose her ideal system *on* history.

Another desire—despite the talk of objectivity, neutrality, and nonpartisanship—seems to be to expand the modern and postmodern canon to include her favorite candidates. This does not really seem problematic here, since according to my historical categories, Mary Wigman is modern (but not modern*ist*, the way the postmoderns of the 1970s analytic phase were), and Pina Bausch represents a local German outgrowth of certain American first-generation postmodern concerns. I say this about Bausch in the 1987 introduction; many second-generation American postmoderns are also mentioned there only in passing.

But what is problematic is Manning's refusal to acknowledge her own partisanship. Many academic disciplines, from literary criticism to art history, now claim that some kind of commitment is necessary to all research. And one could also argue that to be partisan does not preclude being accurate or objective in one's research and analysis. That is, even if one is committed to a certain project, one can still be objective insofar as one remains responsible to the facts and to the methods of one's field of inquiry. Let us, as critics and historians, go ahead and find exemplary choreographers, dancers, and dances. But let us, in all fairness, acknowledge as we write about them our own presuppositions and commitments. And let us discuss them in language that means something.

Susan Manning:

It seems that Sally Banes and I are writing past one another rather than penning a conversation.

Although the editors of TDR decided to place "Modernist Dogma and Postmodern Rhetoric" next to two book reviews, my article was not intended to assess the value of *Terpsichore in Sneakers* as a publication in the dance field. If that had been my intent, I surely would have voiced a sentiment similar to that which concluded my review of Banes' *Democracy's Body*: "That [this volume] raises all sorts of challenges for future work on the Judson Dance Theater to meet only shows what a definitive contribution Banes makes to dance scholarship" (*Theatre Survey* 28, no. 1, May 1987:96–100).

Written as a thought piece, "Modernist Dogma and Post-modern Rhetoric" took off from the juxtaposition of the original 1980 introduction and the new introduction to the 1987 edition of *Terpsichore in Sneakers*. As such, I wanted to locate Banes in a tradition of dance writers from Lincoln Kirstein and John Martin to Jill Johnston and suggest that the critical apologies penned by these writers, when taken as historical studies (as they often are), distort the larger contours of dance modernism.

I use the term "modernism" in the conventional way it is used in the other arts: to refer to a set of related developments that began around the turn of the century and have continued almost into the present. (That "almost" is what occasions such vehement debate.) In some ways, dance modernism parallels other artistic modernisms, most particularly in its formalism ("the reflexive rationalization of movement"). But in other (and more interesting) ways, dance modernism departs from modernism in the other arts, specifically in its self-division ("the dual practice of modern dance and 20th-century ballet") and in its projection of issues related to gender and nationality.

Banes understands "modernism" very differently. As she explains above, she equates modernism with the "Greenbergian gallery aesthetic" and with reflexivity—"that the work not merely be itself but that it be about being the kind of thing it is." If I read her rightly, she sees Merce Cunningham's dances as anticipating a reflexivity achieved by the Judson choreographers. But I can't agree that this reflexivity is limited to Cunningham, Judson, and their legacy. Vaslav Nijinsky's *The Rite of Spring,* Mary Wigman's *Scenes from a Dance Drama,* Martha Graham's *Primitive Mysteries,* George Balanchine's *Serenade*—all were *about dancing* and about other things as well. Ditto Cunningham's *Walkaround Time,* Yvonne Rainer's *Trio A,* and Twyla Tharp's *Push Comes to Shove*. What fascinates me about 20th-century dance is the way the spectator is invited to make associations beyond the dance and at the same time denied the fulfillment of that possibility.

This notion, and my understanding of dance modernism, do not come out of ahistorical theorizing. On the contrary, they come out of the most basic kind of historical research—reconstructing dances from the fragments that remain. My research demonstrated that what choreographers say they're doing often differs from their practice, and this realization in turn made me question the rhetoric of formalism ("modernist dogma") and examine what other issues were at stake. I'm not yet at the end of this inquiry, but it has led me to speculate that just as the body becomes the repressed or the absent "other" in modern Western culture, so too does theatre dance (and not just ballet and modern dance). Within the arena of 20th-century culture, theatre dance traces the imprint of social facts eclipsed by the other arts.

Of course, Banes is right when she insists that all scholarship has an agenda. But she misinterprets my agenda. My polemic is aimed at the overlap between dance criticism and dance scholarship exemplified by Banes' dual introduction to *Terpsichore in Sneakers*. When critical apology is mistaken as historical or theoretical inquiry—and this is as much the responsibility of readers as of writers—then the potential reach of dance scholarship becomes limited, both in terms of audience and in terms of implication. If dance studies is to find a wider audience and larger role within the academy, we must disentangle criticism from scholarship. Of course, history and theory do function as a sort of contemporary criticism, but this does not mean that the dance researcher must become the advocate for one particular choreographer or school. There are agendas for dance scholarship other than critical apology. It's time we pursued them.

Théâtre du Soleil Shines Its Light on the Holy Land

To the Editor:

As an American actor performing with the Théâtre du Soleil at the Israeli Theater Festival in May 1988, I thought you might be interested in the following declaration. It was originally published on 15 April in the following Israeli newspapers: *Ha'aretz* (Hebrew), *Yediot Ahronot* (Hebrew), *Al-Ittihad* (Arabic), *Al-Fajar* (Arabic), and the *Jerusalem Post* (English).

At the festival, the Théâtre du Soleil performed Hèléne Cixous's *The Indiad, or The India of Their Dreams* (directed by Ariane Mnouchkine). The play, which covers the period from 1937 to 1948, describes the Indian struggle for independence from the British. Degenerating into a fratricidal war between Hindus and Muslims, the conflict led to the partition of the subcontinent into two nations: India and Pakistan.

Recent events in Israel, the subject matter of the play, and the varied national and religious composition of the Théâtre du Soleil demanded the following statement of purpose on our part.

Paul Golub
Le Théâtre du Soleil
Paris

The Théâtre du Soleil in Israel

You have invited us and we have accepted your invitation. But before we enter into your house, you should know who we are and what we believe.

We, the author, actors, musicians, technicians, and director of the Théâtre du Soleil, come from 22 different countries (France, Portugal, Chile, Belgium, Italy, Brazil, Algeria, India, Cambodia, the United States, Tunisia, Turkey, Armenia, Lebanon, Iran, Spain, Germany, Switzerland, Argentina, Guatemala, the Dominican Republic, and Togo); we are Christian, Muslim, Jewish, Buddhist, Hindu, and Atheist; we are white, we are black, we are yellow; we come from countries which in the course of their history have at different times played the role of the colonizers and of the colonized, of the oppressed and the oppressors, of the occupied and of the occupying, from countries which have known and continue to know their hours of pride and of shame, of progress and of decline, of dignity and of indignity, of humanity and of inhumanity. That is who we are.

And now this is what we believe:

We believe that it is inadmissible to appropriate territory by force;

We believe that to kill children, whatever the circumstances and whether they be Israeli or Palestinian, is a monstrosity;

We believe that the killing of unarmed civilians violates not only the Geneva Convention but above all Moral Law;

We believe that a nation that oppresses another cannot itself be entirely free;

> We believe that it is madness to try to destroy by force what no force can ever destroy: the love of the native land and the spirit of freedom. The body can be broken, but the soul of a people cannot be crushed. And of all the peoples it is the Jewish people that have immemorially proved this;
>
> We believe that the Palestinian people are right to revolt against the Israeli occupation and that its cause is just;
>
> We believe that the Palestinian people have an inalienable right to self-determination and to a Palestinian State;
>
> We believe that the State of Israel has an unimpeachable right to exist here in peace and security;
>
> We believe that there are two peoples in this Holy Land and that it should be shared and its borders negotiated. In the hope that in days to come, when Time has paved the way to forgetfulness and forgiveness, some kind of association may come to pass;
>
> We believe that there has been enough stubbornness, persistence in crime and error, and that there have been enough blind eyes and deaf ears;
>
> We believe that the leaders that the Israeli people have chosen must accept to negotiate with the leaders that the Palestinian people have chosen, even if these leaders are not to Israeli liking and no matter what their strategy was in the past;
>
> We believe that Israel, being the stronger, must make the first move. The most critical one. Is Israel incapable of this? Could Israel be more afraid of peace than of war?;
>
> We believe that by closing their eyes to those Palestinians who hold out their hand, Israel runs the risk of being faced one day exclusively by those who only know how to raise a dagger;
>
> We believe that Israel and the PLO should come to a mutual recognition of each other at one and the same time, at the very moment negotiations begin, and then the whole world will breathe and hope again.

We have hesitated about coming, we have talked, we have consulted a fair number of you, and we have decided not to add a facile refusal to so many other criminal ones in the past. Nothing can bring us to despair of the strength of words, to renounce our faith in mankind, nor in Art. That we shall never give up.

It is for Peace and for those who defend it that we come, out of admiration and fraternal feeling for all those in both camps who, sometimes at peril of their lives or by braving this or that senseless law of the land, attempt to "build a bridge," to meet and talk together, whether in Paris or Beirut, in Brussels, Bucharest, Budapest, or Tunis, whether on one bank or the other.

By coming we pay homage to all those in Israel—members of the Knesset, intellectuals, writers, artists, lawyers, journalists, or citizens—who untiringly weave and have for decades now been weaving the fabric of Peace which irresponsible leaders are bent on ripping apart.

We come because we believe that men change, that they have already changed, that many Palestinians have changed and that if Israel fails to change, Israel will lose not only blood and lives, but its honor and civil peace. For we believe that the blindness of some is driving the whole people of Israel towards the massacre that engenders massacre and civil war.

We say all this to you because it is not right to enter the house of a friend with a heart full of unspoken anguish and reproaches left unsaid.

On Getting the Message

To the Editor:

In the Spring 1988 issue I was struck by both the similarities and differences between Suzanne Lacy's work and Karen Finley's. Both deal with feminist issues, both are hard-hitting in their messages of alienation in a patriarchal society. Yet, Lacy's work is experienced by many hundreds, her production teams held together by volunteers, grants, corporate donations, and paid positions, while Finley is being denied performance opportunities.

The contrasts between these two artists present a wonderful opportunity to view what form a message is wrapped in. Lacy's larger works are smooth, gentle, and well organized, even while they speak of hardship. Finley's work is filled with anger and outrage. One artist enrolls the audience to consider difficult issues, the other pushes them away, denying them the opportunity to learn.

The essence of any social and political artist is communication, and when the message is wrapped in a form that the audience can't hear, the artist has failed in his or her commitment to teach. Finley would be well served to find a form for her work that will enroll her audience to listen and consider her well-meaning and important message.

Gerry Large
Pasadena, CA

Of Time and Mime

A Polylog on Festivity

Frank E. Manning

Carnival and Theater: Plebeian Culture and the Structure of Authority in Renaissance England. By Michael Bristol. New York: Methuen, 1985; 237 pp. $33.

Carnival! By Umberto Eco, V.V. Ivanov, and Monica Rector. Berlin: Mouton, 1984; vii + 165 pp. $52.50.

Time Out of Time: Essays on the Festival. Edited by Alessandro Falassi. Albuquerque: University of New Mexico Press, 1987; x+311 pp. $17.50.

In a 1983 paper delivered in Baton Rouge during Mardi Gras, James Boon interpreted the phenomenal proliferation of play studies as the voice of Desiderius Erasmus's allegorical Folly speaking through the anthropological amplification of Gregory Bateson, Victor Turner, and others:

> Thanks to Victor Turner and a host of recent interpreters of serio-ludic forms—rites, performances, institutions, texts—Bateson's brand of insight, long rejected in standard functionalist anthropology, has become something of an industry. Parody has been busting out all over: once Trickster is unshackled or Folly unleashed, he/she doesn't know where to stop. And rightly so (1984:157).

The notion of a scholarly industry devoted to studying play is itself parody and paradox. What others enjoy, academics work at understanding. The products of this understanding now constitute a voluminous body of literature, which in turn is the subject of conferences, courses, and reviews—including, of course, my own efforts on these pages. Industry begets industry.

How does one assess the task of assessing play and play studies? Again, Erasmus can be summoned for insight. A scholar and religious humanist whose writing contributed to the ferment of the Renaissance, Erasmus offered *The Praise of Folly* (1511) as a doubly ironic comment on the sophistry and corruption of his time, ecclesiastical as well as civil. Folly, he averred, is a necessary and pleasurable component of life. But all of life is folly, including the pronouncements of those who presume to know the matter. The allegorical Folly praises and condemns herself in a manner that today is termed reflexive; aware of herself as both subject and object, she realizes that she cuts as ridiculous and paradoxical a figure as the targets of her comic satire.

Folly remains the spirit of carnivalism, expressed both in carnival itself and through the "carnivalization" of literature. Folly also inspires the scholarly reviewer dealing with the texts under discussion here: a study of carnival and popular theatre in Renaissance England by the Canadian literary scholar Michael Bristol; a series of three essays about carnival by the Italian semiotician Umberto Eco, the Soviet linguist V.V. Ivanov, and the Brazilian linguist Monica Rector; and a collection of articles on festivity edited by the Italian folklorist Alessandro Falassi. The globe-circling, multidisciplinary character of these three books is itself carnivalesque. One hears from them what one hears from any festive playground: a polylog of voices. Folly's role, as critic, is interlocutory—orchestrating the voices, conversing self-consciously with them, and commenting on the experience to a wider audience.

Folly's Voice in Carnival

Carnival and Theater is the most ingenious and provocative of the three books. It is also the one where Folly is most explicitly acknowledged and given freest reign. "Erasmus's purpose," Bristol contends, "is to recuperate laughter as philosophy" (1985:130). Folly's laughter is amplified in the "fool's paradise" that is symbolically constructed by carnival, described by Bristol as:

> [. . .] a counterstatement to the demands of authority, wisdom, and hard work, which are laughed away by celebratory practice and irreverent spectacle. Laughter exposes the entire Olympian hierarchy as a farcical imposture and at the same time reveals the narrow limits within which ordered reason may function. With reason carefully circumscribed, there is ample scope for living, for surrender to pleasure and communality in the acceptance of weakness, frailty, and imperfection (131).

Bristol's interest in festive laughter draws him toward what he terms the "sociological poetics of Mikhail Bakhtin" (19). With Bakhtin, he views carnival as a plebeian "second life," a positive alternative to the "official" system. This second life is not simply a means of resisting the dominant culture or of taking refuge from it, although it serves both of those ends. It is also a parody which sabotages the dominant culture, exposing the latter's arbitrariness and perishability and rendering it essentially laughable.

Bristol emphasizes the "transformation downward" or "uncrowning" of official culture (22). Exalted truths and values, along with the status groups which represent them, are associated in carnival imagery with the cosmological underworld (hell, devils, death itself) and the anatomical underside (genitalia, buttocks, gross bodily processes). Abstractions are materialized, the eternal is temporalized, the powerful are portrayed as frail and decadent. Conversely, carnival carnivalizes. It is not simply a celebratory event that is bound in time and space (although that is a profound measure of its significance). It is also the source of a popular culture that infiltrates official culture, permeating it with humor, irony, indeterminacy, and unconcludedness.

One will readily recognize the carnivalesque *mundus inversus,* which is often described with reference to such concepts as symbolic inversion and ritualized reversal. Festivals typically transpose a repertory of social, cosmological, and moral polarities in ways that have an observable form and function. Bristol's study, however, does more than provide another example of this familiar pattern. He is concerned as much with reversibility as with reversal. He emphasizes not simply that carnival interchanges semantic opposites, but that in doing so it demonstrates their equivalency, plasticity, and co-conspiracy in a common fiction. Carnival satirizes its plebeian self with the same relish that it lampoons official culture. Here, again, is Folly.

Carnival's capacity for self-mockery is situated in its own transitoriness. It is a temporal event, archetypally poised against Lent, the season to which it gives way. Carnival's emphasis on indulgent consumption is not only the licensing of sensual pleasure, but a reminder of the results of that consumption: defecation, decay, death. Carnival is consumed by its celebrants, and it consumes itself as it expires into the season which is its social undoing and moral renunciation.

Yet true to its reversibility, carnival combines stark temporality with a capacity to transcend other temporal systems:

> One of the functions of carnival is to facilitate the annual transition from celebrations fixed by the solar calendar, including All Souls' and the Twelve Days of Christmas, and ending with Candlemas on

> February 2nd, to celebrations fixed by the juxtaposition of the lunar calendar with the vernal equinox, including Lent and Easter, and ending with Ascension Day. Because it occurs "betwixt and between" these liturgically recognized cycles but is not strictly speaking part of the liturgical year, Carnival's annual arrival is "untimely" and is marked with customs like ringing the church bell at the wrong time or changing the hands on the clock. As the liminal event par excellence, Carnival is the pivotal link in the annual cycle of festivity, and carnivalesque manifestations pervade every celebration, those of May and midsummer no less than the winter observances (Bristol 1985:41).

Bristol's sense of the paradigmatic significance of carnival as an expression of human festivity underlies his political analysis, which is a major concern of the book. Carnival is both social and antisocial, conservative and progressive. As an unselfconscious ritual, it enhances social cohesion and thereby reinforces established patterns of political domination. But for this function to constitute a total explanation, "It would be necessary for festivals to be completely unselfconscious occasions on which nothing was ever learned, and for the participants to cooperate, year after year, in an oppressive routine contrary to their interests" (27). Of course, this is not true. Carnival is also a conscious expression of social protest, a pragmatic performance through which the plebeian classes articulate their immediate aspirations for freedom and abundance as well as their "collective determination to conserve the authority of the community to set its own standards of behavior and social discipline and to enforce those standards by appropriate means" (52).

But while carnival represents and promotes popular resistance against the established political order, its more significant function is that of reminding the powerful that their rule is neither as effective nor as enduring as they would like. Potentates, like plebeians, have feet of clay. As an "idiom of social experimentation" (52), carnival envisions not the toppling and replacement of an elite but the radical regeneration of political society. Carnival in this sense is closer to millenarianism than to ritualized rebellion.

Semiotic Echoes

The theme of comic laughter is echoed by Umberto Eco, whose eight-page musing on carnival constitutes the opening essay of *Carnival!*, a book that general editor Thomas Sebeok describes as a "tryptich of a text" (vii). Yet Eco's approach and conclusions are diametrically contrary to those of Bristol, making the two together an oppositional pairing of carnivalesque proportions. A synthesis of this thesis-antithesis sequence is quite likely futile, but the nature of it reveals much about carnival and even more about the academic industry of interpreting it.

"The idea of carnival," Eco observes in his opening sentence, "has something to do with the comic" (1). This conclusion leads him to probe the nature of comedy, a problem for which he turns to the second book of Aristotle's *Poetics* for help. But, "There is only one minor inconvenience: this book was either lost or was never even written—an irreparable loss, indeed" (1). Nonetheless, he persists doggedly on his Aristotelian course by considering what the Greek philosopher might have said—a methodology that he describes as "the Peircean art of fair guesses or abductions" (1).

Comic characters, Eco tells us, are socially inferior (often animal-like) figures who violate relatively minor rules. We, their audience, laugh derisively at their predicament, while at the same time feeling a sense of relief that the rule was broken. But because of their inferior status we do not sympathize with them, much less develop any sense of human unity. The process, moreover, is cathartic and socially conservative. The rules are reinforced and validated by the manner of their temporary violation. "One should conclude that the comic is only an instrument of social control and can never be a form of social criticism" (7).

Eco subscribes explicitly to the bread-and-circuses theory. The rulers allow comedy (and carnival) in order to maintain the status quo. "To support the universe of business," he says, "there is no business like show business" (3). Eco's elitism is unfettered and rather cynically enthusiastic. "Popular cultures are always determined by cultivated cultures" (7) . . . "Carnival can exist only as an authorized transgression" (6) . . . "The upper classes (through their poets) depicted the peasants as animals (in comedy); then they allowed the same peasants to 'freely' express themselves (in carnival) exactly as they were depicted in theater" (7).

Paired against Bristol's view of an autonomous, influential popular culture and a carnival tradition which is a creative source for theatre, Eco's position is itself (though unintentionally so) a symbolic reversal. Eco seeks to reclaim an affinity with *homo ludens* by balancing his disparagement of the comic with an endorsement of humor. Following Pirandello, he proposes:

> If the comic is the perception of the opposite, humor is the sentiment of the opposite. A case of comic [sic] is the decrepit old woman who smears her face with make-up and dresses like a young girl; facing such a picture, one notices that this woman is the opposite of what a respectable old woman should be. In the case of humor, one asks why the old woman masks herself, to regain her lost youth. The character is still animal-like but in some way one sympathizes with it (7).

This tortured distinction reduces comedy (and carnival) to slapstick, while conceptualizing humor as a more sophisticated sensibility. Interestingly, while comedy is the pastime of the masses, humor approaches the semiotic intelligence.

> Humor is always, if not metalinguistic, metasemiotic: through verbal language or some other sign system it casts in doubt other cultural codes. If there is a possibility of transgression, it lies in humor rather than in comic (8).

Hence significant rule violations, along with the insights that derive therefrom, are the exclusive province of those capable of perceiving the semiotic complexities of humor. Humor is a "true movement of freedom" (8) which offers to a select few what is unavailable to the masses.

> Humor does not promise us liberation: on the contrary it warns us about the impossibility of global liberation, reminding us of the presence of a law that we no longer have reason to obey [. . .]. Very seldom does the business of entertainment display real humor. More

> frequently it sells carnival. When a real piece of humor appears, entertainment becomes avant-garde: a supreme philosophical game (8).

In sum, if Bristol embraces and celebrates the people's second life, Eco contemptuously dismisses it. Its denizens, after all, are animal-like, and "Comic is always racist" (2). Eco's interpretive role is a solipsism, not a dialog with carnival. His bibliography contains only one reference, and that is to his own work. Eco echoes himself, not the voices of festivity.

V.V. Ivanov's contribution to the book provides yet another radical contrast. If Eco talks only to himself, Ivanov attempts an exhaustive survey of ethnological and literary sources on carnival and related (loosely, at times) performative and mythical genres. The text of the article is a mere 12 pages, but it is followed by 36 footnotes and 121 citations.

Ivanov's central theme is accurately announced in his title: "The Semiotic Theory of Carnival as the Inversion of Bipolar Opposites." He traces the inversion perspective to Bakhtin, to whose "eternal memory" (11) he dedicates the chapter. He further proposes that carnival tends to neutralize and mediate its inverted oppositions. To cite a single example, carnival typically includes both transvestism and androgyny; the transvestites reverse the male-female opposition, while the androgynes neutralize the reversal.

Ivanov concludes that, for writers, "The idea of carnival is a fertile source of creativity" (23). This sentiment aligns him with Bristol and against Eco. Yet unlike both Bristol and Eco, he does not probe the broader political significance of carnivalesque festivity, either in general or in the context of particular societies. Soviet ethnology tends to remain smugly aloof from such issues, much like British social anthropology in the days before its colonial empire was aggressively challenged. Instead, Ivanov is content to pile example atop example in litanylike fashion, substituting an inventory of carnival artifacts for focused social analysis. In this sense, ironically, he fails to recall the memory of Bakhtin.

The third and final article, Monica Rector's "The Code and Message of Carnival," extends the disproportionate and disjunctive makeup of the book. While Eco deals with carnival in general and Ivanov with an encyclopedic number of cases, Rector focuses intensively on a single case—the Brazilian carnival. Her contribution, moreover, is four times the length of the other two combined. Rather than Sebeok's "tryptich," this might be described as a book by Rector, with forewords by Eco and Ivanov.

Still, Rector's contribution does have an unsettling consistency with the introductory pieces. It reduces celebration to catharsis, assumes that inversion is an ephemeral social escape, uncritically adopts elitist biases, and speaks with the authority of an omniscient exegete. Again, one listens in vain for the self-parodic criticism of Folly or the populist insights of Bakhtin.

Like her colleagues, Rector raises and salutes a semiotic flag. She begins, "This work is being done from a semiotic point of view; it is an attempt to explain the meaning of carnival by means of the interpretation of several codes" (37). She proceeds in a rather schematic fashion to analyze music, gestures, language, dress, dance movements, and other semiotic elements of carnival. The text is supplemented by 24 pages of color photographs, which feature the two most familiar figures in the Brazilian carnival: *pastoras* (women clad in skimpy, spangled bikinis and feather headdresses) and *ritmastas* (tambourine-playing men who accompany the pastoras in processional dancing). The pictures are striking in both clarity and composition, and constitute one of the highlights of the book.

Regrettably, the essay is marred by glaring reportorial inconsistencies. Color plate 17, which shows a clown made up to look like he is crying, is accompanied by the caption: "The clown, one of the main figures of the carnival, is always sad" (72). Plate 33, showing another clown, bears the caption: "Just a happy clown" (120). Similarly, the word *carnavelasco* is defined as "any situation in which there is a rupture of the social order and a breaking up of moral attributes" (102). But in a glossary that follows a few pages later, she defines carnavelesco (spelled with an "e") simply as a "float maker" (107). The first usage of the term seems generally consistent with that of Roberto da Matta, a leading anthropological scholar of Brazilian carnival, who defines the term as "that which one wants to do or say, along with everything that one does not want to do, during carnival" (1984:230). Why, then, does Rector give us such a limited sense of the term in her glossary, which is meant to be, presumably, a comprehensive reference?

Rector's social analysis is disappointing for the same reasons Eco and Ivanov are disappointing. Like them, she throws her weight primarily behind the notion that carnival is a social inversion which allows the poor to indulge their fantasies by playfully assuming the places of the rich and powerful. Her explanation, however, simply echoes the fatuous safety-valve theory. Carnivalists have "a need to release their instincts, reaching a catharsis that will ease the frustrations of their daily lives" (42). Later in the essay she claims, "The frustration related to an inferior position in the social world is compensated for symbolically by the privileged position in the samba world" (102). This makes the compensation of the poor illusory in the double sense. Once the oppressive frustration is released, the oppressed are ready for more oppression. Carnival's function is psychological only; it is socially innocuous and politically inconsequential.

Apart from all else, this view runs into two ethnographic problems. The first is that the Brazilian authorities seem to disagree. The state's perception of carnival's potential to incite popular unrest has led it to ban political themes from costuming and song, a policy that was particularly explicit during the long period of military rule. While the power structure may of course be paranoid, its suspicions find support in the historical work of Emmanuel LeRoy Ladurie (1979) and Natalie Davis (1975), as well as in more general theories of performative play propounded by Brian Sutton-Smith (1976), Turner (1982), and many others. Like Bakhtin and Bristol, these scholars remind those who dominate the social order that homo ludens has a peculiar power to erode the very foundations of their regime.

The second difficulty comes to light in a discussion of Caribbean carnival by Roger Abrahams and Richard Bauman (1978). Dealing with the island of St. Vincent, they conclude that the notion of inversion provides an important but insufficient understanding of the social dynamics of carnival. More precisely, carnival is an occasion when those segments of the community who are ordinarily the agents of disorder and misrule are given greater license and more positive recognition than at other times. This insight may also apply to Brazil. The suntan patterns on the pastoras shown in Rector's photographs reveal that these women are not shedding their clothes for the first time during carnival. One doubts that they conform to the "established" Brazilian standard of spending their quotidian lives entirely in the *casa* (household, domestic sphere), where they are subject to conservative patriarchal domination. While such evidence is frankly "scant," it raises questions about the adequacy of the academic shibboleth that carnivalists are simply performing a fantasy that is the opposite of their normal—and normative—experience.

Festival Portraits

The theme of inversion is struck again in *Time Out of Time,* Alessandro Falassi's edited volume on festivals. Following the Johan Huizinga tradition of play studies, he views festivity as a meaningful world unto itself, apart from and contrastive to the realities of normal life. On a certain metalevel, his introduction to the volume is consistent with his title. It is "out of time," a discussion of festivity based on a dated European tradition of humanistic scholarship that is clearly anterior to most of the articles in the volume. One wonders whether this anachronism is an intentional piece of carnivalism on Falassi's part or an attachment to a particular conception of folklore studies. Perhaps it is both.

Unlike most of his contributors, Falassi speaks not of festivals but of "the festival"—in effect, a paradigmatic form of which a given occurrence is merely an illustrative manifestation. He defines the festival as "a periodically recurrent, social occasion in which, through a multiplicity of forms and a series of coordinated events, participate directly or indirectly and to various degrees, all members of a whole community, united by ethnic, linguistic, religious, historical bonds, and sharing a worldview" (2). A supplementary sentence removes any doubt about Falassi's understanding of festivity: "Both the social function and the symbolic meaning of the festival are closely related to a series of overt values that the community recognizes as essential to its ideology and worldview, to its social identity, its historical continuity, and to its physical survival, which is ultimately what festival celebrates" (2).

The archaic nature of this definition is twofold. It conceptualizes the festival as a single exemplary form, and it effectively restricts festivity to simple, unitary societies where participation is obligatory. This notion excludes the vast range of festivals in complex contemporary societies, where participation is optional and must be seen in relation to varying degrees of spectatorship among both community and noncommunity members. Festivals in the modern world are popular entertainments as much as social rituals, performed in and by constituencies who often share little in the way of an explicit worldview or value system. The modern situation is not that an established, stable society produces a paradigmatic festival, but that a variety of discrete festive forms produce a plurality of social solidarities (see Manning 1983).

Falassi's brief introduction includes a discussion of what he calls "festival morphology." Following Vladimir Propp's approach to the anatomy of folktales, he identifies several "building blocks of festival" (3), each of them a nuclear and constituent rite. The result is an inventory that includes rites of valorization, rites of conspicuous display, rites of conspicuous consumption, ritual dramas, and rites of exchange. Apart from their particular roles, the collective role of these rites is to segregate the festival from ordinary life and thereby make it a "time out of time."

The 24 articles that follow Falassi's introduction exhibit a healthy diversity. An opening section entitled, "Men of Letters and Social Scientists Reporting from the Scene of the Festival," consists of reprints of classic pieces. Included are selections from Johann Wolfgang von Goethe (the Roman Carnival), Aldous Huxley (the Palio at Siena), Ernest Hemingway (bullfighting), Arnold van Gennep (pilgrimage), William Bascom (a Yuroba festival), and Victor Turner (the Rio Carnival). The following three sections examine, respectively, "Continuity and Change," "Signs and Symbols," and "Social Functions and Ritual Meanings." Most of the articles in these latter three sections are original publications, and all are introduced by a brief editorial synopsis.

Several of the Falassi volume's papers extend themes and orientations developed at greater length in the other books presently under review. Richard Bauman describes the religious aversion of 17th-century Quakers to festivity, following a Weberian interpretation of Reformation Protestantism that nicely complements Bristol's discussion of festivity in the more ambivalently congenial Catholic context. Denise Lawrence examines Pasadena's Doo-Dah Parade, a popular spoof of the Tournament of Roses Parade that has gradually become a version of the people's "second life" in southern California. Beverly Stoeltze's analysis of Texas rodeos illustrates how this performance form embraces fundamental sociocultural polarities: male-female, nature-culture, the wild and the tame, and so on. Other papers exemplify semiotic approaches roughly similar to those presented by Eco, Ivanov, and Rector. In short, the book serves well as a companion piece to other books, which is its intended aim. It is a volume that has what the publishers call "textbook potential," and it may well join the ludic industry identified by Boon.

Peeing on the Altar

What voice can a commentator add to this engaging triad of books? Inspiration comes from Richard Swiderski's *Voices* (1986), an ingenious and unsettling application of Bakhtinian consciousness to the study of an Italian-American festival. Swiderski highlights two poles of symbolic action: the carnival and the altar. The carnival is an American carnival, a complex of mechanical amusements, food stands, games of skill and chance. It is the pole of secularity and commercialism. The altar is the setting of Mass and other religious devotions, and it is where the statue of St. Peter, patron saint of the festival, is temporarily enshrined. It is the pole of spirituality and idealized cultural tradition.

In dialog with his surroundings and his own inner anthropological voices, Swiderski ponders the interpretation of this opposition:

> Not only Turner and Geertz, but the previous generation of anthropologists were with me: Ruth Benedict pointing to the Apollonian altar space next to the Dionysian carnival; Levi-Strauss admiring the symmetry and asymmetry of the one and the other. And, of course, Burke giving me the right to think as a dramatist as long as the materials were present. Try as I may to make it otherwise, I am doomed to take up the enormously suggestive split between carnival and altar, which was the first completed structure of the fiesta. Altar/thesis, carnival/antithesis and the fiesta itself as synthesis. As in Brecht's epic theatre, the plot was deliberately familiar in order to bring greater attention to the drama's dialectical exposition. This fiesta was a good deal like epic theater performed perhaps by a provincial troupe.
>
> I find myself extending the order of the fiesta space throughout the Italian community and willing to believe that it was the intention of the fiesta committee to do exactly this. The order of the public altar is the order of the family altar and the ship's altar challenged by the carnival, which broods on the side. I must devoutly (anthropologically) succumb to this temptation—Turner and Geertz demand that—but never be fully persuaded as they might be that the carnival

> is all the carnival there is, contained in its symbolic opposition to the altar. A higher carnival there no doubt was, one in which carnival and altar were not opposed or joined together but remained terrifyingly separate, the common ruin of a fractured unity: Bakhtin's great carnival crying to get through and dissipate memory (1986:66–67).

But this stream of consciousness is abruptly broken by an informant who happens on the scene: "A man, unzipping his fly, confided to me that he was going to pee against the altar ('not the holy part'), because that way nothing worse could happen to it" (1986:67).

The scholarly industry of play studies is a secular search for a spiritual talisman. The meaning, of course, lies in the search. But we are fortunate if, along the way, we meet those anonymous mimes of Folly who mock our understanding of the world, reduce our narrow interests to comic absurdity, and subversively force us to take time out from our serious business. Peeing on the altar makes it worthy of its more accustomed roles.

References

Abrahams, Roger, and Richard Bauman
1978 "Ranges of Festival Behavior." In *The Reversible World: Symbolic Inversion in Art and Society,* edited by Barbara Babcock, 193–208. Ithaca, NY: Cornell University Press.

Boon, James
1984 "Folly, Bali, and Anthropology, or Satire Across Cultures." In *Text, Play and Story: The Construction and Reconstruction of Self and Society,* edited by Edward Bruner, 156–77. Washington, DC: The American Ethnological Society.

Davis, Natalie
1975 *Society and Culture in Early Modern France.* Stanford, CA: Stanford University Press.

Erasmus, Desiderius
1941 [1511] *The Praise of Folly.* Translated by H.H. Hudson. Princeton, NJ: Princeton University Press.

Ladurie, Emmanuel LeRoy
1979 *Carnival in Romans.* Translated by Mary Feeney. New York: George Braziller, Inc.

Manning, Frank E., ed.
1983 *The Celebration of Society: Perspectives on Contemporary Cultural Performance.* Bowling Green, OH: Bowling Green University Popular Press.

da Matta, Roberto
1984 "On Carnival, Informality, and Magic: A Point of View from Brazil." In *Text, Play and Story: The Construction and Reconstruction of Self and Society,* edited by Edward Bruner, 230–46. Washington, DC: The American Ethnological Society.

Sutton-Smith, Brian
1976 *The Dialectics of Play.* Schorndoff, West Germany: Verlag Hoffman.

Swiderski, Richard
1986 *Voices: An Anthropologist's Dialogue with an Italian-American Festival.* London, Ontario: Centre for Social and Humanistic Studies, University of Western Ontario.

Turner, Victor
1982 *From Ritual to Theater: The Human Seriousness of Play*. New York: Performing Arts Journal Press.

***Frank E. Manning** is Professor of Anthropology at the University of Western Ontario. He has written widely on popular festivity, and is a former president of the Association for the Study of Play.*

Latin America and Beyond

To the Editor:

An important meeting took place in Paris between 18 and 21 May 1988 that the readers of TDR may be interested in: El Encuentro Internacional Sobre Teatro Latinoamericano (The International Congress on Modern Latin American Theatre). Not only was this one of the largest and most successful meetings of its kind on Latin American theatre, it also marked the foundation of the first international body devoted exclusively to theoretical research and critical analysis of Latin American theatre: El Instituto Internacional de Teoría y Crítica de Teatro Latinoamericano (The International Institute of Theory and Criticism of Latin American Theatre).

The encuentro was held at the recently opened Latin American cultural center in the Left Bank area of the French capital, La Maison de l'Amérique Latine. It was run under the auspices of several organizations including: the Departments of Comparative Literature and Spanish at Carleton University in Canada; the Université de Paris III, Centre de Recherches d'Etudes Comparatives Ibéro-Françaises; the Venezuelain Centro Latinoamericano de Creación e Investigatión Teatral; the Département de Théâtre, Centre de Recherches Sur la Théorie et l'Histoire du Théâtre, Université de Paris VIII; and the Spanish-based Instituto de Cooperación Iberoamericana.

The 80-odd participants—including playwrights, directors, and journalists—were drawn from South and Central America, as well as the United States, Canada, and Europe. There were over 60 papers presented and several roundtable discussions led by specially invited guests which, together, covered topics ranging from the work of Latin American playwrights such as Enrique Buenaventura, Griselda Gambaro, and Osvaldo Dragún, to aspects of Puerto Rican, Argentinian, Cuban, Mexican, and Salvadoran theatre, as well as theoretical topics, popular theatre, and Eugenio Barba's influence on the continent's group theatre.

Despite the value of these papers and discussions, the meeting's most important legacy was the foundation of the Instituto Internacional de Teoría y Crítica de Teatro Latinoamericano (IITCTL). During the course of the four-day conference the appointment of IITCTL's first president, Fernando de Toro, was ratified, along with a similar ratification of his administrative staff, a 14-member executive committee drawn from Latin America, the USA, Canada, and Europe, and a group of delegates selected from each country represented at the gathering. These officials were charged with organizing the next encuentro in 1990—to be held in either Cordoba, Argentina, or Washington, D.C.—as well as exploring the logistical problems and sources of funding needed to mount similar gatherings every two years.

In addition to organizing these conferences, IITCTL hopes to produce a bulletin every six months which would include information on current research, recently published books and journals in the field, and information on upcoming colloquia and festivals. Similarly, a semiannual journal is planned that will include theoretical, historical, and descriptive articles on Latin American theatre both on the continent and outside of it.

The fact that IITCTL wants not only to consider theatre within the continent but also to look at what is happening to Latin American theatre when it is presented in other parts of the world is a significant aspect of the organization's charter. Certainly the focus of any gathering or ongoing organization on Latin American theatre will be the continent, but, in broadening its horizons to include Latin America's effect in/on other parts of the world, IITCTL is emphasizing the ever-increasing internationalism of Latin American theatre. The hope of IITCTL's founders is to accelerate the already developing body of world-class theory and criticism in the study of Latin American theatre and, in so doing, to draw Latin America out of its tendency to introversion and toward a realization of its rightful place in world theatre.

Ian Watson
University of Pennsylvania
Philadelphia, PA

(Birth) Announcements

Ed. Note: TDR is pleased to print announcements of upcoming conferences, festivals, publications, etc. Please submit all notices at least 6–8 months in advance of the event.

New International Theatre School in Cuba

The *Escuela Internacional de Teatro de la América Latina y el Caribe* (International Theatre School of Latin America and the Caribbean) will present its first workshop in July and August of 1989 in Cuba. The school, instituted in accordance with a proposal made at the Third Encounter of Latin American and Caribbean Theatre Workers that took place in 1987 at Casa de las Americas in Cuba, will address Latin American and Caribbean theatre workers' needs for training and exchange.

This institution, which will be independent from the government, will focus on pedagogy and training of theatre artists. It will be concerned with the propagation of Latin American and Caribbean cultures, and the liberation and sovereignty of the region's peoples. It will provide a broad range of training to prepare theatre workers for the diversity of conditions under which they must function.

In acknowledgment of its international character, the school will conduct activities in other countries as well as Cuba. These activities will take the form of workshops which will focus on each region's theatrical specialty.

This summer's workshop is entitled "Present Techniques for Theatrical Creation in Latin America and the Caribbean." It will be conducted by members of the following groups: La Candelaria (Colombia), Yuyachkani (Perú), Actoral 80 (Venezuela), and a fourth group or teacher to be chosen at a later date.

The members of the school's planning committee are Atahualpa del Cioppo (Uruguay), Santiago García (Colombia), Miguel Rubio (Perú), Nissim Sharim (Chile), Fernando Peixoto (Brazil), José Solé (México), Enrique Dacal (Argentina), Juan Carlos Gené (Venezuela), and Raquel Carrió and Magaly Muguercia (Cuba).

This committee was chosen at the Third Encounter, which was initiated by Luis Molina, the general director of the Latin American Center for Theatre Creation and Research (CELCIT). The committee requests the support of individuals, cultural institutions, and the governments of Latin America and the rest of the world to realize this artistic project, unprecedented on this continent.

For more information please contact Magaly Muguercia, Director of the Latin American Theatre Department, Casa de las Américas, 3ra. Y G, El Vedado, La Habana, Cuba.

Performance Studies Festival: Call for Papers

Performance Studies International (PSI) will host a festival bringing together both scholars and performers to celebrate the 10th anniversary of New York University's Department of Performance Studies on 14–18 March, 1990. The festival will be a forum for the exploration of contemporary performance studies research and experimentation in performance itself. Crossover between these two areas is encouraged. The festival will include panel discussions, workshops, and papers. If interested in participating, please send workshop proposals and papers to Performance Studies International, Department of Performance Studies, New York University, 721 Broadway, 6th floor, New York, NY, 10003.

Yugoslavian Theatre Festival

A Yugoslavian theatre festival will be hosted by Cankarjev Dom on 31 March–2 April 1989 in Ljubljana. Featuring Yugoslavian theatre and dance performances, the gathering will provide an opportunity for theatre professionals from around the world to become acquainted with contemporary Yugoslavian performance. For more information, contact Andrej Drapal, Theatre Manager, Cankarjev Dom, Cultural and Congress Centre, 61000 Ljubljana, Kidričev Park 1, YU—Jugoslavija.

Editors' Addition

Carol Martin and Richard Schechner are pleased to announce the birth of their daughter, Sophia Martin Schechner, on 28 June 1988.

Etc.

Correction

In Frederick Lamp's article "An Opera of the West African Bondo," vol. 32, no. 2 (T118), plate 16 was printed upside down.

In Memory: Jacques Chwat (1935–1988)

Jacques Chwat, friend and colleague, died on 8 August last year from Kaposi's sarcoma. He chose to make his life *in* the theatre.

Born in Vilna, USSR, Chwat was a connection to the heart of Stanislavski, to certain traditions, which he extended into his life/art. He was a longtime collaborator with and translator of Jerzy Grotowski and participant in the ongoing Theatre of Sources, director in the U.S. and Europe of his own WorkProjects and Runways (Stanislavski: what the director must provide for the actor so that s/he may literally be able to take off), editor of *The Act* (performance art journal), and Visiting Professor of Directing at Hunter College.

A memorial was published in *The Act* last November.

Jeffrey Greenberg
Managing Editor, The Act

Staging the Obscene Body

Elinor Fuchs

> *How can business men and women stand in a room and discuss business without even one reference to their genitals? I mean everybody has them. They just pretend they don't.*
>
> —*Maria Irene Fornes*
> Fefu and Her Friends *(1980:19)*

I

Nearly 25 years ago the conceptual and performance artist Carolee Schneemann created a loft art environment, *Eye Body,* in which she included her own body as one of the materials. Photos of *Eye Body* showing the naked, beautiful Schneemann, flowers painted on her cheeks, her breasts and body covered with splashes of paint, grease, and chalk, or lying on the floor slithered over by live snakes, speak to the shocking but also the erotic and celebratory nature of her performances. Schneemann has written of the "ritual aspect of the process" that could put her in a "trancelike state," and of her later discovery, through the study of Earth Goddess artifacts, of the sacral implications of the body images explored in that performance (1979:52).

In performances created by a number of women in the 1980s, Schneemann's sacred body has been replaced by the obscene body—aggressive, scatalogical, and sometimes pornographic. My purpose here is to gather the scattered evidence of this phenomenon, and to begin to map its location in the fraught contemporary debate over female sexuality, feminism, and pornography. What do these performances say to us about contemporary theatre practice? What does it mean that women are making these performances? And how does one begin to think about these questions: with theories of the avant-garde? Of modernist "transgression"? Of pornography? With the feminist pornography wars? Though only one performance I will write about was unequivocally pornographic (others were borderline, most were "only" obscene—the boundaries smudge instantly), I started this project by trying to find out what people who have thought about it, think pornography is.

At one border of the pornography debate there is a real enjoyment and tolerance of pornography. Its defenders, such as Marxist philosopher Alan Soble, see violent pornography as marginal. Soble makes little distinction

1. *Carolee Schneemann in her 1963 loft art environment,* Eye Body. *(Photo by Erró)*

between most pornography and erotica. He suggests a pornography without offense, gender, or marketplace.

> Pornography refers to any literature or film (or other art-technological form) that describes or depicts sexual organs, preludes to sexual activity (or related organs and activities) in such a way as to produce sexual arousal in the user or the viewer (1986:8–9).

Many feminists defend pornography. The FACT group—Feminist Anti-Censorship Taskforce—was formed in 1984 by scholars and activists such as Anne Snitow, Carole Vance, and Ellen Willis to defend women's right to explore their own pleasure in sexuality, and defeat the antipornography ordinances then being proposed in various communities. Some of the women active in FACT are responsible for the publication *Caught Looking,* a glossy book with a magazine layout in which articles defending pornography or attacking its censorship jostle a large number of nonviolent (porno)graphics (Alderfer 1988). Pro-porn activists include some lesbian feminists, such as the Samois group, who create their own S&M pornography.

At the other end of the debate are the Women Against Pornography (WAP) and other antiporn feminist activists, who supported the Andrea Dworkin–Catharine MacKinnon antipornography ordinance. The ordinance, which was struck down by the Supreme Court in 1986, defined pornography as those representations that showed the sexual "subordination" of women. Women's crushing subordination to male sexual power is also the theme of Dworkin's book *Pornography: Men Possessing Women.* To Dworkin, pornography is literally "the graphic depiction of women as vile whores" (1981:200).

Reading through the literature I start less with a theoretical position than with an almost physical fear. I find I have a horror so deep of being reduced to my sexual parts by men that I can scarcely give a name to it. My lifelong avoidance of exposure to pornography begins to stir my curiosity. I find that pornography is not decidable on the basis of my personal aversion. Still, I am unable at the outset of this piece to fix myself between the pornographies. WAP inevitably colludes with the antifeminist and homophobic right; FACT indirectly encourages the pornography industry. My political sympathies are with FACT nevertheless. But there is still that fear . . . of disappearing.

Encouraged by the editors of this journal on the basis of an earlier draft to "state my own position," I think it is important to state my ambivalence. This article is a journey through that ambivalence. In it "I" will mean just that: a heterosexual female spectator, a feminist groping for her own position on divided theoretical terrain, and a critic whose formalist training did not prepare her for sexual anxiety in the theatre. My starting point is my own discomfort as a spectator to the scenes I will describe, which took place for the most part in "alternative" New York performance spaces where the experimental theatre of the late '60s and '70s was created. Some of this theatre in its first days had encouraged its spectators to join the artists in shedding sexual inhibitions. Then followed new artists and a decade of formal sophistication. The theatre I am discussing doesn't reach out to unify spectator and performer in a mutual emotion, nor does it coolly work on our perceptual apparatus. The scenes I discuss are raw, "dirty" theatre. I think they disturb women in a particular way because they are written, directed, or performed by women before mixed audiences. Here I try to find out what that way is.

Dead End Kids

My chronology begins with the decade. In Fall 1980, Mabou Mines' production of *Dead End Kids: A History of Nuclear Power,* directed by JoAnne Akalaitis and written by Akalaitis with the collaboration of company members, was produced at the Public Theatre. The nightclub scene at the end of the second act was improvised at Akalaitis' behest by actor David Brisbin. Lenny Bruce was the model in a general sense for Brisbin's '50s nightclub comedian. Handling his microphone like a dildo, he leeringly inveigles onto the stage a member of his fictive nightclub audience, a young, female, grade school teacher from "Popular" Bluffs. There is a routine of insulting sexual banter. The comic uses the young woman's seductively exaggerated naivete to degrade her. Finally, the comedian pulls a limp, plucked chicken from the crotch of his trousers. He asks the teacher to manipulate the bird's neck stump ("No head? Well, give it head!") while he reads from a report, "The Effects of Radioactive Fallout on Livestock in the Event of Nuclear War" (Akalaitis 1982).[1]

The female director's "tastelessness" was widely questioned, as it was by the *Philadelphia Inquirer* critic who found the episode "flagrantly obscene" (Collins 1983:4). I squirmed with discomfort throughout the scene, resisting the stereotypes. The scene felt dangerous. Why make the girl so dumb? Why make the man so menacing and vile? Even though I recognized in the scene the most unsettling version of the connection Akalaitis had been making all along between the war state and the sexist state, male nuclear fantasies and the exploitation of women, when I enthusiastically reviewed the play for the *Soho News* I didn't describe the scene because it made me uncomfortable, and wrote around it by describing Akalaitis' method as "coarse and slashing" (1980). The work went on to be performed in many places around the country, and the shock of the scene was obscured in a halo of awards and praise. Most critics, sympathetic with the director's political intentions, finally "allowed" it on political grounds.

In an interesting sequel, the nightclub scene was presented as a single excerpt at a joint anniversary celebration of the War Resisters' League (WRL) and Performing Artists for Nuclear Disarmament in May 1983 which I attended. Like the 19th-century provincials who rushed on stage (or so the story goes) to rescue Desdemona in the last act, women in the hall began to shout to the female character, "Don't do it honey, don't let him do it to you!"[2] Within moments, accompanied by mounting booing and hissing, there occurred a full-scale feminist walkout from the hall led by Grace Paley. The performance was broken off and an angry confrontation with the director followed. It is possible that an audience unaccustomed to the ironic strategies of the alternative theatre lost sight of the common political ground shared with the performers, but perhaps the WRL women would not have tolerated the scene on any grounds. In any event, the episode demonstrates one problem underlying the present inquiry, the difficulty of "reading" sexually offensive material when it is taken out of its usual, politically determined settings—that is, when it becomes unclear for whose pleasure the performance is being staged.

Route 1 & 9

Of all the new theatrical obscenity and pornography under discussion here, the Akalaitis is the easiest to read in the sense that it is the most easily recognized within a right-left and a right-wrong political framework. The Wooster Group's *Route 1 & 9* was more problematical in every way. First performed at the Performing Garage in October 1981, the production created a major theatrical scandal centered on the all-white group's reconstruction of a 1965 blackface routine by the latter-day black American vaudeville entertainer, Dewey (Pigmeat) Markham. Audiences and critics were bitterly divided on whether the piece was racist, in effect if not in intention. In the ensuing controversy over the racial issue, the group temporarily lost its funding from the New York State Council on the Arts.

In addition to the blackface routine with its wild dancing and raucous farce, *Route 1 & 9* included a send-up of a pedantic *Encyclopedia Brittanica* teaching film on Thornton Wilder, portions of Wilder's *Our Town* played as a dolorous all-white soap opera on a high bank of television monitors, and film of the despoiled New Jersey landscape actually shot on Route 1 & 9. Toward the end of the piece, two small television sets, placed at the level of the first row of steeply raked bleachers, began to flicker with a grainy black-and-white silent film scene, not noticed at first by most of the audience, in which a woman performs fellatio on her male partner in extreme closeup. The film ran for several minutes. No faces were visible. There was no sexual climax, only the concentration of the performers' bodies, and the silent intensity of the audience as spectators became aware of the film. As I watched the scene, I drifted into a private, erotic world, almost relieved by the silence and physical contact of the participants after the bruising indictment of the audience as racist that had preceded it.[3] For the moment I did not ask what it meant that an entire theatre audience seemed to have lost its social coherence and slipped into individual, sexual reveries.

Astonishingly, in contrast to the racial furor, the scene was noted only by a single critic in passing, and was barely mentioned in the public debates that took place in the theatre after some of the performances. Asked about the film's purpose at one of these debates, director Elizabeth LeCompte defended the "porn sequence" as "erotic" and one that gave her pleasure.

How to decide whether the scene represented an erotic act between willing partners, or a pornographic image? I was one of those who read the blackface and the *Our Town* sequence as devastating exposures of American racism. To me, the sex scene pointed at, but still seemed to function as an antidote to, a pornography of the American culture, as if to say that sex could at least be depended on to be on the side of life, unlike racism. Why then speak of pornography at all? There is more to the story.

LeCompte has said that in 1978, when working on *Nayatt School,* the company studied pornographic films and imitated their "depthless" performance style in this last work of the *Rhode Island Trilogy* (1988). In the summer of 1980, LeCompte and her company decided to make a sex film of their own with the distanced style and simple story line they found in porn films. LeCompte has said in an interview with me that as with so many other projects the company has undertaken, the suggestion to make

2. Wooster Group performers in blackface during Route 1 & 9 *at the Performing Garage in 1981. (Photo by Nancy Campbell)*

the film originated with others in the company (1988). In the film's rudimentary scenario, a hitchhiking couple is picked up on Route 1 & 9 in New Jersey, taken to an isolated house, given dinner, and enticed by their hosts into making a sex film. The film was actually shot in the LeCompte family home, representing a "middle-class space that becomes sexualized" (LeCompte 1988) and contained a variety of sexual acts, including the scene used in *Route 1 & 9*. The resulting 25-minute film was actually shown at the Performing Garage in a workshop season during the spring of 1981. Company readings of *Our Town* alternated with performances of the film and some of the racial material the company had begun to develop. By the fall of that year, these unrelated projects had coalesced into *Route 1 & 9*, with a few shots of the film footage surviving in the decontextualized images of the "porn sequence."

LeCompte's theatre, unlike Akalaitis's, offers the spectator few interpretative clues. This is a spectator's response theatre; we write our own script out of the "pieces of culture" offered by the company. LeCompte considered her fellatio scene simply "erotic," but many feminists of the theatrical community were convinced that the actress in the film had been abused, and believed that the sequence was indeed in its full context pornographic and misogynistic. Though immersion in commercial pornography provided the background for the film, LeCompte distinguishes this project from porn. "Porn out of context is no longer porn: porn is about money" (LeCompte 1988).

I don't agree that the exhibitionism and voyeurism entered into in this experiment necessarily constituted abuse, but it is clear that LeCompte in some sense had this sequence both ways, as porn, or simulated porn, and as not-porn. This was evident even in the context of the staging, where the erotic image, presented on small monitors placed low, was framed as a kind of peep show. The very unclassifiability of the sexual material, its refusal to take up a position between "bad" porn and "good" erotica, between social commentary and theatrical and even personal license, becomes perhaps its most uncomfortable aspect.

Deep Inside Porn Stars

In January 1984, Franklin Furnace sponsored the work of a seven-woman artist's collective called Carnival Knowledge, which put on a month-long exhibit and performance series titled "The Second Coming," exploring the possibility of a "new definition of pornography, one that is not demeaning to women, men and children" (Carnival Knowledge 1984). (Franklin Furnace and a constellation of downtown and Chelsea performance spaces such as The Kitchen, Dance Theatre Workshop, and P.S. 122 serve a performance world adjacent to the alternative theatres. These venues specialize in performance art, and their performers easily combine fields—theatre and dance, dance and art, art and video, etc.) Eight different performance events accompanied the exhibit of art works and sale/display of adult books and sexual aids, culminating in *Deep Inside Porn Stars*, which promised "live performances with 7 top film stars from the sex industry" (Carnival Knowledge 1984). This performance, however, was not in itself pornographic, as it has been described to me (the Franklin Furnace event is the only one included here that I did not attend). Instead the performance became part *Chorus Line* and part consciousness-raising session about the performers' personal lives and working experiences, inspired by a support group the women had organized the previous year.

3. The cover of the program for Deep Inside Porn Stars *at Franklin Furnace in New York, January 1984. (Program designed by Annie Sprinkle)*

The Birth of the Poet

In Fall 1985, two collaborations took place between female artists and male directors that were more aggressively obscene (in one case) and pornographic (in the other) than those of previous seasons. *The Birth of the Poet,* perhaps better called a coexistence than a collaboration among director Richard Foreman, designer David Salle, composer Peter Gordon, and writer Kathy Acker, was performed in the 1985 Next Wave Festival at the Brooklyn Academy of Music following a production the previous year in Rotterdam.

The three apocalyptic acts of this "opera" were focused on world history at three moments of destruction and violence. In the obscene second act, the text of which was taken almost word for word from Acker's 1982 novel *Great Expectations,* the setting is Rome in 29 BC, when poets must celebrate the newly triumphant empire or be destroyed. Acker drew her characters from literature, as she frequently does. However, in Roman literature we know the Roman "Cynthia," a lady or courtesan whose actual name was Hostia, through the elegies of Propertius. In the second act of *Birth of the Poet,* the point of view belongs to Cynthia, here a raucous and distraught whore.

The assault on the audience is textual. The obscene dialog (which included stage directions) was not matched by correspondingly obscene images. Cynthia and Propertius are engaged in a struggle: each wants to satisfy sexual desire without losing power. At first Cynthia is in control, "pisses on Propertius" (a read stage direction), and thinks the best solution to the problem of men would be a "wife with a cock." He brags he wants only "split open red and black pussy" without a woman attached, but begs at her "little cunt door" and weakly refuses to make decisions. She gives him an ultimatum—sex now: "I've only got five minutes," and "I want it. Flesh is it" (Acker 1987).

A soliloquy of frantic fucking follows, Cynthia celebrating with such lines as, "Sex is public The streets made themselves for us to walk naked down them Take out your cock and piss over me." Propertius leaves her and she is furious. "A twelve-year-old syphilitic named Janey Smith should wrap her cunt around that prick I hate." Now in abject desire she reapproaches Propertius but he has turned against the "open cunt" and will have nothing to do with her.

Acker constructs Cynthia as an animal, first a "raging blonde leopard," then a dog. She is on the "street of dogs," even barking like one (again, a read stage direction), and whining, "I can't help myself anymore I'm just a girl." She "lies down on the street and sticks razor blades up her arms." "I am only an obsession. . . . Do you think I exist?"

In the final scene, titled "On the Nature of Art," Propertius has no more interest in the "goddamn sluts," indeed he has become an utter pornographer. Angela Carter writes,

> [In] pornography [. . .] the self is reduced to its formal elements [. . .] the probe and the fringed hole [. . .] the biological symbols scrawled on the subway poster and the urinal wall (1978:4).

"Take the hole I slept with last night," growls this far from elegiac Propertius. "Sure she moaned hard when I stuck my dick in her. But did she have any idea that I didn't feel?" His only love now is art, gendered female. "Art, you are the black hole of vulnerability." Following the known facts of Propertius's life, Acker has his patron Maecenas make a plea for socially responsible art, but Propertius belongs to a new next generation. To him, art is the "elaborating of violence" and violence is desire. "Desire violence will never stop." The birth of the (male) poet is complete.

Like Cynthia taking to the streets, Acker's language scandalously leaves the privacy of print for the publicly witnessed theatre. Though I had previously read the Acker novel, hearing this language from the stage was an uncomfortable experience, but confusing as well, because the visual production took no notice of it. In an experiment in nonhierarchical stage production, the artistic principals in this undertaking proceeded in their

4. Jan Leslie Harding as Cynthia in The Birth of the Poet *in BAM's 1985 Next Wave Festival. (Photo by Beatriz Schiller)*

disciplines without prior consultation, the only common ground being that all male collaborators had read the Acker text. I almost suspected a conspiracy to keep the unruly Cynthia off the streets and the playwright off the stage, shouting to be heard over the Gordon music, struggling to be seen through the abstract Foreman staging, overwhelmed by the outsize banality of the Salle designs, and finally silenced by the press, where only one critic—Erika Munk of *The Village Voice*—discussed the language and its effect: "I was *upset*. I hadn't heard a woman's voice saying these things. So much the better" (1985:120). I shared Munk's mixed feelings. Acker made me queasy, her out-of-control, lust-ridden, ultimately pathetic Cynthia is a degrading stereotype of woman run amok. But there was also something exhilarating about the obscene force of the text, even if unrealized by the production.

The Birth of the Poet appeared to set into competition two types of theatrical experiment, one social (the testing of female authorial limits in the theatre: how much offense would an obscene text by a female writer be permitted to give); the other structural or formal (the noncoordination of creative elements). Later I wondered whether the first experiment was inhibited by the second. Would a male-authored obscene text have operated on the imaginations of the male collaborators as a form of permission rather than as a signal for control? Did Acker's male collaborators in effect identify with the Propertius side of the play's "birth trauma"? In both cases, it could be argued that male poetry was "born" at the price of female repression.

Prometheus Project

In December 1985, Richard Schechner's *Prometheus Project* was staged at the Performing Garage, the performance space he founded during the avant-garde theatrical explosion of the '60s. Like *Dead End Kids* and *The Birth of the Poet,* the *Prometheus Project* was about apocalypse: its central image was the link between Promethean fire and the destruction of Hiroshima.

The piece was assembled with the combination of quotation, improvisation, and mixed media that has become the familiar idiom of New York performance. However, its second episode put this piece in a category of its own. This episode, containing a clear example of pornography in Dworkin's sense of woman-as-whore, was given over to the "Renaissance woman of porn," 42nd Street burlesque and porno-film star, former prostitute, porn photographer, and porn magazine editor—Annie Sprinkle. Sprinkle had previously appeared in *Deep Inside Porn Stars* at Franklin Furnace.

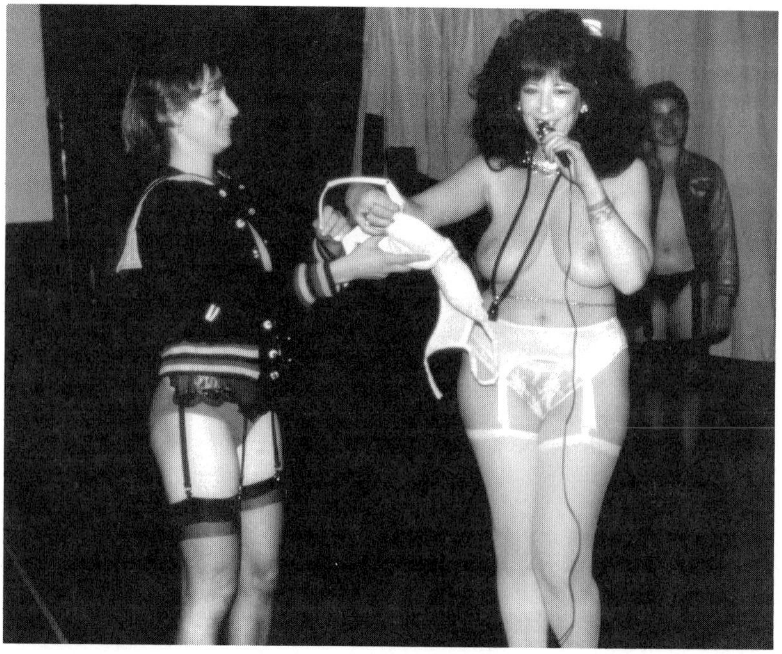

5. *Annie Sprinkle (right) as a school nurse, conducting her "show and tell" sex education class in* The Prometheus Project *at the Performing Garage, December 1985. (Photo by Leslie Barany)*

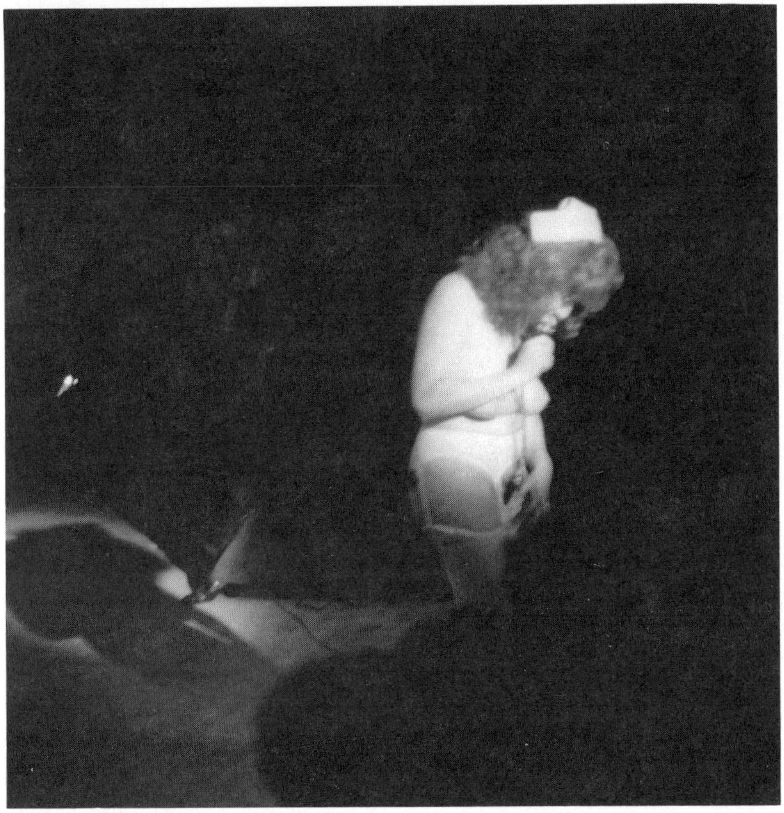

6. Sprinkle invites interested spectators to examine her labia with a magnifying glass and describe their texture and color. (Photo by Leslie Barany)

Sprinkle's show-within-a-show was framed by an onstage audience of four masturbators in trenchcoats, hands in pockets, sitting in for a burlesque house audience. In the first and most elaborate of four scenes, Sprinkle appears in a school nurse uniform and conducts a "show and tell" sex education class, stripping as she goes along. Audience members are invited to touch her nipples, then put their heads between her breasts and describe the feeling. I shared Gerald Rabkin's perception, recorded in *Performing Arts Journal,* that the rhapsodic male responses to Sprinkle's breasts were a "macho pose of knowledgeability" layered over a "general embarrassment" (1986:24). Embarrassment deepens as Sprinkle asks any interested spectator to shine a flashlight at her genitals, examine them with a magnifying glass, and describe their texture and color. Only males volunteer.

This is a moment I won't easily forget in the theatre: Sprinkle's smiling face and robust, cooing voice, her very white and soft body largely exposed, encouraging a spectator to scrutinize and describe her labia. I shrink back from the spectacle in my seat, filled with rage at Schechner, who is submitting me and other women to this *assault on our bodies* via this alien medium, this . . . who is she? Is she a woman like me? Does she smile because she enjoys this or smile because she is encoded by pornography to convince men she "enjoys" this? The act becomes more threatening still when Sprinkle offers to "give a little demonstration of cock sucking." By now blind to objective critical judgment, whatever that might be in such a case, I feel violated and furious at my entrapment here. (The seating configuration of the Performing Garage adds an element of coercion, as it is impossible to recapture our autonomy and walk out of the theatre without crossing the playing area.) When there are no volunteers, Sprinkle starts to demonstrate on a dildo. Interrupted by the actor playing the MC, Sprinkle returns in a traditional burlesque costume to perform a strip act, singing "I'll Fuck Anything that Moves."

Sprinkle goes on to a slide show. One slide wittily poses the Empire State Building, 1,475 feet high, next to an enormous erect prick, representing the number of feet of cock Sprinkle has sucked in her career. Then Sprinkle shows a slide of pie graphics whose "pornstistics" demonstrate that the advantages of Sprinkle's earning capacity in the sex industry ($3,000 a week) "seemed to far outweigh the disadvantages." The last segment shows Sprinkle masturbating on a film loop, one of the many she has made for the peep-show market, with a male voice-over, added by Schechner, directing her moves. But because Sprinkle has already revealed herself as a forceful personality, this doesn't quite give the impression of male exploitation (Sprinkle "spoken" by pornographic codes) that may have been intended.

A subtheme to the Prometheus-Hiroshima line in the piece developed out of the myth of Io, the priestess whom Zeus raped and turned into a cow. In the myth, Io is forced to roam the earth to avoid jealous Hera's stinging gadflies. At the end of her act, Sprinkle put on a cow mask and introduced the Io sequence, the third part of the performance. Here young women similarly masked ran back and forth, stopping to testify to their personal experiences of sexual abuse. The Io story was used to provide a link, also made by Akalaitis, between nuclear aggression and female sexual oppression.

Once during her performance, and again at the end of her sequence, Sprinkle gazed long and accusingly at the audience. Enter: the Gaze. I distantly thought then, and have subsequently confirmed, that the director was interested in the exchange of gazes this performance entailed. Ours at her, hers at us, ours at the little trenchcoated porn audience gazing at her, etc. To me this looked more like an effort to put a feminist "spin" on the routines than to actually explore the role of the spectator's gaze in the performance. In a telephone conversation, Schechner told me that it was Sprinkle's own sophisticated play with the gazing male in the nurse act—her distancing or "deconstruction" of pornography—noted by his performance class on their field visit to the Triple Treat theatre on 42nd Street where Sprinkle performed her nurse show—that attracted him to Sprinkle's work in the first place. And in a paper describing the performance as the "hit of the piece," Schechner writes about the toying with the spectator's view as a sophisticated distancing device: "At each increment of sexual opportunity, Sprinkle interviews the spectator—asking him [sic] to describe what he sees, or how he feels. This automatically distances the action from its own sexual possibilities—making it antiporn porn, or a send-up of porn" (1987:18).[4]

Who and what is being distanced? Is my spectatorship, or any female spectatorship, included in this "automatic distancing"? The "sexual possibilities" that hurt me here are not those the director has in mind, but the visual rape and sexual objectification of my body by identification. I become the Grace Paley of this performance: I cannot subsume it in a self-referential play of ironies. Any theorization of the Gaze, and the more discriminating in a sense the worse, seems to me utterly anemic compared to the crush of gender, class, and performance issues brought down by this performance.

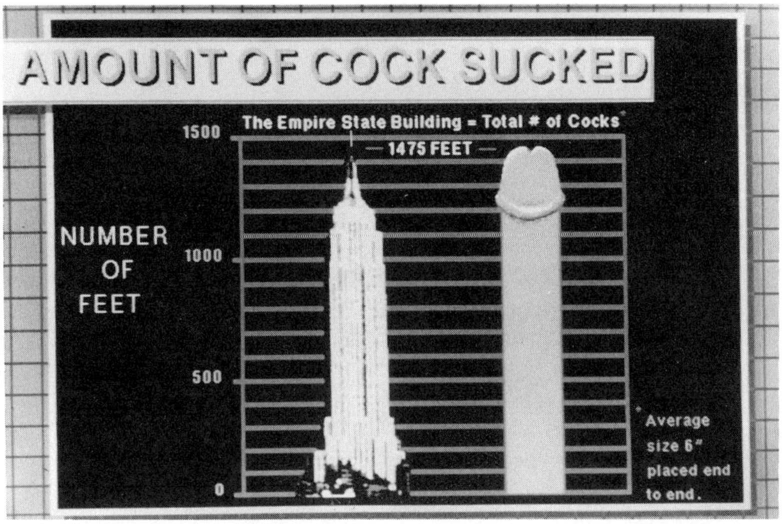

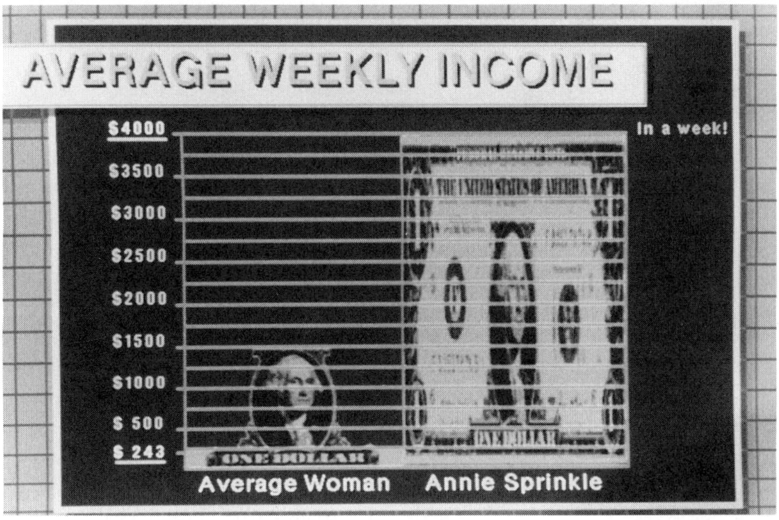

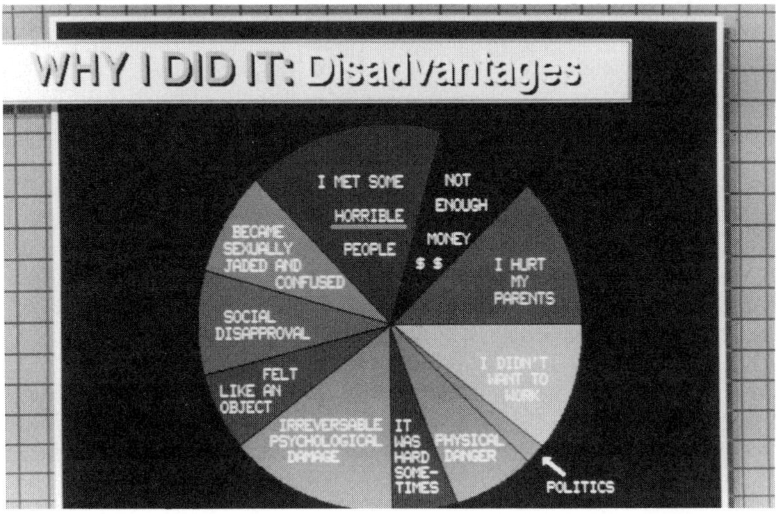

7., 8. & 9. Sprinkle's slide show in The Prometheus Project, *December 1985. (Photos and graphics by Annie Sprinkle)*

10. Nurse Sprinkle among the audience. A woman (partly obscured) reaches for Sprinkle's breast. (Photo by Leslie Barany)

For more than 20 years, Schechner has been a leading theoretician of experimental theatre. He explained the Sprinkle appearance as a kind of satyr play on the Io theme. Critics (all except the writer from *Screw* magazine) fell in with this classicism, and treated the Sprinkle episode with amused condescension, as a diversion from Schechner's serious theme. However, Schechner's interest in pornography and performance was expressed as early as 1966 in an essay, "Pornography and the New Expression," where he speculated that both the live body of the performer and the social nature of theatre, which includes the audience's concern about the actor, makes theatre much less pornographizable, to coin a term, than fiction and film (1970:110–11). Two decades later, Schechner may have been interested in testing the limits of those restrictions, introducing an abrasive "porn modernism" to make the alternative theatre audience rethink theatre's boundaries. Our comfortable status as theatre patrons was shaken by our transformation into peep show and burlesque hall voyeurs.

I considered making this performance a counterexample in my catalog. The male director here controlled the theatrical experience, and male pleasure had governed Sprinkle's creation of her work in the first place. And yet. I was not prepared to take away Annie Sprinkle's voice and deny her female authorship, for this was her material. Also, I could not be blind to my own class discomfort: what was this 42nd Street venue doing invading my performance space?

Despite my turbulence, or perhaps as a deeper cause of it, I became aware again of a disturbing ambivalence, an effect also stirred in different ways by LeCompte and Acker. My problem was, if Sprinkle represented a female "other," she was also not "other" enough. This was not taking place in a barn of a burlesque hall with an elevated stage, where I might fade into the balcony (as I did once in Boston), and become an invisible or masqueraded spectator of a separate male culture with its different kind of female. In this space Sprinkle had entered my world. She was telling me she had made a pretty good bargain in life. She was pushing me to think her as self-respecting worker rather than as victim who could be disposed of by my condescending "pity." Porn magazines edited and published by Sprinkle were displayed at the ticket desk as one entered, evidence of Sprinkle's enterprise in extending her product to a new market. Sprinkle represented herself as independent businesswoman (the theme, incidentally, of the feminist filmmaker Lizzie Borden's feature, *Working Girls,* released within a few weeks of the Performing Garage performance), as subject, as "I" rather than as Io, the abused woman. She made herself undismissable.

Karen Finley

My chronology ends with a number of performances in which female performers such as Karen Finley, Lydia Lunch, Johanna Went, the duo Dancenoise, and others have been exploring a disturbing range of obscenity and scatalogical references. I will discuss briefly only the work of the notorious Karen Finley, who creates a theatre of disgust filled with obscene fantasies. The self of the typical Finley performance is a toxic landfill of throwaway bodies and cynical or psychotic voices, an emblematic figure from the "excremental culture" of the Kroker/Cook "postmodern scene" (1986). Nothing could be farther from Carolee Schneemann's celebration of feminine sexuality a quarter-century ago than Finley's despoiled universe.

I have seen one Finley piece on tape, and three other more recent performances live. This later work may be less raw and offensive visually than the work that created the Finley legend—we don't see her abuse her body anymore—but the texts are filled with abusive, nauseous obscenity. Like Acker in fiction, Finley has been both hailed as an anarchic new female voice on the stage and dismissed as a sick young woman who has "bought into" oppressive male stereotypes. She caused riots in Rotterdam, was closed down in London, and was the subject of an explosively controversial cover feature by C. Carr in *The Village Voice* (1986).

She first became known for her performances on the East Village club circuit in 1979. Her solo performances take the form of discontinuous first-person narratives which alternate a controlled rage with strident, chaotic trances. Sometimes these riffs begin politically: for instance, "LET ME TELL YOU ABOUT PARANOIA. Sixty percent of the world's commercial fish stocks are in danger." But shortly such an opening will slide into excremental fantasies, then a gang rape, then mayhem: "Until they discover my secret of being born without a vagina. They throw me onto the train tracks with their embarrassment and the train rolls over me" (1988:145).

Finley closes her eyes, seems to enter an interior space, and utters forth fragments of stories whose themes are incest, child abuse, rape, torture, death, patricide, along with stories that have the ring of truth—an abortion perhaps, or the known suicide of her father. In earlier performances she would smear garbage over herself, a legacy of her relationship with Brian Routh, one of the Kipper Kids. In *I'm an Assman* (which I saw only on

11. Karen Finley in her I Like to Smell the Gas Passed from Your Ass *routine at the Cat Club in New York, 1986. (Photo by Dona Ann McAdams)*

tape), she poured dog food, cream, and other condiments over her low-necked, ruffled, '50s party dress. In past performances documented by Carr, she actually put yams up her ass on stage; once she performed while periodically emptying her diarrhetic guts into an onstage bucket (1986:17–19).

Finley creates a mass of characters who erupt in jerky schizoid fragments. Stories trail off in midsentence. There are no finished narratives, and more important, as in Acker's fiction, there are no finished narrators: the mutating "I" is in turn woman, man, parent, child, all finding their level in the subterranean miasma of sexual abuse and numbing excess that begins virtually in utero. One such sequence in her 1986 *The Constant State of Desire* opens, "My first sexual experience occurred at the time of my

12. Finley putting yams up her ass on stage during Yams Up My Granny's Ass *at The World, a New York club, in 1986. (Photo by Dona Ann McAdams)*

birth, passing through the vaginal canal." This evolves into two deep incest trances, the first in which a son sucks "my own cum juice outta my own mama's ass," and the second in which a five-year-old's father puts her naked into a refrigerator and "starts working my little hole" with carrots, zucchini, etc. (1988:147–48).

Carr reports near-riots during Finley's club performances in which excited men threw lighted cigarettes at her, dropped their pants or yelled "Whore" (1986:18). In my limited exposure to Finley I felt sickened, but not menaced, probably because she did not threaten to violate her own body. Finley's recent *A Suggestion of Madness* uses other performers, has begun to acquire a theatrical shape and a conspicuously feminist and analytic edge. The most chaotic of her performances may be in the past.

II

> *For, if that view [from "elsewhere"] is nowhere to be seen, not given in a single text, not recognizable as a representation, it is not that we—feminists, women—have not yet succeeded in producing it. It is, rather, that what we have produced is not recognizable, precisely, as a representation.*
>
> —*Teresa de Lauretis (1987:25)*

There is something menacing about this aggregation of marginalia, increasingly so in the later examples, something that stirs a sort of vertigo, as if all the moral categories were beginning to slide. This experience may be Georges Bataille's "crack in the system," the shattering of individual unity he says occurs when the erotic boils up, as in the exposure to pornography (1986:105). In a discussion of Bataille's theories of erotic transgression, Susan Rubin Suleiman writes that this "slipping" of the limits of the self occurs as one senses that a violation has taken place: "Indeed, it is precisely by and through its transgression that the force of a prohibition becomes fully realized" (1986:120). Two apparently different issues can be pursued from Bataille's lead. The first relates to stage practice, the second to gender.

In her important, post-Bataille meditation on literary pornography, "The Pornographic Imagination," Susan Sontag places its effect of "psychic dislocation" within the transgressive tradition of modern art, which has measured its advance through the "dialectic of outrage" (1981:145). Perhaps in these performances theatre is making another of its periodic lunges at the limits of theatrical discourse, an extension of Ubu's historic "Shitr!" The "dirty" performance of Times Square hustles in on the "advanced" "art" of the "experimental" theatre. Such a theatre/class argument acknowledges that theatre is still a preserve of the "slow and unsexy," as Wallace Shawn said in a recent interview, and that it still has the ability to protect its middle-class identity in bourgeois culture, ruling out contamination by the lower elements of burlesque and peep show (in Savran 1988:220). Akalaitis's lowlife nightclub scene is preceded by, among other elements, a scene from part 1 of Goethe's *Faust,* and LeCompte's fellatio scene rubs shoulders with the "classic," very clean, very middle-class *Our Town.* Sprinkle's porn routines take their place next to Beckett and Prometheus. (The class argument would explain, for instance, why Finley's earlier work in the clubs was more incendiary than her work at the Kitchen, a halfway house between the clubs and the theatre.)

So there may be an important element of transgression against the still "legitimate" theatre in these performances. It is the intrusion itself that makes us aware, following Suleiman, that theatre still has firmer boundaries than film or fiction. Yet to receive these performances as merely uncomfortable exhibits of an "avant-garde" practice is itself too comfortable. Art-cultural theory can't help us to resolve the crucial issue: what *value* (besides shock value) to place upon obscenity and pornography in these theatrical contexts. One might use the theory of a Renato Poggioli or a Peter Bürger on avant-garde to "account" for these performances, yet never refer to the fact that they represent a body of women's work in the theatre. Returning again to Bataille's "crack in the system," maybe the question here should be, what "system" is being cracked? Bataille may have had in mind the phallomorphic organization of male subjectivity, threatened with a loss of boundaries and self-mastery. But for the female theatre directors, writers, performers, and female spectators of these performances—and for me—the "system" under stress may be not this selfsame, centered subject, but its distorted "other," the riven female subject that porn constructs.

At this intersection I locate the heart of my discomfort. The ambivalence I experience within and about this work, my sense of danger as a "good" female spectator, results from a crack in *this* system: the systematic division of women into opposed sexual pools, and the replication of that division in an elaborated system of values within each female consciousness. I am helped to see this by an article in *Enclitic* written by Jacquelyn Zita. In a discussion of film pornography she points out that the "pornographic apparatus" constructs two female populations, one to service the fantasies and "secret realities" of male dominion over women, the other "ignorant" and "purified," each operating as a "necessary condition" to keep the system in place. "It is often 'good' women who do the work of separating themselves from female sex workers and maintaining an aura of purity and goodness for themselves" (1987:39). Historian Gerda Lerner sees this systematic division as the controlling condition of female socialization.

> The division of women into "respectable women," who are protected by their men, and "disreputable women," who are out in the street unprotected by men, and agree to sell their services, has been the basic class division for women. It has marked off the limited privileges of upper-class women against the economic and sexual oppression of lower-class women and has divided women from one another. Historically it has impeded cross-class alliances among women and obstructed the formation of feminist consciousness (1986:139).

This fundamental binary division is echoed in the feminist debate over pornography. In an overview of books by women on feminine sexuality and pornography in *Feminist Studies,* B. Ruby Rich writes that the discussion of pornography "still hovers between two inadequate definitions: either a conscious degradation of women, ideologically aligned with misogyny and psychologically linked to actual violence against women, or one of the few expressions of explicit sexuality in a repressive culture" (1986:540–41). The irreconcilability of the terms of female socialization may underlie Mary Ann Doane's despair that "No true feminist theory of pornography [. . .] can be constructed" (1984:53).

I don't assume that the artists here consciously worked to break down this division. In fact, Schechner's *Prometheus Project* functioned to sustain and restate it by pouring Sprinkle and the young women in the show into the mold of Io, who is cruelly punished for her sexual transgressions by the powerful, respectably married Hera. Nevertheless, each in a different way, the performances I have been considering defy the "system" by undecidably intertwining ideologically and iconically opposed female representations. The "good" female subjectivity of the ordered libido and separated boundaries (the woman of autonomy, authority, authorship) slides into the "bad" woman of pornographic male fantasy (the woman of infinite compliance, who pants with desire, who is really, secretly, a "whore").

In an apt performance, perhaps parody, of this division, Annie Sprinkle and sister porn artist Veronica Vera, who now call themselves "feminist porn activists," opened their segment of the Kitchen's February 1988 *Car-*

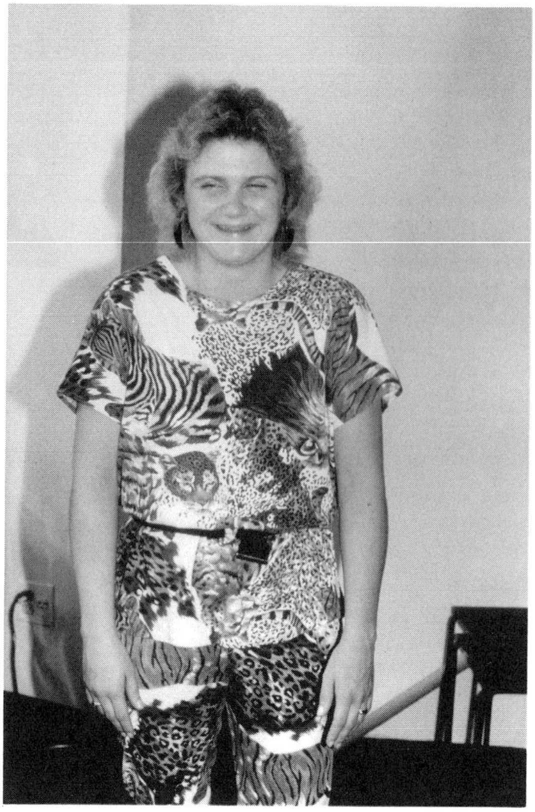

Plates 13. & 14.

nival of Sleaze with a series of "transformation" slides. The slides displayed Sprinkle, Vera, and many other women not associated with the sex industry in alternative poses, first in family or other "clean" roles, then as sex queens. Performance artist Linda Montano was shown in a flashy sex costume; Sprinkle came forward in demure dress under her given name, Ellen Steinberg. Played before a mixed, nonburlesque audience in value-free deadpan, the sequence was a kind of dare to the "good girl" female spectator, if not exactly to enter the sex trade, to examine her own self-division. The female spectator, who energetically defends herself against being projected into a role as the "other" of male fantasy, is shown an

Before and After

Annie Sprinkle

I have been in the sex business for 14 years as a porn star, centerfold model, and most recently as a photographer. (Photography pays the best.)

I've always been fascinated by the dramatic transformation a model took when she came onto the set "a regular person" and was turned into a "sex goddess." All it took was makeup, lighting, a garter belt, some high high heels, a little attitude change, and some decent photography. I personally experienced the transformation when photographers made me look more glamorous and sexy than I ever dreamed possible. It was wonderfully liberating and healing. It helped me get over lots of shyness and insecurity.

Now as a photographer, I get to transform "regular people" into "sex stars." The photos you see here, and others like them, were taken for, and published in, various sex magazines—without the before pictures, of course. Some of the models were professional nude models, and many were amateurs who won a Girl Next Door Photo Contest and would be flown to New York, all expenses paid, for their fantasy come true—a studio shooting. (I prefer shooting the amateurs because the transformation is always more dramatic.) I got into the habit of taking a snapshot of how they looked when they arrived at my studio, so I could marvel their change.

Feminists are always arguing that sex magazines should not glamorize women and make them look "perfect," because very few women can live up to that *Playboy* centerfold image. Thus women are unsatisfied and insecure about their own bodies, and men are wondering why their lovers don't look like pinups. But as you can see clearly here, even the pinups don't really look like pinups. So as a feminist myself I say let's NOT STOP glamorizing women. Let's make them all look glamorous and sexy. Give all women a studio photography shooting with a good makeup artist!

I do not judge whether the before or the after photo of each model makes her look better. I think they are equally beautiful and sexy in both.

Maybe there's a little porn star in you. Maybe not. But I can tell you from experience . . . there's a lot of you in every porn star.

image of her own replication of that pattern, her cooperation with it, in her own deepest terror of being contaminated by the other side of female life. Here she is caught before men with her "other" showing (her other "other").

In an essay on *Histoire d'O,* Kaja Silverman writes that pornography is "a discourse that dramatizes with unusual clarity the disjunction between the speaking (male) subject and the spoken (female) subject" (1985:327). If the obscene imagery and texts show the fascination of its makers with woman as constituted in male pornographic discourse, the performances in context also project a speaking female subject. This was not at first easy for me to see in performance, for this inching together of opposed feminine categories is more a groping symptom of cultural change than an aesthetic or political program in these performances. But it is happening anyhow in these female texts, or intertexts, even when the concerns of the overall performance are not feminist. Ironically, where a conscious attempt was made to use some feminist theory in the *Prometheus Project* (Mulvey et al. on the Gaze), the masculinist assumptions of the production—the central agony of Prometheus, the unexamined implications of the Io myth, and Schechner's simple delight in Sprinkle as a "hit" performer—also made this the most problematic of my examples.

What poet, in *The Birth of the Poet,* is being born? Acker's narrative leads from Cynthia's sexual insatiability to her abasement and humiliation to the triumph of the male Word. The male poet is born out of female desire, perfected by frustrating that desire. But Acker's obscene "graffiti writing" scrawls over the tradition of Roman elegiac writing and allows Propertius's voiceless Cynthia to yell her head off (see Hulley forthcoming). No longer will the artist's model pose. The last section of Acker's obscene second act (titled "On the Nature of Art") virtually exposes the male artist's fetishization of art as a form of sexual dysfunction.

In each of the performances, this double strain can be traced. Finley's images are fished from the very depths of pornography, often violent and deviant pornography, but, in Jill Dolan's acute analysis, "she revises the power balance in traditional pornography [. . .] by claiming sexual power for herself to wield" (1988:67). Unlike Finley, who deliberately turns off male appetite by presenting all sexual exchange on a closed, interior circuit, Sprinkle enthusiastically offers herself as a sexual commodity. At the same time Sprinkle presents herself as manager, controlling her own body-as-business and enjoying her success. All three performances suggest a certain exhilaration, a sense of "mastery" in being on both sides of the production of obscenity, simultaneously its object and author.

The same two lines can be traced in Akalaitis and LeCompte. They overwrite male texts and expose their hidden assumptions, de-idealize the male canon, ironically recycle forgotten sexist or racist performance forms as social critique. While they subvert male-speak they also try on the male gaze. Akalaitis does this through the persona of the nightclub comedian, whose scene with the young woman appears at first to cross the border between subversion and imitation. Similarly, in her more ambiguous affair with porn, LeCompte experiments with the male position of voyeur. But LeCompte stresses that she was not deliberately assuming an inscribed position. "I don't know what porn is, and I'm attracted to things I don't understand well. I've never been able to put my reactions to porn together with a political stance" (1988).

Witnessing these performances in "my" theatres, thinking about and writing this article, I have felt some ancient resistance give, perhaps not to oppressive pornography in Dworkin's sense, which I regard as harmful to women, but to images which, in an earlier period, I would have rejected as dangerously invading me and leading me toward that harm. These performances exposed (Suleiman's comment on Bataille) the privileged and protected social circumstances of most theatre. The violation of theatrical norms, presumably experienced by all spectators, was offensive without being politically or theoretically combustive. The disturbance, the risky melting into each other of the polar conventions of patriarchal female representation, was for me the greater violation. I was forced to see the "crack" in the patriarchal system of female socialization and in my own socially conditioned, deeply inscribed mental formations—literally to confront this abyss in the cracks of the female body.

The two leads I took from Bataille—into theatre practice and into gender—could be seen as a single construction. Both women's bodies and the theatre have traditionally been sites of prohibition, subject to "prophylactic" separations of the clean from the dirty. Indeed, distaste for the theatre has often been couched in terms of fear of the female body. In *The Anti-Theatrical Prejudice,* Jonas Barish's theatrophobes, from the Romans to Prynne, to Rousseau, to Nietzsche, all attack theatrical performance itself (whether performed by women or not) as inherently lewd and "feminine" (1981:42–44, 85, 227, 237, 271, 303, 409). Misogyny appears always to have played a role in the periodic closings or regulations of the theatre. In *The Politics and Poetics of Transgression* (1986), Peter Stallybrass and Allon White discuss the creation of the modern bourgeois theatre in sexual terms. After the reopening of the theatres in 1660, playwrights such as Dryden, Southerne, and Cibber conducted a campaign to socialize audiences to new standards of decorum in the theatres. By the turn of the century the space of theatre was being decisively severed "from the market of sexual liaison," and converted into a "systematically scoured" and "idealized space of consciousness." The 18th-century theatre demanded a "sublimated public body without smells, without coarse laughter, without organs" (1986:92–93). That new theatre is now our old theatre, and today it is under pressure by these same bad manners.

Why make a fuss about manners? It is not so surprising that women would play an important role in desocializing the theatre, which has so prejudicially socialized them, but it would be a mistake to dismiss these gestures as an issue of manners. When Fornes' Emma wants to stand in a room discussing her genitals as well as business, she is contemplating an act of political anarchism that, if generally adopted, would lead to the collapse of business, family, and state. If, as Pierre Bourdieu points out, "the concessions of politeness always contain political concessions," then it is also true that a breakdown of accepted behavior is inescapably political (1977:95).[5]

In "The Discourse of Others: Feminists and Postmodernism"—a still somewhat lonely essay given the mistrust so many feminists bring to postmodernism—Craig Owens utters a kind of manifesto that, theatrical metaphor and all, could almost be taken for a comment on the theatre work I have described. It is at "the legislative frontier between what can be represented and what cannot," he writes, "that the postmodernist operation is being staged—not in order to transcend representation, but in order to expose that system of power that authorizes certain representations while blocking, prohibiting or invalidating others" (1983:59). These performances showed me my own complicated positioning in the "system of power" that divides feminine representation.

In blurring the boundary between "good girl" and "bad girl," the theatre of female obscenity I have been discussing is a kind of "repo theatre." It is possible to sense, on contemplating its terms, the source of power the merged signs of female sexual identity would open for women, a self-repossession that would signify the most profound cultural shift. At a programmatic level, some feminists have been working to break down barriers between the two populations of women and their representations. *Caught Looking* performs the merger by making readers look at "dirty" pictures in order to read feminist texts (or encounter feminist texts in order to gaze at dirty pictures). *Good Girls/Bad Girls* documents a conference in

Toronto in which an open dialog between activist feminists and sex trade workers was attempted (see Bell 1987).

The performances I describe are not programmatic. However they do not need to know about "legislative frontiers" to breach them. De Lauretis characterizes the subject of feminism as the discovery of those spaces in the (male-centered) representation of gender "that representation leaves out or, more pointedly, makes unrepresentable." The semiotic merger would open up one of de Lauretis's "space-offs" in the representation of gender, a film term acknowledging a space already here within the terms of a particular representation, yet "not recognizable, precisely, as a representation" (1987:25–26). It is still virtually impossible to think "heterosexual woman" without sex/class polarities, no matter how sublimated and masked such a crude division has become in an apparently liberal society. The performances I have described seem to me to be working at the edges of the sexual "space-off," seeking through contradiction to find the unrepresented but present terms of a new construction.

Notes

1. Though the text of *Dead End Kids* appeared in *Theater,* the nightclub scene is only acknowledged as an "improvisation" and not printed. The unpublished text is quoted here by permission of David Brisbin.
2. I witnessed this event, which to my knowledge has not been reported elsewhere.
3. When the scene was first presented in 1981, it played entirely in silence. When the production was revived in December 1986, LeCompte added a sparse, intermittent soundtrack which repeated some language spoken earlier by the male actors in the blackface scene.
4. An earlier and slightly different version of the Schechner article here referenced, "Uprooting the Garden: Thoughts around 'The Prometheus Project,' " appeared in *New Theatre Quarterly* (1986).
5. Though it is beyond the scope of the present article, it would be interesting to explore what links might be sustained between the transgressive female of carnival and the transgressive females of the contemporary obscene theatre. In an article modeling such an attempt, "Female Grotesques: Carnival and Theory," Mary Russo draws out from Bakhtin what is only implicit in *Rabelais and His World,* the figure of the female carnivalesque transgressor as a destabilizing force in culture. Russo acknowledges that the Unruly Woman of carnival occupied a "complicitous place in dominant culture," yet also played at least an emblematic role (and here she quotes the work of Natalie Zemon Davis on women and 17th-century European carnival) in the "efforts to change the basic distribution of power within society" (1986:215).

References

Acker, Kathy
1987 *The Birth of the Poet.* In *Word Plays 5,* 305–44. New York: Performing Arts Journal Publications.

Akalaitis, JoAnne
1982 *"Dead End Kids: A History of Nuclear Power." Theater.* (Summer/Fall): 34–42.

Alderfer, Hannah, et al
1988 *Caught Looking.* Seattle, WA: The Real Comet Press.

Barish, Jonas
1981 *The Anti-Theatrical Prejudice.* Berkeley: University of California Press.

Bataille, Georges
1986 "Sexual Plethora and Death." In *Eroticism,* 94–108. San Francisco: City Lights Books.

Bell, Laurie, ed.
1987 *Good Girls/Bad Girls.* Seattle, WA: The Seal Press.

Bourdieu, Pierre
1977 *Outline of a Theory of Practice.* Translated by Richard Nice. Cambridge: Cambridge University Press.

Carnival Knowledge
1984 Press release.

Carr, C.
1986 "Unspeakable Practices, Unnatural Acts: The Taboo Art of Karen Finley." *The Village Voice,* 24 June:17.

Carter, Angela
1978 *The Sadeian Woman and the Ideology of Pornography.* New York: Pantheon.

Collins, William B.
1983 "This Protest of Nuclear Policy is Neither Art Nor Propaganda." *Philadelphia Inquirer,* 25 February, sec. C:4.

Doane, Mary Ann, et al.
1984 "Excerpts from a Forum on Pornography." *subjects/objects* (Spring):51–61.

Dolan, Jill
1988 *The Feminist Spectator as Critic.* Ann Arbor, MI: U.M.I. Research Press.

Dworkin, Andrea
1981 *Pornography: Men Possessing Women.* New York: G.P. Putnam's Sons.

Finley, Karen
1988 "The Constant State of Desire." *TDR* 32, no. 1 (T117):139–51.

Fornes, Maria Irene
1980 *Fefu and Her Friends.* In *Word Plays,* 5–41. New York: Performing Arts Journal Publications.

Fuchs, Elinor
1980 "Too Late for Kidding." *The Soho News,* 19 November.

Hulley, Kathleen
forthcoming "Transgressing Genre: Kathy Acker's Intertext." In *Intertextuality and Contemporary American Fiction.* Baltimore, MD: Johns Hopkins University Press.

Kroker, Arthur, and David Cook
1986 *The Postmodern Scene: Excremental Culture and Hyper-Aesthetics.* New York: Oxford University Press.

de Lauretis, Teresa
1987 *Technologies of Gender.* Bloomington: Indiana University Press.

LeCompte, Elizabeth
1988 Interviews with author, New York.

Lerner, Gerda
1986 *The Creation of Patriarchy.* New York: Oxford University Press.

Munk, Erika
1985 "Cross Left." *The Village Voice,* 17 December:117.

Owens, Craig
1983 "The Discourse of Others: Feminists and Postmodernism." In *The Anti-Aesthetic,* edited by Hal Foster, 57–82. Port Townsend, WA: Bay Press.

Rabkin, Gerald, et al.
1986 "The Controversial 1985–6 Theatre Season: A Politics of Reception." *Performing Arts Journal* 10, no. 1(PAJ28):7–33.

Rich, B. Ruby
1986 "Feminism and Sexuality in the 1980's." *Feminist Studies* 12, no. 3 (Fall):525–61.

Russo, Mary
1986 "Female Grotesques: Carnival and Theory." In *Feminist Studies/ Critical Studies,* edited by Teresa de Lauretis, 213–29. Bloomington: Indiana University Press.

Savran, David
1988 "Wallace Shawn." In *In Their Own Words: Contemporary American Playwrights,* 207–22. New York: Theatre Communications Group.

Schechner, Richard
1970 "Pornography and the New Expression." In *The Perverse Imagination,* edited by Irving Buchen, 103–14. New York: New York University Press.
1986 "Uprooting the Garden: Thoughts Around 'The Prometheus Project.' " *New Theatre Quarterly* 2 (no. 5):3–11.
1987 "Uprooting the Garden: Thoughts Around 'The Prometheus Project.' " Unpublished manuscript.

Schneemann, Carolee
1979 *More Than Meat Joy.* Edited by Bruce McPherson. New York: Documentext.

Silverman, Kaja
1985 "*Histoire d'O,* Construction of a Female Subject." In *Pleasure and Danger: Exploring Female Sexuality,* edited by Carole S. Vance, 320–49. London: Routledge & Kegan Paul.

Soble, Alan
1986 *Pornography: Marxism, Feminism and the Future of Sexuality.* New Haven, CT: Yale University Press.

Sontag, Susan
1981 "The Pornographic Imagination." In *Styles of Radical Will,* 35–73. New York: Delta.

Stallybrass, Peter, and Allon White
1986 *The Politics and Poetics of Transgression.* Ithaca, NY: Cornell University Press.

Suleiman, Susan Rubin
1986 "Pornography and the Avant-Garde." In *The Poetics of Gender,* edited by Nancy K. Miller, 117–36. New York: Columbia University Press.

Zita, Jacquelyn N.
1987 "Pornography and the Male Imaginary." *Enclitic* 9 (nos. 1–2):28–44.

Elinor Fuchs *is a New York theatre critic who contributes frequently to* The Village Voice *and has published numerous articles on dramatic theory and criticism in such journals as* Performing Arts Journal, American Theatre, Theater Three, *and* Comparative Drama. *Her books include the award-winning documentary play* Year One of the Empire, *produced in 1980, and* Plays of the Holocaust: An International Anthology. *She is on the faculty of the Department of Theatre and Film Studies of Emory University in Atlanta.*

Desire Cloaked in a Trenchcoat

Jill Dolan

"Desire Cloaked in a Trenchcoat" is maybe a corny image to inform an investigation of pornography, performance, and spectators. But the man sitting alone in a darkened theatre masturbating under his coat while staring at the screen is an image engraved on our collective imagination. Male arousal by pictures is an accepted part of dominant cultural discourse.

The provocative relationship between sexuality and representation is revealed perhaps most blatantly in pornography. Pornography is an important locus for feminist critical thought because it provides a site for the intersection of feminist sexual politics and the politics of representation.

Whether you are for or against pornography, or straddle the anticensorship fence with "First Amendment" painted on it, pornography has to be dealt with as representation. As Susanne Kappeler points out in *The Pornography of Representation,* "Representation is not so much the means of representing an object through imitation (that is, matching contents) as a means of self-representation through authorship: The expression of subjectivity" (1986:53). Antiporn feminists condemning pornography as both image and educator of male violence against women look for a match of contents by equating pornography and reality.[1] But pornography is more than simple mimesis. As representation, it helps to construct subject positions that maintain the strict gender divisions on which the culture operates.

The subject/object relations delineated by pornography are also paradigmatic of those structured by representation in general. Feminist film and performance critics argue that representation is addressed to the gaze of the male spectator. He is invited to identify with the active male protagonist portrayed in the narrative through voyeuristic and fetishistic viewing conventions. The male spectator shares in the pleasure of the hero's quest to fulfill his desire for the story's passively situated female (see de Lauretis 1984, Kaplan 1983, Mulvey 1975).

If all representation is structured by male desire, then sexuality is as integral a part of constructing spectator subjectivity in a Shakespeare production at Stratford as it is in live sex shows in Times Square. Any representation can be seen as essentially pornographic, since the structure of gendered relationships through which it operates is based on granting men subjectivity while denying it to women.

Kantian aesthetics propose that the only way to contemplate a work of art is through a certain detachment from reality. Disengagement allows the art work a separate, "objective" existence and hides the fact of its authorship within a particular historical moment governed by cultural and economic considerations. Kappeler argues after Kant that the principles of aesthetic distance and disinterestedness motivate pornography as well as art. She suggests that in the peep shows where men masturbate while watching women perform behind glass windows, the goal is not actually to fuck women. Rather, the goal is what she calls the "feeling of life, the pleasure of the subject" derived from aesthetic distance (1986:49–62). Kappeler says that the pornographic representation is even preferable, because it allows the total assertion of a man's subjectivity. Since there is no intersubjective action, the image of the woman behind the glass becomes a screen for the projection of a fantasy over which the male viewer has total control.

In "Bar Wars," written for *Esquire* in November 1986, Bob Greene provides a succinct example of the intersection of sexuality, pornography, and spectatorship on the representational economy. A bar called B.T.'s in Dearborn, Michigan, which usually presents topless female dancing entertainment, also offers what it calls "Rambo Wet Panty Nights." Black plastic Uzi submachine water guns are handed out to the customers. Then a woman—sometimes a regular B.T.'s dancer, sometimes an "amateur" volunteer—mounts the stage dressed in a skimpy T-shirt and underwear and stands covering her eyes and face while the men shoot their water guns at her vagina. Six or seven women perform each evening, and cash prizes are given to the women who do the "best" job of being shot at according to the bar owner's subjective judgments. Greene doesn't describe the critical standards applied (1986:61–62).

This performative exchange is a cultural feminist's nightmare of the conflation of sexuality and violence. But aside from this neat match of contents, it's an overt example of representation proceeding according to a pornographic model. The bar is packed with men drawn by a chance to become Rambo in the flesh. The elements of a prior representation, then, are mapped onto the performance at the bar. Sylvester Stallone and his Rambo movies are missing, but they're implied in the narrative.

In the Rambo films, as in most Vietnam films, the enemy—or the Other—is an Asian race. In the paramilitary ambience of B.T.'s bar, the woman on stage becomes the alien enemy, the Other defined by her difference.[2] The floor manager at B.T.'s encourages the men with guns to think of the woman on stage as Vietnam, or Libya, or even Nicaragua. It's a neat way of eroticizing imperialism and keeping sexuality imperialist.

The men with the Uzis are implicitly identifying with Rambo as they aim, and they experience visual pleasure by projecting their subjective fantasies onto the passive women. One man tells Greene, "I got her. She's hot; I know she likes it. She likes it, and she knows that I know she likes it" (1986:62). But if the woman's eyes were covered, how could this man possibly think the performer was acknowledging and enjoying a spray from his gun, except by fantasizing because he wants it that way?

What do the performers at B.T.'s think about allowing their bodies to be used as substitutes for Third World nations, and becoming screens for projections of male fantasy? One woman tells Greene that "It's a power game." Unlike most, she doesn't cover her eyes when she performs: "I try to look out into the audience and make eye contact with as many of the men with guns as I can. A lot of times, they'll turn away. If a woman looks them in the eye, they'll turn away (1986:62). At issue here is the struggle for subjectivity. These men can't face the intersubjectivity of the woman's gaze. They must maintain the disengagement of desire inspired by the safe aesthetic distance of the representation.

Greene's article, of course, is governed by the exigencies of his own male gaze, and he doesn't mention whether there are women spectators in the bar. But theoretically, where could a woman place herself in relation to this display? How could she position herself in front of a peep show window? The image of a woman sitting in a darkened theatre wearing a trenchcoat is incongruous at best.

Whether or not female spectators can be placed in positions of power that might allow for the objectification of male performers or that might allow for the liberation of both gender classes from the oppressions of the representational gaze is an issue hotly debated in feminist theory. As Kappeler and others have pointed out, simply trading gender positions isn't as easy as it sounds. While women in representation usually signify their gender class, the culturally sanctioned power of male subjectivity makes a similar signification very difficult. Women cannot simply express their subjectivity by objectifying men. A nude male in an objectified position remains an individual man, not necessarily a representative of the male gender class.

For example, Richard Schechner, while pondering these issues, described the activity at several sex clubs in Montreal in which males danced for females as examples of women adopting the male gaze. Schechner says the male dancers

> [. . .] stripped until fully naked. They played with their cocks and displayed the rest of their bodies in a way very parallel to what women do in strip clubs. [. . .] As a new male entered the stage, the dancer who was on stage went from table to table, and danced directly in front of women. The male dancer brought with him a little step stool so that his genitals were face level to the female spectator(s). The women tipped him. There was a lot of flirtation, kissing, and some genital playing (Schechner 1987).

While this situation seems to reverse the traditional paradigm, male sexuality is still active, privileged, and displayed. The women spectators want the male performer to desire them. Similar conditions are implied by female dancers in clubs for male spectators. The female dancers aren't performing their own sexuality—their display implies penile satisfaction, their open legs and wet vaginas imply the possibility of penetration. In both situations, the desire of women spectators or performers is subordinate to male desire.

According to the psychoanalytical model, since male desire drives representation, a female spectator is given two options. She can identify with the active male and symbolically participate in the female performer's objectification, or she can identify with the narrative's objectified female and position herself as an object.

I do not mean to propose a universalism when I use the term "female spectator." For the materialist feminist, women are differentiated along class, race, and sexual orientation lines that make it impossible for them to respond to any image as a unit. Part of the problem with the psychoanalytical model of spectatorship is just this tendency to pose universal "male" and "female" spectators who respond only according to gender. Part of my project here is to suggest that sexuality is as large a part of spectator response as gender, and that by altering the assumed sexuality of spectators, the representational exchange can also be changed.

Mary Ann Doane in *The Desire to Desire* writes, "There is a certain naiveté assigned to women in relation to systems of signification, a tendency to deny the process of representation, to collapse the opposition between the sign (the image) and the real" (1987:1). Women remain part of Lacan's Imaginary realm, completely marginal to the signifying process. Since she cannot separate herself from the image, the female spectator cannot experience the mirror phase through which she might see herself reflected as a separate subject. Because Doane's psychoanalytic reading considers desire as a form of disengagement "crucial to the assumption of the position of the speaking subject" (1987:11), a woman cannot hope to articulate her desire in the representational space.

Since she can assume neither disengagement nor aesthetic distance from the image, she is denied the scopophilic pleasure of voyeurism. Fetishism—which also operates particularly in the cinematic apparatus to provide visual pleasure—is also unavailable to the female spectator, since her ordinary lack dictates that she already has nothing to lose.

Woman as a psychic subject, then, is unarticulated in representation. Doane goes on to propose that women as social subjects are constructed merely as passive consumers invited to buy the idealized, male-generated image of the female body as a commodity displayed in the representational frame.

If the female spectator chooses to accept this passively constructed consumer position, Doane writes, "The mirror/window takes on then the aspect of a trap whereby her subjectivity becomes synonymous with her objectification" (1987:33). Buying the idealized image of herself, she turns herself into a commodity to then be sold, as the performer already has. The positions of the female performer and the female spectator are collapsed into one—they become prostitutes who buy and sell their own image in a male-generated visual economy. They are goods in the representational marketplace, commodities in an exchange by means of which they are both objectified.[3]

The women performing at B.T.'s, for example, are sheer spectacle in a representational exchange constructed for the male gaze. Some of the women admit they do it for the money, prostituting their subjectivity to the demands of the representational space. The owner of B.T.'s, of course, doesn't see it in so mercenary a light. He romanticizes the women's involvement, speculating that they are willing to perform because they come from disturbed backgrounds and need attention—a variation on *A Chorus Line*'s "What I Did for Love."

The idea that specularized, objectified women do it for the love of the male gaze is a concept perpetuated by dominant cultural discourse. In "Confessions of a Feminist Porno Star," printed in a feminist anthology of personal narratives called *Sex Work,* Nina Hartley acquiesces to this view. She says she is an exhibitionist, a woman who is aroused by being looked at. But she also feels she has some control over the production of her image. "In choosing my roles and characterizations carefully," she writes, "I strive to show, always, women who thoroughly enjoy sex and are forceful, self-satisfying and guilt-free without also being neurotic, unhappy, or somehow unfulfilled" (1987:142). Hartley proposes that she can subvert the representational apparatus by adjusting the content of its images and giving the positive, active roles to women.

This is a kind of liberal feminist, matching-contents argument that has been used to justify generating feminist erotica. Some feminists think that if women controlled the means of producing pornography, its representations would be different. But the genderized component of heterosexuality, with its inevitable constant of male desire, problematizes positioning women as the producers or subjects of heterosexual pornography. Heterosexual feminist erotica, such as the magazine *Eidos,* and much feminist performance art indicates that disarming male desire in the representational space requires "feminizing" the represented males or avoiding sexuality as an integral issue. These attempts are for the most part either unsuccessful—since the erect male penis is still a power-filled image even if it's displayed in a feminine, "natural" context—or banal, as sexuality gives way to the obfuscating realm of spirituality (see Dolan 1987:157–61).

Debi Sundahl, in her *Sex Work* essay called "Stripper," acknowledges the subject/object problem inherent in heterosexual representation. Initially, she says,

> The hardest part of the job was dealing with my feminist principles concerning the objectification of women. Dancing nude is the epitome of woman as sex object. As the weeks passed, I found I liked being a sex object, because the context was appropriate. [. . .] I perform to turn you on, and if I fail, I feel I've done a poor job. Women who work in the sex industry are not responsible for, nor do they in any way perpetuate, the sexual oppression of women. In fact, to any enlightened observer, our very existence provides a distinction and a choice as to when a woman should be treated like a sex object and when she should not be. At the theatre, yes; on the street, no (1987:176).

I find this a provocative statement. Sundahl suggests that subject positions on stage can be separated from those assumed in life. But she also suggests that bowing to the demands of objectification in theatre is the only role a woman can play in the heterosexual representational space. Implicit in her argument is the idea that representation is driven by a kind of sexuality in which objectification is constantly assumed. But is all sexuality motivated by objectification? And if not, what might happen to representation if the sexual desire motivating it were different?

There's a twist to Sundahl's story. She is a lesbian; she publishes *On Our Backs,* a lesbian porn magazine; and she started a women-only strip show at Baybrick's, a now-defunct lesbian bar in San Francisco. Sundahl herself makes a distinction between her performance spaces, pointing out that the different cultural mandates of the heterosexual and lesbian contexts make the terms of the performative exchange very different, even if the images used or roles played are the same. Describing the show at Baybrick's, for example, Sundahl writes, "The dancers loved performing for the all-female audiences because they had more freedom of expression. They were not limited to ultrafeminine acts only; they could be butch and dress in masculine attire" (1987:178). In other words, if they wanted to, the performers could assume the subject position rather than objectifying themselves. The butch/femme role play allowed the performers to seduce each other and the lesbian spectators through the constant of lesbian sexuality.

This context allows lesbian desire to circulate as the motivating representational term. The subject/object relations that trap women performers and spectators as commodities in a heterosexual context dissolve. The lesbian subject, according to Monique Witting (1980, 1981) and others, has free range across a gender continuum and, to paraphrase Sue-Ellen Case, her role-playing through a "strategy of appearances" (1987) disrupts the dominant cultural discourse representation mandates. Witting says lesbians are "not women" and not men according to the way these gender roles are culturally constructed (1980:110). Since they are already outside a strictly dichotomized gender context, they are free to pick and choose from both extremes. There are no prostitutes on the lesbian representational economy because the goods have gotten together (see Irigaray 1981).

In *Upwardly Mobile Home,* a production by the lesbian performance troupe Split Britches, Peggy Shaw has a monolog describing her character's trip to see the fat lady at the circus. She says the lights and the posters promised her entertainment, but she got much, much more. When she entered the fat lady's tent, Shaw says, "She knew I had come to see her being fat. She looked at me and I looked at her. I loved that fat lady." Rather than the fight for subjectivity that takes place in B.T.'s heterosexual bar, Shaw's exchange with the fat woman seems paradigmatic of the lesbian viewing experience. The recognition of mutual subjectivity allows the gaze to be shared in a direct way. Shaw tells *Upwardly Mobile Home* spectators, "You have paid to see me"—but the visual economy is now under lesbian control.

Lesbians are appropriating the subject position of the male gaze by beginning to articulate the exchange of desire between women. Lesbian subjectivity creates a new economy of desire. To borrow from Irigaray once again, lesbians "go to the 'market' alone, to profit from their own value, to talk to each other, to desire each other, without the control of the selling-buying-consuming subjects" (1981:110). Rather than gazing through the representational window at their commodification as women, lesbians are generating and buying their own desire on a different representational economy. Perhaps the lesbian subject can offer a model for women spectators that will appropriate the male gaze. The aim is not to look like men, but to look at all.

Epilog

Since reading Teresa de Lauretis's article on lesbian representation (1988), I've been rethinking the issue of desire, and with it, the whole of what Case calls the "psychosemiotic" theoretical endeavor (1988). When I attempt to wrench myself from the psychosemiotic subject considerations that have governed my work on the spectator, and that hinge on the question of desire in representation, I come up with the notion of spectatorial communities. This is where de Lauretis, too, seems to arrive in her exploration of how to represent lesbian differences, how not to reify the lesbian spectator as some new, unbroken, unified idol.

The hint of utopianism that creeps into my thoughts when I write about changing the entrenched gender dynamics of representation comes from my conception of lesbian subjectivit(ies) as one of the most challenging, fruitful areas in this field of investigation. According to the psychosemiotic feminist critical model, of which my argument here makes use, male desire is the variable in the representational exchange that upsets the balance of power, reinforces the gender dichotomy in art and culture, and proscribes heterosexuality as compulsory (see Rich 1983). Male desire is not at all a factor in representations created by lesbians. As a result, the area of lesbian subjectivity seems a place to begin to envision new possibilities for representation.

Shifting my emphasis from the psychological construction of the individual spectator, however, brings me perhaps to a less utopian notion of lesbian spectatorial communities, separated and differentiated by class, race, and ideology. As de Lauretis chastises, changing the shape of desire from heterosexual to lesbian won't get the entire crisis of representation off our backs. There is no universal lesbian spectator to whom each lesbian representation will provide the embodiment of the same lesbian desire. Sexuality, and desire, and lesbian subjects are more complicated than that.

Although I might concede the utopianism of my writing on lesbian desire and am currently working to think within the contradictions, I can't concede or condone what some see as the necessity to "universalize" this model to heterosexual women and men. For instance, Linda Walsh Jenkins mistakenly suggests that "most of the leading [feminist theorists] in the middle '80s are lesbian," and complains that "the heterosexual female position has not been given much attention or articulation" (Chinoy and Jenkins 1987:373). Jenkins fails to acknowledge that heterosexual women are in a more visible, privileged position in the culture than lesbians, and have in fact been given a great deal of attention. The history of theatre and performance studies, as well as its criticism and theory, cloaks its heterosexuality in a universal guise that leaves lesbian subjects invisible in its discourse. I am, as Witting suggests, shifting the axis of categorization (1983).

Placing the lesbian subject at the center of the debate, rescued from the invisible margins, illuminates aspects of the arguments about representation that were clouded or unexamined. But my argument also has a personal and political component that aims toward the liberation of a sexual minority. Heterosexual readers unsettled by their absence from this debate might have to confront their own homophobia, just as I, as a white reader grappling with work by racial and ethnic minorities, am forced to examine my own racism. As the postmodernists insist, the center is constantly shifting. The shock might be finding yourself on the margins.

Notes

1. Antiporn feminism is very much in line with the cultural feminist politic which maintains that the biological differences between men and women are the basis of their psychological and social differences. This stance translates into often prescriptive dichotomies that describe men's behavior as violent, women's as pacifist. Andrea Dworkin is the most vocal and visible antiporn cultural feminist—her book *Pornography: Men Possessing Women* (1979) is the bible of the movement. See Dolan (1987) for a further explication of antiporn feminism in terms of feminist performance and criticism.
2. For example, this link between the eroticization of imperialism and sexual imperialism is drawn in Stanley Kubrick's Vietnam film *Full Metal Jacket* (1987). When the American soldiers get to Vietnam in Kubrick's film, they are immediately initiated into an economy based on the exchange of Vietnamese prostitutes for American dollars. The soldiers' options in the war context are sex or fighting, and the two inevitably blur. The slow motion, orgasmic quality of blood capsules bursting all over soldiers falling in battle is unmistakably sexual. After a series of more or less faceless skirmishes with the Asian enemy, the film climaxes with the face-to-face murder of a sniper who, not accidentally, is a woman. Aggression toward an entire country is signified by what ends up as sexual aggression toward one alien woman, the dark territory incarnate. Substituting a woman for the alien Asian enemy cannot be coincidental. In Kubrick's film, Vietnam is signified by a woman.
3. Gayle Rubin, in "The Traffic in Women" (1978) argues that women have been use-value in a male economy at least since the kinship systems studied by Levi-Strauss. Luce Irigaray, in "When the Goods Get Together" (1981), suggests that

if women refused to "go to market," they could fundamentally disrupt the dominant culture's structure.

References

Case, Sue-Ellen

1987 "Toward a Butch-Femme Aesthetic." Women in Theatre Conference keynote address. 2 August, Chicago, IL.

1988 *Feminism and Theatre*. New York: Methuen.

Chinoy, Helen Krich, and Linda Walsh Jenkins

1987 *Women in American Theatre*. New York: Theatre Communications Group.

Doane, Mary Ann

1987 *The Desire to Desire: The Woman's Film of the 1940s*. Bloomington: Indiana University Press.

Dolan, Jill

1987 "The Dynamics of Desire: Sexuality and Gender in Pornography and Performance." *Theatre Journal* 39, no. 2 (May):156–74.

Dworkin, Andrea

1979 *Pornography: Men Possessing Women*. New York: Pedigree Books.

Greene, Bob

1986 "Bar Wars." *Esquire,* November:61–62.

Hartley, Nina

1987 "Confessions of a Feminist Porno Star." In *Sex Work: Writings by Women in the Sex Industry,* edited by Frederique Delacoste and Priscilla Alexander, 142–44. San Francisco: Cleis Press.

Irigaray, Luce

1981 "When the Goods Get Together." In *New French Feminisms,* edited by Elaine Marks and Isabelle de Courtivron, translated by Claudia Reeder, 107–10. New York: Schocken Books.

Kaplan, E. Ann

1983 *Women & Film: Both Sides of the Camera*. New York: Methuen.

Kappeler, Susanne

1986 *The Pornography of Representation*. Minneapolis: University of Minnesota Press.

de Lauretis, Teresa

1984 "Desire in Narrative." In *Alice Doesn't,* 103–57. Bloomington: University of Indiana Press.

1988 "Sexual Indifference and Lesbian Representation." *Theatre Journal* 40 (no. 2):155–77.

Mulvey, Laura

1975 "Visual Pleasure and Narrative Cinema." *Screen* 16 (no. 3):6–18.

Rich, Adrienne

1983 "Compulsory Heterosexuality and Lesbian Existence." In *Powers of Desire,* edited by Ann Snitow, Christine Stansell, Sharon Tompson, 177–205. New York: Monthly Review Press.

Rubin, Gayle

1978 "The Traffic in Women: Notes on the 'Political Economy' of Sex." In *Toward an Anthropology of Women,* edited by Rayna Reiter. New York: Monthly Review Press.

Schechner, Richard

1987 Personal correspondence, 7 September.

Sundahl, Debi

1987 "Stripper." In *Sex Work: Writings by Women in the Sex Industry*, edited by Frederique Delacoste and Priscilla Alexander, 175–80. San Francisco: Cleis Press.

Witting, Monique

1980 "The Straight Mind." *Feminist Issues*, Summer:103–11.

1981 "One is Not Born a Woman." *Feminist Issues*, Winter:47–54.

1983 "The Point of View: Universal or Particular?" *Feminist Issues*, Fall:63–69.

***Jill Dolan** is an Assistant Professor of Theatre and Drama and Women's Studies at the University of Wisconsin-Madison. Her book,* The Feminist Spectator as Critic, *is available from UMI press. She has published feminist performance criticism in a number of publications.*

Theatre By and For the Deaf

Hilary U. Cohen

At the Tenth Congress of the World Federation of the Deaf in Helsinki in July 1987, 18 performance companies composed primarily of amateur deaf actors from Europe and Japan demonstrated a wide range of performance methods. The performances were part of a week of activities. Two thousand delegates from around the world participated in lectures and discussions on scientific, sociological, and cultural issues of deafness. The performances took place in the evenings, three or four a night, after a full day of scholarly sessions. Groups experimented with mime, formalized gesture, and sign language in performing everything from classical Japanese comedy to Monty Python–like satire to Euripides' *Electra*. With one exception, there was no accompanying spoken text; the focus was entirely on visual performance. Although some groups performed within fairly conventional constraints—translating a word-based narrative into sign or using traditional mime gestures—others experimented with narrative, sequence, and multiple images.

The performances differed in a number of ways from the more familiar type of deaf theatre practiced in the United States. The most widely known technique for making performances accessible to the deaf in the U.S. is sign language interpretation of spoken texts. Through the placement of interpreters either at the side of the stage or within the performance space, deaf audience members are presented with a simultaneous signed/visual translation of the words of speaking actors. In this method, hearing actors and hearing interpreters include deaf spectators in performances that are largely created for the hearing.

A second set of techniques creates performance opportunities for deaf actors. Best exemplified by the National Theatre of the Deaf, a federally funded touring company based at the Eugene O'Neill Theatre Center in Connecticut, these performances feature deaf actors who communicate through American Sign Language and "theatrical signing," that is, alteration or expansion of conventional signs for dramatic effect. The goal of theatrical signing is to create a more dynamic sign or one that incorporates miming of the concept behind the sign. The sign may be extended in a number of ways. Signs made with one hand may be made with two hands, and the path of the movement exaggerated. For example the sign "to view" is a "V" made with the index and middle fingers moving out slightly from the right eye. In theatricalizing the sign, one could use both hands to make "V"s coming from both eyes and move the "V"s well over the head in an arc that ends with the hands pointing toward the object to be viewed. Theatricalized signs can also be made with more than one person, either creating multiple images of the sign or creating a large sign shaped by many hands. The sign for tree is made by resting the right elbow on the left hand with the right arm straight and the extended right fingers moving. A whole group of such trees arranged at different levels creates a forest. Finally, theatricalized signing may include the whole body in a combination of signing and mime. In a play about a young boy dreaming of flying like a hawk, the boy sees himself "wrapped up in wind." The sign for "wrap" is both hands circling each other at chest height. In this instance, because the child himself is wrapped in the wind, the signer might encompass his whole body in swirling arms and hands to show who is wrapped and how.

Although the primary actors in this second type of performance are deaf, hearing actors also take part and provide an accompanying spoken text. While developing a growing deaf following, these performances are intended for hearing audiences in order to demonstrate the skill of deaf actors and to gain acceptance for sign language by the hearing majority.

The Helsinki conference performances fell into the second category of methods described above but were different in two important ways: There was no integration of hearing and deaf actors and no spoken text. There are a number of reasons for both of these choices. One is that the audience for the European performances is largely deaf rather than hearing. This in turn is related to the way theatre has developed in Europe through deaf organizations and social clubs. Theatre has emerged as a means of entertaining deaf friends in clubs, expanding methods of communicating, and fostering an active deaf culture. It is more of a grass roots movement born from within groups of deaf people. By contrast, theatre of the deaf in the U.S. is primarily performed for hearing audiences by hearing theatre companies with well-defined theatre aesthetics. For example, the directors of the National Theatre of the Deaf and Cleveland's Fairmont Theatre of the Deaf are hearing theatre artists who had established theatre careers before helping to found these organizations. Two U.S. organizations more similar to the European models are the theatre programs at Gallaudet College in Washington, D.C., and the National Technical Institute of the Deaf in Rochester, New York.

A second reason for the differing focus on deaf and hearing audiences has to do with political goals. Both American and European deaf performance groups are politically motivated, but their diverging interests have carried them in different directions. For the U.S. companies, the thrust has been to gain acceptance for sign language and deaf performers by the mainstream. Many of the performance companies participating in the conference are more militant. Their work embodies a more direct affirmation of the right to communicate through sign language. Some of the groups will not include a spoken text under any circumstances. They feel that if the hearing want to have access, they will have to learn sign language.

This fierce commitment to sign language must be understood within the current climate of growing deaf identity. In the early '70s policy changes made by the hearing for educating the deaf along with the growing assertiveness of the deaf created a resurgence of sign language as the principal means of communication among deaf individuals. For the previous 50 years, deaf people in most parts of the world had been educated in oral programs that emphasized speaking and lip reading, forbidding manual languages.

The goal of the oral programs was to assimilate the deaf population as much as possible into the hearing world. Among the consequences were some that many deaf people now decry. Education of the deaf was taken out of the hands of deaf educators. Because deaf adults could take no part in the education of deaf children in an oral program, they could neither share their experiences nor provide role models. A poignant example of the consequence of this policy was related by a Kenyan interpreter at the Helsinki conference. She has encountered several groups of deaf children in Kenya who think they will grow up to be hearing because they have never seen a deaf adult. Another drawback of oral programs was that the denial of their language forced the deaf to be more dependent on the hearing world. Since they could not communicate with each other, they could not collectively affect social policy and had to rely on hearing individuals for advocacy. A third consequence was the diminishing of deaf identity and culture which had flourished at the end of the 19th century when the deaf had been educated in sign language.

The performances at the conference reflected a diverse but powerful response to communicating through sign language. As Marjaana Suosalmi, the current secretary of the World Federation, signed in an address to the assemblage, "We will never again allow the hearing world to take away our language." This commitment to sign language was demonstrated in the theatre performances not only through the absence of spoken texts but in content and performance style as well. The subject was often sign language itself, satirizing the hearing world and its ignorance of that language. The most biting satire came from the Deaf Comedians, an English company which presented a kind of deaf version of Monty Python. In various sketches the hearing were taken to task either for their ignorance of sign language or for their commitment to imposing speech on the deaf.

In one sketch, a deaf man was confronted by another deaf man doubled over because of his need for a toilet. The latter signed his question about the location of a bathroom, got his answer, and happily hobbled off to relieve himself. A moment later a hearing man appeared, equally desperate for a toilet. He, however, could not make himself understood. Struggling to ask the same question—though it was perfectly apparent from his physical appearance what he wanted—he finally succeeded in communicating with the deaf man. But by that time it was too late, as the wetness spreading across his trousers attested.

In another piece, three tough cops interrogating a deaf man tried to get him to speak his name. Each time he signed rather than spoke in response to this question, he was beaten—punched in the stomach and head, his arms pulled from the shoulder sockets, and finally his fingers broken. When it was at last physically impossible for him to continue signing, he uttered a sound. The police congratulated each other and went out to celebrate, leaving their victim to enjoy his dubious success.

In the first sketch, the usual problematic circumstances of deaf individuals trying to communicate in a hearing world were turned upside down—it was the hearing person who appeared ignorant and out of place. The second sketch took up the very controversial issue of forcing deaf individuals to speak, a subject that was compellingly explored in the play *Children of a Lesser God* by Mark Medoff. Theatre performances at the conference addressed both the principle of being able to choose one's own means of communicating and the actual physical difficulty that many deaf people have in making themselves understood verbally. In a sketch exemplifying problems of verbal clarity, a man in a bar carefully practiced ordering beer, being coached by a hearing friend who insisted there was nothing to it. When he placed his order, the puzzled waitress complied by bringing him a broom.

Doves Teater Loftet from Denmark also performed a series of vignettes satirizing, albeit more gently, the hearing world and its treatment of deaf individuals. In a performance style that combined mime and sign language, four actors dressed in black leotards and tights with red shorts and bow ties explored experiences deaf people have with hearing people at deaf clubs where everyone is deaf. In one vignette, a young man was the only nonhearing person at a dance. He was anxious to fit in and not be identified as a deaf person. Using visual cues, he began to dance when he saw the band playing and other people dancing. However, as he got involved in the dancing, he didn't notice that the other dancers had stopped with the music and he suffered embarrassment as everyone stared at him. In another vignette, a hearing man, identified by a red clown nose, fell in love with a young woman at a deaf club who suddenly disappeared, leaving behind only her hearing aid. Like the prince searching for Cinderella, the man went from woman to woman, trying to find the woman to fit the hearing aid.

Although the tenor of the conference was generally very political, not all the performances had an overtly political focus. The content of the pieces ranged widely. Classical drama was represented by Euripides' *Electra,* Molière's *Tartuffe,* and Chekhov's *The Marriage Proposal.* More popular fare included an English country house murder mystery and, perhaps the most bizarre choice of the week, a signed version of *My Fair Lady* with actors lip synching to an Italian recording of the music. Many pieces did not use previously scripted material. The Finnish company, Elavat Kadet (Living Hands), performed the "Kalevala," the Finnish creation myth. Kontakte, a group from the German Democratic Republic, created a collection of nonsigned, absurdist image-based pieces.

One of the challenges of theatre of the deaf is to find or create performance material appropriate to the performers and deaf audience members. Although often used, the body of scripted texts available to hearing actors is not always particularly suitable. When hearing audiences are presented with a production that is both spoken and signed, the signing becomes an added dimension to a text that is *heard*—hearing being the form for which it was conceived. Moreover, to both hear and see language seems to have a very powerful effect. Deaf audiences do not share that experience. When a scripted text is used, they only *see* what was written to be heard.

This presents a number of problems. First, because the syntax of sign language is different from written and spoken language, it is not enough to simply translate the written text word for word into sign language. Rather the idea expressed in the written sentence must be extracted and given comparable expression in sign language. For example, the sentences "I have a book. It is interesting," are expressed in American Sign Language with the following signs: Book—Have—It—Like. Moreover, facial expression, body movement, and spatial placement need to be conceived as part of the signs.

Second, although in conventional theatre a good play depends on the action of its plot, it is also distinguished by its language. For example, Shakespeare's dialog is rich in visual imagery that could be made accessible to the deaf, but it is also a metaphorical language full of references to other word-based ideas as well as full of innuendo and double meaning. Moreover, the force of Shakespeare's language is enhanced by its sound: meter, rhythm, rolling r's, hissing sibilants, exploding consonants. When Shakespeare is performed in signed and spoken language for hearing audiences, the signing enhances the production by adding visual expression to the language. It is possible to produce Shakespeare in sign language alone, but whereas signing together with speaking expands the work, signing on its own may actually be constricting.

Some of the translation problems are similar to those experienced when moving from one word-based language to another. Languages vary in their ability to express metaphors and similes, to absorb sound-related words, and to be shaped into poetic constructs. Languages also embody diverging cultural concepts. After the recent producton of *Death of a Salesman* in China, Arthur Miller, in a 1987 lecture at the University of Michigan, related various cultural differences that defied translation. For example, the informal way Biff refers to his mother as "Pal" has no comparable expression in China where respect for elders precludes such familiarity. Sign language shares these difficulties but because it is a gesture-based language it is linguistically different as well. Thus, translating a written text into a signed one entails not only recognized translation and cultural considerations but also special attention to the differences between hearing and seeing language and to the essentially different linguistic structure of sign language.

The Swedish Tyst Teater (Silent Theatre) produced *Tartuffe,* illustrating the difficulty of straightforward translation. This group, affiliated with

1. & 2. Tartuffe *by Molière as performed by Tyst Teater (Silent Theatre) the Swedish National Theatre, Riksteatern. (Photo by Birgitta Rydbeck)*

Riksteatern, the Swedish National Theatre, was one of the more professional companies at the conference in terms of its ability to handle the stylized acting of Molière's comedy of manners. The approach they took to *Tartuffe* was basically to substitute signing for speaking and otherwise use conventional acting techniques. There was no elaboration of the physical performance except for the prescribed facial expressions that accompany particular signs. Although the text was skillfully translated into sign language, the intricacies of Molière's language became labored and dull in the signed version. The metaphors, double entendres, and word plays were lost. Also, many ideas became convoluted when depicted through gesture. The strengths of sign language, its visual beauty and economy of expression were hard to exploit in presenting a text so rooted in verbal language.

The Japanese Deaf Theatre, Tsukumo, fared much better in their kyogen presentation, *Tsuri-Onna (Bride Fishing)* or *The Capricious Magic Fish Hook.* This particular kyogen was adapted to dance in the late 19th century and, as it was performed at the conference, combined dance, pantomime, and sign language. Actors moved or danced in a continuous series of large circles with knees bent and head, arms, and hands expressing a recognizable (to Japanese audiences) set of gestures. In this simple story of a feudal lord and his servant who seek wives from the sea with a magic fishing pole, the pantomimic gestures and poses formed the vocabulary of the piece and were readily extended to incorporate signing as a substitute for the usual

3. The kyogen performance, Tsuri-Ona (Bride Fishing) *or* The Capricious Magic Fish Hook *by The Japanese Deaf Theatre, Tsukumo. (Photo by Hilary U. Cohen)*

accompanying dialog. Thus, a gesture of the hands expressing sorrow was extended to include the sign for that emotion; a downward turn of the head to indicate shame was accompanied by the sign for shame.

The Japanese play lent itself particularly well to the incorporation of sign language. Most Western theatre forms are less hospitable and point up the need for the creation of new kinds of performance better suited to the nature of sign language and more rooted in visual ideas. Directors such as Robert Wilson and Lee Breuer have experimented with compelling visual imagery but have not chosen to codify their work and develop a recognizable visual vocabulary. Some deaf theatre groups are beginning to move in that direction with performances that focus on visual expression, whether it be mime, gesture, sign language, or some combination. At the conference, performances employing these new methods tended to be short or made up of a collection of scenes.

The Greek company produced a piece based on the Greek folktale "O Ποντικος Κ' Η Θυγατερα Του" (The Mouse and His Daughter). Created through improvisation, it was conceived with the syntax of sign language rather than the syntax of Greek, thus obviating some of the translation difficulties. Its scenario was also based on a series of visual images: a mouse father seeking a suitor for his daughter among the sun, the clouds, and the north wind. The characters were portrayed as people with only hints of the animals or natural forces on which they were based. For example, the North Wind, dressed in a dark suit, waved his arms and rapidly moved in circles. Although the acting and staging were rudimentary, the work was illustrative of a shift away from the translation of scripted material.

The Elavat Kadet production of the Finnish creation myth "Kalevala," is a more elaborate example of the development of original material with a visual base. A group of itinerant players enacted several versions of the myth through the experiences of three principal supernatural characters:

Vainamoinen, intelligent but weak; Lemminkainen, emotional and amorous; and Kullervo, honest but destructive. In a meandering and violent saga that moved freely through time and contained several repetitions from different points of view, the creation of the heavens and of human pain and suffering was depicted through a series of images.

The seven Elavat Kadat actors were dressed in ragged tunics and leggings of different colors with circles and stripes of matching colors painted on their faces. After arguing about what they should perform, the group of boisterous traveling actors became drawn into three different versions of the myth. In one sequence, as two male actors took the roles of Vainamoinen and Lemminkainen—Vainamoinen added fringe to his costume, Lemminkainen a gold helmet—while the rest of the cast alternated between serving as natural elements such as trees and rocks and playing various human characters in the violent battle that ensued between the two.

The confrontation began as Lemminkainen strummed a stringed instrument (a tape of pipes which played in the background was a contradiction observed only by hearing audience members). Vainamoinen tried in vain to interrupt Lemminkainen's playing by shouting silent screams with his hands to his mouth. Trying another tactic, he threw imaginary rocks at Lemminkainen which became the moon, stars, and the sun projected onto a screen at the back of the stage. Still Lemminkainen played without acknowledging Vainamoinen. Eventually Lemminkainen used his music to root Vainamoinen to the ground and then began to bury him alive with a mimed shovel, digging, lifting, and pouring the dirt with slow, repetitive shoveling movements. An increasingly terrified Vainamoinen was helpless to resist until reprieved by Lemminkainen at the last moment. In retribution, Vainamoinen shot Lemminkainen with an arrow. Lemminkainen tried repeatedly to pull out the arrow, twisting and writhing and appealing for help to no avail. As he collapsed in death, Vainamoinen shouted silently in victory and then aloud in terror at the realization of his action. The sequence finished with a circling Lap dance, performed by an individual from the chorus, which succeeded in bringing the dead Lemminkainen back to life.

The most experienced and skilled performers at the conference were part of the East German company, Kontakte. Kontakte performed a collection of pieces exploring the theme of human interaction. In several of the pieces, strangely clothed characters portrayed incidents plucked from a surreal landscape. In one, a man and woman dressed in pink ate a meal while perched atop tall stools at an unusually high but tiny table. Eating with enormous silver spoons out of white bowls, they sat side by side without communicating until the very act of the other's eating began to irritate each of them. The meal deteriorated into a violent battle in which the spoons and bowls became weapons. Chasing each other on top of and under the table, striking, smacking, kicking, pulling hair, and sitting on one another, the pair alternated power and control in this tightly choreographed sequence. As the violence ran its course, they returned to their eating with the same lack of communication.

In a second piece, *The Robot,* a lonely man created a female robot for company. He programmed her to perform various services such as filing his nails and rubbing his head. The robot could carry out these tasks if the man got his body into the right position—the only drawback being the robot's frightening persistence. Long after the man tired of these activities, the robot continued to rub or file until the exhausted creator finally found a way to make her stop. Deciding to try something calmer, he managed to

4. *Kontakte of the German Democratic Republic in* The Duel *directed by Volkmar Otte. (Photo by K.P. Olthoff)*

get the robot to sit down to watch television with him but lost heart with this frozen, unresponsive companion. Finally, he attempted to make love to the robot, but her persistence became overwhelming. Steadfastly continuing the "tasks" of kissing and caressing, she pursued him relentlessly as he fell exhausted and senseless to the floor.

An important feature of the conference performances was their nature as "events" encompassing actors and audience members. Together they were a shared celebration of deaf identity, a new art form in deaf culture, with behavioral conventions shared by the largely deaf audience.

There were roughly equal numbers of deaf and hearing participants at the conference. The group of hearing participants was comprised largely of interpreters plus scholars and family members of deaf participants. The interpreters were there primarily to translate the 40 national sign systems used by the delegates during the daytime lectures. An international sign language exists, but it is in its infancy and not widely used. Thus, though it is easier to shift between varying manual than between spoken languages, it was essential for clarity and accuracy to have translators for each nationality to translate both the signed and spoken addresses. There were also audio translations in English, French, and Finnish for hearing participants and for the interpreters who were hearing and needed a spoken version of unfamiliar signing systems. Also, because interpreters needed to face toward their constituencies and away from signing speakers, headsets with a spoken version facilitated receiving information while maintaining a consistent physical orientation.

The theatre performances themselves were given neither audio nor signed translation. They were presented only in the sign system of the originating nationality. Because of the visual emphasis of many of the productions and some similarities among signing systems, this did not seem to present the largely deaf audience with much of a problem (with the exception of literal translations of word-based texts which were problematic on both levels of translation). Many of the groups provided synopses or prefaced their productions with the identification of important signs. There was also a fair amount of informal translation among audience members as they watched.

Generally, the audience conventions at the conference involved more interaction than is common in hearing audiences, a difference due in part to deafness but also to the newness of the activity for many of the viewers. Theatre is after all not merely a recent activity for deaf performers but also for most deaf spectators. As performance for the deaf continues to develop, it is possible that viewing conventions distinct from those already established for hearing audiences will develop as well.

The atmosphere at the conference performances was informal and lively, with a great deal of coming and going between and even during presentations. The cafes in the lobby were often full as food and conversation were

5. The Robot *directed by Volkmar Otte of Kontakte from the German Democratic Republic. (Photo by K.P. Olthoff)*

important parts of these events. Quite a lot of food was consumed inside the theatre as well.

Visibility is of paramount importance when deaf individuals are viewing theatre, as it is for any form of communication among the deaf. At the conference, people were very conscious of seating positions, sending children to sit in chairs drawn up to the front near the stage or even permitting them to lean on the apron. There was also a great deal of signing in the audience during performances, both to provide explanation to companions and as commentary on the activity. Light permitting, conversations could actually take place at quite a distance, several rows apart or even from the ground floor to the balcony, although those long-distance conversations usually took place at pauses in the proceedings. While the signing may have been distracting to hearing audience members used to theatre conventions dictating physical inactivity, it did not seem to interfere with the concentration of deaf audience members for whom signing is an integral part of their daily lives. In fact, many spectators actually mimicked signs and gestures from the stage as part of their way of experiencing the performance, similar to the way Javanese audience members enact physical portions of the ludruk plays.

The audience was also quite noisy by conventional standards, something noticed of course only by hearing audience members. Since all the actors and most of the audience were deaf, vocalizations, laughter, shouting children, scraping feet, and rustling papers and clothing had little effect on the majority of those present. The Japanese company had passed out balloons before their performance so that audience members could feel the vibrations of the drumming accompanying their work. Many of the balloons were subsequently popped during that and later productions. A young man sat rubbing a balloon, completely unaware of the loud scraping sound he was producing. Although available only to the hearing persons, decidedly the minority in these audiences, such sounds of exuberance and pride were part of the fabric of the performance event.

While many sounds were made during performances, no sound occurred afterward. Instead of the conventional clapping, the audience waved their hands overhead, a visible demonstration of their appreciation. Each production concluded with a presentation to the players on behalf of the conference. Many had a signed address prepared in response or presented a flag or gift from the company to the Deaf Associations of Finland, the host nation. These exchanges brought a wildly enthusiastic response as the audience shared with the performers the sense of achievement engendered through the performances. Perhaps nothing received a stronger response than the Japanese invitation to the audience to join them in Japan in 1991 for the Eleventh World Congress, an affirmation and celebration of the future of sign language and deaf culture.

Hilary U. Cohen *is Assistant Professor of Theatre and Drama at the University of Michigan. She is also codirector of Wild Swan Theater, a company that conducts workshops with disabled participants and explores methods of making productions accessible to disabled audience members. She has published articles on theatre and disability in TDR,* The Arts in Psychotherapy, *and* Theatre Journal *and is vice-president of the Association for Theatre and Disability.*

Theatre Rhinoceros

A Gay Company

Erik L. MacDonald

The theatre takes its name from the lavender Rhino, a media device popularized by Boston Gays in the mid-seventies. The Rhino was so chosen because it is a mild and peace-loving creature until provoked.

—Program note, Theatre Rhinoceros

The sixth of May 1984: In San Francisco's Franklin Memorial Hospital, Allan Estes died of complications resulting from the failure of his immune system. Estes was not unique because he had AIDS—there were 1,029 new cases reported during the week ending 24 September 1988 alone[1]—but because he was the founder and first artistic director of Theatre Rhinoceros, the largest and most successful lesbian/gay theatre company in America.

Yet Theatre Rhinoceros is not one man's story. While Estes was the driving force behind its founding, Theatre Rhinoceros is a company which epitomizes a movement's coming of age. No longer hiding in, or hidden by a heterosexual theatre world, these gay-oriented artists actively explore the dimensions of their own sexuality and the dynamics of same-sex relationships in an environment ostensibly free from the hegemony of traditional, heterosexual, "mainstream" theatre.

In 1976 the 22-year-old Estes moved to San Francisco from Boston. He had received his baccalaureate in theatre from Emerson College in 1975, and worked as a directing intern at the O'Neill Theatre Center in Waterford, Connecticut. But until he saw Loretta Lorman's 1975 production of *Trans-Lesbianic Follies* for the Gay Academic Union's national conference at Columbia University, he had not considered committing himself to a gay theatre. Suddenly it became the only choice: "It just seemed like the answer to me on a personal level [. . .] to do theatre that was meaningful to me" (Estes 1980b:42). The need for a gay theatre company, a theatre for and about gays, "not only for the audiences, but for the artists themselves" (1980b:42), seemed of central importance to Estes. San Francisco was the obvious place to establish such a theatre, both because of the burgeoning Castro Street gay scene, and because of the city's theatre tradition.

Innovative and experimental theatre has had an illustrious history in San Francisco. The Actor's Workshop and the San Francisco Mime Troupe both had their roots in the Bay Area, and street performance was a familiar San Francisco phenomenon. In the '60s and '70s there were numerous lesser-known alternative theatres as well, such as the Oakland Theatre Ensemble, Just a Stage, the Berkeley Stage Company, Lillith—A Woman's Theatre, Whole Works Theatre Company, Red Balloon, The Asian American Theatre, Feedback Productions, Bay City Reds, East Bay Sharks, and the Blake Street Hawkeyes, all of which regularly presented "something different."

Gay male theatre, however, had not enjoyed such a prominent position. Traditionally, gay performance in San Francisco had consisted primarily of drag shows at clubs such as Finocchio's on Broadway. In the mid-'60s, boisterous audiences attended camp productions of *Dames at Sea, Hello Dolly!,* and *Little Me* at local venues such as the Chi-Chi Club, also on Broadway. During this period several gay "stars" gained popularity as did a few gay companies, and there were even annual gay theatre awards ceremonies—but none of it was lasting or even concerned with permanence. Occasionally a production went up with an all-male cast, as did *George Washington Slept Here* done at the old Sir center (a gay resource facility in the Castro district). Female roles were played by "queens," double entendres were emphasized, the mood remained light and the style campy (Austen 1977:65).

It was not until the gay scene became more politicized in the early '70s that there was a possibility for serious gay theatre. The stonewall riots in New York City were the cornerstone of a new spirit of liberation. As William Hoffman observed:

> The stonewall riots of 1969 might be viewed as Gay street theatre. Led by tough, effeminate young men and tireless Lesbians, who offered themselves as shock troops against waves of policemen so stinted by their self-image of masculinity that they lacked flexibility, and backed by a motley cast of more ordinary Gays and Greenwich Village housewives, homosexuals took command of the central section of one of New York's largest Gay ghettos (1979:xxix).

The "liberation consciousness" that swept through the gay community in the '70s, especially among the young, was the impetus for more substantial gay theatre. During the mid-'70s several attempts were made at developing a theatre based on gay experiences. In San Francisco a realistic production of *Special Friends* was done at the showcase. *Castro Street,* done at the Sir center, and *Kiss the Sky,* produced at the Intersection (the only one of these venues still operating), also stand out in this early series of attempts at realistic gay drama.[2]

Gay theatre's tradition of frivolity was to haunt these early productions, as it would haunt Theatre Rhinoceros for years. The gay community itself was not as responsive to gay theatre as many of the artists had anticipated. Dean Goodman, who once hoped to form a year-round theatre at the Chi-Chi Club, observed that: "The celebrities and royalty didn't come [to gay plays]. They'd been conditioned to think of a gay show in campy terms, and they weren't prepared to see serious themes treated on stage, and the gay press hardly helped" (Austen 1977:66). Gay artists also stayed away, fearing the presumed "narrowness" of gay plots and preferring the financially lucrative "straight" theatre. Former *Bay Area Reporter (B.A.R.)*

1. *(Left to right) Joe Cappetta, Randy Bennett, and Charlie Hufford in Cal Yeoman's* Richmond Jim *(1979). (Photo by Rink)*

correspondent Roger Austen offered another explanation for the lack of interest on the part of the gay community:

> Why pay for vicarious enjoyment when you can improvise your own dialogue, plot, and climaxes, and turn into the star of your own show? Marvelously crafty in adapting the trappings of the acting profession to suit their personal needs, many Gay men can choose to be either Blanche du Bois or Stanley Kowalski by coming up with just the right combination of make-up, posture, pitch, key chains, and colored hankies, not to mention bedroom decor, music, and lighting. Mannered Gay drama unfolds nightly in San Francisco: surrealistic burlesque in the Tenderloin, blackouts in Lafayette Park, pastoral drama at Land's End, soap opera at the baths, commedia dell'arte on Polk Street, comedies of intrigue on Castro; tragedy (well, terror if not pity) on Folsom, and interludes everywhere (1977:66).

Attitudes toward gay theatre were just beginning to change in 1976 when Estes made his way west. Several groups were attempting to create significant gay theatre, and Estes certainly would not be alone in his work. "Altogether, the competition is keen, producers are wary, critics are cynical, and crowds are fickle, but perhaps the days of impasse are over and a new and enduring type of Gay theatre will blossom in San Francisco" (Estes in Austen 1977:66). This comment was to prove prophetic, for in the next 10 years the gay theatre world would reach a level undreamed of in the early '70s.

While getting set up in the city during the fall of 1976, Estes supported himself by driving a cab. A year later he formed a group with his lover Lanny Baugniet, actor and director Guy Bishop, and writer Anthony Rice Ricco to produce theatre for themselves and their friends. The first production of this fledgling group was a double bill of Lanford Wilson's *The Madness of Lady Bright* and Martin Duberman's *Metaphors,* both directed by Estes.

Contemporaneously, The Gay Theatre Collective was forming and developing as a theatre workshop. Chuck Solomon, who later became studio director for Theatre Rhinoceros, broke into San Francisco theatre as an actor and director with this group. Working with both men and women artists, Solomon and the Collective broke important ground for the gay theatre aesthetic which Theatre Rhinoceros would build upon and also brought together many people who would later work for Rhinoceros. The Collective's collaborative production of *Crimes Against Nature,* which documented the struggles of "coming out" and being gay in a straight society, was immensely successful, running off and on for two years between 1976 and 1978.

After his San Francisco directing debut, Estes attended a workshop held by Jerzy Grotowski in Berkeley during the spring of 1977. Estes' response to this experience was to produce his first performance under the name Theatre Rhinoceros. *Gayhem, a Happening* was a performance installation staged in eight rooms of the Grove Street Gay Center on two days, 11 and 13 December 1977. It was the collaborative nature of Grotowski's work that had the most lasting influence on Estes and Theatre Rhinoceros, though later productions turned away from experimental forms toward much more conventional theatre.

Also produced by the theatre in the winter of 1977/78 were a group poetry reading entitled *Stoned Rhino; The Laundry* by David Guerdon; and a series of six one-act plays, *Gays at Play #1 (six tricks),* which included Robert Patrick's *Fred and Harold* and Philip Real's *Breathing Room.* Produced both at the San Francisco Gay Community Center and at the Black and Blue Bar (now closed but once regularly featuring gay performance), these first productions started out as "very ingrown [. . .] our audiences weren't that big, and we weren't really concerned about it" (Estes 1980b:42). No effort was made at reaching a larger audience except for a small press release for *Gayhem, a Happening.* And no attempt to develop a commercially viable theatre was made until the summer of 1978. The first-season audiences were sparse: *The Madness of Lady Bright* and *Metaphors* were performed 10 times, with a total audience of 292; *Gayhem, a Happening* was produced 4 times, for 180 people; and *The Laundry* played 10 times for an audience of 206 (Estes 1981). But these inauspicious beginnings belie the vital role the group was to play in the gay theatre movement.

Rhinoceros was founded as "a troupe of Gay artists working collectively to express Gay sensibilities and attitudes through the performing arts" (Estes 1981). The goals of the company were set forth in the articles of incorporation: "To provide a supportive working atmosphere for Gay men and women in the performing arts, and to promote an honest and positive image of Gay people and Gay life." Theatre Rhinoceros's community function was enunciated as a two-fold manifesto: "To provide San Francisco's large Gay population (residents and visitors alike) with a theatre experience that enriches their lives; and to provide an educational and cultural experience for all people desiring alternate forms of exposure to the Gay lifestyles" (Estes 1980a). Basing their work on the personal experiences of gay men and women put Theatre Rhinoceros at the forefront of burgeoning free-expression and political movements.

Estes saw a need for a gay-lesbian theatre that was more than merely a gay version of a regional repertory company. Estes' organizational expertise enabled Theatre Rhinoceros to offer gay-oriented plays, play readings, community events, classes, and workshops. But it was not just the drive

Theatre Rhinoceros Chronology

Mainstage Productions

Compiled by Lanny Baugniet, Joseph W. Bean, and Tom W. Kelly

1977 *The Madness of Lady Bright* by Lanford Wilson and *Metaphors* by Martin Duberman; *Gays At Play: Six Tricks* (six one-act plays, later called *Gays At Play I*); Stoned Rhino (group poetry readings and film); *Gayhem, A Happening* (collaboration).

1978 *The Laundry* by David Guerdon, adapted by H. Richardson; *Gays At Play II* (three one-act plays); *Sugar, Honey, and Molasses* (collaboration).

1979 *West Street Gang* by Doric Wilson; *Dianna's Dilemma* by Priscilla Huddleson; *Male Rites* (five one-act plays); *The Haunted Host* by Robert Patrick; *Kennedy's Children* by Robert Patrick; *T-Shirts* and *My Cup Runneth Over* by Robert Patrick.

1980 *A Perfect Relationship* by Doric Wilson; *Three One-Act Plays* by Cal Yeomans, Robert Chesley, and Doric Wilson; *Forever After* by Doric Wilson; *Power Lines* by Joel Schwartz; *The Dear Love of Comrades* by Noel Grieg with music by Alex Harding.

1981 *The Line Forms to the Rear* by Cal Yeomans and *Beer and Rhubarb Pie* by Daniel Curzon; *American Coffee* and *Kitchen Duty* by Victor Bumbalo; *News Boy* by Arch Brown; *Dinosaurs* by C.D. Arnold (three plays); *Fugue in a Nursery* by Harvey Fierstein.

1982 *Pogey Bait* by George Birimisa; *Street Theatre: The Twenty-Seventh of June, 1969* by Doric Wilson; *Design For Living* by Noel Coward; *T-Shirts* by Robert Patrick; *Sins of the Father* by Robert Graham; *My Blue Heaven* by Jane Chambers.

1983 *The Enclave* by Arthur Laurents with music by Stephen Sondheim; *Niagra Falls* by Victor Bumbalos; *King of the Crystal Palace* by C.D. Arnold; *A Perfect Relationship* by Doric Wilson; *Fortune,* book and lyrics by Bill Russell, music by Ronald Melrose; *Vieux Carre* by Tennessee Williams; *A Late Snow* by Jane Chambers.

1984 *Crystal Blaze* by Richard Benner; *A Safe Light* by Adele Prandini; *5th of July* by Lanford Wilson; *Bad Drama* by Richard Gray; *The Quintessential Image* by Jane Chambers and *After Eleven* by Victor Bumbalos; *The Concubine at the Feast* by Paul August Cacciotti.

1985 *Mourning Metro* by C.D. Arnold; *High Hopes* by Julianne Gavin; *Night Sweat* by Robert Chesley; *Unfinished Business: The New AIDS Show* (collection of scenes); *Deathtrap* by Ira Levin.

1986 *And Baby Makes 7* by Paul Vogel; *Levitation* by Timothy Mason; *The Corner of the Eye* by Philip Real; *The Children's Hour* by Lillian Hellman; *Life of the Party* by Doug Holsclaw; *Bearclaw* by Timothy Mason.

1987 *Please Wait for the Beep!* by Margery Kreitman; *Spookhouse* by Harvey Fierstein; *What's a Mother To Do?* by Michael Zimmerman; *Pulp and Circumstance* by Adele Prandini and Sue Zemel; *A Late Snow* by Jane Chambers; *Dancing in the Dark* by D.R. Anderson.

1988 *Quisbies* by Leland Moss; *Going to Seed* by Eve Powell; *See Rock City* by Demece Gareps; *In the Summer When It is Hot and Sticky* by Doug Holsclaw; *Kudzu* by Jane Chambers.

1989★ *Passing* by Robert Pitman; *Queen of Swords* by Judy Grahm; *Soul Surviver* by Anthony Bruno.

★Scheduled as of this writing

and commitment of the 23-year-old that made this possible; one man could not create the kind of revolution that took place in San Francisco in the late '70s and early '80s. Only the collective efforts of a people too long oppressed could generate the changes that were evolving. Estes and Theatre Rhinoceros were able to focus and capitalize on those gains and build a theatre that was responsive to, and a part of, that community.

Once the semblance of a "season" was established, Rhinoceros began a staged reading program of new and unproduced scripts by gay playwrights. Six plays were read that summer and fall of 1978. These readings were the only organized forum for reading gay plays in the Bay Area and nurtured many of Theatre Rhinoceros's future playwrights. Writers who premiered work at these readings during the first two years included Robert Chelsey, C.D. Arnold, Cal Yeomans, as well as Real and Patrick, all of whom have continued working with the theatre through the years.

Theatre Rhinoceros received tax-exempt status as a not-for-profit theatre in the fall of 1978 and five full-length, long-run productions were mounted for the first time on a predetermined schedule. While equipment still had to be rented and actors were paid only token fees, this year was the turning point in the establishment of a gay theatre for the general public. "A year ago we were asking 'can we really do this?' " said Estes in an interview with the national gay newspaper *The Advocate*. "Now we know we can do it, and we're doing it all the time" (1980b:43).

The first production of the second season was a collection of poetry and short skits developed by Leigh Watson, Geryl Saulter, and Guy Bishop entitled *Sugar, Honey, and Molasses*. This production was taken to Los Angeles in October for the regional meeting of the Gay Academic Union and then back to San Francisco for a three-week run, where Ricco's *Postcard from My Libido* was added. It gained enough attention in Los Angeles to warrant a write-up in *The Advocate*. This was the theatre's first such review and it was favorable.

Theatre Rhinoceros opened their first Doric Wilson play at the Black and Blue Bar in February 1979. Despite both the limited facility and the small budget, the West Coast premiere of *West Street Gang* attracted nearly full houses for three months. Done in conjunction with Frank Hoffman's *The State of the World and My Mama's Hair*, this was the theatre's first commercial success. Dealing with violence against gays, this comedy portrayed positive actions by characters who reacted against oppression and "gay-bashing" in such a way as to affirm gay life. Opening right after the Harvey Milk/George Moscone slaying, *West Street Gang* rallied gay men in celebration of their struggles against violence.

The community responded and filled the theatre. The extent of this production's success can be measured by the actual attendance tallies. Whereas 677 people saw the season's first two offerings (477 attended 12 productions of *Gays at Play #2*, and 300 watched *Sugar, Honey, and Molasses* in a 7-performance run), *West Street Gang* had an audience of 1,840 for 33 performances (Estes 1981).

Theatre Rhinoceros's production of *Male Rites*, a series of five one-acts done in the spring of 1979 was another important step in developing the group's voice as a gay company. Three major gay playwrights were represented in this production which included Robert Patrick's *Fred and Harold* and *See Other Side*, C.D. Arnold's *Downtown Local*, and Cal Yeoman's *Richmond Jim*.

Yeoman's play, directed by Guy Bishop, was the centerpiece. The play included a good deal of foreplay and fondling on stage, setting a precedent for tackling the controversial subject of gay sex, at issue within the gay community and taboo on stage. This was the first Theatre Rhinoceros production in which two men kissed with deliberate sexual intentions on stage. *Richmond Jim* openly developed the attraction between two men without flinching from the sexual nature of that attraction and without reverting to crass or exploitative pornography. Theatre Rhinoceros took *Richmond Jim* to New York City to perform in the First Gay American Arts Festival in June 1979. Sponsored by the Glines Theatre and funded by the National Endowment for the Arts, the festival brought national recognition to the company and to its commitment to serious issues of gay sexuality and power roles.

Perhaps the most significant development of 1979 was the leasing of a performance space in the Goodman Building on Van Ness Avenue and Geary Boulevard. Not only did this give Theatre Rhinoceros its first permanent home, but it also allowed the group to acquire their own equipment for the first time. Freed from the financial responsibility of renting lighting equipment and scenery, money was now available to invest in increasingly ambitious productions which attempted to realistically reflect gay life.

After the move into the Goodman Building, a board of directors was founded. Comprised of working artists Jon Finch, Lanny Baugniet, Estes, and others, with a president from the business community, Mike Carter, the original board members were intimately involved in the operation of the theatre and had little time or energy to devote to the board. However, when Theatre Rhinoceros moved to their present location in the Mission District at 16th Street and South Van Ness in the summer of 1981, the need

3. A 1983 revival of A Perfect Relationship *by Doric Wilson, with Thomas Mark and Valentine Houver. (Photo by Dakota)*

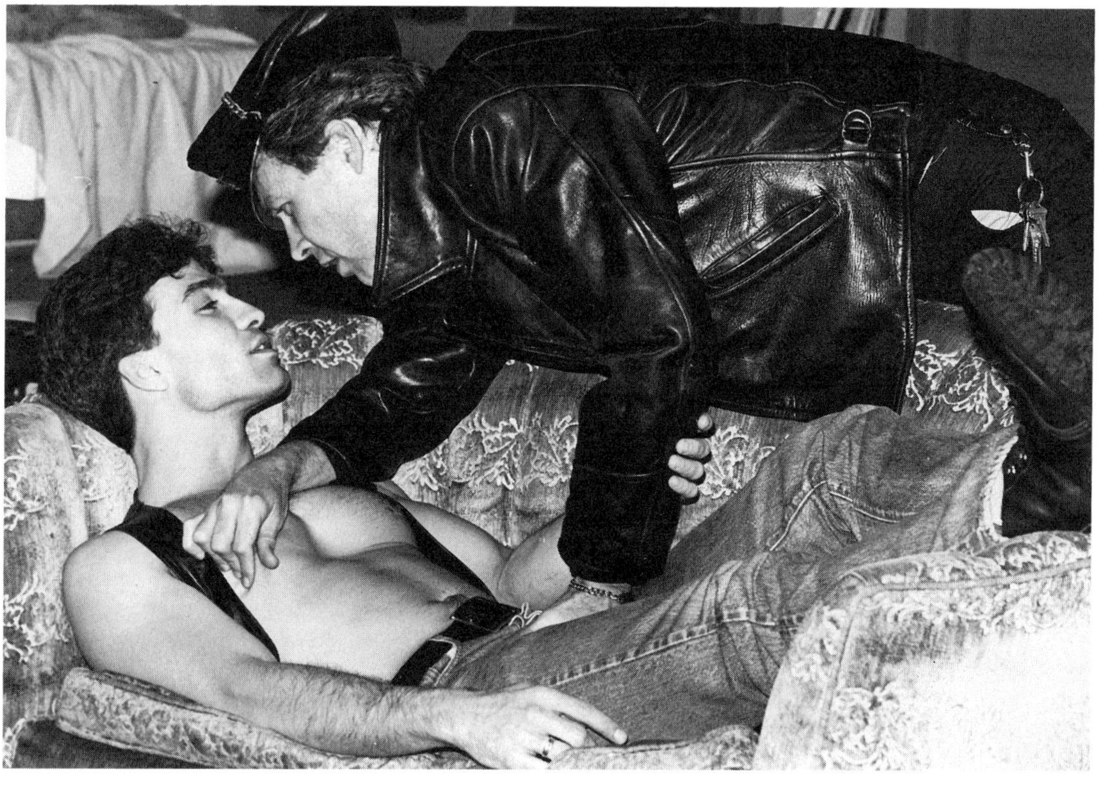

for a working board became apparent. The board was expanded to include more community members and Bernard Pechtor, a local businessman, was elected president. Faced with mounting bills from an ever-expanding production schedule and necessary renovations of the building, Pechtor came up with the idea of starting a subscription season and initiating it with a telethon. Also on the early board was Chuck Tanner, a local graphic artist who designed the current Theatre Rhinoceros logo, and who worked with Pechtor to develop fund-raising projects. Michael Zimmerman, now the financial director for the theatre and successor to Pechtor as board president, was also instrumental in developing a "big-time L.A.-type" fund-raising program (Zimmerman 1987).

Theatre Rhinoceros was the first gay theatre company to receive funding from the National Endowment for the Arts (NEA) and the first gay company in the U.S. to have a subscription season. For the 1980/81 season, a four-play subscription series was funded in part by the NEA Professional Theatre Program and by the San Francisco Hotel Tax Fund, a major source of monies for San Francisco arts organizations. And it was with funding from the California Arts Council that Theatre Rhinoceros moved into the building on 16th Street. With two stage facilities, a mainstage and a studio, the new building offered increased production capacity and finally provided a workable space for the playreading program.

Theatre Rhinoceros obtained national foundation support largely through the fund-raising efforts of Estes. A tireless worker, Estes was perhaps most valuable as a long-range planner and administrator. While he continued to direct plays, his efforts toward procuring funding and developing both the playreading program and the collective spirit were the major reason that the theatre came so quickly to national prominence. In the first three years Theatre Rhinoceros's audience jumped from a total of 744 to 6,284; the budget increased from $2,830 to $25,755 for a total of 117 performances in that same period (Estes 1980b:42). In those three years they went from a workshop of friends to a nationally recognized theatre company with the largest audience base of any West Coast gay theatre.

By the end of the 1980/81 season Theatre Rhinoceros had established itself as a distinct voice in the San Francisco theatre scene. Bay Area gay publications such as the *B.A.R., Sentinel USA, Coming Up,* and *Your Paper,* as well as the *Advocate,* had begun to regularly review productions at the theatre. It was not until two years later, however, that the local straight press, *The Chronicle, The Examiner,* and *The Bay Guardian* began regular coverage of Theatre Rhinoceros productions. Their reportage would begin to bring a larger audience to Rhinoceros, as well as recognition in the larger Bay Area theatre community.

The support and publicity gained by public notice benefited both the theatre and the gay community. However, it also foregrounded the unique and potentially problematic position Theatre Rhinoceros occupied. Put simply, there was no precedent for nor context in which to place a gay-oriented theatre, at least not one with a subscription season and a visible, permanent niche in the local theatre community. Theatre Rhinoceros had the double burden of convincing the public both of gay theatre's legitimacy, and of the theatre's own artistic and administrative capabilities. Even gay audiences had difficulty reacting to the idea of a permanent gay theatre.

This problem was evident in some of the reviews in the gay press. As John Carr, former entertainment editor of the *B.A.R.* put it: "Sometimes gay rags were just inexperienced and unhep [. . .]" (1987). Often gay

4. *Michelle Truffaut directed Jane Chambers'* My Blue Heaven *in 1983. From left to right: Ron Stark, Penny Wallace, and Gail Golden. (Photo by Rink)*

reviewers, even those with the best intentions, were using the gay press as a training ground for learning the trade before graduating into the "slicks." The problem was finding well-trained professionals who could view the theatre with a gay sensibility, finding a critical voice appropriate to a gay institution.

Many of the early reviews in the straight press show a marked homophobia as well as a lack of understanding of gay theatre. Even after five years of successful operation Theatre Rhinoceros would still receive reviews that questioned the concept of gay theatre as a legitimate venue. Nancy Scott of the *San Francisco Chronicle & Examiner* prefaced an interview with Estes:

> We're not talking Oscar Wilde here. We're talking about male homosexual theatre written, directed and produced by male homosexuals for male homosexuals. [. . .] I don't know that gay theatre will ever produce a body of plays with a universal appeal, as ethnic theatre has succeeded in doing. Nor do I know whether gay theatre will produce plays of enduring value commensurate with the classic feminist plays [sic] of Ibsen and Shaw or with those of contemporary feminists, Marsha Norman and Caryl Churchill (1983:4).

This was the exception, however, and most reviews fell somewhere between the extremes of homophobia and unbridled adoration.

In the fall of 1982 Rhinoceros produced its first lesbian play for the subscription season, Jane Chambers' *My Blue Heaven*. Directed by Michelle Truffaut, artistic director of the San Francisco Repertory Theatre, this was also their first play directed by a woman with an all-woman cast. This production was significant for two reasons. First, it raised the issue of lesbian participation in a formerly all-male theatre company. The subscription audience at Theatre Rhinoceros had been running over 90 percent male, as had the production staffs. Even though Estes had always envisioned the theatre as serving lesbian as well as gay audiences, thus far it had remained male. Estes eventually decided that in keeping with the company's original intentions he had no reason not to include lesbian plays and women artists, and began to actively encourage women to participate. The transition occurred without any major problems, except for losing a few disgruntled subscribers who wanted the theatre to remain all male. As a result of this production the theatre expanded its subscription base considerably—the number of women subscribers rose to well over 20 percent during the course of the season.

My Blue Heaven also introduced Kris Gannon to the theatre. Gannon had only recently arrived in San Francisco from the Midwest where she had been active as a director and songwriter for many years. She stage managed this production and stayed on as an administrative assistant, becoming administrative director in the summer of 1983. She directed another Chambers play, *A Late Show,* in the fall of 1983 and continued as administrative director until May 1984 (Gannon 1986).

Enthusiasm and expansion continued on into the spring of 1984. Despite well attended productions and a successful subscription series, the money from the box office was not enough to support the theatre and, without enough fund raising, Theatre Rhinoceros ran deep into debt. Unable to pay creditors, the administration began to lose confidence; expansion plans were shelved and production budgets cut. Then in March 1984, Estes was diagnosed with Pneumocystis pneumonia, an AIDS-related infection.

The Argentine playwright Copi's two plays, *The Homosexual, or the Difficulty of Sexpressing Oneself* and *The Four Twins,* were going into production on 6 May 1984, the day Estes died. Paoli Lacy, who was acting in both, recalled the feeling at the theatre: "People were shocked. No one knew what to do. But there was the sense that the only way to make Allan's life be anything was to keep going and do the best one could" (1987). Gannon echoed this sentiment the next day when she was appointed acting artistic director. "Allan was an amazing and wonderful man who understood life and was wise enough to prepare us to carry on. Our monument to him will be our continuation of his life's work" (1984).

That summer there were major changes not only in the artistic composition of the theatre, but in many aspects of the administration as well. No longer able to depend on Estes' organizational genius, and fighting an overwhelming sense of defeat both in the theatre and in the community due to the ravages of the AIDS epidemic, the theatre had to entrench itself against a flood of debts. While still committed to the original intention of creating a theatre for and about gay life, the theatre had to reassess its goals in light of the AIDS epidemic and the changing political scene of the mid-'80s. The carefree days of the late '70s and early '80s were gone, perhaps forever, and the theatre could no longer rely on that early exuberance. Subsequently, a new board was convened, Gannon was elected permanent artistic director, and many of the previous plans for further expansion were temporarily put aside.

The new board had to fill the immense void created by Estes' death, and toward that end took control of the budget and made Gannon directly responsible to the board for her artistic decisions, something that Estes never was. Zimmerman was hired as financial director, and the staff was put on half-time as a budget-cutting measure. Planning and finance committees were created, and board members took more responsibility for the running of the theatre. To tackle the huge debt left over from the "great rush forward," individual board members were required to organize fund-raising events; each was given a quota to raise and efforts were made to attract wealthy patrons to the board which was thus far composed mainly of self-employed businesspeople (Zimmerman 1987).

In addition to fund raising, new goals included a commitment to improving and expanding the physical facilities, increasing the membership, and expanding the scope of the theatre through new programs that would market video productions, establish a full-time artistic company, and develop a playwrights' workshop (Prandini 1986).

Estes had run a playreading program under the auspices of Theatre Rhinoceros since the theatre's inception, but the program had disappeared by the time the theatre moved to its present space. Estes had continued to support new work, producing seasons composed largely of premieres, but there was no formal development program of any kind until the fall of 1984 when Adele Prandini and Chuck Solomon took on the task of developing plays.

Prandini had had a long career in Bay Area gay theatre. Originally an acting teacher at the Performing Arts Workshop in San Francisco, she grew tired of working on "heterosexist" theatre, and quit to cofound Just a Stage. In the late '70s Prandini was also associated with the Gay and Lesbian Theatre Collective, an offshoot of the Gay Men's Theatre Collective. She left Just a Stage in 1980 to concentrate on writing; her script *A Safe Light* was produced by Theatre Rhinoceros in 1984 (Prandini 1986).

C.D. Arnold, Terry Garner, Paul Caucotti, J.B. Laws, Philip Real, and Prandini comprised the original group. Prandini dropped out when *A Safe Light* opened in New York and Los Angeles. She then returned to San Francisco, worked as production manager at Theatre Rhinoceros, and again took over the playwrighting program in the fall of 1985 when Chuck Solomon retired after contracting AIDS.

One of the first projects of the post-Estes playwrighting program was the production of *Artists Involved with Death and Survival: The A.I.D.S. Show*. In early 1984, Estes, C.D. Arnold, and Robert Pitman proposed to the city arts council a street theatre piece about AIDS for the Democratic National Convention in San Francisco that summer. The proposal was approved and funded by the Hotel Tax Fund, but the project was shelved after Estes' death. Some months after Gannon was appointed artistic director she approached Leland Moss to revive the project. Acting as director, Moss brought together 13 lesbian and gay-male writers, many from the playwrighting program, who composed 21 scenes and 2 songs to express their reaction to AIDS. Rather than presenting a morbid view of death, the project set out to create an event which would be empowering and enlightening to gay audiences, as well as appealing to heterosexuals.

Structured loosely around fragments of New Year's Eve parties from 1980 to 1984, the *A.I.D.S. Show* included scenarios depicting a woman who provides health care for people with AIDS and for her children at home; a woman unsure of everything except her unconditional love for her gay son; and a nostalgic party where the participants come to terms with lifesaving attitudes toward safe sex. Bernard Spunberg in the *B.A.R.* applauded its honesty: "Irresponsibility and self-deception are not glossed over. Neither are humor and heroism" (1984:13). Originally scheduled for four performances in September 1984, the *A.I.D.S. Show* was performed almost continuously for over a year and toured to San Diego and Boston as well.

Theatre Rhinoceros today sits at an unusual crossroads. Like many gay artistic institutions, it is facing a double-barreled scourge. On the one

5. *"To Tell the Truth" panelists Donna Davis, Robert Coffman, and Stacy Cole in Robert Stone's sketch for* Artists Involved with Death and Survival: The A.I.D.S. Show *(1984). (Photo by Joshua Rotsten)*

hand, the extreme New Right has done their best to make funding for gay groups impossible to obtain and has created a political environment hostile to gays and lesbians. From the Supreme Court to the medical profession to arts councils, gay life is facing attacks that yet again threaten to send it underground. An established, visible institution such as Theatre Rhinoceros becomes doubly important in this environment, not only as a place for gay and lesbian artists to explore dimensions of their sexuality, but as a bastion of freedom and openness in a grim world.

The other force threatening Theatre Rhinoceros's survival, as well as the survival of all gay people regardless of their occupation, is AIDS. While the effects of AIDS in the community are well documented elsewhere, a quick list of San Francisco artists who have died in the last five years underscores the severity of the situation: Not only have Estes and Solomon died, but actor John Ponyman, director Raymond Tasco, actor Gerald Duff, and Chuck Tanner are all ill or have died, as have artists Charles Butts, Arthur Conrad, Richard Dhulster, Herman George, James Roy Howell, Bill Kendall, Frank LoBraico, Ed Mock, Tom Morley, and Dennis Yount (Guthmann 1986a:20). Of course these are just the well-known names. For each of these there are a hundred other personal dramas being fought, and lost, in San Francisco General Hospital, in hospices, and in hospitals everywhere.

Kris Gannon, summing up the shocked state of the art scene, said: "I'm at the place where I feel like, who's next? Who's next? And yet every time I'm just devastated. I'm just floored. I'm furious! I'm all those things" (Guthmann 1986b:17). AIDS is a part of everybody's life and yet it has not been passively accepted by anyone. After Estes' death Theatre Rhinoceros produced several shows related to the epidemic. Robert Chelsey's extremely successful *Night Sweat* (1985) is about "a perfectly nice guy who's never really liked himself, who dreams he has AIDS and joins a fancy,

6. Kathryn Knotts and Caitlin Brown in Jane Chambers' A Late Snow *(1987). (Photo by Shari Cohen)*

glitzy suicide club in which he can pick the death of his choice" (Guthmann 1986b:18). *The Life of the Party* (1986) by Doug Holsclaw is a play about four "party boys" accepting restrictions on their lifestyles yet struggling to remain upbeat and positive in the face of death.

The most successful production in the theatre's history was also a response to the AIDS epidemic. *Unfinished Business* was an updated version of the *A.I.D.S. Show* and opened Theatre Rhinoceros's 1985/86 season. A documentary video, *The A.I.D.S. Show: Artists Involved with Death and Survival,* was aired on local station KQED during Gay Pride Week in June 1986, and then shown nationally on PBS in the fall of 1986. The script for this project has also been published and distributed nationally (Hurwitt 1985).

Perhaps more important than the mainstream publicity for gay theatre, gay life, and the AIDS crisis is the pulling together of a battered gay community to celebrate life and freedom even in the face of death. In the summer and fall of 1986 Lyndon Laroche and others in the California legislature were calling for the quarantine of gay men, the AIDS-related death rate was rising with no end in sight, and the Georgia Supreme Court was outlawing gay sex. In this climate of hysteria, projects like the *A.I.D.S. Show* and *Unfinished Business* stand out as examples of hope and light. It is a spirit of resistance confined not just to the theatre community.

The issues surrounding AIDS—media hype, misinformation, political reactions—not to mention the medical facts of illness and death, are a challenge to all gays. And Theatre Rhinoceros has responded in a manner similar to other gay institutions by refusing to lose sight of its purpose despite the death toll and despite the strain on the survivors. Ordinary job stress, combined with the AIDS crisis, have made working conditions at the theatre strenuous. Gannon, who had served as artistic director since May 1984, finally had to leave the theatre in the spring of 1987 to take a

7. Terrence McNally's It's Only a Play *done at Theatre Rhinoceros in September 1988 with Salvatore Bovoso (left) and Doug Holsclaw. (Photo by Steve Savage)*

break. Her departure seemed to mark the end of the rebuilding period after Estes' death. In her absence Prandini has temporarily assumed the artistic directorship.

But the future of the theatre is no longer contingent on the efforts of any one person. By pursuing an aggressive rebuilding campaign over the last three years, and by sticking to its original commitment to create a theatre for and about gays and their world, Theatre Rhinoceros has continued to provide a space for gay artists to express themselves and to offer an honest and positive image of gay people and gay life. Despite the upheavals in the gay community wrought by AIDS and a conservative political environment, Theatre Rhinoceros remains responsive to that community and its irrepressible will to be free.

Notes

1. A total of 22,999 new cases were reported for 1988 up until this date. By way of comparison, there were 13,776 new cases reported for the same period in 1987 (i.e., ending 24 September 1987). Statistics are from the *Weekly Mortality and Morbidity Report* published by The Center for Disease Control in Atlanta, Georgia.
2. Playwrights' names and production dates are not available because, in many cases, those who might be able to provide the information have died.

References

Austen, Roger
1977 "Gay Theatre in San Francisco." *San Francisco Theatre* 1, no. 2 (Winter):65–67.

Carr, John
1987 Interview with author. San Francisco, 18 January.

Estes, Allan
1980a Articles of incorporation, Theatre Rhinoceros.
1980b "In Good Company with a Gay Repertory Theatre." Interview in *The Advocate,* 10 January:42–43.
1981 Grant proposal, National Endowment for the Arts.

Gannon, Kris
1984 Press release, Theatre Rhinoceros. 7 May.
1986 Telephone conversation with author, 30 November.

Guthmann, Edward
1986a "AIDS Artists Remembered: The Faces Behind the Statistics." *San Francisco Chronicle,* 7 December, Datebook:20–25.
1986b "AIDS and the Arts." *San Francisco Chronicle,* 7 December, Datebook:17–18.

Hoffman, William M., ed.
1979 *Gay Plays: The First Collection.* New York: Avon Books.

Hurwitt, Robert
1985 *West Coast Plays.* Vol. 20. Berkeley: California Theatre Council.

Lacy, Paoli
1987 Interview with author. Seattle, 10 January.

Prandini, Adele
1986 Interview with author. San Francisco, 17 December.

Scott, Nancy
1983 "Gay Theatre's Changing Role." *The San Francisco Chronicle & Examiner,* 12 June, Scene:4.

Spunberg, Bernard
1984 "Life and Love." *Bay Area Reporter,* 1 September:13.

Zimmerman, Michael
1987 Interview with author. San Francisco, 18 January.

Erik L. MacDonald *is a doctoral candidate at the University of Washington.*

Summer Saint Camp 1987

With Annie Sprinkle and Veronica Vera

Linda Montano

Annie Sprinkle and Veronica Vera, two bona fide feminist/activist porn stars and SEX NATIONAL TREASURES,* came to the ART/LIFE INSTITUTE, Kingston, NY, for a one-week residency, Summer 1987, becoming the fifth and sixth participants in the reach-out program which is one aspect of 7 YEARS OF LIVING ART (plate 1).

When I designed the 7-year project, I intuited that I would be doing it alone—living alone, that is, in upstate NY. Both aspects were frightening: upstate and living alone. And I knew that a self-imposed isolation would result from the choice. So I wrote into my statement of purpose an invitation for others to "collaborate" with me. After three years of the experiment, my intuition to do this has proven correct . . . so now the somewhat hermetic research project with solo journeys to psychic/psychological places which this kind of structure allows—this self-imposed exile—has visitors and fellow researchers.

Each time is different because of the individual needs and chemistries involved, but in general we do what I do all year—keep a monastic schedule, eat rice and beans, live frugally (a little toilet paper, lights off, cold water baths, etc.) so that structure gets substituted for worldly success, dreaming for TV, walking for cars, and awareness for entertainment.

In 7 days we visualize and experience the 7 chakras, one a day, and then "perform" from that chakra each night, after having spent the day coming from that particular energy. At the end of the residency, participants receive a performance/saint certificate.

ART/LIFE RESIDENCIES

1984/85	Susan Matheson
1985/86	Sylvia Nakkach, Frank Shifreen, Alexandra Montano
1986/87	Annie Sprinkle, Veronica Vera, Helene Aylon, Myriam Abramowicz

*A title I gave them after their one-week residency.

SEX

Annie Sprinkle/Veronica Vera

An interview with Linda Montano

MONTANO: The circumstances of this interview are very different because we are sitting here with crystals in our vaginas and have spent many hours collaborating together in upstate NY, working on chakras during the Summer Saint Camp that you are both attending at the Kingston "Convent." But getting to the question . . . You both, collaboratively and singly, have worked with sex, so the first question is: How did you feel about sex as a child?

VERA: With my fingers! It felt very good and gushy. And when my fingers got slapped, it started feeling bad but still good at the same time, so that became confusing. My mother slapped me but she was motivated by religion so I guess that I can say that the church slapped my hand. But I didn't go looking for that spot—God made it and then let me find it. Daddy's belt became very exciting to me; the idea of any man loosening his pants, taking off a black belt and, as I got older, having a hard cock come out, has been erotic. This doesn't mean that I'm into being spanked, although every once in a while that's OK. But getting back to the source: My mother spanked me with my father's belt and I've thought and written about that at length. The fact that the pants were in the bedroom, that mysterious place closed off to me—that's another element in the drama. And she took the belt from their bedroom, spanked my fingers and bottom, keeping me warm there where I had touched myself. So the belt was a good friend because it made me a good girl again. I was lovable. Suffering made me lovable. What a bunch of baloney!

SPRINKLE: I didn't feel much of anything about sex as a young person; I wasn't a sexual child. My parents never said it was bad. I heard a little about it at school on the playground. I was a very shy child and the only sexual memory that I have is the one of waking up in the morning, needing to pee really badly and at the same time I would actually be having an orgasm. So that's maybe why I got into *Piss Art* [magazine]! So I had nothing to do with sex at all until I was 17 when I lost my virginity. Then it snowballed. My first experience was positive—it was with an older guy and now I see that guys my age were a turn-off. When I met a 26-year-old guy with a hippie coffee shop and motorcycle, I got interested. And then I got turned-on. Maybe it was the motorcycle vibrating between my legs. After I lost my virginity, I immediately dove right in. I thought that it was the greatest—so great that I left him so that I could try every other guy in town. So I left him (we were living isolated in the desert), moved, and made myself available.

I can thank myself and my parents for my being able to experiment so freely. I knew in my heart that sex felt so good—I knew in my heart that it was going to lead me to something. And I had to know everything about sex. I had to do it with everybody, in every combination, with as many or as few people possible. I had to try everything and know everything about this exciting subject. And I knew in my heart that it wasn't a bad thing although sex itself is not always a positive experience. But I knew that I had to do it so I became a hooker, a porn star, and everything but a swinger. Swinger's clubs turned me off although I tried that too. Recently

7 YEARS OF LIVING ART
12/8/84 . . . 12/8/91

an experience based on the 7
energy centers in the body

LINDA MONTANO

PART A. INNER: The Art/Life Institute

Daily, for 7 years, I will:
1. Stay in a colored space (minimum 3 hours).
2. Listen to one pitch (minimum 7 hours).
3. Speak in an accent (except with immediate family).
4. Wear one color clothes.

PART B. OUTER: The New Museum

1. Once a month, for 7 years, I will sit in a window installation at the New Museum and talk about art/life with individuals who join me.

PART C. OTHERS: International

1. Once a year, for 16 days, a collaborator will live with me.
2. Others can collaborate in their own way wherever they are.

I went to an orgy and that was fabulous, so that has changed. I've been around a lot of orgies for various reasons and I think it has a potential, but in general swingers don't turn me on.

As far as sex is concerned, there are three things that I have never tried in 15 years of having sex: I never fucked a horse, never did it with a dead person, and I never ate shit—and that's it! The rest I've done. Sound's like I'm bragging? I guess I am!

VERA: Sex was linked to Prince Charming. The first time I had it, I wanted to have sex all the time, wanted to get married, and it was hooked up to all of that right away. I was shocked when it didn't happen. I went as far as picking out the motel on the Garden State Parkway where we were going to fuck forever. But my first lover only wanted to get into my pants and then he left me. And I bet he's sorry now!

SPRINKLE: I've come up with a new theory about sex. There is a scale and at one end is absolutely total ecstasy and sheer enlightenment. On the other end is abuse, pain, suffering, rape, power-tripping—everything negative about sex. I guess married life or boring, routine sex would be in the middle. I've traveled virtually the entire line, made a stop at every single point. I've experienced everything bad about it—from something I've done or something done to me. And I've experienced incredible ecstasy and beauty, love and peace through sex . . . more than with any other method that I've found. When I was at the low end of the scale and in a

THE SISTER ROSITA SUMMER SAINT CAMP
July 28–August 3 & August 3–August 11 1987

Come to SISTER ROSITA'S SUMMER SAINT CAMP and learn discipline,* how to look for miracles, talk in accents . . . wear a habit (all yellow clothes), get up early, exercise into oneness, take pilgrimages to sacred places (tour Woodstock and swim in the Hudson); take cold showers and prepare for next winter, eat sparingly (rice and beans); fast one day a week, research stories about the saints (performance artists).

*thrift; how to walk and smile like a nun; how to live without hot water, art, or sex; how to remember to turn the lights off when leaving a room; how to make a hair shirt and enjoy wearing one; how to live on air when hungry; how to live without the use of your refrigerator over the Christmas holidays; how to spot a martyr.

At the successful completion of these hardships you will receive saint papers and a performance certificate from the ST. ROSITA ART/LIFE INSTITUTE.

TO APPLY: Send a 2-page bio answering the question: WHY I WANT TO BE A SAINT AND HOW I HAVE BEEN ONE IN THE PAST.
BRING: walking shoes. sleeping bag. swimming suit. your habit (yellow if want). tape recorder tapes and any supplies you'll need.
WHERE: exit 19 (kingston) off thruway. Take broadway to abeel st. right on abeel (in the rondout). Or take a B bus from the Adirondack Trailways station.
DONATION: $250 one week
$520 two weeks
SEND: a self-addressed, stamped envelope with bio, photo, and/or self-portrait to:
SUMMER SAINT CAMP
Montano
THE ART/LIFE INSTITUTE
85 Abeel St.
Kingston, NY 12401

Ed. note: Above is the 1987 camp flyer. THE ART/LIFE INSTITUTE is currently located at 85 Abeel Street, Kingston, New York. The Summer Saint Camp and/or workshop is an ongoing event; for current information and prices write to:

THE ART/LIFE INSTITUTE
c/o 9 John Street
Saugerties, NY 12477

negative place about sex, I stopped in order to cleanse myself and did that for 6 months, once for 8 months, and then a month here and there.

Sometimes I still make mistakes about sex and go to bed with someone and am disappointed, but I can certainly avoid mistakes because of experience—and can also spot an opportunity! When I worked in the whorehouse, I tried to guess what the person was like sexually by looking at their ass or hands. I did face reading, body reading, and I'd also guess what their occupation was and then see if I was right. That was a way of making things amusing. Sometimes I was off. Sometimes I was totally accurate. If the person was crazy or scary, that excited me. Occasionally a trick was a challenge. Miraculously I was never raped or violently assaulted or anything real scary. It's like I walked on hot coals and was totally unscathed. I went into hooking with a heart of gold. I went into it all the way. No one forced me. I loved it. It was something I was very thankful to find. It was wonderful for me and I benefited from it in countless ways. My heart of gold got wounded towards the end because sometimes I got ripped off for my money or a guy would be too rough or unappreciative. Numerous other little hurts.

I try not to put myself in a negative situation anymore. I don't need to experience lousy sex. I've done that. There's a lot of stuff that I don't need to do but I did need to go to that negative extreme so that I could find out what the other side was all about. It's a process of evolution.

VERA: We each go through our own evolution. I went from NO NO NO to YES YES YES to sex. Now, I'm in the middle and I insist on being conscious during sex—and I insist that it's very intimate. Even if it's with a stranger, there's an intimacy going on.

SPRINKLE: There was one point, for about a year in my sexual evolution, where I went to a kinky sex club. I would be in the center of the room, surrounded by 12 guys on their knees, jerking off, then I'd go get fist-fucked by an amputee without a fist, then have a dog eat crisco off my pussy, then I'd fist-fuck a guy up the ass, piss on someone—all in one night. It was the most liberating, mind-boggling, fabulous, fantastic time in my life. It was awesome and felt great. But today, you couldn't get me to do that if you paid me—or at least paid me a lot! Now, that would not excite me. So if I see somebody who's into dumb, stupid S&M, I try not to judge it because at one time, something that's a turn-off to me now was once the most exciting, liberating turn-on in the world.

MONTANO: By following something through to the end, you gain a nonjudgmental mind.

VERA: Yes, definitely. Everything taken in its total context makes sense. Plus, sex feels *good*. Having your pussy eaten by a dog feels *good*. Now I wouldn't do it but all these things really feel good. Sometimes people are afraid to try things so they lay trips on each other. But so many sex rules that don't make sense keep people from experiencing good feelings.

MONTANO: People are afraid of feeling and sex.

VERA: That's OK. Not everyone travels the same route.

SPRINKLE: Not everyone needs to do what I did! Not at all! Not at all! I was curious about sex, that's why I did it. And then I would think about what I had learned—make magazines about it, take pictures of it, talk to other people about it, interview people. So it was a constant study. I would meet a foot fetishist and would want to know what that was about so he would show me his whole trip. Veronica and I once had this experience with a great foot fetishist. Veronica, didn't he work as a pedicurist?

VERA: At one time he did and then he was found out.

SPRINKLE: He did Brooke Shields' toes, Cheryl Tiegs'—celebrities' toes.

VERA: He had watched our cable TV sex show, wrote a letter to us telling us what our exact shoe sizes were and volunteered himself to do anything we wanted. So we invited him over to our house and made a videotape.

SPRINKLE: He put chopsticks between our toes, tied the chopsticks together and when he pulled the string the chopsticks would tighten. It was called the Chinese pedicure. Then we got the hairbrush on the bottom of the foot. It was a whole lot of fun. Very creative. And of course what we learned, we could use on other people. It was going to the source; he could teach us everything.

VERA: We used the Chinese technique recently on the director of a performance art festival and made our way into the festival!

SPRINKLE: That's right, we did.

MONTANO: What are fetishes about?

VERA: With the foot fetishist, I felt that he was looking at my feet but also up my skirt, at my pussy. My foot was a vehicle to get closer. He said, "Anybody can have sex with you but how many men can you find who will want to give you a pedicure?"

SPRINKLE: Didn't we fuck him?

VERA: No, that was another foot fetishist. He jerked off, pulled on the cord tighter and tighter and the chopsticks broke off. We had the vibrators, remember? A lot of people fixated on a particular part of the body are afraid of getting any closer, or sometimes it's a sneaky way of getting closer. If he hadn't offered to pedicure us, we probably wouldn't have invited him over.

SPRINKLE: That's like Frank Moore talking about painting nudes. He's spastic, in a wheelchair, and wanted to see people naked. And he couldn't say, "Will you come over to my house and take your clothes off?" But he could say, "Could you come over to my house so that I can paint you nude?" I bought one of his paintings. It's wonderful . . . like a de Kooning.

Adding cameras, video, lights, and costumes to sex allows things to go much further. You get that camera out and it changes people. I did things for camera that I definitely wouldn't have done! Also money is a nice incentive, too.

I often say that the two reasons I got involved in the sex business are fantasy fulfillment and money. It's well paid given the fact that minimum wage is $3.35 an hour. So a woman making $400 in a peep show plus tips on the side is doing much better.

I never did it for the money. I used money as an excuse to do what I wanted to do. For example, if I needed to pay my rent, I'd go to work in an S&M house. I wouldn't have gone to work there if the money hadn't been there but I think I wanted to work in an S&M house to see what it was about.

VERA: Money was not the number one motive. In my case, what sex was about and what I was taught about sex didn't fit so I've explored everything, done a lot of research. What I've found out is that I am the one who creates the image of living each moment.

MONTANO: You have to be brave and curious to do this.

SPRINKLE: The only hard part was hurting my parents, although they have always accepted what I've wanted to do. My brothers especially didn't want a sister who was a porn star, but after 13, 14 years, they know it's not a passing phase and have become proud of me. I've just had an article published in Penthouse, lectured at Dartmouth, and am writing for a performance art journal so maybe they will be more understanding. But I've always gotten off on being a nonconformist.

Now I've learned how to handle my family. I don't bring it up. If they ask me, I tell them. They express their disapproval and I say, "I have to do what I have to do." And then they say, "As long as you're not being forced or abused."

But going back—getting into porn was perfect for me. I love sex. I also love creativity—making movies, video and photos, acting, making costumes, etc. And it involves a lot of play—the world puts down sex and also play. I am just beginning to accept that to be an artist is fun.

I've seen incredible transformation. I myself have been totally transformed by my years in the sex business. Totally transformed. But I definitely remember one situation: There was this woman who came to a massage parlor where I was working. She had these enormous breasts and her name was Simone. She was very shy, very insecure, and it was her first day as a hooker. I was gentle and helpful, took her under my wing, told her "This might happen, that might happen." She had four kids, was a Hasidic Jew, had worked in the garment district where she made shit money and was always being told to make coffee. Her husband kept her submissive and she generally had a miserable existence. So she left him, had the kids to feed, and ended up being a hooker. After two months she was like a flower blossoming—was making $2,000 a week, was enjoying sex for the first time in her life, was buying her kids everything they wanted, was strong, was becoming happy, looking more beautiful, was getting facials. She was living it up! She was learning about men, learning about women, she was being brave, going against what everyone else told her to do, and became a far better and happier person. It was wonderful to see and I feel like that happened to me also. Up until I got into the sex biz, I was miserable, shy and insecure, totally insecure, and I overcame most of that.

VERA: I remember interviewing this one woman who worked in a peep show. She was 24, had a baby when she was 16, and I asked her if she regretted not having a husband. She said, "I used to feel bad because I could not give my baby things. Then I started working here and now I feel good." As she was saying that, another woman walked into the room and said, "Right on."

SPRINKLE: Of course there is another side of the coin: people getting into drugs, killing themselves—but that's not necessarily because of sex or porn. They sometimes get into prostitution because they need money for drugs.

VERA: For women who become dominatrixes, that's really a transformation. A lot of anger gets expressed toward men. When you put on that outfit and take out that whip, you know what that man is like. I felt very powerful in that role, almost like a witch. I don't do that so often anymore except by telephone for one special person whom I have never met, who also happens to be my mentor. He is 80 years old, a lawyer, a historian, and very wise. He teaches me about life. I teach him about fantasy.

I got into S&M pretty regularly at the Hell Fire Club. I had one lover who I did S&M with and I remember letting out a lot of anger as I whipped him. When I was whipping him, I was whipping every man. I grew up with a lot of love, but even with all that love, there was stuff going on that was confusing. When you are a dominatrix, you work out a lot of that.

SPRINKLE: The idea of whipping someone now is a total turnoff. But lately I've heard something I really like: "Everyone is doing the best they can with what they know and where they came from." And I really like that because it helps me not feel guilty about some of the stupid shit I did because I did it at the time I didn't think it was stupid shit.

To whip someone now doesn't appeal to me because I somehow feel that it hurts them deep down, even though I whipped people with love. I'm in a more soft mode now. I'd like to take somebody who wanted to be whipped and show them what more pure, direct love is like. And Tantra is the image that I have for that—Tantra and loving myself.

VERA: Being spanked while having sex brought pain and guilt and sex together. Now I don't want to associate pain with sex anymore. And I don't want to perpetuate that feeling in other people who get off on it the way that I used to get off on it. I don't want that idea to stay in the world.

SPRINKLE: My motivation was to collect experience and to have fun.

VERA: Yes, I can remember one particular orgy that was quantity sex, not quality sex.

SPRINKLE: I had to experience quantity sex before I could experience quality.

VERA: From not being intimate you learn what intimacy is all about.

SPRINKLE: What I'm exploring in sex now is psychic sex—what's invisible. I feel as if I'm going to be dealing with sex for the rest of my life. I'm totally obsessed with it; I walk down the street and that's almost all that I think about. Or if I'm going to make something, a drawing or a photo, it's always about sex.

MONTANO: What is your collaboration like?

SPRINKLE: Great! We've worked and played together for seven years now.

VERA: We always say that if one of us had a cock, we'd get married. There's someone there to go the distance with you. When we say, "Let's do it, we do it." It's about feeling, loving, and trusting.

SPRINKLE: I love collaborating.

MONTANO: The art world is very excited that you decided to join us. What's happening when you do your thing for that audience?

SPRINKLE: First of all I want to share that you baptized Veronica and me *"artists"* yesterday. That's important to put in here. But the difference between the art world and the porn world is that now I can really tell the truth without prostituting myself. It's being able to have the freedom to express what I really feel instead of worrying about what "they" want. Usually I think, they need to have an orgasm so I'd better write this or photograph that so it can turn them on, although it doesn't turn me on.

Now I want to share my work with my peers who think the way I do. The only place that is open enough for someone like me is the art world. But it's scary. Not many people think the way I do and I might not make a living at it like I can in porn.

VERA: Being in the art world as opposed to the sex world is about taking sex out of a hidden place, out of a ghetto, hidden from the rest of the world. The art world is more open. Now I can feel that I can bring sex out in the open. This means a change in attitude more than anything else.

SPRINKLE: And yes, there is the exciting new challenge of trying to turn on the art world. I mean, I've done it all in porn. There's nowhere else to go. I really need a new audience.

VERA: We love a great dog and pony act!!!

MONTANO: What is AIDS doing to or for your evolution?

SPRINKLE: I'm trying to see it as a positive thing.

VERA: I can't see it as positive because I've been seeing the horrors, too. But I'm concentrating on the positive healing thing that's going on in the world. People are getting closer. And the realization of how much we need each other and are connected is very exhilarating.

SPRINKLE: It changes things because society is jumping on the bandwagon and saying, "See, it *was* wrong and now you're paying the price." So there's a lot of going back into the closet. Negative thoughts and feelings about sex are around. But I'm seeing more intimate and spiritual sex evolving. There's more love in the air. It's not just about cocks going into assholes and pussies anymore.

MONTANO: What about all of the people who missed out and didn't get enough and now feel they can't because of the "health crisis"?

SPRINKLE: That's really a sad thing but we can show them what it was like. I have pictures and stories.

VERA: Safe sex is OK. Sex with rubbers can still be good sex. Everything has its pluses and minuses. Sexual freedom does, sexual abstinance does, jerking off does. We are all still left with a treasure chest of possibilities.

SPRINKLE: I'd rather promote good diet, good health, and self-love instead of condoms. (Use condoms too, of course.) Tantra can be safe. Maybe kids today are going to be happier in a monogamous situation than I was fucking half the world. Maybe they will experience something that I could never experience just because they have that limitation. My limitation was that I had to fuck the whole world because there was birth control and the freedom to do that. I never got to see what it was like to be with one person for 14 years straight.

MONTANO: What will they do to stay monogamous?

VERA: To acknowledge a commitment to one another. To acknowledge that times have changed. We are getting very '50s, very into not having as much sex. Everything has a season and it's not great the way this season has come about. It comes from a plague, but we have to be humbled by the fact that it exists and that we are part of it. We may not understand all of the reasons for it. Hard as it feels sometimes, there is joy in being part of the cosmos.

SPRINKLE: Before, if I wanted to get to know someone, the best way was to just fuck and then you knew each other quite well. I fucked everyone I met. Now that I'm not fucking everyone I meet, I still want that intimacy, I want to know them—so I'm having to find other ways. One great way is the healing circle, which is like the spiritual baths. You go there, get off on the people around you—and it has the same intensity as when 20 people were jerking off on me. But that was a whole big physical show. Now we can relate in other ways.

VERA: Even if you don't find someone to have sex with when you leave the healing circle at night, you still have a feeling that you carry over and can share with other people.

SPRINKLE: We do rituals, chanting, massage, singing, dancing, reading, meditations. It's very erotic. The men are so sexy, too. Unfortunately half of them have AIDS.

VERA: We come together on a consistent basis.

SPRINKLE: Also, working together is very sexual. We've been here at your house for 3 days, haven't had sex, and yet I feel we've gotten very deep, very intense. Whereas if we were just hanging out, it wouldn't be the same. The way we are together allows me to learn, concentrate, experiment, perform, create.

MONTANO: What piece of yours linked sex, life, and art?

VERA: Going on a trip around the world. I went to 15 different cities in 80 days. In all those places, especially India, I got into the feeling of being a woman from that place. In India I wore heavy makeup, dressed in garters, stockings and a leather skirt, a corset, come-fuck-me pumps, and flashed in front of the Taj Mahal and all the national monuments. So it was a chance to take this image of myself around the world through centuries, through different places, and to be women from all those places. Besides I had intense sexual experiences as me/them with the added bonus of taking photos and writing about it afterward. It was complete, unique, and made me happy with myself.

SPRINKLE: This week with you has been a highlight.

VERA: We've done something here that's been good for our friendship and then we get the added bonus of you, so thank you for reaching out and being accessible.

MONTANO: Anything to add?

SPRINKLE: Sex is so cosmic it's undescribable.

VERA: I hope that Annie and I grow old together.

Linda Montano *is a conceptual/life artist and has been teaching herself performance since 1969. Eating disorders, sexual obsession, fear of death, and guilt are themes explored via experiments in duration, altered consciousness, and dream induction. In 1983 she was tied with an eight-foot rope to Tehching Hsieh for a year. They never touched. Now she is experiencing 7 Years of Living Art.*

Annie Sprinkle *is "The High Priestess of the Porn Modernist Movement," a "feminist-porn-activist," and advocate of "New Age Sex" living and loving in Manhattan.*

Veronica Vera *is an artist/propagandist/sexual evolutionary/self-documentarian/animal goddess and native of New Jersey. Her work can be found in* Penthouse, Adam *magazine, the Torch Gallery (Amsterdam), and Fem Video (New York City).*

OUR WEEK AT SISTER ROSITA'S SUMMER SAINT CAMP

STORY BY VERONICA VERA

SCRAPBOOK BY ANNIE SPRINKLE

Our first encounter with Linda Montano was extremely intimate. I was sitting on the toilet at the Franklin Furnace Gallery, N.Y.C. To my left was a bulletin board that contained hundreds of notices, but the one that caught my eye announced: "The Sister Rosita Summer Saint Camp." Having been educated as a Catholic, this immediately appealed to all of my emotions. I read on, "Learn how to spot a martyr, how to look for miracles, wear a habit (all yellow clothes)...

FIRST CLASS MAIL

FIRST CLASS MAIL

The Franklin Furnace bathroom is pretty large. It is one of those toilets where two good friends might easily enter together. I read the notice to my friend and partner Annie Sprinkle. We both agreed that the name "Montano" included in the address must refer to the renowned performance artist. Annie spoke her name with reverence. Luckily, I was not so well informed, because I might have been intimidated and not answered the notice. The next morning my application for sainthood- the story of my sexual evolution- was in the mail accompanied by a photo of me and Annie dressed in crinolines and corsets, she with camera, me with tape recorder and bearing the caption "The High Heel School of Journalism." Linda responded immediately by post card and then by telephone. She explained that part of her "Seven Year Piece" is to invite two people to her home, the Art/Life Institute, each for one week during the summer. We met for lunch, and were accepted to spend a week together at the convent.

ATTICA

Non-profit Org.
U.S. Postage
PAID
Columbus, Ohio
Permit No. 711

USA 25 LOVE

Annie: Thanks for your letter: I'm also
excited about our time together. Loved tantra
article + would like to meet Jarvala someday.
I am contacting High Performance abt an
"exclusive" A week at the Art/Life Institute
with you doing something, Veronica doing some
thing + I would do interview with both of you.
I have read all of your material + am inspired.

Veronica — also read your around the world —
love it. I feel that we all will teach
each other alot — thanks for food.

Be hip,
Be cove
Let the Kundalini rise
I'll call early July to tell
you abt. how to get here
with 2 palms together + a bow also —
Linda, Mother Superior

Annie Sprinkle
+
Veronica Vera
~~10 Lexington Ave~~
#11 F
NYC 10016

TOP SECRET.
SEZ ANNIE

USA 14 Julia Ward Howe

USA 25 LOVE

Prevention
THE MAGAZINE FOR BETTER HEALTH
Subscription $13.97
Single copy $18.00
PRT 12 issues $12.97
FOUR PAYMENTS $3.24

FIRST CLASS MAIL

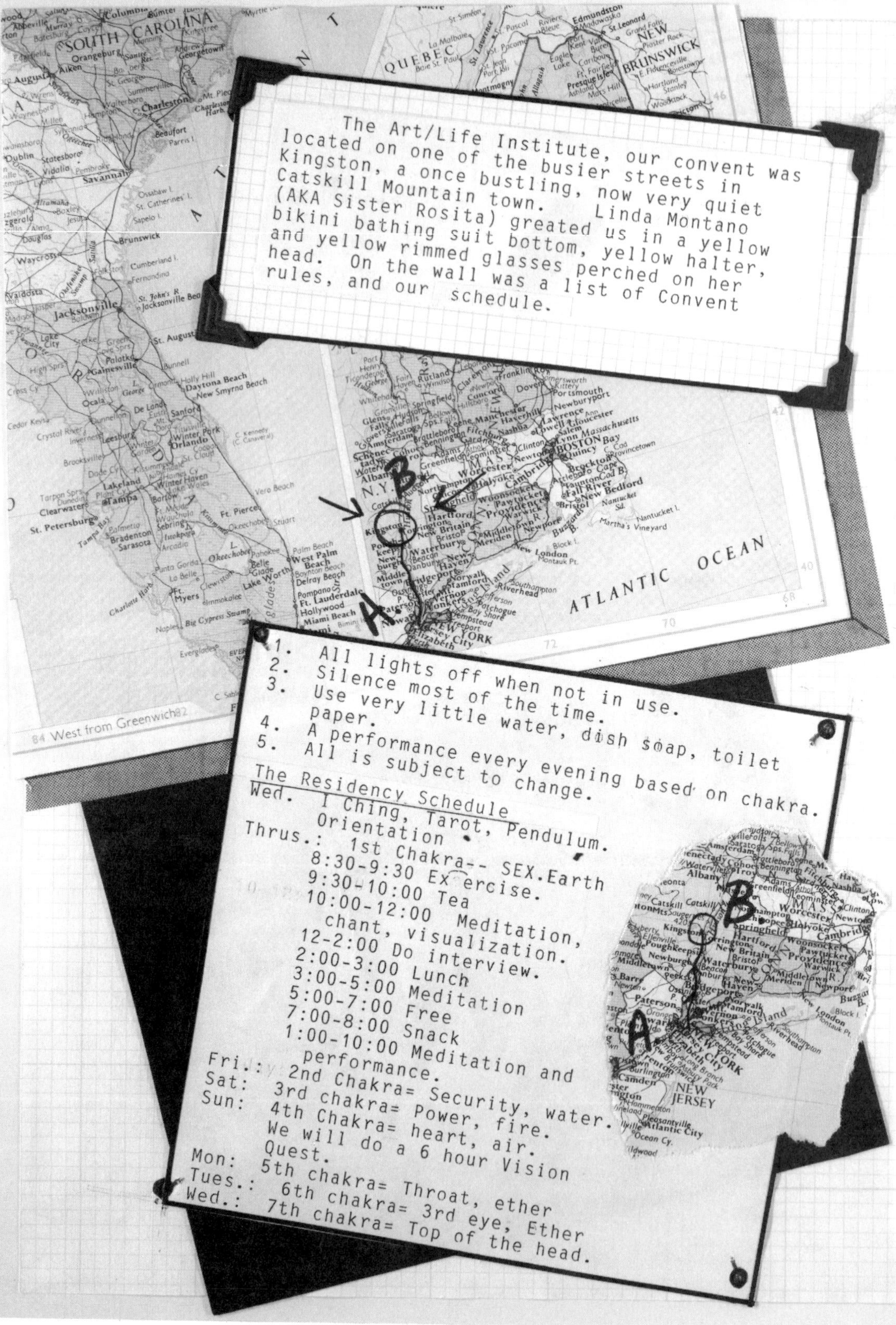

The Art/Life Institute, our convent was located on one of the busier streets in Kingston, a once bustling, now very quiet Catskill Mountain town. Linda Montano (AKA Sister Rosita) greated us in a yellow bikini bathing suit bottom, yellow halter, and yellow rimmed glasses perched on her head. On the wall was a list of Convent rules, and our schedule.

1. All lights off when not in use.
2. Silence most of the time.
3. Use very little water, dish soap, toilet paper.
4. A performance every evening based on chakra.
5. All is subject to change.

The Residency Schedule

Wed. I Ching, Tarot, Pendulum. Orientation

Thrus.: 1st Chakra-- SEX.Earth
- 8:30-9:30 Ex ercise.
- 9:30-10:00 Tea
- 10:00-12:00 Meditation, chant, visualization.
- 12-2:00 Do interview.
- 2:00-3:00 Lunch
- 3:00-5:00 Meditation
- 5:00-7:00 Free
- 7:00-8:00 Snack
- 1:00-10:00 Meditation and performance.

Fri.: 2nd Chakra= Security, water.
Sat: 3rd chakra= Power, fire.
Sun: 4th Chakra= heart, air. We will do a 6 hour Vision Quest.
Mon: 5th chakra= Throat, ether
Tues.: 6th chakra= 3rd eye, Ether
Wed.: 7th chakra= Top of the head.

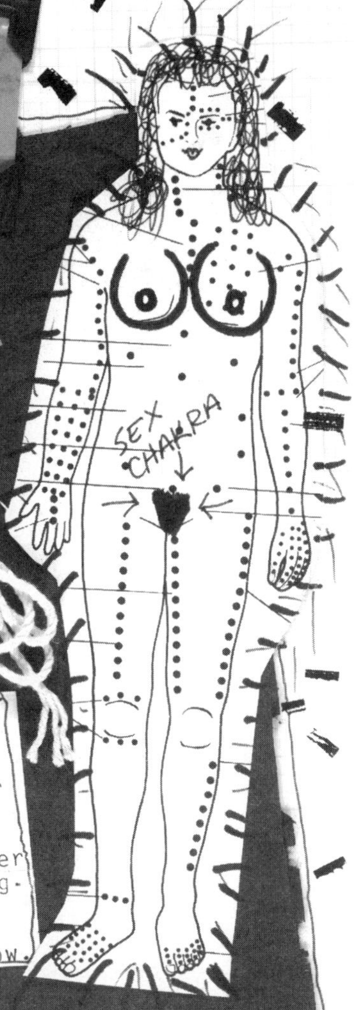

Each day we meditated on a different chakra, chanted its sound, exercised and spent time in the Art/Life Institute's sparsely furnished, floor to ceiling yellow room. We each sat in our space and connected our sex chakras with long strings. The summer was conducive to very little clothing. I enjoyed the chance to get re-connected to my body. The clothing we did wear was like Linda's, all yellow.

Neither Annie nor I had enough yellow clothes for a week's stay. So, on the morning of our departure, we added six boxes of RIT's "Brilliant Yellow" dye to a pile of old but hardly worn white and beige clothes. It was fun to send them to their yellow bath and a new lease on life. This act of preparation made us feel that we were on our way to the convent, an exotic place that required a different costume.

Sister Rosita read Annie's tarot cards and told her that she might have a baby. Little did Annie know, she was at that moment, pregnant. The first night I had what Sister Rose described as a "seven chakra dream." It encompassed art, sex, feminism, money, and love. We were off to a good start. Our psyches were open.

The pendulum spelled out "GO TO THE BEACH" and so we did because we decided that art is both work and relaxation. The beach was refreshing. We bathed with a couple hundred people from the town and this was a reminder that even in our seclusion we were part of the world at large. Annie got excited to think that because we were part of Linda's Seven Year Piece, even our swimming was performance art or as Linda says simply, "Life is art."

B.

A.

Shortly after our arrival in the midst of a heat wave, the clouds parted and big, fat raindrops fell from the sky. "It is a blessing," said Sister Rose. And so it was. I suggested we go out and play in the rain. As we danced around the garden, I felt happy and joyful that we three had chosen to travel on this spiritual, this physical and emotional path together. Then, I got scared. I felt anger and I was not sure why. By the afternoon of day one, Linda had me sitting on the kitchen floor beating up a telephone book with a rubber hose. The phone book and rubber hose were kept within easy reach under the sink. "You can put someone's face in the phone book if you like," she told me. I beat up my beloved father with my frightening anger until I was no longer angry, until I felt ecstasy. When I looked at the torn pages of the phone book, there was my dad smiling back at me. This part of the performance was so powerful for Annie that she was "terrified."

We had a few things to learn about Mother Superior's eccentricities. Convent life was frugal. Linda was not sure if her "rules" restricting such things as the usage of dish detergent and toilet paper were vestiges from her two year novitiate as a Missionary nun or because she was "cheap." Annie ate no chocolate chip cookies. Our meals were simple and cooked in one bowl. But we welcomed Mother Superior's gentle discipline. We nourished ourselves with love, ideas, brown rice, and beans. And today, we still make sure not to waste the toilet paper.

Linda's beloved dog Betty was our constant companion. She was old and made gross noises when she chewed on herself. Her ass was bald but her tail wagged constantly. Betty was a lot like life, not always easy to live with, but full of experience and love. Betty was a found guru.

Day #1 - Sex Chakra

"Hair pie" performance by Veronica Vera. (We loved it.)

Is it *just* more feminist cunt art ?¿?¿

Mud, flowers, pubic hair, yellow pages.

On the back yard of the Art/Life Institute.

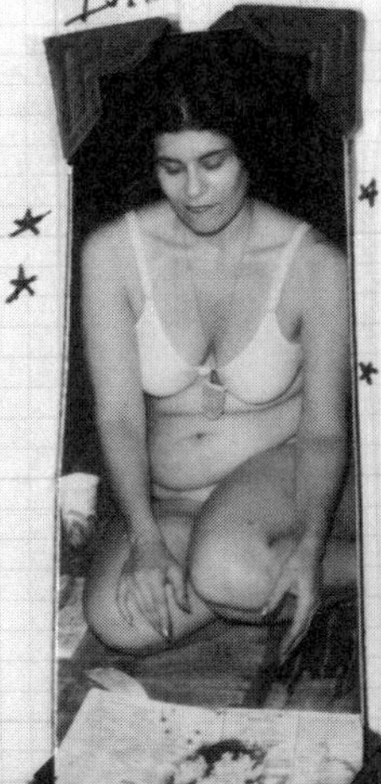

Each night we had a different performance assignment related to the chakra of the day. The first day was devoted to the sex chakra. Annie and I were curious to know what Linda's first year, the sex chakra year, had been like. She told us that she had lots of sex and five lovers at the same time. The element associated with the sex chakra is earth; the color is red. I made a "hair pie" out of mud mixed in a red bowl, flowers, and all of our pubic hair. Linda donated the most fur to the project which was really nice because, being a natural blonde, her hair was a great contrast next to the dark mud. We stuck our fingers in the pie. We tasted it. "Just don't chew it," I warned, remembering the unpleasant experience of gritty teeth. Linda and Annie loved the piece, but I wasn't willing to give myself a break. "Oh," I thought, "It's just another example of feminist cunt art." What I did enjoy about using the mud was that it gave me new material to work with and the understanding that I need not limit myself. I picked the mud because it was the first material I remembered having real fun with as a child and I wanted to return to those early uncivilized, unsocialized feelings. By the end of the week, I understood that I could save myself a lot of pain if I let go of my expectations of what art or I "should be."

A smash Hit!

← Pubic hair

Annie said about her performances:
"I eagerly took a role with Linda of guru/disciple. 'Oh, holy master Linda,' inquired this humble disciple, 'when I do performance art, is it better to work out negative experiences or to get into positive experiences?' 'Work on both,' she answered. 'Perhaps, you could choose one for public and one for private.' Yes. It was simple. I vowed then and there to do performances that make people laugh, feel good, get excited...Maybe one day I would do a performance where everyone has an orgasm...Maybe, I already had! I would work on my negative experiences in private and if I did turn them into public performances, I would make them enjoyable to my audience."

Annie's first performance was a multi- media extravaganza. She created an amazing whole world that travelled the spectrum from gawdy peep shoe to tantric cosmos. She gave Linda and me skimpy yellow outfits to wear and slutty high heels. Then she blasted us with raunchy music and directed us to dance and strut our stuff along with her. Before long

In Annie's performance "SEXWORK", she pays her audience $20 each.

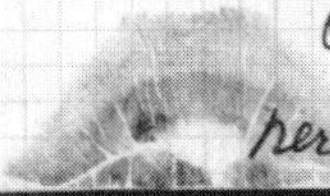

we were rolling over the floor being real nasty and loving it. Linda, who had said she felt uncomfortable in real sexy clothes, had no trouble letting it all out in this performance. As a reward, Annie threw us each a $20 tip. The second part of the performance took place in the garden under the stars. We sat in a circle and chanted OM three times. Then one at a time Linda and I put our head in Annie's lap while she equipped us with a condom and that other most important tool of the trade, ruby red lips. She applied the lipstick very slowly and sensuously. Our heads rose and fell under her breasts as we rode her orgasmically breathing stomach and looked up at the moon.

Later, as we sat quietly in the garden, Linda did a highly emotionally charged piece in which she stabbed the ground with scissors while she expressed anger about sex in a monotone chant. Then she took the clump of earth she'd cut free and threw it into the air. It was breathtaking and we were honored to share such a personal moment and masterpiece performance.

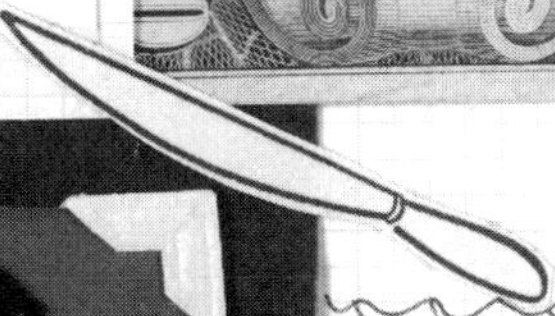

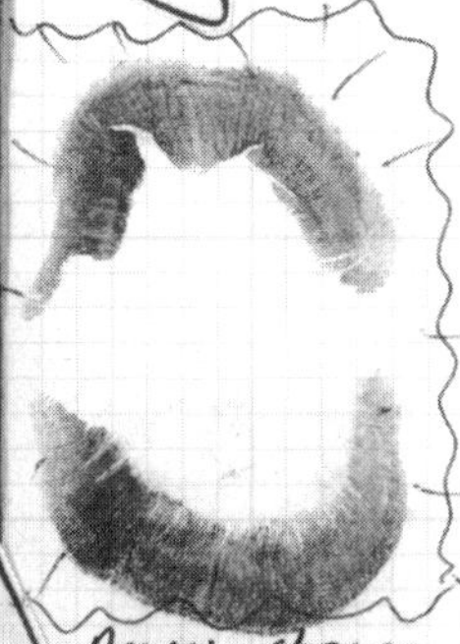

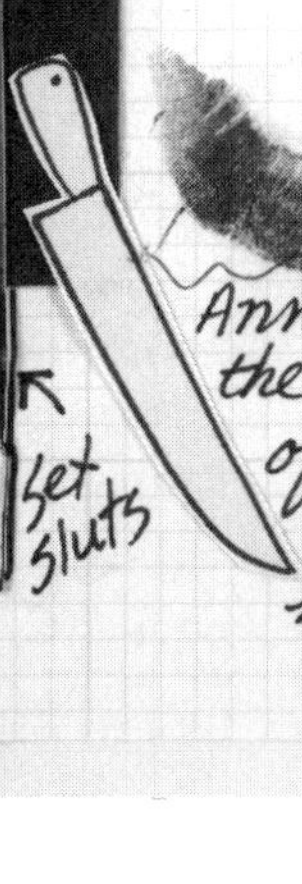

Jet sluts

Annie shares the joys of lip-stick brushes.

Linda Montano blindfolds Veronica.

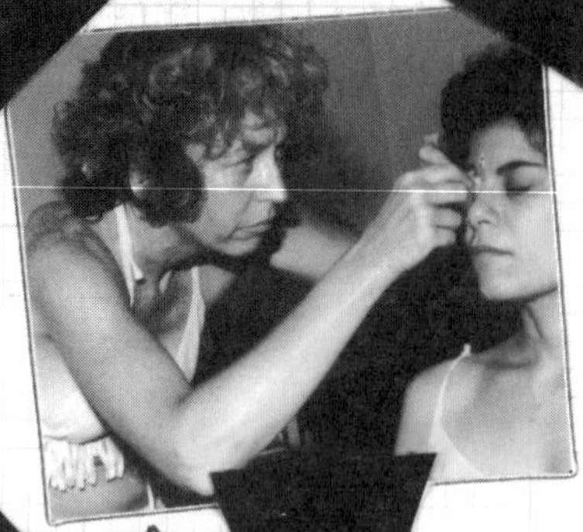

↑ Our teacher Linda

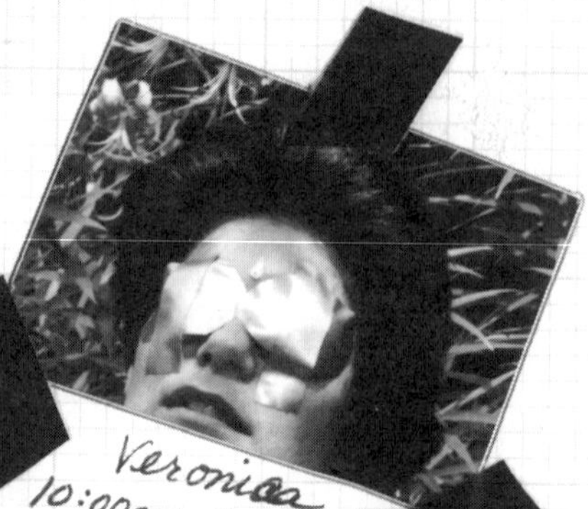

Veronica 10:00am-4:00pm

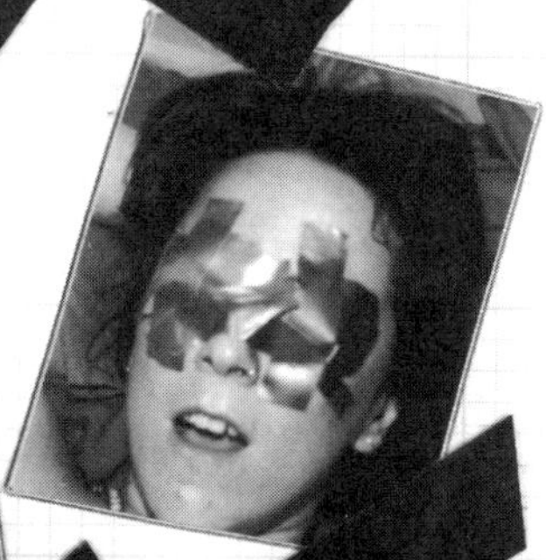

Annie Sprinkle 4:30 a.m-10:30p.m.

Linda described a piece which she had performed while wearing a blindfold and Annie said, "Oh, I'd love to do something like that." No problem for Mother Superior. We decided that Annie and I would each spend six hours under the blindfold. We threw the Chinese coins and I went first. As Sister Rosita applied the mask, I felt like I was being bandaged by a very kind nurse. Annie and I were keeping journals. Under the blindfold I kept my notes very simple. I wanted to be able to read them back, but I knew that even if the notes were indecipherable,that would tell me something. I saw writing in a new, relaxed way. Annie quickly changed her mind about the blindfold. She hated it. She did not like its S/M connotations. She did not like the dark. I enjoyed watching her squirm. She did stay in the blindfold the full six hours, but her favorite part was her release.

1

It was an incredible honor to be baptized an artist by my very favorite artist in the world, Linda Montano.

2

3

I went into a sort of trance;-- high on art/life.

4

I sobbed tears of joy. It was so moving.

The second chakra, located at the base of the spinal cord, related to physical and emotional security. The element was water. Annie quickly came up with the idea that we could be baptized artists by Linda. Much to our delight, she agreed. Together Annie and I wrote our baptismal vow: "I am safe and secure and I prosper as an artist. I accept that Annie Sprinkle/Veronica Vera is an artist." Our baptism was complicated because Annie was at the time blindfolded. We walked to a nearby park and sat in the grass behind a monument. Our mascot Betty watched over us. As Linda poured water over

↑ Photo of Veronica I took while I was blindfolded. I kind of like it!

Sister Veronica Mother Superior (Linda Montano) Sister Sprinkle

Annie's head and named her an artist. Annie burst into tears. "I always wanted to be an artist," she cried. Her sobs came from a place deep inside. Even I who knew her so well was surprised by her intense emotion. I did not expect to cry and I did not. "After all," I told myself, "I have always secretly believed I was an artist." When I was baptized, the event went by so quickly. I was worried because with Annie Behind a blindfold it was not likely my baptism would be documented. For one so confident, I was strangely uneasy. Left to her own devices, blind Annie was taking lots of pictures of trees. That night I went to sleep feeling very frustrated. In our first three days together, Annie seemed to be very clear on questions for Linda. I could not think of one, so I decided just to acknowledge my feeling of confusion. What a relief!

At our first meeting, Linda had said, "I have things to learn from you as well as you from me."
So we shared our expertise with our guru: we turned her into a porn queen. As usual we had brought along our own bag of tricks. Annie applied Linda's makeup in her favorite style, gawdy. I teased her hair to ultimate heights. From among our costumes, we decided the glittery harem outfit and yellow fishnets best suited Linda. She was a golden goddess and a carnival hootchy-kootchy girl. She was definitely Art.
F-Stop Fitzgerald arrived to document the piece.

There were other formal performances: Annie gave herself a humanitarian award for sexual service to the community; I demonstrated a truly motivational form of breast self-exam... We presented a show at a gallery described as "a hotbed of lesbian/feminist political activity" where we encouraged our audience to participate by sharing with us their ideas for an X rated movie. At the conclusion of this performance, Mother Superior surprised me and Annie with our diplomas--cherished hand-written certificates that stated we were "graduated from the Art/Life Institute with honors in performance/sainthood."

Before

I wanted to transform this ex-nun into a pin up girl. She agreed. The photos would only be used in prestigious art magazines, like THE DRAMA REVIEW. So here, folks, is Linda Montano's first all nude photo. Proof that Linda can create life in all genres.

After

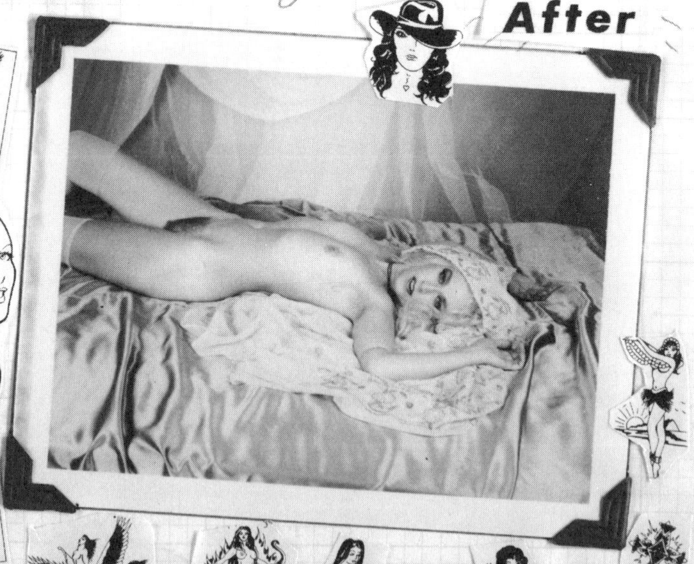

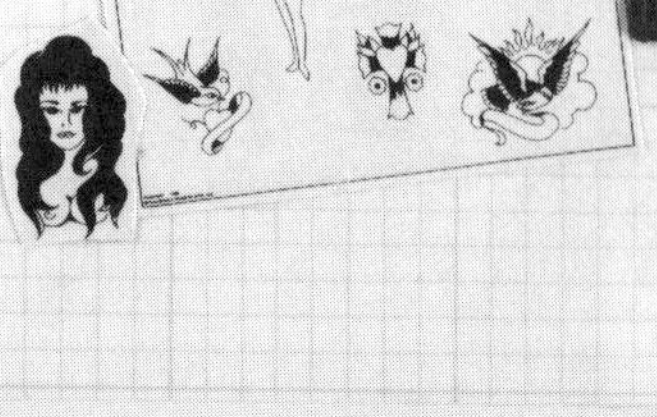

Our GURU, Sister Linda, with symbols of food, sex, money and ritual.

The closer we became, the more we appreciated our differences. It was hard to say good-by to Linda, though Annie and I, fledgling artists, were eager to spread our wings in the world we had left behind. We stood, all three in a circle, at the bus station and bowed, hands pressed together as in prayer. We did not speak, only put our heads together, connecting our energies through our top chakras. I felt so much power surge through my body, I removed my hat before it blew off my head. On the bus, we opened the daily newspaper. There was a big photo of Linda Montano seated cross-legged on the floor of our yellow room. Below the photo, in two inch letters for alll to see, was Linda's bold message, the lesson that Annie and I will always remember, let penetrate our lives, and carry into the world: Life is Art.

EROPLAY

Frank Moore

MY FIRST STROKE OF GOOD LUCK WAS I WAS BORN SPASTIC, UNABLE TO WALK OR TALK. ADD TO THIS GOOD FORTUNE THE FACT THAT MY FORMATIVE YEARS WERE IN THE '60S—MY FATE WAS ASSURED!

YES, I ALWAYS HAVE BEEN LUCKY. I HAVE A BODY THAT IS IDEAL FOR A PERFORMANCE ARTIST. AND I HAVE ALWAYS WANTED TO BE A PERFORMER. WHEN I WAS A KID, MY YOUNGER BROTHER USED TO GET MAD WHEN PEOPLE LOOKED AT ME WHEN HE PUSHED ME TO THE MOVIES OR TO THE TEEN CLUB. HE CRIED. BUT I LIKED PEOPLE LOOKING AT ME. THAT IS WHAT I MEAN BY "I AM LUCKY." I AM LUCKY I AM AN EXHIBITIONIST IN THIS BODY. ONE TIME, I WAS WORKING OUT ON THE JUNGLE GYM OUTSIDE OF OUR HOUSE—A KID CAME BY AND ASKED IF I WAS A MONSTER. I JUST ROARED LIKE A MONSTER. IT WAS FUN.

I WAS LUCKY. I WAS NEVER UNDER PRESSURE TO BE GOOD AT ANYTHING, TO MAKE MONEY, TO MAKE IT IN "THE REAL WORLD," TO BE POLISHED—OR THE OTHER DISTRACTIONS THAT OTHER MODERN ARTISTS HAVE TO, OR THINK THEY HAVE TO DEAL WITH. SO I COULD FOCUS ON HAVING FUN, ON GOING INTO TABOO AREAS WHERE MAGICAL CHANGE CAN BE EVOKED. IN FACT, A MAJOR REASON WHY I AM WRITING THIS IS TO ENCOURAGE ARTISTS WHO HAVE NOT BEEN SO BLESSED WITH BODIES THAT MARK THEM AS MISFITS, TO ASPIRE TO BE MISFITS ANYWAY, TO DO MISFIT ART ANYWAY—EVEN IF YOU ARE HANDICAPPED BY YOUR NORMAL BODY. YOUR ROAD IS DEFINITELY HARDER THAN MY ROAD. BUT THAT'S LIFE.

MY ART IS ROOTED IN BREAKING OUT OF ISOLATION. UNTIL I WAS 17, I DID NOT HAVE ANY WAY TO COMMUNICATE EXCEPT THROUGH MY FAMILY MEMBERS. FOR A COUPLE OF MY TEENAGE YEARS, I WAS VERY HARD OF HEARING. MY HEARING CLEARED UP. I INVENTED MY HEADPOINTER WHEN I WAS 17. MY COMMUNICATION ISOLATION WAS THEN DISPELLED. BUT IT TOOK ME ANOTHER 10 YEARS TO

SHAKE OFF THE ISOLATION CAUSED BY MY ATTITUDES AND SELF-IMAGE. THIS EARLY ISOLATION ALLOWED ME TO OBSERVE LIFE AND PEOPLE AS AN OUTSIDER. I ALWAYS WANTED TO BREAK PHYSICAL, EMOTIONAL, AND SPIRITUAL ISOLATION—FIRST FOR MYSELF, BUT THEN FOR OTHER PEOPLE.

THERE ARE OTHER ADVANTAGES TO MY BODY. PEOPLE PROJECT ONTO ME CERTAIN MYSTICAL POWERS—LIKE SEEING THROUGH THEIR FRONTS TO THEIR REAL SELVES—SEEING THE PAST AND THE FUTURE—AND WHAT THEY SHOULD DO. THEY ARE REACTING TO SOME SYMBOL OF THE DEFORMED MEDICINE MAN. THEY USE ME AS A MEDIUM FOR GETTING THROUGH TO OTHER DIMENSIONS. BECAUSE OF THE SLOWNESS OF MY COMMUNICATION BOARD, THEY ARE FORCED TO SLOW DOWN. THEY CAN PROJECT WHATEVER THEY WANT, MISREAD ME WHEN IT FITS THEM. I AM A SYMBOL. AND BECAUSE THEY GIVE ME POWER AS A SYMBOL, THEY ARE AFRAID OF ME. IT WAS JUST MY LUCK TO BE BORN INTO THE LONG TRADITION OF THE DEFORMED SHAMAN, THE WOUNDED HEALER, THE BLIND PROPHET, THE CLUB-FOOTED "IDIOT" COURT JESTER.

THERE ARE ALL KINDS OF ART. THERE IS ART THAT CALMS, ART THAT PACIFIES, ART THAT SELLS, ART THAT DECORATES, ART THAT ENTERTAINS. BUT WHAT I AM COMMITTED TO IS ART AS A BATTLE, AN UNDERGROUND WAR AGAINST FRAGMENTATION. THE BATTLE IS ON ALL REALITIES. THE CONTROLLERS HAVE ALWAYS TRIED TO FRAGMENT US FROM EACH OTHER. IMPRISON US IN ISLANDS OF SEX, COLOR, RELIGION, POLITICS, CLASS, LABELS, ETC., ETC., ETC., ETC., ETC.—THEY FRAGMENT OUR INNER WORLDS, THEY BLOW OUR INDIVIDUAL REALITIES APART AND PLAY THE PIECES AGAINST ONE ANOTHER. THEY

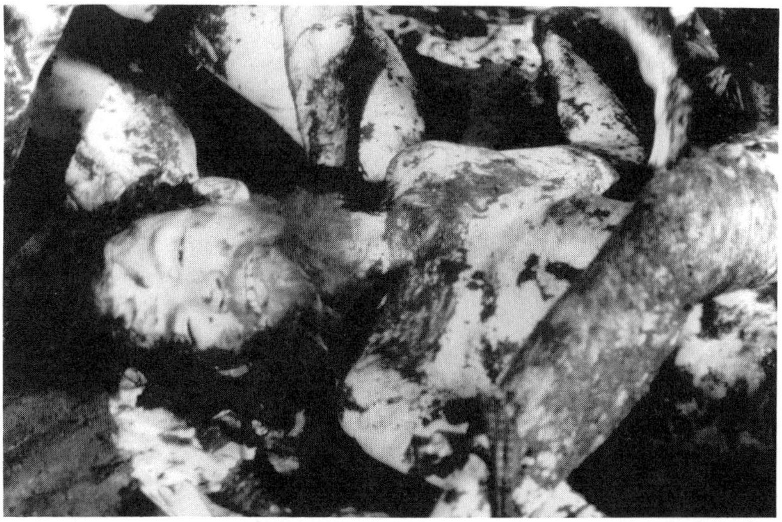

1. Frank Moore in a 12-hour performance, Mud Dance *(1977), at the San Francisco Art Institute. (Photo by K. Jennings)*

2. *"Sonny and Cher" (Frank Moore and Linda Mac) from* Outrageous Road Show *(1984) at New Generic in San Francisco. (Photo by M. Sullivan)*

ARE US, OR A PART OF US. THEY ARE THE CONTROLLERS, THE POLITICIANS, THE SEXISTS, THE WOMEN'S LIBBERS, THE PORNOGRAPHERS, THE CENSORS, THE MORALISTS, THE CHURCH, THE MEDIA, THE BUSINESSMEN, EDUCATORS, THE VICTIMS, AND THE POWERFUL.

THEY ARE US.

I THINK PERFORMANCE IS BEING RUINED BY TRYING TO PACKAGE IT AS ENTERTAINMENT, AS OFF-BEAT CABARET. WHEN SOMEONE GOES TO A CABARET, HE KNOWS THERE ARE CERTAIN LIMITS INVOLVED SUCH AS THAT EACH ACT MUST END BEFORE ANOTHER BEGINS; BUT IN PERFORMANCE, ANYTHING IS POSSIBLE. A PERFORMANCE CAN LAST FOR A MINUTE OR IT CAN LAST FOR DAYS. PERFORMANCE CAN START IN ONE SPACE BUT THEN MOVE TO ANOTHER. PERFORMANCE CAN BE STORYTELLING, IT CAN BE A GUY THREATENING YOU WITH A BASEBALL BAT, IT CAN BE A GUY HANGING BY HIS SKIN, OR THROWING FOOD, OR ANYTHING. IN PERFORMANCE ALL THINGS ARE POSSIBLE. AND THAT IS WHAT GIVES YOU AN EXTRA EDGE TO CREATE DREAMS.

PERFORMANCE, LIKE ANY AVANT-GARDE ART, IS THE WAY SOCIETY DREAMS; IT IS THE WAY SOCIETY EXPANDS ITS FREEDOM, EXPLORES THE FORBIDDEN.

THIS WAS WHAT SEALED ME INTO A PERFORMANCE LIFE.

IN 1972 I HAD JUST FINISHED TAKING A VERY INTENSIVE FILM COURSE IN SANTA FE. I HAD NO MONEY TO MAKE REAL FILMS. SO I STARTED LOOKING FOR A WAY TO WORK WITH PEOPLE. I WANTED TO SEE PEOPLE NUDE, AND TOUCH THEM, AND CREATE AN INTENSITY BETWEEN US. PAINTING WAS THE FIRST ATTEMPT. I USED TO SELL PAPERS ON A CORNER TO FIND PEOPLE TO PAINT. BUT ONCE THE PERSON WAS POSED THE SITUATION WAS STILL, NOT MOVING. SO I DID WHAT I CALLED NONFILMS—FOR WHICH I ASKED PEOPLE I MET WHEN I WAS SELLING NEWSPAPERS TO ACT OUT INTENSIVE EROTIC SCENES WITH ME. ALTHOUGH I HAD PLAYED WITH MY FRIENDS BEFORE IN NONSEXUAL EROTICISM, THIS WAS THE FIRST TIME I TRIED TO USE "SEXUAL" ACTS IN A NONSEXUAL ART FORM. I WAS SURPRISED WITH THE POWER THAT THIS RELEASED. BECAUSE OF THESE SCENES, THE PEOPLE STARTED TALKING ABOUT THEIR LIVES DURING THE SESSIONS AND SAID IT HELPED THEIR OTHER RELATIONSHIPS. NOT ONE PERSON MINDED THAT THERE WAS NO FILM. THESE NONFILMS WERE THE BASE FOR MY CAREER IN RELATIONSHIP COUNSELING IN THE LATE '70S.

BUT I WAS NOT SATISFIED WITH THESE NONFILMS BECAUSE THEY WERE BRIEF RELATIONSHIPS THAT DID NOT GO ANYWHERE. SO I STARTED LOOKING FOR SOME OTHER WAY TO WORK WITH PEOPLE. I TRIED TO CAST A PLAY, BUT I COULDN'T FIND ENOUGH PEOPLE. I STARTED THINKING OF AN INTIMATE THEATRE WHERE THE LINE BETWEEN AUDIENCE AND ACTORS WOULD BE ERASED. I STARTED THINKING ABOUT HOW IF THAT LINE WERE ERASED, IT WOULD PLACE MUCH MORE RESPONSIBILITY ON THE ACTORS. THEY WOULD HAVE TO DARE TO TRICK THE AUDIENCE INTO THE INTENSE MAGICAL STATE.

I DIVIDED MY WORK—THE WORD "WORK" IS WEIRD—IT IS LIKE PLAYING—INTO TWO PARTS. THE FIRST PART IS PLAYED IN "REAL LIFE"—FOR INSTANCE, I GO UP TO A PERSON ON A STREET AND ASK HIM TO BE IN SOME PROJECT WHICH MAY CONTAIN SOME NUDITY AND PHYSICAL PLAY. THE NUDITY AND PHYSICAL PLAY AS AN IDEA IN THIS CONTEXT IS A GREAT TOOL TO GET UNDER THE POLITE CHATTER SURFACE TO THE MORE MEANINGFUL THINGS, AND OFTEN MORE INTIMATE, MORE PERSONAL STUFF—WHICH IS, AFTER ALL, THE AIM OF THE PIECE. I CAN SEE THIS KIND OF PIECE LASTING ANYWHERE FROM A FEW SECONDS TO SEVERAL HOURS.

THE SECOND PART IS A PIECE IN A CONTROLLED SPACE, SUCH AS MY STUDIO, IN WHICH THERE IS A FORM GOING ON, GIVING THE PERSON A REASON TO BE THERE WITH ME.

THIS KIND OF PERFORMANCE IS DIFFERENT THAN NORMAL THEATRE. IN THIS KIND, THERE IS NO REAL SCRIPT. EVEN IF YOU HAVE A SCRIPT, IT REALLY IS A PROP. THE REAL

3. Frank Moore as Fiesto, *July 1986, in Berkeley, California. (Photo by D. Moore)*

COURSE OF ACTION IS SHAPED BY THE PERFORMER SO THE FLOW OF THE PIECE WILL GO FORWARD AND DEEPER.

WHAT IS IMPORTANT IS WHAT HAPPENS BETWEEN ME AS THE ARTIST AND MY AUDIENCE, HOW I CHANGE THEM AND HOW THEY CHANGE ME, THAT MAGICAL STATE IN WHICH WE INTERACT WITH EACH OTHER. I, AS THE PERFORMER, MUST CREATE AROUND THE PEOPLE, BY PLAYING FOR AND TO THEM, BY LETTING THE PERFORMANCE TAKE ME OVER AND GUIDE ME—EVEN WHEN IT LOOKS LIKE THE OTHER PEOPLE ARE DOING ALL OF THE ACTION. THE ULTIMATE GOAL IN MY PERFORMANCE IS TO CREATE A REALITY, NOT AN ILLUSION, WHICH THE AUDIENCE AND I ARE IN—EVEN IF I HAVE TO USE ILLUSIONS TO GET TO THIS REALITY.

THIS RAISES THE QUESTION OF MANIPULATION. ALMOST ANY TIME YOU PERFORM TO AN AUDIENCE, YOU MANIPULATE THE AUDIENCE. LET'S GET BEYOND THE NEGATIVE CONNOTATION OF THE WORD "MANIPULATE." PEOPLE GO TO THE THEATRE, MOVIES, CONCERTS, DANCE COMPANIES, ETC., TO HAVE THEIR EMOTIONS MANIPULATED. THEY COME INTO THE PERFORMANCE AREA WITH A WILLINGNESS TO BE MANIPULATED BY THE ARTISTS WITHIN CERTAIN LIMITS. BUT IN MY PERFORMANCES, THE ONES WHICH ARE NOT DIVIDED FROM THE REST OF LIFE BY A THEATRE OR A STAGE, THERE IS NO WAY TO TELL THE PERSON SHE IS ENTERING A PERFORMANCE. WHEN I HAVE A FORMAL STRUCTURE, A THEATRE SPACE, AND A SET TIME ENDING—WHAT IS REALLY GOING ON IS NOT WHAT IS SAID TO BE HAPPENING. ALSO IT IS A REALITY THAT IS HOPEFULLY BEING CREATED—PEOPLE WILL BE AFFECTED, INFECTED, AND EFFECTED BY THIS REALITY.

PERFORMANCE OBVIOUSLY GOES MUCH FARTHER BACK THAN 1909 WHEN IT BECAME A FORMAL ART FORM. I THINK PERFORMANCE CAME INTO EXISTENCE TO FILL A VOID IN

WESTERN LIFE. THE VOID WAS THE LACK OF MAGIC AND INSPIRATION. THE TWO AREAS OF CREATIVITY, THEATRE AND RELIGION, THAT TRADITIONALLY WERE THE SOURCE OF THIS MAGICAL INSPIRATION HAD LONG AGO MOVED FROM MAGIC TO ENTERTAINMENT AND POLITICS. THIS VOID ALSO GAVE BIRTH TO PSYCHOLOGY DURING THE SAME TIME PERIOD. I OFTEN GET THE CRITICISM THAT MY WORK IS REALLY PSYCHOLOGY AND THERAPY, AND NOT ART. WHEN IT IS REALIZED THAT PSYCHOLOGY AS A FORMAL SCIENCE AND PERFORMANCE AS A FORMAL ART WERE BORN AT THE SAME TIME, THIS CRITICISM CAN BE ANSWERED. PERFORMANCE AND PSYCHOLOGY ARE BOTH INVOLVED IN SPIRITUAL HEALING.

I SEE PERFORMANCE AS EXPERIMENTS IN HUMAN POSSIBILITIES. TO DO THESE EXPERIMENTS, I FORMED IN SANTA FE IN 1972 A WEEKLY DROP-IN WORKSHOP TO DO RITUALS LASTING MANY HOURS. A YEAR LATER, PEOPLE FROM THAT DROP-IN GROUP MOVED WITH ME TO N.Y.C. TO BE THE CORE OF A COMMITTED GROUP. BUT IT WAS IN BERKELEY THAT WE FOUND A PERMANENT HOME IN 1974. THERE, THE WORKSHOP SLOWLY DEVELOPED INTO A GROUP OF 30 PEOPLE.

IN THE LATE '70S WE STARTED OUR PUBLIC PERFORMANCES BY DOING LONG RITUALISTIC PLAYS. OVER THE YEARS, THE GROUP BRANCHED OUT TO DO MANY DIFFERENT KINDS OF LIVE AND VIDEO PIECES, INCLUDING *the outrageous beauty revue* [1978].

THE *o.b.r.* WAS A CABARET SHOW THAT TRIED TO SHORT-CIRCUIT THE CABARET LIMITS OF TIME AND STAGE. IT DID THIS BY BEING A SHOW OF PEOPLE WHO WERE HAVING FUN AND WHO WERE LIVING THEIR FANTASIES—A SHOW THAT

4. An all-day, private performance, Rapture Performance, *on 18 January 1987 in Berkeley, California. (Photo by Linda Mac)*

5. *The audience and cast during the "Intimate Gestures" section of* Intimate Cave *on 14 May 1987 at Franklin Furnace in New York City. (Photo by L. Barany)*

INCLUDED THE AUDIENCE DIRECTLY IN THE ACTION—AN UNPOLISHED SHOW THAT FLAUNTED NUDITY, EROTICISM, AND GORE IN A SILLY, CHILDLIKE PLAYFULNESS—AN EVER-CHANGING SHOW WITH PREGNANT SEX SYMBOLS, NUDE GIRLS, CRIPPLED ROCK STARS, MEN AS WOMEN AND WOMEN AS MEN WITHOUT ANY SEXUAL MEANING. THE *o.b.r.* RAN FOR THREE YEARS AND WAS BY FAR MY MOST POPULAR WORK IN TERMS OF HOW MANY PEOPLE SAW IT. BUT THE SUCCESS OF A PIECE SHOULD NOT BE JUDGED BY HOW MANY PEOPLE SEE IT, BUT BY HOW FAR IT WENT BEYOND THE TABOOS, BY ITS MAGIC POWER FOR CHANGE. BY THIS STANDARD, MY BEST WORK WITH THE GROUP WAS OUR 48-HOUR DREAM PERFORMANCES IN THE LATE '70S.

SINCE 1983, I HAVE BEEN DOING A PERFORMANCE SERIES AT U.C. BERKELEY WHICH HAS GIVEN ME A LAB WHERE I CAN DEVELOP PIECES BY DOING THEM OVER AND OVER WITHOUT THE PRESSURES OF MAKING MONEY OR ENTERTAINING. THESE PIECES ARE WHAT GOT ME THE N.E.A. FELLOWSHIP, AND THEY ARE THE ONES I DO ON MY TOURS.

IN MY WORK, I ALWAYS HAVE USED NUDITY AND PHYSICAL ACTS WHICH MOST PEOPLE WOULD CALL SEXUAL. IT IS JUST ONE OF MY WAYS OF BREAKING NORMAL REALITY INTO NEW WAYS OF COMMUNICATING AND RELATING. I COMBINE THIS WITH BREAKING TIME/SPACE TABOOS, MY UNIQUE BODY, AND OTHER TOOLS. BUT THE "SEXUAL" CONTENT OF MY WORK GRABS MOST OF THE ATTENTION.

6. Wrapping/Rocking *with Frank Moore (right) on 23 May 1987 at the Painted Bride Art Center in Philadelphia. (Photo by L. Barany)*

THERE IS A COMMON MISCONCEPTION ABOUT THE DEFORMED SHAMAN TRADITION—THAT IT GETS ITS POWER FROM THE MENTAL AND THE SPIRITUAL PLANE, SINCE THE PHYSICAL AND SENSUAL ARE ALMOST NONEXISTENT. IN TRUTH, THE WOUNDED HEALER USES HIS PHYSICALITY AS A CHANNEL TO UNITE THE SPIRITUAL WITH THE PHYSICAL.

I HAVE ALWAYS BEEN A VERY PHYSICAL AND SEXUAL PERSON. THIS WAS HEIGHTENED BY MY EARLY PHYSICAL ISOLATION. IN THE EARLY '70S WHEN I WAS NOT YET OUT OF MY SEXUAL ISOLATION, I OBSERVED AS AN INTERESTED OUTSIDER THAT FREE SEX (CONFUSED WITH FREE LOVE) WAS NOT WORKING. IT WASN'T MAKING MY HIPPIE FRIENDS HAPPY. THIS OBSERVATION WAS AGAINST MY PHILOSOPHY OF FREEDOM. BUT I COULD NOT DENY THE FACTS. I STARTED LOOKING FOR NEW WAYS OF RELATING AND TOUCHING. I WAS LOOKING FOR A NEW FREE LOVE. MY PERFORMANCES, BOTH THE PUBLIC EVENTS AND THE PRIVATE NONFILMS, WERE MY RESEARCH, MY EXPERIMENTS.

I EXPERIMENTED IN USING THE EXCITED, AROUSED, PLEASURABLE ENERGY IN THE CONTEXT OF ART, OF PLAYING, RELATIONSHIP-BUILDING—NOT THE CONTEXT OF SEX. THIS RESEARCH REACHED A CLIMAX IN MY BERKELEY WORKSHOP DURING THE YEARS OF *the outrageous beauty revue*.

IT WAS FAIRLY CLEAR TO 30 OF US THAT THERE WAS A DIFFERENCE BETWEEN PLAYING AND SEX. WE SAW IT HAD

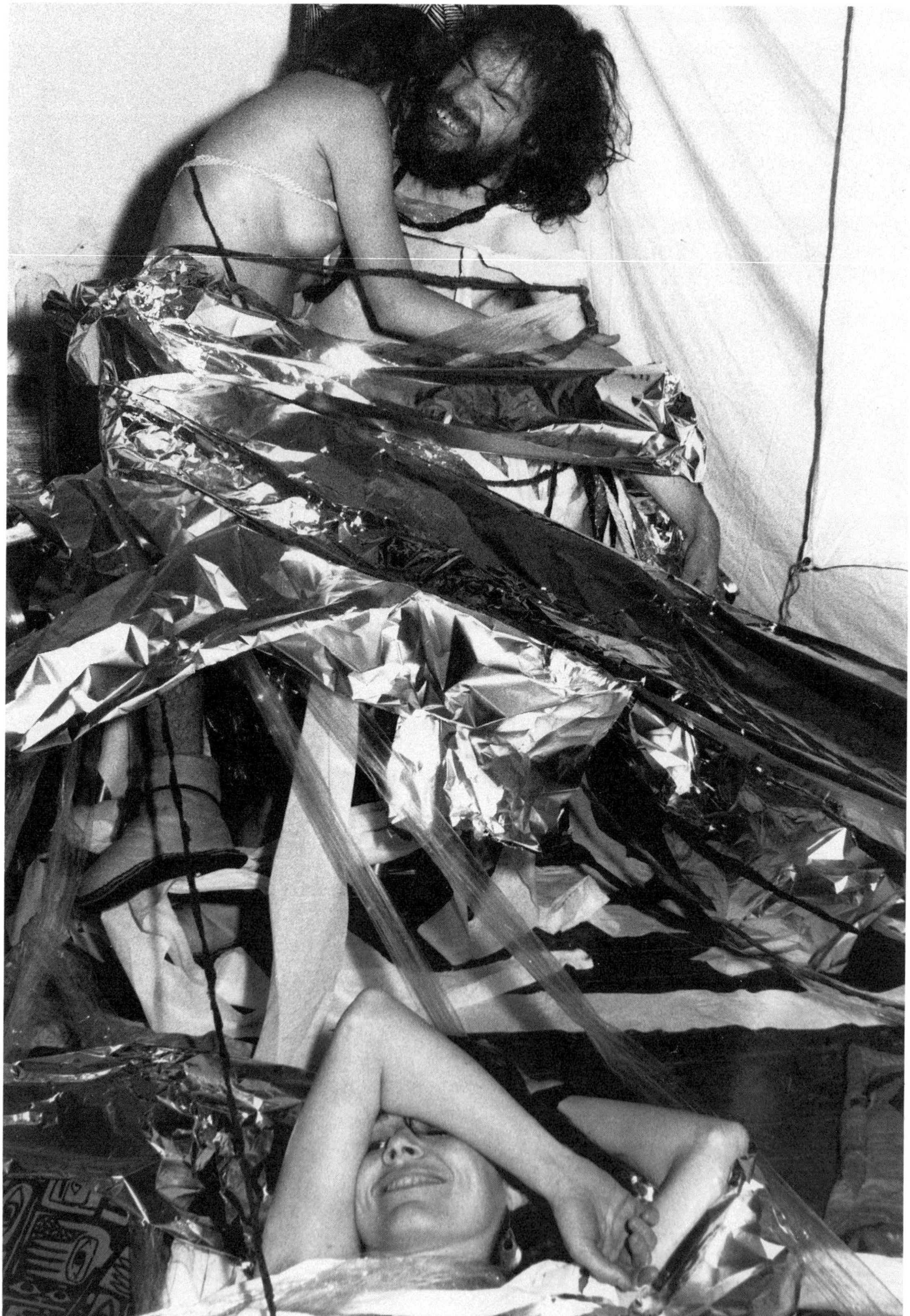

SOMETHING TO DO WITH SEX AND "MARRIAGE" (THE WORD marriage IS ANOTHER WORD THAT HAS NEGATIVE CONNOTATIONS HIDDEN WITHIN IT). SO WE DECIDED TO COMMIT OURSELVES TO HAVING SEX ONLY WITH THOSE TO WHOM WE WERE MARRIED. BUT WE EROTICALLY PLAYED (FOR LACK OF A BETTER TERM FOR IT) WITH ALL OF THE PEOPLE IN THE GROUP.

THE EROTIC PLAY GOT WACKIER, MORE PHYSICAL. IT GAVE US A GREATER FREEDOM NOT ONLY WITHIN OUR GROUP, BUT IN SOCIETY IN GENERAL AS WELL. EROTIC PLAYING INTENSELY BUT PLAYFULLY RELEASED CREATIVITY WHICH WE USED IN MANY WAYS. SUCCESSFUL BUSINESSES WERE ESTABLISHED. WE DID SEVERAL PUBLIC PERFORMANCES, AND A WEALTH OF PRIVATE PERFORMANCES. THERE WAS NO JEALOUSY OR POSSESSIVENESS BECAUSE IT WAS CLEAR THAT SEX WOULD NOT BE INVOLVED. THIS WENT ON FOR THREE YEARS.

AT A CERTAIN POINT, WE STARTED QUESTIONING THE CONCEPT OF MARRIAGE. WE DID NOT SEE ANY DIFFERENCE BETWEEN WHAT WE 30 HAD TOGETHER AND BEING MARRIED. NOT SEEING ANY DIFFERENCE BETWEEN MARRIAGE AND WHAT WE HAD AS A GROUP, THE NEXT LOGICAL QUESTION WAS, "WHY NOT HAVE SEX?" SO WE STARTED TO HAVE SEX OUTSIDE MARRIAGE, WITHIN THE GROUP. ALMOST IMMEDIATELY CHANGES APPEARED IN THE GROUP. JEALOUSY AND POSSESSIVENESS APPEARED. THE GROUP QUICKLY BEGAN TO FALL APART.

AFTER THIS BREAKUP, I FOCUSED MY WORK ON DEFINING THE UNIQUE PHYSICAL-SPIRITUAL ENERGY WE HAD USED, FORMALIZED IT IN MY ART TO TAP AGAIN INTO THE INTENSE, PURE PLAY WITH PEOPLE, USING THE RESULTING CREATIVENESS IN ART WITHOUT BEING DERAILED BY SEX.

I REALIZED THAT ONE OF THE THINGS THAT WAS UNDERMINING MY WORK WAS THE ENGLISH LANGUAGE. THERE WAS NO WORD, NO NAME, FOR THE FORCE I WAS DEALING WITH. MY FIRST TASK WAS TO CREATE A NEW WORD: eroplay.

OUR MIND NEEDS LABELS. THERE IS SUCH A FORCE OR ENERGY, WHICH I HAVE LABELED EROPLAY. BUT THERE HAS NOT BEEN A WORD FOR IT. THE WORD sex HAS BEEN THE DUMP FOR EVERYTHING SENSUAL, ROMANTIC, PHYSICAL, OR FOR SHOWING MORE SKIN THAN USUAL. CARS ARE CALLED SEXY. POSES THAT DO NOT SHOW THE SEX ACT ARE CALLED SEXUAL. WEARING CERTAIN THINGS, MOVING CERTAIN WAYS ARE ALL CALLED SEXUAL, EVEN WHEN IT IS NOT LEADING TO THE SEXUAL ACT—EVEN WHEN THERE IS NO INTENT TO HAVE SEX.

7. Frank Moore in Passion Underground, *4 December 1987, at Artists' Television Access in San Francisco. (Photo by Kevin Rice)*

EROPLAY IS INTENSE PHYSICAL PLAYING AND TOUCHING OF ONESELF AND OTHERS. EROPLAY IS THE FORCE OR EN-

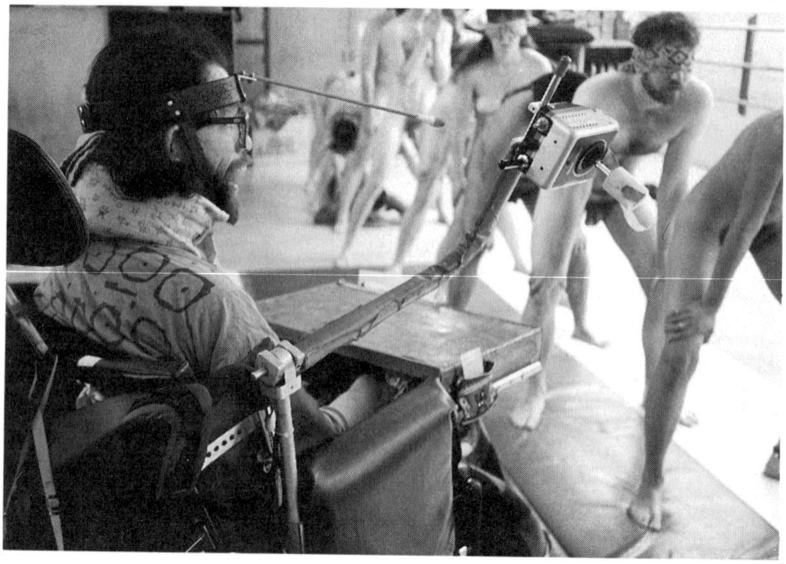

8. Playing with Reality, *Frank Moore's nine-hour private performance on 20 February 1988 in Berkeley, California. (Photo by Linda Mac)*

ERGY RELEASED BY SUCH PLAY. IT IS ALSO THE HAPPY, PLAYFUL ATTITUDE TOWARDS LIFE THAT COMES FROM SUCH PLAY. EROPLAY IS NOT FOREPLAY, EVEN THOUGH FOREPLAY IS EROPLAY.

FOREPLAY LEADS TO ORGASM—EROPLAY LEADS TO BEING TURNED-ON IN MANY DIFFERENT WAYS AND IN ALL PARTS OF THE BODY—INCLUDING, BUT NOT LIMITED TO, PHYSICAL AROUSAL. IT CAN BE DIFFERENT EVERY TIME. SKIN TOUCHING SKIN SEEMS TO BE WHAT RELEASES THE FULL IMPACT OF EROPLAY. EROPLAY CAN BE INTENSE. IT IS LIKE WHEN YOU RUB A PUPPY ON ITS BELLY AND THE PUPPY GOES INTO A STATE OF RAPTURE, BOTH TOTALLY TURNED-ON AND RELAXED. EROPLAY IS THE BLISSED-OUT, WARM, RELAXED, TURNED-ON, TOTALLY SATISFYING FEELING OF A GOOD HEAD RUB.

EROPLAY IS FUN!

EROPLAY IS INNOCENT AND CHILDLIKE.

EROPLAY'S FOCUS IS ON PHYSICAL ENJOYMENT.

EROPLAY DECREASES ISOLATION AND ALIENATION. IT INCREASES SELF-TRUST AND TRUSTING OF OTHERS. IT MAKES YOU HARDER TO BE CONTROLLED. EROPLAY LEADS TO A LIFE-STYLE WITH ALL THESE CHARACTERISTICS. THE LIFE-STYLE LOOKS STRANGELY LIKE THE LOVE GENERATION, BUT WITHOUT DRUGS OR FREE SEX.

IN RECENT YEARS, OUTSIDE FORCES HAVE AFFECTED MY WORK. EDWIN MEESE'S POLITICAL WAR OF SEXUAL SUPRESSION AND THE BLANDNESS OF YUPPIES HAVE GIVEN MY ART SOCIAL ISSUES AGAINST WHICH I CAN DO BATTLE.

BUT IT IS AIDS THAT HAS STARTED PEOPLE SEARCHING FOR NONSEXUAL WAYS TO FIND, TO SHOW, AND TO GIVE PHYSICAL INTIMACY. EROPLAY IS A SAFE, FUN, LUSTY CHANNEL FOR FREE PHYSICAL TOUCHING. IT IS SAFE BECAUSE THERE IS NO PHYSICAL INTERCOURSE. IT IS NOT AN AVOIDANCE, AS CELIBACY IS. IT IS NOT SOMETHING SECOND RATE. EROPLAY IS SATISFYING IN ITSELF.

I HAVE DEBATED WITH MYSELF ABOUT NO LONGER RESISTING THE LABEL sexual. BY INSISTING WHAT I AM DOING IS NOT SEXUAL, I AM OPENING MYSELF TO PEOPLE QUESTIONING MY HONESTY AND INTEGRITY. IF I ACCEPT THE SEXUAL LABEL, PEOPLE WOULD JUST HAVE TO DECIDE WHETHER OR NOT THEY LIKE SEX IN ART—DECIDE WHETHER IT IS ART OR NOT. THAT WOULD BE THE DEPTH OF THE QUESTIONING. THEY MAY FEEL UNCOMFORTABLE SEEING SEX AS ART—BUT THAT UNCOMFORTABLENESS WOULD BE JUST FROM BREAKING THE TABOO OF SEX—WHAT'S THE BIG DEAL? WHAT I AM DOING IS TAKING NUDITY AND ACTS THAT ARE USUALLY CONSIDERED SEXUAL AND GIVING THEM A NEW, NONSEXUAL CONTEXT. THAT CREATES A TENSION, A CONFLICT, AN EXAMINING, A LEAP INTO SOMETHING NEW. THAT IS WHAT I AM AFTER. THIS LEAP INTO NEWNESS IS WHY PEOPLE WHO ARE NORMALLY COMFORTABLE WITH CASUAL NUDITY AND CASUAL SEX SOMETIMES GET VERY UNCOMFORTABLE WITH THE NUDITY AND EROPLAY IN MY WORK. BY TAKING "SEXUAL" ACTS AND SINCERELY PUTTING THEM INTO A DIFFERENT CONTEXT, I CREATE ANOTHER REALITY, ANOTHER WAY OF RELATING. I ALSO CREATE CONFLICT WITH THE NORMAL REALITY—AND THAT CONFLICT MAY CHANGE, IN AN UNDERGROUND SORT OF A WAY, THE NORMAL REALITY. I THINK ART—OR AT LEAST THIS KIND OF ART—SHOULD CREATE CONFLICT AND CHANGE. AND I LIKE RELATING WITH PEOPLE IN THIS "UNNORMAL" WAY. THIS IS WHY I DO PERFORMANCE.

Frank Moore *started doing private, erotic performances and nonfilms in the early '70s. Developed from a workshop, his performance group began doing long ritualistic pieces then public events and experimental theatre. This period peaked in the late '70s and early '80s with the* Outrageous Beauty Revue. *Since then he has run a bimonthly series at the University of California, Berkeley, developing intimate rituals for clubs, galleries, and college performances. In 1985 he received an NEA fellowship and in Spring 1987 did a national tour, including a five-hour piece at Franklin Furnace in New York City.*

Dress Suits to Hire

A collaboration between Holly Hughes, Peggy Shaw, and Lois Weaver

---

Written by Holly Hughes
Directed by Lois Weaver
Performed by Peggy Shaw and Lois Weaver

(DEELUXE and MICHIGAN are seated as the lights come up. DEELUXE's chair faces upstage, MICHIGAN's downstage. They are facing each other as DEELUXE begins to sing. Gradually, DEELUXE's attention becomes focused on dressing herself, specifically on putting on nylon stockings as she sings. MICHIGAN faces upstage, mouthing the words silently.)*

DEELUXE: Gonna fill my mouth with red wine
Gonna fill my head with cement
Gonna fill my ears with cotton wool
Gonna fill my nose with cocaine
Gonna buy myself a diamond ring
Gonna get me on a fast train
Gonna pack my soul in a handkerchief
But will you be there when I come back again?

I will go where you will never find me
I will change so you won't recognize me
Everything I know I'll leave behind me
A distant memory of all the things there used to be
When there was only you and me

*"Run Run Run" by Peggy Shaw.

I'm gonna run run run
Catch me if you can
I'm gonna run run run
Catch me if you can
I'm gonna run run run so far away
But will you be there when I come back again?

You're gonna sit down in your easy chair
You're gonna look out of your window
You're gonna fill your lungs with nicotine
You're gonna bite your nails down to the bone
You're gonna buy yourself a diamond ring
You're gonna get you on a fast train
You're gonna pack your soul in a handkerchief
But will I be there when you come back again . . .

(DEELUXE's right hand starts to choke her neck until she falls to the floor, apparently lifeless. In fact she is dead for the rest of the play. It seems rigor mortis has set in rather early. MICHIGAN is facing upstage. In her lap a small white dog of a mechanical species—LINDA—begins barking. MICHIGAN turns around to see what LINDA's barking at and discovers DEELUXE.)

MICHIGAN: *(Addressing the right hand of DEELUXE.)* I suppose you know what this will mean. There will be no show. She will be unable to do the show. You're not going to like this. *(MICHIGAN begins searching through the suit coats. She pulls out a phone receiver. Pink, plastic, sans cord—it should be as phony as possible.)* Hello? Ninth precinct? Yes, I'll hold. *(To DEELUXE's hand.)* You're asking for this. *(To phone.)* There's a man in here. I can't say if he's dangerous or not. I don't know any other men so I can't compare. Through the door! He lives with us. More with her than with me. Me, this man, and the body. Yes there certainly is a body. Did I discover it? Many years ago. I first discovered the body in the Hotel Universal in Salamanca. A single light bulb. The light came in through the window. The streets were lit by little oranges. The oranges were perfect and bitter. In this light I lay down on the bed and discovered the body. Especially the legs. She's part palomino. In the legs, pure palomino. Do you know what a palomino is? A race horse covered with Parmesan cheese, yes. That's her. And after that first time I would discover the body again and again. And even when I hate her, I love the body. Who does the body belong to? Partly to me. It belongs to her. I usually say she's my sister and most of the time we are sisters. Sometimes we're even worse. I don't know the address. I don't go out much. I don't go out at all, so I don't need an address. I could describe the place. We live in a town. I've forgotten the name. In the bad part of town. We live in a rental clothing store. It doesn't look like much from the outside. But we have too many clothes for our own good. Is that enough of an address? Could you find us based on what I've just said? You're not there anymore, are you? She's not there anymore either. She's dead. Do you understand? Never mind, I understand. She probably won't be able to perform anymore. And I will never again lie down in the afternoon and discover the body. *(MICHIGAN replaces the phone in the suit coat. She begins speaking to LINDA.)* Is it cold in here or is it me? *(To DEELUXE.)* Oh, it's you. You should relax. You know there are worse things in New York than being killed by someone who loves you. Like trying to cash a check! Are you mad at me because I said your body belongs to me?

(MICHIGAN kneels down and opens DEELUXE's robe.) Remember the night we became sisters? I looked out and there were no more stars. The sky was full of teeth. Blue and sharp and they were falling towards us. We were already in the wolf's mouth and it was closing in around us. Our only chance was to become twins. To be swallowed whole. But being twins slowed us down. People don't rent dress suits from twins. But then there was always the body to come back to. I'm not going to look at you any longer. I got to look where I'm going. I never thought I would have to go anywhere.

(MICHIGAN crosses to the stereo and puts on a scratchy version of Frank Sinatra singing: "A Lover Is Blue." While the record plays, MICHIGAN paces, drains her drink and, looking at DEELUXE, polishes off hers as well. The stereo cuts off abruptly. MICHIGAN starts. A small wall sconce comes on. When MICHIGAN turns around to look at it, the light cuts off. The stereo comes on suddenly, it's the beginning bars of "Temptation" by Perry Como. MICHIGAN backs away from it. DEELUXE's dress falls off its hook. MICHIGAN stands still, afraid. Lights slowly crossfade up—it's morning. MICHIGAN begins talking to LINDA again.)

MICHIGAN: Born in that cold snap spring won't come time of year. Under the sign of Go Fish. My Venus was stuck in the mud. Mud a' the Bad River, she's acting up again. Outgrowing her banks. Slipping through locked doors, spitting up coffins and dead Cheverolets. Leaving turds in the hope chest. Stores running outta Birdeye's Frozen Vegetables and everything plaid. People getting nervous they'd have to eat fresh food and wear solid colors. Thought the end of the world had come to Michigan. Nobody's hair would hold a set. Forsythia blooms so hard and sudden she cracks the plate glass windows and then freezes all the way back to the ground. And they blamed my mother. She was full of too much bad river water. The end of the world, not spring, was coming to

1. Michigan kneels down and opens Deeluxe's robe. Lois Weaver is Michigan, Peggy Shaw is Deeluxe. The photos accompanying the script are all from the May 1987 production at P.S. 122 in New York. (Photo by Dona Ann McAdams)

Michigan. And I was the first robin of disaster. When I started breathing on my own the doctor went and beat me anyway and Momma she's screaming, "What is it? Is it a girl?" And the doctor's screaming, "She's an animal!" Animal, doc, you said it! I do the Rin-tin-tin, I get down on all fours. Being a girl is just a phase I'm going through. I feel my own ass up and it's ticking like a time bomb. I am the end of the world after. Tick tock through the teacher's lounge where Mr. Science pins you against the wall in the name of higher. I like being pinned down, an' what do you think of that? An' he says, "I bet you wish you hadda father," an' I say, "Nope, I wish I had his clothes though," and I play with his tie and he's screaming to stop it o please stop it but we don't stop it we both want it till his tie is exploding in my hand like a trick cigar and he slaps me hard and says: "You're an animal!" Bomb on outta there. By now I'm sweating hard and I break out in titties. See the girls in the hall and my milk drops down. I got what they want, and I wanna give it to them and I do. Right on the pink plastic floor. Ever seen a bunch a lamprey eels up close? Well they're everywhere in Michigan now and there're these girls too, their mouths are little oohs. Just made to suck. Go on, suck the life outta me, I wanna feel my life in somebody else's mouth. Makes me know what Jesus feels. At communion. He feels good. We take communion to make Jesus feel better. Jesus feels like a big rare roast beef on a platter squirting blood and fat on a platter and lifting his hips to heaven beggin' for it! "O God, yes! Yes, I need it, this is my body, hurry up and take it! Take me! Ketchup, Mustard, and the Holy Ghost are with me! Please god, o my god, O my god EAT ME!" Then the girls get what they want, what we both want and they stop being eels and go back to being girls again and I'm just barely ticking when they slap me hard an' say: "You're an animal!" I don't want nobody anymore. I wanna be myself, just me and moon. I feel her before I see her. The moon pulls something tight in me. I get that ocean feeling. Ol' Michigan she was an ocean before she was anything else. A blue-green bottomless pit, that's what's in me. The moon she could be anything she wants. She's a bigger prize than you can win bowling, she's that white bread women keep between their legs. She's a mirror, I'm not afraid to look. Oh, yoo hoo! Mrs. Moon? *(Piano music up—"Amato Mio." French windows swing open.)* You're so smart and Italian. Tell me what I am.

(DEELUXE begins to sit, opening a giant fan as she does. She's singing "Amato Mio" a la Bela Lugosi, i.e., lots of rolling eyebrows. At the end of every phrase DEELUXE strikes another pose against the fan. She looks like a singing Art Deco vase. MICHIGAN strikes poses of terror in unison with DEELUXE. At the song's end, DEELUXE picks up the illuminated tulips and offers them to the horrified MICHIGAN.)

MICHIGAN: Why did you come back?

DEELUXE: The car.

MICHIGAN: The car?

DEELUXE: The keys!

MICHIGAN: They won't let you. Expired!

DEELUXE: Why? My license is good!

MICHIGAN: Not your license! You're no good. You're expired! They won't let a dead woman run around in a Cheverolet!

DEELUXE: I'm taking the Cadillac! Kiss me and say you're sorry.

MICHIGAN: You'll make me sick! Your kisses are more ice water down my neck.

DEELUXE: You're my sister. I got rights.

MICHIGAN: I'm not your sister. I'm a White Christmas. I'm the wrong age for you. The age when you can't be sick. The Ice Age! *(Pause.)* Close the window. *(DEELUXE crosses and closes the window. She remains facing upstage, her back to MICHIGAN.)* We need more sherry.

DEELUXE: I've had all I want.

MICHIGAN: We've exhausted the reserves.

DEELUXE: I'm sick of sherry.

MICHIGAN: There's money in the pocket.

DEELUXE: Is that a threat?

MICHIGAN: Get enough.

DEELUXE: I've had enough.

MICHIGAN: We need more.

DEELUXE: *(Turning around to face MICHIGAN.)* We? You! You need more. More of what?

MICHIGAN: You know.

DEELUXE: More of the same. More of the same conversations. More of the same air. Well not me. I want.

MICHIGAN: What?

DEELUXE: I don't know. But it's not in this shop. It may not even be on this block. I may have to cross Second Avenue to get it. I know I don't want the same thing because day after day I have the same thing and at the end of the day I still want.

MICHIGAN: Hurry.

DEELUXE: You can't tell me what to do anymore. Well, I'm going. And I'm taking the money. *(DEELUXE removes a piggy bank from a suit coat pocket.)* Not for sherry. I'm getting what I want. *(She moves toward the exit.)* And if I come back and I'm not saying that I will, I'm not telling you a thing. I need a secret. Well, my mind's made up. Nothing you can do or say can stop me. *(Pause.)* Well, this time I'm really going. Don't try to get in my way. Goodbye.

MICHIGAN: Go on.

DEELUXE: *(Turning around and recrossing the room.)* I'm doing what I want and I want to stay. *(DEELUXE hunts through the boxes to find her clothes. She begins dressing. MICHIGAN and LINDA observe.)* They said a lot of things about us. 'Cause of where we lived. You know that swamp. Used to be a river running through there but the river got lost and turned belly up. Went dark and stinky and we called it "home." Said we must be a lot like that lost river. Backed-up. Scum. Living there in that place mutts went to die. Most people don't like mud. That's 'cause they don't know anything about it. And they said we went to the Dairy Queen any chance we got. Just climbed outta the mud and went down and grabbed a Mr. Softee. But not them. Dairy Queen wasn't good enough for the MacDonald's crowd. And that was just another reason for them to hate us. Us. Me and my mother, talk of the town. And my talk stank worse than their mud. About my mother they said she wasn't a full-time woman. That other times she was a mud puppy and a river pussy. That we lived in quicksand and ate outta cans. That she had every single Petula Clark record and had to play them up full every night before she could get to sleep. That she looked right into men's crotches and if she didn't like what she saw she gave them a facefull of her muddy spit. Nasty talk about my mother. But it didn't hurt me none. Because it was all true. Every stinky last word of it, true. And the truth can't hurt you. Not if you're a young girl with mud on the brain. And everywhere this young girl went the talk went too. Most of it about me and the new one. Me, you know my story by looking at me once. And her, that two-bit, small-town Pekinese. About her and me being lesbians. And that talk didn't hurt either. I coulda laughed. Lesbians. If it was that simple, that easy. Muff-divers. They didn't know the half of it. *(DEELUXE is fully dressed in her satin strapless gown. LINDA begins barking in MICHIGAN's lap.)*

MICHIGAN: *(Placing LINDA on the floor.)* What is it, Linda? You want to go out? You don't want to go out. I went out once. Five years ago. There's nothing out there. What do you smell? Pussy! No, Linda, no! No more pussy for us. That's just Little Peter. You know him, Little Peter from across the street. He had a nice thing going till he got his hands on that wildcat. No man can handle a wildcat. Nothing cuts as deep as mean pussy.

LITTLE PETER: *(Spoken by DEELUXE. LITTLE PETER occasionally possesses DEELUXE's right hand.)* That's it. We're closed! Scram! Everybody but you sweetheart. *(To DEELUXE.)* Let me see your face. Hmmm. I like the eyes. Let's see the teeth. Nice. I like the face. But I don't like your song.

DEELUXE: Nobody likes it, that's why it's so good.

LITTLE PETER: Ooooh, honey, you're what's good.

DEELUXE: Deeluxe.

LITTLE PETER: *(Slaps DEELUXE.)* Guess again, sweetheart, you don't got a name. You don't need a name. You work for me now. Only name you got to remember is Little Peter. All you got to do is let him, love him. Let him touch your hair. How you make your hair do that? The way it comes out of your head like your brain's on fire. *(LITTLE PETER's hand reaches for DEELUXE, who flinches.)* What started that fire in you? You can tell Little Peter.

MICHIGAN: That tiger was getting the best of Little Peter and he didn't even know it. We just called her a tiger 'cause there weren't words for what she was. Half woman, half something weird. French, maybe. All cat.

LITTLE PETER: You think I want to hurt you? I want to be nice to you. It's you that makes me hurt you. You hurt yourself. Look at me. Not the eyes. At the hands. Don't the hands tell the truth? They want to be nice to you. Think of them as your own hands. Think of me as a part of you. Hmm, there. What's your name now?

DEELUXE: Deeluxe.

LITTLE PETER: Forget it! That part is over. Got it? Put some clothes on. Some, but not too many. And honey. I don't like girls who cry about their mother. Don't sing that song again.

MICHIGAN: Maybe I was as big a sucker as him. Even a dog's got sense to be afraid of cats. One look at her pelt and I went stupid. Maybe I was as big a sucker as him. I knew what a hundred-fifty pounds of killer pussy'd do to a man. What I didn't know is what it could do to a woman. *(MICHIGAN crosses to DEELUXE. The spirit of LITTLE PETER seems to have left her, but DEELUXE is wary of MICHIGAN.)* We need more sherry to tide us over.

DEELUXE: You can see into the future, can't you?

MICHIGAN: *(Reaching for the LITTLE PETER hand.)* Give me your hand.

DEELUXE: You know how it ends, don't you?

MICHIGAN: I need your hand.

DEELUXE: Why this hand?

MICHIGAN: That one you were born with and this the one you made for yourself. Give.

DEELUXE: It's not mine to give.

MICHIGAN: What?

DEELUXE: It's not MY hand!

MICHIGAN: What could it be then?

DEELUXE: It could be anything. It works against me. I have no feeling in it. And it's not an "it." It's a he. He does what he wants and when he wants. He's an underground river that empties into my heart. I know what my heart is. It's a red whirlpool and I got to watch so I don't fall in. And this hand is proof. Proof I was hit. Heat lightning. My own fault. Storks like trailer parks. I could never stay put when the pressure drops.

MICHIGAN: You look fine. *(Still trying to get the hand.)*

DEELUXE: I'm far from fine. I'm a tree and I been hit bad. Still look like a tree on the outside but on the inside there's just animals and disease and no tree left. *(MICHIGAN is finally able to get DEELUXE's hand.)* What's he say?

MICHIGAN: He says your head line and your heart line split early on. He says you have a long life.

DEELUXE: How does it end?

MICHIGAN: It doesn't end really. Your life line runs into your veins.

DEELUXE: It's not forever I want!

MICHIGAN: OK. It ends with you getting sherry.

DEELUXE: That's not how it ends. It ends with me leaving and never coming back! And then my life will start. You can't stop me!

(DEELUXE crosses to the rack of tuxedos and begins rifling through them as

though she were going to get dressed and leave. MICHIGAN watches without concern. DEELUXE pulls an innocent-looking scarf out of a suit pocket but the scarf is a huge backdrop of a desert scene. At this point, real time stops. That is, time stops moving only forward. The following scene works in two ways: as a flashback—a la Billy Pilgrim in Slaughterhouse Five, *the characters become unstuck in time—and also as a ritualistic reenactment of a past event. MICHIGAN begins to loosen her robe, and DEELUXE pins up the scarf-backdrop like a sheet hung out to dry.)*

DEELUXE: *(Without conviction, as MICHIGAN throws over her robe.)* I'm going anyway.

(In unison, the two begin to dress for the ritual. MICHIGAN holds up a pair of pink high-heeled cowboy boots as DEELUXE removes a pair of rhinestone earrings with fetishistic attentiveness. DEELUXE picks up a toothpick while MICHIGAN sticks a wad of bubble gum in her mouth. They reach behind the hanging suits to pull out a pair of day-glo hula hoops. As MICHIGAN begins to cross downstage center, DEELUXE puts on a cowboy hat.)

MICHIGAN: *(Addressing the audience and slinging her hoop).* Thirteen years old. Mama called me a woman and slapped me hard and gave me a silver dollar with a Bible verse. "Ask and you shall receive." I put my Bible verse into the candy machine, pull hard, nada. Being good don't buy you sweet things anymore I'm thinking when the foreign car pulls up and snake pops out. A real señor monsieur type a snake: cologne, real leather shoes coiling down the sidewalk. No offer a candy just gives me one hard bite and he's off. Greases back his hair with mother's milk and takes off with those other too-handsome kind a guys. Nothing showed on the outside but I was bleeding bad on the inside. Skin goes the color of flophouse sheets. Poison's working on me and all I wanted was some more poison. Mama taught us to feed a fever and I got a hot python squeezing that little girl's heart. All that sugar and spice running down my legs and staining up those spanky pants. My heart was sweating and contagious with that secret dirt and I ripped those panties off and went without underwear. Hoping for an accident and soon. Poison's gotta work itself outta you and the only way outta you is into somebody else. Felt like touching my new wound, but didn't dare. Knew somebody would lose a finger in there and it wasn't gonna be me. Disguised myself with a cross around my neck and a kilt on too. Let that skirt ride up and my bare ass rose like a wet moon over the candy store. Snake on down to the mall. Coiling and uncoiling in the dust. Looking for somebody to infect. Poison's gotta work itself out. Staring at all those girls that never got bit. The blonde that would bring out the blonde in me. Take my sweet meat out behind the cheap shoe stores and lay her down in the astroturf and make her mine. Carve my initials on the insides a her thigh with my tongue. Gonna give her a little scar to remember me by, gonna match mine. I'm shaking, I'm rattling, baby needs a new way to sing the blues, come on, come on, let's go, snake eyes.

(MICHIGAN drops her hoop. Music up, it's the instrumental theme from "A Man and A Woman." DEELUXE crosses to center stage moving as much like a cowboy as you can in a strapless gown and heels. DEELUXE snaps her hula hoop over to MICHIGAN so that it rolls past her, then boomerangs back. MICHIGAN catches it. Music fades out as they begin to speak.)

MICHIGAN: Filler up?

DEELUXE: Just five dollars, thanks.

MICHIGAN: Oil OK? Water? Small engine.

DEELUXE: Checked it this morning in Tulsa.

MICHIGAN: Oh, the big city, huh? And they didn't tell you about me in Tulsa? They didn't tell you this was your last chance?

DEELUXE: Every place on this road says that.

MICHIGAN: Well I am flattered. You know what they say about imitation! Everyone wanting a piece of my action. Maybe they can sucker a few but they can't improve on reality. Believe me, I've tried. I'm the only real thing for 50 miles around, I'm it. I'm the end of the line.

DEELUXE: OK, keep the change, just give me the keys.

MICHIGAN: Just where you think you going in such an all-fired hurry? California?

DEELUXE: So what?

MICHIGAN: California! Whatcha gonna do in Cala . . . ha, ha, fornia?

DEELUXE: Look around.

MICHIGAN: Oh, there's a lot to see out there in California, all right. Man-size mice dancing with movie stars with missile-sized tits. Or is it tit-sized missiles? Two-stepping through the mud slides. No, you sure don't want to miss that. You'll never make it.

DEELUXE: I'm gonna see California.

MICHIGAN: You're gonna see California but you're not leaving this station. 'Cause I already seen California and I'm gonna show you my shots. I got all the best places. *(MICHIGAN begins to display her tattoos as though they were souvenirs.)*

DEELUXE: Disneyland? Knott's Berry Farm? Universal Studios? Marineland? *(DEELUXE's hand is resting on MICHIGAN's crotch.)*

MICHIGAN: Sorry about Marineland. Dropped my camera into the killer whale tank. Didn't dare go in after it. Sharks are terrified of me. Are you ready to see California? *("A Man and A Woman" theme music up, DEELUXE takes out her toothpick as MICHIGAN spits her gum out into her hand. They kiss. After the kiss, they replace the toothpick and gum. Music fades as they begin to speak.)*

DEELUXE: So that's California, huh?

MICHIGAN: Yeah.

DEELUXE: So we should do something.

MICHIGAN: So.

DEELUXE: Why stay here?

MICHIGAN: So what and just because.

DEELUXE: That's what I thought.

MICHIGAN: So what if I got no friends and no money. There's no snakes here. I could go someplace and get friends and money but then I might get snakes. Besides, my nothing is better than your something.

2. *"Marineland?" (Photo by Dona Ann McAdams)*

DEELUXE: Well, I was just thinking . . .

MICHIGAN: Don't start. Just shut up and be happy. *(She picks up her hula hoop and begins to rattle it.)*

DEELUXE: What's that?

MICHIGAN: A snake.

DEELUXE: You promised no snakes! *(MICHIGAN slips the hoop over DEELUXE's head.)*

MICHIGAN: Quick!

DEELUXE: What?

MICHIGAN: Here!

DEELUXE: How?

MICHIGAN: Suck! *(They kiss. The hoop drops.)* I'm beginning to like this desert air. So refreshing. *(Pause.)* You spit it out didn't you?

DEELUXE: What?

MICHIGAN: The poison.

DEELUXE: What poison?

MICHIGAN: My poison. You spit it out?

DEELUXE: I swallowed it. *(MICHIGAN crosses upstage and begins folding up the backdrop. DEELUXE faces the audience.)*

DEELUXE: She's got a bad heart. The kind you die from. Runs in the family. I gotta bad heart too. Just not the kind you die from. The kind that makes you wear too much eye makeup. She's my cousin, come up from one of those sweaty states. She wouldn't sweat in a forest fire. Ice wouldn't melt in her mouth. I make a little bet with myself. I can make her sweat. The first time I know for sure I got heart problems is when my cousin came to visit. Heat spell. Bad heart and bad heat spell couldn't keep my cousin from pitching pop-ups in the garden. Takes everything she has and makes it into a ball. Something in me follows that ball up, and it hangs in the air a moment seems like forever then into the dirt. I can't throw, can't make a fist. She can throw and stay cool. She's a little bit Catholic. So yellow her hair it hurts my teeth. I sneak her weenies on Friday and I don't tell on her forbidden patent leathers hoping they'll reflect up to that place she's got muscles girls don't, got heart places boys don't. Don't want to do nothing about it yet, still that bad heart of mine wanna bite. She's still not sweating but I get to sleep with her because there's not enough beds. I iron my father's shorts and bleach his stains to send her roses. Downstairs with her, the fake wood, the pump straining to keep us from going under. The earth sweating through the fake wood. Lip syncing to 45s. I got the aspirins she got the cokes waiting for it to happen. And the sweat is all over us now, hers and mine together tasting like a memory of a place I never been. Waiting for it to happen, for one heart to give out, for the rattler to strike. *(LITTLE PETER begins to invade DEELUXE. Her hand begins twitching and finally, singing.)*

LITTLE PETER: She may be weary,
Women do get weary,
Wearing the same shabby dress.
And when she's weary,
Try a little tenderness.

(To DEELUXE.) Yeah, go on and try it sucker, see what it'll get you.

DEELUXE: I can do it.

LITTLE PETER: We aren't talking about an "it" here to do. We are talking skirt, a woman, a Jane.

DEELUXE: So?

LITTLE PETER: So you don't do a woman. You handle her.

DEELUXE: Like you used to handle me, huh.

LITTLE PETER: Correction, carrot brain, like I did, do, and will handle you.

DEELUXE: Stay outta this.

LITTLE PETER: I'll sit out this fox-trot, but I'll be around. *(DEELUXE crosses to MICHIGAN and takes off her hat.)*

DEELUXE: I'm back. I'm sorry.

MICHIGAN: No you're not.

DEELUXE: I know you said you wanted to be alone.

MICHIGAN: Did I?

DEELUXE: You said I shouldn't see you again. *(MICHIGAN starts laughing.)* What's so funny?

MICHIGAN: You should laugh. Be happy. I thought tall people laughed a lot.

DEELUXE: What about?

MICHIGAN: About me being such a liar. I didn't want to be alone. Did you want me to be alone?

DEELUXE: No.

MICHIGAN: And wouldcha leave me alone?

DEELUXE: No.

MICHIGAN: Until?

DEELUXE: No until. I won't leave.

MICHIGAN: Period?

DEELUXE: Period.

MICHIGAN: Wouldcha leave if I asked you to go?

DEELUXE: I would try.

MICHIGAN: You would.

DEELUXE: If you asked.

MICHIGAN: Oh.

DEELUXE: But I couldn't leave.

MICHIGAN: Well if you can't leave then I guess you can stay. *(MICHIGAN starts laughing.)*

DEELUXE: This time it's really not funny.

MICHIGAN: Show me. Make me stop laughing if you don't like it.

DEELUXE: *(Addressing her LITTLE PETER hand.)* Help me. I don't know what to do.

MICHIGAN: *(Singing.)* You won't regret it,
Women don't forget it,
Love is their whole happiness.

Aren't you glad I stuck around? OK, now let's try a little tenderness. *(DEELUXE displays an invisible key to MICHIGAN. Then she mimes locking the door with it and swallowing the key. It's as though her entire body has been taken over by LITTLE PETER.)* Did you see what I did with that key?

MICHIGAN: So what?

LITTLE PETER: That's what I'm going to do to you.

MICHIGAN: Huh.

LITTLE PETER: I'm gonna swallow you whole. There's a part of you nobody sees. A part I know is there. Like I know that white stuff is in the middle of those black cookies. But you gotta twist open the whole rotten thing to get to it. *(He/she begins caressing MICHIGAN more fiercely than tenderly.)* That's what I'm gonna do to you. It's your secret now but I'm going to know it too. Make your cream the glue between us. No matter what it costs me. Or you. *(He/she yanks MICHIGAN to her feet. LITTLE PETER addresses DEELUXE.)*

MICHIGAN: Aren't you afraid?

DEELUXE: No.

MICHIGAN: You should be. You're lucky you're so dumb.

DEELUXE: You're afraid.

MICHIGAN: Of what? I'm the scariest thing going.

DEELUXE: There's something even worse.

MICHIGAN: Yeah?

DEELUXE: The cold.

MICHIGAN: What's that? I ain't been cold a day in my life. You afraid?

DEELUXE: Yes I got no feeling anywhere.

MICHIGAN: So?

DEELUXE: So I could die and not even notice it. *(French windows blow open. Howling wind is heard.)*

MICHIGAN: Shut it!

DEELUXE: You shut it!

MICHIGAN: You're closer.

DEELUXE: Closer to what?

MICHIGAN: The window.

DEELUXE: I wasn't talking about the window! *(MICHIGAN closes the window. Howling stops.)* I thought you were hot enough for both of us. I guess I was wrong.

MICHIGAN: I got the heat sweetheart, I just don't give it away. *(MICHIGAN pulls a long black flashlight out of a suit coat pocket.)*

DEELUXE: What's that for?

MICHIGAN: Stars.

DEELUXE: It's aimed down at the street. That's a funny place to look for stars. There's no stars on this part of Second Avenue. Just three bums pissing on a futon. Hey! You can see right into my bedroom! You been looking at me!

MICHIGAN: No.

DEELUXE: Yes you have. This is proof.

MICHIGAN: I been more than looking. I been watching. That's looking with a reason.

DEELUXE: What's the reason?

MICHIGAN: 'Cause you're my kind of star.

DEELUXE: What's that?

MICHIGAN: A falling star. Wanna see one? It's a nice night for viewing. Rare to see so many binaries.

DEELUXE: Binaries?

MICHIGAN: Doubles. A pair of stars so close they cannot escape each other.

DEELUXE: Close as sisters?

MICHIGAN: Closer. Like twins.

DEELUXE: How come they stay together?

MICHIGAN: Gravity.

DEELUXE: I don't see anything like that.

MICHIGAN: And the closer they get the worse it gets.

DEELUXE: What?

MICHIGAN: The pull, and then it's . . . kaboom. But there's that moment right before the end when they're the brightest thing on Second Avenue. Just a big red nova.

DEELUXE: I hadda one of those once. Not fancy but a good car.

MICHIGAN: 'Course even the brightest star can get stuck with a black hole.

DEELUXE: What's that?

MICHIGAN: Something so dense you can't imagine it. You wait and wait and the bang you counted on never comes.

DEELUXE: Is that what makes a star fall?

MICHIGAN: Almost anything can make a star fall. Here's one now, about to fall. *(MICHIGAN directs DEELUXE's flashlight so it shines on herself. Throughout the following monolog. MICHIGAN strikes different peep show poses while DEELUXE observes her as attentively but asexually as a nerd looking at an ant farm.)*

DEELUXE: I see it. Looks familiar. Looks like me. That was the year I was living alone in Bad Axe. Just wouldn't move in with him. "What's the difference?" he'd say. Then he'd go off and leave me trying whether to decide whether to be a lesbian today or put it off till tomorrow. And then I'd put on plastic nurse's shoes. Wait on tables. Getting tips in Bible verses. People with one eye ate at this place a lot. I guess it was just about the favorite place of one-eyed people to eat. Down at the mall. Not even a real mall, fucking shopping center. One day I get up with him and alla sudden I'm falling. And I tried to break my fall by reaching out for him. But it didn't come out that way. I socked him once, twice in the jaw and kept falling. Falling into the Chevy with the bad plates with a cat and a raincoat. I don't know what started it and what I'm falling into.

MICHIGAN: *(Directing flashlight so it falls on her breasts.)* Probably the moon.

3. Bound together in Michigan's pearls, the "sisters" begin a slow circle dance. (Photo by Dona Ann McAdams)

DEELUXE: I dunno. Is the moon that strong?

MICHIGAN: Take a look and see.

DEELUXE: Wow. Get a load of that moon. She's so full. There's two moons and they're both full.

MICHIGAN: Don't tell me she's not strong enough to pull you off course. *(MICHIGAN takes the flashlight out of DEELUXE's hands.)*

DEELUXE: What's going on here?

MICHIGAN: I got nothing to hide. *(MICHIGAN grabs DEELUXE's bodice.)* What about you?

DEELUXE: Don't get me naked. I get so Italian when I'm naked.

MICHIGAN: Thought you wanted that secret. Wanna touch it? Touch me the way you touch him.

DEELUXE: I don't!

MICHIGAN: Don't lie. Just tell me you love me.

DEELUXE: I can't say that.

MICHIGAN: *(MICHIGAN wraps DEELUXE in the strand of pearls.)* There, does that make it any easier? *(The two are bound together and begin a slow circle dance.)* Soon as they start to shine they start to change. The center contracts. Pressure at the center rises. And the center can't hold up. *(DEELUXE backs away. The pearls break. DEELUXE and MICHIGAN face each other for a long beat. Then DEELUXE turns away. MICHIGAN sinks to the floor and begins picking up the pearls.)* You take care of something, it grows. You can see I got the knack. Too big? Is there such a thing as "too big"? Besides it's just the way I am. Too damned juicy for my own good. With you around gets wicked. One look at you and my pink pulp starts pounding. *(DEELUXE begins to unzip her gown.)* Wanna know something? They're gonna get bigger. That pink is gonna go all the way into red. Then you watch out. My sap's running from the heat of your eyes. That special blue heat outta the eyes gets the pink ocean stirred up. That's when you squeeze them. Put the muscle on those peaches till my bucks are bucking like I'm riding an invisible palomino. *(DEELUXE is in her underwear, black tap pants and a corset. She reaches out for MICHIGAN. Pause.)* Well, I dunno, I might let you. These peaches getting mighty tight. But I gotta decide. What you ever done for me except make me cry? Right now I'm sobbing bad. Just look, I'm crying for you. You look hungry. Come on get it, squeeze it outta me, suck it outta me. I wanna be totally Spain when you're done with me. *(MICHIGAN begins to put on a filmy peignoir as she sings the following song. Her actions are as flirtatious as if she were stripping. MICHIGAN sings.)*

Bugs are bitin'
Fish are jumpin'
When my baby starts a humpin' me
Hot cross buns
Always beg for jam
Every beaver
Needs a beaver dam
Taste of fish
Taste of chicken
Don't taste like the girl I'm lickin'
She puts the cunt back in country
Pulls the rug out from under me
In case you are wondering
She can put what she wants in me.
Hot sweet cream
Dripping from my pet
How I scream
When she gets me wet
With her finger
On my sugar plum
There she lingers
Till I start to cum
'Cause she puts the cunt back in country
Pulls the rug out from under me
In case you are wondering
She can put what she wants in me.

(DEELUXE is tired of the tease. She dons a black tuxedo jacket. It's a magi-

cian's jacket: There are scarves, paper flowers, etc., in the pockets. During the following monolog, DEELUXE fumbles with the jacket and the objects seem to fly from her pockets. DEELUXE is facing the audience.)

DEELUXE: Alotta people ask me: What about Ohio? And I have to tell them what I know. Because I'm part buckeye. Not that you would know. That's why I never take all my clothes off all at the same time so you can never see the Ohio in me. But I haven't forgotten about Toledo and I won't. The very mention of the word "Toledo" makes me wanna puke. Toledo used to belong to us. We went to war to save it. People always ask: "Why'd you bother to have a war in Toledo? Aren't the winters there war enough?" Things got pretty bad between me and Toledo and a pig was killed. The government came in like they always do but the fighting went on when no one was looking. They took away Toledo. Gave us this little chunk of perpetual January that used to belong to Minnesota. Don't even get me started about Minnesota. When everybody else is dead I'm going to get a nice slab of Ohio. Right now it's my Uncle Bert's asparagus patch. I hate asparagus. I'm afraid of it. Especially at night when the stalks look like dead people from Toledo giving you the finger. We'd take these trips to visit the land. Going as fast as we could, pretending to be going someplace else. I guess that's the only way to live through a trip to Ohio: Pretend to be going someplace else. And keep the window rolled up tight. Ohio air can make you dizzy if you're not used to it. Remember: In the winters here they set the rivers on fire. We get to the land and they break out the asparagus and put on the ham. Aunt Helen is fat and she waits on the skinny people. We do things that way in Ohio: The fat people wait on the skinny ones. 'Course everyone in my family is fat. Except for Bert. But then he's not one of us. The only reason they let him stay in Ohio is he porked Aunt Helen back in that freak thaw last leap year. After dinner Bert helps Helen up the stairs. I do the dishes and they do it. When a three-hundred-and-fifty-pound woman has sex in a wood-frame house in Ohio, you know about it. Bert liked to get her right after the ham when she still had mayonnaise on her arms. Helen died before Bert learned what to do about asparagus. He just went out back and lay down in the mud. Face down. We left him that way. Very polite. And then I read in this magazine about this man that loves mud. Loves it better than he loves his dead wife. "Mud is better than any woman. You don't have to wait till after dinner. And it's romantic. After a rain. During a sunset. You just find a place and stick it in." And the letter was signed. Bert from Ohio. And that's Ohio.

(MICHIGAN crosses to the stereo and puts on a record—"Temptation." They do a tango which ends with MICHIGAN dipping DEELUXE. Suddenly, LITTLE PETER appears and begins talking to DEELUXE. MICHIGAN watches the dialog like someone watches a seizure or a crazy on the IRT.)

LITTLE PETER: We gotta talk.

DEELUXE: Leave me alone.

LITTLE PETER: Alone, who's alone? You're not alone. You probably couldn't even spell it. Always had me on your side. Don't sleep alone. Don't take a shit alone. Little Peter holds your hand. I seen alone and it's not for you. Maybe I know the wrong kind of alone. You wanna be alone alright, alone with her.

DEELUXE: *(To MICHIGAN.)* Would you like some more sherry? *(MICHIGAN shakes her head no.)*

LITTLE PETER: Why don't you ask her if she wants to be alone with you? Maybe she'd like a chaperon. Go ahead, ask her.

DEELUXE: I'm not going to ask her.

LITTLE PETER: Maybe she'd like me better, huh?

DEELUXE: She won't like you. She can't see you.

LITTLE PETER: She can see me. You're the one who can't see me.

DEELUXE: We're over. I'm not talking to you anymore.

LITTLE PETER: What?

DEELUXE: I said I'm not talking to you anymore. You're not real.

LITTLE PETER: You're doing it sister. Not real. What kinda thing is that to say to a friend? Hey, if I'm not real what does that make you?

DEELUXE: Keep your hands off me.

LITTLE PETER: Deeluxe, please!

DEELUXE: One minute. Just one. But don't go touching me. *(To MICHIGAN.)* There's this guy I know, um—outside. He's outside. That's why you can't see him. I gotta go give him some money. I'll be right back. *(DEELUXE crosses to the stage right window and pulls down the shade. The area is backlit so her shadow appears. The LITTLE PETER hand comes out from behind the shade. DEELUXE's hand follows, grabs LITTLE PETER and "strangles" him. After the LITTLE PETER hand is limp, DEELUXE crosses to MICHIGAN.)* You got to show them. They never believe you till you show them.

MICHIGAN: Is he gone?

DEELUXE: He's gone. Don't think about him. *(Pause.)* What you looking at?

MICHIGAN: You.

DEELUXE: Quit it.

MICHIGAN: You quit it.

DEELUXE: Me? What am I doing? It's not coming from me. I heard about you. What you do to women, what you make other women do. I'm not going to let you do that to me. I'm going to open the window and cry for help. I'm going to get the National Guard, the Marines, the *New York Times,* the Weight Watchers. I'm going to tell the world that evil is alive and well and living on Second Avenue. I'm going to—

(French windows blow open. Sound of howling wind. MICHIGAN stands up and crosses stage left. She puts on a fox fur stole. It's a larger, more gory version of the type with the head clipping onto the tail.)

MICHIGAN: Tell me again. What are you going to do? That's what I thought you were going to do. Nothing! And what did you say you thought I was? Tell me.

DEELUXE: You. You're an animal.

MICHIGAN: And what do you think you are? A fucking zucchini?

DEELUXE: Stop. Why don't you stop?

MICHIGAN: Because you don't want me to stop.

DEELUXE: I could make you.

MICHIGAN: Go ahead. Make me.

DEELUXE: Cross this line.

MICHIGAN: I already crossed that line a long time ago. And this line. Go on honey. Do it to me. Do it to me before I cross this line too.

DEELUXE: That's enough.

MICHIGAN: Sure it is. When you're really good you don't have to touch. She walks in the room and you don't touch. You don't even talk. But you feel her on every inch of your body like a suit of clothes you put on and can't take off. Feels like silk. But tight. Like a silk straight jacket. You're in deep and getting deeper. It's like being buried alive. And you like it.

DEELUXE: I won't . . . *(DEELUXE attempts to exit, but MICHIGAN grabs her breast.)*

MICHIGAN: There's nothing you won't do. This is what you wanted all along and no one has to know. It'll be our secret.

DEELUXE: What will?

MICHIGAN: Our secret will be what makes you tick. *(DEELUXE's bodice rips. Pearls and magic flowers explode out of it as she breaks away from MICHIGAN.)*

DEELUXE: I was never right
Look into my eyes
See the trouble
See the fire under water
See my brain's too big
See my heart's too small
I gotta pump it
That's why I gotta pump it.
I tried to make my heart move another way
But the blood's too thin
Like the see-thru blouse
Momma puts on when Daddy leaves the house.
My body's too fat like Crisco in the pan
It smokes it steams it cries out for meat.
There's no other way your ham sure hits my spot
And if that don't grease the clock
You gotta pump it.
I call my private Jesus on the pay telephone
Down on my knees in a booth filled with piss
Asking the King O'Love won'tcha please
Strike me dead.
I can't live a life with a head too big
I can't get a laugh with a shrunken love pump
My too big head's filled with a too bad thought
It stinks it bites it goes straight to the brain
Till I pump it.
It's not just bad
It's more than bad it's wrong
In the wrong place
My heart got stuck between my legs

You wouldn't think I wouldn't think
Such a tiny thing could put the muzzle on the brain
On those full moon nights the way it beats so bad
No top 40 drum machine
More a solo with a shake
I gotta bad heart but I'm a nice girl, girl.
I'm not a girl at all, I'm more like a car.
A nice new car, why don't you thumb me down.
I'll let you take the wheel
A woman with a bad heart gets lonely when she drives her-
self insane
Take the wheel and I'll let you bite my ham.
Turn the key over quick, put your boot to the floor
If you don't get the power first
Gotta pump it.

MICHIGAN: I'm getting out of here!

DEELUXE: I'm dying, you can't do that! Rip somebody's heart out and leave them to die!

MICHIGAN: I do it all the time.

DEELUXE: Then it's true!

MICHIGAN: Yes, it's true, let me go!

DEELUXE: If you go I'll die.

MICHIGAN: If I stay you'll be worse than dead. You'll be like me.

DEELUXE: What are you? *(DEELUXE collapses.)*

MICHIGAN: There's a word for it in Michigan. From the early days of Michigan. Before Michigan was Motown, or Ford four-doors, or Gerald Ford or Chevy hatchbacks, and before the soybeans, sweet cherries, and mint fields went in. Before they started burning the sugar beets and soaking the kirbies in barrels of brine. Before they opened the Keewanah for copper pennies. Before all that when all Michigan was was cold. Mooneye, steelhead, alewife, all of that. A coupla shriveled spits of land shivering in glacial puddles that'd lost their salt, that's what Michigan was. All she grew was protection from the cold. Beaver protection, and weasel, fisher, marten, mink, red fox, gray fox, catamount, muskrat, lynx, and bobcat too. Fur. Pelts. And all of a sudden, Michigan was full of Frenchmen. They set their trap lines out on the ice. Along the Manistee, the Ausable. But the animals they caught didn't die right away they lay out on the ice freezing and snarling and bleeding until the stars, most of them, fled to Canada. And Orion bent down out the January sky and put a silver bullet in their brain. Silver on the brain, they changed. Became monsters out on that ice. Until the Frenchmen came back and the monsters became hats. Fancy hats and pocketbooks. But there was something else out there. Another sort of animal. Or a woman. They always called her a "she." She came along the trap lines before the Frenchmen. She ripped open the steel and tossed it into the Tittabawassee. She set free the monsters. Whatever she was, she had a mean head on her shoulders shaped like a wedge of Pinconning extra sharp cheddar cheese gone bad and a fat ass. She was always about fifty-six years old. And the monsters crashed through the split-level prefab houses of the Frenchmen and fucked their wives and got them full of baby monsters. They don't say this anymore in Michigan. No one knows what happened to the woman who set the monsters free. The woman who was an animal. Loup Garou. They said that women were monsters. Because they had teeth in their parts. And now they say we're not like that. We're not dangerous anymore. But it's a lie. We are monsters. We got teeth in our parts and we're so hungry. If you stay here, I'll eat you alive. Do you understand? Do you still want to be like me? *(MICHIGAN turns upstage and crosses to hang up the fur. While she is still turned upstage, DEELUXE slowly sits up.)* Why did you come back?

DEELUXE: I live here.

MICHIGAN: Lived here. I liked it when you were dead because I got to do all the things I always wanted to but you kept me from doing.

DEELUXE: Like what?

MICHIGAN: Redecorate.

DEELUXE: It's the same.

MICHIGAN: It's not the same. *(DEELUXE moves toward MICHIGAN who is seated.)* This is my chair.

DEELUXE: *(Sitting down in her chair.)* I only been gone five minutes. *(A blue airmail letter falls out of the skylight. MICHIGAN rushes to pick it up, then hands it to DEELUXE.)*

MICHIGAN: It's for you.

DEELUXE: *(Reading the letter.)*

> "Dear Deeluxe,
> You asked about the future. Here's the deal: it's gonna be just like the past. In the past the heart of the world was filled with carbon and water and that is why we had life on earth. When everything got heavier the world started collapsing in on itself, an old heart in a fat body. Aunt Helen collapsing in Cleveland. After the baby was born. The one who couldn't talk. Or get up to go to the bathroom by herself. The one who's being born killed Helen's only daughter. And Aunt Helen, she just collapsed. Carbon and water into diamonds. And in the future, women will replace the world. In a woman's heart there is rice and water and that is why there is life on earth. But in the future, women will start collapsing the world thick with babies who can't talk and only daughters who live alone on Oreos. And rice and water will be crushed into tears. But no one will cry. The tears will stay inside. They will be the hardest things known to man. Women's tears will be used. In the future, women's tears will put a man on the moon. And in the future, all the men who kill for a living will wear pinky rings with women's tears.
> Love always,
> Little Peter."

(Pause.) So that's the future, huh?

MICHIGAN: *(Pouring sherry for a toast.)* Don't worry. We'll never see it.

(MICHIGAN starts to raise her glass to DEELUXE's, but the upstage window shade flies up. There is a hand at the window with a pinky ring. DEELUXE and MICHIGAN continue staring at the hand as the lights fade down and out.)

Reading Past the Heterosexual Imperative

Dress Suits to Hire

Kate Davy

Lesbians should be mistresses of discrepancies, knowing that resistance lies in the change of context.

—*Joan Nestle (1984:236)*

When Holly Hughes, Peggy Shaw, and Lois Weaver embarked on the collaboration that resulted in *Dress Suits to Hire,* all three artists had a history of creating work to be performed in the WOW Cafe, a lesbian theatre space in Manhattan's East Village.[1] An unmistakable specificity is evident in pieces performed at WOW—the address is clearly lesbian. Freely borrowing from popular culture forms, WOW artists produce pieces based on scenarios from familiar, recognizable entertainment genres. In this work, they construct subcultural, under-the-text imagery, metaphors, and conventions derived from lesbian culture. Making work for this context assumes a certain coherence of exchange between performance and spectators that cannot be presumed in other arenas. Meanings shift radically when a site-specific work is taken out of its production context.

From its inception, *Dress Suits* was made to be performed at P.S. 122, an East Village venue for new, or nonmainstream, theatre, dance, music, and performance art.[2] Hughes, Shaw, and Weaver understood that the tacit assumptions operant when making work specifically for WOW and its audience—assumptions that inform the nature and shape of the work—could not be taken for granted outside WOW turf. Working toward performance in a sociologically (if not artistically) mainstream, predominantly heterosexual space influenced the narrative and performative strategies developed for *Dress Suits* in an attempt to resist dominant culture readings of the piece. While the objective remained the same as that of WOW productions, *Dress Suits* marks a significant departure from the style and some of the strategies that distinguish WOW theatre work.

A basic tenet of reception theory is that a production and its audience are not separate. A performance text intersects with individual audience mem-

1. In a publicity shot for Dress Suits to Hire, *Michigan (Lois Weaver) gazes at the viewer through the gartered leg of Deeluxe (Peggy Shaw). The photos accompanying this article are from the May 1987 P.S. 122 production in New York. (Photo by Eva Weiss)*

bers who, in turn, intersect with it—producing meaning in terms of their own relationships with discourses and practices in society. Meanings do not reside exclusively in the work of art, nor solely in individual readings. Moreover, the context in which a work and its audience are positioned materially influences reception. For instance, under certain conditions a work that attempts to subvert dominant culture's system of representation can instead be assimilated into it, thereby reinforcing, rather than disrupting, its codes.

The WOW Cafe is a context that presumes a lesbian worldview. In this context, WOW artists create a theatre *for* lesbians, a theatre that responds to lesbian subjectivity. *Dress Suits* attempts to maintain this stance in a context that presumes a heterosexual worldview. Hughes, Shaw, and Weaver devised strategies of resistance for this context that manifest a fierce struggle to thwart the assimilation of their discourse. My purpose in this essay is to examine the dimensions of this struggle and, through my reading of the work, indicate some of the wider implications for lesbian performance in particular and feminist performance in general.

When misreadings of lesbian work occur even within WOW space—as they did in WOW's Spring 1988 production of Lisa Kron's *Paradykes Lost*—the difficulty of resisting an appropriation by the spectator into dominant, heterosexual cultural readings is apparent. Two critics reviewing the performance eschewed the play's lesbian perspective by imposing a heterosexual worldview on the work and reading the performance through this worldview, thereby misinterpreting a crucial dimension of the piece.

A closer look at the response to *Paradykes Lost* informs the project of *Dress Suits*. Set in the parlor of an English manor during the 1920s, *Para-*

dykes Lost loosely follows a conventional murder mystery formula. Among the cast are a detective, an ingenue, a couple, a butler, and an assortment of eccentric singles. All the characters have women's names, all are explicitly identified as lesbian in the dialog, and all the roles were played by women. Yet in her review for *The New York Native*—a gay newspaper—Amy L. Eddings writes about "the all-woman cast who play male characters and refer to each other as 'she' " (1988:29). This represents a fundamental misreading of a butch/femme dynamic that is the M.O. of this detective spoof, as well as the modus operandi of most WOW work. The cast of *Paradykes* most definitely did not play male characters—they refer to each other as "she" because they play lesbian characters.

Writing for *The Village Voice,* Robert Massa also read *Paradykes* as drag performance: "As in men's camp, the characters refer to each other as 'she' regardless of gender [. . .]" (1988:97). Although WOW productions are similar to male camp performances and Theatre of the Ridiculous in their farcical style, there are important differences. Male drag emphasizes the illusionistic qualities of impersonation. The actor attempts to simulate that which he is not, the "other." Instead of foregrounding dominant culture's fiercely polarized gender roles, men's camp assumes them and plays them out. Like much of men's camp, WOW artists use scenarios from popular performance forms as sources for their narratives, but WOW performers do not adopt the heterosexual imperative operant in these scenarios. They do not impersonate women and men in heterosexual couplings. Ironically, male camp tends to reinscribe, rather than undermine, the dominant culture paradigms it appropriates for its farce and means to parody.

Men—both gay and straight—are the intended audience for male camp, while the projected spectator in WOW productions is lesbian—a subject who, as defined by Monique Witting, stands outside dominant culture categories as not-man, not-woman.[3] WOW performances efface a heterosexual address by constructing a spectator who is neither man nor woman but lesbian—a subject defined in terms of sexual similarity. Same-sexuality is the model and organizing principle from which WOW artists work.

Massa goes on in his review to describe a dimension of his own position as spectator—"As a gay man, I feel less left out at WOW than at straight burlesque"—and then singles out one performance in *Paradykes* to critique: "Kate Stafford as the detective manages to suggest Cary Grant without caricature. Even I swooned" (1988:97). Could there be any clearer evidence of the role desire plays in reception? Here, a gay man appropriates a lesbian character by reading her performance as "in drag," then swoons over the male character he constructs. Unfortunately, in appropriating the character, Massa deprived himself of the radical experience of the play.

Given such misappropriations, it is useful to examine how butch/femme as a system of representation in lesbian theatre differs from drag performance. The iconography and dynamics of butch/femme culture present in WOW productions is not, as it is often described, about cross-dressing. Wearing the gender of the "other" sex, in dominant culture terms, is not the point. Nor is it about drag in the sense of simulation. No attempt is made to hide the lesbian beneath a mask of male or female gender identity. To fool the audience, even momentarily, is not the objective. In their essay "The Misunderstanding: Toward a More Precise Sexual Vocabulary," Esther Newton and Shirley Walton wrote:

> The terms 'butch' and 'femme' refer to gay erotic identities, derived historically from dominant gender categories but now distinct. Thus

> 'butch' is a gay erotic identity in which symbols from the male gender category play a significant part, and 'femme' is the complementary gay identity, drawing on feminine gender symbols (1984:245).

As a dimension of erotic identity, butch/femme is about sexuality and its myriad nuances. It is also about gender in that it appropriates gender in its social articulation and representational construction, but not as it functions in material social relations in dominant cultural terms.[4] In butch/femme iconography, attributes which in dominant culture are associated with strict gender roles are not sex-class specific. Worn by lesbians, these attributes have meanings for lesbians in a same-sex, lesbian culture that do not necessarily symbolize conformity to rules of gender behavior and the oppositional dynamics of polarized gender roles.

Femme and butch constructions exist outside of these paradigms and foreground the problem of confusing sexuality with gender. When sexuality and gender are mistakenly conflated and collapsed into one "sex/gender" concept and assumed to be social facts according to a binary opposition (one sex/gender being male; the other sex/gender being not-male), the effect is to construe sex and gender as the same phenomenon. Moreover, it is to construe sex and gender as "natural"—a law of nature enforced by a law of culture. Compulsory heterosexuality. Sexuality and gender are discrete, albeit linked, phenomena in what Gayle Rubin has described as the sex-gender system (1978). Butch/femme as a social dynamic in lesbian culture is a manifestation of the separation of sexuality from polarized gender constructs and imperative heterosexuality.[5]

Each WOW artist mines the material, social terrain of butch/femme culture somewhat differently in her theatre work. In *Paradykes Lost,* Lisa Kron's use of butch/femme iconography must be largely overlooked in order to read her production in heterosexual terms. For instance, although Kate Stafford's detective "costume" was butch, her makeup and hair were femme in style. The stance and deportment of another butch character in *Paradykes* echoed the femme. When dominant culture notions of man and woman are "present" it is *not* because they are presented as such—they are read into the performance.

The title *Paradykes Lost* is rich in canonical connotation. It critiques the absence of lesbian work in the canons of theatre and dramatic literature. Ironically, a lesbian perspective is (re)found, recuperated, and given a voice in productions like *Paradykes,* only to be obfuscated in heterosexual readings of the work. The dykes are lost once again.

For the makers of *Dress Suits,* then, the project is to insist that the lesbian represent herself on her own terms, through strategies that thwart rather than facilitate the propensity to read her signs and symbols from a heterosexual perspective.

Dress Suits to Hire is set in a cramped storefront room of a cheesy New York clothing rental store where two women live and where clearly no one ever comes to rent anything. Before the performance begins, the audience can see the set. It is constructivist in style—its back and side walls comprised of empty frames that delineate two large windows and a door. Another empty frame is positioned downstage. It faces front, suggesting a window through which the audience can look into the private space of the room. Positioned in this vertical plane it echoes both the illusionary fourth wall of frontal staging, and the proscenium "opening" of theatrical space—the theatre's keyhole through which the voyeuristic gaze of the spectator is engaged.

Because the stage embodies the "to-be-looked-at" dimension of the theatrical apparatus—the site of the spectacle, the artificial, the histrionic, the site of deceit, conceit, and disguise—it is sometimes linked metaphorically with "the feminine." Of course, ultimately, "woman"—woman as sign, as the collective essence of femininity—is conflated with spectacle itself, *woman as spectacle,* woman as object of the spectatorial gaze. This gaze, the looking itself, is male. As E. Ann Kaplan explains in her book *Women and Film,* "The gaze is not necessarily male (literally), but to own and activate the gaze, given our language and the structure of the unconscious, is to be in the 'masculine' position" (1983:30).

In their collaboration on *Dress Suits to Hire,* Hughes, Shaw, and Weaver created a production in which this configuration—one that constitutes the gaze as masculine and locates both the site and recipient of the gaze as feminine—is played out with a vengeance and a twist. The apparatus is made aware of itself—woman looks back. And she is femme.

As the lights come up at the beginning of the play, two performers sit across a small table looking into each other's eyes. Their bodies are covered with identical floor-length boudoir robes made from sturdy fabric that hangs from them in a way that hides their bodies. Deeluxe (played by Shaw) sings a song quietly to herself as she pulls nylon stockings onto each leg, fastens them to garters, and puts high-heeled shoes on her feet. The song is a list of things she is going to do for and to her body—"Gonna buy myself a diamond ring / Gonna stuff my nose with cocaine"—which she sings as she dons the clothing and accessories that are the trappings of femininity. She pulls on long, black evening gloves and, still singing, crosses to the downstage window. Just as she starts to look out the window at the audience, she is attacked, mid-song, by her own right hand which—like a separate, possessed being—grabs her throat and strangles her. She staggers backward and dies noisily center stage.

As Wittig suggests, lesbian as a category may sidestep dominant constructions and classifications of woman and man in the economy of the sex-gender system, but the lesbian performer nonetheless confronts the complex significative workings of the female body as sign the moment she sets foot on stage. From the outset, Shaw and Weaver, in their identical, body-concealing garb, begin the arduous process of interrupting the dynamics of signification that in dominant culture conflate women exclusively with the body.

In theatre, as in the rest of culture, women as speaking subjects are missing from representation. In their place, "woman" appears as a construction that signifies a (feminine) essence intrinsic to all women. This construction is anathema to women as historical beings and social subjects because it reduces them to "nature," "mother," and ultimately, the object of (male) desire. The absence of women as speaking subjects in representation is central to what feminist scholars have described as the crisis in representation. For practitioners who work in forms that have a visual dimension, the central issue is how to image the female body without engendering "woman."

Feminist filmmakers and theorists have accomplished much in the project of dismantling "woman"; from identifying and articulating the male gaze and the ways in which the female body is placed in the service of that gaze through operations of voyeurism and fetishism,[6] to manipulating the narrative and cinematic mechanisms that produce meaning in film through strategies that subvert or disrupt the cinematic apparatus. While it is not possible to adequately describe here the many important ways feminist filmmakers work, a brief description of a crucial dimension of Yvonne Rainer's film *The Man Who Envied Women* (1985) serves the purpose of this discussion by demonstrating a significant approach to grappling with the problematic of imaging the female body.

Working against the dynamics of the male gaze, Rainer constructs the female protagonist in her film by means of a voice-over. The spectator hears the protagonist but never sees her, for Rainer refuses to embody her voice in a single, coherent image of a woman's body. Rainer removes the object of the cinematic fetish (the fetishized female body) from the screen, thwarting the operations of voyeurism. This strategy produces a kind of "radical absence" that echoes the nature of filmic representation itself. For, unlike theatre, film by definition is marked by absences—the objects the camera "sees" are not in fact present at the moment of screening.[7]

Since some of the mechanisms operant in cinema are similar to those at work in live performance, feminist theatre scholars and practitioners have turned to film theory and practice for insight and direction. Although this research continues to be enormously fruitful, there are obvious limitations. In theatre, for example, the mechanisms of voyeurism, fetishism, and scopophilia (pleasure in looking) work in analogous ways to film, but not in the same ways. Feminist filmmakers work both with and against the (inter)mediating "eye" of the camera which, together with editing, create the illusion of point of view, temporal continuity, and in general what Stephen Heath terms "narrative space" (1986). If Mary Ann Doane (1982) is right when she suggests that the absence of the live body in filmed images makes it possible to fetishize that body (precisely because of the extreme distance from the image/object this absence engenders and permits),[8] then the very presence of the performing body in live, three-dimensional, theatrical space suggests a venue for undermining the mechanisms that contribute the fetishism in representational systems that have a visual dimension.

Indeed the conditions of the theatre—the very *presentness* of the theatrical apparatus, and the *immediacy* of theatrical representation—are key to the subversion of "woman" within *Dress Suits*. Just as Rainer takes filmic absence to its logical extreme in her film, Hughes, Shaw, and Weaver seize the theatre as an "arena of presence," over-constructing the performative dimensions of their piece, to produce a kind of "radical presence." By over-constructing the body in *Dress Suits,* the operations of theatrical representation are over-determined, foregrounded, and made visible, thereby undermining, paradoxically, the construction of *woman as body*.

A number of devices are employed repeatedly and cumulatively in *Dress Suits* to undercut the illusory dimension of theatre and insist on the material presence of the body. Opening the performance with Shaw dressing on stage, literally putting on femininity, foregrounds gender as "man-made." Wearing the reference marks of femininity under her robe—referents that inscribe the body as female and, conversely, the female as body—Deeluxe sings the body's pleasures before killing it off. Significantly, the script's first stage direction states that the body is "dead for the rest of the play."

After Deeluxe collapses, the audience hears the high-pitched yapping of a small dog. Michigan (Weaver), with the dog in her lap, has been seated with her back to the corpselike Deeluxe, who lies between her and the audience. The dog—a battery-operated toy—rouses Michigan. (Significantly, it is the mechanical dog that bears a woman's name, "Linda"—the characters do not.) Michigan turns, sees Deeluxe, and begins frantically to search for a telephone. She pulls out a pink, plastic receiver, puts it to her

2. Linda yaps in Michigan's lap as Deeluxe lies dead with Little Peter still at her throat. (Photo by Dona Ann McAdams)

ear and says, "Hello? Ninth Precinct?" The cord on the receiver has been cut and the rest of the telephone apparatus is missing. As in *Lady Dick*, Hughes' 1985 production with WOW, a character calls on the "authorities" for help.[9] The obviously cut cord signals that this attempt "to get outside" is futile. The action of the performance literally and figuratively remains within the confines of this small room, circumscribed by the nature of theatrical representation. The challenge is to find a way out from within, to articulate another kind of author(ity), one inside the discourse of *Dress Suits*, but outside the Law.

Michigan's monolog that follows is a kind of micro-articulation mapping the terms of the rest of the performance. In her phone conversation, Michigan refers only to "the body," emphasizing that the murder she calls to report is not the death of Deeluxe. This distinction between the speaking subject and the body is further complicated when Michigan speaks of her desire. In answer to questions from the Ninth Precinct officer (as a matter of course, or better, as a matter of gender, we presume the officer on the other end of the line is male), Michigan smiles seductively and says slowly and suggestively,

> Yes there certainly is a body. Did I discover it? Many years ago. [. . .] I lay down on the bed and discovered the body. [. . .] And after that first time I would discover the body again and again.

She suggests a distinction between the (dead) body and the lesbian body that is the object of her desire. A repeated and insistent articulation of lesbian desire within the piece positions it outside heterosexuality both as a social institution and representational model, by realigning what Jill Dolan describes as the "dynamics of desire" between performance and its spectators. Dolan writes, "desire is not necessarily a fixed, male-owned commodity, but can be exchanged, with much different meaning, between women. When the locus of desire changes, the demonstration of sexuality and gender roles also changes" (1987:173). *Dress Suits* breaks the "heterosexual contract" that Teresa de Lauretis identifies as "the very site in which the social relations of gender and thus gender ideology are reproduced in everyday life" (1987:17).

Of course the heterosexual model in representation is not dismantled simply and unproblematically, especially outside a lesbian performance context. In *Dress Suits* a narrative/performative strategy addresses the dilemma in the form of "Little Peter"—an entity that resides in the right hand of Deeluxe. Although the spectator doesn't learn his name until later in the piece, "Little Peter" as a performative "figure of speech" is identified almost immediately. Michigan doesn't report a murder to the Ninth Precinct, she says,

> There's a man in here. [. . .] He lives with us. More with her than with me. Me, this man, and the body.

The hand that strangles the body represents the male economy that "the body" was constructed to serve. If "the body" signifies women as trade, commodity, and use value in the sexual marketplace, and "woman" in the representational marketplace, then it is significant that the murdering hand is an extension of that body for it belongs to the male economy that inscribes and appropriates it.

The not-so-subtle phallic signifier, Little Peter, is the force that repeatedly attempts to contain what de Lauretis calls the "trauma of gender—the potential disruption of the social fabric and of white male privilege [. . .]" (1987:21). That he resides in Deeluxe acknowledges poignantly the great complexity of imagining a different order while immersed in the current sociosymbolic order.

During the opening monolog-cum-monodrama, Michigan "redecorates." She performs a seemingly senseless series of actions over the ostensibly dead body. She covers the waist with a small table, for instance, and then removes it; she spreads the arms out away from the body and then moves them back—all the while relating in explicit language the history of her lesbian erotic desire, identifying herself as an "animal" ("Being a girl is just a phase I'm going through"). It's as though she performs some transformative ritual designed to (re)articulate and transform this dead body, resurrect it, into the lesbian body.

In grappling with the problematic of the body, this opening monolog also establishes exhibitionism both as subject matter and an identifying dimension of theatre itself. Shaw and Weaver are performers who present performers that move from one showbiz "turn" to another, using recognizable bits—the stand-up-comic routine, the song-and-dance number—that foreground the theatrical nature of live performance as well as the voyeur/exhibitionist relationship it engenders. Michigan says to Deeluxe's murderous right hand:

> I suppose you know what this will mean. There will be no show. She will be unable to do the show. You're not going to like this. [. . .] She probably won't be able to perform anymore!

Hundreds of narratives, from *Antigone* to *'Night Mother* and *Fatal Attraction,* end with the physical death of a woman, or her psychological death or, as in (romantic) comedy, her recuperation through marriage. *Dress Suits* inverts narrative closure by beginning the play with a death, the momentous event that is usually the target of narrative suspense, the resolution of processes of expectation. Hughes' play also undercuts those narratives that begin with a murder which propels the action toward an eventual resolution—ten minutes into *Dress Suits* the body is resurrected.

As befits her name, Deeluxe is resurrected "in spectacle." Pulling herself up from the floor, she "over sings" (forcefully and very dramatically) the song *"Amato Mio"* from *Gilda,* a Rita Hayworth film. At the same time, she pulls a large, gold, gaudy accordion fan up behind her. It is as tall as she is and frames her still-robed body, à la Cecil B. de Mille. Michigan hands her a bouquet of tulips attached to an electric cord. As Deeluxe strikes a finale pose against the fan, the tulips light up. Deeluxe is "in spectacle"—decorated, lit-up like a Christmas tree—a performance within a performance.

It is significant that in this micro-extravaganza musical number—one that refers visually to the genre of Hollywood spectacle—Deeluxe is posed against the fan still wearing a shapeless robe. The curvaceous female body, conventionally associated with this Hollywood image, is hidden. Hence, an image that invites a fetishistic response is deconstructed by "displaying" a hidden body. Throughout *Dress Suits,* iconic expectations are repeatedly thwarted by images that are consistently skewed: there is always something wrong with the "picture."

Resurrected, Deeluxe grabs a piggybank and threatens to leave home. While it seems as though this scene is one she's enacted many times before, like everything in the play, it's unclear. Nothing in *Dress Suits* is stable, not the time in which the action takes place, not the characters, not the actions. Even dialects and idioms shift in style from lofty theatrical monolog to lesbian bar-culture slang to underworld gun moll to Midwestern twang. The linguistic, behavioral, and gestural signs indicative of a core character from which all else is merely a departure, are repeatedly subverted. Michigan and Deeluxe change clothes and personas frequently.

Although smacking of vaudeville and burlesque in its humor and presentational style, the ambiance of *Dress Suits* is definitely not an upbeat, playful one of "let's make a show" for each other. Instead, there is a seemingly random, fragmented exploration of the dark side of sexuality. The atmosphere is heavy, private, subterranean. The spectator can feel the weight and import of a private symbol system without necessarily being able to decipher, decode, or complete it. Gone is the butch/femme play that is a hallmark of WOW productions, but that threatens to reinforce rather than subvert gender polarizations. Gone, too, are conventional narratives (like those based on romance novel formulas, or television sitcoms) that can be parodied in lesbian performance contexts. Instead, throughout *Dress Suits'* roughly 75 minutes, there are continuous shifts narratively and visually as the artists attempt to create, moment-to-moment, points of identification with the potential for engaging their subjectivity as lesbians, as women, as girls, as femme, as butch, as femme fatale. And as "animal," nonhumans (the cat, palomino, werewolf) who transgress the boundaries of the body and conventional femininity.

These points of identification are continuously, almost breathlessly, constructed and then dissolved and are not to be confused with a single, coherent "point of identification" related to some unproblematic notion of identity with which all well-meaning spectators can identify. Manipulating the operations of identification through an articulation of many different and rapidly changing points of view creates a continuously shifting subject field. Spectators are invited to repeatedly (re)engage with shifting subject positions, intermittently activating certain kinds of subjectivity. Narrative episodes in *Dress Suits* interrupt narrative coherence—the "flowing with" narrative that ostensibly comes "naturally" but is in fact manufactured by the processes and organizing principles of narrative itself (see de Lauretis 1984).

Within *Dress Suits'* shifting subject field, power relations are repeatedly redistributed. Both women in "Dress Suits" are "suited" with femme iconography, so that when one emerges as more powerful than the other, the action is played out in the context of sameness—same sex partner, same erotic identity. If power is understood as distributed according to "difference," then, again, the "picture" is out of kilter. The "difference" is in erotic role, which is not fixed—power positionings change, slide back and forth, throughout the performance. Power is exchanged between the two performers.

The underlying assumption is that power and sexual desire are deeply connected. Power is not denied women in *Dress Suits*. Lesbian theatre artists refuse to agree that power belongs solely to male constructs. But because power dynamics and gender identity are fiercely linked in dominant discourses (in positionings that in heterosexual culture are seemingly inextricably grounded in the configuration "male/female," construed as active/passive, powerful/powerless, and prescribed according to gender) the butch/femme play that works so subversively in lesbian performance contexts it not employed in *Dress Suits*. Outside of lesbian venues, butch/femme can too easily be read as male/female. *Dress Suits* scrambles the signals, the processes of identification, when it "unhooks" power from polarized gender relations and heterosexual desire.

The butch, however, is not erased—she appears within the femme construct. Once Deeluxe removes her concealing robe, an iconographic process is begun whereby meaning is layered upon meaning, establishing an increasingly complex iconicity. When Deeluxe "disrobes," she is seen wearing a black, strapless, waist-length corset, black satin panties, and a black garter belt. Her back to the audience, Deeluxe faces Michigan who, as spectator, watches while Deeluxe dresses herself in a strapless, full-length, satin evening gown, gartered nylon stockings, heels, long black evening gloves, and dangling earrings. Deeluxe bends over, throws her mane of curly red hair forward, and brushes it. Standing, she throws her head back suggestively, and extends her arms to suggest she is displaying herself for Michigan.

She is in full masquerade, that is, she has *made a spectacle of herself.* She has, in Mary Russo's words, "put on femininity with a vengeance" (1986:224). But what prevents this flaunting of femininity from being recuperated back into "woman"? Shaw's demeanor, the performative quality of her work, is important in understanding how this problematic is worked out in the complexity of Deeluxe as an iconic sign. Michigan refers to Deeluxe as, "Half woman, half something weird. French, maybe. All cat." Shaw's masquerade hints at the butch, but she does not fully play it at this point in the performance.

Having presented herself for Weaver's attentive gaze, Shaw slowly turns to the audience and sinuously walks downstage to sing another Rita Hayworth song—"Put the Blame on Mame" from *Gilda*—in her own version as "Put the Blame on Me." The relationship between performer, character, and spectator that Elin Diamond delineates in her reading of Brecht (1988) is multiplied and problematized as Shaw performs Deeluxe performing Rita Hayworth performing still another character, Gilda. Shaw culls bits of gesture, stance, and attitude from Hayworth's performing style in *Gilda,* and then overstates and overplays them in her own performance, projecting an ironic, knowing attitude about what she is doing. It's as if she's winking at the audience, sharing a private understanding. The critique of objectification is clear. Shaw plays the fetishized object of the male gaze and at the same time critiques that position.

The articulation and circulation of the gaze is further complicated when Shaw looks back at the spectators and interacts with them directly. With Weaver positioned as "onstage spectator" watching her from behind while the audience watches her from the front, Shaw is caught in the fourth wall. In the P.S. 122 production and on tour in Milwaukee, Wisconsin, the audience seating section was so close to the performing area that spectators seated on the floor in front of the first row were literally at Shaw's feet. During the "Blame" song, she played the vamp, the femme fatale, transforming the theatre into an intimate cabaret, choosing individual women in the audience to address seductively—teasing them with the possibility of tossing out one of her gloves. Not only are the dynamics of same-sex desire absolutely clear in this sequence—the address lesbian—but the physical separation and psychological distance provided by the fourth wall of proscenium staging is breached.

The enormous influence on reception of this crucial dimension of distance was apparent in performances at the University of Michigan, Ann Arbor, where the production circumstances were especially skewed. A physical distance of several yards separated the performing space from the audience seating sections, establishing a kind of Wagnerian "mystic gulf" that produced a certain "lesbian theatre under glass" aura. Because Shaw could not close the gap and indicate precisely the spectators she was addressing, it was not difficult to apply a dominant culture model, read from that perspective, and engage in fetishizing the image.[10]

Shaw plays the femme utterly in her "Blame" song so that when she shifts to the butch, during the play's one blatantly conventional seduction scene, her masquerade becomes so (over)loaded with seemingly contradictory meanings that it virtually "vibrates" and threatens to rupture. The scene ostensibly takes place at the pumps of a desert filling station. Weaver wears a white full slip that clings to her body, and pink high-heeled boots that zip to her ankles. Shaw ties a bandana around her neck, puts a cowboy hat on her head, a toothpick in her mouth and, as the theme song from the film *A Man and a Woman* swells up, crosses the stage to Weaver, moving (according to a stage direction) "as much like a cowboy as you can in a strapless gown and heels." Weaver "comes on" to Shaw who plays the butch fully while still embedded visually in femme iconography.

On stage, Shaw and Weaver are frequently described as "hot," and the stage in this seduction scene is exceedingly sexually charged. The femme and femme-cum-butch tease each other, seduce each other, until Shaw pulls Weaver to her in a long stage kiss—the music from *A Man and A Woman* swells again. Like the sentence "This is not a pipe," that Magritte scrawled in French under his careful drawing of a pipe, the sound track in this scene states, "This is *not* a man and a woman." Taken together, the elements of this scene conspire to skew the potential for gender polarization in butch/femme play by over-determining femme iconography and inserting the butch into it—creating an especially ironic distance from the body, or masquerade.[11]

In her essay entitled "The Technology of Gender," de Lauretis argues persuasively for what she describes as "the movement in and out of gender as ideological representation." She writes,

> [A] movement between the (represented) discursive space of the positions made available by hegemonic discourses and the space-off, the elsewhere, of those discourses: those other spaces both discursive and social that exist, since feminist practices have (re)constructed them, in the margins (or "between the lines," or "against the grain") of hegemonic discourses. [. . .] These two kinds of spaces are neither in opposition to one another nor strung along a chain of signification, but they coexist concurrently and in contradiction. The movement between them, therefore, is not that of a dialectic, of integration, of a combinatory, or of *difference,* but is the tension of contradiction, multiplicity, and heteronomy (1987:26).

It is from this other space that *Dress Suits* attempts to exist in contradiction with dominant discourse. Especially (although not only) in the seduction scene, played out in terms of lesbian desire, a palpable tension between dominant discourse and lesbian discourse is created, and a voice emerges from under the masquerade: a voice-under that articulates a nonrecuperable discursive space. Little Peter, of course, reappears at the scene's conclusion, the ever just-around-the-corner phallic principle that, when threatened, surfaces. The two discursive spaces coexist, the tension of the female-body-in-contradiction delineates their respective positions.

The issue of objectification is repeatedly addressed directorially and narratively in scenes that foreground, throw into relief, the meaning-producing mechanisms of the theatrical apparatus. In what could be called "the stargazing scene," the performers look back through the proscenium opening, creating a kind of reversed voyeurism that—like Shaw's "Blame" number—addresses concretely the issue of the gaze. Michigan stargazes out the window through a prop that represents a telescope but is not one—it is an unusually long, phallic flashlight turned on the audience. Its beam of light metaphorically projects her gaze and literally traces it visually. Unlike the receptive nature and passive activity a telescope suggests—the gazer receiving images—a flashlight is aggressive, its beam is visible across space and its spot of light hits and reveals its target. In this scene, the target of the gaze is the audience, individual spectators are "spotlighted." The distance separating performers from spectators is effaced as the "object" of fetishistic gazing assumes an active stance and looks back.

Deeluxe takes the flashlight from Michigan, looks out the window "through" it, and says to Michigan, "Hey! You can see right into my bedroom! You been looking at me! This is proof." Michigan responds, "I been more than looking. I been watching. That's looking with a reason." By virtue of their "looking with a reason," with lesbian desire, the gaze is reinscribed, detaching the scopophilic drive from its association, or sole alliance with masculinity.

Just as Michigan and Deeluxe, with a beam of light, take the gaze both literally and metaphorically into their own hands, Hughes, Shaw, and Weaver take the theatrical apparatus in hand and, through *Dress Suits to Hire,* make every dimension of it resonate with meaning for lesbians and women. The set, for example, suggests meanings anyone can read: the

3. Stargazing with a flashlight. (Photo by Dona Ann McAdams)

walls that separate public (male) from domestic (female) space; the division between the outside world of "social reality" and the interior realm of subjectivity, and so forth. But the physical space, like nearly every other element of the production, also generates meanings that resonate in ways that bear significance especially for lesbians and women—a private experience in a public, gender-mixed and gender-inscribed, arena. When the characters perform a sweeping, à la '40s-movie-musical dance number in the small space, they nearly smash into the walls and crash into the furniture. It is a very funny number ("hysterically" funny?) during which the room seems smaller, even more claustrophobic. Like the destroyed illusion of backdrop scenery painted in perspective when performers move too close to it, Shaw and Weaver appear too large to be contained by the space. Whether received at a conscious level or not, the experience of this dance number carries the potential for engendering a resonance for lesbians and women that describes the entire project of *Dress Suits to Hire*.

As if to punctuate finally and emphatically the artificiality and meaning-making nature of the theatrical apparatus, the production employs one of theatre's most unconvincing mechanisms—the "deus ex machina" ending. Deeluxe has killed Little Peter. In a hilarious struggle with herself, she strangles him, until her left hand holds nothing but a limp right hand. The two women then sit quietly across from each other, robed as they were at the beginning, when "out of nowhere" a letter falls from above into the room. Michigan picks the envelope up off the floor, looks at it and says, "It's for you." Deeluxe opens it and reads a letter from Little Peter in which he describes the future. It is a sober narrative on the uses to which men will put the tears of women. Deeluxe says, "So that's the future, huh?" Michigan responds, "Don't worry. We'll never see it." As the lights fade out, a certain residue, a certain resonance, hangs in the air.

In the theatre, artists like Holly Hughes, Peggy Shaw, and Lois Weaver have consistently pushed at the boundaries of a seemingly monolithic representational system in order to re(image)ine a subject position for lesbians and women. The ultimate aim is social change, but in order to achieve a different position in the social order, it is crucial to reconceptualize this position in the symbolic order.

What does it mean, then, when lesbian theatre is performed in venues outside of lesbian performance spaces? It doesn't necessarily mean assimilation into the mainstream, a virtually automatic appropriation by dominant culture. We need to be aware, however, that even when lesbian artists organize the narrative, visual, and symbolic dimensions of their work to address other lesbians, the theatre as a social technology that includes its spectators is still firmly embedded in the sociosymbolic systems and discourses of dominant culture. *Dress Suits* confronts this challenge and grapples with it.

When signals are crossed in every dimension, increased effort and attention are required on the part of spectators to "read" the performance, scanning and rescanning the production's visual and narrative fields. The additional effort prompted by this kind of performance attempts to dissolve the conventional filters through which spectators usually receive theatre—as a matter of custom, habit, and gender—to suggest new meanings, new ways of seeing, and foreground how those readings and meanings are produced. *Dress Suits to Hire* does not set out to reinvent the wheel, only to puncture and deflate it long enough to create a space in which to imagine lesbians and women differently in the symbolic order.

The production's performance context influenced this project in ways that cannot be ignored. In Ann Arbor where *Dress Suits* was performed in a conventional theatre setting, in the legitimate (and legitimizing) institutional setting of a major university, the work's potential to subvert dominant ideology was seriously undermined. In Milwaukee, where *Dress Suits* was performed in an unconventional, marginal, "illegitimate" theatre space for audiences made up almost entirely of working- and middle-class lesbians,[12] the exchange of meaning between performance and spectators was arguably different. Still, the struggle to critique objectification and interrupt the processes by which theatrical representation inscribes and prescribes meaning was no less intense. Having experienced the production in several contexts, I could argue with conviction, if not without contradiction, both sides of an ongoing debate: the importance of *Dress Suits* as an instance of lesbian discourse outside of lesbian performance contexts, and the importance of segregating pieces like *Dress Suits* in spaces where lesbians and women are the only spectators.

By mainstream theatre standards, *Dress Suits to Hire* was successful. It received favorable reviews in New York's major newspapers, and Peggy Shaw won an Obie award for her performance of Deeluxe. The political implications of this success for lesbian theatre are more complex and difficult to measure. As I write, a group of WOW artists are making a full-length piece that will open at WOW. At least at this point in their improvisational rehearsal process, they intend to play heterosexual couples. How will such a piece differ from men's camp and Theatre of the Ridiculous? And, extrapolating further, what would it mean for the project of feminism if the next wave of lesbian performance were to enter the mainstream in drag?

Notes

1. For an excellent introductory history of this performance venue see Solomon (1985), Davy (1985), and Dolan (1985), all published in an issue of TDR devoted to East Village performance.
2. *Dress Suits to Hire* was first produced at the May 1987 Veselka Performance Festival at P.S. 122. In December 1987 it was presented by Split Britches at Women's Interart on West 52nd Street where it played through February 1988.
3. See Witting (1981). Jill Dolan was the first critic to apply Witting's theoretical position to lesbian performance and articulate its implications for the exchange of meanings between performers and spectators (1984). See also Dolan (1988).
4. The distinction between gender as a social and representational construction and its role as a *system* of representation is a vital part of recent feminist debate. See de Lauretis (1987:1–30).
5. I am, admittedly, overstating the case here, relating a butch/femme performative strategy back to lesbian culture, that is, in the way it is played out by some, not all, lesbians. See de Lauretis (1988) for a different theoretical argument and far-reaching analysis of lesbian representation. She refers to an essay by Sue-Ellen Case entitled "Towards a Butch-Femme Aesthetic" unavailable at the time of this writing but forthcoming in *Making a Spectacle: Feminist Essays on Contemporary Women's Theatre*, edited by Lynda Hart (Ann Arbor: University of Michigan Press).
6. Laura Mulvey's 1975 essay is so central to an understanding of how voyeurism, fetishism, and scopophilia (pleasure in looking) apply to cinema that nearly every theorist working from a feminist psychoanalytic perspective continues to refer to it, even though new work (including Mulvey's own) rethinks some of her initial positions. See also Mayne (1984) for an analysis of the structures of voyeurism in relation to women as filmmakers and film voyeurs.
7. For a different theoretical approach and in-depth analysis of Rainer's film, see Phelan (1988) and the chapter entitled "Strategies of Coherence: Narrative Cinema, Feminist Poetics, and Yvonne Rainer" in de Lauretis (1987:107–26). See also Silverman (1984) for an analysis of how filmic strategies, like the voice-over and intertitles, are employed to "denaturalize" the female voice.
8. Doane (1982) discusses, among other things, how distance from the body functions in representational forms, especially distance from the female body on the cinema screen.

9. For an analysis of how the spectator is constructed in Hughes' *Lady Dick* see Davy (1986).
10. In Ann Arbor all the dimensions of material context conspired to undermine *Dress Suits* as an act of resistance. Strategies designed to subvert dominant culture codes tended instead to emphasize them. The critique of objectification was erased and the production became another, albeit different, instance of objectification.

    Feminist theatre scholars Sue-Ellen Case and Elin Diamond were invited by the university to respond to *Dress Suits* and lead a discussion with the audience. One of the issues that surfaced in the discussion following the first performance centered on assimilation: Is lesbian theatre's political import and impact neutralized when it is produced in a major university? Is it assimilated by virtue of its very acceptance in the academy—academe being the storehouse and (re)manufacturer of dominant ideologies and epistemologies? And what are the implications if lesbian performance is perceived as entertainment for predominantly straight audiences? Since some felt the university context radically reshaped the reception of *Dress Suits,* it was suggested that the piece be performed exclusively in lesbian or women-only performance spaces. *Dress Suits* was created by Hughes, Shaw, and Weaver as a way to move lesbian theatre out of the ghetto of lesbian performance spaces. The production circumstances in Ann Arbor made manifest the risks involved in that move.
11. For the original work on masquerade, see Riviere (1986)—her essay was first published in 1929.
12. The only publicity for *Dress Suits'* three performances in Milwaukee was a promotional mailing to approximately 1,700 names on the list of a local organization that produces women's music concerts, an annual Kate Clinton (a lesbian stand-up comedian) show, dances, and other events for the lesbian community. The piece was performed in a warehouse that had been converted into a makeshift theatre by a local performing group. Because this group was using the theatre part of the warehouse, *Dress Suits* was mounted in the large "lobby" area of the space—literally on the margins of an already marginal space.

References

Davy, Kate

1985 "*The Heart of the Scorpion* at the WOW Cafe." *The Drama Review* 29, no. 1 (T105):52–56.

1986 "Constructing the Spectator: Reception, Context, and Address in Lesbian Performance." *Performing Arts Journal* 10, no. 2 (September/October):74–87.

Diamond, Elin

1988 "Brechtian Theory/Feminist Theory: Toward a Gestic Feminist Criticism." *The Drama Review* 32, no. 1 (T117):82–94.

Doane, Mary Ann

1982 "Film and Masquerade: Theorizing the Female Spectator." *Screen* 23, no. 4 (September/October):74–87.

Dolan, Jill

1984 "Lesbian as Refuser, Lesbian as Creator: An Anti-Aesthetic." Paper delivered at the ATA conference. August, San Francisco, CA.

1985 "*Carmelita Tropicana Chats* at the Club Chandalier." *The Drama Review* 29, no. 1 (T105):26–33.

1987 "The Dynamics of Desire: Sexuality and Gender in Pornography and Performance." *Theatre Journal* 39, no. 2 (May):156–74.

1988 *The Feminist Spectator as Critic.* Ann Arbor, MI: UMI Research Press.

Eddings, Amy L.

1988 "Comic Interludes." *The New York Native* 258 (28 March):29.

Heath, Stephen
1986 "Narrative Space." In *Narrative, Apparatus, Ideology,* edited by Philip Rosen, 379–420. New York: Columbia University Press.

Kaplan, E. Ann
1983 *Women and Film: Both Sides of the Camera.* New York: Methuen.

de Lauretis, Teresa
1984 "Desire in Narrative." In *Alice Doesn't: Feminism, Semiotics, Cinema,* 103–57. Bloomington: Indiana University Press.
1987 *Technologies of Gender: Essays on Theory, Film, and Fiction.* Bloomington: Indiana University Press.
1988 "Sexual Indifference and Lesbian Representation." *Theatre Journal* 40, no. 2 (May):155–77.

Massa, Robert
1988 "Sightlines." *The Village Voice* 33, no. 12 (22 March):97.

Mayne, Judith
1984 "The Woman at the Keyhole: Women's Cinema and Feminist Criticism." In *Re-Vision: Essays in Feminist Film Criticism,* edited by Mary Ann Doane, Patricia Mellencamp, and Linda Williams, 49–66. Los Angeles: American Film Institute, University Publications of America.

Mulvey, Laura
1975 "Visual Pleasure and Narrative Cinema." *Screen* 16, no. 3 (Autumn):6–18.

Nestle, Joan
1984 "The Fem Question." In *Pleasure and Danger: Exploring Female Sexuality,* edited by Carole S. Vance, 232–41. Boston: Routledge & Kegan Paul.

Newton, Esther, and Shirley Walton
1984 "The Misunderstanding: Toward a More Precise Sexual Vocabulary." In *Pleasure and Danger: Exploring Female Sexuality,* edited by Carole S. Vance, 242–50. Boston: Routledge & Kegan Paul.

Phelan, Peggy
1988 "Feminist Theory, Poststructuralism, and Performance." *The Drama Review* 32, no. 1 (T117):107–27.

Riviere, Joan
1986 "Womanliness as a Masquerade." In *Formations of Fantasy,* edited by Victor Burgin, James Donald, and Cora Kaplan, 35–44. London: Methuen.

Rubin, Gayle
1978 "The Traffic in Women: Notes on the 'Political Economy' of Sex." In *Toward an Anthropology of Women,* edited by Rayna Reiter, 157–210. New York: Monthly Review Press.

Russo, Mary
1986 "Female Grotesques: Carnival and Theory." In *Feminist Studies: Critical Studies,* edited by Teresa de Lauretis, 213–29. Bloomington: Indiana University Press.

Silverman, Kaja
1984 "Dis-Embodying the Female Voice." In *Re-Vision: Essays in Feminist Film Criticism,* edited by Mary Ann Doane, Patricia Mellencamp, and Linda Williams, 131–49. Los Angeles: American Film Institute, University Publications of America.

Solomon, Alisa
1985 "The WOW Cafe." *The Drama Review* 29, no. 1 (T105):92–101.

Witting, Monique
1981 "One is Not Born a Woman." *Feminist Issues* (Winter):47–54.

Kate Davy *is Dean of Fine Arts at a women's college in the Midwest, and formerly an associate editor of* The Drama Review. *She is the author of* Richard Foreman and the Ontological-Hysteric Theatre *and the editor of* Richard Foreman: Plays and Manifestos.

Holly Hughes

Polymorphous Perversity and the Lesbian Scientist

An interview by Rebecca Schneider

Dress Suits to Hire won Holly Hughes the distinction of having authored her own genre. When the play opened in May 1987 at P.S. 122 in New York City, C. Carr of *The Village Voice* heralded Hughes as queen of her own "Dyke Noir Theatre" and broadcast her reputation as bad girl of the bad girls. "She's hell on heels, a twisted sister—a character from the timeless, tasteless world of dyke noir as imagined by Holly Hughes." Where is Hughes' dyke noir since *Dress Suits*? If Carr is right, "Wherever she goes it's the wrong side of town" (1987:32).

I found Hughes close to midnight in the East Village. She was popping out of a glaring pink, plaster-of-paris pig at performance space P.S. 122. It was 16 September 1988, the beginning of *World Without End,* Hughes' latest work-in-progress. The pig bore the name "Trojan Pig" because, Hughes told me, she wanted to appear as "some kind of Sappho reincarnate." Hughes stood with her naked back to the audience as four lovely negligee-clad attendants helped her don a pinkish bra to complete her garish girdle outfit. The beauties guided her to a pink scallop-backed chair center stage where, for the rest of the night, like some kind of Venus on her shell, Hughes told it all—from her own version of Genesis in which Eve and Adam ride the IRT subway, to the particularly smutty Gospel According to Mona, Hughes' mother. In the course of her raunchy tales, spicy asides, and sometimes painful personal sagas, Hughes, with a winsome smile, proclaimed herself the "preeminent lesbian playwright of my generation."

The campy butch-femme role playing of Hughes early *Well of Horniness* evolved through *Lady Dick* and *Dress Suits* to receive quite a bit of critical attention, especially from those interested in ways lesbian theatre disrupts traditional constellations of gender and power on stage (see Davy 1986; Dolan 1988). Hughes' latest "dyke noir" appears in new garb as the sinuous and long-winded monolog *World Without End,* a piece which pays a surprising amount of attention to the specifics of Adam's anatomy:

This is the start of history,
starting with my hand wet, on your wet dick.
Which is wetter: Adam or Eve?
Which is closer to the sea?
And then Adam says:
"I dunno about you, but let's just take it up against the wall."
And that hero spreads Eve's legs like, um, like um, nothing else could,
be cause, *recuerda,* remember:
This is the beginning
Beginning with Mr. Adam sliding in that cock kinda slow kinda real slow a bit too slow for our heroine,
So we have to give our hero a little credit here! Maybe Mr. Adam is no dumbo afterall!
He knows that shame didn't just ram its way into the newborn human mind!
Tragedy takes time!
More time and care than the 16 thrusts average for average coitus.
O la la.
Eve is happy, Adam is happy too there's sheetrock surrounding her Garden of Eden. And Mr. Adam is happy too cause he's all the way inside her and he feels her feel him hit—
paydirt.
When alla sudden Eve's gotta say: "Do you have any idea who you're porking?
I'm the preeminent lesbian playwright of my generation!"
(Hughes 1988)

It may be that this dyke-noir-in-progress is in some ways flavored by the recent appearances of lesbian theatre before more diverse audiences. When *Dress Suits* moved from downtown P.S. 122 to midtown Women's Interart in 1987 to a 1988 guest appearance at the University of Michigan, its steamy scenes between lesbian lovers were suddenly playing for the "general" public. Questions as to the reception of that sexual dynamic took on a certain urgency within the lesbian theatrical community: Outside of the framework of "women for women," will lesbians displaying sexuality automatically read as women displayed for men? In *World Without End,* Hughes puts herself on display and seems to invite some of those questions. Her sultry theatrics are an elaborately devised tease: "Do you love me? Are you faithful? I'm faithful to you," Hughes says to her audience. But who is this "you"? To whom is she faithful? And who is being teased—the performer or the spectator?

Packaged in her stiffly gartered get-up, Hughes is both pushing and resisting an easy reading. The sexual testimony dripping off her tongue is consistently qualified by her commanding image as sexually autonomous—her bevy of beauties, we suspect, are dutifully waiting in the wings. Autonomy and the expression of sexual desire are an unusual mix for a woman to so adroitly control on stage, especially one as slight and spritelike as Hughes, but in *World Without End* Hughes attempts to twist the gaze of the spectator through the tangle of her tease, playing for control of the pink bon-bon body she wields on stage.

In the following interview Hughes talks about her evolution as a playwright and addresses some of the issues facing lesbian theatre. Though she says she doesn't write with a particular audience in mind, she's found a

1. Holly Hughes in World Without End, *September 1988 at P.S. 122 in New York City. (Photo by Dona Ann McAdams)*

way to negotiate her position in the gaze wars. "I'm a lesbian scientist," she says, experimenting with something she fondly calls "polymorphous perversity."

SCHNEIDER: Talk a little bit about how you became involved with WOW Cafe.

HUGHES: I came to New York and I was a painter—I was going to be a big feminist painter and I was going to build giant vulvas that were going to topple the corporate structure and I wanted to work with a community of women. I found a community of women who were making giant vulvas—they were also bashing each other's heads in with words like sisterhood and trust. They weren't able to find a language to deal with things like competition and other things that women aren't supposed to have—balls—you know, things that are phallic values that of course we're trying to lop off.

I stopped painting after a while and was just a waitress living in Queens. Things looked pretty bleak. One day I was walking down East 11th Street and bumped into WOW. I came in to WOW when it was at 330 East 11th Street and started volunteering there. I had gone to a few WOW events before that. They were having double-XX-rated Christmas parties at Club 57 [the original "East Village Club" on St. Mark's Place, see TDR 29, no. 1]—it was just a whole different kind of approach to feminist performance than I had ever seen before.

SCHNEIDER: As opposed to sisterhood?

HUGHES: Yes. Sisterhood. . . . We had women like Diane Torr trouncing around in negligees and kissing booths and lingerie shows. It was *for* women. People would come in there and strip off their clothes and put on lingerie. It had a lot of the drag theatre flavor and permission. And everybody became a performer—it was so *avant*. And it was a great time. So I started serving coffee there as a volunteer and within two weeks—two months—I had seized the reins of power because everyone else had left to go on tour to Europe and I was the only one left with the keys. So I didn't know jack shit about performance or about running even a tiny theatre space, I didn't even know how to turn the lights on, but we just booked Jane Doe Feminist to come in with her rocks and crystals and abortion stories—like, "Hey, you can have a show here!" Then it began to evolve into a repertory theatre company.

SCHNEIDER: In and around performers Peggy Shaw and Lois Weaver?

HUGHES: Peggy and Lois were . . . how should I say it? They were role models in a sense in the beginning because they'd been doing this work a lot longer than anyone else and at that point they had more recognition. They encouraged people like Carmelita Tropicana and Alice Forester and myself.

SCHNEIDER: There were a lot of dress-up parties, right? Military drag and medical drag parties?

HUGHES: Yeah and "I Paid the Rent in my Maidenform Bra" parties. They usually revolved around taking clothes off.

SCHNEIDER: How does *Dress Suits to Hire* respond to that? There's all those clothes back in the closets and lots of dressing up and stripping down.

HUGHES: I think girls just like to dress up and take it off. *Dress Suits* actually came into being because after I'd done *Lady Dick*—which Peggy had been in and Lois had been real supportive of—they asked me to write something for them. They had the idea that it would be in a tuxedo rental shop and based on some rumors surrounding an actual rental shop on Second Avenue. And the idea evolved that there would be these two sisters in there—I use the word sisters euphemistically—I mean like two lesbians living together presenting the fact that they were sisters to the rest of the world, but also in that way that lovers become sisters, that they become a family.

SCHNEIDER: The energy between Shaw and Weaver is very highly charged and sexual, but there's also a real claustrophobia of the space—a very small shop crammed with lots of things, yapping Linda [the mechanical dog]—

HUGHES: —It's a microcosm of the whole lesbian situation!

SCHNEIDER: You answered my question.

HUGHES: It's about relationships in general, in the way that you form a binary unit. It becomes a little world unto itself. I think that two people always have some kind of a baby. The relationship is the baby. It becomes a whole world, a whole system of reality between themselves.

SCHNEIDER: A lot of crying in the night, a lot of shit to clean up?

HUGHES: A lot of shit to clean up. And stories of the past. Stories about how you met start out as the actual fact, then become a story, then become a ritual—in the way that you repeat the stories of Exodus to reinforce a sense of identity.

SCHNEIDER: Michigan and Deeluxe's hoola-hoop ritual in the gas station scene, for instance?

HUGHES: In the gas station scene.

SCHNEIDER: Time here is irrelevant. Past and present slide in and out of each other in your narratives. In this intimate space that the characters say they're trying to leave, but never do, the present is almost entirely spent maintaining these ritualized memories of the past.

HUGHES: Yes, I thought about how older people, or people who are really isolated, think. Past and present—there's not really a distinction, time is not always moving forward. My grandmother had Alzheimers and would slip into her childhood and be experiencing things the way she did as a young girl.

SCHNEIDER: But what's interesting about this is that two people are consciously performing the act together. Michigan will get out the boots and she'll get out the hat and they know what's coming. One of the most erotic points is when Shaw just grabs Weaver and kisses her in the middle of this gas station ritual. They know the road and they've been there before—it's mapped out on a geographic space. A geography which turns out to be Weaver's body. Weaver says, "You're gonna see California but you're not leaving this gas station."

HUGHES: Yeah, it's real elaborate foreplay. But it's also about lesbian relationships, about the desire to make a lesbian culture, to try and isolate it from mainstream culture. But there's problems in isolation—you are still part of the culture. There's Little Peter cropping up in all of us. [Little Peter is Deeluxe's errant hand that speaks like a pimp and is referred to as "he."]

SCHNEIDER: I want to get to Little Peter later, but before we go on, can you briefly say how *Dress Suits* moved from WOW to P.S. 122 to Women's Interart uptown?

HUGHES: Well we did a reading of the script in February of '87 at WOW and it was in a real raw state. C. Carr of *The Village Voice* came and was *real* supportive. Then I did extensive revisions in the text and we did it in May '87 at P.S. 122 at the Veselka Performance Festival. And in December 1987 it went uptown to Women's Interart and ran through February '88.

SCHNEIDER: *Dress Suits* was your first piece written with the awareness that a general audience would see it—written to be performed at P.S. 122. It was an attempt to bring lesbian theatre to a broader audience, right?

How did that affect the collaboration? Were you and Peggy and Lois expecting a potentially different reception when putting the piece together?

HUGHES: I would have written the same play if I thought only women were going to see it. I absolutely didn't alter it, I just planned to have it be in a different venue. I feel real strongly about putting lesbian work out. I want to make it as kinky, dirty, specifically women-oriented—as true to myself as I can make it. But I really feel like I don't want to preach to the converted. I really feel that it's very important for women's work to be seen in a more general context. It's scary.

SCHNEIDER: Yes, it's scary. When *Dress Suits* was at Michigan University in Ann Arbor, there was a discussion afterward in which Sue-Ellen Case made the point that perhaps the piece would be better served performed exclusively for women. The argument was that the context of academia—in the lap, so to speak, of dominant ideology—undermined the radical content of the play. And that for straight audiences it became . . . entertainment; that straight audiences and specifically males in that context couldn't somehow "read" the piece correctly.[1] What do you think?

HUGHES: Well, first of all, I don't feel like there is a correct reading. I really don't. If I felt that there was a correct reading for something I'd be Jesse Jackson. Jackson is great, but the kind of writing he does is rhetoric and it's political, didactic writing. This is not that. People will approach my work in different ways. People have thought that *Dress Suits* is about incest because of the mention of sisters. People have thought all sorts of things. And those things could be there! I really believe in art and I believe in allowing the audience to have their own personal subjective view. I give the audience a lot of credit—I think people are really bored with a straight white male perspective in theatre and can relate to the story in a lot of ways. A lot of people have experienced being an outsider. Everybody feels queer in some sense of the word. I think that there are various windows into an experience . . . all of a sudden they're inside of an experience that's formed by a lesbian.

SCHNEIDER: Some say that art, or representation, is always political and that lesbian theatre has a chance to really provide a way out of the mainstream economy of male desire which appropriates the female image for its own. Case, for instance, has written that butch-femme roles are the answer for feminist theatre. For her, butch-femme couples on stage—and on the street—defy the patriarchal gender-biased power structure by creating and outwardly symbolizing a woman-controlled economy of desire (1987; see also Davy this issue). Jill Dolan, after Luce Irigaray, writes of lesbian theatre as the goods getting together and redefining the market (see Dolan this issue). I guess my question is: What happens when lesbian theatre enters the mainstream theatrical market? After all, when Michigan gives a "peep show" for Deeluxe, she's also giving one for the audience. Considering Case's butch-femme argument, and given the fact that the Michigan University issues were such a problem for some people, what does it mean that this lesbian play has two femmes on display, or—

HUGHES: I don't think Michigan and Deeluxe are two femmes. I think its really about role playing on all the different levels. Look at Peggy Shaw! She's wearing a dress but look at her body, man! She's like drop dead Martina! It's a comment on drag performance—

SCHNEIDER: Oh no, that's true. By femme I meant that for the most part it's a female iconography they're playing around with—the negligees, the gown, the boa . . .

HUGHES: Yeah they are playing with it. So you're saying that what's difficult about it is that it's not using the traditional understanding of butch-femme?

SCHNEIDER: I don't know. I'm trying to get at the problem of reception, to find out what was difficult about the show in terms of its reception for a heterosexual audience. Why the question of keeping *Dress Suits* a women-only show would come up? We would like to believe that desire, in the hands and eyes of women, fully resists traditional reading. But in *Dress Suits* it's almost as if you're saying that the hands of women are complicated—look at Little Peter. What is it about the piece that makes it uncomfortable for some or too easily appropriated in a straight context?

HUGHES: I don't know why they have a problem. I think it really comes down to the fact that I really feel that I am a theatre artist first and a lesbian second. And that to grow as a theatre artist I have to put my work in challenging venues. It has to stand up as art and I don't believe that it's something so fragile that people will—I mean, it's not going to be performed in the middle of Independence Plaza—but I feel like . . . I don't know that there is a straight male audience. I think that you can be noticed by the mainstream and not coopted. Irene Fornes—she's absolutely her own person and she's gotten attention, I mean she's not a household word like Sam Shepard, she's really remained true to her vision, and her work comes from a very female-identified place. But she's putting it out there. And the whole butch-femme thing—I don't think anything is that black and white.

I think the problem these chicks are having with the show is that I'm just refusing to make this lesbian feminist fairy tale that only affirms what women want to know about themselves and that we're better than everyone else and that we're this and that and that lesbian relationships are perfect. Are they really any better than any other relationships? They're just as twisted. And they're twisted in specific ways that have to do with homophobia and sexism in the culture and the desire to create something new and the frustration of not really being able to construct something new. I want to explore things that are actual as opposed to posing some sort of utopian solution. I don't think that it's all so beautiful and that women's desire is so completely different from men's desire. There's desire to possess and voyeurism and objectification. Hopefully, the object becomes a subject in women's desire, but it's not all clean-cut and whole wheat berries. I hate that stuff. Where are they hanging out that they get these ideas? Its like creating a lesbian utopia, a lesbian Disneyland.

SCHNEIDER: I think that part of all the energy put into the various forms of feminist theatre is just to open up the boundaries of women's expression and open the lens on its reception. Kate Davy writes in her article on *Dress Suits* [in this issue] that there's an infinite flexibility suggested in the role playing—in the scarves and the boots and the different things that they put on, like the frames of past and present they slip in and out of. There's no one essential, riveting identity or role at all. But it's not merely a happy playful arena. There's also a sense of frustration with the games and with the rituals. And so there's a tension, an ambiguity in the fun of the masquerade.

Still, despite the flexibility of the roles, there is a significant difference between Deeluxe and Michigan and its far more evident on the stage than in the text. It has to do with two things, I think. One, with Shaw's history playing butch roles in WOW, a reputation that travels with her that the audience really responds to. The other thing is that Shaw is the one who gets to lose the feminine iconography in the show—she goes back to what she does best, with the cowboy hat and the toothpick between her teeth. Weaver is at home with the "feminine wiles," whereas, in that hilarious song number with the fan, Shaw is awkward and definitely in drag. As Deeluxe, Shaw is putting on the costume. But for Michigan the femme seems more than a costume. Michigan is a "state" after all—maybe a state of being. And Deeluxe is spectacle, as Davy writes. Could you speak about that difference a little bit?

HUGHES: Deeluxe is a stripper who performs for an audience of maybe two, if you count the dog. There is this cat and mouse game. Michigan is the desirous one and Deeluxe is the love object. It's some sort of a role reversal because she [Michigan] is a femme, but of course she's not really femme. If you think of butch in terms of looks then she's femme, but if you think of the roles in the way they conduct their lives—being sexually aggressive and stuff like that—she's definitely butch.

SCHNEIDER: What I was getting at in terms of Michigan and the state, is the sense of "stuckness," of restless unhappiness with the "state" of her desire. She's the female body as landscape, the terrain, the "state" of California and the site of desire. She's "Marineland." Deeluxe is the one that gets to go there, to take a ride. Michigan performs the "peep show" with the flashlight/spotlight shining on her body. But at the end, Michigan sadly talks of the repressed she-monster, of women's voracious desires and the insatiable toothy vagina. She, the femme, kind of pathetically asks the butch in drag, "Do you really want to be like me?" It seems that little is "liberated" or "satisfied" for Michigan. Why is that?

2. Peggy Shaw performs Deeluxe's fan dance. Lois Weaver as Michigan looks on during the May 1987 production of Dress Suits to Hire *at P.S. 122 in New York City. (Photo by Dona Ann McAdams)*

HUGHES: Well I think that's really about terror. Right now—being out there performing and being sexual in my new piece *World Without End*—I'm experiencing that there's an absolute terror in this culture of women's sexuality. It's absolutely frightening. And I don't think it's any less frightening for women than it is for men. But it's like, yeah, women are multiorgasmic, they're insatiable. There have been so many constraints put on our sexuality and so many blinders by every possible institution in the culture that we're just beginning to notice that there's this volcano beneath the surface. I'm not a sociologist; I'm just a "mere artist." All I can say is that I sense this absolute terror—a terror that comes up in women when they realize that they're sexual. So many women are so castrated. I think it's interesting that castration is a fear of men, but when you think of the ability to pursue desire to satisfaction, castration is a fact of life for women—they're not allowed to be empowered sexually. And I don't understand why the most insulting thing a man can say to a woman is probably to call her a cock-sucker, when it's probably the thing that he wants the most. It has to do with becoming the receptacle of his filth, you know—

SCHNEIDER: A man's bad self-image?

HUGHES: Yes, and she becomes the screen that he projects that on. But women do that too, I mean we internalize that idea.

SCHNEIDER: That's another thing I could bring up at this point. We talk about men's self-image and women as the receptacle. One of the things feminists have reacted against has been the constant representation of woman equaling sexuality and the body of woman signifying sexuality. And yet, in the theatre, that's your terrain.

HUGHES: It doesn't mean that there aren't other things to talk about. I just can't get out of bed in terms of my writing. The worst thing in our life is that our life ends. We're given two things to deal with that fact: one is creative work and the other is love, specifically sexual love. It's like one of those little sets of elephants that you keep pulling smaller and smaller elephants out of, or something that has endless layers you keep peeling back. It's something that you could endlessly observe, like Cezanne realizing that apples could be a fine subject to paint for the rest of his life, that even the space between apples is endlessly significant. There are other things to talk about, but I think that sex is so much the kernel of your self-esteem and your sense of empowerment. It's no accident that I use male terms like "impotence" and "flaccid" because there aren't any female terms. There's no positive terms for a strong, sexual woman. Whore or slut do not equal stud.

SCHNEIDER: Whenever Michigan and Deeluxe come close against that really hot, or strong desire, either Little Peter comes in or Michigan will start talking about poison and she-wolfness and then put herself down.

HUGHES: It's very much the position that I see women in. We're just beginning to see that we have this desire, but it's terrifying to us. We back down from it all the time. There's just something monstrous about it, it's so unnameable and unknowable and you know you're going to go off the main drag if you pursue this—

SCHNEIDER: —Or get derailed by the larger culture.

HUGHES: Right.

SCHNEIDER: Talk a little bit about why you use camp in your productions as a theatrical strategy.

HUGHES: Camp is a style of humor that seems dated in a way. It seems TV-oriented. It's a post–World War II kind of thing and/or it has a gay sensibility. It's about a love/hate relationship with popular culture. I like the artiface of theatre a lot. Naturalistic theatre really bores me. The reason I use camp is sheer pleasure, it's like a spice. Stuff that's completely camp, and there are few really good camp performers, is a style that gets really wearing, like eating nothing but hot fudge. I tend to use camp in my work as a spice, except for the *Well of Horniness* which is nothing but campy and trashy. Also, camp is an outsider sensibility, kind of commenting and exaggerating and ironic.

SCHNEIDER: What about Little Peter?

HUGHES: This play is really not about men at all except in the fact that a lesbian relationship exists in a larger culture. The whole inside-outside kind of tension that exists in the play—are they going to go outside; the windows keep blowing open; they never leave the space—we're not completely free of a culture that has a bias. Little Peter is a lot of different things. I always liked the goofy hand-choking-your-throat kind of convention. I mean what is that? That some part of yourself would turn against the rest of your body. And I'm also inspired by *Dr. Jekyll and Mr. Hyde*. There's an unknowable part of yourself that—call it dark, evil, whatever—is something we're not comfortable with. In Dr. Jekyll's desire to get rid of that he actually allows that part of himself to take over. There's some part of Deeluxe, whether it's her masculine side in a Jungian sense, or whether it's a certain part of herself that's aggressive or dark, there's a part of herself that she has not accepted. She obviously associates that part with male values. It's a lot about what we've internalized from the culture.

SCHNEIDER: I'd like to talk about your new piece, *World Without End*. There's a great deal of time devoted to penises, among other things. I'm interested in this because penises are, as you say in the piece, an interesting subject for the "preeminent lesbian playwright of our day." We were discussing before whether a woman looking at another woman, full of desire, as Michigan looks at Deeluxe, disrupts traditional female passivity, traditional one-way objectification. But what happens when a woman looks at a man? That's where we get sluts, femme fatals, she-monsters, whores, and the "vagina dentina" you're so fond of. Some feminists say that women looking at men with desire cannot "disarm male desire because the erect male penis is still a powerful image" (see Dolan this issue). When Deeluxe strangles Little Peter—

HUGHES: —Well, Little Peter may be a dick but he's not a penis.

SCHNEIDER: OK, but in *World Without End* a great deal of juicy description is devoted to the penis and heterosexual sex. Are you moving on to a new frontier? Are you trying to manipulate penises to be less of a power-filled image—to rewrite the penis? Basically, what is this penis stuff?

HUGHES: What *is* the penis all about?! Well, the work's real personal, real autobiographical and it's about at some point coming to terms with, for lack of a better word, the fact that I was bisexual. I was trying to figure out some things about that. I'd like to think of it not so much as bisexuality that I'm exploring as polymorphous perversity.

3. World Without End, *September 1988 at P.S. 122. (Photo by Dona Ann McAdams)*

SCHNEIDER: And bringing it to the stage—

HUGHES: I have a piece that I didn't include where I said that I have a lot of rules in my life and having a lot of rules convinces me that I'm still a lesbian even though I might fuck a guy. In fact, I'm a lesbian scientist and I'm just going through this stagnant glass-bottom boat, gazing and going "Uh-huh, Uh-huh."

First of all I feel like women should be really free to explore their sexuality in whatever form it expresses itself. And it may change and permutate in their lifetime. I'm really anti anyone other than individuals defining their own sexuality. I don't have any conclusions about what to say about being a powerful woman sexually vis-à-vis men. It's absolutely terrifying to men. Absolutely terrifying. They like it, but it's absolutely terrifying. But it's interesting—it's material for my plays.

SCHNEIDER: You mention Karen Finley in *World Without End,* alluding to the fact that your work is similar.[2]

HUGHES: I like Karen Finley a lot. She's exploring from a female perspective what Burroughs and Henry Miller and those people talked about from a male perspective. She's really going into the dark part of sanity and the wackier side of sexuality. She's like some sort of theatrical proctologist—she's pokin' around in there. I think she's amazing in a lot of ways in that there's this absolute meshing of presentation and text, like I can't imagine Meryl Streep doing one of her monologs. It comes out of this sort of Cassandra wail, in a very primeval way. One of the differences in our writing is that I find that in a lot of women's art that deals with sexuality—and I'm thinking of Karen Finley and Kathy Acker and others—I tend to find that the dominant mode of sexual expression, sexual relationship, is rape and violation. I know that exists. I am interested in talking about sexual pleasure and what it could mean for women. I'm also not interested in exploring sex as a form of alienation. There's a whole East Village literature—gay, straight, whatever—that has a kind of mindless fucking, where you feel like fucking is just the manner in which our alienation and dehumanization is revealed. I'm interested in talking about sexuality as a return, and a way of re-creating your life as a powerful thing, as a positive force. I'm interested in trying to invent new images for women sexually.

You know, someone interviewed me and asked why there wasn't more lesbian theatre. And I said, there's not very much theatre produced by women. Seven percent, less than seven percent, of all "legitimate" theatre productions in the last year were women's productions. And of that, well . . . what percentage will be lesbian?

SCHNEIDER: What do you see in terms of the future of WOW?

HUGHES: WOW is just growing by leaps and bounds. Five years ago there were about four of us. Now there's tons of people there that I don't know. Last year we did 18 original shows. This year I have no idea how many shows but there's more than that. WOW is basically a developmental theatre, both in the sense of developing new women theatre artists and in the sense of people who have more experience using it as a place to develop new work. It's really an incubator. It's just not set up to take things to full bloom.

SCHNEIDER: Because of the space?

HUGHES: The space and the fact that it's a cooperative.

SCHNEIDER: What about funding?

HUGHES: There's no funding. There's no funding.

SCHNEIDER: Why is that?

HUGHES: Some people have gotten individual grants. I got a Franklin Furnace grant this year. But there aren't very many funding organizations that are set up to fund something developmental. It's not systematized enough in terms of lengthy resumes and stuff. People, women, can come to WOW and work for a year on other people's shows and then do their own show—they don't have to have any credentials. I think that's really important. You don't have to prove anything other than your willingness to work.

Notes

1. I was not in Ann Arbor to hear the postperformance discussion of *Dress Suits to Hire*. I formulated my questions from the description of the event in Kate Davy's article in this issue.
2. See TDR 32, no. 1(T117) for Karen Finley's script *Constant State of Desire* and interview with Richard Schechner. See also Elinor Fuchs' "Staging the Obscene Body" on Finley in this issue.

References

Carr, C.
1987 "The Lady is a Dick: The Dyke Noir Theater of Holly Hughes." *The Village Voice*, 19 May:32–34.

Case, Sue-Ellen
1987 "Toward a Butch-Femme Aesthetic." Women in Theatre Conference, keynote address. 2 August: Chicago, IL.

Davy, Kate
1986 "Constructing the Spectator." *Performing Arts Journal* 10, no. 2 (PAJ29):43–52.

Dolan, Jill
1988 *The Feminist Spectator as Critic.* Ann Arbor: UMI Research Press.

Rebecca Schneider, *managing editor of TDR, has published criticism and analysis in* High Performance *and* Women and Performance.

STATEMENT OF OWNERSHIP, MANAGEMENT AND CIRCULATION
(Required by 39 U.S.C. 3685)

1. A. Title of Publication: The Drama Review
   B. Publication No.: 00125962
2. Date of Filing: 9/23/88
3. Frequency of Issue: Quarterly
   A. No. of issues published annually: Four
   B. Annual subscription price: $23.00/Ind $52.00/Inst
4. Location of known office of publication (not printer): MIT Press, 55 Hayward Street, Cambridge, Middlesex, MA 02142-1399
5. Location of Headquarters of General Business office of the publisher (not printer): same as item 4
6. Names and Complete Addresses of Publisher, Editor, and Managing Editor:
   Publisher: MIT Press, 55 Hayward Street, Cambridge, MA 02142-1399
   Editor: Richard Schechner, TDR, 721 Broadway, Rm. 626, New York, NY 10003
   Managing Editor: Rebecca Schneider, TDR, 721 Broadway, New York, NY 10003
7. Owner (if owned by a corporation, its name and address must be stated and also immediately thereunder the names and addresses of stock-holders owning or holding 1 percent or more of total amount of stock. If not owned by a corporation, the names and addresses of the individual owners must be given. If owned by a partnership or other unincorporated firm, its name and address, as well as that of each individual, must be given. If the publication is published by a nonprofit organization, its name and address must be stated.): New York Univ., Tisch School of the Arts, 721 Broadway, New York, NY 10012 and MIT Press, 55 Hayward Street, Cambridge, MA 02142-1399
8. Known bondholders, mortgagees, and other security holders owning or holding 1 percent or more of total amount of bonds, mortgages, or other securities: None
9. For completion by nonprofit organizations authorized to mail at special rates: Has not changed during preceding 12 months
10. Extent and nature of circulation:
   A. Total number of copies printed (not press run):
      Average number of copies each issue during preceding 12 months: 5464
      Actual number of copies of single issue published nearest to filing date: 5714
   B. Paid and/or requested circulation:
      1. Sales through dealers and carriers, street vendors and counter sales: Average number of copies each issue during preceding 12 months: 642
         Actual number of copies of single issue published nearest to filing date: 623
      2. Mail Subscriptions: Average number of copies each issue during preceding 12 months: 3638
         Actual number of copies of single issue published nearest to filing date: 3644
   C. Total paid circulation: Average number of copies each issue during preceding 12 months: 4280
      Actual number of copies of single issue published nearest to filing date: 4267
   D. Free distribution by mail, carrier or other means—samples, complimentary and other free copies: Average number of copies each issue during preceding 12 months: 152
      Actual number of copies of single issue published nearest to filing date: 165
   E. Total distribution (Sum of C and D): Average number of copies each issue during preceding 12 months: 4432
      Actual number of copies of single issue published nearest to filing date: 4432
   F. Copies not distributed:
      1. Office use, left-over, unaccounted, spoiled after printing: Average number of copies each issue during preceding 12 months: 797
         Actual number of copies of single issue published nearest to filing date: 1031
      2. Returns from news agents: Average number of copies each issue during preceding 12 months: 235
         Actual number of copies of single issue published nearest to filing date: 251
   G. Total (Sum of E and F—should equal net press run shown in A): Average number of copies each issue during preceding 12 months: 5464
      Actual number of copies of single issue published nearest to filing date: 5714

I certify that the statements made above by me are correct and complete.

Dorothy Devereaux
Circulation Manager

Photo: Helma Klooss

"The play's the thing"

M. BUTTERFLY

By David Henry Hwang. "A brilliant play of ideas...a visionary work that bridges the history and culture of two worlds," wrote Frank Rich in *The New York Times* of this play based on the true story of a French diplomat and a male spy disguised as a Chinese diva who became his life's obsession. Winner of the 1988 Tony and the Drama Desk Award for Best New Play.

Ⓟ PLUME 0-452-26230-5 $7.95

100 MONOLOGUES
An Audition Sourcebook from New Dramatists

Edited by Laura Harrington. From New York's outstanding forum for talented playwrights comes this collection of fresh, riveting monologues selected from a wide range of contemporary plays with parts suitable for a variety of actors. Includes monologues from regional, Off-Broadway and Broadway productions including *The Complaint Department Closes at Five, Living at Home, Fences, The House of Blue Leaves, I Never Sang for My Father,* and many more.

Ⓜ MENTOR 0-451-62688-5 $4.95

A SHAYNA MAIDEL

By Barbara Lebow. "Two sisters—one a survivor of Nazi concentration camps, the other brought up as an American—meet in 1946 after a separation of almost 20 years...they achieve an intimacy that transcends the theatrical event. Lebow's play is about the horrors of the Holocaust; it is also a deeply personalized study of sisterhood, family and a crisis of faith."—*The New York Times*

Ⓟ PLUME 0-452-26150-3 $6.95

A WALK IN THE WOODS

By Lee Blessing. "Witty, polished and absorbing," said *The New York Times* of this dramatization of a Soviet and an American diplomat's "walk in the woods" together during arms control talks in Geneva in 1983. "Best new American play of the season." —John Simon

Ⓟ PLUME 0-452-26199-6 $6.95

JOE TURNER'S COME AND GONE

By August Wilson. From the author of *Fences,* the Pulitzer Prize-winning blockbuster of 1987, comes this drama of the tumultuous experiences of American blacks who are the children of slaves. "August Wilson continues to rewrite the history of the American theater. *Joe Turner* is his most adventurous piece of writing."—*The New York Times.* Best Play of the Year by the New York Drama Critics Circle.

Ⓟ PLUME 0-452-26009-4 $6.95

SCENES AND MONOLOGUES FROM THE NEW AMERICAN THEATER

Edited by Frank Pike and Thomas G. Dunn. For students and professionals, thls invaluable new anthology features scenes and monologues for men and women from almost 70 of the best contemporary American stage productions, including works by John Guare, Sam Shepard, David Mamet, August Wilson and Marsha Norman.

Ⓜ MENTOR 0-451-62547-1 $4.95

PLAYS FROM THE CONTEMPORARY AMERICAN THEATRE

Edited by Brooks McNamara. Representing the changes in American theater in the past 20 years, this collection includes *Streamers,* Rabe; *Marco Polo Sings a Solo,* Guare; *Wings,* Kopit; *Sister Mary Ignatius Explains It All for You,* Durang; *Crimes of the Heart,* Henley; *The Dining Room,* Gurney; *Painting Churches,* Howe; and *Ma Rainey's Black Bottom,* Wilson.

Ⓜ MENTOR 0-451-62580-3 $4.95

Prices subject to change. Write to the NAL Education Department at the address below for a free Literature & Language catalog.

NEW AMERICAN LIBRARY
1633 Broadway, New York, NY 10019
NAL

COMING IN TDR

James Brandon
Asian Theatre in the West Today

Philip Auslander
Performance Art in Mass Culture

Anna Halprin on her Recent Works

Beijing Roundtable on
Chinese Experimental Theatre

Qu Liuyi
Chinese Nuo Theatre

Yu Qiuyu
Looking at Chinese Performance in Context

Patrice Pavis on Interculturalism

ISSN 0012 5962

TDR

blished by MIT Press
w York University/Tisch School of the Arts

Chinese Spoken Drama
Skipitares's Performing Objects
Anna Halprin: A Life in Ritual
Asian Theatre in the West Today
Performance Art and Mass Culture
The Carnival of Guinea-Bissau
Simulating *Potemkin*
The Global Voyage of Robert Lepage

icles by: James R. Brandon, Philip
slander, Anna Halprin, Daniel J. Crowley,
niel Gerould, *and others*

TDR

The Drama Review *a journal of performance studies*

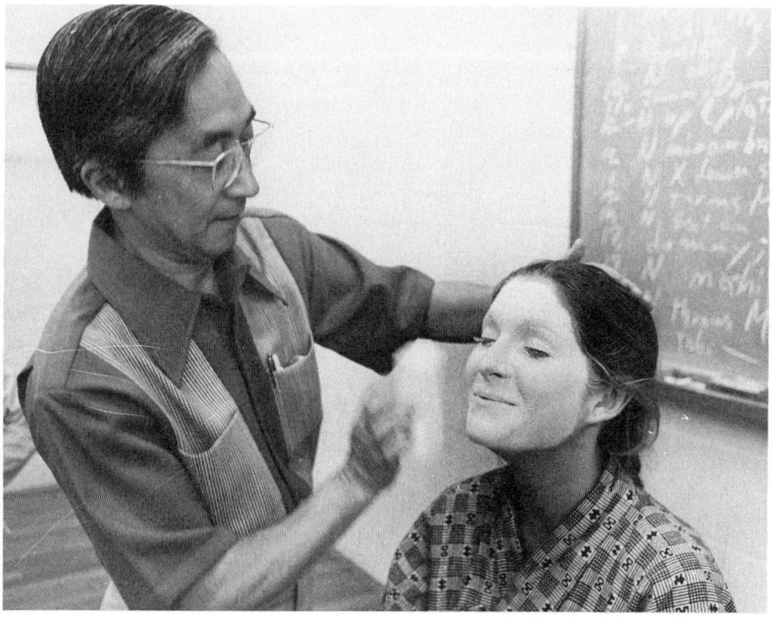

Nakamura Matagoro II, Chief Instructor, Kabuki Training School, National Theatre of Japan, teaches actress Barrie Moss proper makeup technique for the role of Lady Taema in Narukami the Thunder God *at the University of Hawaii in 1973. See "A New World: Asian Theatre in the West Today" by James R. Brandon in this issue. (Photo courtesy of University Theatre, University of Hawaii)*

Front Cover: *Instilling a "sense of community," Anna Halprin's* City Dance *was performed once each year from 1976–78 in diverse neighborhood streets of San Francisco. Here, a bystander joins the dance—"interacting with her environment." See the interview with Halprin and her article "Planetary Dance" in this issue. (Photo by Buck O'Kelly)*

Back Cover: *A performer in* Le Bord Extreme *(1986) by writer/director/actor Robert Lepage. See Nigel Hunt's article "The Global Voyage of Robert Lepage" in this issue. (Photo by Claudel Huot)*

TDR

TDR Comment:
PAJ Distorts the Broad Spectrum 4

Letters, Reports, Etc.

Site-Seeing in London: Observing Edge 88 10
LINDA FRYE BURNHAM

Auslander Wins Last Word 15
a letter from PHILIP AUSLANDER

Announcements 19

Editors' Choice: Books We Recommend 20

Etc. 24

A New World: Asian Theatre in the West Today 25
JAMES R. BRANDON

Planetary Dance 51
ANNA HALPRIN

Anna Halprin: A Life in Ritual 67
An interview by RICHARD SCHECHNER

The Carnival of Guinea-Bissau 74
DANIEL J. CROWLEY

Speaking About China's Spoken Drama: 87
A Roundtable with Chinese Directors and Playwrights

The Global Voyage of Robert Lepage 104
NIGEL HUNT

Going With the Flow: Performance Art and Mass Culture 119
PHILIP AUSLANDER

Skipitares's Performing Objects 137
JOAN DRISCOLL LYNCH

Historical Simulation and Popular Entertainment: The *Potemkin* Mutiny from Reconstructed Newsreel to Black Sea Stunt Men 161
DANIEL GEROULD

Volume 33, Number 2 (T122), Summer 1989

The Drama Review *(ISSN 0012 5962) is published quarterly (Spring, Summer, Fall, Winter) by The MIT Press, 55 Hayward St., Cambridge, MA 02142, and London, England, for the Tisch School of the Arts, New York University. Editorial correspondence:* The Drama Review, *NYU, 721 Broadway, 6th fl., New York, NY 10003. Subscription and business correspondence:* The Drama Review, *Journals Dept., The MIT Press, 55 Hayward Street, Cambridge, MA 02142. Subscriptions: $17.00 per year for students; $23.00 per year for individuals; $52.00 per year for institutions. Subscribers outside the U.S. and Canada add $9.00 for surface mail, $17.00 for airmail. Current single copies, $7.00; back copies, $13.00. Back volume rates available. Circulation Dept.: 617-253-2889.* *Second class postage paid at Boston, MA and additional mailing offices. Postmaster: Send address changes to* The Drama Review, *55 Hayward Street, Cambridge, MA 02142. For advertising information please contact the Advertising Manager, MIT Press Journals (see business correspondence; telephone: 617-253-2866). This publication is made possible, in part, with public funds from the New York State Council on the Arts and the National Endowment for the Arts.*

TDR Comment

PAJ Distorts the Broad Spectrum

In an editorial titled "Critical Positions" Bonnie Marranca and Gautam Dasgupta, the editors of *Performing Arts Journal,* attack my proposals for the development of performance studies, what I call the "broad spectrum approach" (see PAJ 11, no. 2 [PAJ 32]:4–6 and TDR 32, no. 3 [T119]: 4–6). Ironically, however, what they finally come up with in opposition is a mirror of the broad spectrum approach. What annoys me, provoking this Comment, is how often in their editorial—before they make proposals that sound like mine—Marranca and Dasgupta misrepresent what I have been developing over the years. They also display an elitist and ethnocentric bias.

"We disagree," say Marranca and Dasgupta, *"with this purportedly 'broad spectrum' proposition on several grounds [. . .]. Perhaps the most important of them is that his approach shifts performance to the realm of the social sciences, rather than that of art. To make performance a means of cultural analysis is to substitute a kind of Performancism for Marxism in the analysis of societies and their means of production. The twentieth century has taught us plenty about ideology and the arts in the guise of a benign cultural politics."*

"Performancism" (the PAJ editors' ugly word, not mine) is not what I have in mind. Marxism is a way of understanding historical process, but not the only way. As the new historians, feminists, deconstructionists, and others have compellingly argued, all forms of analysis are inscribed with definite, historically locatable value systems or, if you will, ideologies; and all develop within specific historical contexts. So if the goal of PAJ's editors is to remove the study of theatre from the arena of ideology, forget it.

Actually their aim is elitist: to erect a special "art for art's sake" ivory tower controlled by a select group of (patriarchal) collectors, critics, and academicians who, while apparently "helping" or even "protecting" artists, actually collaborate in their exploitation. By isolating art and artists from participating in social and political process, art is reduced to "collectables" (objects, people, styles) and artists are only weakly able to resist cooption, exploitation, and subjugation. Theatre and dance are especially vulnerable because their "products" are evanescent, what people do, labor if you will, with no residual object financially appreciating in the attic of its possessor. Of course, this owner is usually not the artist, as the history of Vincent Van Gogh's paintings, and the auctions at Sotheby's, so poignantly narrate.

"Theatre, the idea of the theatrical, is a long great theme in the history of civilizations, but it belongs in the wider humanist intellectual tradition that encompasses

literature, philosophy, architecture, history, music, painting. It is wrong to reconceive performance or theatre, or whatever one wants to call it, in the realm of the soft sciences (sociology, anthropology, speech/communications) which have increasingly moved to value-free positions."

The metaphors speak. Are "hard" sciences and the humanities (erect, respectable, male) preferred over the "soft" sciences? Are academic disciplines contained within various "realms" (royal domains of elitist privilege)? Who gets included in the "history of civilizations" and who excluded—are the ancient Greeks in and the modern Apaches out, for example? What are "values" as distinct from "value-free positions"? Surely there are values (also called "truths"), temporary and slippery, always in need of debate and redefinition, hedged by contexts and historical processes. But talk of "value-free" . . . what is more desirous of being value-free than the "art for art's sake" ideology whose proponents want to rid themselves of the social, political, and economic circumstances circumscribing the production of art? I prefer the scientific method where truth is revised as new data is taken into account. These changing truths are locatable only by vectoring a number of different analytic systems—where does Marxism cross the methods of the new historians, or how does a Buddhist's view of the cosmos intersect that of Stephen Hawking? Just now there are a number of useful analytic methods: Marxism, psychoanalysis, semiotics, linguistics, feminism, deconstruction. As time goes on, some methods are no longer helpful so others will come into use. A key task of education is to help students acquire several methods while arousing in them a robust skepticism regarding them all.

What is dangerous is the call for the establishment *of any single system* of values. The attempt to position and fix performance (theatre, dance, music) in the "realm" of art is a move toward such an establishment. Theatre and dance are arts, certainly, but they are also social, political, and personal acts. They deserve to be studied not only as art, but as behaviors and actions, from varying and possibly conflicting perspectives (dialectics).

"Schechner offers no secure place for the dramatic text in his 'broad spectrum' of things. Like it or not, the main purpose of theatre is founded on the staging of texts, just as the main purpose of the music world is to acknowledge the playing and singing of musical texts."

Such blatantly ethnocentric nonsense hardly deserves comment. It is only from the Euro-American perspective that one can possibly say that the purpose of theatre and music is the staging or "acknowledging" of texts. And even in the Euro-American tradition there is a long and notable history of popular non–playscript-based theatre (see Allardyce Nicoll's *Mask, Mimes, and Miracles,* 1963). Do the editors of PAJ really believe that Sanjukta Panigrahi's odissi dancing can best be understood by studying the poetry of the *Gita Govinda* or that kathakali dance theatre is reducible to an analysis of the narratives of the *Ramayana* and *Mahabharata*? Are Christopher Walken's Coriolanus or Ruth Maleczech's Lear "founded on the staging of [Shakespeare's] texts" or on some more complex interaction?

And what do the PAJ editors mean by "text" anyway? If they mean dramatic text, that is plays, then the comparable music text would be written scores. But anyone who knows anything about music knows that most of the world's musicians, including many very great ones, do not read music or play from a written score. If they mean performance text (as defined by Pavis 1982 or Schechner 1973, 1988) then written dramas are not necessarily the foundation of theatre. The PAJ editors slide uncritically from one meaning of "text" to another.

Similarly they accuse me of offering "no secure place for the dramatic text." But I have never argued that students of performance should be ignorant of the literature of *world* theatre. The emphasis is on "world" because even if drama begins with Aeschylus it certainly doesn't end with Beckett, nor is it limited to the European canon. Playtexts (scripts, plays) can be studied separate from their enactment but they achieve their fullest meaning and impact by means of acting, mise-en-scene, design, and so on—the whole bundle that comprises theatrical language. This is no new position—it was championed by Gordon Craig nearly 90 years ago, and repeated by Meyerhold, Artaud, and Grotowski among many others. It claims for theatre studies—and now for performance studies—an autonomy, an existence separate from the study of literature and philosophy (or any other discipline or field). Parallel claims can be made for dance and music.

What the "broad spectrum" approach addresses is the need for performing arts departments to recuperate what rightly belongs to them. Steadily over the past 25 years theatre and dance departments, obsessed with "professional training," have let the intellectual aspects of performance studies—historical, political, philosophical, theoretical—pass into the hands of social scientists, literary scholars, and historians. The editors of PAJ are apparently unaware of this slippage. To correct these imbalances, the scholarly study of performance must not shrink further but expand to include an awareness of the full range of performative genres, an understanding of the various historical and cultural contexts (non-Western as well as Western) in which performance occurs, and a familiarity with several methods of performance analysis.

"[Schechner refers] to theatre as a subgenre of 'performance' and elevat[es] 'performance studies' to a discipline. (One can compare it to the uneasy field of 'American Studies'—is it History, Literature, Folklore? An entirely made-up field looking for justification of its existence, it too is trying to be pluralistic—here one can just as well study or write on quilts, postcards, the Catskills, or parades.) These kinds of "studies" cut knowledge up into too many pieces, making academic life look sillier and sillier."

Just the opposite. The motive for establishing "studies" is more often to integrate, to knit together disciplines which if kept separate isolate and segment knowledge. In belittling the emergence of performance studies and American studies the editors of PAJ expose their ignorance of the history of universities in the Western tradition. *All* modern academic disciplines with the exceptions of classical languages, philosophy, and theology, were "made-up" since the Renaissance. Some disciplines—like theatre and dance—are very recent, barely more than 50 years old. What would the PAJ editors have said in the 1920s, '30s, and '40s?—that there is no room for such an uneasy and "made-up" field like theatre? What constitutes an academic discipline is not an event "out there" in the world (people acted in and wrote plays long before there were theatre departments, and they performed rituals and played sports long before there were performance studies departments) but the felt need among a community of scholars to gather people who are concerned with a particular set of questions, data, and methods. It is this confluence of concerns that is creating performance studies at this time.

What can be said regarding the elitism expressed in rejecting the study of quilts, the Catskills, postcards, or parades? Ought entomologists not study *blattidae* or archaeologists the midden heaps of extinct cultures because they feel roaches and garbage dumps beneath academic inquiry? Are PAJ's editors unaware of Jacques Derrida's *The Postcard* (1980)? Do they know Malek Alloula's *The Colonial Harem* (1986) which shows how French postcards depicting Algerian women reveal colonial racism and fantasies of the "oriental woman"? In rejecting parades as an object of scholarly attention are PAJ's editors disparaging TDR's issue on processional performance (T107)? Can the editors of PAJ know so little concerning how researchers put together big stories out of small details? In this vein, later on in their editorial the editors of PAJ say:

"[W]e cannot take seriously Schechner's view that studying healing, conversation, rituals, job interviews, sex shows, or sports can be a means of saving theatre departments. Neither do theatre people have to be saved from oblivion by placing their field of study in other departments on a campus."

The editors of PAJ hope to nail me by implying that certain subjects are irrelevant, trivial, or dirty. Their objection is beside the point. Any human action can be studied "as" performance (or "as" physics, sociology, etc.). What is crucial is to study actions that may not be theatre according to orthodox Western aesthetics. In what ways do healing, everyday behavior, rituals, sports, and so on follow a particular society's performance conventions? Whatever is being studied needs to be examined interculturally, as it occurs in Melanesian, native American, African, Asian, and other cultures as well as in the Western traditions. As for the diaspora of theatre faculty, the editors of PAJ read me backwards. The reach of performance studies must be expanded by having its specialists teach courses outside of (as well as within) theatre and dance departments.

Throughout their editorial, the PAJ editors enact the myth of the individual by referring to no person but me in their discussion. It is not modesty that makes me want to emphasize the collective nature of the emergence of performance studies. New York University's performance studies department was so named in 1980 though we in the "drama department" had been doing performance studies since the late-'60s.

The performance studies paradigm came to the fore in the mid-'50s. Gregory Bateson's "A Theory of Play and Fantasy" was published in 1955, the same year as J.L. Austin's Harvard lectures on the "performative" (*How to Do Things With Words*). Erving Goffman's *The Presentation of Self in Everyday Life* was published in 1959; Albert B. Lord's *The Singer of Tales* in 1960; and Roger Caillois' *Man, Play, and Games* in 1961. My "Approaches to Theory/Criticism" was published in 1966; Dell Hymes' "Models of the Interaction of Language and Social Setting" in 1967. Victor Turner's *The Ritual Process* came out in 1969, his *Dramas, Fields, and Metaphors* in 1974. Milton Singer's *When a Great Tradition Modernizes* appeared in 1972. *Folklore: Performance and Communication* (editors, Dan Ben-Amos and Kenneth Goldstein) was published in 1974 as was Barbara Myerhoff's *The Peyote Hunt*. *Secular Ritual* (edited by Myerhoff and Sally Moore) appeared in 1977, the same year as Richard Bauman's *Verbal Art as Performance*.[1] Since the mid-'70s there has been an immense body of performance studies work. It is not possible to name even a fraction of the scholars—some well known, some just emerging—currently working the field.

Long before scholars took an interest, artists had an expanded view of performance. Futurism, dada, surrealism, the writings of Artaud, the practice of Meyerhold, Okhlopkov, Brecht, Grotowski, Halprin, Kaprow—to name only some. Many non-Western artists in many cultures have traditionally enacted such an expanded view integrating their arts with rituals and the practice of everyday life.

The question of "art" deserves a little more attention all by itself. I am a working artist and have been for most of my life. I know what it means to "make art." But "studying art" is quite another matter. One can train people to master certain techniques necessary to being an artist—though that won't guarantee them success in the art field any more than, say, what training as a lawyer, doctor, or engineer guarantees to a graduate. So what does it mean to study art in the "realm of art," as the editors of PAJ put it? Does it mean to grapple only with a work's aesthetic dimensions—what makes it beautiful? what its internal structures are? As early as 1966 and then again in 1973 I wrote that the performing arts are continuous with a wide range of "communicative behavior [such as] ritual ceremonies, public gatherings, and various means of exchanging information, goods, and customs" (1973:3); I suggested a formal and practical continuity among play, games, sports, theatre, and ritual (1966:28–39). It seemed to me then, and I continue to believe so now, that the "realm of art" is a phony country, an elitist cover-up for making art (both works and artists) into consumer objects and capitalist fetishes.

What troubles me most about the PAJ editorial is this narrow-mindedness and class bias. Behind the high-sounding pomposity—"This issue finds PAJ in a contemplative mood"—slouch some very reactionary ideas. The editors of PAJ want to establish a "value system" (their own, no doubt), make the written text boss, and retreat within an art-for-art's-sake ivory tower where those delighting in dramatic literature and eschewing popular culture can contemplate "the life of the mind." When the PAJ editors celebrate what they call "the history of civilizations" they are invoking nothing other than the old racist/colonial distinction between "civilized" and "savage" with you-know-who determining what's right for all.

Having said or implied all this, PAJ's editors, near the end of their editorial, accept what they have spent most of their essay rejecting.

"There is room in any serious, expansively conceived theatre program—and we hope universities will begin immediately to create them—for study of the dramatic text, ritual, theatrical paradigm in everyday life, Western and non-Western contributions, for criticism, theory, and history. This is our vision of what constitutes a broad spectrum approach."

Wrong. It is TDR's vision—and the vision of those who over the years have been developing the field of performance studies. After distorting my enunciation of performance studies, the PAJ editors end by appropriating my proposals. What impoliteness—and more. For some time now the contents and concerns of PAJ have followed TDR's lead—to wit, theatre anthropology, ritual studies, and interculturalism. So why not performance studies? I'm glad PAJ's editors are seeing the light, but who wouldn't be a little unhappy that Marranca and Dasgupta feel compelled to call the light dark.

Richard Schechner

Note

1. I am outlining the emergence of performance studies in America. Different lists—with some significant overlaps—could be constructed for other parts of the world. The question remains, is performance studies a Western invention?

References

Alloula, Malek
1986 *The Colonial Harem.* Minneapolis: University of Minnesota Press.

Austin, J.L.
1962 [1955] *How to Do Things With Words.* Cambridge: Harvard University Press.

Bateson, Gregory
1955 "A Theory of Play and Fantasy." *American Psychological Association Psychiatric Research Reports* II. Reprinted in *Steps to an Ecology of Mind* by Gregory Bateson, 77–93. New York: Ballentine Books, 1972.

Bauman, Richard
1977 *Verbal Art as Performance.* Rowley, MA: Newbury House.

Ben-Amos, Dan, and Kenneth Goldstein
1974 *Folklore: Performance and Communication.* The Hague: Mouton.

Caillois, Roger
1961 *Man, Play, and Games.* New York: The Free Press.

Derrida, Jacques
1980 *La Carte Postale.* Paris: Aubier-Flammarion.

Goffman, Erving
1959 *The Presentation of Self in Everyday Life.* Garden City, NJ: Doubleday.

Hymes, Dell
1967 "Models of the Interaction of Language and Social Setting." *Journal of Social Issues* 23 (no. 2):8–28.

Lord, Albert B.
1960 *The Singer of Tales.* Cambridge: Harvard University Press.

Myerhoff, Barbara
1974 *The Peyote Hunt.* Ithaca, NY: Cornell University Press.

Moore, Sally F., and Barbara Myerhoff, eds.
1977 *Secular Ritual.* Amsterdam: Van Gorcum.

Nicoll, Allardyce
1963 *Masks, Mimes, and Miracles.* New York: Cooper Square.

Pavis, Patrice
1982 *Languages of the Stage.* New York: PAJ Publications.

Schechner, Richard
1966 "Approaches to Theory/Criticism." *The Drama Review* 10, no. 4 (T32):20–53.
1973 "Drama, Script, Theatre, and Performance." *The Drama Review* 17, no. 3 (T59):5–36.
1988 *Performance Theory.* New York: Routledge. (Revised edition of *Essays on Performance Theory,* 1977.)

Singer, Milton
1972 *When a Great Tradition Modernizes.* London: Pall Mall.

Turner, Victor
1969 *The Ritual Process.* Chicago: Aldine.
1974 *Dramas, Fields, and Metaphors.* Ithaca, NY: Cornell University Press.

Letters, Reports, Etc.

Site-Seeing in London

Observing Edge 88

Linda Frye Burnham

As the performance community rounds the corner into the next decade, the old form-vs-content arguments have given way to talk about context—the importance of the who-what-when-where-and-why surrounding an art object or event. Culture-watchers are excited to point out that a frame doesn't just bind a picture, it alters it; and in performance a radically unusual setting or a repositioning of the physical relationship between artwork and audience can add fresh perspective to issues that have been media-battered and hyperanalyzed. Site-specific performance is certainly not a new idea, considering the history of Happenings, but one that is rightly being reconsidered.

These were my thoughts while experiencing a number of performances and installations that explored unusual sites during the Edge 88 festival in London last fall (13–25 September 1988), particularly while witnessing a live work by an eminent Belfast artist in a dark, musty warren of subterranean cells that once held Irish prisoners. The political rhetoric, republican drama, and terrorist belligerence around the centuries of struggle between Ireland and England were infused with something quite new for me during my hours there in the terrible dark. Because I was physically involved, the experience opened realms of feeling and perception that would not have been available if I had been safely removed from it in a theatre seat.

Edge 88 was characterized by the careful search for interesting sites where the artists of this international festival might create new pieces. Edge 88 founder/director Rob La Frenais (founder and former editor of England's *Performance* magazine) and staff members Alison Ely and Tracey Warr chose the urban village of Clerkenwell, hard by the downtown financial district of London referred to as The City, and scoured it for locations for performances, installations, and site-specific sculptures. Festival-goers got to know this section of the old town by walking the 30-plus square blocks to visit and revisit contemporary works mounted in an art-deco swimming pool, a cloistered garden, a converted slaughterhouse, an empty warehouse, and a tiny hospital chapel, in addition to the local AIR Gallery and other artspaces in the area.

I found this contextual framing device far more interesting than the festival's stated focus—"Britain's first biennale presenting artists working on the experimental edge of the visual arts." Likewise, the issues that the festival was to address, which included "the use of the body in art, the development of women's performance, artists' use of technology and large-scale spectacle," were not as compelling to me as the focus on community sites.

Just as important was the attention to process works (some performances lasting for weeks) and live art dominated by a visual art perspective. Based on what I saw in London, the English art community has not abandoned an interest in, patience with, or reverence for those forms of performance developed in the '70s and tossed aside by the U.S. art community in its relentless search for the new and hip. Here, in addition to more theatrically formed or tech-oriented works by Nigel Rolfe (Ireland), Carolee Schneemann (U.S.), Paul Wong (Canada), Roberto Taroni (Italy), Carles Santos (Spain), Marcelle van Bemmel (Holland), Told by an Idiot (Australia), Silvia Ziranek (U.K.), and Tina Keane (U.K.), and installations that stretched visual art and video by Ian Breakwell, Helen Chadwick, Mona Hatoum (all U.K.), and Vera Frenkel (Canada), we were able to explore the mature performance work of process artists like Stuart Brisley, Ulrike Rosenbach, Alistair MacLennan, and Zbigniew Warpechowski in events that defied the tightening grip of theatrical convention.

Brisley, the grand old man of English performance, appeared locally for the first time in ten years with *Bourgeois Manners No. 2—Brute Force and Bloody Ignorance—May the Sheep Safely Graze.* The piece was performed over a two-week period in an industrial warehouse with a lengthy text posted on the door that referred to the "structural violence" concealed within the essential makeup of bourgeois society "so as to oppress particular classes." During certain hours open to the public, Brisley labored in the old workspace for eight days with an array of found objects (chairs, ply-

1. Marcelle van Bemmel in Peeneewally*—the Jamaican word for "firefly."*

wood, rope, birdseed, sheep's heads, and carpenter's worktables), pacing, arranging, setting and controlling fires, and meditating on the grisly construction as it balanced upon and consumed itself. No costumes, lights, or actors—just an industrious figure building and destroying a metaphor for careless exploitation and waste of natural resources. It was possible to stand for hours watching the piece form and reform, and to observe one's own responses at length.

German feminist Ulrike Rosenbach brought a similarly meditative work, *In the House of Women,* to the Cloister Garden beside Grand Priory Church. The religious overtones imposed by the site were exaggerated by the common knowledge that Rosenbach is now a supporter of the Indian guru Bagwan Shree Rajneesh. Entering the garden wearing a circular red skirt, Rosenbach spun in a circle for half an hour, intersecting with red strings that were stretched across the garden from the limbs of trees to the limbs of the large crucified Christ figure on an adjacent wall. A representation of linear male constructions of reality, versus more circular or central female orientation? A confrontation of the female against male constraints? An animistic link between the trees and the Christ figure? A comparison of Eastern and Western religion? The exhausting work was not literally accessible, but was oddly enhanced by the presence of a number of children of color (possibly of Indian or Pakistani extraction) who had climbed the garden wall and anxiously observed the performance. The art audience treated this piece with unexpected reverence, possibly due to Rosenbach's considerable reputation.

A Polish artist of renown relatively unknown to Americans, Zbigniew Warpechowski, presented, in the basement of a slaughterhouse, two performances that appeared to approach issues of political repression. Raw imagery and demanding physical tasks probed personal responses to the

2. A chair and several sheep's heads burn in Stuart Brisley's Bourgeois Manners No. 2—Brute Force and Bloody Ignorance—May the Sheep Safely Graze. *(Photo by Maya Balcioglu)*

3. Ulrike Rosenbach spinning in a red skirt in In the House of Women. *(Photo by Steven Durland)*

restraints of contemporary Polish life. There on the old killing floor, Warpechowski moved among and manipulated images of animals out of their elements: a chicken carcass strung up like an elaborate puppet, a water frog beached on concrete. Costumed like the frog and trying to breathe and sing through water, then having blood leeched out of his back and poured onto the chicken, Warpechowski identified his own body with these handicapped natural creatures. In his second performance, he simply held a stick in the air between his two hands, his shadow creating a cross with a line he had drawn on the wall, until he could no longer stand. Here again, these performances were carried out in a completely packed house of people squashed into the cold concrete space in rapt attention. (I arrived at the festival too late to see a performance by Poland's Jerzy Beres, a sculptor who works with ritual and magic.)

Among interesting festival works not so site-oriented, I very much appreciated Mona Hatoum's *Reflections on Value.* Presented in the warehouse, her work explored the divide between two worlds by juxtaposing a photographic image of a protest demonstration in a Third World country with a large platform covered with gold leaf. Equally as impressive was Rose Garrard's (U.K.) installation in the slaughterhouse, *Out of Line,* a display of clothing dipped in plaster and a bank of telephones which, when lifted, played tape-recorded interviews with hospital patients. The piece pointed to Garrard's recent hospitalization in a fractures ward where she noticed that the ecology of the place—young men injured in motorcycle accidents and older women injured in falls—was sharply dominated by the men.

By far the best use of site as context was Alistair MacLennan's piece, which brought the viewer directly into the heart of the Irish troubles. *Bled Edge* was an installation and five-day continuous performance beneath Kingsway Princeton College, which in 1867 was the Middlesex House of Detention. A plaque in the college courtyard told us that on Friday the 13th of December of that year, 9 people were killed and 40 injured when an explosion ripped the walls apart during an attempt to rescue Irish prisoners awaiting trial on charges of "Fenian conspiracy."

Throughout the week of 19–23 September, MacLennan lived in the cells, neither eating nor sleeping, lit only by sunlight falling through a

4. Costumed to resemble a frog and suspended above a pan of water, Zbigniew Warpechowski created an image of an animal out of its element. (Photo by P. Barker)

small grating in the school playground above. Forbidden to remain in the cells at night, he simply walked around the block in the dark. During the days, a visit to the installation revealed little visually. Sometimes the small cells along the wall were lit by candles and a barbed wire cage erected in the space was dimly observed, strewn with torn Irish and English flags. A tape haunted the space with the sounds of soft keening and a faraway baby's cry. After a few minutes the eye could barely discern a human figure standing in the passage or against the wall, presumably the artist.

For this tourist the despair and grief apparent in this circumstance was decidedly painful, and having listened privately for many hours to the artists of England and Ireland spelling out their frustration, anger, sadness, and regret over the seemingly insoluble problem of England's presence in Northern Ireland, I can imagine the depth of what was going through their hearts and minds standing in that chamber. As I moved through London, my heart swelled with new pain every time I saw graffiti slashed across an English wall reading "Kill All Irish." *Bled Edge* came back to me as I watched English television reports on the investigation of the assassination of three IRA members by the British SAS on Gibraltar. And it gripped me again in the airport the day I left when I read the newspaper account of the new U.K. broadcast ban on the voices of "terrorists," meaning essentially that England and Northern Ireland might see images of IRA and Sinn Fein members on television, but their voices will be silenced and a voiceover will deliver the acceptable, official version of what is being said.

For me, MacLennan's piece was art that was deeply real, touching courageously on a tragic issue of daily life for the audiences who witnessed it. It is so hard to find art of these spiritual and political dimensions in the U.S., obsessed as our culture-brokers have become with opaque, minimalist spectacle enshrined in opera houses. I felt really privileged.

These days the most progressive cultural workers are talking about the importance of art that relates to the community where it resides. True, the festival organizers can be faulted for choosing an apparently lily-white community and including almost no artists of color. But in its presentation of the opportunity for artists and audiences to explore the whole village and history of Clerkenwell, and particularly such loaded sites as the prison, the cloister, and the slaughterhouse, Edge 88 may have taken a bolder step toward contemporary experiment than its designers realized. One indication that the festival was truly on the edge was the complete lack of coverage in the local press—except for the *Financial Times* report noting that the festival was good publicity for Clerkenwell.

Linda Frye Burnham *is the manager of the 18th Street Arts Complex in Santa Monica, CA, and the cofounder, with Tim Miller, of Highways—a new performance space in the complex. She is also the founder and former editor of* High Performance.

Auslander Wins Last Word

Ed. Note: "Ways of Speaking, Loci of Cognition," Richard Schechner's Comment in TDR 31, no. 3 (T115), *was a response to Philip Auslander's "Toward a Concept of the Political in Postmodern Art"* (Theatre Journal *39, no. 1 [1987]). We published several letters in response to Schechner's Comment in TDR 32, no. 2 (T118). What follows is a final rebuttal.*

To the Editor:

I would like to say a few words in response to the letters published as "Debating 'Ways of Speaking, Loci of Cognition,' " particularly Richard Schechner's contribution.

First off, I don't think that either Nancy Fraser, the deconstructivist philosophers she was reporting on in the essay I cited (Fraser 1984), or myself is suggesting that artists and intellectuals should absent themselves from political discussion and engagement—as Schechner states, I wouldn't be trying to figure out what "postmodern political art" might look like if that were my position. My main purpose in making that point was simply to say that deconstruction in and of itself is not a basis for a politics. The point the French philosophers ultimately found themselves addressing was not *whether* artists and intellectuals should engage in political debate, but rather on what terms. From the deconstructivist perspective, it became clear that the *nature* of politics itself as a network of institutions, social practices, and discourses needs to be the central issue, not whether particular interests are being served by a given system. Jean-Francois Lyotard says something similar when he states that "politics as representation" is the issue (1984:78): if politics is representation, to respond to political representations with still more representations is to participate in the system of politics as representation. Therefore, I don't accept Schechner's implication that representation is simply a given to be discussed no further—the whole point of my essay on the Wooster Group (1987), and of other essays I've written since, is that postmodern political art must find ways of both occupying the structures of representation and resisting them; must, in short, undermine its own representations even as it presents them.

Schechner states that my rhetoric suggests that I am weary, resigned, and willing to "seek out the traces of resistance within hegemonic discourses." I'm not sure that my writing provides direct access to my emotional state, but I assure anyone concerned about that state that the contrary is true. Until I began to be able to perceive the work of the Wooster Group and others as a new kind of political art, I was pretty much ready to give up on the whole project of political art, for precisely the reasons I stated in my original essay: the models from the historical avant-garde and the '60s are by and large no longer useful, and most self-consciously political artists seem hampered by an inability to move beyond them. I'm afraid that John Bell's letter did nothing to dissuade me of that belief, although I would be willing to concede that work that descends from the strategies of the 1960s may succeed under certain local conditions. For example, R.G. Davis recently took note of the Bread and Puppet Theatre's work in Nicaragua, saying that Peter Schumann's "big puppets, religious homilies, and encouraging rural religiosity unite sympathetically with liberation theology in Central America." Following a brief survey of the fate of radical theatre in the United States in the same essay, Davis goes on to deplore a cultural situation in which "a few tiny protest theatre groups are acceptable as left culture—when they are so illiterate, unintelligent, hysterical, and, at best, naively agitprop" (1987:606–7).

I'm afraid that my experience of most recent art (not just theatre) that is self-consciously "political" accords with Davis's. He and I look in different directions for alternatives, however. Davis wonders whether the work of leftist theatres in Colombia and Italy might provide models for American radical theatre, but notes that "Before we can take on the question of how to deliver 'the new political insight,' or what audience or constituency should be addressed, we have to face up to corporate culture and corporate imperialism [. . .]" (1987:608). I feel pretty certain that Davis, Bell, and I all agree on this: my main point in my essay on the Wooster Group was that the deconstructive modality of postmodern theatre is a valid mode for political art. As Fredric Jameson and many other left-oriented writers have argued, postmodernism, for better or worse, is a symptom of a corporate culture. The orthodox Marxist position is that postmodernism is *only* a symptom of advanced capitalism, and that postmodern art therefore cannot do anything but reflect that pathology. My own position is simply that art which acknowledges its own complicity with corporate culture, the ways in which it is always already caught up in it even as it seeks sites of resistance, may ultimately offer more insight into the nature of that culture, and thus bring us closer to the point at which we may be able to "deliver 'the new political insight,' " than art which posits itself as an alternative to corporate culture.

I would have been more interested if Bell had offered some real arguments for the continued efficacy of '60s models rather than accusing me of adopting positions that I do not take. (For example, I do not claim in that article or anywhere else that there is a " 'gap' [. . .] between the historical avant-garde and our status as postmodern North Americans." In fact, I specifically leave open the question of whether postmodernism represents a historical or epistemological "break" with the modern.) I hope that Bell will provide the "consideration of both the work and the economic strategies of the Bread and Puppet Theatre over these past seven years" that he mentions. In short, far from being weary, I am energized by the belief that we are on the brink of conceiving a vital, new kind of political art that takes the politics of representation as its primary subject.

As for seeking out traces of resistance within even hegemonic discourses, Schechner asks: "Is this all that's left?" If by posing that question he means that the ambitions of the postmodern political theatre as I describe it are less global than those of, say, the Living Theatre, he is absolutely right. I found Johannes Birringer's letter very interesting in this connection: he says that his experience in Dallas left him and the other participants with "a sense of empowerment." Compared to the aspirations of modernist political art, whether Berlin Dada or the Living Theatre, "a sense of empowerment" is pretty small potatoes, a far cry from the idea that art can actually *cause revolutionary change*. However, I don't see any of this as problematic; the abandonment of that particular "grand rècit" is simply a realistic response to the world as it is. I don't consider the project of seeking out sites of resistance to be a diminished one ("all that's left"); rather, it requires some very close and careful analysis of the processes of representation and their links with power. I would cite the work of Hans Haacke as an example. It strikes me that Bell seems disinterested in precisely this kind of analysis. His description of the political theatre that takes place "on the *hashigakari* between the presidential helicopter and the back door of the White House" is vivid and to the point. It may be true that "this political theatre is probably being produced without any conscious effort to position its theorizing within dominant or nondominant discourses [. . .]," though it is also probable that those who seem to have achieved hegemony are concerned with maintaining it. However, if they do not conduct such analysis, it is because they do not need to, which cannot be said of those who are interested in constructing resistant or counterhegemonic discourses.

I don't think Schechner and I are particularly far apart in our political beliefs, though I am a bit less sanguine about "unity" than he. When I think of "disparate entities" coming together "in response to an issue or cluster of issues," I think for example of the coalition of radical feminists and reactionary antifeminists around the issue of pornography. That kind of coalition doesn't seem very healthy: it is not clear to me who ends up "empowered" as a result. As Gayle Rubin suggests, one result of such a coalition is that the more powerful interest simply coopts the less powerful one, which it is then in a position to undermine:

> The right wing opposes pornography and has already adopted elements of feminist anti-porn rhetoric. The anti-S/M discourse developed in the women's movement could easily become a vehicle for a moral witch hunt. It provides a ready-made defenseless target population. It provides a rationale for the recriminalization of materials which have escaped the reach of current obscenity laws (1984:298–99).

I think I'm more attracted to Lyotard's utopian vision of "a multiplicity or diversity" each member of which is essentially autonomous, yet somehow relates to the others justly. I don't know that this is possible, as I said in my first response (T118), but I'm not at all convinced that using an issue as the rallying point for unity creates a just situation. I am thinking about all this once again, trying to find a way through the thickets of "totalizing" and "micropolitical" discourses. Truthfully, I'm not satisfied with either end of that spectrum, which veers toward totalitarianism and terrorism on both ends. I don't think that loose and temporary coalitions are the answer, because the forces to which we must respond are neither loose nor temporary. Some kind of totalizing vision is necessary, but a totality of multiplicity, whatever that would be. I'm also continuing to think about the relation of the cultural to the political in all this. I have found the discussion in the pages of TDR very valuable in thinking through these issues, and hope it will continue and develop in new directions.

Philip Auslander
Georgia Institute of Technology

References

Auslander, Philip
1987 "Toward a Concept of the Political in Postmodern Theatre." *Theatre Journal* 39 (no. 1):20–34.

Davis, R.G.
1987 "Rethinking Guerilla Theatre, 1971, 1985." In *American Media and Mass Culture: A Left Perspective,* edited by Donald Lazere, 599–609. Berkeley: University of California Press.

Fraser, Nancy
1984 "The French Derrideans: Politicizing Deconstruction or Deconstructing the Political?" *New German Critique* 33:127–54.

Lyotard, Jean-Francois
1984 "Notes on the Critical Function of the Work of Art." In *Driftworks,* translated by Susan Hanson, 69–83. New York: Semiotext(e).

Rubin, Gayle
1984 "Thinking Sex: Notes for a Radical Theory of the Politics of Sexuality." In *Pleasure and Danger: Exploring Female Sexuality,* edited by Carole S. Vance, 267–319. Boston: Routledge and Kegan Paul.

Announcements

Ed. Note: TDR is pleased to print announcements of upcoming conferences, festivals, publications, etc. Please submit all notices at least 6–8 months in advance of the event.

Renaissance Drama to Order Disorder

Renaissance Drama is seeking submissions for a 1990 issue to be titled "Disorder and the Drama." Essays that discuss Renaissance dramatic representations of violence, crime, public strife, and political mayhem, and essays that explore the ways in which chaos is ritualized to contain and/or encourage social, political, and religious disorder will be considered. Manuscripts should conform to the conventions of the *MLA Style Manual* and be sent to Mary Beth Rose, Newberry Library, 60 West Walton Street, Chicago, IL 60610, no later than 1 December 1989.

The Reincarnation of *Southern Folklore*

Southern Folklore, continuing *Southern Folklore Quarterly* and incorporating *Kentucky Folklore Record,* will resume publication in 1989 with Camilla A. Collins as editor. Beginning with volume 46, *Southern Folklore* will be published three times a year and will be available from The University Press of Kentucky, 663 South Limestone Street, Lexington, KY 40506–0336, at $20 per year ($22 outside the U.S.). Direct editorial inquiries to Camilla A. Collins, Program in Folk Studies, Western Kentucky University, Bowling Green, Kentucky 42101.

Performance Studies Festival: Call for Papers

Performance Studies International (PSI) will host a festival bringing together both scholars and performers to celebrate the 10th anniversary of New York University's Department of Performance Studies on 14–18 March, 1990. The festival will be a forum for the exploration of contemporary performance studies research and experimentation in performance itself. Crossover between these two areas is encouraged. The festival will include panel discussions, workshops, and papers. Those interested in participating, please send workshop proposals and papers to Performance Studies International, Department of Performance Studies, New York University, 721 Broadway, 6th floor, New York, NY 10003.

Contest Continues

The TDR Student Essay Contest is still underway. We would like to encourage young performance scholars to submit essays dealing with *any aspect of performance*—any genre, any culture, any approach. We want to see what the best younger minds are thinking. The first prize is $500, and there are two $250 second prizes. Winners will be announced in Spring 1990, and the first- and second-prize essays will be published in TDR soon thereafter.

The deadline for submission is 15 December 1989. If possible, keep your essay to 25 pages, though there is no official limit; let the subject and your treatment of it determine its length. Please mark clearly that you are submitting your manuscript to the TDR Student Essay Contest. To show that you are a student, include a photocopy of your student ID.

Editors' Choice

Books We Recommend

The following list was compiled by our contributing editors and the editorial staff. It represents professional and personal judgments regarding books brought to our attention within the past year. Although books are selected by the editors, we appreciate suggestions from readers.

Aslan, Odette
1988 *Roger Blin and Twentieth Century Playwrights.* New York: Cambridge University Press.

Badawi, M.M.
1988 *Early Arabic Drama.* Cambridge: Cambridge University Press.

Banes, Sally
1987 *Terpsichore In Sneakers: Post-Modern Dance,* 2nd edition. Middletown, CT: Wesleyan University Press.

Beacham, Richard C.
1987 *Adolphe Appia: Theatre Artist.* New York: Cambridge University Press.

Betsko, Kathleen, and Rachel Koenig, eds.
1987 *Interviews with Contemporary Women Playwrights.* New York: Beech Tree Books.

Blau, Herbert
1987 *The Eye of Prey: Subversions of the Postmodern.* Bloomington: Indiana University Press.

Bogard, Travis, ed.
1988 *O'Neill: Complete Plays,* 3 vols. New York: Literary Classics of the United States.

Bowers, Jane, and Judith Tic, eds.
1986 *Women Making Music.* Chicago: University of Illinois Press.

Bratzher, Joe W., III, and Elzbieta Szoka, eds.
1988 *Three Contemporary Brazilian Plays.* Austin, TX: Host Publications.

Brecht, Stefan
1988 *The Bread & Puppet Theatre,* 2 vols. New York: Routledge.

Case, Sue-Ellen
1988 *Feminism and Theatre.* New York: Methuen.

Casini Ropa, Eugenia
1988 *La danza e l'agitprop.* Bologna: il Mulino.

Ceballos, Edgar
1988 *El Actor Sobre la Escena.* Mexico City: Grupo Editoral Gaceta.

Clifford, James
1988 *The Predicament of Culture.* Cambridge, MA: Harvard University Press.

Dahl, Mary Karen
1987 *Political Violence in Drama: Classical Models, Contemporary Variations.* Ann Arbor, MI: UMI Research Press.

De Marinis, Marco
1988 *Capire il Teatro. Lineamenti di una Nuova Teatrologia.* Firenze: La Casa Usher.

Dolan, Jill
1988 *The Feminist Spectator as Critic.* Ann Arbor, MI: UMI Research Press.

Dort, Bernard
1988 *la Représentation émancipée.* Toulouse: Actes Sud.

van Erven, Eugène
1988 *Radical People's Theatre.* Bloomington: Indiana University Press.

Foster, Stephen
1988 *"Event" Arts and Art Events.* Ann Arbor, MI: UMI Research Press.

Frith, Simon
1988 *Music for Pleasure.* New York: Routledge.

Gordon, Mel
1987 *Dada Performance.* New York: Performing Arts Journal Publications.
1988 *The Grand Guignol: Theatre of Fear and Terror.* New York: Amok Press.

Gray, Spalding
1985 *Swimming to Cambodia.* New York: Theatre Communications Group.

Greenblatt, Stephen
1988 *Shakespearean Negotiations: The Circulation of Social Energy in Renaissance England.* Berkeley: University of California Press.

Harrison, Paul Carter, ed.
1989 *Totem Voices: Eight Plays from the Black World Repertory.* New York: Grove Press.

Hart, Lynda, ed.
1989 *Making a Spectacle: Essays on Contemporary Women's Theatre.* Ann Arbor: University of Michigan Press.

Hartog, Francis
1988 *The Mirror of Herodotus: The Representation of the Other in the*

Writing of History. Translated by Janet Lloyd. Berkeley: University of California Press.

Helbo, André
1987 *Theory of Performing Arts*. Philadelphia, PA: John Benjamins Publishing Co.

Holland, Patricia, Jo Spence, and Simon Watney, eds.
1987 *Photography/Politics: Two*. London: Comedia Publishing Group.

Howard, Jean E., and Marion F. O'Connor, eds.
1987 *Shakespeare Reproduced: The Text in History and Ideology*. New York: Methuen.

Issacharoff, Michael, and Robin F. Jones, eds.
1988 *Performing Texts*. Philadelphia: University of Pennsylvania Press.

Izenour, George C.
1988 *Theater Technology*. New York: McGraw-Hill Book Co.

Jenkins, Ron
1988 *Acrobats of the Soul: Comedy and Virtuosity in Contemporary American Theatre*. New York: Theatre Communications Group.

Jowitt, Deborah
1988 *Time and the Dancing Image*. New York: William Morrow & Co., Inc.

Kennedy, Adrienne
1988 *People Who Led to My Plays*. New York: Theatre Communications Group.

Kersenboom-Story, Saskia C.
1987 *Nityasumangali: Devadasi Tradition in South India*. Delhi: Motilal Banarsidass.

Kiebuzinska, Christine
1988 *Revolutionaries in Theater: Meyerhold, Brecht, and Witkiewicz*. Ann Arbor, MI: UMI Research Press.

Kirby, Michael
1986 [1971] *Futurist Performance*. New York: Performing Arts Journal Publications.

Leabhart, Thomas, ed.
1986 *Mime Journal: Canadian Post-Modern Performance*. Claremont, CA: Pomona College Theatre Department.

Maclean, Marie
1988 *Narrative as Performance: The Baudelairean Experiment*. New York: Routledge, Chapman & Hall.

Marcus, Leah S.
1988 *Puzzling Shakespeare: Local Reading and Its Discontents*. Berkeley: University of California Press.

Meister, Charles W.
1988 *Chekhov Criticism, 1880 Through 1986*. Jefferson, NC: McFarland & Company, Inc.

Mizruchi, Ephraim H.
1987 [1983] *Regulating Society: Beguines, Bohemians, and Other Marginals.* Chicago: University of Chicago Press.

Munoz, Diego, et al.
1987 *Poetica de la Poblacion Marginal: el Teatro Poblacional Chileno: 1978–1985 (Antologia Critica).* Minneapolis, MN: The Prisma Institute.

Nagrin, Daniel
1988 *How to Dance Forever: Surviving Against the Odds.* New York: William Morrow & Co., Inc.

Napier, A. David
1986 *Masks, Transformation, and Paradox.* Berkeley: University of California Press.

Nunley, John W., and Judith Bettelheim
1989 *Caribbean Festival Arts: Each and Every Bit of Difference.* Seattle: University of Washington Press.

Ochsenius, Carlos y otros
1988 *Practica teatral y expresion popular en America Latina.* Buenos Aires: Ediciones Paulinas.

Osborn, M. Elizabeth, ed.
1987 *On New Ground: Contemporary Hispanic-American Plays.* New York: Theatre Communications Group.

Osborne, John
1988 *The Meiningen Court Theatre 1866–1890.* Cambridge: Cambridge University Press.

Parkin, David, ed.
1985 *The Anthropology of Evil.* Oxford: Basil Blackwell Ltd.

Pfister, Manfred
1988 *The Theory and Analysis of Drama.* New York: Cambridge University Press.

Plett, Nicole, ed.
1988 *Eleanor King: Sixty Years in American Dance.* Santa Cruz, NM: Moving Press.

Raven, Arlene
1987 *Crossing Over: Feminism and Art of Social Concern.* Ann Arbor, MI: UMI Research Press.

Sanders, Leslie Catherine
1988 *The Development of Black Theater in America.* Baton Rouge: Louisiana State University Press.

Scarry, Elaine
1985 *The Body in Pain: The Making and Unmaking of the World.* New York: Oxford University Press.

Schaef, Anne Wilson, and Diane Fassel
1988 *The Addictive Organization.* San Francisco: Harper & Row.

Schor, Naomi
1987 *Reading in Detail: Aesthetics and the Feminine.* New York: Methuen.

Simonson, Rick, and Scott Walker, eds.
1988 *Multi-Cultural Literacy: Opening the American Mind.* St. Paul, MN: Graywolf Press.

Sparshott, Francis
1988 *Off the Ground: First Steps to a Philosophical Consideration of the Dance.* Lawrenceville, NJ: Princeton University Press.

Strasberg, Lee
1988 *A Dream of Passion: The Development of the Method.* New York: Plume.

Temkine, Raymonde
1988 *Le Theatre au Present.* Lectoure: Contrastes.

Wainscott, Ronald H.
1988 *Staging O'Neill: The Experimental Years, 1920–1934.* New Haven, CT: Yale University Press.

Willett, John
1988 *The Theatre of the Weimar Republic.* New York: Holmes & Meier Publishers, Inc.

Zurbuchen, Mary Sabina
1987 *The Language of Balinese Shadow Theater.* Princeton, NJ: Princeton University Press.

Etc.

Where Are You, Characters?

Last Fall, TDR announced a playwriting competition sponsored by a group of retired media and theatre professionals who called themselves "The Characters" (vol. 32, no. 3 [T119]:21). Soon after the announcement appeared, reader Gerard A. Cox informed us that The Characters had moved and left no forwarding address. Where are you, Characters? If you have relocated, there are authors in search of you. Please provide us with a current address.

A New World

Asian Theatre in the West Today

James R. Brandon

The new world I am referring to is not, I hasten to say, the new American world—north, central, or south. The advent of a new world in our relations to the theatres of the East is not a matter of geography. It is a matter of attitude, of intention, and, in the end, of values. I believe that within the past decade the influence of Asian performing arts on Western cultures has indeed changed so greatly, and for the better, that we can speak of a "new world." This is not a scholarly review of all that has been written on this topic, but rather my thoughts and reactions presented on a rather personal level.[1]

For perspective, let me reminisce for a moment about the world of East-West theatre when I was a college undergraduate in the mid-1940s. In brief, there was no such world. No university in the country offered even a single course devoted to the theatre of non-Western cultures. Indeed, I don't remember seeing the words "kathakaḷi," "kabuki," or "wayang" in any book that was a part of the university curriculum. When the terms "world drama" or "world theatre" occasionally were used, they meant European plus American drama or theatre. The situation was certainly no different in other Western countries. World War II changed our international theatre scene as drastically as it changed so many other aspects of our lives. If World War I expanded American cultural horizons to include Europe, World War II and the years following saw more than a million Americans temporarily living in Asia. World War II, the Occupation of Japan, the Korean War, and the Vietnamese War (1941–73) constitute a third of a century of continuous large-scale American involvement in Asia, something that was unique in our national history. In addition, Fulbright exchanges, teaching exchanges, and jet-age tourism had the effect of opening Asian cultures and arts to a varied group of Westerners. Among them, theatre-trained professionals saw performances of nō in Kyoto, Chinese opera in Beijing and Taipei, khon dance drama in Bangkok, kathakaḷi in India, barong and topeng in Bali. On one level, these Western-Asian theatre contacts provided an impetus for commercial theatre, musicals, and films—*South Pacific, The King and I,* and others—in which the East was an exotic background. In doing this, a long tradition of orientalism in Western art was being continued, to which I will return in a moment.

More significantly, influential descriptive studies of theatre in Asia, carried out by Western theatre scholars during occupation and post-occupation times, were published in the 1950s. Today hundreds of books and articles detail Asian theatre forms, plays, and even specific performances. So it may be a bit difficult to realize that such books as Earle Ernst's *The Kabuki Theatre* (1956), Faubion Bowers's *Japanese Theatre* (1952) and *The Theatre in the East* (1956), and A.C. Scott's *Kabuki Theatre of Japan* (1955) and *The Classical Theatre of China* (1957) were audacious in conception. These were landmark works that "legitimated" theatre forms of Asia by approaching them on the same level that theatre in the West was studied. (In prewar years only Noël Péri's *Cinq Nō* [1921] is comparable.) By happenstance, I first saw performances in Asia in 1951 before these books were written, so I received my initial impressions as a tabula rasa. Those images of kabuki and bunraku performances are clear and vivid after 37 years, but for all I knew then I could have been seeing Martian theatre. Even in 1955, when I went to Southeast Asia for two years, I saw performances of genres whose names were unknown to me.

Most of these books appeared during an eight-year period in the 1950s when I was living in Asia. I hunted them out and read them avidly with great admiration. Using many Asian sources, they established the canon of drama, provided firm histories of the development of major theatre genres, offered analyses of aesthetic characteristics unique to each country's cultural setting, and began discussions of the complex relations between genres of theatre and their political and social milieus. A direct link can be

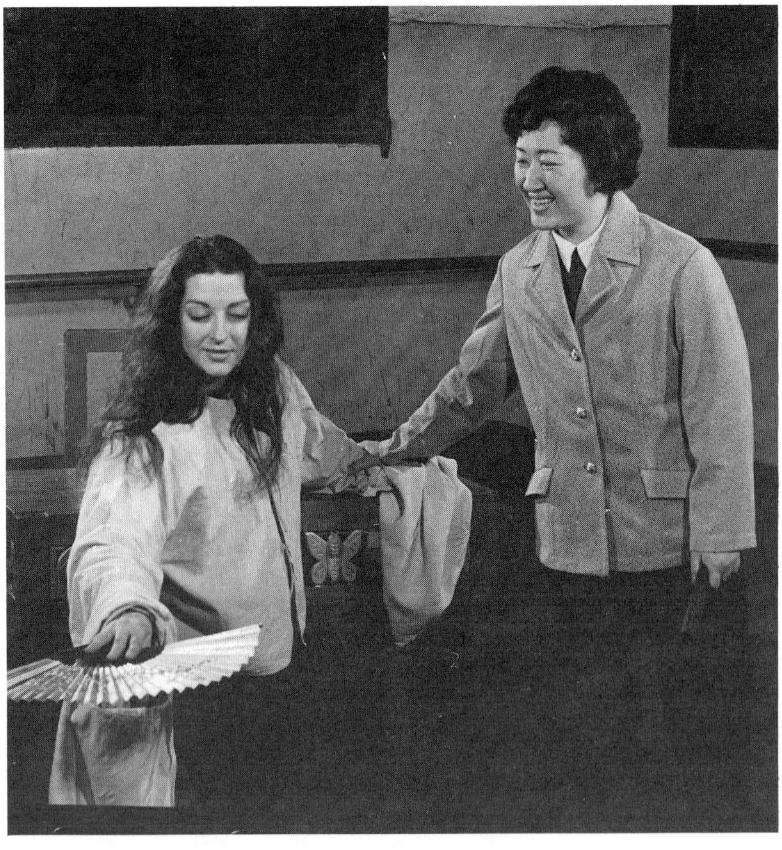

1. *American Elizabeth Wichmann in 1980 being taught by the Beijing opera actress Shen Xiaomei—one of Mei Lanfang's last pupils. Wichmann now teaches Beijing opera techniques at the University of Hawaii. (Photo courtesy of Jiangsu Province School of Traditional Theatre)*

2. *Elizabeth Wichmann performing the leading role in the Beijing opera,* The Favorite Concubine Becomes Intoxicated, *with fellow students in Nanjing, 1980. (Photo courtesy of Jiangsu Province School of Traditional Theatre)*

traced between the scholarly interest and research which produced these books and the beginning of academic instruction in Asian theatre in America.

The first such course, a "Seminar in Oriental Theatre," was created by Earle Ernst at the University of Hawaii in the Fall of 1954 as a result of his study of Japanese theatre during the Occupation (by 1977 the Asian Theatre Program at the University of Hawaii had grown to 13 courses). I taught my first course in Asian theatre in 1961, at Michigan State University. In the following decade and a half other teacher/directors introduced courses or Asian performance at other institutions: A.C. Scott, University of Wisconsin (1963), Leonard C. Pronko, Pomona College (1965), Andrew T. Tsubaki, University of Kansas (1968), Benito Ortolani, Columbia University (1969) and Graduate Center at the City University of New York (1971), Samuel L. Leiter, Brooklyn College (1977). Today, I think 50 to 60 schools in North America and Europe offer instruction in the theatre of some area of Asia. And at even more institutions, Asian-influenced productions are being conceived and staged in English. Asian performance, in other words, is entering our Western world from within the educational system; that is a fundamental change from the situation I knew at the University of Wisconsin some 40 years ago when the only theatre performance and the only theatre literature that mattered was that of our own culture.

What is happening in academic institutions is only one aspect of the contemporary picture. One indication of our great change of attitude is that we can all recite the litany of our Euro-American theatre artists who

3. American Kathy Foley performing a clown scene with her wayang golek troupe. Shae Unisna and Michael Schuster, who have studied wayang with her, flank her to pass puppets. (Photo by Victor Schiffern)

are directly indebted to Asian theatre—starting with Jerzy Grotowski, Ariane Mnouchkine, Peter Brook, Robert Wilson, and David Henry Hwang. I want to make the less obvious point that academic institutions—notoriously conservative and resistant to change—are accepting Asian theatre seriously today and that this has profound implications for the future. (There is resistance, too, which I will take up in a moment.) Let me turn now directly to consider Western attitudes toward the theatre of Asia, which I believe lie at the heart of the changes that have occurred and are continuing to occur, in both the professional theatre and in the academic world.

The earliest Western attitudes toward theatre in Asia were derived from the type of contact we had with Asian theatre. The earliest knowledge Europeans had of Asian theatre came through the publication, in European languages, of translations and then adaptations of Asian plays. Leonard C. Pronko describes some of these early translations in detail (1967:35–42, 115–26). I will mention just two. In 1736 the Jesuit Father de Prémare translated the Chinese opera *The Orphan of the House of Tchao* into French. The song lyrics were ignored and went untranslated. In 1755 Voltaire, intrigued by this translation, rewrote the play and had it staged for audiences at the Comédie-Française. In the following century and a half, it became common to rewrite and adapt Chinese, Indian, and Japanese plays until all that remained Asian about them was their exotic locales. Second, Kālidāsa's famous drama *Śākuntala* was translated from Sanskrit into English by the British Indic scholar William Jones in 1789. This scholarly translation was retranslated into a German version which Goethe read, influencing him to write a prolog, such as appears in Kālidāsa's play, in his *Faust*. We can note that Asian theatre was first perceived as being very distant ("other") culturally, that it was first encountered as literature (which is not the way a Japanese or an Indian first encounters their theatre), and that people not trained in theatre did the translating. It bears repeating that nontheatre Europeans mediated our understanding of Asian drama in the beginning.

Somewhat later, starting around the middle of the 19th century, descriptions of various Asian theatre forms began to be written in European languages. Like the translators mentioned above, the authors were not connected to theatre work in their home countries. Typically they were long-term Western residents in Asia—diplomats, merchants, advisors to Asian governments, and Christian missionaries. Coincidental to living in Asia for career reasons, they fell in love with some form of theatre that they discovered in the culture around them (or they polemically opposed the "evil" of the theatre profession) and in the course of time became self-taught experts, usually through a good command of the vernacular language. I am particularly impressed by the devotion to Asian theatre shown in the pioneering works of four long-term residents of Asia: Lewis Arlington in China (*The Chinese Drama From Earliest Times Until Today,* 1930), Emily G. Hatch in India (*The Kathakali,* 1934), Zoe Kincaid in Japan (*Kabuki, the Popular Stage of Japan,* 1925), and Walter Spies in Bali (*Dance and Drama in Bali,* with Beryl de Zoete, 1938). Perhaps the books contain some romantic excesses, but overall they are closely observed, factual, multifaceted descriptions of theatre based on personal attendance at hundreds of performances. Published over 50 years ago, they are still useful.

On a profound level, however, these theatre pioneers present two problems of attitude. First is the ambivalent position they held in the culture in which they lived. They were always Western observers, standing psychologically outside of and, because of their special status, above Asian cultures. At the same time they were trying to penetrate into and interpret those cultures' theatres. (Most Western observers today—including my-

4. Kathy Foley's teacher, the noted dalang *(puppeteer) A. Sunarya. As part of her training, Foley lived for six months at Sunarya's home, and followed him nightly to performances given by himself or his sons. (Photo by Kathy Foley)*

self—share this ambivalent position; to an extent it is unavoidable.) Spies lived his entire adult life in Bali and was assimilated into local life as much as any Westerner of this period, yet he could not help being treated as a distinguished foreign resident of a European colony. Second, none were theatre practitioners. These lovers of Chinese, Balinese, Japanese, or Indian theatre present the paradoxical case of studying theatre in situ, often for scores of years, without entering the world of theatre themselves. They not only stood outside the culture they lived in, they stood outside the theatre they wished to describe. I don't say this as a criticism, but to clarify that they and their work were part of the larger Western colonial experience in Asia. (I would argue that because of Japanese sensitivity to Western criticism, Kincaid, an American woman in 1920s Japan, was accorded the same privileged treatment received by the others.)

The decades of the 1920s and '30s saw a second important development in Western attitudes toward Asian theatre, this one occurring within Europe. At the same time that Western expatriates were living and writing in Asia, traditional Asian troupes began touring Europe and America. This new circumstance allowed Western theatre professionals—especially actors and directors—to see and hear Chinese opera, Japanese kabuki, Cambodian classic dance, and Balinese dance dramas performed by the finest artists of Asia. The kabuki star Ichikawa Sadanji and his troupe toured Russia in 1928. Eisenstein noted the independent strands of performance and the stop-action *mie* pose, and wrote afterwards about how these correspond to film montage and close-ups (Eisenstein 1963:20). Mei Lanfang's highly acclaimed tour of the United States in 1930 and performances in Europe in 1935 are well known. Mei's virtuosic artistry impressed Eisenstein, Meyerhold, and Brecht, stimulating and reinforcing the Europeans in their search for nonrealistic performance. The theory of alienation owes much to Brecht seeing Mei perform in Moscow (it seems Brecht attended a single performance and witnessed an impromptu demonstration by Mei at a party). The Chinese theatre provided a concrete model of a nonrealistic theatre which, nonetheless, was profoundly human and emotionally moving (see Banu 1986:159–61). William Butler Yeats, knowing the Japanese dancer Michio Ito in London and reading the new Pound-Fenollosa translations of nō plays (1917), was inspired to write impressionistic plays in nō style, including *Four Plays for Dancers* (see Quamber 1974:60; Jacquot 1961:275–77).

European interest in Asian theatre in the 1920s and '30s was only a part, and a relatively late and small part at that, of a half-century craze for "things Chinese" and "things Japanese" that had begun as early as the 1870s. Woodblock prints, scroll paintings, porcelains, cloth, and decorative objects of all kinds from the Orient had long been popular and had influenced the styles of painters as varied as Whistler, Manet, Pissarro, Cassatt, Klimt, and Beardsley, the sculptor Rodin, and even operetta composers Saint-Saens and Gilbert and Sullivan. From around 1902 through 1920, pseudotraditional Japanese performances by the geisha dancers Hanako and Sada Yakko had impressed Loie Fuller, Isadora Duncan, Ellen Terry, and even Queen Victoria (see Pronko 1967:120; Savarese 1988: 66–67). Theatre critics in Vienna, London, and Berlin raved "*extraordinaire [. . .] merveilleuse*" (Brandon 1988:97). Let me leave the subject of the interweaving of East and West in Europe and America by noting that the process was subtly complex and at the same time superficial. What is of greater interest is a comparison of the situation within the West (primarily Europe) with that of the expatriates in Asia.

When we look at how Western artists viewed Asian theatre within Europe, two points are inescapable. First, theatre artists in Europe had at best brief and sporadic contact with Asian performances. True, Rodin spent several weeks sketching the Cambodian royal dancers when they performed in Marseille in 1906 and he sketched Hanako in his studio in Paris any number of times (see Savarese 1988:71–72). Artaud and Brecht, whose interest in Asian theatre was as great as anyone's, saw few kinds of performance and these a limited number of times. Further, they saw performances in an unnatural Western context, as special "shows" filtered through the expectations of foreign hosts and of sponsoring governments. While they read as much as they could about what they were seeing and hearing, it did not occur to them to visit Asia to see performances in their true settings. And so they never experienced the actor-audience dynamic that infuses performance in Asia. Artaud, who got as far as Mexico, didn't go to Asia. (George Bernard Shaw visited India, China, and Japan in the 1930s, too late in his career to have any real effect.)

Second, I think it is fair to say that European theatre professionals were not interested in Asian theatre per se; the theatre of Asia was not a consuming, lifetime's passion for study and total comprehension. In this respect they were very different from, say, Spies or Arlington. Paul Claudel was the only practicing Western theatre artist of this period who lived in Asia for a protracted stay; his playwriting was deeply colored by residence in Japan, where he attended nō and kabuki and studied them extensively (see Gillespie 1983:58–59). Asian theatre was a source of inspiration for Western playwrights and directors in writing or directing plays for Western audiences. In a good sense, they "used" their Asian experience as one element in their own creativity. It was not the intention of these professionals, working wholly within Western culture, to study or reproduce Asian performances themselves. They had neither the time, the circumstance, nor the inclination to do so.

Brecht's "Chinese plays," such as *The Caucasian Chalk Circle* and *Good Person of Szechuan,* are good examples. It is unlikely that Brecht could have conceived these mature works if he had not had the personal experience of observing Mei's acting and subsequently reading about Chinese theatre. These experiences fascinated him and he returned to them again and again. They sparked his native genius. But Brecht's plays are not "Chinese theatre" or "Chinese drama" and they do not in any way describe "China." Brecht's interest wasn't different from that of Byron, Goethe, and Hugo before him: "At the most, the 'real' Orient provoked a writer to a vision; it very rarely guided it" (Said 1978:22). Nor do we turn to Brecht's essay "Alienation Effects in Chinese Acting" (1964) for an understanding of Chinese opera aesthetics. Brecht's responses to Chinese acting are impressive, intuitively brilliant. But it would be absurd to imagine that Brecht had the knowledge to explain "what Chinese theatre is."

The same can be said of Artaud. When Artaud saw performances of classical Cambodian and Balinese dance in France in 1922 and 1931, they seemed living embodiments of the kind of nonverbal, emotional, physical performance that he was developing in his mind. They validated what he was already thinking and doing. Artaud was inspired especially by the Balinese and some of his observations are percipient:

> One of the reasons for our delight in this faultless performance lies precisely in the use these actors make of an exact quantity of specific gestures, of well-tried mime at a given point, and above all in the

> prevailing spiritual tone, the deep and subtle study that has presided at the elaboration of these plays of expression, these powerful signs which give us the impression that their power has not weakened during thousands of years (1958:55).

But he had no way of knowing details of Balinese performance. Artaud projected onto the Balinese performance his own powerful beliefs and expectations. Disentangling observation from subjective conjecture in his writing is not easy, but he drew many wrong conclusions; for example, that Balinese spectacle required a powerful director, that improvisation could not occur, and that movements were "ritual gestures" conveying direct meanings (Artaud 1958:53–57). Today if we want to understand Balinese theatre we read Bandem and deBoer (1981); we read *The Theater and Its Double* to understand Artaud.

The number of Western theatre people whose work was colored by attending Asian performance in Europe or America before World War II extends beyond these examples. The seminal professionals I have mentioned are significant for bringing some aspects of Asian theatre into the mainstream of Western performance—no small achievement in ethnocentric Europe. Yet, I have mixed feelings about these icons of our modern theatre. Isn't Brecht demonstrating Western hubris when he announces "one must accept the fact" that he, Brecht, knows how a Chinese performer functions? Brecht writes:

> [The Chinese performer] makes his own mystery from the mysteries of nature (especially human nature): he allows nobody to examine how he produces the natural phenomenon, nor does nature allow him to understand as he produces it (1964:96).

How can Brecht presume to know what goes on inside a Chinese performer's head? Isn't it a sense of cultural superiority that supports our Western habit of instant explanation and consequent appropriation of power over the object? It's not extreme to suggest such discourse is "a Western style for dominating, restructuring, and having authority over the Orient" (Said 1978:3).

This article and my attitudes are inescapably part of that discourse; I hope with a difference, however.[2] What led Brecht and Artaud and Eisenstein and Yeats, among others, to imagine that after limited contact with a genre of theatre from China or Indonesia or Japan they could speak about its most complex aspects, its aesthetics, and the religions which undergird Asian performance? Working wholly within their own Western culture, these artists cannot be faulted for their creative borrowing and reworking—imaginative playwrights and directors do this. But they didn't have continuing or deep relations with people who made theatre in Asia. They were outsiders and they were dilettantes.

Both cases I've outlined above—the expatriates and the Europeans at home—show an imbalance, an incomplete coupling, of experience in Asia with training in theatre. The former group, primarily translators and chroniclers, had long Asian experiences but little or no theatre training; the latter group of professional directors and playwrights were first-rank theatre artists, but had only brief exposure to Asian performance (and not in Asia).

Neither of these two circumstances proved very satisfactory for mutual theatre exchange between Asia and the West. The attitudes of the Western participants in both cases were formed within the larger context of Euro-American relations with Asian culture. Edward Said (1978) has shown, conclusively in my opinion, that the fundamental dominance of West over East in political, military, and economic affairs extends into Western artistic and literary representations of the East. (Said wrote about the Middle East, where the situation is perhaps more extreme, but his analysis applies to Asia as well.) India, Pakistan, Sri Lanka, Burma, Malaysia, Hong Kong, Goa, Macao, Kampuchea, Laos, Vietnam, Indonesia, and the Philippines were colonies of England, Portugal, France, Holland, and the United States (Thailand and Japan alone were independent; China was a virtual cryptocolony of various European nations). Foreign, white, Euro-American males ruled; the "native" population served the rulers. "Native" arts certainly had little to do with the dominant thrust of Euro-American political-economic policies; theatre of any kind was peripheral, while modern theatre, often nationalistic, could be a threat to colonial rule. At best traditional theatre was an exotic fruit of colonial rule that could be shown off, as it was at the Colonial Expositions in Paris (1931) and Marseille (1922), not so different from the way the Caesars of Rome paraded foreign captives before the plebes to demonstrate their imperial power.

Individual Western government officials may have loved and supported indigenous theatre (Arlington, for example), but colonial policy in Asia never permitted Asian art to be placed on an equal footing with Western art. Euro-American rulers established Western educational systems that taught Western subjects, including Western systems and values of art. A tragic heritage of colonial mentality is that even today public school children in Japan (which was not even forcibly colonized), India, and elsewhere in Asia hear less about their own arts than they do about Shakespeare and Rembrandt. The special communal and ritual nature of Balinese folk theatre and the minimalist aesthetic of Japan's Zen-inspired nō impressed many Western admirers 50 years ago, but with rare exceptions Western artistic values were applied willy-nilly to Asian genres, regardless of appropriateness: Why isn't kabuki realistic? Why isn't perspective scenery used in Chinese opera? Why do bunraku chanters sing with guttural voices, instead of "correct" pure tones? Why is there no tragic flaw in *Śākuntala*?—and so on. Of course, I'm reducing more sophisticated attitudes to parody, but the parody expresses a bitter truth.

The brute fact is that until World War II, few in the West doubted that our culture was inherently superior to all other cultures. A handful of Orientalists, in fine arts and religious studies in particular, counted for little overall (Artaud was a voice crying in the wilderness, his canonization recent). Theories of Western supremacy and the white man's burden were proclaimed God-given verities that justified colonial rule. Western artistic principles were simply assumed to be superior. Ferdinand Brunetière wrote in 1886:

> Between our theater and the Chinese theater the only real difference I find [. . .] is the difference between the mumbling of a baby and the words of a grown Man. The Chinese theater [. . .] has remained in its infancy; or if you prefer, it was immobilized very early into rigid forms from which it has not succeeded in freeing itself (in Pronko 1967:40).

Pronko notes that in the first Western book devoted to Japanese theatre (written in 1889), the Frenchman A. Lequeux ridiculed kabuki as the art of a "nation of children" (in Pronko 1967); while in an earlier (1874) article Georges Bousquet showed undisguised contempt for the theatre of a non-white race:

> The Far East, we must recognize, has not known the simple, naked beauty of the Greeks: a prerogative of the Aryan race, the conception of a superior world has, for the Oriental, always taken the shape of a formless exaggeration of reality. Beyond daily triviality he has found only the monstrous (in Pronko 1967:119).

Judgment was easy to reach: since a Sanskrit play, a nō drama, a Chinese opera didn't fit a Western dramatic model (Aristotle, Shakespeare, realism—whatever standard was applied), it was, ergo, inferior. To Western ears Chinese opera singing was "the meowing of a cat whose larynx was particularly badly organized," and so on (in Pronko 1967:40).

Even when admiration for some aspect of Asian theatre was possible, it was assumed that an unbridgeable gap separated our cultures. Gordon Craig was able to rhapsodize over the enthralling mysteries of Indian theatre in *The Mask,* but he took pains to make clear that Western theatre and Eastern theatre had nothing to do with each other, each had its own principles and they were unalterably opposed (1918a:31–32). It was a restatement, for theatre, of one of the West's favorite fables about the "Orient," which Kipling merely summed up in his famous 1889 line, "Oh, East is East and West is West" (1956:425).[3] The study of an Eastern art, Craig argued, would contaminate the inherent qualities of the West. Craig was no interculturalist in spite of his love for the Orient. From that perspective, Brecht's and Artaud's use of Asian theatre was daring and commendable.

Today, I suggest major changes have occurred in our attitudes and values. In theory, at least, we believe in cultural and artistic equality. Given the end of Western colonial rule it is no longer possible to cling to the absurd notion that Western culture is superior, that Sophocles is greater than Zeami, that Judeo-Christian values are inherently better than Buddhist or Hindu or Islamic or Shinto values. Even in our economies, the final bastion of Western advantage, we are no longer all-powerful (and therefore superior): Japan, Korea, Taiwan, Hong Kong, and Singapore provide alternative models of economic success. In the practical theatre world and the world of theatre scholarship, we cross paths constantly in New York, Tokyo, Calcutta, Beijing, Paris. We know so much more about each other's theatre than we used to. International theatre conferences occur every year and at international theatre festivals kathakaḷi is seen side-by-side with ballet, butō with Molière, Balinese wayang with Shakespeare. Within our own theatre world, dissatisfaction with realism has continued, with little resolution, for three-quarters of a century. Our avant-garde is essentially an ongoing attempt to find alternative forms of theatrical expression that are able to address new issues and reach new audiences. In this quest, Brecht and Artaud pointed the way to Asia, where alternative models exist; Asian genres are living examples of how varied the possibilities of performance are.

Internal imperatives within Western societies coupled with a changed international political order have led to changed attitudes on the part of Western theatre artists toward Asian performance. Japanese, Chinese, Indonesian, and Indian theatres are now widely recognized as independent, powerful sources of theatrical knowledge and techniques. For the first time in the long history of contact between East and West, it is possible for large groups in Western theatre to agree that the study of Asian theatres per se—for their intrinsic qualities and on their own terms—is desirable, because their value is equal to Western theatre. The wholly heretical thought can now be imagined: Asian theatre may be *better* than Western theatre. (This is not my view, but it inspires some.)

Here theatre meshes with larger cultural and political agendas. Part of what I am saying is a polemic about what should be. The current controversy at Stanford over including nontraditional books as part of the "Western culture" course required of all students shows that there is a kind of desperate resistance to actually giving non-Western cultures equal time in the American academic marketplace. All that happened, Stanford president Donald Kennedy said placatingly, was that some works by "women, minorities and persons of color" were added to the canon of "Great Books" in order to reflect "the diversity of contemporary American culture and values" (Atlas 1988:26). This blandly innocuous explanation roused the fury of many, including Secretary of Education William J. Bennett, who traveled to Stanford to denounce the action of its faculty senate. On what grounds? Because, Bennett said, "the West is the culture in which we live. [. . .] It has set the moral, political, economic and social standards for the rest of the world" (Atlas 1988:26). The comment would be laughable if it weren't so callously insulting. In maligning the beliefs of three-fourths of the world's people Bennett said more than Kipling's myth is alive and well in the 1980s. Bennett reminds us that our Western superiority complex is deep-seated and that it draws sustenance from an ethnocentrism which asserts that we are "special" simply because we are of

5. Acting students of nō master actor Nomura Shirō at the University of Hawaii following the traditional practice of cleaning the dancing stage before receiving instruction. (Photo by James R. Brandon)

the West. Jews as the chosen people, born-again Christians as converters of heathens, Western-derived schemes of economic development applying to all societies, American military versus "gooks," Western scholars' penchant for "universalizing" from Western data—each is a manifestation of the notion of Western uniqueness and the special moral authority we are prone to show in our dealings with non-Westerners.

But let us set aside polemics (Bennett arguing for Western cultural centrality and me urging cultural equality) to look at what is indisputably happening. I believe the feature of our new world that will have the most profound effects on the future is the training which young Western actors, musicians, singers, puppeteers, and maskers are now receiving while living in China, Japan, India, Korea, Thailand, Indonesia, and elsewhere in Asia. They are enrolled in Asian theatre schools; they are the pupils of Asian master artists; they are learning to perform specific genres of Asian theatre. In such master-pupil relationships the centuries-old idea of Western political and cultural dominance of Asia is shattered, displaced, rendered obsolete. I cannot express too strongly how significant it is that Western performers apprentice themselves to Asian masters. They learn the intrinsic values of the performing system by assimilation, directly and without the intermediacy of a Western interpreter (Brecht said what Mei "meant," Mei did not explain himself). They function within the language of the performance and the performer. They enter that cultural world, not solely as scholars or observers as in the past, but as "doers" (the literal meaning of *shite* in nō). They do so as learners, as pupils, as followers. In the process they inevitably shed a lot of Western conceptual baggage. To greater or lesser degree, their success in learning depends upon their ability to become accepted "as if they were Indian" (Japanese, etc.). Granted, the period of study is often one or two years, in comparison to the decades that traditional Asian performers spend. But I also know American actors who have been studying in Asia under master teachers for 20 years and more, and some who return again and again. All of this process, I submit, represents a profound shift of attitude on our part. When Brecht made the rules and the theories, he was responsible to himself alone; the Western student training in Asia must accept the rules of an art established by others and run by others. Here the two parts of our puzzle come together: today these students have lengthy experiences with Asian performance and they are theatre artists themselves. This combination provides them with exceptional capabilities.

Of course, Westerners have studied performance in Asia before. Ruth St. Denis comes to mind as well as Asian theatre specialists of my generation (Leonard C. Pronko and myself in kabuki, Andrew Tsubaki in nō and kyōgen, A.C. Scott in tai chi). But we were adults already occupying privileged positions when we studied in Asia—we were "outside" the art, whether we wanted to be or not. The student today is not just younger, but able to gain greater personal entry into the social fabric of theatre and the teaching-learning system. The impact upon Western performance, as these younger people become teachers, performers, and directors in the United States is already considerable and is bound to become greater. A defining test is whether they return with the capability of maintaining (within limits) the Asian performing tradition they have learned.

In the 1960s I used to say that Asian theatre will have truly arrived when we can drop "Asian" as a term and just talk about theatre as theatre, regardless of where it is from. I now think this was a utopian idea. The problem is not that comparisons stated in terms of East and West are

6. Master actor Nomura Shirō teaching complex nō dance movements at the University of Hawaii in 1988. The students learn by observing (mi narai) *and modeling themselves on their teacher. (Photo by James R. Brandon)*

always reductive and invidious and therefore must be avoided (see Said 1978:28). The problem is having superficial knowledge and applying Western standards to everything. It seems more valuable now to emphasize the specialness of theatre in other cultures and grapple directly with learning their unique features. We don't think it strange that Seiji Ozawa masters Western symphonic music and becomes a conductor in the West. Why not value the Western actor who performs Asian theatre in Asia? It is already happening. Don Kenny regularly performs kyōgen in Tokyo. John Emigh has performed topeng in Bali, Elizabeth Wichmann has sung Chinese opera in Beijing, Kathy Foley has done wayang golek in Bandung.

The change of attitude in the West that accepts Asian as equal to Western theatre is reflected in other ways as well. At the University of Hawaii we regularly bring professional kabuki, nō, kyōgen, and Chinese opera actors for periods of up to one year to teach students to perform in the traditional manner. After intensive training, we "replicate" a Japanese or Chinese production as closely as possible. Music is played and songs are sung live by students and faculty. We follow traditional acting techniques. We perform in English because we have an English-speaking audience—parallel to opera being sung in English (or German or French) to suit its audience.[4] We can note, too, that new theatre groups are forming in which perform-

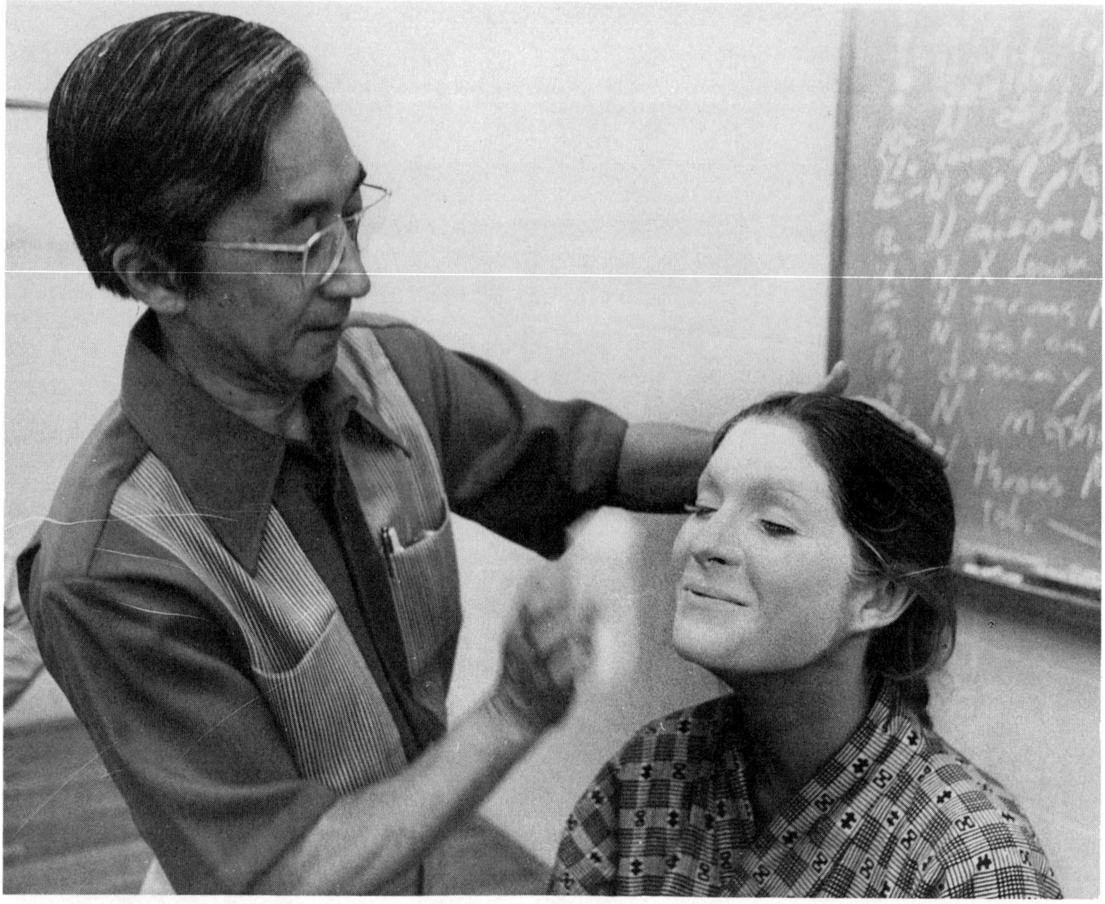

7. Nakamura Matagoro II, Chief Instructor, Kabuki Training School, National Theatre of Japan, teaching actress Barrie Moss proper makeup technique for the role of Lady Taema in Narukami the Thunder God *at the University of Hawaii in 1973. (Photo courtesy of University Theatre, University of Hawaii)*

ers' knowledge of Asian acting technique is utilized to create innovative performing styles—Theatre of Yugen in San Francisco, East West Fusion Theatre in Connecticut, and Islene Pinder's Balinese American Dance Theatre in New York only suggest the range of work being undertaken. The *Asian Theatre Journal,* now in its sixth year of publication and sponsored by the Association for Asian Performance, is a product of this new world. It is dedicated to mutual and equal interchange between Asian and Western theatre artists and scholars. The many articles on Asian theatre published in TDR and the occasional ones in *Performing Arts Journal* and *Theatre Journal* reflect the same interest.

What is the basic nature of Asian performance that appeals to us in the West today? Why acceptance, though perhaps not by everyone, of what was once exotic? You can make an argument based on economic power: Japan receives respect and attention because it is a superpower the West can't afford to ignore. (When and if Japan attains hegemony over us economically, will we recoil from its arts or embrace them more?) But power doesn't explain the appeal of theatre of Bali or Kampuchea or India, lesser players in the world power game. Like Brecht, Artaud, or Yeats, we can find in the Asian experience concrete examples of alternative ways of making theatre. First, the body of the actor is the source and medium of performance. This idea was deeply impressed on European viewers by Mei

Lanfang and Ichikawa Sadanji and is obvious to anyone who sees Asian performances today. To take kabuki as an example:

> The overriding emphasis upon the person of the actor in kabuki is usually attributed—by Japanese commentators—to the desire to show off the actor's "physical attractiveness" (*nikutai miryoku*). [. . .] Yet, there is, it seems, more to it than this. Kabuki acting style is legitimately based on using the physical possibilities of the human body. Its aesthetic of performance is centered on projecting human character and feeling through the total physical form (Brandon 1982:128).

The actor, not the playwright's text and not the outside director, is the source and origin of performance. It follows from this that the persona of the actor, as well as that of the fictive character, interests the audience. In Chinese opera, kabuki, popular Thai likay, Indian kuchipuḍi, and other forms, audiences respond to what the "actor" does. The kabuki "actor" announces his name during a scene. The "actor" drinks a cup of tea to clean the "actor's" throat. Asian performance provides countermodels to set against psychological realism, where the actor's persona is expected to become invisible within the character's persona.

Second, Asian theatre forms have highly developed "codes" of performing—song, declamation, chant, dance, movement, and gesture—and of visual iconography—makeup, costuming, masking, and puppetry.[5] These artistic codes are performative languages, shared by performers and spectators. So Asian theatre provides scores of different models of connoisseurship, where an audience's knowledge of the theatre form contributes to the depth and subtlety of that audience's response. Western audiences and performers share knowledge of performance codes in classical ballet and, to an extent, in opera. But in straight Western drama there are virtually no codes of artistry that actors learn and transmit to future generations. The fundamental theory of Stanislavskian acting is that the audience should perceive the action on stage "as if" occurring in ordinary life. So not only should the actor's persona be subsumed into the character's persona (that is, not observable to the audience), the behavior of the actor-character should be indistinguishable from daily behavior. People do not converse in song or walk via dance codes in real life; as a consequence, artistic codes of performance have no place. Asian models show alternative ways of structuring play content and alternative ways of projecting character.

Eugenio Barba uses the terms "daily" and "extra-daily" to distinguish acting techniques from natural behavior from techniques created by the actor (1986:268); Barba equates the latter with what I call codes of acting. Barba's formulation is useful to the Western actor searching for a personal acting style, for it points the actor to developing both representational ability (conveying life as we know it) and a theatrical skill (however that may be defined). The concepts parallel, I think, the two categories of movement within classical Indian dance: *nṛtya* (mimetic dance that expresses actions, feelings, and human relationships drawn from life) and *nṛtta* (pure dance that doesn't have meaning but is pure form). The way I would describe what happens in most Asian performance is that some recognizable daily action—walking, weeping, killing—is patterned by the actor through codes into an expressive unit that is, to use Barba's terms, daily and extra-daily at the same time. Every action in Asian performance is encoded; every movement or sound, regardless of whether it is derived from daily life or not, is expressed through culturally agreed-upon patterns or codes of performance. For these reasons, I prefer the concept of codes when discussing Asian performance.

Asian performance has a special relevance to some forms of contemporary Western theatre. Performance art incorporates "signifying practices as varied as dance, music, painting, architecture, and sculpture" (Féral 1982:170) as does traditional Asian performance. Both are opposed to straight Western theatre practice. There are points of divergence, as well. The "non-narrative and nonrepresentational" aims of performance art (Féral 1982:171) are far from a theatre that is based on codes. Codes relate to narrative and characterization, and codes add to and enhance textual meaning. Certainly there is no natural affinity between an Asian genre based on codes of performance and a piece of Western performance art in which "having no set form, every performance constitutes its own genre" (Féral 1982:174). What JoAnne Akalaitis has said about the rehearsal-creative process of Mabou Mines is similar: actors create a "new performance style" for each play they develop (1982). In this actor-centered approach a significant problem is how to clue in an audience to each performance's unique form. This is the opposite of the audience as connoisseur of performing codes.

Codes are learned by performers through rigorous, disciplined training. The training results in a flexible, conditioned acting instrument, with a wide range of potential in any acting situation. Disciplined practice makes "the physical eye and body steady" (Zarrilli 1984b:205). Particularly in the current Western theatre situation, where early spontaneous, inner-focused acting is prized, Asian models demonstrate the value of training the expressive body over time. Grotowski and Barba are obvious admirers and beneficiaries of traditional Asian actor training systems. Barba in particular continues to explore Balinese, Indian, and Japanese acting principles in workshops at various meetings of his International School for Theatre Anthropology. The contemporary actor training of the Suzuki Method, developed by Suzuki Tadashi and the Waseda Little Theatre group (now called the Suzuki Company of Toga [SCOT]), has excited imitation in the United States (see Suzuki 1986; Brandon 1978b; Beeman 1982). Each summer a dozen young Western actors are invited to Toga Village in the remote mountains of central Japan to train under Suzuki's rigorous tutelage. Training in specific Asian acting techniques regularly goes on at Pomona College, Emerson College, University of Wisconsin, University of Kansas, University of Hawaii, and in other places as well.

Third, Asian performance provides models of close ties between audience and performance which many in Western theatre are seeking. When traditional Asian theatre genres are performed, audience and performance spaces are closely related. In Bali, symbolic bamboo poles at four corners of an acting area and sometimes a cord of woven leaves can be all that separates spectators from performers. Audiences of men, women, and children crowd closely around puppet performers in Indonesia; usually the veranda of a house is turned into a temporary and informal stage. In traditional Japanese theatres, the architecture is quite different from the peephole proscenium arch that evolved in Western countries. The nō stage is a simple platform that thrusts forward into an intimate seating area. In the past it simply faced a temple or residential courtyard; today the same arrangement is retained inside a modern building.

Look carefully at the inside of a traditional kabuki house—even the cavernous Kabuki-za in Tokyo—and you see that the enclosed area is a simple rectangular box that has a raised stage at one end. Stage width is virtually the same as auditorium width (88 feet at the Kabuki-za) and we scarcely notice the sides and top of the stage opening (i.e., the proscenium arch). Stage action is not tucked back away from the audience: spectators in the house and actors on stage are occupying different portions *of the same space*. As a result, the actor is constantly aware of what is happening in the audience. Because the house lights are up, the actor can see the faces of the spectators clearly. No one plays into a dark hole. Zeami's advice to the nō actor, written in the 15th century, could well apply to any genre of Asian theatre: the actor must always be aware of and respond to the mood of the spectator, he must see himself as the audience sees him (*riken no ken*) and adjust his performance accordingly (Zeami 1984:100–102). From Asia we have both theory and practice for audience-actor interaction that we say we want in the West.

Finally, we can see in numerous examples of Asian performance concrete evidence that the artistic codes of performance are in no way inimical to expressing human and social concerns. "Stylization" is often a pejorative in Western performance, bringing to mind artificiality, preciousness, and a lack of truth and reality. Some of the strongest critics of stylization were the supporters of socialist realism in the Soviet Union (and for a time in China), for whom theatrical "formalism" was antirevolutionary and a crime against the state (see Banu 1986:167–70). Meyerhold, committed to a labor camp in 1938 for the crime of formalism, died there. But these objections to nonrealistic performance are based on the false premise that a choice must be made between what is real (theatrical representation that reproduces phenomenal reality) and what is nonreal (formalistic or stylized abstractions that depart from observable reality). Asian theatre provides endless examples that this choice doesn't have to be made. The either/or dilemma is artificially imposed. Images of the real world abound in such a highly codified and abstract art as nō. In kathakaḷi, hand gestures (*hasta* or *mudrā*) convey explicit meanings as precisely as do words. How can we explain Japanese audiences weeping during a bunraku puppet performance, if not by our human ability to filter perceptions of reality through the most rigorous performing codes? Codes carry messages, and those messages can relate to the real world. *Kata,* usually translated as "form" or "pattern," in Japanese traditional theatre is far more than an outer, meaningless form. Mark Oshima makes the interesting observation that in Japanese culture kata function like Kanji ideograms: the form is readily identifiable and in itself contains meaning apart from context (Oshima 1987). I argue that the strongest audience responses in theatre occur precisely when the strongest emotions are expressed through sophisticated performing codes.

It isn't new to say there is freedom in form, or that creative potential can be heightened through a discipline of training. Jerzy Grotowski spoke to this point in the 1960s:

> There is no contradiction between inner technique and artifice (articulation of a role by signs). We believe that a personal process which is not supported and expressed by a formal articulation and disciplined structuring of the role is not a release and will collapse in shapelessness.
>
> We find that artificial composition not only does not limit the spiritual but actually leads to it. (The tropistic tension between the inner process and the form strengthens both. [. . .]) The forms of common "natural" behavior obscure the truth (1968:17).

Yet, the fact is that Western theatre lacks both theories and established practices which integrate form with content, or which integrate discipline with spontaneity in performance. And it lacks audiences trained for such performances.

In our present circumstance, Asian performance provides an additional and useful perspective on such concerns as textual interpretation. Take the deconstructionist argument that the director needs to be totally free to interpret a written dramatic text, for the text has no "privileged stability" (Rabkin 1983:55), no unchallengeable authority based on its "translucent and free-standing autonomy" (Felperin 1985:110). I am not concerned here with the applicability (or nonapplicability) of this theory in our text-oriented Western theatre, nor with the debate over whether or not deconstruction as a theory is "elitist [. . .] a reactionary force [. . .] dandyist aestheticism [. . .] apocalyptic irrationalism" (Felperin 1985:111–12). What I want to do is look at the reasoning behind this position as it applies to theatre practice.

The unspoken premises, the givens, of the argument are: first, that text exists separate from performance; second, that the written text—no matter how deconstructed or reconstructed—is the beginning source material of performance; and third, that an outside force (the director) is necessary to give shape to an otherwise unknowable performance. To a great extent, these premises don't apply to traditional Asian theatre. Some years ago I wrote:

> Because theatre in Asia is conceived of primarily as a performing art, the text is not accorded priority, and there is little tendency to look first at a play in terms of its meaning. The theatrical art is regarded as a whole. Thus the meaning of a play may be stated through elements of form (1972:4–5).

Zeami was a nō actor who wrote plays to suit his performing style and at the same time he developed performing codes and theories of theatre to match the play texts he was composing. The great kabuki playwrights of the 19th century, Tsuruya Namboku IV and Kawatake Mokuami, spent their lives in the professional theatre, writing for actors in their troupe and within the codes of kabuki acting which had been created by previous generations of actors. You don't have a written text for a Balinese or a Javanese wayang kulit "play": a *dalang* (puppeteer) extemporizes, within certain parameters, story, dialog, narrative, and action, and makes music and song choices in the process of giving a nine-hour performance. Each performance reveals its own "text," which is unknown beforehand, is different from any other, and will not be performed again. These three Asian genres show different ways of joining verbal text and performing codes, they show different fusions. You cannot say the written (or even oral) text "comes first"; looked at historically, performing codes had to be in place (though changeable) before any particular performance—or text—could be created. This is the opposite of the way we perceive Western theatre.

A tenet of deconstruction is that the critic (and in theatre the director) is a coequal creator with text-makers (see Rabkin 1983:56–57). This can make sense in the West, where the prime text-maker is a playwright. But in most Asian theatres, no director exists, because only performers know all the performing codes—a director is not competent to tell actors what to do nor how to do it. Sanskrit theatre troupes, the exception in Asia, had director/producers who were skilled in all aspects of performance. As Bharata wrote in the *Nāṭyaśāstra* (c200 BCE:):

> I shall speak of the qualities of a Director. First of all, he should possess knowledge of characteristics (of everything concerning the theatre), desirable refinement of speech, knowledge of the rules of Tāla [rhythm] and theory of notes and instruments. [. . .] One who is an expert in playing the four kinds of musical instrument, has various practical experience [. . .] knows the various conventional Gaits and movements, thoroughly understands all the Sentiments [*rasa*] and the States [*bhāva*], and is an expert in producing plays, acquainted with all arts and crafts, with words and the rules of prosody, and proficient in all the Śāstras [treatises] [. . .] should be made a teacher and Director (1961:vol. II, 222).

Usually the natural interpreter of Asian dramatic texts is the performer. Just as the natural teacher of theatre in Asia is the performer. The performer knows in his/her body, and through constant doing and practice, what the play text is and what the performing codes are. In traditional Asian genres an experienced playwright will have learned a lot of this, too. But a director is not needed and the critic remains an outsider to the world of performance. I don't quarrel with deconstruction in Western theatre. I do point to Asian theatre practice to illustrate what theatre is like when the Western rent between text and performance isn't operating. Dialectic absolutes are part of the Western scholarly tradition: if the text is dead, destroy it and make (reinterpret, reconstruct) a new one. The yin-yang principle of East Asia says something different: opposites coexist, therefore strive to find an appropriate balance, between light and dark, soft and hard, male and female. Traditional Asian theatre follows the yin-yang principle in balancing, constantly, the pull of text and the push of performing codes. And the agent who maintains that balance is the performer, either entirely or primarily, depending upon the genre.

Gerald Rabkin expresses a not uncommon view that the best contemporary directorial interpretations of classic dramatic texts result from a "strong" clash between director and text, and he quotes the deconstructionist critic Harold Bloom in support of his argument: "Only strength is memorable; only the capacity to wound gives a healing capacity the chance to endure, and so to be heard" (1983:60). The idea isn't new (although the method is), it's an updated vision of Artaud's theatre as plague "created to drain absesses collectively" (Artaud 1958:31), which in turn brings Aristotle's cathartic function of theatre to mind. I don't doubt that radical interpretations of classic Western dramatic texts have value. The deliberate clash between text and performance, the commenting of one upon the other, may be necessary if we imagine the usual Western audience is bored with the standard *Hamlet* (if there is a standard *Hamlet*). Artaud, an artist, incites us to enter and share his apocalyptic dream (and we may refuse) but Rabkin/Bloom are critics laying down rules. Their vision is too narrow. Theatre has valid functions other than to wound. Performance may be affirmative, it may be gentle, it may be exultant, it may be raucous, it may do many, many things besides inflict wounds. Whatever else the Rabkin/Bloom discourse may be, it is parochial and arrogant in not considering the evidence of theatres other than of the contemporary West. I repeat: if contact with Asian performance is good for anything, it is that it can provide models of "other" theatres from which we can learn. It is time for

Western theorists to recognize that other patterns of theatre exist, in short to become intercultural.

One common practice underlying theatre training in Asia is that you enter a process that has no end. You do not aim for a goal: you enter a stream or flow that began long before you joined it and will continue after you are gone. Although most Asian actor training is not "person" centered (it is first skill centered and then audience centered), the actor enters into a personal relationship with his/her teacher. Learning an Asian acting discipline, even for a short time, can help a Western actor develop habits of focus and concentration, and encourage the actor to understand the larger structure of performance, including personal relationships with a teacher and other performers within which the ego of the actor can find its place. It is crucial for any actor to be noticed by spectators and this means balancing the fixed elements of the codes and text with individuality.

I am sometimes asked if learning formal Asian acting techniques doesn't hinder a Western actor's own creativity. I don't think so (and there is some research evidence to support my view).[6] But the question has been around for a long time. Seventy years ago, when Gordon Craig was insisting the Western actor had no business learning Asian theatre and should not "wish to capture a single trick of its technique" his reason was you would "never come back" (1918a:31–32). With fine asperity he chided his followers to improve their own theatre, for "it's not on the road to Mandalay that we are moving. [. . .] Europe and America look to us, remember, to remain ourselves" (1918a:32). Craig had his reasons for not wanting direct intercourse between Eastern and Western theatre artists. He wrote, in some despair it seems to me, that hardly two in a thousand of the young people for whom he was writing were followers of his New Movement for an artistic theatre. We can understand why, to keep these few, he didn't want them to "gad about pretending to understand Chinese" (1918b:3–4). This was before Brecht and Artaud encountered Asia in Europe.

Even more basic, Craig's split attitude—praising Asian theatricality while warning against the folly of Westerners actually trying to *do* Asian acting, or dancing, or music—is still around. As recently as 20 years ago, when William J. Bruehl first reported on Asian (and African) theatre studies in the United States in TDR, he almost exactly repeated Craig:

> The arrogance of supposing that we have nothing to learn from the theatrical forms of Asia and Africa is arrogance born of ignorance. We have no business trying to imitate Kabuki or Nigerian dance, but we can relearn things we have lost in our own tradition—stylization, movement, visual effects, techniques of playwriting, music, and song (1968:175).

The belief that Western performers "have no business trying to imitate" Asian performance can stem from good motives—wish to preserve some realm of Asian art from Western predation, abhorrence of amateur Chinoiserie or Japonisme in theatre, and concern for the practical difficulties of Asian training systems. But also, at heart there is the sense that it is an impossible task.

I can only say I disagree with Craig. I think he was wrong then and he is wrong today. We learn what we set out to learn, and to say it can't be done is self-defeating. Twenty-two years ago (1967) I said about kabuki training:

8. The author learning kyōgen from teacher Nomura Mansaku at the University of Hawaii in 1988. During training, the master actor's voice and body are the sole legitimate models, and the pupil must focus all his/her attention on the teacher. (Photo by Katherine Mezur)

> Looked at in broad perspective, a *kabuki* actor travels "a way of art," or *geidō. Geidō,* in the world of Japanese performing arts, is parallel to *shintō,* or "way of the gods," in Japanese religion and *bushidō,* or "way of the warrior," in Japanese military science and ethics. In each there is a known path to knowledge and the initiate is guided in his steps along the path by a master already proficient in its secrets. In *kabuki,* this means the actor learns a total "way of art" which, while it encompasses specific forms of *kata* [pattern], looks beyond them to a total approach to *kabuki* acting. [. . .] At each step of an actor's development, there is the dual knowledge that one level of artistic skill has been achieved, with its concomitant satisfaction, and that a yet higher level of attainment lies ahead, stimulating further study and improvement. Learning existing *kata* then does not pit pupil *versus* teacher's conception, or creation *versus* tradition (as we would expect in the West). The ideal pupil so completely absorbs the totality of the way, that his approach and his master's are one. [. . .] Change is not denied in this view, only its importance is. It is assumed that change will take place and that when it occurs it will be incorporated into the broad stream of the actor's way of art, causing no more than a ripple on its surface (1978a:124–25).

While this is quite different from the way young American actors usually work, it is not an impossible model in our culture. You can come back. I believe that young American actors will benefit by studying Asian performance—here or in Asia—and these performers will find their own way to incorporate the specific Asian experience into their Western theatre experience. It is not the skill or technique per se that matters, although performers like John Emigh, Islene Pindar (see Snow 1986:206–218), Monica Bethe, Yuriko Doi, Mark Hoffman, and others do use their Asian-

9. Precise replication of choreography, music, vocal patterns (in English), and characterization was the goal of kabuki actor Nakamura Matagoro II in training and directing University of Hawaii students to perform The Forty-Seven Samurai *in 1979. Pictured here is a* tachimawari *(group battle) in the "Fugitive Lovers Travel Scene." (Photo by Donald Kozono)*

learned techniques directly in performance. These are the raw materials out of which theories, projects, training other performers, and performance have evolved and may be expected to evolve in the future.

The new players in the new world of East-West theatre are the performers. Playwrights and directors have been involved, to one degree or another, for a long time. Now performers are committing themselves to long-range training and long-term relationships with Asian performers. They are plunging into alien cultures and into alien theatres—all contrary to Craig's advice—and I for one think much has already come of it. Let me end on a personal note, as I began. What I would like most to see at this time is receptivity, openness, willingness to try the different (even if different is not "new"). Can we look past the moment and imagine the long haul. Can we, like Zeami, value the mature performance that eventually will result from constant training and continual learning. Can we, in time, come to appreciate "the flower blossoming on the old tree."

Notes

1. Parts of this article were presented at the International Symposium on Theatres East and West ("Translation, Mutation and Betrayal") in London on 14 November 1987, and have been published in French translation in *Jeu* 49, no. 4 (December 1988).
2. The personal misuse or exploitation of Asian performers, raised by Zarrilli (1986) and Foley (1988), is a related issue that I cannot take up here.
3. Kipling did not end "The Ballad of East and West" with "never the twain shall meet," but continued "but there is neither East nor West [. . .] when two strong men stand face to face, though they come from the ends of the earth" (1956:425).

No one remembers the latter lines; the equality implied in them did not fit the age.

4. Elsewhere I have written about how directorial goals, training methods, and interaction with audiences have changed over the course of directing (in one case producing) eight English-language kabuki productions at the University of Hawaii between 1970 and 1987 (1981:73–91).
5. The topic of acting "codes" in general has yet to be written about, but acting techniques and training systems of specific Asian genres can be found described in a number of works, including: Kabuki: Brandon (1978a); Leiter (1967, 1979 [introduction]); Pronko (1971). Nō: Kunio (1983); Bethe and Brazell (1982); Berberich (1984). Bunraku: Adachi (1978). Chinese opera: Scott (1956, 1957). Indian dance drama: Vatsyayan (1968); Zarrilli (1984a, 1984b). Indonesian shadow theatre: Long (1982). Thai classical dance-drama: Yupho (1952). Intercultural training: Schechner (1985).
6. During the academic year 1978–79, three professional kabuki actors, led by Nakamura Matagorō II, taught 40 University of Hawaii students kabuki acting techniques and directed them in the play *The Forty-Seven Samurai* (*Kanadehon Chūshingura*). In a sophisticated multivariant study of the effects of this extensive kabuki training (two to four hours a day for nine months), Robert Bethune (1985) found that students ranged as high as 80 percent in their ability to learn and perform kabuki movement and voice in short kabuki scenes as measured on 54 indicators (eye tension, gesture amount, weight transfer, torso units, posturality, flow, space, expansion, axial and planar orientation, kinespheric size and zone, vocal mode, noise, accent, pitch width and center, vibrato, slide, volume width and change, etc.). Even the poorest students could reproduce 40 percent of the kabuki techniques they were taught. Bethune found that kabuki movement was learned more readily than voice, which matches my personal experience. Finally, Bethune found that the "actors do not assimilate what they can find little use for" (428) and "none of the well-known devices of the kabuki theatre were shown by the student actors in their Western work" (434). Bethune surmises that well-trained actors are capable of drawing upon just that part of the acting experience required for a given acting task and that kabuki acting did not "bleed into" Western acting unnoticed or unbidden.

References

Adachi, Barbara
1978 *The Voices and Hands of Bunraku*. Tokyo: Kodansha.

Akalaitis, JoAnne
1982 Lecture at the International Symposium on Theater and Ritual. The Asia Society, New York City, 26 August.

Arlington, Lewis Charles
1966 [1930] *The Chinese Drama From Earliest Times Until Today*. New York: B. Blom.

Artaud, Antonin
1958 *The Theater and Its Double*. Translated by Mary Caroline Richards. New York: Grove Press.

Atlas, James
1988 "The Battle of the Books." *The New York Times Magazine*, 5 June: 24–26, 72–74, 85, 94.

Bandem, I Made, and Fredrik Eugene deBoer
1981 *Kaja and Kelod: Balinese Dance in Transition*. Kuala Lumpur: Oxford University Press.

Banu, Georges
1986 "Mei Lanfang: A Case Against and a Model for the Occidental Stage." *Asian Theatre Journal* 3, no. 2 (Fall):159–61.

Barba, Eugenio
1986 "Ingmar Bergman's *King Lear.*" *Asian Theatre Journal* 3, no. 2 (Fall):261–69.

Beeman, William O.
1982 "Tadashi Suzuki's Universal Vision." *Performing Arts Journal* 6, no. 2 (PAJ 17):77–87.

Berberich, Junko
1984 "Some Observations on Movement in Nō." *Asian Theatre Journal* 1, no. 2 (Fall):207–16.

Bethe, Monica, and Karen Brazell
1982 *Dance in the Nō Theater: Vol. III, Dance Patterns.* Ithaca, NY: Cornell China-Japan Program.

Bethune, Robert William
1985 "The Effect of *Kabuki* Training on the Western Performances of Western Acting Students." PhD dissertation, University of Hawaii.

Bharata-Muni
1961 [c200 BCE] *The Nāṭyaśāstra: A Treatise on Hindu Dramaturgy and Histrionics,* Vol. II. Translated by Manomohan Ghosh. Calcutta: Asiatic Society.

Bowers, Faubion
1959 [1952] *Japanese Theatre.* New York: Hill and Wang.
1960 [1956] *Theatre in the East.* New York: Grove Press.

Brandon, James R.
1972 *Traditional Asian Plays.* New York: Hill and Wang.
1978a "Form in Kabuki Acting." In *Studies in Kabuki: Its Acting, Music, and Historical Context,* by James R. Brandon, William P. Malm, and Donald H. Shively, 63–132. Honolulu: University Press of Hawaii/East-West Center.
1978b "Training at the Waseda Little Theatre." *The Drama Review* 22, no. 4 (T80):29–42.
1981 "Kabuki in English: Toward Authenticity." In *Japanese Tradition: Search and Research,* edited by Judith Mitoma Susilo, 73–91. Los Angeles: College of Fine Arts, University of California at Los Angeles.
1982 "The Theft of *Chūshingura:* or The Great Kabuki Caper." In *Chūshingura: Studies in Kabuki and the Puppet Theatre,* edited by James R. Brandon, 111–46. Honolulu: University of Hawaii Press.
1988 "On *Little Hanako.*" *Asian Theatre Journal* 5, no. 1 (Spring):92–100.

Brecht, Bertolt
1964 "Alienation Effects in Chinese Acting." In *Brecht on Theatre: The Development of an Aesthetic,* edited and translated by John Willett, 91–99. New York: Hill and Wang.

Bruehl, William J.
1968 "A Survey: African and Asian Theatre Studies." *The Drama Review* 13, no. 2 (T42):175–77.

Craig, Gordon
1918a "Asia America Europe." *The Mask* 8, no. 8 (September):31–32.
1918b "Review of Sheldon Cheney's *The Art Theatre.*" *The Mask* 8 (no. 1):31–32.

Eisenstein, Sergei
1963 *Film Form: The Film Sense.* Edited and translated by Jay Leyda. New York: Meridian.

Ernst, Earle
1974 [1956] *The Kabuki Theatre.* Honolulu: University of Hawaii Press.

Felperin, Howard
1985 *Beyond Deconstruction: The Uses and Abuses of Literary Theory.* London: Oxford University Press.

Féral, Josette
1982 "Performance and Theatricality: The Subject Demystified." *Modern Drama* 25, no. 1 (March):170–81.

Foley, Kathy
1988 "Hanako and the European Imagination." *Asian Theatre Journal* 5, no. 1 (Spring):76–85.

Gillespie, John K.
1983 "The Impact of Noh on Paul Claudel's Style of Playwriting." *Theatre Journal* 35, no. 1 (March):58–73.

Grotowski, Jerzy
1968 *Towards a Poor Theatre.* New York: Simon and Schuster.

Hatch, Emily Gilchriest
1934 "The Kathakali: The Indigenous Drama of Malabar." PhD dissertation, Cornell University.

Jacquot, Jean
1961 "Craig, Yeats et le théâtre d'orient." In *Les théâtres d'Asia,* edited by Jean Jacquot, 271–83. Paris: Centre National de la Recherche Scientifique.

Kincaid, Zoe
1977 [1925] *Kabuki, the Popular Stage of Japan.* New York: Arno Press.

Kipling, Rudyard
1956 "The Ballad of East and West." In *Kipling,* Vol. II, edited by John Beecroft, 425. Garden City, NY: Doubleday.

Kunio, Komparu
1983 *The Noh Theater: Principles and Perspectives.* Tokyo: Weatherhill/Tankosha.

Leiter, Samuel L.
1967 "The Frozen Moment: A Kabuki Technique." *Drama Survey* 6, no. 1 (Summer):74–80.
1979 *The Art of Kabuki.* Berkeley: University of California Press.

Long, Roger
1982 *Javanese Shadow Theatre: Movement and Characterization in Ngayogyakarta Wayang Kulit.* Ann Arbor, MI: UMI Research Press.

Oshima, Mark
1987 Personal conversation. Tokyo, 19 December.

Péri, Noël
1921 *Cinq Nō.* Paris: Bossard.

Pound, Ezra, and Ernest Fenollosa
1959 [1917] *Noh or Accomplishment.* New York: New Directions.

Pronko, Leonard C.
1967 *Theater East and West.* Berkeley: University of California Press.
1971 "Learning Kabuki: The Training Program of the National Theatre of Japan." *Educational Theatre Journal* 23, no. 4 (December):409–30.

Quamber, Akhtar
1974 *Yeats and the Noh.* New York: Weatherhill.

Rabkin, Gerald
1983 "The Play of Misreading: Text/Theatre/Deconstruction." *Performing Arts Journal* 7, no. 1 (PAJ 19):44–60.

Said, Edward W.
1978 *Orientalism*. New York: Pantheon.

Savarese, Nicola
1988 "A Portrait of Hanako." *Asian Theatre Journal* 5, no. 1 (Spring):63–75.

Schechner, Richard
1985 "Performer Training Interculturally." In *Between Theater and Anthropology*, 213–60. Philadelphia: University of Pennsylvania Press.

Scott, A.C.
1956 "Students of the Pear Garden: Some Notes on the Training of the Peking Actors During the Last Hundred Years." *Journal of Oriental Studies* 3:69–74.
1966 [1955] *The Kabuki Theatre of Japan*. New York: Collier Books.
1978 [1957] *The Classical Theatre of China*. Westport, CT: Greenwood Press.

Snow, Stephen
1986 "Intercultural Performance: The Balinese-American Model." *Asian Theatre Journal* 3, no. 2 (Fall):204–32.

Suzuki Tadashi
1986 *The Way of Acting: The Writings of Tadashi Suzuki*. Translated by J. Thomas Rimer. New York: Theatre Communications Group.

Vatsyayan, Kapila
1968 *Classical Indian Dance in Literature and the Arts*. New Delhi: Sangeet Natak Akademi.

Yupho, Dhanit
1952 *Classical Siamese Theatre*. Bangkok: Hatha Dhip.

Zarrilli, Phillip B.
1984a *The Kathakali Complex: Actor, Performance and Structure*. New Delhi: Abhinav.
1984b " 'Doing the Exercise': The In-body Transmission of Performance Knowledge in a Traditional Martial Art." *Asian Theatre Journal* 1, no. 2 (Fall):191–206.
1986 "The Aftermath: When Peter Brook Came to India." *The Drama Review* 30, no. 1 (T109):92–99.

Zeami, Motokiyo
1984 *On the Art of the Nō Drama: The Major Treatises of Zeami*. Translated by J. Thomas Rimer and Yamasaki Masakazu. Princeton, NJ: Princeton University Press.

de Zoete, Beryl, and Walter Spies
1938 *Dance and Drama in Bali*. London: Faber & Faber, Ltd.

***James R. Brandon,** Professor, Department of Drama and Theatre, University of Hawaii, has translated and directed 13 kabuki and other Asian plays. Among his books are* Chūshingura: Studies in Kabuki and the Puppet Theatre *(1982),* Kabuki: Five Classic Plays *(1976),* On Thrones of Gold: Three Javanese Shadow Plays *(1971), and* Theatre in Southeast Asia *(1967). He is the founding editor of* Asian Theatre Journal. *During 1988–89 he is codirecting a "Nō and Kyōgen Performance Project" at the University of Hawaii.*

Planetary Dance

Anna Halprin

Because the world is round, it is always sunrise somewhere and sunset somewhere else, always noon and also the middle of the night. When my phone rang on 17 April 1987 it was midday in California. I was about to leave for the final rehearsal of *Circle the Earth,* a two-day dance ritual which was to culminate at sunrise on the 19th with our participation in a planetary dance.

It was Amanda Levey calling from New Zealand and she sounded very excited. "We have just done it. We danced the *Earth Run* at sunset. I think we have started the worldwide dance!" On the other side of the planet it was April 18th and night. And while we were still rehearsing our turn of *Circle the Earth,* the dance had already begun.

When I arrived at rehearsal and told the performers of Levey's call there was stunned silence, some quiet tears, a sense of awe, and then a spontaneous celebration. The *Planetary Dance* was moving in a wave around the globe, going west with the sun while the news had reached us coming east by the telephone. In these split seconds of joy we understood that the world was indeed round and also connected, each part to the other. Inspired, we went on with the rehearsal, preparing for our part in the ritual.

I felt especially fired inside. I had been rehearsing and preparing for this kind of dance for over 60 years but only seemed to be realizing it now. A dance that mattered, a dance that could contribute to the quality of life; a dance of power.

I have always called myself a dancer and called my work dance because that was my own training and history and, if you really look into it, also the history of dance. Dance has a magical and transforming power. Some cultures understand this; so do some people in cultures that don't. But I have found the dance world in the U.S. sadly ignorant, even disdainful, of this power. The head of a dance department at a major university once told me that I had set dance back 100 years. I am sure he meant it as an insult but I found it flattering. The Western notion of "progress," of "later is more developed than earlier," is barely tolerable in science, and completely out of place in art.

So many artists seem to think that the whole history of their art form leads up to them . . . never down. It doesn't seem to occur to most that their particular discipline may, like violin making, be in a state of decline. You cannot rank artistic form or experience by carbon-dating them. Sometimes important practices are ignored or forgotten, carried on only by remnant groups which may be viewed as backward or cultist. Often,

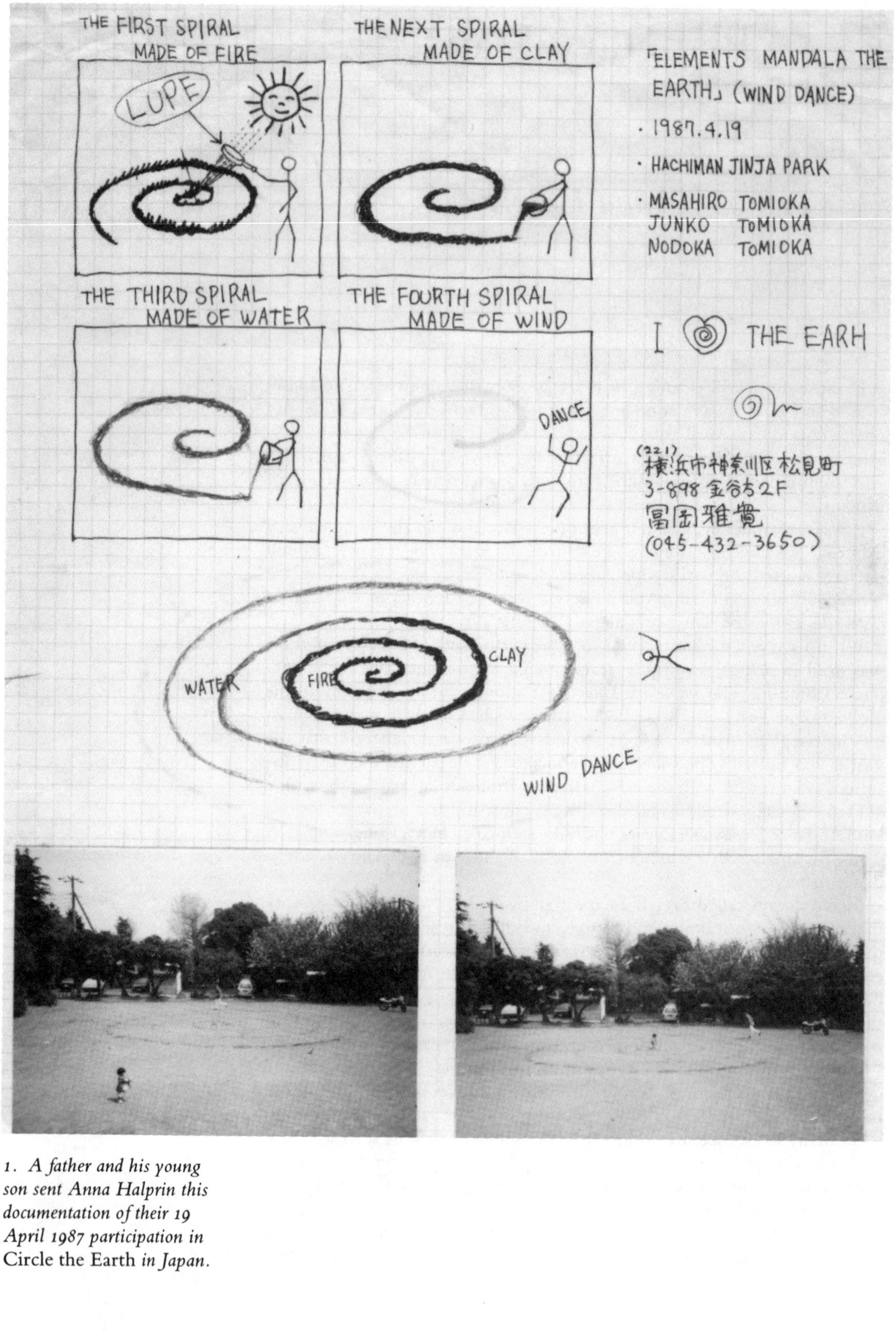

1. A father and his young son sent Anna Halprin this documentation of their 19 April 1987 participation in Circle the Earth *in Japan.*

things have to be rediscovered. Once you begin to view time in a cyclic instead of a linear way, you understand that kindred artistic visions and spirits exist discontinuously. There is no logical and orderly development.

The all-too-common practice of identifying what you are doing by its place in some nonexistent, smooth time-continuum creates false categories and false understandings of interrelationships. I began as a "modern" dancer. But how long can anything keep calling itself modern, or post-modern?

Books on the "history of modern dance" sometimes lay out an elaborately constructed family tree based on who came before and who came after and who studied what technique with whom. As firmly entrenched as I sometimes am in these modern dance histories, my fall off the family tree took no more than a small breeze. All I had to do was create a dance (*Apt. 6, 1965*) in which the performers wore shoes (horrors!) . . . and not even ballet slippers or jazz shoes, or bare feet, but high heels! I had not realized that being barefoot was already such a sacrosanct tradition. Suddenly I was no longer modern. And soon, not even to be considered any longer a dancer.

2. In 1965 dancers wore shoes ("horrors!") for Halprin's Apt. 6. *Here, John Graham and A.A. Leah enact their relationship using a radio as a prop. (Photo by Warner Jepson)*

When an artist begins to work outside the officially recognized context of her discipline, the established artistic community will often ignore her. If this doesn't work (because the artist is either persistent or good, or both) she may be called "avant-garde," meaning that she is ahead of the times or so far behind that she seems to be ahead (which is what happens when things move in circles).

The dance community in the '60s was too conservative to have an official avant-garde; the theatre world, however, was not. So my work began to be thought of as theatre and my strongest artistic rapport was with theatre people like Jerzy Grotowski, Lee Breuer and Ruth Maleczech, Julian Beck and Judith Malina, Richard Schechner, San Francisco's Actors' Workshop, and the San Francisco Playhouse on Hyde Street. In the '60s much of the work I did was innocently avant-garde, which is to say that it was controversial, but I was not always certain why. At times there was enormous hostility from audiences.

In Italy they threw things at us, but asked us to come back (*Four Legged Stool,* 1962). They said they had never had such a gorgeous scandal. Everywhere the San Francisco Dancers' Workshop went something violent would happen: shoes were thrown at us; spectators screamed and shouted; we were arrested in New York City because we undressed on stage (*Parades & Changes,* 1965); an audience member broke a glass lantern

3. The audience performs scores in Mutual Creations *(1967) at the Dancers' Workshop Studio-Theatre, San Francisco. (Photo by Bob Machover)*

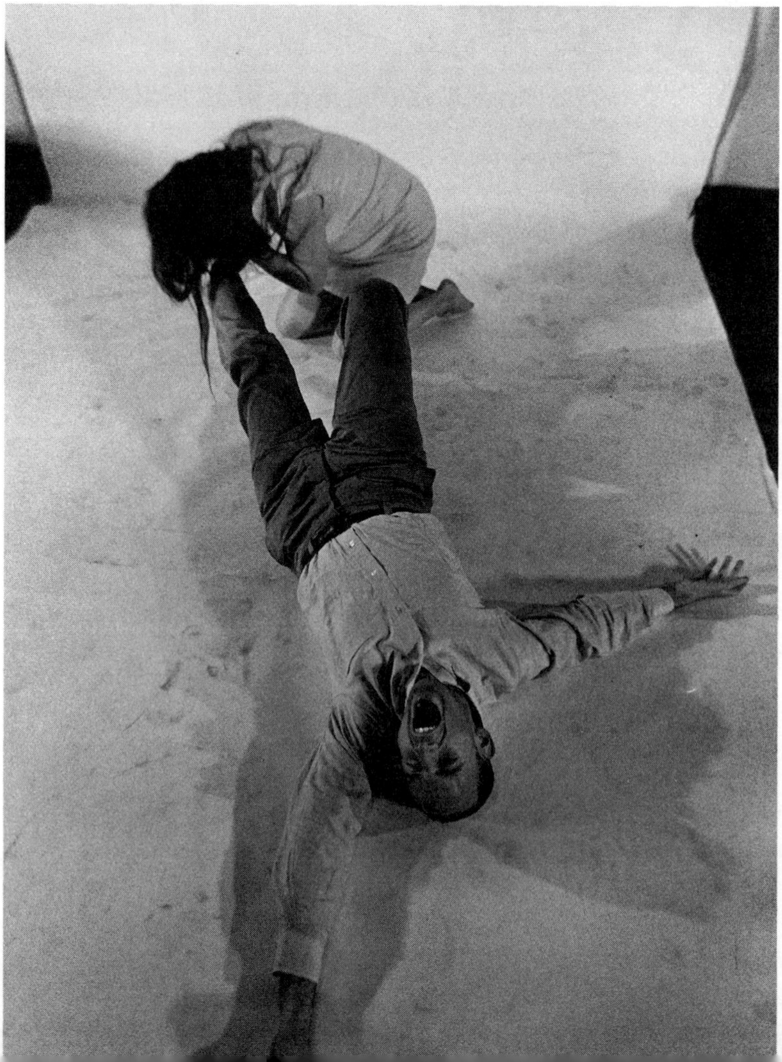

4. *In a 1973 Cleveland College workshop the audience performs* Trance Dance *(1971–1973). (Photo courtesy of Anna Halprin)*

on stage and drew blood from a performer (*Parades & Changes,* 1966, U.C. Berkeley).

I was concerned that we had some kind of power that stirred people up. If we could generate this kind of magical power in dance, how should we use it? This power came from within the dance and also from that space between the spectators and the performers. The power was not contained and, in fact, could not be contained within the confines of a stage that was separated from the spectators. Not only could it arise from the whole of life and affect the whole of life, it was most powerful when it did so.

So we were tapping into some source, but did we really know what to do with the connection once we made it? I don't think so. The resulting hostility and confrontation with audiences, although exciting, often fun, and sometimes dangerous, was not what I wanted.

I wanted to know what else we could channel the power toward and how to channel it. So when the riotous atmosphere of the '60s calmed down, we continued a steady exploration based on those two questions. For several years I made no distinction between audience and performers. I preferred designing structures for all kinds of people who would become performers. These structures, or scores as we later call them, explored notions about a group mind, male and female separations and rejoinings, environmental influences, ritualistic initiations, interpersonal relations, and others. Some structures were improvisational while others were formal.

As a result of these explorations, my work was linked with the social sciences; I was interested in using creative processes to achieve concrete social changes. What follows is a summary chronology of some of those works [the place listed is the location of the first performance]:

Mutual Creations (1967)
Ten myths with scores designed for large group audiences to perform. Intention: to explore archetypal themes with nondancers and to reverse audience/performer roles. Performed at Dancers' Workshop Studio-Theatre, San Francisco.

Ceremony of Us (1968)
A dance developed between a group of blacks from Studio Watts in Los Angeles and a group of whites from the San Francisco Dancers' Workshop. Intention: to use the real-life issue of racial conflict and to use dance as a vehicle for change. Performed at the Mark Taper Forum, Los Angeles.

Animal Ritual (1971)
Intention: to create a new dance based on the stylistic diversity of the multi-ethnic performers. Performed at the American Dance Festival, New London, Connecticut.

Trance Dances (1971–73)
Intention: to have large groups explore group mind and archetypal movement with no separation between audience and performer. Performed at Dancers' Workshop Studio-Theatre, San Francisco.

Initiations and Transformations (1971)
Animal Ritual recycled with *Trance Dance* as a closure. Audience and performers joined. Performed at New York City Center.

New Time Shuffle (1972)
A multi-ethnic musical drama for prisons. Intention: to interact with prisoners to lessen racial tensions. Performed in Soledad Prison, Southern California.

City Dance (1976, 1977, 1978)
Intention: to unify performance, environment, and people to achieve a sense of "community." Performed once each year in diverse neighborhood streets of San Francisco.

The chief intention of these works was to understand how the process of creation and performance could be used to accomplish concrete results: social change, personal growth, physical alignment, and spiritual attunement. This necessarily involved studying the relationships between audience and performers, between a person's life issues and the performance content, between performance skills and life skills. In other words, developing an integrated life/art process.

While in the middle of this, in 1972, I got cancer. For ten years I withdrew from public performance. I didn't stop working, but the work became internally oriented. This was only natural: I was working to regain my life and using the work process in my own healing.

During this time, whatever remained of my classical, external aesthetics were of little concern. How a dance looked or how it might be received by an audience was not on my mind. More important was how it felt to the performers and how they were able to use the experience of its creation and

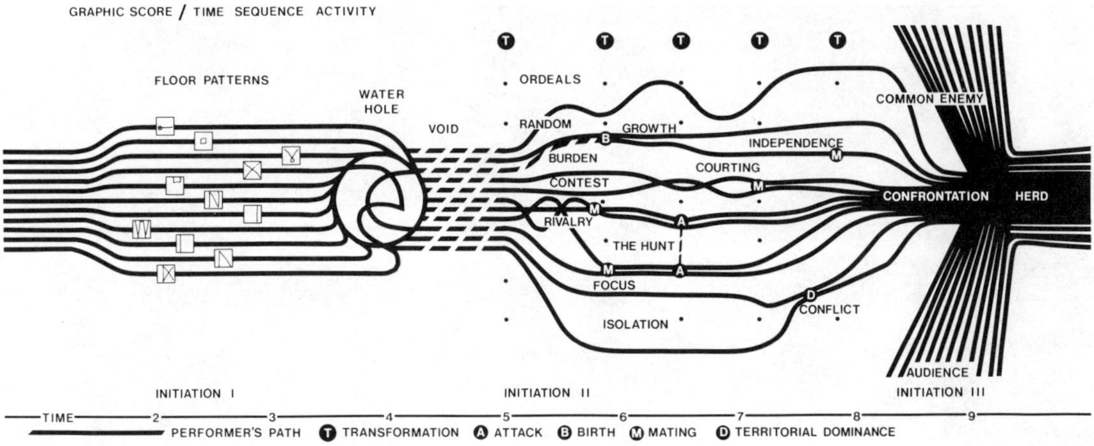

5. *The score for* Animal Ritual *performed at the 1971 American Dance Festival in New London, Connecticut. (Graphics by John Muto)*

performance in furthering their own personal, artistic, and communal growth.

When I gradually began to return to public works I had different interests. First, I wanted to create dances that would influence change. I wanted to apply what I had learned about healing myself to other people and to whole communities. From 1972 to 1986 I explored this idea with an intimate group in a training program. Secondly, I had a strong interest in working with the general public, with large numbers of people who were untrained in dance or any type of performance. I had an opportunity to do just that in a series of community dance classes I led. Each session was attended by 60 to 100 people.

In these large group dances I noticed an exceptional phenomenon occurring time and time again. When enough people moved together in a common pulse with a common purpose, an amazing force, an ecstatic rhythm took over. People began to move as if they were parts of a single body, not in uniform motion, but in deeply interrelated ways. This recurrence of spatial and interrelated movement is no accident. It is an external version of the geometry and biology of our inner life—our bodies extended in space. In this sense, such movement is contained within us. People form circles. They make processions. Spirals. Entrances and exits. They orient themselves in space by using the four directions. They create a central axis. They move linearly in processions. In the same way we move from one to the many, from alone to couples, to family, to tribe—leading, following, blending.

In these archetypal movements people seemed to be tracing out the forms and patterns of a larger organism, communicating with and being moved by a group body-mind or spirit. This phenomenon of tapping into a deep collective force needs 50 to 100 people to break through individual limitations and even cultural preconditioning. The time it takes to generate such a dance depends on the diversity of the people, their purpose, and the guidance they are given. It can take as little as 30 minutes to all day or night.

Had I discovered something new? Of course not! This large-scale group movement is an ancient phenomenon in dance. Cultures everywhere in the world have channeled the power of such a group spirit to help them bring rain, hunt, raise crops, and initiate the young. It is a power that can renew, inspire, teach, create, and heal. What was exciting was that we were learn-

6. Initiations and Transformations *(1971) at New York City Center. (Photo by Raymond Macrino)*

ing how to generate this same tribal spirit and energy, this same sense of group ritual, with people whose culture contains little of such tradition in dance performances. We were learning how to return to performers and spectators power which in this culture had often been taken from them and placed in the hands of scientific experts and official artists.

The point has been raised that this collective power can be destructive, as it was for Hitler, Jim Jones, or any fanatical cult leader. I have gone to considerable lengths to develop a process that safeguards participants from this potential.

By virtue of making a score (scenario) visible, learning and evaluating it, and then modifying it with their own images, the performers become empowered as cocreators of the dance. In other words, the leader does not require obedience but rather creative involvement. Furthermore, it's crucial that the purpose of the score is clearly stated so that each performer can agree to the purpose and can determine whether the score realizes that purpose. If it doesn't, there is a mutual responsibility to recycle the score until its purpose is fulfilled.

More and more, in both workshops and public rituals, I encouraged people to work with their own lives as material, to use real-life issues so that the transforming power of dance would have the opportunity to effect real-life changes for them. On a personal level my experience in ridding myself of cancer showed me that it was possible to use the power of dance for a higher purpose, that we could channel the power to experience interconnection with a life force, and that this experience was nourishing and necessary—the right of all living beings, not just artists. This power could be channeled for healing, of our bodies, our psyches, our communities, and for the healing of the planet . . . for peace (see Halprin 1969).

It was in this context in 1980 that I began a project called *Search for Living Myths and Rituals through Dance and the Environment.* I didn't know then that it was going to last five years. It started as a community workshop in Marin County, California, led by my husband, Lawrence Halprin, and myself.

At this time a trailside killer had committed a series of brutal murders on nearby Mount Tamalpais, terrifying the community. In response to feelings of grief, rage, and impotence caused by the killings, the participants in the *Search for Living Myths* workshop decided to perform a dance to enact a positive myth—reclaiming the mountain. The dance, performed in 1981, was called *In and On the Mountain.*

This was not the kind of dance I had done in the past. The idea for it had emerged from the six workshops Larry and I had led during the year. In these workshops hundreds of people from the community had taken part—exploring the environment, moving together, sharing reactions to their experiences. They had drawn pictures of images that came to them, and what was amazing was that Mount Tamalpais kept reappearing. When we noticed this recurring image we knew we had found the myth we were searching for. It wasn't only that the trailside killer had terrified the people in the community—he had defiled, denied, threatened the very heart of our community. We could no longer walk the trails of our mountain—the mountain was off-limits. For the community the mountain became a symbol of our spiritual identity—our responses to the mountain individually and collectively became our story or myth—and how we would enact our myth would become our dance, our ritual.

Guided by the participants' shared experiences, a two-part ritual was created: The text below was the dedication used in the narration at the beginning of the dance. It was addressed particularly to the family and friends of the women who had been murdered on the mountain.

7. Soledad Prison's New Time Shuffle *(1972). (Photo by Barbara Renan)*

For the spirit of the mountain, we dance
For those who consider her a Holy Place
For the Miwoks who lived beneath her
Who gathered her herbs
and sang her songs, we dance
And quietly we dance
for those who were among us and who lost
their lives on her trails
Quietly we dance for them.
For the trails that lead us
back to the mountain
and life, we dance.

—*Jim Cave*

In and On the Mountain took place in the theatre at the College of Marin, overlooked by Mount Tamalpais. The theatre became the symbolic cave, like a native American kiva.[1] The dancers invoked the spirit of the mountain and enacted the killings. The urgency and the realness was intense. Friends and family of the women who had been murdered were in the audience. Someone called the police because they imagined the killer was present. During the night after the performance a series of ceremonies and events took place in preparation for the second part—*On the Mountain*. The next day witnesses and performers went to the mountain peak and walked down the trails where the killings had taken place. For the first time in two years a group of people returned to the mountain and reclaimed it.

A few days after the ritual, the police received an anonymous phone tip and the killer was captured.

Often people get upset when I tell this story because they get caught up in "cause and effect" or "who gets credit/blame for what." Am I really saying that the ritual caused the capture of the killer? If I say yes, then the discussion immediately moves to the question of how. But it is of no use to quarrel about how the two events are related; it is important to understand that they *are* related. In one sense we performed a prayer and our prayer was answered. Why argue about the power of prayer? Rejoice and try prayer again. Which is exactly what we did.

And in any event, it seems to me that the real miracle was not the capture of the killer but what happened with the people who performed the ritual, what happened in the community. They found a meaningful myth, and reclaimed the mountain. That was their purpose. Catching the killer was an added bonus. The performers felt that they had taken an active part in bringing the terror to an end. They had transformed themselves from victims of violence to creators of peace. It was no less and no more than an act of magic.

Inspired by this, we continued to dance on the mountain each spring for five years, not just for peace on the mountain but in the world. *In and On the Mountain* (1981), *Return to the Mountain* (1982), *Run to the Mountain* (1984), *Circle the Mountain* (1985), and then *Circle the Earth* (1986, '87, '88). During those years many people came from other parts of the country and the world to participate. They returned home eager to share the experience with their own communities.

So the rituals began to "go on tour." Of course this was not a tour in the ordinary sense because there was no permanent company. What traveled from place to place was not the performers or even a particular performance, but the scores, the recipes for creating the rituals. In the beginning I was always present as a facilitator and I brought along some of the ceremonial objects which had been used in San Francisco as a kind of material continuity. After a while the rituals began to take on lives of their own. People wanted to take them back to their own communities. I began to receive letters and calls asking permission to do all or parts of *Circle the Earth*.

Out of this response grew the idea of the *Planetary Dance,* of uniting, on 19 April 1987, all the groups touched by *Circle the Earth*. This letter went out in 1987:

Dear Friend of Circle the Earth,

You are invited to help create a very special event this Spring: our first Planetary Dance of peace. On April 19, 1987 all the people and places that have touched Circle the Earth are invited to join in the world-wide performance of this special score. Hopefully, over 2,000 people in 25 countries around the world will participate in this event, gathering the family of Circle the Earth in the spirit of peace, unifying us in dance, prayer, and meditation.

THE SCORE:

We will be performing the Earth Run portion from Circle the Earth. In Marin, we will begin at sunrise at the foot of Mt. Tamalpais. You can join us by performing the Earth Run in your own community at any time between sunrise and sunset on April 19th—the time of Easter, Passover, and especially Spring, the time of renewal and hope. The Earth Run has been called a moving mandala of peace. Since the time of performance will vary from place to place, our Planetary Dance will "ripple" or "run" around the world with the passage of the sun.

A DANCE WITH VARIATIONS:

Although the performance will focus on the Earth Run, there is also ample room for you to create a unique event—one that will express the character and imagination of your culture. You can do this in two ways:

1) Frame the score (preparation and closure) in different ways—a ceremony, ritual, blessing, or dance pertaining to something special in your community or culture; a group of spiritual leaders of different backgrounds offering inspiration; processions, spontaneous group dances and singing, meditations, etc. Many groups are planning to do a preliminary workshop.

2) Change some of the resources used in the Earth Run score—within the score, we encourage you to explore narrations appropriate to your group or culture.

SHARING THE EVENT:

We would like as many groups as possible to photograph their performances. Document your community's participation in the Planetary Dance—slides, photographs, writings, graphic scores, valuactions, visualizations . . . any way you can think of. Send a copy of this documentation to us at Tamalpa and we will combine and edit them. This rich set of resources can also serve to stimulate growth for a world-wide awareness of dance as a powerful expression for people's visions for peace.

8. The City Dance *was performed once each year from 1976–78 in different San Francisco neighborhoods. (Photo by Buck O'Kelly)*

We know that for many people it may be difficult to organize a Peace Run. For this reason, we invite you to do the Peace Dance Meditation, either alone or with family and friends. In this way your participation will add to the power and magic of linking together with the Planet for Peace.

That's the basic idea. Your questions and ideas are important in shaping this event, so I eagerly await your response. I am very excited about our first Planetary Dance, excited about what we will create together and what we will learn about creating peace from each other. Please let me know how you and your friends or community can take part.

Yours,
Anna

We had very little sense of how many people and places would do it. So when Amanda Levey called from New Zealand, that was the first hint that it was happening on a global scale. Slowly, over the next few days, we began to receive phone calls, letters, and other materials from these "peacemakers around the world." Sometimes from people we had never heard of who had learned of the Planetary Dance from intermediaries. My letter became a kind of chain letter finding its way to unexpected places. After six months, we still received documents of these events. Some of the events were large, with hundreds of people; some were small and private, like the father and son in Japan who sent us a stunning graphic design of their dance.

I am still amazed at how easily it all happened, so easily that it is obvious that *Circle the Earth* and the *Planetary Dance* must in some way embody something already at work. We did not create the wave that moved around the globe on 19 April, we simply rode on it.

Is there not a growing vision in the world today? More than ever before, people all around are uniting to express their highest aspirations for life, and in the process learning that they have both the power and the responsibility to create a world without war, free of hunger, respectful of each other, of all life and of the environment. We have Live Aid, Hands Across America, a marathon run around the world, Instant Cooperation, and Harmonic Convergence.[2] This spontaneous and popular movement has its parallel in theatre and dance. Call it Global or Planetary Art.

What I find new and particularly challenging in this global art is its scale. That scale is largely unexplored. For now the biggest artistic problems seem to be the logistics of working over great distances. There isn't room for a lot of other considerations at the moment.

So we continue to work by the principles developed on a smaller scale, though we know that they will be transformed, even abandoned, once we come to understand the potentialities of the global scale. The scale is new, but newness of form does not mean that it is unconnected to the past. It is the latest—and not the last—stop for us on a continuous trail. The *Planetary Dance* was a natural outgrowth of *Circle the Earth*. There was nothing new about *Circle the Earth*, it was a natural outgrowth of *Search for Living Myths*. And *Search for Living Myths* was not new either, that was an outgrowth of societal art developed with our multiracial dances in the '70s. And that wasn't new either, that was an outgrowth of the '60s when we were busy breaking every boundary we could find to redefine our values and rediscover authenticity. And did we find new values or just rediscover old ones?

Of course art on a global scale is developing in many different directions and embodying many different values. The arts merchants of the world, who deliver symbols and images in much the same way and for the same kinds of profits that they manufacture and deliver other commodities, recognize that there is a global market. They visualize global art as a one-to-many configuration. The central source is also characterized by assumptions about superior creative abilities, technologically and culturally. This is just a large scale version of "artist-as-elitist."

The global art I am interested in developing does not take a one-to-many configuration. It has many sources or centers and no audience. It is completely interactive and difficult to characterize because there is no separate stage from which to view it and no neutral, cultural stance from which to criticize it. It may appear at times to be shaped as many-to-many; it may at moments take the form of many-as-one. It is a highly flexible form because

9. A bystander joins the City Dance *(1976, '77, '78) in a San Francisco neighborhood. (Photo by Buck O'Kelly)*

it is not sharply defined by cultural bias. In many respects it has the same shape as the nuclear nightmare: all will be involved and it will not be confined to a single moment in time or a single place. All our seeming differences will seem inconsequential in the face of our overwhelming commonalities.

So what's the next step in developing *Circle the Earth* as a global or planetary dance? Letting go of it. Re-creating it. Realizing that as exciting, inspiring, exhilarating as its many performances have been, it is still full of racial and cultural bias and necessarily so. It was created from a very specific, local concern and gradually enlarged in scope and intention. And there is certainly no single artist, nor any one community or culture that can alone redefine the score to make it fully work on a global scale. There is no one among us with that much vision. The vision must arise from the interaction of many different sources. A new score for *Circle the Earth* must

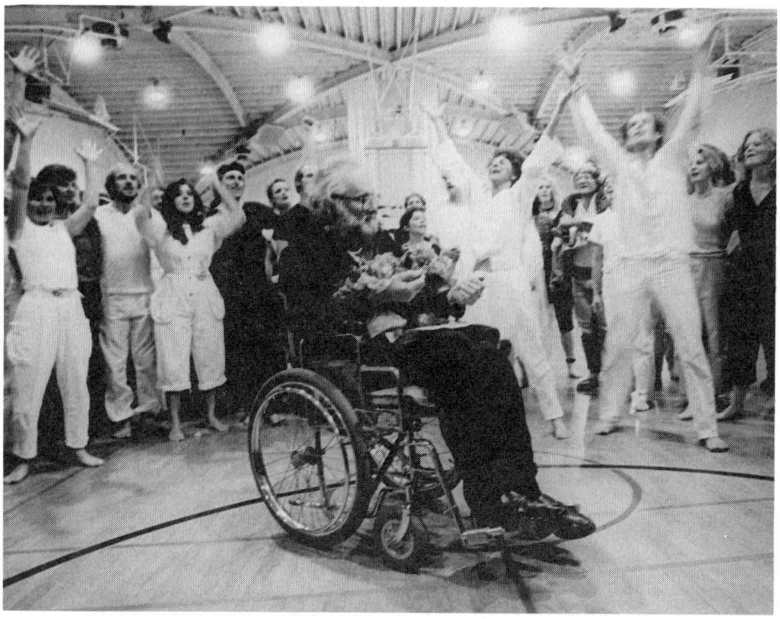

10. A witness coming through the "bridge and passages" during Circle the Earth *(1986) at Redwood High School in Marin County, California. (Photo by Paul Fusco)*

be collectively evaluated and re-created by diverse participation. And it probably won't and shouldn't even be called *Circle the Earth* anymore. Even the title implies traveling, going from one location to another, a separation of the planet and her many people. *Circle the Earth* was where the dance was going, the direction it took. Now it is the time for a new direction.

In 1987, 75 groups in 35 countries took part in the *Planetary Dance*. In 1988 there was more, and in new and unpredictable forms.[3] The global expansion of the score inspires a new vision: the creation of a world dance, a dance that transcends national boundaries and political machinations. This was to take the form of a U.S.–Soviet exchange in 1989. We had geared ourselves up for the exchange and had even done a preliminary trial-run with the *Earth Run* at the American–Soviet Peace Walk in November 1988. But midway in our plans we made a sudden shift. The following announcement was sent out:

> For eight years, *Circle the Earth* has danced for the well-being of the planet. During those same eight years, a shadow has fallen across all of our lives: the shadow of AIDS. Within this circle of health, peace, and trust which we want to embody, there has emerged a parallel circle of death and isolation, ignorance and fear. To survive this crisis, the first circle must be strengthened; the second circle, broken. This year we ask you to dance with those among us who are fighting for life, to support the commitment and honor the courage of your brothers and sisters who are challenging AIDS.

Now we are planning a global conference in the San Francisco Bay Area in 1990 to create the first dance of a planetary scope. People can take part by writing to me at Tamalpa Institute, P.O. Box 794, Kentfield, CA 94914. Three ways to take part:

1. Write for the *Earth Run* score.
2. Come join *Circle the Earth* either in Marin County (Spring 1990), Zurich (July 1989), or Sweden (*Planetary Dance*, July 1989).
3. Write for information about the conference in 1990.

The immense challenge of the global conference is to mutually create with a sense of maximizing our differences, honoring and respecting our unique cultural heritages, while also finding universal commonalities that connect us to all life. Participants will create a score for the dance which they will take back to their own local communities.

There is a discernible trend for people to bypass governments, cross over boundaries, and unify for the common good—for survival. *Circle the Earth* is my contribution to that process.

Art and dance can take a lead. It is necessary for art to express visions that political systems resist. In a world where war has become a national science, peacemaking must become a community art, and even more importantly, a planetary art in the deepest sense of the word: An exemplification of our ability to cooperate in creation, an expression of our best collective aspirations, and a powerful act of magic.

References

Halprin, Lawrence

1969 *The RSVP Cycles: Creative Processes in the Human Environment*. New York: George Braziller, Inc.

Notes

1. A native American ceremonial structure that is usually round and partially underground.
2. These were all large-scale popular events initiated by a variety of people with the purpose of mobilizing people around the world to speak out about peace in a nonpolitical manner.
3. In 1988 *Circle the Earth* moved the entire nine-day workshop/performance to an outdoor site in the Marin Headlands, across the Golden Gate Bridge from San Francisco. The environment offered a variety of settings: sand, ocean, fields, forests, cliffs, sun, sky, fog, as well as the cement ruins of a military barracks. Sixty people camped out at this site, becoming totally integrated with the environment. The theme of *Circle the Earth* was a dance of our peaceful nature. We had a serious drought in 1988, and it seemed appropriate to connect directly with the earth. In our 1988 announcement we wrote:

> When we imagine ourselves separate from nature, we lose our balance, if we think ourselves opposed to her, we find the earth to be a wild, uncertain, and unfriendly place. Only technology offers us protection. If we think ourselves exiled from nature, we see her romantically, utopian, fragile, and benevolent. Only the abandonment of technology can redeem and return us to the garden.
>
> But is the earth either adversary or paradise lost? To recover our balance, to honor our connection with nature, we must create a vision appropriate to our awesome technological capacities and yet capable of sustaining a reverence to our good green earth.

Anna Halprin

A Life in Ritual

An Interview by Richard Schechner

SCHECHNER: Why do you feel more comfortable in the theatre world than the dance world?

HALPRIN: The theatre world is more inclusive than dance in Western culture. Particularly when it comes to using movement connected to feelings. In the dance world the reaction I often get is that "this is therapy, not dance." I've never found this prejudice in the theatre world. I search for real-life-as-art. I want the personalized self-body to become the metaphor for the big collective body. I don't like the way ballet, modern, or even postmodern dance armors the body personality by abstracting feelings, content, and physical movement. It becomes formalized art, feels distant from life, and doesn't involve me. I can be momentarily entertained, excited, even elevated like anyone else that goes to dance performances, but it doesn't last.

I often visit the Native American Pomo Roundhouse. The Roundhouse is partially underground—the entrance is a narrow passage that opens up into a round space with a dirt floor, an open fire, an opening in the roof for the sky to enter and the smoke to leave, a center pole, and a rhythmically pounded drum made from a log over a resonating hole in the ground. It's a mystical theatre. The people dance their prayers, their stories, their healings, and their dreams. They joke and feast, the young and old. Some dances outsiders can join; other dances are only for the initiated. When Loren Smith, a Pomo Healer, comes to *Circle the Earth* he understands what is happening, even though it's nothing like his dances, and he is a great critic. He knows when the power is present, when it isn't, and why. I'm comfortable, at home so to speak, with this kind of "theatre" as well. What interests me is how completely interwoven the many threads of cultural life are—social, political, spiritual, and aesthetic. It's more than just dance.

SCHECHNER: What is it that puts you where you are?

HALPRIN: Everything that has happened to me in my life puts me where I am. My interest in social issues may very well come from my background as a Jew. Particularly since my impressionable years of growing up were during the time the Nazis ruled most of Europe. Or my enchantment with my grandfather—my first dance experience was seeing him pray when I was four years old. He was a Hassidic Jew who would pray by singing, jumping up and down, and flinging his arms in the air. He had a long white beard and I thought he was GOD, and that GOD was a dancer. To this day, I still have vivid memories of his religious ecstatic dancing.

Fritz Perls, pioneer gestalt therapist, was interested in theatre and my whole company worked with him. He would often conduct sessions around the pieces we were doing. He made a tremendous impact on me and broke the barriers between the "artist" and the "person." He showed me ways to humanize, if you will, the artist and art. My dance professor at the University of Wisconsin was Margaret H'Doubler. She was originally a biologist and taught dance objectively from a scientific perspective. That was a wonderful eye opener. I could learn an approach to movement based on the nature of movement and its inner operation. This released me from learning a set vocabulary of movements based on imitation or copying my teacher. Instead, to the degree movement was objectified, I could subjectify, creating my own movement experience according to my own expressive mind. From her teachings I think I got a real strong foundation on how to generate creativity. She instilled in me a passion for true movement, and a fierce dedication to dance that people can do in their own way.

My husband, Lawrence Halprin, an environmental architect, has impacted on me in so many ways I have lost track of our mutual boundaries. But certainly one area is an appreciation of the environment. Raising a family in the country kept me well-grounded, and led me to teaching children for years, and eventually brought me into community interaction. My battle with cancer has been an ever present lesson in my life. And this has been reinforced by the work I'm currently engaged in with people challenging AIDS. Someone summed it up with the expression: "Enlightenment—at gunpoint."

SCHECHNER: What makes you angry when people freeze you in a historical box? How do you feel?

HALPRIN: It has taken me a long time to find my place, my location in the arts, in dance, in theatre. It has been a long journey. I get angry when people take one or another episode in my journey and use that episode to locate me. It prevents them from experiencing the work that I am doing now. They want me to keep doing what I was doing then. Sometimes they get angry and feel betrayed. Sometimes they try to interpret what I am doing now as if it were what I was doing then, only worse. I want them to understand where I am now and to engage me in a healthy challenging dialog.

SCHECHNER: I want to know who in the performance world and outside the performance world you feel close to. I don't want to embarrass you and have you tell me who your enemies are but who your friends are. Not your personal friends so much as the people whose work you admire.

HALPRIN: When I was in New York City in June 1988, the International Arts Festival was going on. I saw several pieces that intrigued me. Among them were two that I'll mention: Martha Clarke's *Miracolo d' Amore* and the Gardzienice Theatre Association's *Avvakum* and *Gathering* [see TDR 31, no. 1 (T113)]. In Clarke's dance I liked the exquisite, lyrical, sensuous beauty of the images contrasted by the horror of the content; the skills of the performers in integrating movement, voice, imagery, in highly creative ways. I tolerated the proscenium arch but would have preferred the performance to take place in the plaza in Venice. Uptown at St. John the Divine, in one of the small chapels, the Polish group Gardzienice was performing. I felt the rage and intensity of Poland in political crisis in their bold, violent, gross, crude, and raw power. The women took the same physical risks as the men. Certainly the opposite of a ballerina who depends on men to support her. The women not only supported themselves but asserted themselves as they took giant attacking steps, like warriors, across the floor.

As I felt a strong female quality in Clarke's piece, I admired the powerful masculine thrust of the Polish piece. The men in Clarke's work were able to express femaleness just as the Polish women expressed maleness. This yin and yang is important to me. I want to see that balance and the ability to embody both male and female.

Just this past July at Redwood High in Marin County, California, Joseph Chaikin did a 30-minute monolog called *The War in Heaven* that he and Sam Shepard wrote. He performed this piece after his crippling stroke which affected his vocal chords so that his speech must be formed very consciously. The piece was profound in itself but the eloquence, courage, and nobility of Chaikin's performance was inspiring—to see him use his illness as a teacher was a truly spiritual experience.

I read about Robert Wilson featuring a deaf and dumb boy in one of his pieces and I recall attending a rehearsal of his and being so pleased that he was incorporating a very large heavy-set woman in his dance. I was im-

1. During a workshop-rehearsal of Circle the Earth *(1986) participants confront their fears of death and destruction as part of this dance in the spirit of peace. (Photo by Paul Fusco)*

pressed that he showed no stereotypical, cliché attitudes about what a dancer's body should look like.

I missed Peter Brook's *Mahabharata* but I like the idea that he has a company of performers from many different cultures because I think this is a challenging concept, attempting to maintain cultural identity while moving toward some kind of universality. I identify with Jerzy Grotowski and Eugenio Barba because I believe they too are continuing to explore new ways to create a living theatre—one connected to real life in a cultural context.

I like the idea that Liz Lerman has a dance company of elders and that they go to schools performing for children. That kind of diversity is a wonderful social statement of respect. Suzanne Lacy's work sounds great—I like her social, visual, and environmental connections [see TDR 32, no. 1 (T117)]. I feel deeply connected and have a sense of reverence for nature when I view the dances of Eiko and Koma. I admire their adherence to what is true for them in their Japanese culture. It's important to me that dancers be true to their culture, whatever that may be. When I had our multiracial company with Asian, Chicano, Latino, black, white and native Americans creating and performing together, the conflicts and creative resolutions we encountered came from a place of cultural diversity. It was incredibly exciting. The excitement led to unexpected new forms.

SCHECHNER: Say a young person of 18 comes to you and says, "What should I do with my life?" and they won't take "I don't know" as a response. What response would you give them?

HALPRIN: What a huge question! My response would be: Go on a vision quest in the wilderness. Stay there alone until an answer comes. If the answer is to dance, then find a way to dance that is purposeful. If you choose dance in your life, then make sure your life is integrated into your dance. Go other places and witness the great ceremonial dances of India, Bali, Africa, or, closer to home, American Indians, and get a broad perspective. Then find a teacher or teachers who inspire you. Don't forget that you are being nurtured from life itself and, if that is cut off, ultimately what's left is just a flashy technique, usually imitative of someone else's idiosyncratic style.

SCHECHNER: Which dancers are you talking about?

HALPRIN: I really don't like any way of training the body that is based on some preconceived stylization.

SCHECHNER: But where do you see that? Do you see that, for example, in Martha Graham's technique?

HALPRIN: Yes. The movement was real when Martha Graham, Doris Humphrey, Charles Weidman, and Hanya Holm revolted against ballet and the Denishawn, and developed another style. It was a major breakthrough. But because it was based on their personalities, it was subjective and idiosyncratic. Their followers imitated them and soon we had companies of look-alikes. When the next generation of modern dancers began to imitate them and blend ballet into their technique it became slick and glitzy, losing all the original intention. Now we have postmodern, the newest fashion. Dance styles are like skirts that go up and down.

Imitating someone else's personal style produces an army of clones. This offends me—it offends my fierce loyalty to the uniqueness of the individual. Even those I consider the very best of our dance artists today—some who have made a major contribution and who, by the way, happen to be good personal friends, are examples. They have evolved a beautiful personal style—like Merce Cunningham, Trisha Brown, Steve Paxton, etc.—but their companies are full of look-alikes.

I prefer to have people told *what* to do but not *how* to do it. Certainly there are many ways to find our commonalities and to explore the basic principles of movement. I feel very encouraged that so many dancers are now turning to the work of Bonnie Cohn, Moshe Feldenkrais, Mabel Todd, and others who approach movement from the point of view of origin, evolution, and structural integration.

SCHECHNER: I'd like you to deal with what I think are some difficulties with your work. One difficulty is the gap between the actual experience of doing your work and how that feels for the performer in contrast to how viewing your work feels for the spectator.

HALPRIN: I don't want spectators. Spectators imply a spectacle that takes place to entertain and amuse and perhaps stimulate them. I want witnesses who realize that we are dancing for a purpose—to accomplish something in ourselves and in the world. We are performing our best attempts to create authentic contemporary theatre rituals.

The role of the witness is to understand the dance and support the dancers who have undertaken the challenge of performing. Spectators often come with their own personal aesthetics. They sit back and watch and judge to see if what is done lives up to their preconceived notion of a particular, very culture-bound idea of a certain kind of "art."

If they have a hard time with my work it is because they don't belong. They don't know what they are supposed to do. They tend to get confused and embarrassed. I deal with this by doing my best to tell people what we are trying to accomplish and how they can help—what role we want them to perform. We have clear standards, clear values, but they are the values of a community engaging with an idea, seeking to accomplish something. Playing the role of witness in this kind of ritual is deeply engaging but very different from being a spectator.

In the end I just have to tell people what I'm up to and what I want, and hope for the best.

SCHECHNER: Another difficulty is trying to create an efficacious act, a dance that really makes rain, saves the world, or catches a murderer.

HALPRIN: I don't really know whether dancing produces results per se, but I'm willing to find out. It brings out awareness and focuses us on issues of human need and concern, that much I do know.

SCHECHNER: Well, that's not the way it sounds. You talk about the capture of the Tamalpais killer. You say, in effect, "Look, it worked for my cancer, it worked for Tamalpais, and it will work for the world." I have no problem with you believing that—but do you? You seem to waffle on this question of efficacy.

HALPRIN: What I care about is that a group of people focus on something of mutual concern—on the effort.

SCHECHNER: Is that "mutual concern" a shared belief that dancing is a ritual act that can do something? When a group of business people get together it's not just a "mutual concern" that they can make money but they believe certain actions will make money. If they make money they're happy—if they don't, they're fired. I really want you to face this head on.

2. *Witnesses don masks to protect themselves from the demonic dances of fear and destruction during* Circle the Earth *(1986). (Photo by Paul Fusco)*

HALPRIN: I don't know whether dancing will work or won't. Maybe it will—and in this threatening world it's worth a try!

SCHECHNER: But I want to know when you ask people to come together, is it in order to enjoy dancing, making dances, or is it to "change the world"?

HALPRIN: I don't know the answer to this question yet. We are engaged in an experiment and we are by no means finished with it.

There is a very basic principle that underlies traditional rituals. The people enact in the ritual what they want to have happen in their lives. This principle has been around for a lot longer than our more recent notions of how to make things happen.

I'm just going back to this hypothesis and testing it out again, only with contemporary rituals. This is almost a scientific perspective and so I feel very reinforced by what has happened.

If a collection of communities dances together in a planetary dance all around the world—releasing their fear of war and enacting their desire for peace—and then if all these people agree to take specific actions for peace in their own lives and in the life of their community, this is pretty likely to help and not likely to be harmful.

And who knows, it may even turn out that there is some truth to the belief of traditional cultures that an unseen—energy—dimension does play a role in causing—or at least clearing the way for—manifestation in the physical dimension, and that ritual dance is a way to make an energy pathway to guide physical reality. That certainly would offer an explanation for how dance could help capture "the killer on the mountain" and cure cancer.

If this were even partially true, it would become even more significant and important for us to keep up this ritual of dancing for peace and for healing.

SCHECHNER: I'm asking you to go one step beyond that. Look into your heart, and answer: If you found out it wouldn't change things, would you stop dancing?

HALPRIN: No, because whether it rains or not isn't the purpose.

SCHECHNER: What is the purpose?

HALPRIN: For me, dancing can be a prayer. Would the Hopis stop doing the Snake Dance every August if it didn't rain? They would do it again next year. Do we stop praying if our prayers aren't answered, or do we pray again?

Efficacy in this sense is not cause and effect. The purpose is to awaken people to peace and move them to action—to concrete peaceful actions in their lives. For *Circle the Earth* there is a score designed for performers and witnesses alike to do the next day as a closure—*Peace Bird*. They mold a huge bird image in the sand by the seashore and then, one by one, place a rock in the circle as, aloud, they make a commitment to do a specific act for peace during the year. Like-minded people come together to do this dance because they care about peace and they have chosen dance as a way to give voice to their feelings; to take an active stance, to be counted as it were. Some people do civil disobedience, protest marches, whatever—we dance!

The Carnival of Guinea-Bissau

Daniel J. Crowley

Unquestionably "the greatest show on earth," the pre-Lenten secular Christian carnival has its roots in the classical Mediterranean and took shape in early Medieval times. Today distinctive traditional street carnivals exist widely in German towns and villages, in Basel and elsewhere in Switzerland, in Nice and Cannes, and in Binche in Belgium. The famous but moribund Venetian carnival has been successfully revived, and new carnivals have been introduced in such cold Protestant northern cities as Copenhagen and London, the northernmost one I have yet observed being Akureyri, Iceland, on a fjord facing the Arctic Sea. Private carnival festivities take place in homes, schools, and clubs in virtually every Latin city, both in the Old World and in the New, where the Spanish, Portuguese, and French introduced carnival a half-millennium ago, one of the few aspects of colonialism that was welcomed by the aboriginal peoples.

The greatest of all contemporary carnivals is in Rio de Janeiro, with Salvador da Bahia, Recife, and virtually every other Brazilian city also mounting impressive week-long festivities. Buenos Aires, Montevideo, Caracas, Panama City, Oruro Bolivia, and even Communist Havana have large carnivals, although the latter has been transferred to July to celebrate the 1958 Revolution. Similarly, carnivals in the Caribbean have been changed in date to attract tourists and/or celebrate historic events, but the greatest of them all in Port-of-Spain, Trinidad, is still held on the traditional February-March dates, as is the Mardi Gras in New Orleans, other Louisiana Creole towns, and in nearby Mobile, Alabama. Curiously enough, Ash Wednesday is the big day when Martiniquaises "bury" carnival, and the Haitian Rara carnival breaks all the rules by taking place during Lent. Although equally hit by the onslaught of European colonialism, Asian cultures resisted with their own festival traditions, even in the Christianized Philippines, but a lively carnival did develop and still survives in the ex-Portuguese enclave of Goa on the western coast of India.

In Africa, too, strong local traditions minimized the importation of European festival life, but one carnival has been reported, that of Guinea-Bissau, an ex-Portuguese colony on the curve of the West African coast between Senegal and ex-French Guinea. Living in a small triangular nation of 14,000 square miles of river estuaries, swamps, and savannah, the Bissauan population of less than a million is deeply divided by religious, ethnic, linguistic, and ecological differences. Of the one-third who are

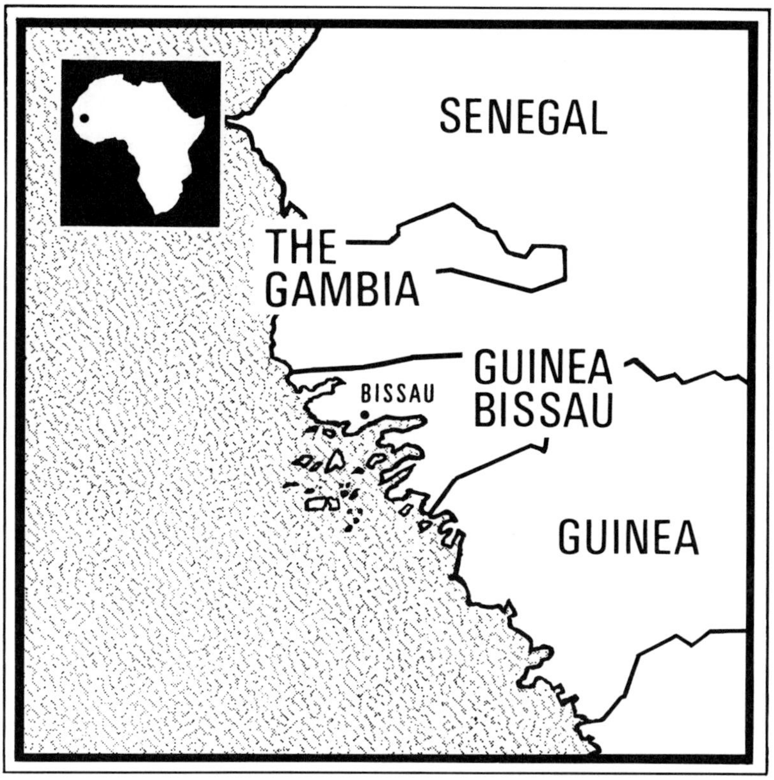

1. Map of Guinea-Bissau on the western coast of Africa. (Graphic by Caroline J. Kavanagh)

Muslims, the aristocratic Fulani pastoralists and the Malinke farmers and traders belong to two distinct sects of Islam and speak unrelated languages. The four percent population of Christians are largely the urban Creoulo descendants of Cape Verde mulatto civil servants and their local wives, and speak Portuguese Creole as their first language. Of the remaining two-thirds who are "pagan" traditional religionists, half are Balanta, a stateless people known for their individualism and prowess as warriors, and the rest are evenly split between the Manjaco who farm extensive palm groves, and some nine other ethnic groups who live by fishing and subsistence agriculture.

First sighted by the Portuguese in 1446, Guinea-Bissau did not become a colony until 1879, and "pacification" was not completed until 1915. A war of liberation led by the charismatic Amilcar Cabral began in 1961 but ended only in 1974 with the Portuguese withdrawal and the establishment of a "nonaligned" state, first in union with the offshore Cape Verde Islands, and then alone. In spite of considerable improvement in education, communications, and health, Guinea-Bissau today remains one of the poorest and least developable nations on earth, and also one of the least known.

The research on which this paper is based was initiated by my daughter Eve Crowley in 1983 when, as an anthropological graduate student at Yale, she spent three months in Bissau, returning there in early 1986 as a Fulbright scholar studying three traditional religious shrines in their inter-ethnic, medical, psychiatric, and political aspects. She also researched the organization of the Guinea-Bissau carnival and interviewed maskmakers and participants in preparation for the arrival of our team.[1]

But before we arrived in Africa, I tried to project what this unique African carnival would be like. Conscious of Africa's great heritage of music and dance, I felt sure that brilliant rhythmic effects produced on local instruments would inspire some spectacular dancing comparable to the samba, frevo/passo, and calypso dance of other carnivals. And remembering the marvels of African masquerade festivals, I envisioned carved and painted wooden bull masks derived from the local tradition of the offshore Bissago Islands, as well as the themes and characters universal in carnivals such as clowns, Indians, and transvestites. I was less certain that I would find the equally widespread mock battles with flour, powder, cologne, or urine sometimes called *entrudo* and deriving from Medieval Iberia. I especially expected that the Bissauan carnival would be strongly localized, not only because the Portuguese are long gone and the country has always been isolated both from its neighboring countries and from outside influences, but even more so because African festival traditions are so powerful and overwhelming. I was about to learn once more the folly of projection and the infinite human potential for unexpected creativity and variability so often demonstrated in carnival.

The carnival began on the Sunday preceding Ash Wednesday, with an afternoon parade of children's groups through the residential streets and the small business district of Bissau, with judging stands set up at appropriate corner locations. The "parade" hardly deserved that name, since it was totally unplanned and uncoordinated, being nothing more than the occasional and casual marching of groups of masked children past the judges. These groups were always segregated by gender, and at least 90 percent of them were made up of boys and young men in their teens. About 40 groups appeared, ranging in size from family bands of 6 or 8 brothers, cousins, or friends, to bands of 50 or so varying in age from about 6 to 18. The female groups had similar range in age, but the largest numbered only about 25 members.

What was so astonishing about these groups was neither their numbers nor their ages, but their masks. Where we had expected carved wooden helmet masks representing bulls deriving from the local Bissago tradition—which previous interviewing had indicated was the traditional carnival form—we found even larger helmet masks made of papier-mâché formed over impromptu sculptured molds made of the ample local swamp clay. What was totally unexpected was the subject of these masks. Monsters shared the characteristics of Mephistopheles, dragons, the occult, and sea creatures, resulting in something like the 1950s film monster "The Creature from the Black Lagoon," whence indeed the original clay had come. Goggle eyes, beetling eyebrows, tongues, sharp shark's teeth, horns protruding from foreheads and jaws, barbed tails, weblike wings and ears, fish scales, beaks, and skull and crossbones were all featured in every possible permutation and combination, and painted in shiny lurid enamels, sometimes with the help of spray guns. Where do such unexpected and nonlocal subjects come from? Interviewing soon uncovered the most likely sources: old foreign comic books brought in ever since Portuguese times and much appreciated by the local youth. Comic books and newspapers with comic strips still come in from Senegal, Portugal, and elsewhere, although few could be found amidst the drab propaganda for sale in the nearly empty local bookstores, probably because of the shortage of exchange. Another possible source suggested by one informant were the dragon masks used for Chinese New Year street dancing in Portuguese Macau near Hongkong, known to Bissauans through films and photographs.

2. A group of Bissauan monster maskers during carnival. (Photo by Eve L. Crowley)

3. A monster mask surmounted by a heraldic lion from the Portuguese crest. (Photo by Eve L. Crowley)

In their gruesome way, the masks were of consistently high quality. An estimated 90 percent were either new or repainted, so that very few showed the signs of wear inevitable in so fragile a material as papier-mâché—cracked paint, disintegrating material, or loose or broken parts. One local tradition that came through was the occasional tipping back of the mask so as to expose the wearer's face, the front of the mask's neck then being across the wearer's forehead. This allowed the wearer to cool off, smoke a cigarette, and see his surroundings and fellow maskers better than he could through the interstices in the mask, but of course it also revealed the wearer's identity. In most cases, secrecy is no issue here, since the maskers can often be recognized by the parade observers on the basis of their masks alone, which are made in the crowded yards under full public scrutiny. However, in some *bairros* (neighborhoods), strict secrecy is the rule during the manufacture of the masks in order to keep the theme concealed and thus increase its impact during the judging.

The next day, Monday, the adult maskers joined the children and we saw many more even finer and larger masks. Following another African tradition, the children never retreated from the carnival, but were in evidence everywhere and at all times during the three days of the festival.

We also noticed another subject, sometimes as a mask but more often as an effigy atop a helmet mask, or in several cases as a drawing on a placard carried by a masker. This was Nturi Palan, a black boy with large ears, a protruding abdomen with umbilical hernia, and large feet—the cartoon character invented by 28-year-old twin brothers Fernando and Manel Julio (their school name, their African "title" being Nanti). The brothers' cartoons have appeared for over a decade in the local press and Nturi Palan has come to represent the Bissauan Everyman, and indeed a personification of the country itself. *Nturi* means "deceiver" in the local Balanta language, and *Palan*, from Portuguese *"planear"* or English "plan," implies plotting, so that this likable underdog is the local manifestation of the classic Trickster known throughout world folklore. The most striking representation we saw of Nturi was by a masker wearing a full helmet mask, bare chest with carefully tinted brown papier-mâché body-mask to represent the protruding belly, dirty shorts, and bare legs with huge splayed papier-mâché feet tied on around the ankles. Nturi shambled around, ostensibly helping another masker representing a doctor.

This doctor represented the third theme of Bissau carnival—the official government theme, "Vaccination Protects Health." Understandably, dour "nonaligned" one-party states are innately leery of unrestrained and undirected frivolity, especially when it derives from the culture of the only-recently-defeated colonial overlord. At the same time, the carnival in Bissau has always been relatively local in form and flavor, and the Portuguese in any case are no longer a threat. So we can envision some earnest government officials pondering how best to use this living, popular festival in pursuit of national and even international goals. Certainly it ought to be used to educate, and to push national policies—hence the vaccination theme.

The results must have been edifying to the carnival organizers, since at least 15 groups chose to portray the theme. Of course it was widely rumored among the maskers that these groups knew that the highest prizes would go to groups glorifying national policy. Even so, their creativity was impressive. Several groups came out as doctors and nurses in white smocks, starched caps, mirrored headgear, suitcases marked with Red Cross symbols, and of course large papier-mâché injection needles, some

4. A masker as Nturi Palan with a loudspeaker. (Photo by Eve L. Crowley)

5. Following the official vaccination theme, Nturi Palan sits atop a mask and wields a large injection needle. (Photo by Eve L. Crowley)

6. Another masker's entire head has become an injection needle. (Photo by Eve L. Crowley)

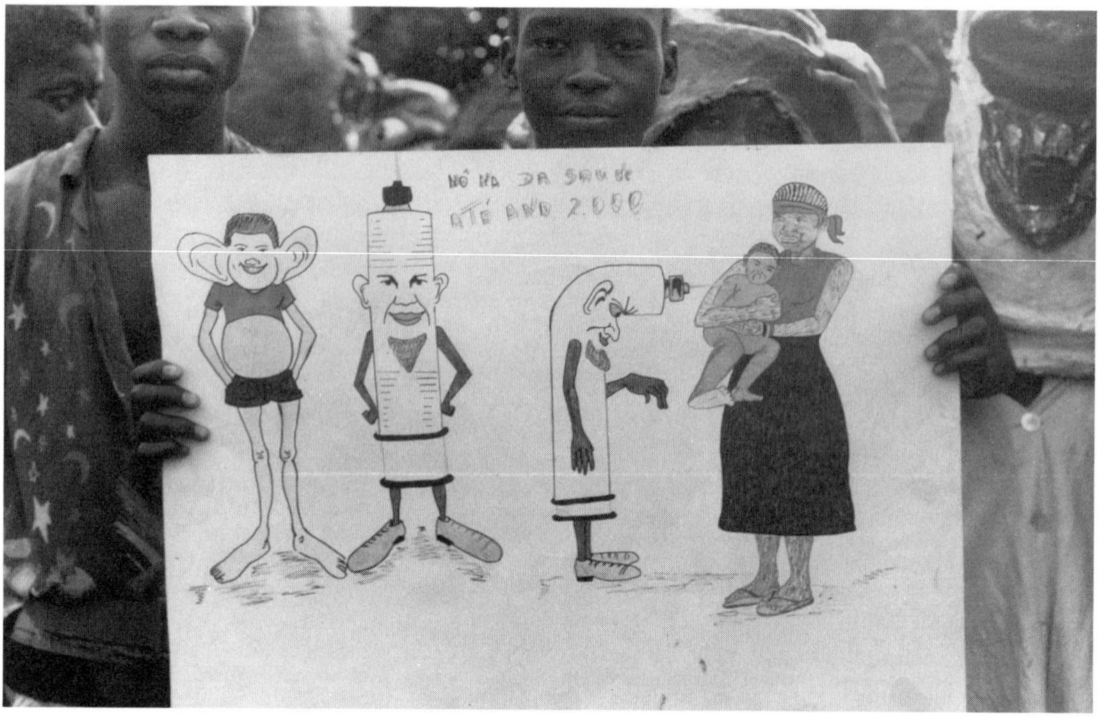

7. A Nturi Palan placard recommends innoculation, but some think the lurid displays actually set back the cause of vaccination in Bissau by some years. (Photo by Eve L. Crowley)

of which (built around bicycle pumps) shot streams of bright red liquid. (Doran Ross, Africanist art historian and assistant director of the Museum of Cultural History at UCLA, remarked that these lurid displays actually *set back* the cause of vaccination in Bissau by some years.) A few maskers also became animated syringes or injection needles, and one group was inspired to represent the various diseases to be cured by the vaccination campaign, with headmasks and accoutrements representing leprosy, tuberculosis, smallpox, polio, cholera, and yellow fever, all horribly graphic, with open sores of sticky red enamel, huge pustules oozing bright yellow paint, distorted faces and gnarled bodies not unlike some traditional African masks representing disease. One helmet mask representing polio was even topped by a papier-mâché wheelchair. While such grim subjects would seem to be utterly inappropriate for the merry mood of carnival, they fit in perfectly as the maskers capered around leering and grimacing at the audience. The horrible subjects and earnest preachiness of the theme did nothing to dim the carnival spirit.

As Monday and Tuesday wore on and we had more chance to observe the groups, we realized that the festival was considerably larger than we had expected, with at least 1,000 participants in the streets, 500 of them in elaborate masks and costumes, and the others in clownlike or other traditional festival costumes. As it turned out, the papier-mâché helmet masks have "traditional" costumes connected with them, perhaps derived from comic-strip characters but freely interpreted using local resources. This costume includes coveralls or monkey suits locally termed *farda da mecanica* (mechanic's uniform), galoshes or high rubber boots used for working in the swamps, finely braided short or long grass skirts which were sometimes oiled or stained in bright colors, sashes and crisscross panels of the beautiful and expensive local Papel or Manjaco narrow-strip-weave textile

8. The masker at right wears the expensive Manjaco sash, white gloves, a grass skirt, and a large papier-mâché mask. (Photo by Eve L. Crowley)

(often shot with imported gold or silver Lurex thread), white cotton work gloves, a cloth cape sometimes painted or embroidered, and often a wooden staff, cane, musket, or sword. The Manjaco cloths, a type of which is used in funerary rituals, are highly valued heirlooms costing from $30 to $100 or more, and are now beginning to be avidly sought by foreign collectors. Combined with the large and heavy helmet mask, this costume represents a considerable burden for any masker under the hot West African sun.

As the carnival continued, several large village groups appeared numbering between 75 and 100 people, including adult men, a few women, and large numbers of boys and girls, all wearing the local festival dress of finely braided short or long grass skirts, sometimes dyed orange-red or black, headbands of the same material, leis and hair ornaments of white cowrie shell sometimes replaced with much lighter bits of Styrofoam packing material, shell ankle and wrist rattles, and red and white face paint. These groups came on like the proverbial gangbusters, the men and boys shouting and running, then dancing ecstatically in such a way as to kick up the ample dust in the streets, surrounding themselves with clouds of it. Little

9. A troupe of village girls, chanting and dancing in the street. (Photo by Eve L. Crowley)

girls were topless while older women wore carefully tied bandannas as they sang or chanted in unison between the periods of wild dancing. As is so often the case in the Third World, they gave no inkling of stage fright as they sashayed through the crowded city streets. In fact, one member of the dance troupe commented that it was about time the urban Creoulos saw some good dancing for a change.

And this brings up one of the biggest surprises of the carnival: the papier-mâché masked groups do no dancing or singing whatsoever, but merely shuffle, bent forward, through the streets without any pretense of ordered formation or any kind of pattern. There were no musical instruments in evidence, much less any musical or rhythmic effects. Imagine an African festival with no music or dance! Evidently, the relatively recent introduction of the monster theme has not yet generated music or dance forms. In contrast, the ecstatic dancing of the few traditional bairro or village groups was accompanied by several types of local slit gongs and drums including both square and round tambourines similar to the famed *pandeiros* of the Rio de Janeiro carnival, and two groups also had ear-piercing police whistles equally popular in New World carnivals. But since these groups were literally few and far between, much of the carnival was relatively quiet, if not exactly silent. To liven things up, the Ministry of Culture broadcast taped music, some of it Brazilian, during the judging on Thursday, and a small group of light-skinned locals and foreigners (one bystander referred to them as *Libaneses*) carried placards reading "Festival Carioca, N'Kassa Cobra Produção," played Brazilian-type drums, and danced in an approximation of the street samba while singing Brazilian songs in Portuguese.

After the 500 or so monster maskers, the next largest category was that of individual maskers, who probably numbered 200 or more. They

10. An individual masker smeared with clay and carrying night soil. (Photo by Eve L. Crowley)

strolled around the edges of the parade and occasionally joined in, but again without music or dance. The variety of their costumes was impressive: small groups or couples dressed as clowns with painted faces and red plastic balls on their noses; pirates in torn clothes and upturned hats painted with skull and crossbones; very dirty and nearly naked little boys smeared with red mud rather like Brazilian *sujos* or Trinidadian "living dead"; a shabbily dressed man carrying baskets of night soil; a running group cracking whips like Caribbean "Jab Molassis"; a man wearing a large plastic funnel upside-down on his head like a character from the U.S. "Viking" comic strip "Hagar the Horrible"; an American Indian woman with long braids, face paint, and a fringed costume; a man with a punk Mohawk coiffeur; a teenage boy with a large, pink, wooden or plastic red-tipped phallus which he concealed in a large pair of shorts and periodically exposed to the delight of the crowd (one of the oldest carnival antics, documented back to ancient Greece); other uncostumed boys who "mooned" the crowd in unison; little girls in Styrofoam leis, grass skirts, and red face-paint; children wearing kimonos and Chinese conical paper "coolie" hats; and uncostumed boys playing Nturi by wearing their fathers' shoes.

Among all these individuals, a few stood out. A mock diviner wearing a long Muslim robe and turban threw cowrie shells as in Yoruba Ifa Divination and practiced fake Arabic writing. Called "Mouro" (Moor), he wisecracked silly answers to questions from the crowd. When an old woman asked, "Why can't I have more children?" he answered, "You put your eggs in a pot and they broke." A more spectacular individual was "Pelican Man," a nearly nude young man who arrived running and yelling. He was wearing an apron and large "angel" wings of rather ruffled brown and white feathers, had a yellow chain design painted around his arms and legs, eyes painted on his knees, and was wearing a beakless face mask that resembled a fish more than a bird. He carried a long staff on which was impaled a small, headless stuffed pig with which he did a ten-minute-long skit including screams, runs, falls, mock rituals, and a resuscitation of sorts.

Judging by audience response, the hit among the individual maskers was a very skillful stilt dancer who would have been immediately recognized throughout the Caribbean by the good old West African name of "Moko Jumby." Standing at least 14 feet high, he wore long red trousers, yellow and green earflaps, and a mirrored and brimmed hat not unlike the *Torchon* (lufa or sea cucumber) hat of Trinidad carnival's Moko Jumbies. He displayed his considerable skill by dancing delicately through gates and over cars, then going down on his back doing breakdancing steps, mimicking death and resurrection, and managing to right himself again.

In contrast to such elaborate performers were those in minimal costumes of faded and used T-shirts emblazoned with "University of Notre Dame," "I survived Motorcycle week at Daytona Beach," and a somewhat enigmatic salute from my natal city, "Heart of Illinois Chili Shootout, Peoria." More traditional minicostumes included a shirt simply worn backwards, a homemade paper hat, or a conical basketry Manding herder's hat from the interior.

After a very, very quiet Wednesday—the Catholics went to Church to receive an anointing with ashes and the maskers rested—Thursday was again busy. In the courtyard of the Casa da Cultura, the Director General of Culture, Wilson Barbosa, presented some 200,000 pesos ($800) in prizes to the maskers from funds donated by various governmental agencies. Here we saw performers we had never seen in the streets: for instance, a group of drummers, three with cylindrical European military drums, the fourth playing a long tapered "Congo" drum; a noncostumed group miming agricultural work with hoes and shovels under banners reading "Support the Development Process" and "Plant Lovers, The Ending of the Burning of the Bush," and singing original songs entitled "Children Need Peace," "Give the World a Chance," and even, "By Way of Carnival, We'll Get There"; a group consisting of doctors and nurses with real mothers and real babies receiving real vaccinations before the judges while a masked Nturi encouraged the crying babies then fell into the courtyard fountain; a masker wearing a poor version of a traditional Baga Nimba mask and grass fringe costume; two expert fire-eaters; a group of Balanta dancers with small metallic drums; a masker wearing an overturned basket made into a seemingly traditional Balanta bull mask with holes for eyes and added horns; and other skits designed to please the politically chosen judges. It was a pleasant afternoon, with soft drinks served on a large patio decorated with papier-mâché masks collected in previous years.

Prizes in various categories ranged from about 8,000 pesos ($32) plus 10 meters of trade cloth to about 20,000 pesos ($80) plus 35 meters of trade cloth in three designs. The biggest prizes were a large electric fan and a "Walkman" cassette player. Interviewing soon revealed that the traditional bairro dance groups of adults and children, entirely African and local in costume and dance, were from nearby non-Muslim, non-Christian neighborhoods and were specifically recruited by government officials to encourage their participation in the national life while showcasing their skills in a city that otherwise knows little about them. The papier mâché masked groups proved to be largely urban and Creoulo, meaning detribalized and/or racially mixed urban people whose first language is the local Portuguese

11. The hit masker—a skillful stilt-dancing "Moko Jumby." (Photo by Eve L. Crowley)

Creole. Numbering only about four percent of the total national population of one million, the Creoulo city-dwellers may be Catholic but more often they practice the traditional religion (or both). A few are part Portuguese in ancestry, but more are descendants of the Cape Verdean mulattos from the offshore island nation once united with Guinea-Bissau. A few masking groups were made up of local still-tribalized Papels who speak Creoulo as a second language but are not Christian.

The audience for this carnival proved to be almost as odd as the comic-strip maskers. Largely made up of technicians, medics, teachers, agronomists, and the like—locally termed *cooperantes* (cooperators)—these were people sent from various countries to help this poor and long war-torn nation. One can envision the Swedish nurses, tight-lipped in the dusty streets, the broad beamed Bulgarian couples strolling by, and the North Korean women looking lonesomely down from their embassy balcony.

If political stability continues, and the economy develops enough to provide steady supplies of gasoline, electricity, food, and water, this carnival could become the centerpiece of Bissauan nationalism and a unifying force badly needed in so divided a country. In the same way, like all carnivals, it is a natural lure for tourists, the simplest source of foreign currency. With fine beaches, the picturesque offshore Bissago Islands, the moldering colonial ghost town of Bolama, and strong traditional woven cloth and wood sculpture, Guinea-Bissau has the beginnings of a tourist industry, if only because it is so unknown. Nearby Senegal and Gambia have done very well with minimal facilities in attracting North Europeans, and in my crabbed opinion at least, their cultures have not suffered perceptibly by the mass influx of sun-seeking Swedish nude bathers nor by tourist shoppers buying up the incomparable batiks, tie-dyes, and weavings of the cloth markets of Dakar and Banjul.

Although Bissau is the only carnival yet studied in Africa, another exists in the market town of Ziguinchor in the nearby Casamance district of Senegal, and still another is rumored to persist among Brazilian-descended residents of Cotonou in the Republic of Benin (ex-Dahomey). Others with greater European influence survive in such offshore islands as Terceira in the Azores, Sąo Vicente in the Cape Verdes, and in a post-Franco revived form in Tenerife in the Spanish Canaries.

Note

1. I take this opportunity to thank my wife Pearl, our daughters Eve and Magdalene, student Marie Durquet, Rui Ribeiro and his family, the Ministry of Culture, Philip Ravenhill, and my UCLA colleague Doran Ross for their help in the research on which this paper is based.

Daniel J. Crowley *, Professor of Anthropology and Art History at the University of California at Davis, has been studying carnival for 30 years.*

Speaking About China's Spoken Drama

A Roundtable with Chinese Directors and Playwrights

The following discussion took place at the Beijing headquarters of the Chinese Theatre Association in January 1988. Attending the roundtable were (in order of speaking):

Wang Zheng, playwright and critic, executive secretary of the Chinese Theatre Association and chief editor of the China Theatre Publishing House.

Chen Yong, director and first vice-president of the China Youth Art Theatre of Beijing. Since this roundtable she has become artistic director of the same theatre.

Wen Xingyu, director and vice-president of the Central Experimental Spoken Drama Theatre in Beijing.

Wang Xiaoying, director with the China Youth Art Theatre and director of *Guazai Qiangshang de Lao B (The Old B Hanging on the Wall)* by Sun Huizhu (see TDR 30, no. 4:84–105).

Xing Yixun, playwright at the China Youth Art Theatre.

Qu Liuyi, director of research for the Chinese Theatre Association and chief editor of *Chinese Theatre Yearbook.*

Sun Zhongshu, deputy director of the foreign liaison office at the Chinese Theatre Association.

In January and February 1988 Richard Schechner traveled in China observing performances and meeting artists and scholars. He spent five days in Beijing before going to Shanghai and then on to various places in Guizhou, Guangdong, and Fujian provinces. In China, he was hosted by the Chinese Theatre Association, the Shanghai Drama Institute, the Shanghai Peoples Art Theatre, and a number of organizations in Guizhou, Guangdong, and Fujian. The Asian Cultural Council paid for Schechner's trip. In May and June 1989 Schechner, funded by the United States Information Agency (USIA), returned to China to direct Sun Huizhu's *Miangri Jiuyao Chushan (Tomorrow He'll Be Out of the Mountains)* (in Chinese) at the Shanghai People's Art Theatre.[1]

The Chinese Theatre Association is what the Chinese call a "nonofficial organization." But because the CTA is China's only association for theatre artists, it is influential in presenting theatre festivals, conducting cultural exchanges with foreigners, and publishing journals and books containing both theories and scripts. Its members include professional directors, playwrights, actors, designers, and technicians as well as some theoreticians from China's two schools of theatre, the Beijing Central Academy of Drama and the Shanghai Drama Institute. The CTA has branches in all provinces.

The China Youth Art Theatre was founded in 1949, the year the People's Republic of China came into existence. It is one of the biggest spoken drama theatres in China (the others include the Central Experimental Spoken Drama Theatre in Beijing, the Beijing People's Art Theatre, and the Shanghai People's Art Theatre). The Youth Art Theatre is well known for its innovative productions, although for quite some time it has not been a "youth" theatre.

SCHECHNER: What is the current state of today's Chinese spoken drama?

WANG ZHENG: Richard Schechner is in China looking at nuoxi[2] and other kinds of traditional performances. After watching some traditional performances—Chinese operas, folk and ritual performances—Schechner felt that some of his ideas about theatre were very much in keeping with Chinese traditions. He is making a survey of these connections. Sun Huizhu also did something similar when he came back from the USA and went to Ding county for his research.[3]

But Schechner specializes in spoken drama, that's why we invited him to come here and discuss the current state of Chinese spoken drama. You can say whatever you want. Schechner hopes that, in the future, the works of more Chinese playwrights can be produced more often in the USA and that writings by Chinese artists and scholars will more regularly appear in American journals.

I want to mention that spoken drama—European theatre—was introduced to China from Japan in 1907, 81 years ago. Before 1949, Chinese spoken drama developed from the embryo stage to maturity. Some great playwrights such as Tian Han, Cao Yu, Ouyang Yuqian, and Xia Yan[4] appeared during that period. Some great novelists such as Guo Moruo and Mao Dun also wrote plays.[5] After the founding of the People's Republic of China [PRC] in 1949, spoken drama became more popular and therefore more people began to work in it. Many playwrights emerged—most of these are more than 60 years of age now.

In the 1950s and '60s we mostly learned from the Soviet Union and we followed Stanislavski's methods. There were some good plays written in that period. Lao She wrote about ten plays after Liberation, *Chaguan (Tea House)* being the most famous.[6] But most of the plays from that period were political propaganda.

Later on, during the Cultural Revolution [1966–76], spoken drama was almost completely destroyed.

After the Cultural Revolution, spoken drama flourished as never before. Performances revealed the crimes of the "Gang of Four."[7] Spoken drama appealed to people because they had not seen any for ten years and also because people had suffered a great deal during the Cultural Revolution.

In 1978 and '79, China began to open its doors[8] and great changes took place in our society and in the life of our people. With these changes certain questions arose concerning how our theatre would adapt itself to the new

1. China's first Shakespearean Drama Festival took place in 1986. Li Jiayo directed a kungu opera production of Macbeth, *which went to the Edinburgh Festival in 1987. (Photo by Ji Cheng)*

era. If we still promoted a drama that served politics then the stage would remain closed and people would not like it anymore. Therefore, artists tried to create something new—and experimental theatre came into being.

During recent years Chinese theatre has twice been at a low ebb. In 1983 and '84 people didn't go to the theatre very much because popular music, movies, and TV captured their attention. Later, due to the efforts of theatre people to create new works, things improved in 1985 and '86. But since 1987 the situation has gotten bad again. What on earth is the problem?

In my opinion, old-fashioned techniques were used too much in the past, but now experimental theatre seems too abstract. How can we make our works relate to the people, reflecting their life? This requires great effort.

SCHECHNER: In the Western theatre at this time, the director has emerged as the most important person—more important even than the writers and the actors. This has happened largely because of the influence of films where the director is the primary creator, the shaper of the images seen on the screen. The screenwriter is "part of the team," not the leading figure. The language of the theatre or film is the mise-en-scene, not the playtext. Has something similar happened in China?

CHEN: The question you raise is being discussed in China today just as it is in all the countries of the world. Theatre can't exist without either the playwright or the director or the actor or the stage designer. Theatre combines all of these aspects. What is dominant may vary from country to country, period to period. There may be a literary theatre where the playwright is dominant, an action theatre where the director is dominant, a visual theatre where the designer is dominant, or a performance theatre where the actor is dominant.

In the history of the Chinese classical theatre, the actor has dominated. That is the major characteristic of Chinese classical theatre. Our acting may be regarded as a marvelous mixture of playwrighting, directing, and literature. Acting included all the other aspects of theatre.

During the 80 years since spoken drama was introduced into China, it has been affected by social changes in China and it has also assimilated some Chinese ways of thinking as well as some traditional Chinese aesthetics. At first, spoken drama in China was still literature-oriented—because it came into China as something based on the system of Western drama which is very different from our traditional drama. Many Chinese got involved in spoken drama because they admired the works of certain playwrights. For a long time, Chinese spoken drama had a literary tradition, the theatre companies served "good writers." It didn't matter where these writers came from—Japan, Europe, Russia, or China. Moreover, whatever the political and social situation, the main principle guiding the selection of plays was to have our theatre closely related to social reality. A large number of directors, actors, and playwrights were produced according to this tradition.

But now social progress makes us realize the necessity of breaking this tradition. Especially after the Cultural Revolution our way of thinking has changed. The rapid changes occurring in our social, political, and economic system—as well as the influences coming from the open-door policy—have resulted in a change in our attitudes toward art. This is not surprising because there is always a necessary relationship between art and the general cultural background.

Thus, in theatre, auteurism has emerged. Attempts have been made to break the tradition whereby the performance was based on staging a play, on playwriting. In recent years, there have been many different approaches in directing which have broken with spoken drama tradition. These new approaches were mostly directed by young and middle-aged directors. This is in keeping with the law of the development of society and it also suggests that the future will disclose more changes. In the future, we will move away from the single-mode tradition into a wider field. I think the emergence of auteurism is a good thing—before, we didn't pay enough attention to this aspect.

SCHECHNER: Can you give some examples?

CHEN: I am eclectic.

SCHECHNER: How? What's your technique?

CHEN: Because I specialize in directing, I feel the director's work is very important. I don't respect any performance that does not respect the director's creation. But at the same time I think those great directors who can really create a mise-en-scene without taking playwriting as the basis of their productions are not really mainstream directors. I mean there aren't many directors who can work this way—without a play at the bottom of it all.

SCHECHNER: But for those who do work this way, how does it happen in China? Do the actors and directors work alone to create a new mise-en-scene? Do you always work on a stage or do you sometimes work in what I call an "environmental theatre"? Does the audience ever participate?

CHEN: We take everything into consideration. The director is the main force in any theatre. Before, the playwright was thought of as the key person—because a play cannot start without a script. But if we want the theatre to survive, and if we want theatre to relate to the audience and to society, the director will have to be the key person.

SCHECHNER: Do you change—rearrange, rewrite—scripts during rehearsals?

CHEN: Certainly, to some extent. But I haven't finished what I was saying. I said the director was the key person, but I also want to say that I respect playwriting which is the basis of my creative work. Only when my creation is based on the script can I work harmoniously with the playwright. I don't like the idea that the director can entirely ignore the playwright and change the script however she wants. This way, the director's creation and the playwright's creation get confused. Of course, there are directors who are playwrights themselves. This kind of director exists in the West and is now appearing in China too. But when the division of work is unclear, the director becomes a jack-of-all-trades. That can be confusing.

SCHECHNER: Can you say all you want to say on a proscenium stage—do you find the picture-frame stage limiting?

CHEN: No, I can't portray everything I want to.

SCHECHNER: How do you overcome this limitation?

CHEN: We try many different ways—thrust stage, arena stage. Our staging of *The Old B Hanging on the Wall* was exactly this kind of experiment. When I directed *Hong Bizi [Red Nose]*[9] we were confined to the proscenium but we got the audience directly involved. Our productions of *Ah-Q Zhengzhuan [The True Story of Ah-Q]* and *Heshi Bi [The Jade of He]*[10] both went beyond the proscenium. A director can choose what kind of stage and what techniques she wants to use—this is already very common in China. And many directors do not follow the playwright entirely. This is also a good thing. I love this new wave but, at the same time, I still think that the theatre cannot have a solid base without good playwriting. No matter how wonderful and creative the director might be, it is the script rather than the directing that will be handed down to the next generations.

2. Chen Yong's production of Red Nose *at the China Youth Art Theatre in February 1982. (Photo courtesy of the China Youth Art Theatre)*

In this sense, any great director has respect for and pays attention to the development of playwriting.

SCHECHNER: One of the problems we have in America in regard to developing new kinds of theatre is that actors are not trained to perform in any kind of theatre except that based on realism, on a Stanislavskian conception of theatre. They are also trained to act behind the picture-frame stage. Do you have the same problem in China?

CHEN: This is a very controversial issue in China now. Many actors were trained traditionally, but young directors attempting to break with tradition need a different kind of actor. There are many actors who are experiencing a painful confusion when encountering both old and new styles. Actors are complaining that they are at a loss—they don't know what's expected of them. Directors are also complaining not only about the actors but about the scripts.

As a producer as well as director of the Youth Art Theatre I face this kind of problem: it's hard to find good scripts. Once we get one, the playwright is worried that no good director will be available. Then the actors say, "The script is terrible and the director's a jerk!" The director replies, "The script is as bad as the actors. I want to fix it so that it goes this way, but the actors aren't up to it." But I guess this is normal for theatre. It's the same, isn't it, in America, Japan, Hong Kong, the Soviet Union—everywhere.

SCHECHNER: Yes, there is a crisis about who controls the means of expression.

CHEN: In China, this crisis is very confusing.

SCHECHNER: Many people around the world are recognizing that information, communication, and the means of expression are the core of tomorrow's cultures. Whoever controls these will own the future. It used to be that whoever controlled the factories controlled the country, but it really is whoever controls the manufacturing of expression—and so artists are becoming very important because they are specialists in expression. In my country, we're not prepared for this. So there is a crisis about how to manage, how to shape, expression. Not simply words but the kind of holistic system of expression that theatre is.

One small aside on all this. This morning I was at the museum looking at some examples of early Chinese writing. I recognized one very simple detail: Western writing is based on the ear, our alphabets are phonetic, while Chinese writing is based on the eye, the writing is imagistic. Now I believe that the director is more an eye artist than an ear artist. I know that many people would disagree with me—but I am not talking about what should be, but about how directing has evolved in the West. But imagistic directing should be "natural" to the Chinese because your classical literature is a literature of the eye.

WEN: Director Chen has said something that I want to comment on. The situation is as she describes it. It has a lot to do with the director's personality. If the director is strong-minded, he wants everything under his control so that he can get what he wants. I am strong-minded myself—actually, I am an unconscious auteur. However, I combine traditional and experimental techniques.

Some scripts are not sophisticated enough but basically provide subject matter. As a director, I can use these scripts to experiment with. For

3. The Jade of He, *directed by Wen Xingyu at the Central Experimental Spoken Drama Theatre. (Photo courtesy of the Central Experimental Spoken Drama Theatre)*

example, last year I directed a musical spoken drama in Anhui and tried to make it different from a Western musical. I tried to incorporate some of the music and acting techniques from traditional Chinese operas. There were only two young actors in the play.

The story is about two Red Guards who were buried in the basement of a big building when two groups were fighting. The audience can see how they struggle for survival until they die and how, in the meantime, their distorted personalities are restored to normal humanity. During this whole process, we used an orchestra of percussion instruments from traditional Chinese opera. This orchestra was on stage throughout the whole performance—just as in earlier days the traditional Chinese opera orchestra was placed at the back of the stage.

Not everybody likes this kind of thing. *The Jade of He* was liked by some people, hated by others. This kind of staging often creates conflicts among audiences. And also these kinds of plays are sometimes rejected by actors, especially ones trained for the realistic theatre.

SCHECHNER: Yesterday I ate at an excellent, very small, private enterprise restaurant. Are there any private theatres in China?

WEN: All our theatres are big proscenium houses modeled on those in the Soviet Union.

CHEN: For more than two years we've had a small theatre in Nanjing.[11] In September 1988 experimental theatres from all over the country will meet in Nanjing. Some plays will be performed there for this meeting: *Rensheng Budengshi [The Inequality of Life]* from the Guangzhou military theatre, *Yuwang de Hangcheng [The Voyage of Desire]* from the Harbin theatre, *Chang Yi [Long Chair]* from the Shenyang City Theatre, *Juedui Xinhao [Absolute Signal]* from the Beijing People's Art Theatre, two plays from Nanjing, and possibly plays from some other areas. So small theatres are growing in China. And though we don't have many larger modern theatres, we can find thousands of places for small theatres. It all depends on the idea being accepted by theatre people and audiences.

Personally, I think small theatres will be an important aspect of Chinese theatre in the future. Therefore, the first important thing for my own theatre company to do is to open up small theatres.

Because the construction of our big theatre is not finished, we have turned a rehearsal hall into a small theatre, one that doesn't yet meet fire safety standards. We are trying to renovate it and get it approved before Spring Festival [February 1988]. We are rehearsing three plays for the small theatre. *Juedi [Land of Desperation]* is the first, a play from the Northwest.

WANG XIAOYING: I think the director's creation is a very interesting aspect of theatre—something different than what the actor or playwright does. What is critical for the performance is the lively exchange between actor and audience—that is, the space shared by the actor and the audience. This communication involves literature and philosophy as well as visual and oral art forms. In my own work I use all kinds of techniques to create a space for the communication between the audience and the actor to occur.

For example, I'm directing *Juedi*. The story takes place in a desert where a group of travelers get lost and face death. In this desperate situation they realize something they can't understand in their daily lives. But how are we to create the atmosphere of a desert in our small theatre? By putting the actors and the audience very close to each other, and also by means of lighting and sound, we can make the audience feel what the actor feels in the play—including a storm in the desert. We even want the spectators to feel the wind. I think that this would be very hard to convey in a large theatre because there the proscenium stage excludes the audience. In *Juedi* we are trying all kinds of things to put the actors and the audience in the same space.

SCHECHNER: Yes, I am very sympathetic to that kind of approach. In the age of movies and television the theatre has to be an art of many small theatres instead of a few large ones. And these theatres must offer experiences instead of spectacles—something that draws spectators in, not just gives them something sumptuous to look at. Actually, I have nothing against big theatres, they should exist too, but my heart is with the small theatres.

Who wrote *Juedi*?

WANG XIAOYING: A young writer from the Gansu Beijing Opera Theatre.

SCHECHNER: I have a few more questions—but first I want to give everyone who wants to talk a chance to speak to the basic questions we've been discussing.

XING: I would like to talk about one point. As a playwright, my work has passed through three stages. During the first stage life was diversified but theatre was monotonous. Life was very rich but in our scripts we were only allowed to write about workers, peasants, and soldiers, not about intellectuals, businessmen, Chinese overseas, and so on—people who actually do exist in real life. And there were also very rigid rules about how to write. Characters had to fit certain stereotypes.

The second stage, in the '80s, was when our theatre began to seek variety while our life became monotonous. People complained that our plays were not realistic, but I thought that our life itself was so monotonous that our plays were unreal if they sought variety. During this period, form was more important than content. The rich techniques we used were not convincing because they were not based on life.

Now I think we are moving into a third stage. Today the variety in theatre reflects the variety in life because our life has become richer and more open. For example, there is one type of life in the Northwest, another in Beijing, and another type in the special regions along the East Coast.[12] When a journalist came here from Taiwan he said there were several types of societies in China. Peoples' minds are more open now, philosophy has become more diversified, and so have our lives and our theatre.

With the reform of general culture, our theatre—including playwriting, directing, and acting—is showing the kind of diversity necessary to keep up with life. Moreover, Chinese movies such as *Lao Jing [The Old Well]* and *Huang Tudi [Yellow Earth]* have won international awards. These movies represent a backwardness which is certainly true to our reality. Nevertheless, while we are moving toward modernization, advanced ideas do not show up often enough in our works. As writers we are to blame for this.

SCHECHNER: Are you working on something to correct this?

XING: I intend to. My writing is more traditional. I write about social problems and social life, my style is Ibsen-like. Since life is so rich, and there are so many types of life, new ideas of theatre have begun to stir in me. I want to try something new. As far as information is concerned, our society is full of information with the open-door policy. But it is regrettable that the information in our plays is not keeping up with society. Our plays do not reflect enough of our society.

SCHECHNER: This leads to one of the questions we've been talking about. Someone spoke of the musical drama that took advantage of traditional Chinese theatre. There are hundreds of traditional Chinese theatres. What is the relationship between spoken drama and traditional theatres?

CHEN: This is a question almost all directors in China are thinking about. We have a very long, rich cultural tradition. We have seen that Western people are paying attention to Eastern aesthetics in theatre, including Japanese and Indian theatre. However, spoken drama in China has always paid more attention to Western culture and theatre than to our own theatres. Many of our playwrights, directors, and designers were trained that way. In literature and the performing arts, the West is paying attention to us, but we are not paying attention to ourselves—and that is not a rational attitude.

That the West pays attention to the East and the East pays attention to the West should be a natural law in the development of the history and culture of humankind. Different cultures should affect each other. Before, the West paid very little attention to the East and that seemed to make us disregard the East. We should be more conscious of this problem; we should pay more attention to the study of our own culture.

To compare Eastern with Western culture on a higher level and on this basis to develop modern Chinese theatre is a question which all contemporary Chinese directors should consider seriously. This has aroused a lot of interest and has been seriously discussed.

SCHECHNER: Could you give me some examples?

CHEN: There is a director by the name of Wang Gui. He is working on a play called *Zhou Lang Bai Shuai [Young Mr. Zhou Takes Command]* in which he is trying to deal with the relationship between ancient Chinese and Japanese culture and how this relationship can be applied to the theatre.

The Jade of He which Wen Xingyu is working on is another example. In this play Wen is trying to draw a comparison between the Western way of using symbols and our traditional techniques in theatre.

In the *Caucasian Chalk Circle* I am directing, I examine the relationship between the aesthetic principles of Chinese traditional opera and the aesthetic principles of Brechtian theatre. Many other directors, such as Lin Zhaohua and Hu Weimin,[13] are also studying this relationship.

It is not possible to establish a new school of directing in modern Chinese theatre without paying attention to the relationship between our own theatre and world theatre.

QU: In the first years after the founding of the PRC, a strange phenomenon occurred. At that time, Chinese traditional opera was trying to follow the model of spoken drama but just on a very superficial level. For example, opera started to use a curtain which it never had before and also started to use sets like those in spoken drama. Consequently, traditional opera is still using what spoken drama has abandoned.

In my view, spoken drama outstripped traditional opera because it borrowed from traditional opera. What spoken drama has learned from opera is not forms of performance but ideas about theatre, aesthetics, and some techniques unique to our tradition. I think this is where the real vitality for the future of spoken drama lies.

SCHECHNER: Will the time come when there will be a festival bringing together both spoken drama and traditional operas?

QU: That happened at last year's Art Festival of China.

SCHECHNER: Tell me a little about that. And are there any actors who work in both spoken drama and opera?

CHEN: Many opera actors have worked in spoken drama, but very few do the reverse. Some spoken drama actors can sing songs from traditional opera, and also understand the opera's aesthetics, but they do not know how to act in it.

QU: Ouyang Yuqian started out as a spoken drama actor. He could work in both.

4. & 5. *In her 1985 production of Brecht's* Caucasian Chalk Circle *at the China Youth Art Theatre, Chen Yong borrowed techniques from opera and blended them with spoken drama. (Photos by Cao Zhigang)*

CHEN: We have many directors who can direct both. Hu Weiman directs kungu and some other traditional operas as well as spoken drama.

SCHECHNER: What about plays that use both? I'll give an example: A spoken drama begins—and in it a battle is fought. For that scene the techniques of opera are used, and then the production goes back to being a spoken drama.

WANG ZHENG: I would like to talk about the production of two Brecht plays. One is *Caucasian Chalk Circle* as directed by Chen Yong. This director borrowed techniques from opera and blended them with spoken drama. The other is *The Good Woman of Sichuan.* The director borrowed techniques from Chuanju, Sichuan opera, and produced a fantastic combination of traditional opera and spoken drama. The German Embassy wants

6. Music and acting style were borrowed from Chinese opera for Yu Cun and Wen Xingyu's The True Story of Ah-Q *(1983). (Photo courtesy of the Central Experimental Spoken Drama Theatre)*

to have the production seen in Germany. This is no mere superficial combination as in the early days after Liberation, but a combination of artistic spirit as well as aesthetic principles.

SCHECHNER: I can foresee the use of the two in the same play from both the playwright's and the director's view. At a moment of high poetry one kind of physical language gives way to another. For example, at a moment of great passion, instead of just speaking, the actor begins to sing, and then later goes back to speaking. I tried something like that in my production of *Don Juan* (1987) which combined Molière's drama with Mozart's *Don Giovanni*.

CHEN: In 1986 we had our first Shakespearean Drama Festival. In the performances, some spoken drama troupes used traditional realistic techniques and others used abstract symbolic techniques. At the same time, many traditional forms such as jingju, huangmeixi, kungu, and yueju were used in performing Shakespeare. For Chinese traditional opera, this was the first attempt to approach Western drama—to perform Shakespeare with techniques from traditional operas.

SUN: It worked so well that the British invited the huangmei opera's *Macbeth* to Britain.

CHEN: No, it was kungu's *Macbeth* that went to England and played there for three months. In that performance, there were scenes similar to what Schechner was describing. As Macbeth was talking he began to sing and then started to act like a warrior in Chinese opera.

SCHECHNER: I think it could also work with certain scenes from modern dramas.

CHEN: In our own spoken drama we have also started to use a lot of expressive techniques taken from opera, such as body image, body movement, chanting, singing. In *The Jade of He* the actors speak their dialog and move their bodies in ways like that of Beijing opera.

WEN: Also in *The True Story of Ah-Q* the music and a lot of the acting are taken from opera.

CHEN: In the battle scene in *Wusheng de Liaoliang [Silent Loudness]* directed by Gong Xiaodong[14] techniques from opera suddenly appear. However, we don't necessarily agree with all these mixtures. Some are artistically harmonious and consistent, but others are not. I hope the time is coming when a playwright from traditional opera will write a play for spoken drama.

SCHECHNER: Actors will have to be trained in both techniques, right?

CHEN: At the Central Drama Institute there is a course on traditional opera for the acting students.

WANG ZHENG: There are still demarcation lines in our theatre. Spoken drama is spoken drama and traditional opera is traditional opera. We have 300 types of theatre and they are all different from each other and cannot be confused. Although we can combine techniques from different types of theatre, each one has to keep its own basic characteristics.

CHEN: I have another example. In Guangzhou, Hu Weimin is directing *You Youan Jing Meng [A Dream in a Park]* by Bai Xianyong.[15] In that play, he uses singing in the traditional opera style because the play is about traditional opera actors.

7. Because the play is about traditional opera actors, Hu Weimin's production of A Dream in a Park, *with the Guangzhou Spoken Drama Troupe in 1987, used singing in the traditional opera style. (Photo by Hu Weimin)*

SCHECHNER: I'm talking about a situation in which there would be three kinds of theatre flourishing side by side: traditional operas, all 300 types, traditional spoken drama, and this new hybrid form we've been talking about—and maybe more than one kind of combination, maybe lots of types. Many of these new forms would not be staged in proscenium theatres.

CHEN: I totally agree with you. In our theatre this has appeared in embryo. Some people call it "neither fish nor fowl" because it's not like either spoken drama or traditional opera. It even uses some Western techniques.

SCHECHNER: Right. You are lucky in China to have so many possibilities to draw from and to make new things out of.

WEN: In fact, the model operas from the Cultural Revolution period were like this.

CHEN: It means combining all kinds of techniques from both traditional operas and spoken drama. It is too conservative to reject the use of music and dance in spoken drama.

QU: I agree. In Shanghai, huajiju [Shanghai farce] dialog is used as in spoken drama, while other techniques are taken from Beijing opera and local opera traditions. They even use folk songs.

SCHECHNER: Huajiju is a popular form—and popular forms are often ahead of the intelligentsia.

WEN: I just want to add that although spoken drama came from the West, it is definitely influenced by Chinese traditional opera. Opera is our basis. All of us as youngsters saw opera first and only later went to spoken drama.

CHEN: I don't agree. Chinese spoken drama doesn't necessarily borrow anything from traditional opera.

WEN: I mean the influence is in our subconscious, it doesn't matter whether we admit it or not.

CHEN: I still don't agree. For many years we were trained in the tradition of Western theatre. Our ideas about spoken drama are based on this training. The plays we staged were performed in this Western tradition.

SUN: Not only didn't we borrow enough from our own traditional operas, but also we didn't know enough about them. Before, people were saying that the acting in the traditional opera was basically unrealistic. I don't think this is true. In the operas there is also something very realistic. I have two examples.

Yueju [Cantonese opera] was introduced to America through Vietnam in 1852. The yueju stage sets were very realistic even then. And once, in Hebei Province, in order to make a set for a performance, people dug a ditch in front of the stage and filled it with water and even built a bridge over the ditch.

CHEN: But the mainstream of our theatrical aesthetics was not realistic. The opera introduced to America from Vietnam was actually transformed due to the influence of 19th-century Western realism just as our traditional opera was influenced by spoken drama after Liberation.

QU: Nationalism has been a very important question in the history of Chinese spoken drama, raised as early as the '50s. If we compare our spoken drama of the '50s with today's spoken drama, we see that they are very different. Our present-day spoken drama has borrowed a lot from Western modern drama, but it has also borrowed theatrical ideas, techniques, as well as a national aesthetic spirit, from traditional opera. This change indicates that Chinese theatre has generally been nationalized.

To complete this process may take a long time and our nationalized theatre cannot be of just one type. Something may emerge similar to what people are experimenting with—something like the mixture in the Shanghai farce; or something like a complete mixture of spoken drama and traditional opera. It is also possible to have something "neither fish nor fowl" which is neither opera nor spoken drama. I think this "neither fish nor fowl" has more vitality than anything else. I believe it will appear some day.

CHEN: The situation in China now is very diversified, very lively, and also very unstable and confusing.

SCHECHNER: Theatre history all over the world tells us that the most creative things arise out of instability.

CHEN: We are also encountering a serious threat. Our audience is very hard on us now.

SCHECHNER: Why's that?

CHEN: They don't come to see our performances. How can we get them back into the theatres?

SUN: Let me answer that. Go to the audiences!

SCHECHNER: Have lots of small theatres. Audiences like small theatres. And the liveliness around this table—if half of that were on the stage, your theatres would be packed. Why not stage a dialog called *The Future of Chinese Theatre* the way Brecht staged his *Messingkauf Dialogues*? And illustrate the arguments with scenes from different productions, including "neither fish nor fowl" scenes. And end by inviting the audience to join the discussion.

WANG ZHENG: For about 70 or 80 years spoken drama has been frozen in one mode. Now if we want to transform our theatre, we can no longer rely on the playwright alone or the actor alone. Even if there are new playwrights such as Gao Xingjian[16] from the Beijing People's Art Theatre or Sun Huizhu, the director is the one who has to bring about the transformation of our theatre because it is the director who is in charge of the whole performance.

In China there is an idea about spoken drama that says that this kind of theatre is something very intellectual and can only be appreciated by an educated audience. I used to agree with this. But since I started to work in the Chinese Theatre Association, I have changed my mind. From the standpoint of an artist—a writer or director, or even a theatre company—this might be true, but not from the standpoint of the whole country. In China today, popular art prevails. Popular songs and popular novels have large audiences. Eighty percent of our people have only an elementary school education. A popular novel may have millions of copies in print. But a script by a brilliant playwright can only expect a few hundred or at most two-thousand copies. Therefore, the question is whether we can make our works relate to the life and thinking of millions of people and also make our works interesting to them. Moreover, the artistic techniques we use should include things they appreciate. When a director talks about nationalization, he should take into account what the aesthetic judgment of the people might be.

CHEN: Today's audiences have a preference for Western styles. That was not only an artistic but a social phenomenon.

WEN: Even if a play is popular, it can't be performed thousands of times—millions of people can't see it, as they can read a novel or go to a movie or watch television.

XING: *Da cuo Che [Taking the Wrong Bus]*, a musical adaptation of a Taiwanese film, was an exception. It toured all over the country and was performed 1,095 times.

WANG ZHENG: I am in favor of diversity. But how to make our theatre popular is the question.

CHEN: If there's no audience, there's no passion.

Transcribed and translated by Zhang Jia-Xuan
Translation edited by Richard Schechner

Notes

1. For Schechner's account of parts of his journey see "Notes from Abroad: China" in *American Theatre,* March 1989. For a discussion of experimental theatre in China and selections from Sun's *The Old B Hanging on the Wall* see TDR 30, no. 4 (T112):84–105. Sun Huizhu (William), a TDR contributing editor, is a playwright and scholar currently working on his PhD dissertation at NYU. His other plays include *China Dream* with Faye C. Fei.
2. See the next issue of TDR (T123) for Qu and other Chinese scholars on nuoxi and dixi—genres of Chinese folk performance.
3. Ding county in Hebei Province near Beijing was the model for a large-scale rural reconstruction project in China during the 1930s. Experiments—involving audience participation and environmental theatre—were important parts of the project which was ended in 1936 by the Japanese invasion of China.
4. Tian Han was an important playwright, director, and theatre organizer from the 1920s to his death during the Cultural Revolution. Tian was chairman of the Chinese Theatre Association from its establishment just after Liberation until his death in 1966 or 1967. Cao Yu is the best known spoken drama playwright. His plays include *Leiyu (Thunderstorm), Richu (Sunrise),* and *Beijing Ren (Peking Man).* At present he is chairman of the Chinese Theatre Association. Ouyang Yuqian, who died in the 1950s, was an important playwright, director, and theatre educator, the first head of the Central Academy of Drama. He was also an excellent jingju actor, comparable to Mei Lanfang. Xia Yan is a playwright and screenwriter, author of *Shanghai Wuyan Xia (Under Shanghai's Eaves).*
5. Guo Moruo was a prolific social scientist, archaeologist, historian, poet, and playwright from the 1920s to the early 1960s. He was president of the China Academy of Science from Liberation to his death in 1978. Mao Dun was China's most renowned novelist and essayist from the 1930s until his death in the early 1980s. His best known work is *Ziye (Midnight).* Mao was the chairman of the Chinese Writers Association from the Liberation until his death.
6. Lao She was an outstanding novelist and playwright from the 1930s to his death in 1966 when he committed suicide at the start of the Cultural Revolution. His play *Chaguan (Tea House),* which premiered in 1958, is generally considered the best Chinese spoken drama.
7. The Gang of Four—Jiang Quing (Mme. Mao), Zhang Chunqiao, Wang Hong Wen, Yao Wen Yuan—"guided" Mao Zedung after the death of Lin Biao in

1971. The Gang of Four are considered to have been the architects of the most extreme events and brutalities of the Cultural Revolution. After the Cultural Revolution the Gang of Four were convicted of crimes against the people. They are presently in jail.

8. In December 1978 the Chinese leadership decided to "open" China, embracing (in the words of Nicholas D. Kristof of *The New York Times*) "a process of pragmatic development that would come to include private ownership, stock markets, foreign-managed enterprises, and other innovations that repudiated much of Communist ideology" (1989). Along with the changes in economic policy came a more open attitude toward cultural exchanges.
9. The author of *Hong Bizi* is Yao Yiwei, born on the mainland and presently living in Taiwan. *Hong Bizi* premiered at the China Youth Art Theatre in the early 1980s—it was the first play from Taiwan to be produced on the mainland since Liberation.
10. *Ah-Q Zhengzhuan* is an adaptation of Lu Xun's modern novella. *Heshi Bi,* a Taiwanese play by Zhang Xiaofeng, is a dramatization of an ancient historical anecdote.
11. By "small theatre" the Chinese mean houses seating up to 400 persons. In addition to the small theatre in Nanjing, a "black box" theatre seating 150–200 persons opened in Beijing in the early summer of 1988. The small theatre of the Shanghai People's Art Theatre opens in May 1989 with Sun Huizhu's *Miangri Jiuyao Chushan (Tomorrow He'll Be Out of the Mountains)* directed by Schechner.
12. As part of the "open door" policy certain zones along the East Coast of China are given freer rein in determining economic policies. The areas close to Hong Kong in Guangdong province and in Jiangsu province northwest of Shanghai are particularly active areas of private ownership and "free enterprise." Although the people in these areas are better off now than before, labor conditions are often harsh with 12-hour, 7-day weeks and child factory-workers. But people are eager for the work because the pay is high. The difference in living conditions between the relatively well-off coastal regions and the very poor interior of China is extreme. The leadership hopes that a "trickle down effect" will raise living standards for the rural masses. Whether or not the current policies—a kind of Chinese Reaganomics—will lead to such an upswing remains an open question.
13. Lin Zhaohua and Hu Weimin are excellent spoken drama directors. Lin is with the Beijing People's Art Theatre and Hu, the director of the Shanghai Youth Spoken Drama Troupe, is currently guest artistic director with the Guangzhou Spoken Drama Troupe. Hu has also directed traditional operas in various places.
14. *Wusheng de Liaoliang*, written and directed by Gong Xiaodong, was performed in the People's Liberation Army Spoken Drama Theatre in Beijing in 1985. It featured stylized movement drawn from modern Western mime as well as techniques from traditional operas. Gong was one of the two directors of Sun's *Old B.*
15. Bai Xianyong is a playwright who was born on the mainland, moved to Taiwan, and is currently living and teaching in California.
16. Gao Xingjian is a playwright with the Beijing People's Art Theatre. One of his plays, *Chezhan (Bus Stop),* which premiered in 1983, has been compared to *Waiting for Godot.*

Reference

Kristof, Nicholas D.

1989 "China Celebrates Ten Years Along the Capitalist Road." *The New York Times,* 1 January, sec. 4:3.

The Global Voyage of Robert Lepage

Nigel Hunt

Under a wash of pale blue light an actor in a tuxedo walks to the middle of the stage and steps into a sunken swimming pool filled thigh-high with water. A piano bench is lowered from the ceiling. The actor, playing Fréderic Chopin, sits on the bench and is transported 40 feet straight up to a waiting grand piano which is suspended in midair and surrounded by enough chairs and music stands (painted blue to match the piano) for a small orchestra. Calmly, Chopin starts to play a piece by Chopin. This bold and playful image begins *Tectonic Plates,* the latest project of Quebec writer-director-actor Robert Lepage. As a work-in-progress (with collaborator/designer Michael Levine) the piece was seen in its first stage of creation at Harbourfront's du Maurier World Stage theatre festival in Toronto in June 1988.

A native of Quebec City, Lepage graduated from le Conservatoire d'Art dramatique de Quebec in 1978. He then studied in Paris under Alain Knapp, a Swiss director who emphasizes the idea of the acteur-createur—his students learn acting, directing, and writing. Lepage, who often acts in, directs, writes, and designs a piece, terms this approach "global."

Lepage has also enjoyed great success as an improv comedian in Quebec's Ligue Nationale d'Improvisation (LNI), where teams of improvisers dressed in hockey sweaters play off one another. This type of theatre, too, demands a multiplicity of talents. Lepage says: "When you do the improvs you have to be a writer, an actor, a set designer, and a director. All at the same time. Before doing the improvs I was an actor *or* a playwright *or* a director" (Hunt 1987:25).

Another large influence on Lepage's work has been the "REPERE" cycles. Le Théâtre Repère, founded by Jacques Lessard in 1980 (Lepage joined in 1981 and is now artistic director), was inspired by the "RSVP Cycles," a creative method developed by Anna and Lawrence Halprin.[1] The name Repère stands for: REsource, Participation, Evaluation, and REpresentation. The process begins by locating the resource for the creation. For example, in *La trilogie des dragons* (1985–1988), the initial idea was to do a show about the different Chinatowns across Canada; the resource was the parking lot in Quebec City which stands where that city's Chinatown once was. This resource was transformed into the set for the play. Three tons of sand and fine gravel were spread in a rectangle with a lamppost at one end and the parking lot attendant's booth at the other—a replica of what remains of Quebec City's Chinatown. Lepage and his cocreators reconstructed and explored the possibilities inherent in their resource, creating characters, their relationships, and their stories through collective improvisation, and eventually producing a show which incorporated many levels of history and humanity buried beneath the surface idea of "Chinatowns across Canada." Unlike typical play creation where the text precedes other aspects of production (often by years), Théâtre Repère's creative method sees the characters, the text, the design, and the mise-en-scene all evolving together from the start through the work of the entire creative group.

Lepage's one man show *Vinci* premiered in Montreal in 1986. It has since been seen all over Quebec as well as in Toronto, Calgary, Paris, and Avignon, where it won the 1987 Coup de Pouce prize. *Vinci*'s nine scenes, which the program refers to as an "Itinerary," are:

1. Take-Off
2. Big Ben, London (jet-lag)
3. Virgin and Child with St. Anne, National Gallery, London
4. Burger King, boulevard Saint-Germain, Paris
5. Mona Lisa, Oil on canvas 77 × 53 cm, Louvre, Paris
6. Camping in Cannes
7. Duomo, Firenze
8. Shower room, Firenze
9. Vinci (A hillside of Olive Trees)

1. Robert Lepage as the blind Italian narrator in the original production of Vinci *at Théâtre de Quat'Sous in Montreal (1986). (Photo by Claudel Huot)*

Lepage performs two versions of the play, one for English-speaking audiences (translated by Linda Gaboriau) and one for French. Each version uses English, French, and Italian. The English version lasts about 80 minutes, the French, 90. The performance is accompanied by musician Daniel Toussaint, who supplies synthesized music and sound effects throughout.

Vinci starts with some of Leonardo da Vinci's drawings projected onto a large screen at the rear of the stage, accompanied by a taped introduction:

Stain on the eye
Left by the sunlight
All contrasts fade
Too dazzling to remember

Stain on the soul
Left by the death of a friend
The meaning of life fades
Too devastating to remember

Voyage:
Back and forth through the eye,
Through the soul

Vision:
To see the stain on the eye, on the soul,
Again and again

Victory:
To overcome or to perish with the eye,
or with the soul

To come
To see
To conquer
Vini
Vidi
Vinci

Next the sentence "Art is a Vehicle" is projected as a toy train circles at the foot of the screen. Lepage enters wearing dark glasses and carrying a white cane. He is a blind narrator, lecturing the audience in Italian on the subject of art, while translations into English or French (as the case may be) are projected onto the screen above him. He explains that since "the plot follows the creative evolution of a visual artist" he has been asked to talk about the visual arts, even though he is neither an artist himself nor a well-known critic, but merely a fictional character. He continues:

> But since I speak a foreign language
> And am played by an immensely talented actor,
> The production crew felt you would take their artistic preoccupations more seriously if they were exposed to you by someone speaking with a European accent.

He goes on to explain that the train which we have been watching is a visual way of communicating the message "Art is a Vehicle." He compares the construction of a train to the form of a sentence: "At the outset, the cars of a sentence, like those of a train, are empty. They must then be loaded with meaning. And to transmit the sentence, it must be motivated." He concludes that as the subtitles in a film allow us to follow what is going on, and as "art also serves the function of casting light on the chaos of our society, [art] is, to a certain extent: A SUB-TITLE."

In the first section of the Itinerary, "Take-Off," we meet the main character, Philippe, who is seated on a swivel chair. Tilting himself on the chair, and accompanied by the taped sounds of an airplane's engines, he simulates flying an airplane as it lands. At the same time, Philippe reveals his problems to an invisible psychiatrist about various matters: Disillusionment with his career as a photographer; the coldness of his art and its poor critical reception; the fear of letting go, exemplified by his recent inability to jump off a small cliff into a snowbank as his friends were doing; and depression over the suicide of his friend Marc, a filmmaker with the very integrity which Philippe feels he lacks. At the end of his session, Philippe decides that since his psychiatrist hasn't made any useful suggestions, he is going to follow his friends' advice and spend his money on a trip to Europe instead. The sounds of the airplane's engines amplify. Lepage holds his chair, pushes it swiftly across the stage, and lifts it smoothly upwards.

For the second section, "Big Ben," Lepage goes behind the screen (lit so we can see only his silhouette) and plays a British tour guide, narrating a fast-paced musical bus trip around London. A diorama of the London skyline, visible at the bottom of the screen, has come slowly into view during the scene change. This section is full of visual tricks. What appears to be a rear-view mirror dangling above the guide, angling with him from side to side as he points out various highlights of the city, suddenly turns out to be a model World War II fighter plane that Lepage uses to dive-bomb while he describes German attacks on London. A description of Big Ben and the nature of time is illustrated by a mechanical toy boxer punching his way around the ring. The feeling of jet lag, nausea, or "décalage," which the French-Canadians on the bus tour are said to experience from driving on the "wrong side" of the road in London, is compared to the paradox that Leonardo da Vinci abhorred human suffering and yet invented war machines, that he drew "diagrams of divine proportions" but was twice accused of sodomy.

In the next scene, Philippe arrives at the National Gallery of London. The sensation of being inside the museum is conveyed by amplifying Philippe's camera clicks and footsteps. He attempts to be discreet about photographing some of the pictures, but his every move produces a loud echo, an effect created by the cordless microphone which Lepage wears. Philippe then takes a glass film-processing tray from his pack and pours water into it, placing the tray on top of a flashlight. When he lays the prints in the tray, we see slide projections of the paintings he has photographed, as if we are watching the photos actually develop. When he exits, he puts the tray at the foot of the screen and launches a small toy boat into it. As the boat "sails," the diorama of London disappears, and that of Paris approaches. The electric train then resumes its circle.

Lepage reenters, dressed as a woman bearing an uncanny resemblance to the Mona Lisa and parodying a Parisian accent. The entire scene is backgrounded by a banal disco beat. "Mona" and Philippe are in a Paris Burger King. She addresses Philippe and waits for his responses, unheard by the audience. She praises fast-food burgers, calling them "ze last step before ze capsule . . . zo concentrated zat is no more food, it is ze idea of food." After rebuking Philippe for the sterility of his photographs—he admits to her that he photographs bathroom fixtures—she tells him that she is fed up

2. "Mona Lisa" (Robert Lepage) at Burger King in Vinci *(1986). (Photo by Claudel Huot)*

with her work in the Louvre as a simultaneous translator for guided tours and seeks a new freedom. She smiles—a striking likeness of the Mona Lisa.

Next, in a short interlude, Lepage as the blind Italian narrator gives a "Brief Anthology of Artistic Creations Which Have Defied the Rigid Rules of the Tape Measure," using a retractable tape measure and his body to suggest such things as the Great Pyramid, a Picasso painting, television, jazz, *Jaws,* and Michael Jackson's moon walk. For example, the pyramid is formed by bending the tape measure into a triangular shape; the Picasso by twisting the tape to suggest the shape of an extra jutting nose and eye beside Lepage's own features. He ends by commenting upon how sad it is for an artist to die before reaching full potential. "In fact, the difference between art and death is simply a question of . . . speed."

The fifth section, a story on tape about a 1911 theft of the Mona Lisa supplemented by a few slide projections of names and dates, takes place with Lepage off stage, preparing for the following scene. The tape ends with a challenge to Philippe: To create great art you must be prepared to "jump into ze light."

In "Camping in Cannes" Philippe fumbles around, struggling to pitch a tent in the dark. Once the tent is finally up, he goes to pee in the woods, treading on a sheet of plastic bubble packing material to make the sound of snapping twigs; water sprayed from a plastic bottle, seen in the dim light from Philippe's flashlight, completes the effect. Returning to his tent, he plays with the flashlight, making shadows of animals on the side of the tent before finally settling down in his sleeping bag. Once asleep, Philippe relates a nightmare he is having during which he confesses to Marc that he can't finish Marc's film for him because Marc failed to leave him a film script. Rising above the form of Philippe asleep, Lepage appears as Marc, creating an ominous shadow inside the tent as he threatens Philippe in his dream. "Marc" tries to slit Philippe's wrists and it appears as if the two are struggling inside the tent. Lepage then holds the flashlight low to the ground and propels his body over the light, creating the illusion that he is jumping off a cliff, falling through the air. Philippe screams, awakens, and goes outside to pull himself together. He sees the electric train circling near him.

Next, the blind Italian guide takes the spectators on a tour of the Dome of the Cathedral in Florence, creating the sensation of the acoustics inside the cupola by alternating live amplified sound (by means of the cordless microphone) with his unamplified voice. The guide compares the ability to imagine such great architecture with the talent of a Leonardo, "for imagination allows you to soar to liberating heights and, in the final analysis, the difference between flight and the force of gravity is simply a question of speed." At that moment he waves his white cane rapidly back and forth beside him so that it picks up several projections of Leonardo's paintings, causing them to appear out of thin air.

In the penultimate scene, Philippe is in a public bath wearing only a towel around his waist. From time to time, hot water falls from above onto tiles at the side of the stage and steam rises. As he shaves, Philippe cuts himself. The blood reminds him of Marc's suicide. He covers half of his face with shaving cream, forming white hair and a beard to resemble Leonardo da Vinci. Showing first one side of his face and then the other, Lepage creates a dialog between Philippe and Leonardo. Philippe asks about the nature and contradictions of art. Leonardo replies that Philippe has been monopolizing the mirror, preventing his discreet viewing of the good-looking naked men in the bath. Leonardo then forces Philippe to look into the mirror himself, to recognize this own contradictions as necessary for creativity:

> What do you see? On one side, there's a young Quebecois intellectual who pisses everyone off with his big ideas about art and integrity and who thinks he has a stain on his soul. And on the other side, there's a dirty old man who likes to get it while he can. Sometimes it's the young intellectual who gets the upper hand, but other times it's the dirty old man.
>
> Sometimes you're a British guide who keeps a cold, critical eye on society.
>
> And other times, you're an imitation Mona Lisa searching for freedom in the middle of a Burger King.

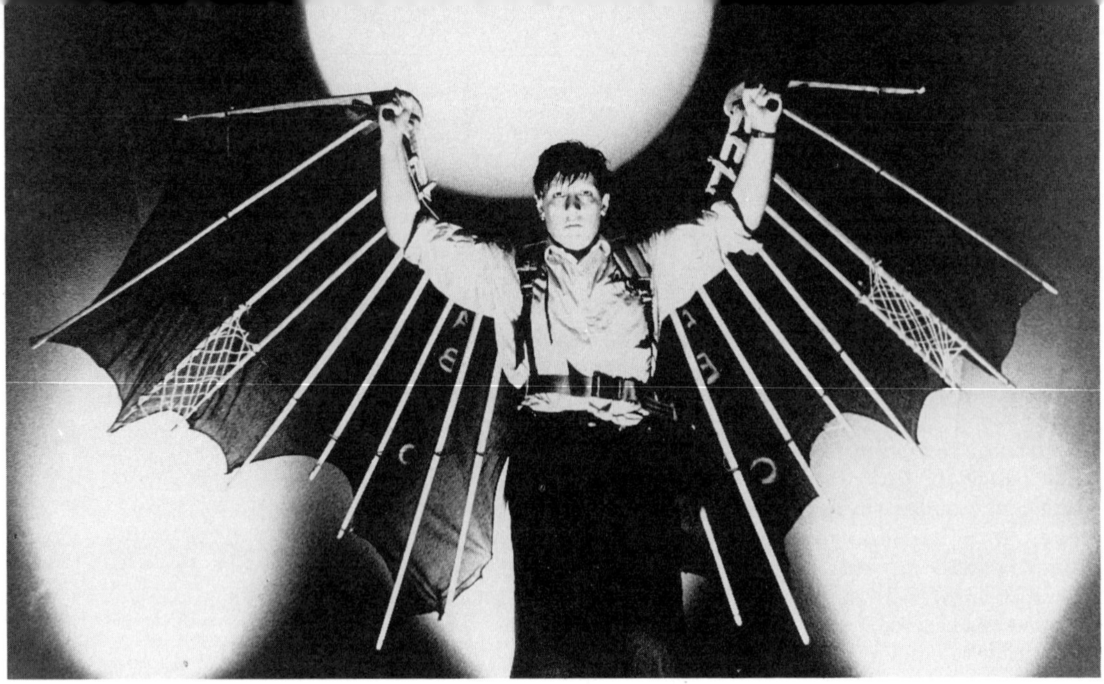

3. Robert Lepage in Leonardo's famous wings in the final tableau of Vinci *(1986). (Photo by Robert Laliberte)*

> When I've gotta stain, Philippe, I let time and the clear water of lucidity wash it away. Art is the result of a conflict between your heart and your head. Art is a conflict. If there's no conflict, there's no art, Philippe, no artists. Art is a paradox, a contradiction. Now, go and wash yourself, Philippe.

In the final scene, Philippe constructs a tiny village by placing several guide books on their sides so that viewed from above they look like roofs. He has finally arrived in the town of Vinci, Leonardo's birthplace. Philippe's journey has taught him that the problems he faces cannot be left behind: they are based upon his own attitudes. By facing up to this, Philippe finds that he can accept both his friend's suicide and his own fear of letting himself go. Da Vinci's birthplace serves as a location for Philippe's own personal renaissance (rebirth). Wearing a backpack, Philippe runs toward the side of the stage as if to jump off the edge of a cliff above Vinci and disappears. He reappears at the back of the stage, in silhouette behind the screen. Still running, Lepage vaults over the light source located on the floor behind the screen, again appearing to have jumped off the cliff. As soon as his feet disappear downwards, Philippe's silhouette reappears, replete with huge wings (as in Leonardo's famous diagram) spread out from his outstretched arms. For a brief moment he is still—then continues his flight out and over the cliff as Lepage again vaults his entire body over the light, as if he is truly flying.

Philippe's journey in *Vinci* is very much the journey of today's Quebecois. In the 1960s and '70s Quebec was resolutely insular and introspective, in reaction against the cultural and economic domination by Canada's English-speaking majority. By the '80s this struggle had largely paid off. Having fought to secure its own French identity, Quebec could now afford to look beyond its own borders with renewed interest. Lepage exemplifies this new attitude. *Vinci* details the journey outside one's own personal and provincial borders, as well as Lepage's own life history. "Before I decided to be an actor, I wanted to be a geography teacher. If I wasn't an actor or writer, I probably would have been a teacher or a tour guide somewhere" (Lepage 1988).

La trilogie des dragons (The Dragons' Trilogy) has been even more successful than *Vinci.* It began as a 90-minute piece performed in Quebec City in 1985, then grew to a 3-hour version for its 1986 Toronto presentation. The *Trilogie* toured to Montreal, Ottawa, Stony Brook (New York), the London International Festival of Theatre (LIFT), Ireland, the Festival des francophonies de Limoges in France, and the 1988 Adelaide Arts Festival in Australia. At the 1987 Festival de théâtre des Amériques in Montreal, the *Trilogie* was presented in a six-hour version and awarded the Grand Prix as well as the Quebec Theatre Critics Association Award for Best Production that year. The six-hour version was remounted in Montreal in 1988.[2]

The *Trilogie* is a journey through three Canadian Chinatowns, beginning in Quebec City in 1910 and ending in Vancouver in 1986. Because it is in three languages (French, English, and Chinese), the audience must piece the story together like a puzzle. Lepage comments on this:

> What I like to do is use words as music. People's talk becomes music and what they do are the real verbs, the real actions, the real phrases. The meaning of the shows has to be what's up front. And the way we get there is by the different languages, to treat them as objects. I have an idea. I say it in a language that people don't understand so they're interested to know what it's all about. I say it again, but in another language they don't understand. But they understand a little

4. Marie Brassard and Lorraine Côté in La trilogie des dragons *(1986). (Photo by Claudel Huot)*

> more of it. They start to build up the show with me. It's very active. It's like saying the same thing over and over again, but with different images. People associate words and senses and objects and imagery. They associate all of that on the same idea, the same theme (Hunt 1987:28).

This creative process, and the way it involves its audience, reminds us that the French word for watching a show is *"assister"* (to assist).

The pivotal characters are Jeanne (Marie Michaud) and Françoise (Marie Gignac), two French-Canadian women played throughout by the same actresses. At the beginning of the play they are children; by the end, they are old women, and the focus of the story has shifted to their children. Accompanying this transformation of character is a transformation of location. The parking lot of today's Quebec City becomes the vanished Chinatown of years ago. The two girls play with shoe boxes, pretending that they are the houses in their neighborhood, imagining relationships and reconstructing conversations they have overheard. The parking lot attendant becomes Wong (Yves-Érick Marier), a Chinese launderer, and the booth, the entrance to his laundry room. William Crawford (originally played by Lepage), the British owner of a shoe store, arrives in Quebec City from Hong Kong to set up business. Both Wong and Crawford (like many Canadians) are displaced from their natural language and culture. Neither speaks French, and so, in order to communicate, they resort to mime, using the available physical objects to convey their stories and situations. Crawford employs his suitcase to show Wong how he has arrived in the New World by boat and how he plans to set up his own shoe store. Eventually, with some sort of friendship and understanding secured, they retreat to the basement of Wong's laundry business, where Wong gives Crawford hashish and insists that Crawford teach him poker.

These characters continue to cross paths throughout the play. Concerned about his advanced age and future financial security, Wong engages the local barber in a poker game. The scene takes place in the dimly lit basement of Wong's laundry. The scene is done with few props. The poker table is a large steel drum; the players hold their hands upright as if holding cards. The sizes of the bets are indicated by the loud booms as Wong and the barber repeatedly slam their fists down on the drum. Crawford and another character, watching in horror as the drunken barber gambles and loses all, mark the start of each round with the percussive tapping of short sticks—a variation on traditional Chinese instruments. Desperate, the barber gambles his business, signified by placing his barber's chair on top of the drum. When he loses that, and has only his pregnant daughter Jeanne left to gamble—she is brought in and placed in the chair, still on top of the drum. She too is lost, and Wong's future is secured as he now has gained not only wealth, but a bride for his son, Lee. After they are married, Lee and Jeanne relocate to Toronto's Chinatown.

The second section takes place during World War II—according to Lepage, the most important period for Toronto's Chinatown. Françoise, on leave from the service, meets Crawford on a train as she journeys to Toronto to visit Jeanne. Chairs are brought out and set back-to-back in the sand to indicate the compartments on a train. Crawford borrows a match, then introduces Françoise to hashish. She asks Crawford for directions to help her find her friend who, it turns out, is working in Crawford's shoe store in Toronto's Chinatown. The chairs are rearranged in a row, a few shoe boxes are brought out, and, voila, Crawford's shoe store on Toronto's Spadina Avenue in the heart of Chinatown.

Unlike *Vinci,* which depended on an abundance of technological gadgetry, *Trilogie* uses only the most basic materials. For instance, in the second section, children's shoes are lifted out of the shoe boxes. A soldier on ice skates marches around the perimeter of the playing space and is joined by other soldiers as the pace quickens. Robert Caux's music builds to a crescendo when the soldiers kick their way through the sand, trampling the children's shoes. Helpless civilians scramble to save the shoes, screaming with terror. The scene is an effective and innovative evocation of the destructiveness of war.

The final section is set in Vancouver (1960–1986), which is, according to Lepage, the most modern and thriving of Canada's Chinatowns (Lefebvre 1987:33). Now a middle-aged woman, Françoise has been visiting her son Pierre, who has left Quebec to live in Vancouver. She introduces Pierre to Yukali, a young Japanese woman she met while trying to decide what to buy her relatives from the airport gift shop. Yukali is an aspiring artist and Pierre runs a small art gallery, so Françoise, ever the meddling mother, tries to matchmake.

In this section the action moves fluidly from scene to scene as events take place one on top of the other. One moment we are in the art gallery where Pierre is dismantling *Constellation,* his conceptual installation piece consisting of strings of Christmas lights strewn about the floor. The lights fade and we are back at the airport where Françoise, waiting for her flight home to Quebec, meets an Air France pilot. When the pilot leaves for his flight, the scene moves to the airport runway as the airplane—played by the pilot laying flat on his stomach on top of an upright suitcase with his arms spread—takes off as the pilot makes the appropriate announcements. The lights of Pierre's *Constellation* flick on, becoming the lights of the city as

5. Françoise (Marie Gignac) and her son Pierre (Robert Lepage) at the airport in the 1986 Toronto production of La trilogie des dragons. *(Photo by Claudel Huot)*

seen from the plane. The lights fade on the pilot and, back in the gallery, Pierre continues to dismantle his artwork. Yukali arrives to show Pierre her drawings—pictures of the three dragons which symbolize the *Trilogie*: the green dragon of the sea, the red dragon of the earth, and the blue dragon of the air.

The motif of Yukali's drawings sums up the *Trilogie's* symbols. The performance began with Crawford's arrival in Quebec City by boat; the Toronto section takes place on a train; and the *Trilogie* ends in the Vancouver airport. The three dragons correspond to the three modes of transportation (water/boat, earth/train, air/plane) as well as the season of each setting (spring, summer, fall). These connections with Chinese dragon mythology (the fourth Chinese dragon, white, representing the interior, was left out by Lepage because from the start he wanted a play divided into three parts, locations, and times) are explained by Lepage as coincidences which occurred during the creation of the piece, but which carry confirmation of the power of intuition in his work (Lefebvre 1987:33).

Near the end of the *Trilogie,* Pierre, enchanted with Yukali, discovers in conversation that his name means "rock" and hers means "emerald," so, they believe, they are like two stones in a Zen garden. As they fall in love, Pierre describes to her a Japanese fertility rite he has heard about. As he describes it, the other actors appear in traditional Japanese costume and reenact the ritual. The men, in one group, hold an enormous rope with one end knotted; the women also hold a rope formed in a large loop—representing yin and yang. The success or failure of the two groups to make a connection is said to determine the prosperity of that year's harvest. The ritual complete—and successful—the actors exit, leaving Pierre and Yukali alone, surrounded by Pierre's *Constellation*. They make love as the lights cross-fade.

The scene moves back to the airplane, where we learn from an in-flight announcement that Crawford is on board, on his way to visit Hong Kong, his birthplace. As the pilot describes the view to his passengers, noting the rise of Vancouver's Chinatown and comparing the setting of the sun in Vancouver and its simultaneous rise in Hong Kong with the eternal balance of the Eastern philosophy of yin and yang, he announces that Halley's comet has just come into view. Then, inexplicably, the airplane loses altitude and crashes into the Pacific.

The final scene brings us back to Quebec City where Françoise and her son Pierre visit the parking lot in the hope of a good view of Halley's comet. Françoise's own mother had seen it from this point in 1910 (the year the *Trilogie* began), and she tells Pierre that when she used to play there as a small girl, the lot was Quebec City's Chinatown. The cultural collage of the *Trilogie,* and the struggle for a balance between cultural identity and assimilation, is, in fact, Lepage's version of the story of Canada.

I spoke with Lepage and Marie Gignac, actress and cocreator, in January 1988 while they were working on *Tectonic Plates,* which had its world premiere in Toronto in June 1988. This show, which is scheduled to be seen in later phases in New York, Montreal, and Glasgow (in 1990 during that city's tenure as the European City of Culture), concerns itself with the coming together and breaking apart of continents and cultures in order to explore the relationship between the New World (the Americas) and the Old World (Europe). When I spoke with Lepage and Gignac they had

6. *Yukali (Marie Brassard) and Pierre (Robert Lepage) surrounded by his* Constellation *installation in* La trilogie des dragons *(1986). (Photo courtesy of Théâtre Repère)*

already come up with three related resources: tectonic plates (as in the theory of continental drift), dinner plates, and boats.

LEPAGE: My shows are usually about traveling, about culture clustering, and things like that. It's very geological, as a starting point, but it will probably evolve into something more metaphorical. It's a lot about continents that used to be one big continent and have separated into two, and then four, and six. Until they became the continents we know now. And they're still drifting apart.

I thought it was a good starting point to talk about differences between Europe and North America, the fact that we used to be very close and now we are separated. Revolutions are parting points where pieces of earth are sliced and separated, then are reunited again in a different way. The tectonic plates separate and oppose themselves. Sometimes they get closer again, but in another shape. They bang and they produce mountains and things like that. Then they move away again and meet somewhere else. So the relationship between the plates resembles the relationship of France to Canada—they colonized French Canada and then went away when the English defeated them in war. The American Revolution also separated Europe from the New World. The metaphor is about people moving close and going away. And about collaboration . . . .

We work with plates, dishes, dinner plates because in dinner plates you can read different levels. For example, you could break a plate so it suddenly looks like the continents, fractured like a big puzzle. If you put them all back together again you could get a sense of what it used to be. It is also very archaeological. The archaeologist finds all sorts of things, but the puzzles that they have to put together are usually dishware because the richest thing an archaeologist can work on is a latrine. What they used to call a latrine is not what it is today. It was a place where everybody would throw away what they didn't use anymore. All of the food perished, but the porcelain, the steel, the utensils are still there. You have all these different layers of history. So when someone finds a latrine, it's a big event because it informs you about all of the periods and styles—how people lived, how fashion and culture evolved, and how much time it took.

We saw the show as a big puzzle. You put pieces together to get information. Instead of taking a puzzle and just building it, we thought of trying to reconstruct dishes since it has to do with human beings eating. Everything happens at the table: big discussions, the family.

Also, the broken dishes are a miniaturization of tectonic plates. They also mean divorce, separation. So it's a show about things being separated, moving away. Probably somewhere in the story line there will be a divorce, or people breaking dishes. We haven't finished exploring that object, but at this point there are about 15 significations to that small plate. It indicates some of the characters that will be there, some of the situations, what some characters do for a living. There probably will be an archaeologist.

We also have another metaphor, another object: the boat. The boat is, in some way, an island that's drifting away—again, like tectonic plates, like a society. A continent is a very big boat, a society that floats away. Even if we have the impression that everything is still, it isn't, it's moving away. Also the boat is a very important starting point because that's the first link between Europe and North America—Christopher Columbus discovering America. So that is the other object we intend to develop. The idea is about these islands that float around, coming from somewhere and going to somewhere.

HUNT: What interests you more, traveling to other places or the cultures that you find there?

LEPAGE: It's all linked together—the language, the traveling, the tourist side of it. But the human side also: finding your roots in someone else's culture. Also because Quebecois have strange roots. I don't know where I came from. A lot of people in Toronto know that their family came from Ireland, or somewhere. You could go back more than 200 years. We [Quebecois] always have an idea that we came from somewhere in the North of France, but it's not precise. It's not very clear. We're looking for our roots.

GIGNAC: Theatrically, what is interesting about looking at people who are very different from you, and doing a show about that, is that it's a very good starting point for your imagination. If you just talk about yourself, your imagination does not go very far. If you look at your near or far neighbor and try to imagine what's happening in his or her life—the sky's the limit. It's very stimulating.

HUNT: Is looking at another culture a way of examining yourself, or is it just an interest in the other culture?

GIGNAC: We are examining ourselves. Like in the *Trilogie,* we were talking about ourselves through our vision of China.

LEPAGE: It was a pretext for us. We said, we're going to do a show about the Chinatowns. But we knew what really concerned us was the people we knew, our families, our intimates.

HUNT: Are you just pretending to be interested in the Chinese as a way of being interested in yourselves?

LEPAGE: That would be a strange way to put it. We don't pretend. We're very interested in the Chinese, Chinatowns, and all of that. But while we are searching and digging to find answers about that, most of the answers that come back to us are about ourselves, about how we are, how we look.

It's the opposite of a documentary. It's as if we would've said: we're going to do something about China, so we take this camera and we go to China and we bring back images, and we say, you see how Chinese people are different from us. Look at how their eyes are, the color of their skin. Listen to their speech. Look at this. Listen to that. That's documentary. Sometimes people in the theatre approach these kind of things and think they make us learn a lot about the Chinese by showing us how they are. But we try to work the other way around. We try to say, we've been to China, now look at how we look, how we are made.

GIGNAC: The way you look at somebody is the way you are. It's all you, all your culture.

LEPAGE: You get a very good idea of what Quebec is about if you go to France, to England, Switzerland. There is a clearer image of Quebec, now that people are going away and coming back. Our old attitude was to be secluded. That was very important for us to do, but we were looking at ourselves a lot.

HUNT: What about your consistent use of three languages in your work?

LEPAGE: There's a lot of reasons. The geography side of it. Also, language is a costume. An actor who decides to do a character will find the clothes of the character very important. Speaking with an accent, or not, speaking in another language, or speaking in your own language is a costume you put on. I don't think people are very conscious of it. Also, there's the metaphor of theatre or art as another language.

And even if we speak of seemingly unimportant things that only concern two little girls in a small place in Quebec, using other languages to translate what they are saying or to refer to it implies that this is happening all over the world. It's a way of universalizing small things that seem unimportant, but are important. It helps you to focus on humanity instead of regionalism. For a long time in Quebec our theatre has been about our national colors: the way we spoke, the way we lived, our folklore. Now we're saying that we're talking about humankind, and this is what we feel about it.

GIGNAC: Also when you improvise in another language, in English or in Chinese, it keeps you nearer to real things. You often hide behind your maternal language because you're so comfortable in it. In another language, you're forced to go straight to the right thing.

LEPAGE: It makes improvising more essential.

GIGNAC: When you perform in another language you have to play the emotion. You can't hide behind your diction or speaking abilities. So you have a chance of getting more truth.

LEPAGE: It is also a way of "imposing" poetry. For example, if I spoke very few words in English, the way I would be expressing myself would be more essential, more poetic, because I have only very few materials to express everything I have to say. It's like writing poetry or working in art. You are very limited, you have only few tools. The way you put them together is poetry. You're talking about something very important, but you have only this table, and a few glasses.

Notes

1. "RSVP" stands for Resources Scores Valuaction Performance: "these describe the procedures inherent in the creative process" (Halprin 1969:2). The Halprins developed the idea of "scores" as a means of communicating the creative process in any art form "to allow many people to enter into the act of creation together" (1969:1).
2. See *Cahiers de théâtre Jeu* (1987) for several articles devoted to this play. See also TDR 32, no. 1 (T117) for a report on the 1987 Festival de théâtre des Amériques (MacDougall 1988).

References

Cahiers de théâtre Jeu
1987 Vol. 45, no. 4 (Winter):37–210. Several articles devoted to *La trilogie des dragons*.

Halprin, Lawrence
1969 *The RSVP Cycles: Creative Processes in the Human Environment*. New York: George Braziller, Inc.

Hunt, Nigel
1987 "The Moving Language of Robert Lepage." *Theatrum*, no. 6 (Spring): 25–28, 32.

Lefebvre, Paul
1987 "New Filters for Creation." *Canadian Theatre Review*, no. 52 (Fall): 30–35.

Lepage, Robert
1988 Interview with author. Toronto, 22 January.

MacDougall, Jill
1988 "Le Festival de Théâtre des Amèriques: Montreal 1987." *The Drama Review* 32, no. 1 (T117):9–19.

Nigel Hunt *is a playwright and critic in Toronto. He is also editor of* Theatrum.

Going with the Flow

Performance Art and Mass Culture

Philip Auslander

[E]very performance ultimately meets the video screen, where the demystified subject is frozen and dies. There, performance once again encounters representation, from which it wanted to escape at all costs and which marks both its fulfillment and its end.

—*Josette Féral (1982:173)*

To graduate from the art world into real life—into television or into video discs, into feeding the industries that in turn feed the art and allow artists to live on revenue from their own work—has been the goal of many young artists now performing [. . .].

—*RoseLee Goldberg (1984:75)*

These two quotations encapsulate virtually the entire history of American performance art over the last 20 years or so, the transition from the generation of conceptual performers to what Goldberg has called "the media generation" of performers (1988). Whereas the earlier generation was concerned with the body's raw, physical presence, the current generation is more concerned with the word than the body. Whereas the earlier work is austere, often threatening in its emphasis on physical risk, and largely eschews theatricality and concern with audience, much current work is marked by a return to versions of narrative and characterization, and appropriations of the conventions of stand-up comedy and other popular entertainment forms. One of the major concerns of performance in the late '60s and early '70s (the era of body art and conceptual performance) was to serve as an alternative to the work of art as commodity; many current performance artists happily embrace the commodified world of mass entertainment.

The relation of the new work to photography, film, and video is intriguing in itself. The function of these media in earlier performance was primarily documentary—an ephemeral performance would be photographed or taped to serve as a record of its occurrence. This record could be exhibited or even sold in galleries and thus functioned as a sort of commodity by-product of an art form that itself intentionally resisted commodification. Féral notes the irony in the fact that conceptual performance constructed its own history by means that are antithetical to its integrity as performance: "With the help of the video camera with which every performance ends, it has provided itself with a past" (1982:175). Today, videos, photographs, and sound recordings, which represent the commodification and objectification that conceptual performance resisted, are no longer documents of ephemeral performances, but often constitute virtual performances in themselves. Douglas Crimp has in fact argued that performance has become the informing epistemology of much contemporary visual art (1984). Cindy Sherman's movie–still photographs of herself, which often reproduce typical screen representations of women, do not document a performance, but constitute a performance which exists only in them. In his early videos, especially those he made with his dogs, William Wegman plays on the whole idea of performance documentation by producing technically unsophisticated videos which have the look of crude documents made on the spur of the moment, but are in fact records of carefully rehearsed events which could never be duplicated in a live performance. Wegman also plays on the whole idea of "the demystified subject," for it is a bit difficult to determine the status of the dog as performing subject in the economy of desire that Féral sees as constitutive of theatricality. Like performance, these performative modes of recent visual art are merging with mass culture and entertainment. Jenny Holzer, for example, is reportedly exploring ways of translating her textual art into the format of the 15-second television commercial (see Howell 1988:127).

The rapprochement between performance and entertainment described by Goldberg has been fairly successful. Thanks in large part to public and cable television, at least some performance artists have gained considerable mass exposure. Performance is a staple of PBS's "Alive From Off Center"; Eric Bogosian and Spalding Gray have had cable specials, as has Ann Magnuson, whose performances derived from television initially. All three also have fledgling careers as film actors because of the notoriety they have gained as performance artists.

Other cultural institutions besides television are engaged in the dissemination of performance as entertainment. Laurie Anderson's performances occupy the cultural position of rock music more than of performance art, as do the records she has made for Warner Brothers. One can see Wegman's videos on "Saturday Night Live," or at the museum. Gray's *Swimming to Cambodia* has been available, in different forms, at the Performing Garage in New York's Soho, in more mainstream theatres, in movie theatres, and at local video and bookstores. Bogosian too has published his performances in book form; Anderson, like Gray, has translated her performance works into both film and print. Work that we once might have expected to find only in vanguard cultural contexts is now available in both vanguard and mass cultural contexts.

This is hardly the first time that experimental performance artists have participated in mass cultural entertainments; even the Living Theatre appeared in its share of commercial films. But the assumption behind such crossovers was always that they were merely expedient, a way for oppositional artists to finance their "real," socially critical work. As Goldberg has suggested, neither the distinction between the expedient work and the real work nor the need to justify the former in terms of the latter exists for the current generation of performance artists (1984). The present relationship between art performance and mass culture is one of mutual support—each "feeds" the other.

1. Ann Magnuson in her 1987 Cinemax special "Cinemax Comedy Experiment: Ann Magnuson's Vandemonium." Eric Bogosian stands at the rear. (Photo by Paula Court)

In making these observations, I am not suggesting that these artists have necessarily "sold out" or that performance art has become the current equivalent of Hollywood's Schwab's soda fountain; anyone who has ever had to support her/himself as a performance artist will attest to the continued marginality of most performance (see Burnham 1986). Several performance artists have foregrounded their new-found marketability in their work. In *United States,* Laurie Anderson draws attention to "the highly sophisticated (very expensive) state-of-the-art gadgetry" she uses in her performance, making a point of saying "this stuff does not grow on trees." The next segment of the performance sees her negotiating with Warner Brothers Records:

> And I said: Listen, I've got a vision. I see myself as part of a long tradition of American humor. You know—Bugs Bunny, Daffy Duck, Porky Pig, Elmer Fudd, Roadrunner, Yosemite Sam [all Warner Brothers "artists," of course].
>
> And they said: "Well actually, we had something a little more adult in mind."
>
> And I said: "OK! OK! Listen, I can adapt!" (1984).

In *Swimming to Cambodia,* Spalding Gray recalls various of his experiences auditioning for television and films. One anecdote, which perhaps encapsulates an aspect of the relationship between vanguard and mass culture, involves a representative from "Late Night with David Letterman" calling Gray and saying, "David wants to know what's going on with that funny guy behind the table downtown. And he wants to know, Spalding, if you could *say something funny to me over the phone*" (1985:67). Obviously such self-conscious references to the artist's participation in a commodity economy can be read as either ironic or self-serving.

Whether performance remains marginal or gains mass exposure seems to have little to do with the nature or content of a particular artist's work. Even performance work that cannot for whatever reason be showcased in its own cable television special can still find a home in a variety format, such as the recent "Mondo Bizarro" special on HBO, hosted by Bette Midler, herself a performer whose background includes a long stint on the margins. The relative success of performance in the mass media attests to the ability of a mass-mediated culture to convert almost anything into "entertainment." If a particular mode of performance cannot be marketed on television as high culture or mass entertainment, it can still be recuperated as oddity or freak show. Admittedly, it is hard to imagine Hermann Nitsch or Karen Finley doing cable specials. But given that cable television, in its network and local access forms, has provided venues for such ostensibly antisocial cultural expressions as pornography and fascist political rhetoric, one wonders if there really is a content which exceeds television's institutional tolerance.

Goldberg's conflation of the "real world" with the television industry thus gives a very clear picture of the culture that performance art now engages, a culture in which the economy of mass communications has a decisive impact on artistic production, and in which the distinction between "high" or even "vanguard" art and "mass culture" is no longer clear, from either the producers' or the consumers' point of view. At this moment in cultural history, when one literally can obtain the same cultural object at The Performing Garage in Soho, at the neighborhood video store,[1] at the museum, or on network television, any clear-cut distinction between "advanced" art and mass culture has become untenable. I believe that the situation of performance today is extraordinary, for the recent incursions performance has made into mass culture are not questions of the unannounced absorption of its aesthetic strategies by mass-market art forms, the pattern that the "mainstreaming" of vanguard aesthetic innovations usually follows. Rather, performance works are presently available under their own names in a variety of cultural contexts oriented toward different cultural markets.

Commentators who saw in earlier performance art an aesthetically and politically radical alternative to both theatre and mass entertainment are discouraged by these flirtations of performance art with commodity culture. Linda Frye Burnham takes solace in the idea that there are still "performance artists of all generations who oppose theatrical and cabaret performance," whose "work cannot be termed entertainment in any traditional sense (nor can it be easily consumed, digested, and swallowed by the Conspiracy)" (1986:45–46). Ultimately, Burnham argues, performance can retain its integrity only by choosing to remain on the margins. Burnham's idealism is admirable, and might lead one to conclude that postmodernist performance work like Anderson's and Gray's simply lends itself too easily to cooption to be taken seriously as alternative art.

But, as Jeanie Forte observes in a recent essay on feminist performance art, even performers who do not exactly "go commercial," whose work would seem far too radical to be coopted easily, and who have not achieved anything like the degree of mass cultural acceptance that Anderson and Gray have, can find themselves in a compromised position as soon as they venture even a short distance from the margin. Forte cites Karen Finley, whose "being catapulted into a higher degree of visibility hastened her assimilation into a more commercial audience. In venues other than New York, beer-drinking fraternity boys came to see the naked woman shove yams up her ass and throw obscenities at the crowd. Her work became reinscribed in the fetishistic process associated with striptease or live sex, and not at all the feminist or subversive strategy that theory might endorse" (1988:234). What is the limit past which marginality gives way to marketability? The questions Forte poses are important ones for those concerned with the practical politics of performance:

> [J]ust how much does the work retain any potentially subversive impact once it has achieved commercial viability? To what extent do those commercial endorsements render any radical politics impossible? Yet, if performance artists are doomed to relative obscurity, playing only to audiences of "the converted," how will societal consciousness be raised (or abrased) on a larger scale? Should this even be a conscious goal? (1988:234).

These questions admit no easy answers. It is equally facile, and equally incorrect, to insist that performance work automatically loses its subversive potential (if it can ever be said to have possessed such potential) when it enters a mass cultural context as to insist that its new-found position inside of mass culture places performance art in the perfect posture to undermine it from within. In any case, as Forte also points out, performance artists themselves welcome their new opportunities: the general trend in performance art at the moment is away from the margins, toward greater exposure. "In general, the mid 1980s has brought about a regrouping, perhaps in response to a reactionary political climate, perhaps in the perceived failure of 1970s strategies to achieve more measurable, visible effects" (1988:233).

It may be that the questions Forte poses must be addressed from a new perspective. The assumptions underlying Burnham's and Forte's observations derive from the traditional theoretical opposition of vanguard culture and mass culture which sees mass culture as necessarily "hegemonic" and only vanguard culture as potentially "non-" or "counterhegemonic."[2] As Dana Polan, Tania Modleski, Andreas Huyssen, and others have argued in detail recently, such a dichotomy ignores the fact that there are few distinctions one can make at the levels of form, content, even, possibly, ideology between current vanguard and mass-cultural work. So, on the one hand, a "highly mainstream artform" such as television may bear "the very same formal traits which are often taken to constitute a challenge to the mainstream" (Polan 1986:170)—disruption of narrative, refusal of closure, etc.

On the other hand, mass culture itself has emerged as a site of possible resistance to the mainstream. In her essay on slasher films, for example, Tania Modleski observes that certain forms of mass culture are becoming "increasingly adversarial": "Many of these films are engaged in an unprecedented assault on all that bourgeois culture is supposed to cherish—like the ideological apparatuses of the family and the school" (1986:158). One striking example of mass culture serving a valuable political function, though not precisely an adversarial one, is Huyssen's account of the impact of the American television miniseries "Holocaust" when it was broadcast in West Germany. In Huyssen's view, "Holocaust," which many American viewers saw as trivializing the historical events it represented by conveying them in the limited, sensationalistic format of the miniseries, enabled Germans to confront their history in a way that previous, more experimental dramas had not succeeded in doing (1986:94–114).

We should hesitate, therefore, before concluding that entrance into a mass-cultural context is in and of itself a sign that performance art is compromised as a critical practice. Indeed, several critics writing on the performance artist who has had the greatest success in the mass-cultural context, Laurie Anderson, point, admittedly somewhat hesitantly, to a progressive content in her work. Forte entertains the possibility that "Anderson's gender-bending appearance and performance style continues to evoke a deconstructive process, however subliminal" (1988:234). Craig Owens argues that in *United States,* Anderson momentarily effects communication between "divergent series"—male and female, emission and reception, sexuality and language. Owens stresses the fragility of this communication, but concludes that it is "at least [. . .] a beginning" (1984a:55). Fred Pfeil also sees, in a different moment of *United States,* a fragile, momentary emergence of "a new sense, a new kind of relationship to the Real, which neither I nor Laurie Anderson nor anyone else in the hall was as yet able to live or name" (1988:400). The emphasis on subliminality, the taking of first steps, and the value of a single moment in these descriptions signals the difficulty of assessing the political potential of postmodern performance, the sense that we may require a new concept of the political in art to make sense of this work.

One reason for this difficulty is that these descriptions are all based on the traditional critical procedure of reading a single work for its political or social content, in relation, perhaps, to a real or imagined audience, but separate from the cultural context in which the work itself appears (Huyssen's account of "Holocaust" in Germany points up the importance of one kind of contextual study). Polan has recently suggested that such a procedure is itself inadequate to grasp today's cultural reality, noting that:

> [W]e need to understand how each text, and each moment in each text, is part of a larger *intertextuality*—pieces in a montage that robs each piece of any enduring sense or value. In this perspective, each part of mass culture needs to be studied as part of that flow that Raymond Williams suggested was part of the specific operation of commercial television. Flow involves the transcendence of meaningful units by a system whose only meaning is the fact of its global non-meaning (1986:183).[3]

Here, Polan invokes Raymond Williams's well-known concept of "flow," which Williams considers "the central television experience" (1974:95). Williams suggests that there are three levels of flow on television: the overall flow of an evening's programming on all available sources; the flow of images and topics, including any commercials and announcements that may appear, during a particular period of time on a particular programming source; and the flow of specific words and images within any programming sequence, again including commercials and announcements (1974:86–118). Williams indicates that the effect of flow can be disorienting: the interposition of "real" and "fictional" images (news items interspersed with commercials, for example); the appearance of the same visual styles, even the same actors, in both programs and commercials; and the intercutting of scenes from different films, can blur critical distinctions (1974:91–92). Jane Feuer, who emphasizes that television narratives cannot be seen as self-enclosed narratives separate from the overall flow of programming, provides a further example of the disorienting potential of flow: tie-ins between television movies and news programs, in which an issue treated as fiction in a movie may be followed by a news program which treats the same issue as real (1986:105).

Williams has recently reemphasized the impact of flow upon the content and meaning of the individual work: "I have always argued that [commercials] don't interrupt the programs, they help to constitute them" (in Heath and Skirrow 1986:15). While watching the network telecast of the film *The Killing Fields* recently, I was struck by a sequence in which a segment of the film ended as the main character, the Cambodian Dith Pran, who was doing enforced agricultural labor under the watchful eye of the Khmer Rouge, grabbed surreptitiously at a tiny lizard, which he killed and stored away to eat later. This moment was followed by a commercial for breakfast cereal. Clearly, the meaning that emerges from such a sequence is neither that of the film nor that of the commercial, nor the sum of the two meanings. It is also not at all clear that the commercial simply supercedes the film in meaning, or that the meaning of the entire sequence is that television can convert anything into a sales pitch. Rather, the sense of the sequence is relational: the meaning (or, more likely, *meanings*) lie in the juxtaposition of two very different discourses. Polan carries Williams's concept of flow beyond its application to television, suggesting that it may serve as a good description of our culture as a whole, a culture in which any particular cultural manifestation is part of an extended and disorienting "montagist social text" (1986:183), a culture whose blurring of distinctions extends out from television programming to encompass entire cultural discourses. This is the culture *of* television understood *as* television, a culture defined in large part by the impact of mass media. Richard Schechner has codified that impact in a way that accords with Williams's and Polan's observations: "A world that was securely positional is becoming dizzyingly relational" (1985:322).

It may, then, be worthwhile to try to understand postmodern performance as part of the dizzyingly intertextual mass culture it seems determined to enter, rather than as a set of individual texts which somehow respond to social contexts from which they are detached. Most often, performance art is discussed in a "high art" context, usually as part of the history of visual art; more occasionally, as part of the history of theatre. In the remainder of this essay, I would like to sketch a few ideas that result from seeing current performance art as a form of mass culture which, like the culture it is part of, has taken on some of the salient characteristics of mass media, especially television, in its modes of discourse, and in its relation to other cultural discourses. I chose, for several reasons, to focus on the work of Laurie Anderson and Spalding Gray, whose work exemplifies the "crossover" from vanguard to mass cultural status that many current performance artists seem to hope for. Both Anderson and Gray possess impeccable "downtown" credentials, yet have achieved a significant level of success on television and in other mass-cultural arenas. The relationship between their work and television is not obvious at the level of content, as it is in the work of, say, Ann Magnuson or Eric Bogosian, whose relationship to television and other mass media is largely one of image appropriation, often with satiric or parodic intent. That Anderson and Gray work in different, in some ways opposing, styles permits me to make some generalizations about postmodern performance art without limiting those generalizations to one type of performance or to treat the polyglot term "performance art" monolithically.

2. Eric Bogosian, a performance artist whose images are often appropriated from television and other mass media, in his 1987 Talk Radio *at the Public Theatre in New York. (Photo by Paula Court)*

Consider the following description of a performance:

> Each individual bit [. . .] may have a certain sense, a certain message [. . .], but the whole effect of the show comes from the incongruous confrontation of each bit with the other, the ongoing flow that forces each scene to give way to the next.

Taken out of context, this passage sounds like a description of a Wooster Group or Squat Theatre performance, even of a piece by Robert Wilson or Richard Foreman, or perhaps of a Laurie Anderson concert. In fact, it is Polan's description of "The Tonight Show" (1986:182). As Polan emphasizes, the meaning or content of any particular segment within the flow is subsumed by the whole experience, which is indeterminate in meaning, or perhaps finally meaningless. This seems to constitute a useful description of the discursive strategies of much performance art—Féral in fact defines performance as "the absence of meaning" (1982:173).

The relation of any individual image to the whole of an Anderson performance could be characterized by the concept of flow, even in the way longer segments are punctuated by shorter ones. Owens has described Anderson's work in terms very similar to the succession of images, each meaningful in itself, that yield to a larger sense of meaninglessness in Polan's description of "The Tonight Show": "[Anderson] is not concerned with ambiguity, with multiple meanings engendered by a single sign; rather, two *clearly defined but mutually incompatible* readings are engaged in blind confrontation in such a way that it is impossible to choose between them" (Owens 1984b:219–20).[4] Pfeil analyses Anderson's song, "O Superman," in related terms:

> [T]he lyrics of "O Superman" and the electronically distorted timbres of Laurie Anderson's voice alter abruptly, without transition. [. . .] Despite these inexplicable shifts in speaker and tone, we may sense the slim possibility of a narrative of sorts, but Anderson is an expert at tempting us with such mirages and then erasing them (1988:386).

If the discursive structure of an Anderson performance can be compared with that of a television talk show, the narrative structure of Gray's monologs is very close to that of the television serial. Like the typical serial, the recent monologs feature a central couple, Gray himself and Renée Shafransky. The recurrence of these characters makes it possible to follow the successive monologs the way one might follow the lives and adventures of a couple on one's favorite soap opera. Like those on the nighttime soap, these characters are essentially static; as Feuer notes of characters on continuing dramatic serials, "they perpetuate the narrative by continuing to make the same mistakes" (1986:112–13). Spalding is always afraid of commitment, seeking out utopias in unlikely places, naive in practical, worldly matters. Renée, on the other hand, seems always to be demanding commitment of one kind or another, trying to keep Spalding grounded in the real world, and far more aggressive and pragmatic in her dealings with that world than he is. As a couple, Spalding and Renée seek what every television serial couple seeks—"integration into a happy family"—but the need to continue the flow of narrative prevents the story from ever achieving any kind of stable closure (Feuer 1986:113). The possibility that these characters will ring yet one more change on their characteristic behaviors in yet another somewhat different set of circumstances must always remain open, accessible to the flow, conducive to "television's dual ideological compulsions: the need to repeat and the need to contain" (Feuer 1986:114).

Anderson's quasi- or antinarrative structures strongly resemble the flow of television programming in their successive negation of stable meanings and in their creation of an "endless antivista of unrelated presences, surfaces, voices, in an autoreferential succession without consequence" (Pfeil 1988:386). Gray's more straightforward narrative style, like the television serial, remains static and essentially conservative in that it permits no change in the characters or their basic relations. However, we cannot ignore the different circumstances under which information and narrative are presented in television and performance art. Unlike television, "live" performance is still framed by its occasional nature: we have to go somewhere to see Anderson or Gray in person, and the experience is bounded by that specific effort. Live performance is not continuous with our everyday experience the way television, whose flow of programming spills over into "household flow," can be (see Altman 1986). However, this frame has been rendered porous by the spillover of performance art into cultural settings other than the live performance. Anderson's and Gray's respective live performances exist side by side with the films, videotapes, records, and books derived from them—each object takes its place in the overall *cultural* flow described by Polan.

As Polan suggests, this flow robs each individual object of its specific value and meaning; when the same object is available in several mediated forms, the meaning of each one as an experience is likely to derive from its relation to another. When I referred above to the recordings and books as "derived from" the live performances, I was privileging the live performance as the origin and source of the other cultural objects, to which they inevitably refer. It is not at all clear, however, that such a privileging accords with the cultural facts. One assumes that a spectator might buy the book in order to be reminded of the live performance, but in the case of *Swimming to Cambodia,* the spectator might buy the book in order to be reminded of the film, or vice versa, referring one mediated version of the performance to another. The fact that Gray's transcribed monologs have been reviewed as literature suggests that their link back to performance is not necessarily irrevocable.

Discussing the relationship between rock concerts and recordings, Adam Parfrey has argued that "the live concert recapitulates and reemphasizes the recorded text (which must have an *a priori* existence if the concert is to be successful). [. . .] The live concert, then, supports the recorded text, advertises its presence, and holds congregation with the text's believers" (1985:218). Parfrey is right about rock concerts. Presumably Anderson, whose recordings resulted from her performances, has already encountered audiences whose primary interest is in a reification of her recorded texts. It is not, however, implausible that Gray, whose performances do not occur within the cultural context of the rock concert, has encountered audiences whose interest in his performance derives from their experience of Gray on film or videotape, or in print, and who also see the live performance as a reification of a recorded one. In such cases, the traditional privileging of the "original," "live" performance over its "adaptations" is reversed and undermined: the recorded performance has become the referent of the live one.

Unlike the television executive who wanted Gray to be funny over the phone, I am not suggesting that there is no difference between Anderson or Gray live and in mediated form, only that the live performance has no greater or different cultural authority than its "adaptations."[5] I would further argue that in the marketplace of cultural commodities, the live performance and the tape, despite their phenomenological differences, do have fundamentally the same thing to sell: the performer's persona. Here is another link with television, which depends for its authority on persuasive personae, like the "personalities" on talk and game shows, and most particularly, on the news (see Morse 1986 and Schechner 1985). Here again Anderson's and Gray's respective artistic practices are quite different: the persona Gray has created through his performances is overtly autobiographical, narcissistic, possessed of a defined personality. Anderson's persona, on the other hand, is a nonpersona, a straight-man or, as she has said herself, a "moderator between things" (quoted in Rockwell 1983:126). These personae are not confined to the performance context, or even to its adaptations, but are highly mobile within the cultural flow.

Anderson has moderated on KCTA's "Alive From Off Center" as well as in her own performances. On the television program, she has appeared accompanied by a short, male, bearded character (played by Anderson herself) whom she describes as her "video clone"—the television equivalent of the electronic distortions of her own voice that she uses in her concerts and recordings. Gray has demonstrated the mobility of a performance persona more extensively. The Gray persona can crop up anywhere—as character and narrator in Gray's monologs, whether live or recorded; as a television or film actor (I would insist here that when we see Gray acting on television or in film, what we are seeing is the Gray persona as actor); as a character in, and the author of, a book. When Gray reviewed the writings of another monologist, Garrison Keillor, for the *New York Times Book Review*, his persona as reviewer was an extension of his performance persona: the scene of the review, a dispute between Spalding and Renée over the value of Keillor's work, is entirely continuous with the scene of the monologs (Gray 1987). In this regard, the Gray persona is no different from that of Pee Wee Herman, who has appeared alternately as a character in live performances, the host of a well-received children's television program, the occasional host of a late-night interview program for adults, an actor and a character in films and videotapes (as with Gray, when Pee Wee Herman acts, it is the persona who acts), the subject of numerous interviews, and a "real-life" contestant on "The Dating Game."

The blending of real and fabricated personae and situations that occurs when performance personae assume the same functions as "real" people in the media has much the same disorienting effect as the flowing together of various levels and types of meanings on television, but on a larger scale. One effect of this flow is that the differences between live and mediated performance have been destabilized, especially for an audience which can obtain the same cultural objects and commodities (e.g., performance personae) in live or mediated forms, or both. In a discussion of the relation of television to live performance and the social realm, Schechner predicts that "There will be more 'in-between' performative genres. In-between is becoming the norm: between literature and recitation; between religion and entertainment; between ritual and theatre" (1985:322). Postmodern per-

3. Laurie Anderson and her video clone introducing a performance for KCTA's "Alive From Off Center." (Photo from video by Paula Court)

formance is already between vanguard art and mass culture; is it too much to suggest that it can also be between live and mediated performance, at least from the point of view of an audience for which, as Parfrey would have it, the mediated experience is increasingly the referent for the direct one? The further performance art ventures into the realm of mass culture, the more this promises to be the case. It is no longer simply a question of whether or not to go on TV—one may already be there, even in live performance.

So far, my analysis probably has not warmed the hearts of those who are disturbed by performance art's entry into mass culture, for I seem to be suggesting not only that performance has found its way into commodity culture, but that it has become a discourse almost indistinguishable from other mass cultural discourses. Above all, I have suggested that performance's most defining characteristic, its presence or "liveness" (Goldberg refers to performance as "live art"), is on the verge of being subsumed within a cultural flow that renders the distinction between live and mediated performance virtually irrelevant. I do not in any way dismiss such concern, but only reiterate my earlier point that mass culture is no more necessarily repressive than vanguard culture is necessarily liberating.

I shall attempt, however, to recuperate a small space within performance art as a mass cultural discourse as the space of a potentially critical practice. To do this, I shall refer to Jean-Paul Sartre's theory of mass media, discussed in his *Critique of Dialectical Reason* (1960). Using the radio broadcast as his example, Sartre emphasizes the ability of mass media to isolate the subject (in this case, the listener). The mass media create collectives in the form of audiences, but the relation of each member of these collectives to each other is a relation of absence rather than presence, despite their common participation in the collective:

> [T]he mere fact of *listening to the radio,* that is to say, of listening to a particular broadcast at a particular time, establishes a serial relation of *absence* between the different listeners. In this way, the practico-inert object not only produces a unity of individuals outside themselves in inorganic matter, but also determines them in separation and, in so far as they are separate, ensures *their communication through alterity* (and the same applies to all mass media) (1960:271).

The mass-media audience exists as a collective only by virtue of each individual member's relation to the medium; that relation in itself ensures that the collective will never be more than a grouping of isolated individuals whose only common bond is their relation to the medium, and who will never be able to respond collectively to the medium. "In this way, the voice [on the radio] becomes *vertiginous* for everyone: it is no longer anyone's voice (even if the broadcaster is named), since reciprocity has been destroyed" (1960:274). Just as the relationships amongst the individuals who make up the media audience will always be defined by separation, so the relation of any individual to the medium itself is one of alterity, regardless of whether or not she agrees with the message being conveyed. Even those who agree with the message will always hear the radio voice as the voice of an Other, just as they can only conceive of their fellow members of the media audience as absent Others (1960:274–75).[6]

At first glance, one might suppose that Sartre's description has little to do with performance art, again because it is a live medium. The audience at an Anderson or Gray performance resembles the traditional theatre audience—a group of people assembled at the same place, at the same time, theoretically capable of responding to the performance in a way that Sartre's serialized media audience is not.[7] While the point is well taken, it is also contingent. For example, the rock concert audience, for whom the referent of the experience is a recording, recapitulates an experience of absence and alterity through an experience one might traditionally have assumed is an experience of presence. Sartre defines presence "as the maximum distance permitting the immediate establishment of relations of reciprocity between two individuals" (1960:270). No matter how physically close two individuals are, theirs is not a relation of presence unless reciprocity is possible. Clearly, no reciprocity is possible between a performer and an audience that perceives the performer's presence primarily as a reminder of his absence, or amongst members of such an audience. Nor is it clear that the work itself promotes reciprocity. Pfeil has described postmodern art (drawing examples from the work of Anderson, Robert Wilson, Talking Heads, and Philip Glass) as creating "a closed solipsistic universe," arguing that the manipulation of codes characteristic of such art leaves the spectator with two possible routes of understanding:

> We may allow ourselves to drift into that space and accept its mutating babble as the very image of consciousness; or we may confront that same babble [. . .] as a distilled representation of the whole antagonistic, voracious world of Otherness, engaged in an endless struggle to engulf, colonize, and devour the self, to scribble its graffiti on our every surface, to precode and appropriate the spot of Being that still permits us to stand. [. . .] But the result of either point of view is that experience becomes a matter of *pure internality* (1988:385).

Like Sartre's mass-media audience, whose collectivity is defined by the very agency which guarantees the failure of the collective, the audience of postmodern art is engaged in a collective experience which converts even the experience of collectivity itself into an experience of isolating internality. I believe that it is this lack of reciprocity in postmodern performance—understood as a relation between audience and performance, not literally as the audience's ability to "talk back" to the performers—that Schechner finds so disappointing in his account of postmodern performance work in "The Decline and Fall of the (American) Avant Garde" (1982:27–29).

The figures on the stage in Anderson's and Gray's works are themselves representations of alterity. In his description of the voice on the radio quoted above, Sartre notes that "the voice becomes *vertiginous* for everyone: it's no longer anyone's voice (even if the broadcaster is named), since reciprocity has been destroyed. [. . .] it produces me as an inert member of a series and as Other in the midst of Others [. . .]" (1976:274). There is no better representation of this social effect and its relation to mediatization than Anderson's use of electronics to distort her own voice into those of her characters. These voices are no longer her own, yet they do not belong to an identifiable Other—they belong to no one; Anderson's voice becomes vertiginous even for herself. Anderson becomes both the radio voice and the listening subject: no reciprocity is possible amongst her various voices because they cannot all exist simultaneously, except through further mediation (recording). Anderson's many voices form an image of Sartre's media-produced collective as a series of Others which constitute a collective only by virtue of their relationship to a medium, which in turn determines their relation to one another as a relation of absence. The voices produce Anderson as an "Other in the midst of Others": each voice is but one of the unlimited number of versions of her own voice that can be produced by mediation. Anderson herself, as "moderator," has no "real" voice, assumes no privileged position in the series. On television, Anderson's video clone is an Other which is also her self-in-alterity, with which she coexists only in a medium which constructs both the clone and the "real" Laurie Anderson we see beside him.

Gray achieves the same effect without the aid of literal mediation. Gray, too, is a moderator; Schechner has described his style in the monologs as "very cool—cooler even than Johnny Carson. In fact, Gray is more like a TV talk-show host, a Dick Cavett, than any stand-up comic. Except that Gray's guests are his own personae, his multiple selves" (1982:47). Here again is the voice (self) vertiginous before itself, and vertiginous for the audience as well. Even though Gray is ostensibly present before us in his own person, we get the sense that the figure we are seeing is the performance persona Spalding Gray, which is caught up in a complex and reversible relationship with the performer Spalding Gray. "It has gradually become Gray's chosen lot simultaneously to live his life and play the role of Spalding Gray living his life, *and* to observe said Gray living his life in order to report on it in the next monologue" (Leverett in Gray 1985:xii). This is the self caught up in the reflexive flow of culture-as-television described by Polan, in which it is no longer clear what the differences amongst these various, mediated and nonmediated versions of the self are, or if there are any differences anymore. What Anderson and Gray offer us in their performance personae are representations of the self after it has internalized its own relation to a mediatized environment. Reciprocity with these figures is impossible, for they are not present, even to themselves.

I am clearly not arguing, then, that postmodern performance takes on the trappings of mass culture/mass media but reestablishes the relation of presence, of reciprocity, between itself and its audience that is the antithesis of Sartre's mediatized collective. Postmodern performance offers no antidote to alterity; rather, it accepts alterity as its condition of being. I am arguing that it is important to see the figures of alterity in postmodern performance art as *representations* of the relation of alterity that characterizes mass-mediatized society, not simply as symptoms or products of that alterity. I return to my formulation of the figure of alterity in postmodern performance as a *representation of the self after it has internalized its own relation to a mediatized environment.* In this way, such performance demonstrates the "impossible complicity" Owens sees in postmodernist art that adopts a critical position, "the unavoidable necessity of participating in the very activity that is being denounced *precisely in order to denounce it*" (1984b:235; original emphasis). "Denounce" is perhaps the wrong word to describe the critical element of postmodernist art, an element for which, as I have already suggested, critics have yet to find a vocabulary. Nevertheless, Owens's point is an important one: postmodernist art does not position itself outside the practices it holds up for scrutiny. It *problematizes,* but does not *reject,* the representational means it shares with other cultural practices. In the small space remaining between simply being the self-in-alterity produced by a mediatized culture and representing that self, the space some postmodernist performance occupies, lies the possibility for a critical perspective on the culture of flow.

Notes

1. In referring to live and mediated versions of the same performance work as "the same cultural objects," I am not suggesting that there is no difference between live and mediated performance. The cultural relationship of live to mediated performance is an issue to which I shall return in this essay.
2. Andreas Huyssen makes the following observation on the relation of the historical avant-garde to mass culture:

   > It was the culture industry, not the avant garde, which succeeded in transforming everyday life in the twentieth century. And yet—the utopian hopes of the historical avant garde are preserved, even though in distorted form, in this system of secondary exploitation euphemistically called mass culture. It seems preferable for cultural theory today to address the contradictions of technologized mass culture rather than pondering over the products and performances of the various neo–avant gardes, which, more often than not, derive their originality from social and aesthetic amnesia (1986:15).

3. Neither Polan nor I suggest that the interpretation of individual works should be abandoned; ideally, the meaning of the work must somehow be constructed through both an intrinsic reading and a consideration of how the cultural flow constructs that particular work.

   The present situation of interpretation suggests the need for such an approach. In his essay on postmodernist art, Pfeil argues skillfully that from a Marxist perspective, postmodernist art possesses no "revolutionary potential" but merely illustrates a "capitalist pathology." He goes on to show that from a materialist feminist perspective, the same qualities which appear pathological to the orthodox Marxist acquire "revolutionary potential" (1988:395). This is but one of many recent examples in which critics have had to acknowledge that interpretation depends an awful lot on where the interpreter sits, a perspective which clearly problematizes the whole question of art as critical practice. While the question of "totalizing" versus "micropolitical" discourses is much too large to take up here, I will at least suggest that Polan's notion of cultural flow may be useful in providing a framework for interpretation that is totalizing, but suggests that the social production of meaning is a complex, frequently self-contradictory phenomenon.
4. The Owens essay (1984b) from which I have quoted here was originally published in *October* in 1980. In another, later essay (1984a), Owens recants this position, calling it "a case of gross critical negligence" because he had not taken into consideration the representation of sexual difference in Anderson's work (1984a:48). In the earlier essay (1984b), he asserts that Anderson sets up "blind confrontations" between "mutually incompatible readings." In the later essay (1984a), he begins to see momentary convergence and communication amongst images he previously saw as purely confrontational. Owens's change of heart is important, but tentative: its tentativeness further points up the difficulty of interpreting images whose relation is defined by flow.
5. In his provocative, conservative estimation of postmodern culture, *The Post-Modern Aura,* Charles Newman states that adaptation, by which he means primarily the adaptation of works of fiction for television, "has become the primary literary convention of the age." He goes on to say: "This development should not be reduced to a question of 'high' versus 'low' art. With the scenario and the adaptation, we are simply dealing with a willfully inferior form of cognition" (1985:129). Although I share Newman's belief that the adaptation is an extremely important cultural convention of our time, I do not think that simply falling back on a privileging of the "original" as cognitively superior to the "adaptation" (and, implicitly, of literary fiction as superior to television or film) enables the critic to understand the actual operation and implications of that convention.

6. In many particulars, the foundations of Jean Baudrillard's media theory, as defined in his early essay "Requiem for the Media" (1972), recapitulate Sartre. For Baudrillard, the essence of the mass media is that they constitute "Speech Without Response" (1972:169): "they speak, or something is spoken there, but in such a way as *to exclude any response anywhere*" (1972:170). The power of the media derives, in this view, from their ability to speak without ever having to negotiate with a response from the audience. The effect of speech without response is the social isolation of the spectator, isolation which is a function of the form of the medium, not its message:

> As an extreme case, authority would provide every citizen with a TV set without preoccupying itself with programming (assuming an authority that was not also obsessed by content and convinced of the ideological force of media "persuasion," and thus of the need to control the message). It is useless to fantasize about state projection of police control through TV [. . .]: TV, by virtue of its mere presence, is a social control in itself. There is no need to imagine it as a state periscope spying on everyone's private life—the situation as it stands is far more efficient than that: it is the certainty that people are no longer speaking to each other, that they are definitively isolated in the face of a speech without response (1972:171–72).

Because the power of the media derives from the socially isolating effect of their form, not their ability to transmit content, neither intervening at the level of content nor taking possession of the media apparatus can turn the media to revolutionary ends. Only a practice that "radically checkmates the dominant form" (1972:184) has value as a counterhegemonic media strategy. In later writings, Baudrillard has extended this analysis to suggest that mediatized reality has superceded "the real" and that the only critical response to a world of simulacra is to undermine the power of forces which seek to impose meaning by refusing all meaning. I am not ready to follow Baudrillard down this path, which essentially removes performance and other artistic discourses which depend for their very existence on *representation* not simulation (or repetition of simulation) from the picture, and denies the value of *any* kind of actively critical practice.

7. Of course, the notion of a "traditional theatre audience" as a certain kind of collective or community can no longer be taken for granted. Herbert Blau has explored this question extensively and provocatively in the two parts of his "Odd, Anonymous Needs: The Audience in a Dramatized Society" (1985/86).

References

Altman, Rick

1986 "Television/Sound." In *Studies in Entertainment: Critical Approaches to Mass Culture,* edited by Tania Modleski, 39–54. Bloomington: Indiana University Press.

Anderson, Laurie

1984 *United States.* New York: Harper and Row.

Baudrillard, Jean

1981 [1972] "Requiem for the Media." In *For a Critique of the Political Economy of the Sign,* translated by Charles Levin, 164–84. St. Louis: Telos Press.

Blau, Herbert

1985/86 "Odd, Anonymous Needs: The Audience in a Dramatized Society." *Performing Arts Journal* 9, nos. 2 & 3 (PAJ 26/27):199–212, and no. 4 (PAJ 28):34–42.

Burnham, Linda Frye
1986 "*High Performance*, Performance Art, and Me." *The Drama Review* 30, no. 2 (T109):15–51.

Crimp, Douglas
1984 "Pictures." In *Art After Modernism: Rethinking Representation*, edited by Brian Wallis, 175–88. Boston: David R. Godine.

Féral, Josette
1982 "Performance and Theatricality: The Subject Demystified." *Modern Drama* 25 (no. 1):170–81.

Feuer, Jane
1986 "Narrative Form in American Network Television." In *High Theory/Low Culture: Analysing Popular Television and Film*, edited by Colin MacCabe, 101–14. New York: St. Martin's Press.

Forte, Jeanie
1988 "Women's Performance Art: Feminism and Postmodernism." *Theatre Journal* 40 (no. 2):217–35.

Goldberg, RoseLee
1984 "Performance: The Golden Years." In *The Art of Performance: A Critical Anthology*, edited by Gregory Battcock and Robert Nickas, 71–94. New York: Dutton.
1988 *Performance Art: From Futurism to the Present*. New York: Abrams.

Gray, Spalding
1985 *Swimming to Cambodia*. New York: Theatre Communications Group.
1987 "Plenty Wholesome and a Little Perverse." *The New York Times Book Review*, 4 October: 9.

Heath, Stephen, and Gillian Skirrow
1986 "An Interview with Raymond Williams." In *Studies in Entertainment: Critical Approaches to Mass Culture*, edited by Tania Modleski, 3–17. Bloomington: Indiana University Press.

Howell, John
1988 "The Message is the Medium." *ARTnews* 87 (no. 6):122–27.

Huyssen, Andreas
1986 *After The Great Divide: Modernism, Mass Culture, Postmodernism*. Bloomington: Indiana University Press.

Modleski, Tania
1986 "The Terror of Pleasure: The Contemporary Horror Film and Postmodern Theory." In *Studies in Entertainment: Critical Approaches to Mass Culture*, edited by Tania Modleski, 155–66. Bloomington: Indiana University Press.

Morse, Margaret
1986 "The Television News Personality and Credibility: Reflections on the News in Transition." In *Studies in Entertainment: Critical Approaches to Mass Culture*, edited by Tania Modleski, 55–79. Bloomington: Indiana University Press.

Newman, Charles
1985 *The Post-Modern Aura: The Act of Fiction in an Age of Inflation*. Evanston, IL: Northwestern University Press.

Owens, Craig
1984a "Sex and Language: In Between." In *Laurie Anderson: Works from 1969 to 1983*, edited by Janet Kardon, 48–55. Philadelphia: Institute of Contemporary Art, University of Pennsylvania.
1984b "The Allegorical Impulse: Toward a Theory of Postmodernism." In

Art After Modernism, edited by Brian Wallis, 203–35. Boston: David R. Godine.

Parfrey, Adam
1985 "The Pre-Recorded Audience in Two Dimensions." *Performing Arts Journal* 9, nos. 2 & 3 (PAJ 26/27):213–18.

Pfeil, Fred
1988 "Postmodernism as a 'Structure of Feeling.' " In *Marxism and the Interpretation of Culture,* edited by Cary Nelson and Lawrence Grossberg, 381–404. Urbana: University of Illinois Press.

Polan, Dana
1986 "Brief Encounters: Mass Culture and the Evacuation of Sense." In *Studies in Entertainment: Critical Approaches to Mass Culture,* edited by Tania Modleski, 167–87. Bloomington: Indiana University Press.

Rockwell, John
1983 *All American Music: Composition in the Late Twentieth Century.* New York: Alfred A. Knopf.

Sartre, Jean-Paul
1976 [1960] *Critique of Dialectical Reason.* Translated by Alan Sheridan-Smith. Atlantic Highlands, NJ: Humanities Press.

Schechner, Richard
1982 *The End of Humanism: Writings on Performance.* New York: Performing Arts Journal Publications.
1985 "News, Sex, and Performance Theory." In *Between Theater and Anthropology,* 295–324. Philadelphia: University of Pennsylvania Press.

Williams, Raymond
1974 *Television: Technology and Cultural Form.* New York: Schocken Books.

Philip Auslander *teaches Contemporary Drama in the English Department of the Georgia Institute of Technology. He is the author of* The New York School Poets as Playwrights *(forthcoming from Peter Lang) and is currently working on a book to be titled* Presence and Resistance: Essays on Postmodern Performance and Culture.

Theodora Skipitares's Performing Objects

Joan Driscoll Lynch

In an evocative image from an early work, *The Venus Cafe* (1977), a masked Theodora Skipitares sits on a high stool dressed in 20 layers of men's white cotton shirts and pants, with dinner plates of different patterns hanging from her neck by multicolored ribbons. She rises and does a slow, clunky dance of the plates, prefiguring the lyrical dance of the women in Conestoga wagons in *The Age of Invention* (1985), and the dance of the noses in *Defenders of the Code* (1987). Thematically, personal and universal concerns merge in this image of woman repressed, restricted and bound by traditional household duties; formally, the image raises a number of aesthetic issues that will develop throughout the artist's work. In *The Venus Cafe,* Theodora Skipitares is both humanoid and manipulator, both puppet and puppeteer.

Andrea Balis, Skipitares's longtime friend and collaborator, says of the artist's early work:

> These were intensely personal performances by the person who made the piece, out of whose life the piece had been made, who at the same time was being as alienated, dispassionate, and non-there as possible and who wasn't necessarily wearing clothes all the time. This was a very curious combination that gave the pieces a very special savor and an odd tension (Balis et al. 1987).

Skipitares rejects the notion that she is a performer in the traditional sense; that is, a person who needs to express herself to an audience. Rather she sees herself as a maker of physical objects which she needs to display, an artist who creates artifacts in order to give life to them.

This impulse to treat herself as a mannequin for the display of weird, exotic costumes and headdresses began as early as junior high school. At that time, she worked with her mother—her earliest collaborator—to create outfits and then had her sister drive her to Golden Gate Park in her hometown, San Francisco, where she would display herself masked. These one-woman shows broadened to include friends at Berkeley, where she studied at the University of California during the '60s. Using signs, they staged agitprop shows—propaganda pieces. Skipitares's signs now are electrified, dancing in the dark of the theatre, commenting ironically on a character, as do the signs with quotations from *Poor Richard's Almanac* which comment on Benjamin Franklin in *The Age of Invention.*

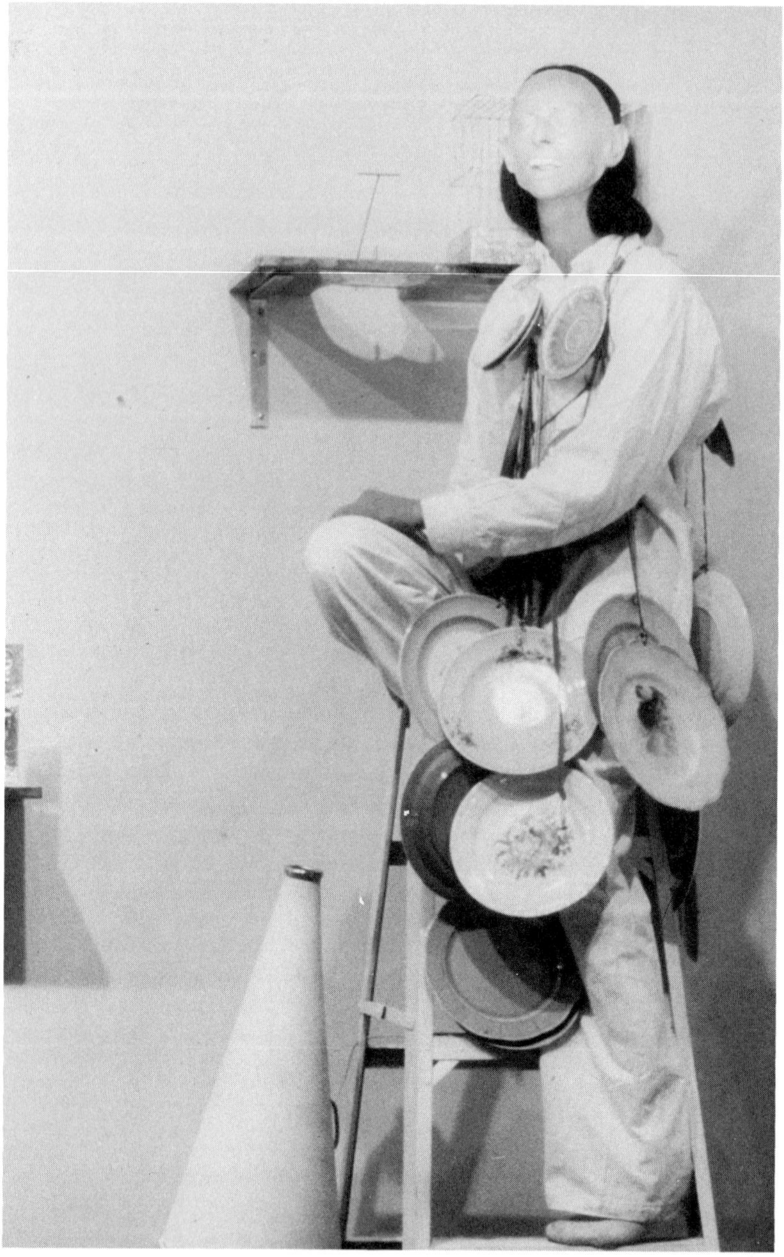

1. Theodora Skipitares, masked and festooned with dinner plates in The Venus Cafe *(1977). (Photo by Richard Heinrich)*

"God helps them that help themselves"

"No gains without pains"

"Riches to the careful, power to the bold"

"Mine is better than ours"

At Berkeley Skipitares was first a premed student, an interest that explains her preoccupation in *The Age of Invention* and *Defenders of the Code* with science and scientists. In her sophomore year, which was also the year her father died, she transferred to the art department to major in painting and sculpture. These years, 1964 to '66, were years of political activism that tore the California campus apart and Skipitares became involved in this politicized and permissive environment. The art department encouraged experimentation blurring the boundaries of performance, text, and sculpture—a confirmation of what she had already been doing intuitively. She left Berkeley to spend two years in Greece investigating her roots (her parents were born there) and studying theatre in Athens and Delphi, paying particular attention to masks and mask construction. She sees this as an important step in her development, the conjunction of experimentation and tradition. This period is richly represented in her early works, *Mask Performance* (1975), *The Venus Cafe,* and *The Mother and the Maid* (1979).

In 1968, Skipitares finished her degree at Berkeley and enrolled in the graduate theatre department of the Tisch School of the Arts, New York University, to study design. To say that she didn't fit in there is an understatement. Skipitares recollects, "Other divisions of the theatre department were doing breakthrough stuff at the time; the department of design was reactionary (1987). So she spent as little time as possible in her own department, preferring to "eavesdrop" on what was happening in others. She watched the work of Richard Schechner and Omar Shapli, who were teaching directing, acting theory, and improvisation, and attended workshops given by Jerzy Grotowski. The graduate film department was also very active and she spent hours there. If she was uninterested in what her design teachers had to offer, the feeling was mutual. The costumes she designed were headless, armless, legless puppets—a dress made of 3,000 walnut shells, a suit of woven newspapers, a footman's costume out of hundreds of tiny pencils, a dress made of glass that weighed 90 pounds. "The actress who wore it had to be padlocked into it nightly by two assistants, and once dressed she couldn't move" (Balis 1980:1). In an era of physical theatre when actors were exploring the plasticity of their bodies, she was offering a theatre of objects. Why did she stay three years, finishing the degree in stage and costume design in 1972? "I don't know what kept me going on, except that I always finish what I start. I think the usefulness of NYU—after all that fighting and all that resistance—was that I really learned how to forge a totally independent artistic identity" (1987).

Was she influenced by the major theatre theorists of the time?

> Everyone was making very eclectic use of ideas from Artaud, Grotowski, and Brecht and these influences have no doubt permeated my work, but I was not interested in understanding theory; it was not my realm, my realm was making things with my hands. Most of the theories I read, absorbed, and really cared about were theories I read in *Artforum* rather than what I would see in *TDR* or somewhere else (1987).

She claims her best inspiration came not from theory but from watching her colleagues' work. She mentions particularly Meredith Monk's sound and movement experiments, Spalding Gray's approach to performance art, and Elizabeth LeCompte's strong visual sense.

> I would say that in the early and mid-'70s the performer who knocked me out the most in every way was Meredith Monk. Meredith was walking a line between music, dance, and the spoken

> text that was astonishing. Then Liz's work came along and there was an eye there that I knew I really loved, I felt a kinship to it. I saw someone in Liz who was visually constructing something radically different. Liz's second piece with Spalding was *Rumstick Road* [1976]. I had an epiphany. I saw it about 17 times. I was obsessed with *Rumstick Road* because it was for me all the major intersecting points of what great performance art should be. It was incredibly powerful autobiography, which a lot of other performance artists were trying at the time, but this was tragic on a major level. It was about Spalding's mother's suicide. It was magnificently done. The actors were first-rate. The eye, the visual take on it was astounding. So they were real important to me. They were like an artistic family for those years (1987).

From 1972 to '78 Skipitares was a practicing costume designer, first at Villanova University Theatre (1972/73), then with Shapli and Balis's Section Ten (1973/74), and finally with Schechner's Performance Group (1974–78). She was sought out for these positions for precisely the same reasons that she was rejected by the NYU design department. In her words, "Experimental theatre at the time was seeking radical notions of all aspects of theatre including design, so my desire to use and work with unusual materials was welcome" (1987). For a production of *Electra* at Villanova she made a cape out of hundreds of nails and another from small squares of plywood hooked together. For a production of *Great Hoss Pistol,* a piece about the American Revolution performed by Section Ten, she used found material: a textile factory in the East Village had burned and many bolts of damaged fabric were thrown onto the sidewalk in front; Skipitares hauled charred polyester back to the theatre and used it to form the basis of every costume in the show.

All three of the groups she worked with approached texts as stimuli for improvisation. They created scripts using experimental material and a collagist method of assembly—a way of working which has strongly influenced her own improvisational methods of juxtaposing materials from different sources.

> There was this incredibly open framework, really wide open—the word is "permission," permission to work a certain open way that was very important then. I employ that kind of license when I go out and look for scraps of research material. I am in a sense a one-person improvisation team (1987).

In the early '70s, performance art exploded onto the visual art scene with tremendous energy. But there was little connection between the visual art world and the vigorous experimental theatre movement of the time. Skipitares feels that she had her feet in both camps: "My soul was with the painters and sculptors; my feet were in theatre" (1987). Her first piece of performance art was called *Mask Performance* and was presented at the Artist's Gallery on Wooster Street in New York City in 1975. Seventy-five masks of her face set in different expressions were fixed to one wall of the gallery (plate 2). One of the audience members who saw this early work wrote:

> [S]he stood in front of a wall peopled with rows and rows of masks, all of her own face. Each mask portrayed a slightly different expres-

2. *Skipitares amid dozens of masks in* Mask Performance *(1975), each portraying a slightly different expression. (Photo by Valery Taylor)*

> sion. Hilarity. Smugness. Determination. Despair. I wonder if we even have names for all the tiny movements that shift the meaning of a face. Skipitares stood, silent and still, contemplating the flesh-toned masks. Finally she chose one, put it on, and slowly assumed its character—sounding, giving voice to the emotion frozen on the face. Her performance still haunts me. The solemnity, the not-quite-human quality of the unchanging mask. The disjunction of the real sounds, the real gestures. And then Skipitares re-emerging, taking off the mask—just there, a quiet presence. Someone given license only behind a mask (Heinemann 1980:3).

Skipitares's next piece, *The Venus Cafe,* was unabashedly autobiographical. The title echoed the name of her father's cafe and bar in San Francisco where she and her sister would go every day after school while her mother worked. As with *Mask Performance,* the gallery wall provided a mural of objects, but now the objects were also a notation system for a story line, the story of a woman caught between two cultures, Greek and American: "Being conflicted about a twofold point of view became the motif for all of my pieces after this one" (1987). The conflicts in this piece were intercultural but also feminist—freedom/repression; virginity/promiscuity; responsibility to others/need for self-expression. Masks once more adorned the wall, three of them, each on its own shelf with objects, each with its own story. One of the stories, about a flamboyant American girl who is transformed into a staid Greek matron, was on tape. As it was told, Skipitares covered her body, which was nude from the waist up, with layer upon layer of white clothing. The story was repeated, this time by a male voice with a Brooklyn accent. At the climax of the transformation, a slide of the Byzantine empress Theodora, who had once been a prostitute, was projected onto Theodora Skipitares's mask. The ancient myth resonated against a modern dilemma. The "cleansing" of both women was completed.

A film about the real Venus Cafe was shown and a voice on the sound track narrated: "His name was Demosthenes Skipitares, but they called him 'Jimmy.' " A great cultural heritage was trivialized and reduced to a projected menu, an endless list of choices—moussakas, spinach pie, avgolemono soup. Skipitares donned a necklace of plates and her dance perfectly evoked the noisy clatter of the Greek restaurant. A puppetlike figure first appeared in this piece banging her arm against the wall as slides of Athenian ruins flashed on and off. The piece ended with Skipitares sitting on top of a ladder shouting the gossip-history of her family in their Athenian village through a megaphone. A reviewer who labeled most performance art of the period "confessional" and "voyeuristic" described Skipitares's work as being exceptional:

> Playing off the ambiguities inherent in both material and format—the contradictions arising from the clash of two cultures; the use of Greek theatrical techniques (the mask, the megaphone) in a chamber situation; the several ways that the information is detached from the author's personal presence; the one story repeated with two separate meanings—Skipitares transcends the cult of personality to create a mythic geography filled with a panoply of objects and signals that range from the familiar to the bizarre (Banes 1977:21).

The Mother and the Maid again dealt with the transformation of women. Stories of two of Skipitares's neighbors, who left honored places as craftswomen in Greece to assume menial jobs in this country, were set against the ancient myths of Arachne and Penelope. Arachne was transformed into a spider, condemned to perfecting her stitches forever; Penelope wove a tapestry by day and unraveled it at night—to finish it would mark her betrothal and her doom. All four women were trapped by their circumstances. The costumes Skipitares wore to present these stories, told on slides and audiotapes, were symbolic of women's entrapment—skirts of dead fish, wooden treadles, and armorlike, trapezoidal stainless steel. Ritual acts were associated with each of these costumes—lemon juice was squirted on the fish miniskirt which encircled her, her hair (beneath a hat of wooden spoons) was cut in a gesture of self-mutilation, and rows of altar candles welded to the long, unyielding, metal skirt were lit. All of these were powerful metaphors for the suppression of women's desires for creativity, autonomy, and self-realization.

The opening section began with a conversation between Skipitares and her mother:

> "Are you going to be naked again?" her mother asks, ignoring the success or esteem Skipitares earns by her performances. Equating nakedness with shame, the artist's mother unwittingly places her daughter in the same brave tradition as Arachne—embracing her craft over public disapproval. Complex stuff for a relatively short piece, but *Mother and the Maid* combines all those elements precisely, at a fast-clipped, entertaining pace (Perlberg 1980:80).

Skipitares toured Europe with *The Venus Cafe* and *The Mother and the Maid* and was encouraged, particularly in Amsterdam where she performed the pair together at the Mickery Theatre for three weeks. Then a gallery and theatre in Frankfurt—galerie ak and Teatra am Turm—commissioned a new piece. She entitled it *Skysaver* (1980), and then named her company Skysaver Productions. Why "Skysaver"? "Skysaver was the name of the airline that took me over to Germany," she said. "It was also an apt name for a piece about life, madness, and artists" (1987). Skipitares had been doing art therapy with the insane and had some strong feelings

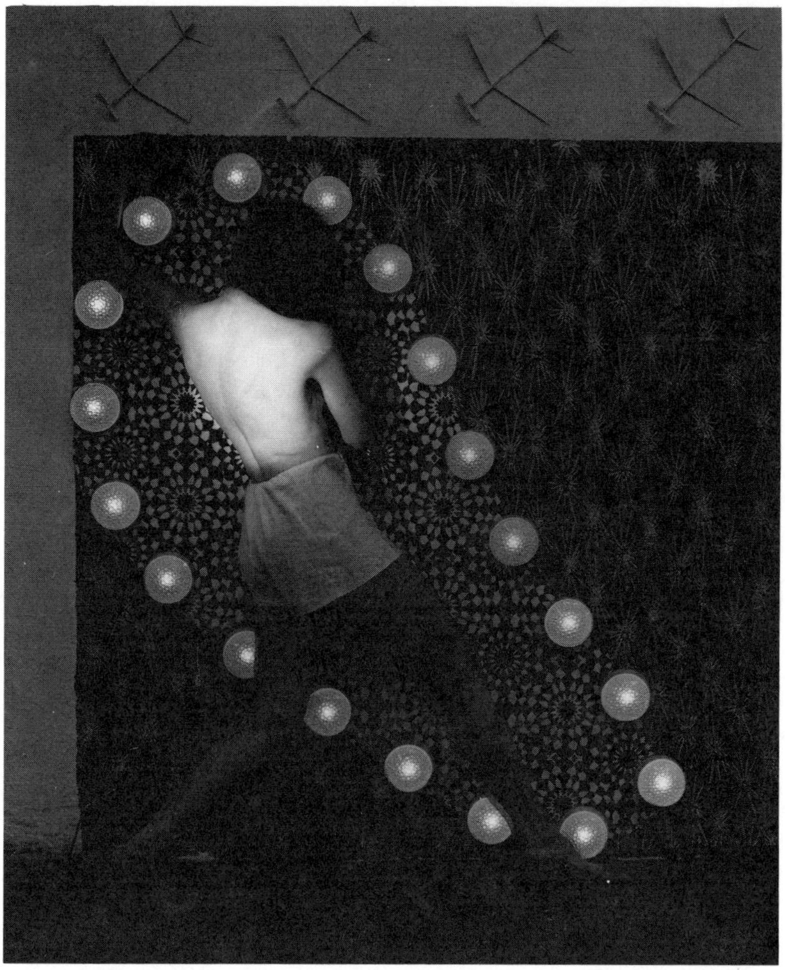

3. Skipitares's growing interest in mechanical effects was apparent in Skysaver *(1980). (Photo by Jimmy Lindner)*

about their treatment and how it is affected by socioeconomic issues; she also took great interest in their artworks, which in many cases resembled "some very well-respected works of modern art" (in Shewey 1981:49).

Skysaver is the piece that burst the narrow confines of its gallery space and forced the artist back into the theatre (plate 3). As the piece evolved it became far more complex than the previous ones and it forced some significant changes—the need to be serious about the text in terms of editing and juxtaposition of material, the need for characters other than the artist herself and for mechanical effects. The text was taken from tracts on mental illness, mythology (the Icarus legend), Christian lore (the story of Saint Lucca), a conversation between two blind people overhead on a bus, and excerpts from the lives of several of her patients.

Skipitares didn't want to use actors in her work, so she stumbled on the notion of using animated figures—puppets if you will, though the word with its connotation of children's theatre is one she dislikes. Her first figures were a two-foot, pompous psychiatrist and a chattering lamb that functioned as a Greek chorus commenting on the action. Skipitares herself stepped even further into the background of the piece. Her body was still a reference point for moving the narrative along but now she saw herself as merely a special stagehand, a facilitator, who saw to it that the show worked, "like a bunraku puppeteer who is on stage but relatively invisible" (1987). Jan Schall offered a descriptive analysis of a portion of *Skysaver* in *Art Papers*:

> Three vignettes relate events which specifically involve the plight of New York's emotionally disturbed. In the first of these, a blindfolded Skipitares with fluorescent light bulbs strapped to her shins moves awkwardly about the center of the tableau as the taped voices of a man and woman express the handicapped person's fear of being lost within the "normal" milieu of a dance hall. Another finds the artist limply draped over a sawhorse amid red and yellow flashing lights while a voice relates an episode in which sane and insane behavior merge within the context of a "disco day out" at the Roseland Ballroom. The third sequence is further subdivided into the three case studies, each of which is immediately followed by a focus on the lamb and a section of the Daedalus story. Additionally, the learned oracle of mental fitness speaks thrice through the absurd and repetitive gestures of a ceramic puppet, heralded by thunderous roll and climactic crash. The substance of these lectures, drawn from a textbook history of mental illness, reflects naive and simplistic attitudes once associated with this malady (1981:23).

After *Skysaver,* Skipitares began making puppets of herself—Theodora dolls:

> The first one is the figure which became Sylvia in *Micropolis.* I did a sculpture, about one-third life-size, which was a very carefully made self-portrait of my whole body. It just sat around my studio for the longest time. For *Micropolis,* I made a mold and I turned out these female forms. I used my face on the dinosaur in the last scene, too. Even the male puppets were adjusted Theodoras (Jenner 1983:109).

Micropolis (subtitled *Seven Portraits and a Landscape*), which premiered at the Performing Garage in New York City in 1982, represented a drastic break in Skipitares's work. Instead of autobiography or stories of acquaintances, most of the minidramas originated from newspaper or magazine articles. "Sylvia," a portrait of a schizophrenic, was taken from a dazzling piece of investigative journalism first published in the *New Yorker* by Susan Sheehan. "Wild Ducks" was loosely based on the widely publicized story of murder victim Kitty Genovese; it was a surrealistic piece "reminiscent of Magritte or Ernst" (Neff 1982), which featured neighbors voyeuristically peeping into a bathroom window to watch a woman who has been shot bleed to death (plate 4). The pieces echoed the topicality of the headlines, but resonated with a poetry that bespoke a bleak vision of the human condition.

Each scene was set on a miniature stage five feet wide and three feet high and mounted on a platform with castors which Skipitares compared to the ancient Greek *ekkyklema,* a device for revealing tableaux. The minisets were highly realistic, painted with acrylics and oils, and had their own internal lighting and audio systems. All the objects on the sets were proportionate to the 28-inch-high puppets and were either mechanized or, like the puppets, manipulated by Skipitares and her assistants; the narrative was both taped and spoken by the puppeteers.

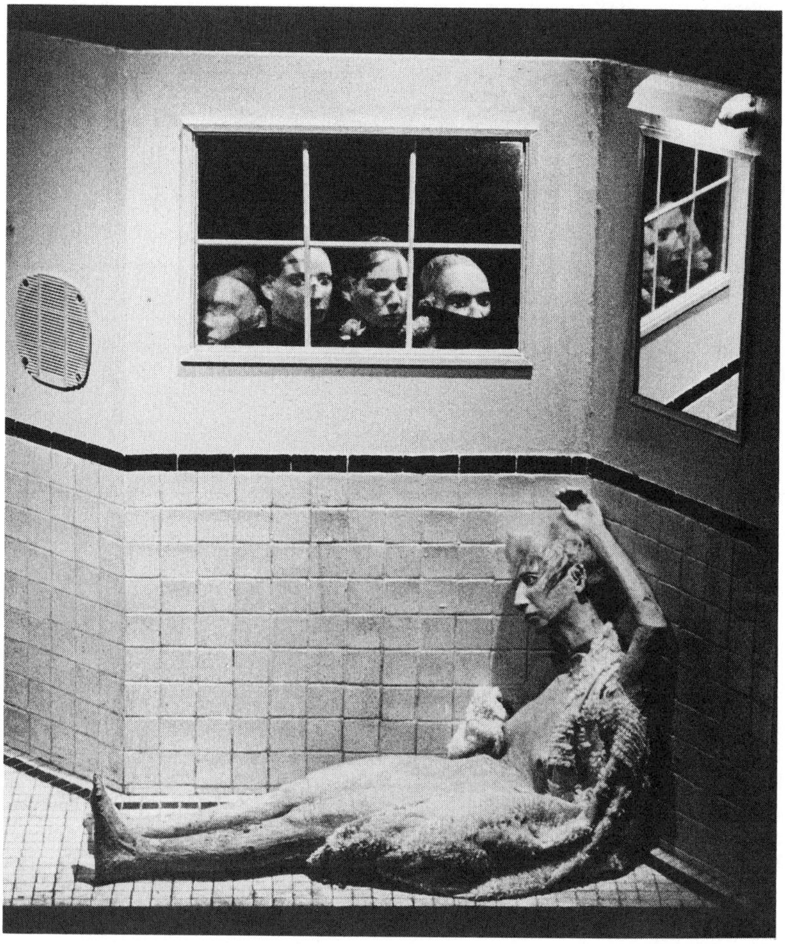

4. "Wild Ducks," one of a series of minidramas that comprised Skipitares's Micropolis *(1982), was loosely based on the widely publicized story of murder victim Kitty Genovese. Here, puppet neighbors peep through a bathroom window to watch a woman who has been shot bleed to death. (Photo by Eli Langner)*

For the first time Skipitares employed a technical assistant, Eli Langner. His mechanical abilities helped to anthropomorphize the puppets by adding flexibility and enabling them to perform human functions such as bleeding, vomiting, and maintaining gargantuan erections.

The puppets began as clay figures from which plaster molds were made; the molds were filled with liquid latex and then drained, leaving a thin coat of rubber. For puppets such as Sylvia Frumkin which performed human functions, plastic tubing was inserted inside her mouth, through her torso, and out her back; the tube then extended behind her through the wall where a rubber bulb containing yellow liquid was squeezed to make her vomit. A tiny microphone was placed in her throat which caused the very human "aargh" sound as the upchucking began. Polyurethane foam provided rigidity, and the puppet was cut at the waist and furnished with a cloth hinge for articulation. The puppets were painted with acrylics, their hair was fake fur, and their costumes were meticulously sewn and fitted. They were fixed into their miniature environments with dowels inserted into their legs (see Jones 1984:47).

Micropolis also brought together two other longtime Skipitares collaborators: Virgil Moorefield, who composed the music, and Andrea Balis. Balis, one of several writers who contributed to the project, has worked on each of Skipitares's pieces since *Mask Performance*. They began collaborating in 1972 when they both worked with Omar Shapli and they continued the relationship when Balis formed her own company, The Cutting Edge, in 1976. Balis is also credited with being the dramaturg of *The Age of Invention* and *Defenders of the Code*.

Micropolis was Skiptares's first popular success in America. It attracted large audiences and garnered excellent reviews from both theatre and art presses. What is very striking in reading the reviews is the emphasis on audience response:

> One vignette, entitled "Urban Landscape," offers us the writing on the wall of the puppet-box. The words: "Capitalism offers no future for you or your children" flash on and off in hazy red lights. The intermittent humor ranges from tongue-in-cheek to bizarre and heavily ironic, and the outburst of audience laughter is always joyous and spontaneous (Dicker 1982:4).

> Clearly a puppet with a past, Sylvia engages us with demented intimacies and shares a sex fantasy of Mick Jagger, but beneath the dry surface of the skip-jack banter, there is a detached, mild-mannered rage. The soliloquy abruptly concludes when Sylvia vomits. Amazing to see such behaviour from a puppet; and so engrossing was her

5. *Appealing to the child in everyone, the puppet has direct access to the viewer's subconscious. Shown here is a puppet of Charles Darwin from* Defenders of the Code *(1987). (Photo by Adam Bartos)*

> crazily fragmented chatter, a collective gasp . . . surprise? shock? disgust? . . . went up in the audience (Neff 1982:10).

> One of the most riveting moments takes place when Skipitares stands by an illuminated jar of formaldehyde in which floats a romantically decomposing figure of herself. The figure stirs slightly as Skipitares almost abstractedly agitates the surface of the liquid. A somnambulistic taped voice-over which accompanies this scene drifts to its conclusion with Rimbaud's words, "I dream of a war of unthinkable logic." But the emotional effect owes nothing to logic; its rightness is visceral (Flood 1982:77).

None of the reviewers mentioned the sense of awe and childlike wonder the piece evoked, the feeling that in this world of mechanical objects and beings anything could happen. Preston Foerder, the head puppeteer for *The Age of Invention* and *Defenders of the Code,* who studied with Philippe Genty at the Institute of Marionettes in France, quotes Genty as saying, "You can express things through a puppet that you couldn't through another means. The puppet appeals to the child in everyone which breaks down the spectator's barriers toward what is being presented and allows the work direct access to the subconscious" (Balis et al. 1987) (plate 5).

For all its technical virtuosity, *Micropolis* was produced for only $900. This was the cost of the materials; no one was paid a salary and the Performing Garage very generously rented the space for a percentage of the receipts. With the exception of *Skysaver,* which was commissioned in Germany, Skipitares paid for her productions out of her own pocket. She earns money teaching art at Pratt Institute and is an artist-in-residence in a Bronx high school program administered by the Guggenheim Museum. She has never taken a salary for her own efforts, preferring always to put the money into the production.

In 1982 she received a grant of $1,000 from Creative Time of New York City for *The Age of Invention,*[1] a piece that was to be performed at 65 Liberty Street—then the New York Chamber of Commerce building. This was her first big-budget work and the piece that propelled her into being a producer/business manager/grants-writer as well as an artist. She raised the $75,000 production cost by applying for and getting grants from the National Endowment for the Arts (NEA), the New York State Council on the Arts (NYSCA), the Henson Foundation, and a few other private foundations.

On the way home from viewing the space at the Chamber of Commerce, she found a book in a bin for 99¢ entitled *Portrait of a Salesman* which told the story of a medical parts salesman who illegally performed 900 operations with surgeons who were using his products. This became Act III of *The Age of Invention.* As in *Micropolis,* Skipitares used a documentary approach in which narrator Tom Costello told the story of Mike Connors, the salesman, using Connors's own words. The scenes which intercut the puppet's monolog were commentaries or illustrations, displaying Skipitares's customary inventiveness and quirky humor. One scene, for instance, which occurred after Mike talks about acquiring bodies from Third World countries for his research, showed cadaver-filled trucks decorated with flashing, colored signs which blinked greetings from different Asian and African countries (plate 6).

The theme of *The Age of Invention*—that Yankee ingenuity can easily be perverted and corrupted by greed—is made chillingly clear by Connors's words in the final lines of the play:

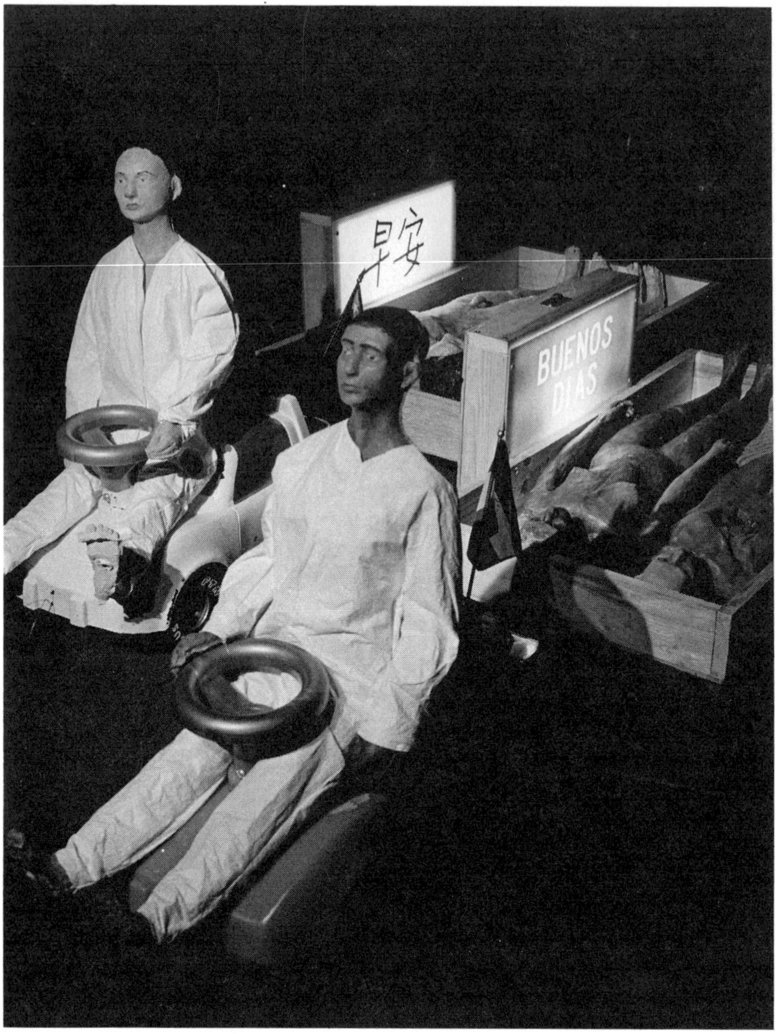

6. Trucks bring cadavers to the U.S. from Third World countries in The Age of Invention *(1985), Skipitares's critical examination of science and scientists. (Photo by Eli Langner)*

From then on, doctors began increasingly to consult me about new prostheses and surgical problems in implanting them. Other times, they asked for help in correcting their errors. Unfortunately, errors were all too frequent. I started worrying when I began to get calls insisting that I attend certain operations. They began to be orders, not requests. I could have refused, but frankly, I was concerned about losing business at the hospital. It was one of my major accounts.

Surgeons promise that a certain procedure will relieve a painful leg, restore a stiff arm, or enable someone to dance at their daughter's wedding. In my business, this is called selling. Indeed, many doctors I encountered "sold" hip and knee surgery, even though they totally lacked experience to perform it, even though these devices are highly experimental, with high rates of failure. But these doctors were selling surgery, and there was virtually nothing they would not undertake, especially if they had me standing by (Skipitares 1985:15).

The Mike Connors story was the third act in a trilogy about Yankee ingenuity. Ben Franklin and Thomas Edison were Skipitares's choices to represent the 18th and 19th centuries respectively for acts I and II. Skipitares read all of the biographies of Franklin, and then all of Franklin's own writings which she found in the rare book room of the New York Public Library. When researching Edison she had as additional sources the newspapers of the day which recorded his exploits in minute detail. Fidelity to the writings was an important consideration as she assembled the material on these men. She quoted them exactly, in proper contexts. Making up scenes seemed wrong to her: "Maybe it's because I'm not working with real people. Puppets are such a sensational lie of their own—but a very innocent lie—that I don't think you can ask them to support anything but the truth" (in Harris 1985:17). If there was anything unscholarly in her approach she feels it might have been her selectivity: "I get so carried away with eccentricities that I let them glare out at me and I flock to them, finding obscure pieces and fashioning them into a picture rather than constructing what might be a more temperate portrait of someone" (1987).

Act I featured Franklin against the backdrop of his times, the wave of immigration from England and the Revolutionary War. The scenography in this section was complex. Immigration was shown by a large magnetized map that featured boats crossing the Atlantic from Europe to America. Three 24-inch-high tableaux represented the Revolutionary War: soldiers fighting the Battle of Lexington, Washingon crossing the Delaware, and the citizens of New York City toppling the statue of George III. Through mechanization and/or the manipulation of the puppeteers, soldiers were shot down in battle, boats rocked in stormy seas, and the statue fell.

Franklin's monolog revealed his strengths but also his weaknesses. The platitudinous nature of the aphorisms from *Poor Richard's Almanac* were pointed up by juxtaposition. "God helps them who helps themselves" echoed, for instance, during the Battle of Lexington. His simplistic approach to diplomacy drew a laugh when he leaned over the dead on the battlefield and said, "What should be done to settle the dispute between Great Britain and the colonies? Why, they should kiss and be friends."

Franklin's racism, so extreme that it is genuinely funny, was exposed as well. He proposed that all blacks and "tawnys" be excluded from America. "Tawnys" he defined as Spaniards, Italians, French, Russians, Swedes, and Germans, "the Saxons only excepted." Skipitares's purpose in creating this portrait was to give viewers "a different look at American heros, an inside look at Yankee ingenuity. It's really the flip side of what we were told as children" (in Harris 1985:17).

Edison articulated the similarity between himself, Franklin, and the huckster salesman: "An inventor is essentially practical. Anything that won't sell, I don't want to invent." Their research efforts and inventions were motivated by the desire for profit, with sometimes grisly results. Edison and Franklin, for instance, both experimented with electrocution using live animals.

Act II was tight and integrated, and therefore the most absorbing to watch. For example, while Edison talked about how he made his first fortune selling papers during the Civil War, a large map populated with moving heads and flashing eyes which made telegraphlike clacking sounds illustrated the population's eagerness for the news. The map finally split in two indicating the Civil War.

Edison's electrification of New York City was shown through the gradual lighting up of a detailed, accurate scale model of Wall and Broad Streets, the section he first converted to electricity (plate 7). Commenting on the fact, Edison the inventor instantaneously became Edison the businessman: "After this I will make electricity so cheap, only the rich will be able to afford to burn candles." Juxtaposed to this miracle of light was his film *Electrocuting the Elephant* (1889), an image which merged his contribution to the advancement of moving pictures and his cruel experiments. Conflicting feelings about the "supreme tinkerer" were expressed again in the final scene of Act II, an animated remake of *The Wizard of Oz*. Frank Baum, the author, modeled the wizard on Edison, "The Wizard of Menlo Park." Oz/Edison's hucksterism was implied in the selection in which he gave the Scarecrow a brain made of bran, pins, and needles, and in his cavalier attitude toward suffering as demonstrated in the line to the Woodsman, "I shall have to cut a hole in your breast, so I can put your heart in the right place. I hope it won't hurt you."

Hucksterism and cruel experiments are the themes which segue the piece into the 20th century, which is typified by Mike Connors, the con man. Skipitares comments:

> I think *Age* is really talking about the rise and fall of Yankee ingenuity, not a straight historical progression of great inventors. There are a few elements of the hustler in Franklin and Edison, but by the time you get to our century, that's become the main feature of the salesman. Ultimately, those three figures became really interesting expressions of facade. The puppet mechanisms served them well (in Harris 1985:16).

Each of the three sections of *The Age of Invention* was introduced by a prolog: the Buffalo Gals represented the 18th century, the Pioneer Women the 19th, and Rosy the Riveter the 20th. Women as a group were juxtaposed to single male figures: "My point was that traditionally history has been this big, blustery affair basically acted out by important men. But these ordinary women provide a throughline, a mainstay of history" (1987). The Buffalo Gals were buffaloes with women's faces: dispossessed, powerless, exploited. Their song, written by Martha Wilson, opens the piece:

> Living' with the white man
> Stead of livin' with the Indians
> Sorta like the landlord
> Who's bought the place from under you (Skipitares 1985:6).

The image of women in Conestoga wagons crossing the frontier was haunting and provocative. The wagons, seen in forced perspective (the furthest from us was the smallest), were carried by four puppeteers; their slow, rhythmic dancing provided the motion, their voices the song. The fact that their voices were untrained lent a note of authenticity to the plaintive cry of the obviously pregnant woman in the first wagon:

> To civilize the savage plains
> Is called our destiny
> I know I'm slowing progress down
> But I always have to pee (Skipitares 1985:9).

7. A six-foot-tall Thomas Edison overlooks a scale model of Wall Street in The Age of Invention. *(Photo by Bern Boyle)*

The pioneer women's true destiny was to endure and to raise their voices only in lament.

Rosie the Riveter reminded the viewer that the women who kept this country going throughout World War II were conveniently shifted back into the home when the men returned, sowing the seeds for the women's movement which arose in the '60s. Feminist concerns are a throughline of Skipitares's work: "It was important to me that the prologs show the quiet, ordinary, everyday life of women who were busy making history, only it wasn't called that because we were brought up thinking history was major, larger-than-life events enacted by important men" (1987).

The Age of Invention was a critical and popular success within the parameters of the avant-garde, "though there were some people who didn't think it was a play or even theatre," according to Skipitares (1987). Since it was about Americana and used life-sized puppets, it aroused popular interest; Skipitares subsequently received invitations to appear on television. However, because of its size and large cast, *Age* was expensive to tour, so it was only shown for three weeks in Europe and in two cities in the U.S.—Atlanta, GA, and New York City.

With *Age* Skipitares assumed another new role, that of director. The first stage of working with the puppets involved playful experimentation to test their physical limits. At this stage they break a lot, technical designer Michael Cummings notes ruefully. When the actor is a puppet, the puppeteer must literally find the so-called spine of a character. "Character isn't built in the traditional way," according to puppeteer Preston Foerder, "a lot comes out of what the puppet can do" (in Balis et al. 1987). Can it pick up a pen, for instance? If it needs to be a fidgeter, as the eugenicist Charles Davenport was in *Defenders of the Code,* how much can be done with hand, head, and body gestures (plates 8 & 9)?

Once the capacities and limitations of the puppet are explored, the work of scoring movement to the text begins. This is done word by word. The next step occurs when the live narrator is used with the inanimate character. The manipulators (two and sometimes three), whose actions are already tightly choreographed, must now adapt to changes in the narrator's intonations and also be aware of any line changes she or he might make.

One of the major aesthetic choices to be made involves the relationship of the puppet to the manipulator. Should the puppeteer react to what the puppet is doing, be expressionless, or be hidden? Foerder answers these

8. & 9. Drawings by technical designer Michael Cummings show the complexity of the knee and eye mechanisms for the puppet Davenport in Defenders of the Code.

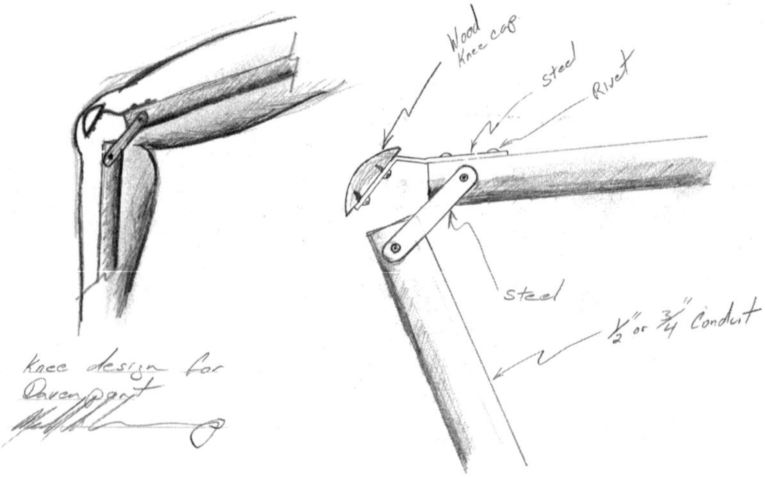

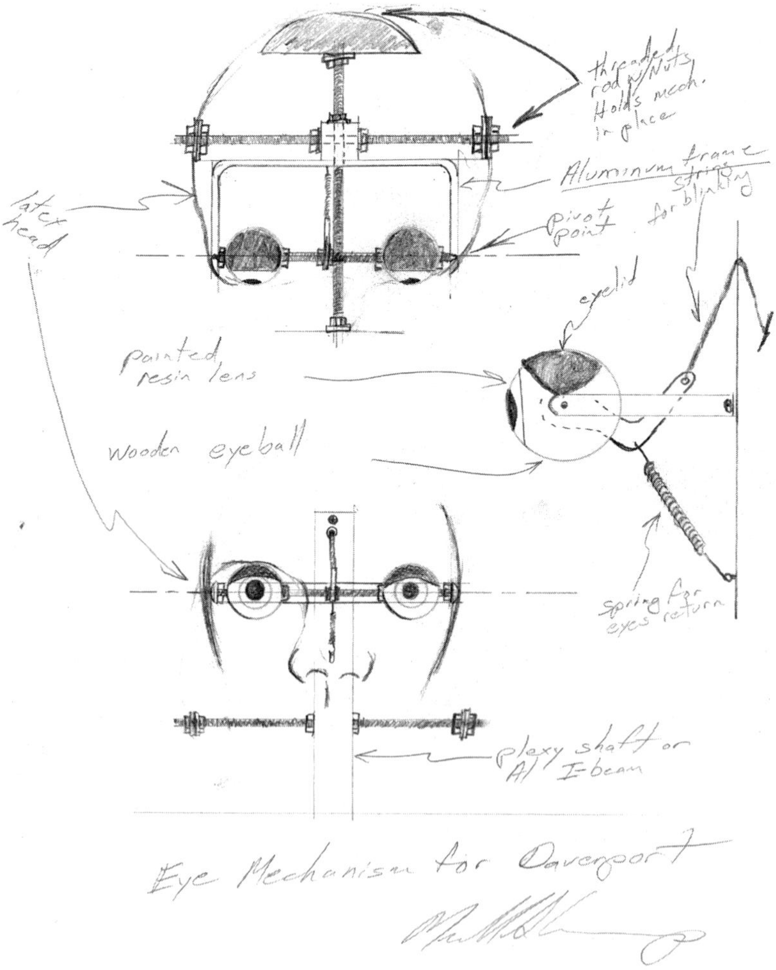

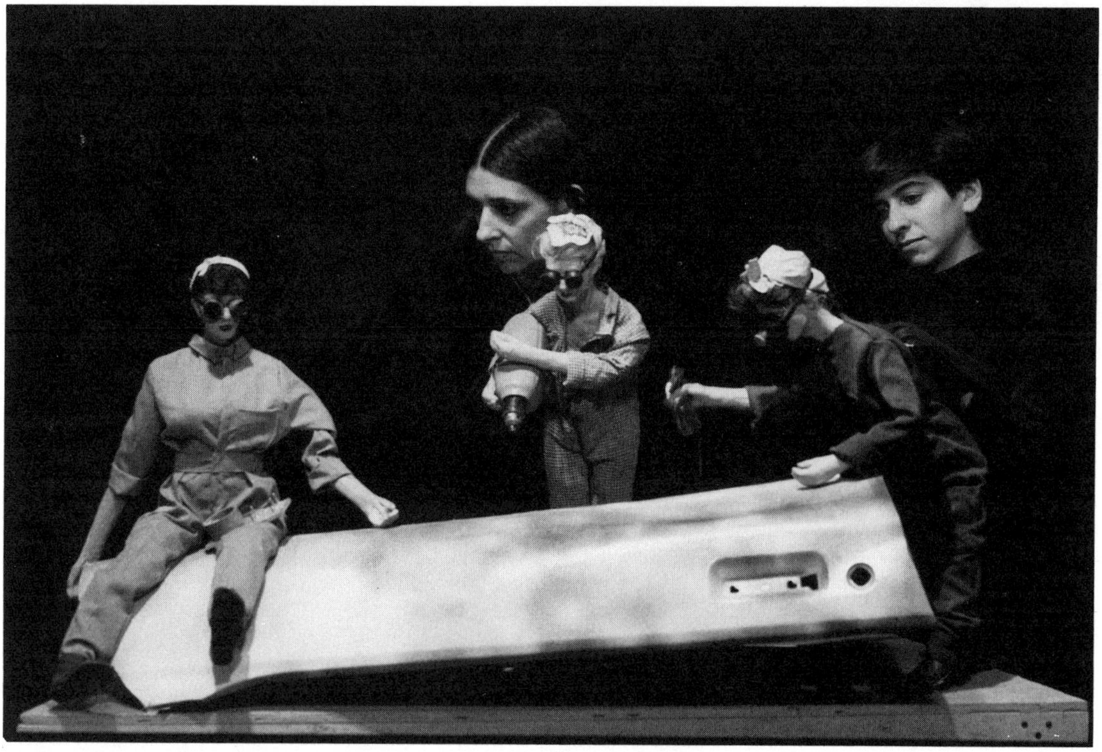

10. Skipitares (left) and Debby Lee Cohen manipulate Rosie the Riveter puppets in The Age of Invention. *Skipitares leaves her puppeteers unmasked to remind the audience of the artificiality and illusionism of the theatre. (Photo by Peter Volkart)*

questions in relation to Skipitares's work. "We are very much a presence. We are there to be seen as facilitators manipulating the characters, but we are not involved in the drama" (in Balis et al. 1987). Skipitares elaborates:

> The puppeteers wear black. However, their faces are visible [plate 10]. I have made a conscious choice to leave the puppeteers unmasked as a constant reminder to the audience of the artificiality and illusionism of the theatrical experience. I also like seeing the emotional connections that develop between the live performers and the puppets (in Balis et al. 1987).

This question of audience involvement/distanciation recurs throughout Skipitares's work. Puppetry is a distancing device, but it can be undercut by expressive manipulators. Skipitares's puppeteers look at their characters with love and reverence, so that the action takes on an almost ceremonial quality.

As with *The Age of Invention,* grant money was available for *Defenders of the Code* from its inception. The foundations that contributed to *Age*—NEA, NYSCA, and the Henson Foundation—supported the new production, giving the same amounts as they had previously. Skipitares also received a $22,000 Guggenheim fellowship. The additional money allowed a lengthier preparation period for designing and building the puppets, permitting a wider range of artistic choices.

The research process was an evolutionary one. Skipitares began studying Marie Curie, feeling that the piece would be about her (plate 11), and then she looked into Barbara McClintock, which led her to the idea of doing a piece on the history of heredity (the subtitle of *Defenders* is *A Musical*

History of the Uses and Abuses of Heredity). Stephen Jay Gould's works became pivotal to her, particularly *The Mismeasure of Man* (1981). Gould, an expert in evolutionary theory at the organismic level, is a Darwinian who believes that science is not the heartless pursuit of objective information but rather a creative human activity. In *The Mismeasure of Man* Gould wrote about how 19th- and 20th-century scientists, while under the illusion that they were being scientific, literal, and unbiased, were actually using science to support all kinds of prejudices. This dichotomous link between true scientific achievement and charlatanism became the central theme of *Defenders*. The process of demythologizing, so crucial to *The Age of Invention,* also operated in *Defenders*. In Skipitares's words: "I wanted to show that it is a myth, a masculine notion, that science is neutral and deals

11. A Marie Curie puppet, one of the main characters in Defenders of the Code. *(Photo by Adam Bartos)*

only with cold, objective truth rationally, logically, and without emotional investment" (1987).

The decision to make *Defenders* a musical increased the need for collaboration. Balis, who had functioned as Skipitares's dramaturg since *Micropolis* and wrote the "Birth of a Nation" song for *Age,* was engaged to write both music and lyrics for *Defenders.*[2] Skipitares began by doing voluminous research in heredity, genetics, and eugenics and roughed out the scenes which she and Balis then shaped and sequenced. To prepare Balis for writing the lyrics, Skipitares gave her honed down material from her research. For instance, a 300-page book on DNA was summarized in 5 pages. While the lyrics were original, the dialog, as in *Age,* was taken directly from the subjects' own works.

Having money available meant that the designer, Michael Cummings, would be involved from the start in all of the designs. It took him and Skipitares four months, working five days a week, to build the puppets. Drawings were developed first and in several cases working prototypes of the puppets were built. The puppets were more complex than earlier ones and had greater capabilities. Skipitares: "For the first time we began to create puppets with realistic hands whose fingers could lift objects and put them down. One of the most challenging problems Michael faced was how to design a mechanism for a family of genetically engineered cows who would be doing a tap dance" (1987). Cummings even experimented with making a puppet that could be filmed (Davenport), one with a sufficient range of subtle movements to withstand the scrutiny of the camera. Due to Cummings's expertise, the piece had a more finished look than *Age.*

Defenders looked like a primitive fantasy and engaged the viewer on a playful, even comic level. But at the same time, it dealt with one of the most serious, complex issues of our time—the ability of humans to genetically engineer animal and human life, even to create new forms of life. On the surface *Defenders* was about scientific fact and fallacy; subtextually it grappled with painful issues of racism and classism, making megaleaps from scientific thought to social reality. Viewers I spoke with were left disturbed, unsettled, questioning their own beliefs and prejudices.

In *Defenders,* as in *The Age of Invention,* changes in scale furthered the theme. In *Age,* Edison and Franklin were 6 feet tall when portrayed as mythic heroes, but only 28 inches high when shown as human beings. In *Defenders* Curie and Darwin were of mythic proportions. They stood six feet tall, unassailable in their integrity and devotion to science. *Defenders* opened with Madame Curie bending over her test tubes and notebooks, the periodic table as it was in 1911 lit up behind her. She was portrayed as a complex figure—both real and symbolic, a woman recorded in history (unlike the women in *Age*) who won the Nobel Prize for her discovery of radioactivity. Dipping her hands in the primordial stew which links the chemical elements to organic evolution, she raised the question, "What is life?" Scientific inquiry was then pitted against three myths of creation, which Curie narrated: the Greek, the White Nile, and the native American Crow.

Marie Curie also symbolized the artist herself. Just as Curie cooked tons of pitchblend to get her ounce of radium, so Skipitares read voluminously, reducing and transforming her research into images and action which expressed her vision. *Defenders* deals with the relationship between science and art, the scientist and the artist. Skipitares, referring to the discovery of the structure of DNA by James Watson and Francis Crick in 1963, stated,

"Watson's account showed scientific discovery as being hot, turbulent, passionate, vindictive—very much like what I know as making art. Certainly not a cold, detached, neutral process" (1987).

Darwin was deified by being presented as a distinguished old man, with his white hair and beard lit by radiant light from above. His central line from *On the Origin of Species* pointed up peoples' inhumanity to each other, which has been a recurring theme in the artist's work from *Skysaver* to the present:

> I would as soon be descended from some heroic little monkey or from some old baboon who carried away his comrade in triumph from a crowd of astonished dogs as to trace my ancestry from a savage who delights to torture his enemies, offers up bloody sacrifices, treats his wives like slaves, knows no decency and is haunted by the grossest superstition.

Gregor Mendel, the third giant in the history of heredity, was shown 30 inches high in a friezelike tableau watering his 15-inch peas as if to imply that the peas in their regularity had as much to do with the discovery as he did.

In *Defenders,* the seriousness of scientific discovery was lightened with mordant hilarity. Socrates' proclamation to the citizens of Athens about their worth, recorded in Plato's *Republic,* was accompanied by a sardonic

12. In Defenders of the Code, *medieval midwives insist that a woman in labor wait to give birth until the stars are in her favor. The woman, in response, sings "Who cares! So what!" (Photo by Adam Bartos)*

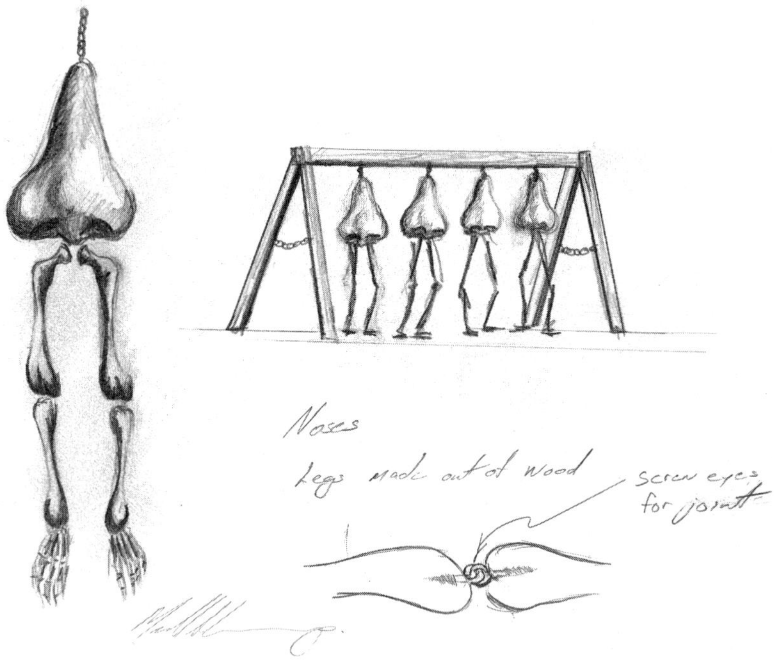

13. A design for the dancing noses in Defenders of the Code. *(Drawing by Michael Cummings)*

slave auction. A medieval text, which dictated when women should give birth based on the positions of the stars, was illustrated with midwives singing to a woman in labor as her fetus madly revolved in her belly, "Real soon! Real soon! Jupiter aligns with the moon to guarantee his riches and fame" (plate 12). The laboring woman answered "Too bad! Who cares! So what! Big deal!" Funniest of all was a discourse on noses taken from an 1848 phrenology textbook. The noses were displayed like meat on hooks as their qualities were ironically described in a scholarly voice by narrator Tom Costello (plate 13). The scene ended with the noses doing an animated, comic dance.

The use of science to support personal prejudice was the theme of the first half of Act II. Creationism was pitted against evolutionism, and distortion against reality, as the respected 19th-century naturalist Louis Agassiz explained that there had to be multiple Adam and Eves, because to believe otherwise would be to posit equality among the races. As he spoke, four separate Gardens of Eden, looking like medieval friezes and containing white, Asian, black, and native American couples, were animated, each in turn, to a song called "The Four Faces of Eve." Paul Broca, the biologist who first identified the specialized parts of the brain, took his ideas into the realm of the ridiculous by positing that the size of the brain determines intelligence: "It is larger in superior races than in inferior races, larger in men than in women. Their inferiority is so obvious that only its degree is worthy of discussion." Skipitares's answer to this was a dance of brains with glowing eyes that moved sprightly in the dark. Charles Davenport was linked to the genetically engineered Beta babies of Aldous Huxley's *Brave New World* (1932). The babies moved rhythmically in their cradles to the refrain "Betas are the best." Earlier in the play Darwin had argued against selective breeding: "The more diversified the descendants become the better their chance of success in the battle for life."

The fallaciousness and unreliability of IQ tests was shown in the satiric "Chitling Test" in which a white polyurethane mouse was forced to answer questions that a black ghetto child would find a snap. The mouse tapped his fingers as he tried to decide among choices, leaned forward with discouragement, played "eenie, meanie, miney, moe," jubilantly kissed a letter when he got a correct answer, cheered when he was assured that he wasn't a complete idiot, and slumped with discouragement when he was told he was a moron.

The centerpiece of Act II was Watson and Crick's discovery of the double helix structure of DNA, which elucidated the genetic code. Previously, science had only theories as to how genes transmitted their information.[3] The discovery of how DNA works was made possible in part by Rosalind Franklin's work in crystallography. Watson acknowledged Franklin's contribution in his book *The Double Helix* (1968), but she was not awarded the Nobel Prize along with Watson, Crick, and Maurice Wilkins. She died at age 37 as the result of her experiments; thus her ghost hovered over Watson and Crick during the play—another woman whose contributions were overlooked.

Scale was linked to importance in *Defenders*. Thus, DNA, which in reality can't be seen without the use of a sophisticated electron microscope, lit up beside its discoverers and was many times their size. The shift in scale had been used earlier in the play for Darwin's "Train of Life"; each of the phyla in the train was on a car of a different height, reflecting its relative complexity on the biological chain—a female homo sapiens stood in the last car (plate 14).

The last half of Act II returned to the theme of selective breeding and raised the problem of genetic engineering. William Shockley, a Nobel Prize winner, explained his voluntary sterilization bonus plan which seemed clearly aimed against minority groups, and talked about his donation to the Nobel Prize–winner sperm bank. The implications of his ideas were heightened by the reading of a newspaper article about the merchandising of sperm and embryos in the cattle business. A cow and her calves danced a comment and the vocalist sang "Moo Cow Moo":

In bovine business dealings
Babies are a big cash crop
Genetic engineering
Means the profits never stop (Balis 1987:8).

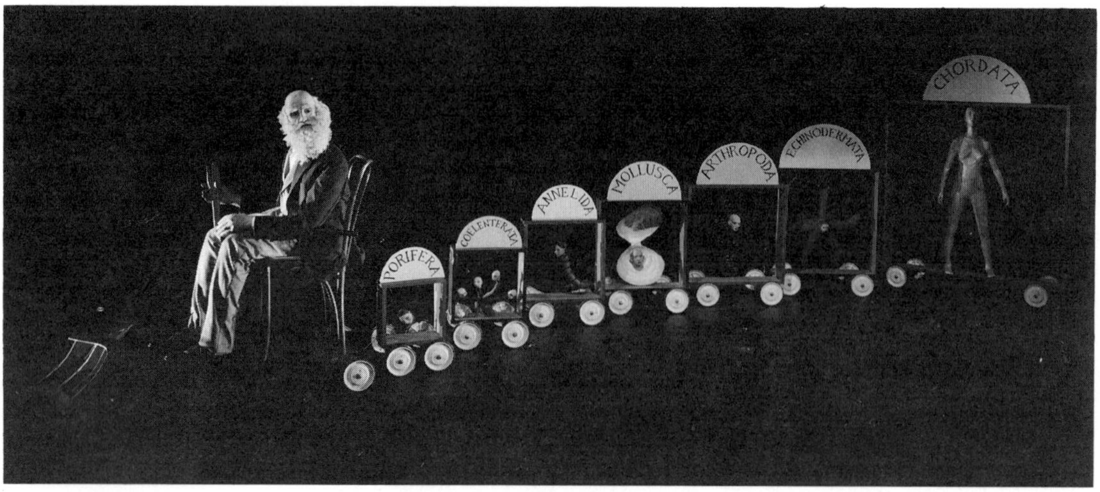

14. Charles Darwin's "Train of Life" in Defenders of the Code. *(Photo by Adam Bartos)*

The piece ended with a model of Einstein's brain and the comment that on examination it was no different from anybody elses.

Darwin stated in *On the Origin of Species,* "If it could be demonstrated that any complex organ existed, which could not possibly have been formed by numerous, successive, slight modifications, my theory would absolutely break down" (1859:189). The complexity and brilliance of *Defenders* was made possible by Skipitares's growth through successive stages—sculptor, performance artist, theatre designer, fund-raiser, researcher, playwright, director. The next step may be to filmmaker. She is currently exploring the aesthetics and mechanisms of cinematic puppetry in preparation for making film versions of *The Age of Invention* and *Defenders of the Code.*

Notes

1. The production of *The Age of Invention* that was analyzed for this article was presented in January 1985 at the Theatre for the New City (New York City); that of *Defenders of the Code* was presented in February 1987 at the Apple Corps Theatre (New York City).
2. Virgil Moorefield composed the music for *Defenders of the Code,* Gail Conrad choreographed, and Tom Costello narrated.
3. Information on the scientific aspects of *Defenders of the Code* was given to me by Dr. Mary Desmond, Professor of Biology at Villanova University, during an interview in Berwyn, PA, on 22 July 1987.

References

Balis, Andrea

1980 "Theodora Skipitares." Catalog of the Wake Forest University, Southeastern Center for Contemporary Art, North Carolina School of the Arts:1.

1987 "Moo Cow Moo." *Defenders of the Code* program:1–8.

Balis, Andrea, Michael Cummings, Preston Foerder, and Theodora Skipitares

1987 Interview with author. New York City, 8 July.

Banes, Sally

1977 "New Mysteries." *Soho Weekly News,* 2 June:21.

Darwin, Charles

1859 *On the Origin of Species.* London: Murray.

Dicker, Shira

1982 "In a Nutshell." *Otherstages,* 15 July:4.

Flood, Richard

1982 "Theodora Skipitares, Three Portraits and a Landscape: Inroads." *Artforum* 20 (no. 8):76–77.

Gould, Stephen Jay

1981 *The Mismeasure of Man.* New York: W.W. Norton, Inc.

Harris, William

1985 "An Interview with Theodora Skipitares." *Theatre* 17, no. 1 (Winter):16–18.

Heinemann, Sue

1980 "Theodora Skipitares: Review." Catalog of the Wake Forest University, Southeastern Center for Contemporary Art, North Carolina School of the Arts:3–4.

Huxley, Aldous
1932 *Brave New World.* Garden City, NY: Doubleday.

Jenner, C. Lee
1983 "Working with Puppets—Theodora Skipitares." *Performing Arts Journal* 7 (no. 1):107–11.

Jones, Jeffrey M.
1984 "Elusive Idiosyncracies: The World of Puppeteer Theodora Skipitares." *Theatre Crafts* 18 (no. 3):20–23, 47–48, 50–51.

Neff, Renfreu
1982 "Puppets With a Past Fear Bleak Future." *The Villager,* 22 April:10.

Perlberg, Deborah
1980 "Theodora Skipitares, the Performing Garage." *Artforum* 18 (no. 7):78–80.

Schall, Jan
1981 "Theodora Skipitares." *Art Papers* 5 (no. 3):22–23.

Shewey, Don
1981 "At the Performing Garage." *The Soho News,* 10 June:49.

Skipitares, Theodora
1985 *"The Age of Invention." Theatre* 17, no. 1 (Winter):5–15.
1987 Interviews with author. New York City, 17, 23, 25, and 30 June.

Joan Driscoll Lynch *is an Associate Professor of Communication Arts at Villanova University. She is the author of* Film Education in Secondary Schools *and has written articles on film, video, and theatre in such journals as* American Theatre, *the* Journal of Film and Video, *the* Literature/Film Quarterly, *and the* Journal of Popular Culture. *She is currently writing a book on women in the avant-garde that is tentatively titled* Women's Creations.

Historical Simulation and Popular Entertainment

The *Potemkin* Mutiny from Reconstructed Newsreel to Black Sea Stunt Men

Daniel Gerould

Modern man [. . .] is continually having a world-panorama unrolled before his eyes by his historical artists. He is turned into a restless, dilettante spectator, and arrives at a condition when even great wars and revolutions cannot affect him beyond the moment. The war is hardly at an end, and it is already converted into thousands of copies of printed matter.

—*Friedrich Nietzsche (1957:29)*

Appearances have always played a much more important part than reality in history, where the unreal is always of greater moment than the real.

Crowds being only capable of thinking in images are only to be impressed by images. It is only images that terrify or attract them and become motives of action.

For this reason theatrical representations, in which the image is shown in its most clearly visible shape, always have an enormous influence on crowds. [. . .] The unreal has almost as much influence on them as the real. They have an evident tendency not to distinguish between the two.

—*Gustave Le Bon (1960:68–9)*

In striving to produce deceptively lifelike changes in their presentation of nature, the panoramas point ahead, beyond photography, to films and sound films. [. . .] The panoramas, which declare a revolution in the relation of art to technology, are at the same time an expression of a new feeling about life.

—*Walter Benjamin (1978:149–50)*

Revolution, war, and natural disaster were converted into spectacle and simulated news became a form of entertainment for mass audiences after 1789. Gigantic paintings and panoramas as well as their animated counterparts in theatrical representations were in vogue during the French Revolution and the Napoleonic era, but pictorial simulation of news events reached its largest public 100 years later at the turn of the next century when the mechanical means of production offered by cinema enabled the show to be inscribed on celluloid, copied, and endlessly replayed. Land engagements, naval battles, shipwrecks, fires at sea, explosions, volcanic eruptions, and earthquakes were popular spectacular reconstructions in the 19th-century entertainment industry that were quickly taken over by early film.

The catastrophic defeats of the Tsarist forces in the Russo-Japanese War, the wave of assassinations and anarchist attacks, and then the revolution of 1905 provided exciting material for these reconstructed newsreels. The revolt aboard the battleship *Potemkin* that took place in late June 1905 in the Black Sea was given its first cinematographic incarnation as a French *actualité reconstituée*—or simulated news event—almost as it was happening and exactly 20 years before Eisenstein's film, *The Battleship Potemkin,* a mythologized version of the same episode from Russian history. Before looking more closely at this first documentary simulation about the *Potemkin,* I must briefly reconstruct the history of the historical reconstruction.

The Masses on the Stage of History: Supernumeraries as Protagonists

The French Revolution was the first great European political and social upheaval that its creators immediately perceived as a spectacle to be enacted and reenacted. The Fall of the Bastille, the Meetings of the Convention and Committees, the Sessions of the Revolutionary Tribunal, and the Terror and the Guillotine were all history theatricalized which could be constantly

1. *The real battleship* Potemkin *after the surrender in Constanta. (Photo courtesy of Daniel Gerould)*

replayed. In the festivals and rites staged by revolutionary choreographers to celebrate and commemorate these events, audience and performers became one. "The most magnificent of spectacles is that of a great people assembled," Robespierre declared; "the spectacle of the spectators themselves" was the essence of the show (in Brown 1980:76–7).

These mass spectacles and popular rituals expressing the unity of the people sometimes took the form of reenactments, such as *La Prise de la Bastille,* a musical *hiérodrama,* presented in the Cathedral of Notre Dame on the eve of the first anniversary (see Carlson 1966:44–5). More often they were pageants and processionals in authentic outdoor settings involving the participation of hundreds of thousands. Such was the *Festival of the Supreme Being,* devised and directed by the painter David in celebration of a deistic god, with Robespierre officiating (see El Nouty 1978:43–4; Billington 1980:45–6). Later, the revolutionary ceremonial might be repeated in simulated form in professional theatres, as was the case with the *Festival of the Unity and Indivisibility of the Republic.* Originally organized by David on the first anniversary of the overthrow of the monarch (10 August 1793) and staged processionally with chariots and floats moving from the Place de la Bastille to the Champs de Mars, this *fête* was subsequently transformed into a dramatic *sans-cullotide,* or revolutionary show in five acts to be performed in playhouses by actors taking the parts of the real people who had played themselves in the earlier version.

The spectacles reflected the new role of the masses in the making of history. A collective act of the people, the taking of the Bastille marked the advent of the French Revolution. On the London stage it was reenacted as early as 1789 with *The Triumph of Liberty, or the Destruction of the Bastille* at the Royal Circus, and *Paris in an Uproar, or The Destruction of the Bastille* at Astley's Amphitheatre (see Booth 1965:93; Nicoll 1962 III:54). But it was military history that brought the masses on stage and provided the greatest impetus for new forms of pictorial journalism in the popular arts. Never before had there been such huge mass-conscripted armies or battles on such a vast scale. French attempts to defend—and export their revolution—against the foreign intervention of a British, Austrian, and Prussian coalition, and then the ensuing Napoleonic Wars, engulfed all of Europe in conflict. Military campaigns in far-off places became of interest to the general public everywhere (see Meisel 1983:204).

Large numbers of people were curious to see with their own eyes the events of the day involving large numbers of people like themselves; simulated news became a form of entertainment. Large-scale history painting portraying current happenings flourished. At the same time there appeared a new pictorial genre of popular entertainment, the panorama, which placed the spectator in the center of an immense circular painting shown in a special rotunda. Invented and named by an Irishman, Robert Barker, the panorama came into being at the time of the French Revolution. Its vogue spread from London to Paris, Berlin, and St. Petersburg and its popularity lasted throughout the 19th, and even into the early 20th century, when it was supplanted by cinema.

The new mass public that followed the warfare in the newspapers was willing to pay admission to look at the latest military paintings on view in galleries and special exhibition sheds or to visit one of the panoramas—at first fixed, later moving through the use of canvas on rollers—that were "the newsreels of the Napoleonic era" (Altick 1978:174–5, 136). Battle artists on assignment accompanied the armies; panoramas were painted from drawings made at the scene of battle, while details were adjusted according to late dispatches.

London theatres competed with historical paintings and panoramas in representing current events, although the historicity of the staged versions of military and naval exploits was less exact than in the graphic arts. With its huge tank of water in which scale models of warships floated, the Sadler's Wells specialized in nautical drama—an imitation of the *naumachia* of the ancient Romans—such as *The Battle of Trafalgar* (1806) and *The Battle of the Nile* (1815) (see Rayhill 1967:133; Booth 1965:100). With its stable of trained horses, sometimes numbering up to 90, Astley's was a hippodrome in which action could move back and forth from ring to stage. It featured cavalry engagements, such as *The British Glory in Egypt* (1801) with "REAL CAVALRY and INFANTRY" and *The Battle of Waterloo,* the greatest favorite of all, which in a number of different versions was constantly revived. Cavalry charges, bugle calls, cannon fire, and military music lent authenticity (see Saxon 1968:46, 137; Booth 1965:93–4; Altick 1978:175). The presence of a special spectator could also serve to authenticate the representation of a battle in which he had been a leading participant, as when the Duke of Wellington attended *The Battle of Waterloo* or Nelson praised Robert Barker for keeping alive the memory of the Battle of the Nile by the creation of his commemorative panorama of 1815 (see Altick 1978:136).

Simulated pictorial representation on canvas was often combined with real objects in three-dimensional space. Panoramas could be incorporated in theatrical pantomimes or used in pleasure-garden settings behind lakes and free-standing models in something approaching a motion picture set (see Altick 1978:325). Such was the case when the Battle of Waterloo was reconstructed as a total event at the Vauxhall Gardens in 1827 with the participation of 1,000 soldiers.

In France during the reign of Napoleon, the imperial ceremonies were the outstanding historical spectacles, and would subsequently be simulated in the theatre. After Waterloo and the Restoration of the Bourbon Monarchy, the huge popular theatres on the boulevards, like the Cirque Olympique with its more than 50 horses and complex stage machinery permitting simultaneous action in the ring and on the stage, satisfied the popular longing for former military glories with mass spectacles. Despite censorship forbidding the presentation of Napoleon on stage, homage was paid to the Emperor by means of plays glorifying his generals and the French army, such as in *La Morte de Kleber, ou Les Français, Cadix et la France* (1819) and *La Prise de la Flotte, ou la Charge de Cavalerie* (1822) in which the French cavalry made a charge across the frozen North Sea to attack and capture the Dutch fleet (see Winter 1964:176; El Nouty 1978:56). Military spectacles like *Les Pyrénées, Cadix et la France* (1824) celebrating the French forces in Spain were given special performances for soldiers (including the disabled) newly returned from the Spanish campaign. A contemporary observer wrote in 1821, "A few years ago the people of Paris went to battles as to the theatre; now they go to the theatre as to a combat" (in El Nouty 1978:46). At the Cirque Olympique the smell of smoke and of horses made veterans imagine that they were back on the battlefield.

After the revolution of July 1830, with the installation of Louis Philippe as king and the lifting of censorship, the Napoleonic myth flourished in the popular theatres, achieving pictorial authentication as history through iconic evocation of the best-known images of Napoleon in historical paintings (see Meisel 1983:215–7). Different aspects of the heroic life and campaigns of the Emperor were shown in over 500 melodramas and military spectacles, whose acts were sometimes called "Epochs." In *L'Empereur,* staged at the Cirque Olympique in 1830, the entire career of Napoleon was presented, ending with the obligatory apotheosis in heaven. "It was no play, it was reality," wrote a spectator (in Saxon 1968:123–4). Every theatre now had its own Napoleon and contests were held to choose the actor who best simulated the Emperor; one performer finally came to believe that he actually was the great man whom he portrayed.

Claims of authenticity extended to the costumes and properties. The director of the Ambigu consulted with Napoleon's old valet for the design and measurement of the Emperor's small hat and gray cloak to reproduce the right texture and exact color (see Saxon 1968:121). In London, British dramas on the Emperor's life, although less chauvinistic than their French counterparts, were equally concerned with scrupulous historical reconstruction. For the "Grand Historical and Military Spectacle" entitled *Napoleon* at Covent Garden in 1831, the management claimed that the costumes, imported from France, had actually been worn by Napoleon and his staff (see Meisel 1983:219–21).

Panoramists were not to be outdone. As an attache in St. Petersburg, Jean-Charles Langlois (1789–1870), an ex-colonel who had served with Napoleon at Waterloo, made on-the-scene studies near Borodino and Moscow for his panoramas, *The Battle of Moskva, The Battle of Borodino,* and *The Burning of Moscow* (see Sternberger 1977:187). For his panorama *The Battle of Navarino,* shown in 1830 at the rotunda he established in Paris, Langlois bought the poop of the *Scipion,* a vessel of 74 cannons which had taken part in the naval engagement on the Ionian Sea, and made it the platform for the spectators, who entered by corridors replicating those of the battleship. When they reached the deck, the spectators found themselves in the midst of the battle, confronted by an approaching Turkish fireship that the sailors of the French, English, and Russian coalition attempted to drive off (see El Nouty 1978:56).

Chronometrically, topographically, and logistically exact, the panorama of *The Battle of Sedan,* first shown in Berlin on 1 September 1883 with the Kaiser in attendance, represented the moment on the afternoon of 1 September 1870 between 1:30 and 2:00 that proved to be a turning point in the engagement leading to the Prussian triumph over the French. To achieve such an effect of reportorial accuracy, the artist—Anton von Werner (1855–1927)—used strategic maps, went on maneuvers, and studied the amount and extent of smoke emitted by different caliber guns, assisted in his research by a staff of weapons experts. Bismarck approvingly viewed himself meeting Napoleon III for the French capitulation, commenting on the lifelikeness of his horse, Rosa. The artist, however, was to complain of the impermanence and disposability of the panorama as an art form undervalued by the cultural establishment.

> All these works, spatially and artistically powerful, vanished after the sight-seers had seen their fill—and the stockholders had no further prospects of high dividends. I wonder if some future book on art history will mention any of them as a characteristic phenomenon of the last third of the nineteenth century? (von Werner in Sternberger 1977:15).

It is precisely this constant unrolling of a world-panorama before the glazed eyes of the passive spectator that lead Nietzsche to assail the hypertrophy of the "historical sense" and "historical culture" in the new democratic age (1957:48, 49).

Projected on Smoke and Imprinted on Wax

Impermanence was characteristic of the popular arts. Two other genres of visual simulations of historical personalities, important in determining how the 19th century perceived itself and imagined its heros and villains, were the phantasmagoria and the waxworks. For six years, starting in 1789, Etienne Gaspard Robertson, a Belgian inventor and balloonist, presented his *Fantasmagorie,* or optical illusions, in an abandoned chapel on the grounds of an Old Capuchin monastery in Paris. By means of a magic lantern he projected ghostly apparitions onto smoke or semitransparent screens (see Barnouw 1981:19–27). In addition to luminous images of Gothic specters and skeletons—fashionable in an age enamored of sorcery, magic, and phantoms—the fantasmagorie included famous figures from the French Revolution and its aftermath, such as Marat, Danton, Robespierre, and Napoleon—specters still haunting Europe (see Robertson 1985:13). A mobile lantern and adjustable lens allowed the images to be enlarged or contracted, creating the illusion of ominously advancing or retreating figures who seemed to approach the spectators and almost touch them, spreading terror among the audience (see El Nouty 1978:51; Altick 1978:219). These shows, presented in London and New York in the first decades of the 19th century, also featured re-creations of eruptions of Mt. Vesuvius and spectacular fires currently in the news. They placed the spectators directly at the center of the spectacle.

When Madame Tussaud established her waxworks in London in 1802 at the Lyceum, her museum was located next to Paul de Philipstal's Phantasmagoria (see Altick 1978:333). Waxworks offered three-dimensional dramatic representations of current events and personalities in the news, and since Madame Tussaud insisted on keeping up with the headlines, the exhibits changed with the times. Rigorous authenticity was proclaimed. For her French Revolutionary figures, such as Charlotte Corday, Marie Antoinette, and Robespierre, the effigies were modeled either from death masks or from casts made of the severed heads brought directly to the cemetery from the guillotine (see Leslie and Chapman 1978:70–5).

Where possible, the figures were dressed in their actual clothes. The Effigy and Personal Effects of Napoleon was one of the special attractions, particularly admired by the Duke of Wellington, a frequent visitor at Madame Tussaud's. Seeing him contemplating his defeated enemy, the Tussaud brothers commissioned George Hayter to paint this scene, thereby obtaining a historical painting—which subsequently hung in the waxworks—that reflexively comments on simulation. One great historical player, now aging, admiringly confronts a replica of his former rival, fixed by death at an earlier moment that has been captured forever by the art of the waxworker. Two time frames co-exist and several layers of simulation intersect, producing a modern perspective (not unlike that present in the Mabou Mines' 1983 historical reconstruction, *Cold Harbor,* in which General Grant is brought out of his museum case) pleasing to those with an increasingly democratized interest in the makers and making of history (see Altick 1978:222–3; Meisel 1983:234–5). Whereas, given present technologies, the Iron Duke would be interviewed on television and shown footage of his former adversary to be commented upon, in the silent Victorian simulation each viewer is required to read Wellington's reflections according to the expression on his face and his stance vis-à-vis the fallen foe.

War by Correspondence in the Crimea and in India: Imperialist Entertainment

An expanding mass-circulation press, financed by advertising and furthered by new telegraphic technology, set out to create and then satisfy curiosity about current events. In its reliance on the power of visual effects, the new pictorial journalism transformed politics and war into entertainment. The Crimean War (1853–6), the bloodiest in Europe between Waterloo and Sarajevo, was the first to be covered by eyewitness reporters. The foreign correspondent of the *Times* of London wielded such power in mobilizing popular support for the war that it was said that the country was actually being governed by the *Times* (see Billington 1980:314–17, 337–8). War correspondents watching from hillsides sent telegraphic dispatches, but photographers actually present still posed and staged battle scenes which would not shock the public. Langlois created a striking photographic panorama of the devastated countryside around Sebastopol, but avoided battle scenes altogether. The gallantry of war, not the spectacle of death, was the subject of patriotic journalism that aimed at pictorial distraction (the American Civil War photographer Matthew Brady was ruined when he showed genuine horrors and atrocities) (see Cogeval 1986:71–4).

At Astley's hippodrome, *The Battle of Alma* was presented in October 1854, less than a month after the event. With 400 extras, brass bands, and vast processions of troops, it put on stage a *Times* correspondent as a character who assists in defeating the barbarian Russians, killing one and capturing several others himself (see Bratton 1980:129–33; Saxon 1968:144). For the first time a historical simulation placed within its frame the newsgatherer who was the source of its existence. It was not until Karl Kraus's vast drama of World War I, *The Last Days of Mankind* (1922), that war correspondents were portrayed not simply as reporters of what happened, but rather as major causes of the war. Kraus indicts journalists as instigators of hatreds responsible for the bloodshed.

Newspapers in the mid-19th century offered enthusiastic support for imperial and colonial wars, and no one questioned the inspiration provided by chauvinistic journalism for popular entertainment. The playwright Dionysius Boucicault records in his memoirs (talking of himself in the third person) that while visiting New York in the 1850s he found in the accounts of historical events in the popular press new subjects for his dramas.

> Boucicault had used these three years in the study of the American people, their tastes, and the direction of their intellectual appetites. The poetic and romantic drama had no longer its old charm; the actual, the contemporary, the photographic had replaced the works of the imagination. It was in turning over the *Illustrated Journal* that the idea struck him that the stage might be employed in a similar manner to embody and illustrate the moving events of the period. The Russian war, the Indian mutiny, the adventures of Dr. Kane in polar regions, the slave question, were all live subjects of the period. But the most immediate and burning matter in the public mind was the Indian mutiny. The news of the massacre at Cawnpore had filled the world with horror, when we learned that a small garrison of Europeans were shut up in Lucknow, besieged by an overwhelming

> force of Indians. This article was seized on by Boucicault when he wrote "Jessie Brown, or the Relief of Lucknow," and this play was produced in New York while the siege was still in progress (Boucicault 1889:230).

All the major battles of the Crimean War—Inkerman, Balaclava, Sebastopol, as well as Alma—had military spectacles devoted to them. Indian and Afghan wars and mutinies were the subjects of panoramas and spectacles in London: *The Battle of Kabul in the Afghan War,* a panorama in 1842 commemorating a defeat; *The Afghanistan War; Or, The Revolt at Kabul and British Triumphs in India,* a huge spectacle of 1843, making use of elephants as well as horses; *The Storming and Capture of Delhi,* at Astley's in 1857, as well as panoramas on the Sepoy Mutiny and the Mutinies at Delhi and Lucknow; and *The Fall of Khartoum and the Death of General Gordon* at the rebuilt Astley's in 1885 (see Nicoll 1962 V:579, 675; Saxon 1968:144, 205, 221).

At the Great Paris Exhibitions of 1890 and 1900 reconstructions of battles and naval engagements continued to be popular, as were panoramas showing scenes from the French Revolution, the battle of Austerlitz, and other episodes in French history (see Rearick 1985:208). But it was the many "little wars" of the early 20th century that provided the best material for the entertainment industry. In 1901 the Cirque d'Hiver presented a military pantomime, *The Allies in China,* while the Nouveau Cirque in 1905 gave a pantomime of the Russo-Japanese War. At the Châtelet, where the Cirque Olympique had moved in 1862 when the theatres on the Boulevard du Temple had been razed, the sinking of a Russian battleship by the Japanese was staged as late as 1911. At the end of the old century and the beginning of the new, news as visual entertainment still took the form of picture postcards, figures at the wax museum, panoramas, and theatrical spectacles; film, the product of the latest technology, would enter into competition with these earlier forms of news simulation and the power of its pictures was such that it eventually supplanted all others.

Reconstructed Newsreel

Almost immediately the new film studios which appeared in the mid-1890s went into the news business. Louis Lumière sent cameramen throughout the world to make newsreels and documentaries, but George Méliès, a magician by training, chose to follow the earlier traditions of spectacle and panorama and to reconstruct current events in his studios (see Hammond 1975:34). Actually, the mass-circulation papers, such as *Le Petit Journal* and *Le Monde Illustré,* were doing much the same thing at this time when they had graphic artists copy or re-create photographs; because of difficulties in photographic reproduction, engravings were preferred for use as illustrations (see Deslandes 1963:62).

Méliès began his pioneering work in reconstructed newsreels with scenes from the Greco-Turkish War of 1897: *War Episodes, Massacre in Crete,* and *Sea Fighting in Greece.* In 1898 he reconstructed scenes of the American intervention in Cuba and the Philippines: *A View of the Wreck of the Maine* and *Divers at Work on the Wreck of the Maine,* in which a painted backdrop representing the sunken battleship was photographed through a large aquarium containing real water and fish (see Hammond 1975:36; Deslandes 1963:62–3). Lumière had shot a brief simulated Dreyfus Affair in 1897. During the summer of 1899, Méliès made a 13-minute *Dreyfus*

Affair with 11 sets that reconstructed the illustrations in the weekly papers (see Hammond 1975:42). Because of the passions these reconstructions aroused, the government prohibited the filming or showing of works about the Dreyfus case (see Kleeblatt 1984:276–7). Using actors and painted sets based on a published photograph, Méliès prepared *The Coronation of Edward VII* in the studio at Montreuil in 1902 several days before the event itself took place so that the film could be shown on the evening of Coronation Day at the Alhambra music hall in Leicester Square (see Hammond 1975:53–4).

We should remember that Méliès was making his famous fantastic "trick" films—such as *A Trip to the Moon* (1902) and *The Impossible Voyage* (1904)—at the same time as his actualités reconstituées. The distinction between true and false, then as now, was hard to draw and for many nonexistent. In certain Third World countries today people believe that the film of the 1969 moon-landing is "simulated"—a kind of Méliès trick film.

The ten years from 1897 to 1906 were the high point in the reconstructed newsreel. In 1906 a cinema was opened which was devoted entirely to authentic actualitès, or so it was advertised. Once techniques of photographing and developing had become sufficiently advanced, current events were increasingly filmed on location rather than in the studio. Starting in 1900, the *Pathé Journal* or newsreel appeared on a regular basis.

But for a number of years at the turn of the century audiences were most deeply moved and affected by simulations which effectively dramatized events that could not be captured or adequately filmed while in progress. Starting with their own six-part *Dreyfus Affair* in 1899, Charles and Emile Pathé began to create a series of actualités reconstituées under the general direction of Ferdinand Zecca, a young Corsican in charge of the studios at Vincennes on the outskirts of Paris. Although Zecca continued to produce comedies, trick films, and adventure and crime stories, special emphasis was placed on the increasingly popular simulated documentaries about disasters, such as *The Great Chicago Theatre Fire* and *The Catastrophe in Martinique* (about the volcanic eruption that killed 40,000). The ancestor of this simulated disaster newsreel was a theatrical spectacle, *The Earthquake in Martinique,* given at the Porte-St.-Martin and Gaité theatres in 1840.

Using eyewitness accounts, photographs, and drawings from newspapers and magazines such as *L'Illustration* and the picture supplement of *Le Petit Journal,* the Pathé artists (already experienced in historical reconstructions such as *Quo Vadis* and various lives of Jesus) were able, in the course of only a few hours, to prepare painted backgrounds of cities and ports so precisely detailed that they could be taken for the real place. For *The Catastrophe in Martinique,* the painted backdrop represented the town and the volcanic mountain Pelée, in front of which a large trough of water served as the ocean. One studio assistant burned sulphur behind the mountain, another on a ladder out of view of the camera manipulated a large tray so as to bring smoke down upon the set in imitation of lava, while yet another, perched on a ladder, threw sawdust to create a rain of cinders. A fourth assistant shook the trough of water to simulate waves and at the end of the film hurled the entire contents at the backdrop to produce a gigantic tidal wave (see Jeanne 1965:127; Mitry 1967:219–20).

The New York studio, Vitagraph, filmed a tabletop battle of Santiago Bay—with cigar smoke, explosives, and cardboard ships going down in inch-deep water—because actual footage of Theodore Roosevelt going up San Juan Hill was dull and disappointing. Such practices cause the documentary film historian Erik Barnouw to talk of fakery and deceit. He cites as further evidence of fraud the work of the British filmmaker James Williamson whose *Attack on a Chinese Mission* (1898) was shot in his backyard, and whose Boer War scenes were filmed on a golf course, while Biograph's *Battle of Re Yalu* and Edison's *Skirmish Between Russian and Japanese Advance Guards* were reconstructed on Long Island and New Jersey (Barnouw 1974:24–5).

Although the British painter John Constable had said of the panoramas and dioramas, "It is without the pale of art, because its object is deception" (in Osborne 1986), the very nature of the 19th-century media for news simulations kept the audience from being truly deceived. No matter how spectators standing at the center of the rotunda exclaimed that the panorama seemed reality itself, no one believed that s/he had been transported from London or Paris back in time to the battlefield at Waterloo. Likewise, for all its three-dimensionality, smoke, noise and smells, real water and real horses, and hundreds of authentically costumed soldiers at the Cirque Olympique or Sadler's Wells, the immediacy of the theatrical representation, the audience's knowledge that the performance was happening here and now limited the possibility of any complete illusion. That the film reconstructions—flat, silent, without color, often involving only several dozen performers, and lasting one or two minutes—seemed so real as to deceive audiences and raise charges of fakery is due to the reportorial nature of cinema. Film portrays something that purportedly happened somewhere else at an earlier time; its record of distant events can be played over and over again in other places and at other times. Its very essence is deception.

Lucien Nonguet, who was the *chef de figuration*—director in charge of supernumeraries and crowd movements—at the Châtelet, Ambigu, and Renaissance theatres in Paris, at first only provided his friend Zecca with extras and supervised their placement and grouping (see Mitry 1967:216). Soon, however, Nonguet undertook the mise-en-scene himself and became Zecca's principal co-worker at Pathé. In 1902/03 the two filmmakers collaborated on a lengthy *Life and Passion of Our Lord Jesus Christ* in 18 tableaux, and Nonguet alone produced a number of spectacular fairy tales, such as *Puss-in-Boots* and *Sleeping Beauty*, as well as a version of Zola's *Germinal* (without acknowledging its source). But it was in the field of actualités reconstituées dealing with nihilists and assassinations, war and revolution, that Nonguet demonstrated his skill in handling crowds (see Jeanne 1965:131).

Starting in 1903 with *The Assassination of the Royal Family of Serbia*—followed by *The Assassination of the Minister Plehve* and *The Assassination of the Grand Duke Serge*—Nonguet began to reconstruct, in a series of carefully researched films, the bloody events taking place in Eastern Europe and Russia. The Russo-Japanese War in 1904 offered spectacular opportunities to make front-page news come alive. *The Catastrophe of the Petropavlovsk in the Roads of Port Arthur* used small-scale models and a theatrical setting to present the sinking of the Russian flagship, whereas another of the *Scenes from the Russo-Japanese War* was filmed outdoors, making use of 150 extras costumed and armed as Russian and Japanese soldiers; alternate titles in six languages proclaiming either "Long Live Russia" or "Long Live Japan" were available, to be chosen according to the political sympathies of the audience, and attesting to the objectivity and neutrality of the representation (see Sadoul 1978:302; Laurent 1967:4).

The revolution of 1905 provided Nonguet with his most important subject. *The Disturbances in Saint Petersburg* dealt with Father Gapon and the

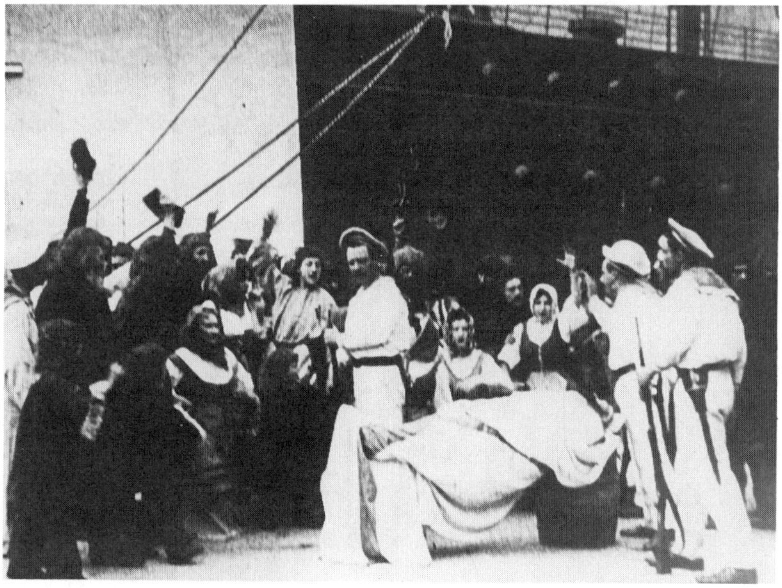

2. *The body of Vakulinchuk, the martyred hero, in Lucien Nonguet's film version of the* Potemkin *mutiny,* The Events of Odessa *(1905). (Photo courtesy of the National Film Archive/Stills Library, the British Film Institute)*

workers' march to the Winter Palace to petition the Tsar on 9 January, known as Bloody Sunday because of the massacre which took place when troops fired on the unarmed demonstrators. In July 1905, 20 years before Sergei Eisenstein commemorated the revolt, the first film about the *Potemkin* mutiny was shot at the Vincennes studio of the Pathé brothers. This two-and-one-half-minute documentary, a part of the series "The Revolution in Russia," is called *The Events in Odessa.* It tells the story of the mutiny aboard the largest and newest warship in the Russian navy, the *Potemkin,* and the impact of the rebellion on the port of Odessa.

Like all the Pathé reconstructed newsreels, Nonguet's *Potemkin* is based on journalistic reports and designed to compete with the illustrated newspapers by means of painted backdrops that are skillful copies of photographs; it strives to be factual and give the spectator the impression that s/he is witnessing actual historic events. Its fast-moving narrative represents the principal stages of the revolt and its effects in all their concrete particularity, quite unlike Eisenstein's attempt to universalize and create a symbolic ship of revolution. Rather than mythos, the French filmmaker offers montage—in its embryonic state to be sure, but nonetheless montage—and herein lies the innovation of *The Events of Odessa* (see Mitry 1967:222).

In this brief one-reel film, Nonguet creates a panoramic series of images that include many of the well-known episodes that now make up the *Potemkin* legend given definitive shape by Eisenstein. Reconstructed in short scenes lasting no more than a few seconds are the sailors' refusal to eat the soup made of spoilt meat, the murder of the sailor Vakulinchuk, the throwing of the officers overboard, the display of the martyr Vakulinchuk's dead body on the pier to the emotional crowd, the shelling of the city, and the cossacks' assault on the people. As the title indicates, the focus of Nonguet's reconstructed newsreel is not upon the battleship itself (we never learn what happens to the crew), but rather upon the impact of the mutiny on Odessa and the inciting of violence there.

Montage results as the camera alternates between ship and shore during the bombardment of the city. First we see the mutinous officer, who has

3. Nonguet's montage device, the telescope iris, shows a view of the shore as cossacks attack the citizens of Odessa. The mound of earth and the fence are real, not a painted set. (Photo courtesy of the National Film Archive/Stills Library, the British Film Institute)

assumed command of the ship, directing cannon fire against Odessa from the side of the deck; next we witness the consequences of the shelling on the people in the burning town, as perceived through the telescope of the now jubilant officer. The point of view of the mutinous commander is juxtaposed to that of his victims, as the camera moves rapidly from his enthusiastic gesticulating to the suffering of a family driven out of their flaming home.

Next the authorities order the massacre of the citizens of Odessa in reprisal for the uprising. Nonguet's documentary ends unresolved, at the moment when a band of cossacks, armed with whips, beat a group of women and children trapped against a wall; this scene of Tsarist repression is comparable—on its own small scale—to Eisenstein's famous Odessa steps sequence, arousing the same feelings of pity and indignation. A sense of lively reality is imparted to the scene when the women fight back furiously and a small dog bites at the heels of one of the cossacks.

Nonguet's primitive montage device of the telescope iris enables the filmmaker to show repercussions in the community caused by the presence of the revolutionary ship in the harbor. The final nine-second sequence reveals much of the city engulfed in flames. Uncertainty remains as to who is responsible for the disorder: the officers, the mutineers, or the cossacks—but the people are clearly the ones who suffer. The *Potemkin* mutiny was chosen as a reconstructed newsreel because it was topical and sensational, capable of arousing feelings of outrage in French audiences at the shocking events in Russia. The reconstructed newsreel had no room for interpretation; the events were all that mattered.

In 1907 Nonguet directed a remake of the Pathé *Dreyfus* (see Sadoul 1975:302), but gradually the actualités reconstituées died out as a film genre, unable to survive the competition posed by the new illustrated newspapers and the authentic news films (*actualités veritables*) which were coming into vogue. During World War I newsreels of battles and atrocities were sometimes simulated in the service of propaganda, further discrediting simulation as deceptive manipulation.

Eisenstein's Battleship Potemkin *as Actualité Reconstitutée and Mass Spectacle*

Like Nonguet's works for Pathé, Eisenstein's film, *The Battleship Potemkin,* displayed the concern for pictorial authenticity characteristic of the reconstructed newsreel; the director and his assistants went to French and Italian illustrated newspapers of the time and reproduced as faithfully as possible the pictures and drawings of Vakulinchuk's body in the tent on the pier and the crowd on the steps looking out to sea at the ship. Eyewitness accounts by the French journalist Gustave Babin—"The Revolt of the *Potemkin* and the Rioting in Odessa" and "The True Adventure of the Battleship *Potemkin*"—appeared on 15 and 22 July in *L'Illustration,* and there were also newspaper articles and published memoirs by a number of the leaders of the revolt as well as a commemorative volume of historical documents for the 20th anniversary of the mutiny, all of which Eisenstein consulted (see Rostovtsev 1962:78–81).

Commissioned for the anniversary of the 1905 revolution, Eisenstein's *Battleship Potemkin* is part of the tradition of the mass spectacle that goes back to the festivals of the French Revolution. Soviet mass spectacles, inspired by the theories of Romain Rolland in his *Le Théâtre du peuple* (1913), had flourished after the October Revolution; thousands of workers, soldiers, and citizens joined professional actors, circus clowns, and acrobats to reenact revolutionary scenes from Russian and world history in the great historic squares of Petrograd and Moscow [for descriptions and photographs see František Deák's 1975 article in TDR 19, no. 2 (T66)]. These huge pageants were staged on major dates in the history of world revolution according to a new revolutionary calendar of holidays designed to replace old Christian celebrations. Where possible, as in the case of the 1920 *The Storming of the Winter Palace* (with 8,000 participants and 100,000 spectators), the mass spectacle was enacted in the original setting of the historical event with the participation of those who had shaped history. In *The Overthrow of Autocracy,* staged in Petrograd in 1919, the revolution of 1905 was presented as the first important step in the crumbling of the Tsarist monarchy; Bloody Sunday, which had taken place in the same city 14 years earlier, was the episode chosen for dramatization. In June 1920, there was staged in Odessa, along Maritime Boulevard overlooking the port, a grandiose concert-meeting entitled "The Revolt of the Battleship *Potemkin,*" in which actors played the roles of the heros of the rebellion.

In the Petrograd mass spectacle, *Toward a World Commune,* staged in 1920 in front of the former Stock Exchange and played partly on the broad steps leading up to the building, the first section devoted to the Paris Commune showed a group of communards trapped on the stairs by the Versailles troops. Moving upwards from below in detachments, soldiers fired a volley into the crowd; the writhing bodies of the wounded and dying communards fell on the steps, while others leapt off the stairs in frenzied attempts to escape.

The aesthetics of the mass spectacle had enduring impact on later dramatic versions of the *Potemkin* mutiny, including Eisenstein's. The aim of these commemorative pageants was to celebrate and strengthen feelings of unanimity and indivisibility by means of ceremonies and processionals, religious in nature but seeking to replace Christian belief with socialist faith, while often retaining the old iconography. In *The Battleship Potemkin,* Eisenstein, long attracted to religious art and the pathos of spiritual ecstasy as found in the paintings of El Greco, stresses themes of martyrdom and brotherhood through repeated religious motifs and imagery.

4. An Italian newspaper photograph (retouched?) of the Odessa crowd looking out at the Potemkin *(1905). (Photo courtesy of Daniel Gerould from Kleiman and Levina 1969)*

Filmed almost entirely in Odessa, in the places where the actual events took place, Eisenstein's *Potemkin* made use of a huge cast of several thousand, composed of a few professional actors and larger masses of local inhabitants, some of whom would actually have witnessed the happenings they were re-creating. The student agitator Konstantin Feldman—one of the key figures in the real drama—was played by Feldman himself in an early example of autoperformance; he also served as an advisor on historical detail and authenticity. Like the mass spectacles, *The Battleship Potemkin* is a reenactment of a famous episode in the revolutionary calendar, in which historical facts are subordinated to the central idea of glorifying revolution. Eisenstein inscribes history into eternal time and transmutes the events in Odessa into myth. As Adrian Piotrovsky (the formalist critic, scenarist, and director of mass spectacles) observed, Eisenstein's *Potemkin* is a film without plot or psychology, devoid of stars or heros, and glorifying only a collective protagonist, the sailors and the people of Odessa (see

5. Eisenstein's Odessa crowd looking out at the Potemkin. *From his film* The Battleship Potemkin *(1925). (Photo courtesy of Daniel Gerould from Kleiman and Levina 1969)*

6. The student agitator, Konstantin Feldman, playing himself in Eisenstein's The Battleship Potemkin *(1925). (Photo courtesy of Daniel Gerould from Kleiman and Levina 1969)*

Piotrovsky 1969:218). Rather than the division between ship and shore as in Nonguet's neutral, ironic actualité reconstituée, Eisenstein imposes a wholeness upon history, eliminating all signs of discord and violence among the people and the sailors, still slightly discernible in the scenario but absent from the film. In the scenario, the rabble-rouser from the reactionary Black Hundreds who cries, "Beat the Jews," is himself beaten by the angry crowd, but in the film he is only driven away—in reality, he was killed on the spot.

In 1925 there was already a sizable body of prose, poetry, and drama about the *Potemkin* and an evolving tradition of imagery and motifs upon which the filmmaker could draw. Eisenstein makes extensive use of the general store of poetic images that the now legendary battleship invariably called forth and gives us the breaking waves, the mist, spray, and fog, the soaring seagulls, and the inevitable revolutionary flag—tinted red by hand for the black-and-white film.

Eisenstein's own attitude toward reconstructed actuality was ambivalent. He both affirmed his film's historicity by his use of sources and consultants and then later denied that some of the famous episodes had any basis in fact. But the innovative spirit of the film is best revealed by how the artist handles the now conventionalized and almost obligatory episodes and themes rather than in claims to original invention. Eisenstein himself is responsible for confusion as to how much of the *Potemkin* legend is the creation of his film. Thus even an event as strictly historical (found in all the eyewitness accounts) as the covering of the sailors with a tarpaulin before the order is given to have them shot was, according to the filmmaker, an artistic fabrication shocking to a naval officer present at the filming who declared that such a procedure was absolutely impossible (see Rostovtsev 1962:100–01).

Likewise, it has been implied that the massacre on the Richelieu Steps never took place and was Eisenstein's invention. Despite some conflicting testimony, the evidence clearly indicates there was a terrible slaughter on the famous stairs leading from the town to the port. The Social Democrat and Menshevik, Kirill (one of Eisenstein's sources), reports that the sailors who went to army headquarters to arrange for Vakulinchuk's funeral saw bodies on the steps: "In the port and on the stairs leading to the sea-front, they had to pick their way through piles of workers killed during the night" (1934:90). During the "red night" of 28 June, extensive looting and burning by an unruly mob took place and the cossacks and soldiers shot those trying to escape from the burning port by the only possible route, the stairs. Eisenstein's originality lies in his skill in dramatizing an authentic element of the historical reality through the transformation of its details. He staged the attack in the daytime with the innocent and unsuspecting people in a festive mood—descending the stairs, rather than trying to escape up them—and falling suddenly victim to the relentlessly advancing, machinelike cossacks. Here Eisenstein has appropriated the basic situation of Bloody Sunday, in which Tsarist troops opened fire on a peacefully assembled crowd of men, women, and children. The Soviet filmmaker absorbed and synthesized the most diverse ideas, suggestions, and raw materials to create a "song" or hymn to revolution.

All that did not further the revolutionary pathos and heroic grandeur of the mutiny was judged irrelevant. The "eccentric" elements in the scenario—grotesque or satirical incidents of overt theatricality, related to the circus numbers in the mass spectacles and similar to the stunts that dominated Eisenstein's staging of Alexander Ostrovsky's *Wiseman* at the Proletkult Theatre and his first film, *Strike*—were rhythmically and tonally disruptive and were cut from the final version of the film. One of these eccentric numbers introduces two journalists, dressed in black and wearing derbies, who stand back to back on the pier and lean against each other as they jot down the words written on the placard on Vakulinchuk's chest as he lies in the tent: "On account of a spoonful of borscht." These bourgeois newsmen, with their music-hall costumes, do not make news, but prey upon those who do; ultimately they are irrelevant to the revolutionary event and were discarded in the cutting room (see Kleiman and Levina 1969:85).

Eisenstein's most striking intervention in the historical record was his turning a humiliating defeat into a great revolutionary victory by ending his film with the triumphant meeting of the battleship *Potemkin* with the squadron sent to attack it. The *Potemkin* cuts directly through the fleet without a shot being fired—the rebellious battleship sails on.

In his essay "Constanta (Where Does the Battleship *Potemkin* Go?)"—written in 1926, but not published until 1969—Eisenstein explains why he decided not to show the desperate and futile wanderings of the *Potemkin* across the Black Sea, its flight to Rumania and final surrender to the Rumanian authorities in Constanta. Because the meeting with the squadron was the "high point representing the maximum of revolutionary spirit conceivable under the circumstances," the Soviet filmmaker chose to conclude his drama at that moment, fixing forever a triumphant image (Eisenstein 1969:290–2). By treating a momentary success rather than an ultimate defeat, Eisenstein was able to show the *Potemkin* as moral victor over the Tsarist forces.

The Red Admiral and the Singer Sewing Machine Company

Revolutionary dramas are always in quest of heros, but the *Potemkin* mutiny could produce no candidates, except for the dead martyr, Vakulinchuk. Afanasii Matiushenko, the haunting, enigmatic leader of the revolt, refused to fit neatly into the heroic mold or to play his expected part in the legendary pageant. In Nonguet's reconstructed newsreel, there is no such protagonist developed as leader of the revolt, and in Eisenstein's scenario he remains unnamed and scarcely visible. In the film, however, Matiushenko assumes a major role as a generalized and idealized representative of the entire crew, forcefully expressing their harmonious will—the perfect revolutionary sailor.

Such is the picture of Matiushenko that appears in a characteristic Soviet form of reconstruction: the retouched photograph of the revolutionary hero, with all blemishes removed. In Boris Pasternak's short poetic epic on the *Potemkin,* "Mutiny at Sea" (1926), which takes place on the first glorious day of freedom (before complications and contradictions set in), Matiushenko strides into view for a moment, "towering tall." In fact, he was small and exceptionally short, as unretouched photographs taken in Rumania show.

After crisscrossing the Black Sea for a week—frantically searching for a friendly port—and failing to kindle the spark of revolution elsewhere, the demoralized crew of the *Potemkin* returned to Constanta (their first port of call) and capitulated on Saturday, 8 July 1905 at 3 A.M. sailing under the Tsarist Saint Andrew Flag. The red flag had been buried at sea the day before. Over 600 members of the crew elected to stay in Rumania, where they were given asylum but kept under strict surveillance. The remaining 117 returned to the ship and swore allegiance to the Tsar once again. They were immediately arrested and imprisoned on the ship, soon to be returned to Russia where they were given summary trials and sentenced to labor camps. A Russian fleet under Rear Admiral Pisarevsky towed the *Potemkin,* which had been partially sunk, back to Sevastopol.

The French journalist Gustave Babin gave the following portrait of the leader of the revolt:

> All those who, at Constanta, have come near Matiushenko remain as it were haunted by this alarming brute of a man, with the prominent cheekbones of a Kalmuck, with hate-filled eyes, with a stupid, gloomy countenance teeming with cruel ideas. [. . .]
>
> He ruled by terror. He went back and forth along the passageways on the bridge and in the batteries, always frenzied and enraged, clutching his revolver, constantly threatening. Every one trembled on seeing him appear (1905:56–57).

In his dramatic poem, *The Battleship Potemkin* (written in 1922 and thus the first Soviet version, performed in 1927 by the TRAM theatre in Perm), the poet Georgii Shengeli gives an unorthodox portrait of Matiushenko as a bitter, disillusioned man confronting a passive, fearful, and disunified crew, threatening to shoot anyone who disagrees with him (an account supported by the memoirs of Feldman and Kirill). After throwing off the Tsarist yoke, there is immediate need to reintroduce even harsher authority; Matiushenko must use revolutionary terror if he is to maintain order. In the final moment of the dramatic poem Matiushenko contemplates suicide and reflects on the failure of the mutiny, while members of the crew have gone to find solace and distraction in the brothels of Constanta. This Matiushenko—with his revolver in hand, his need to assert authority, his hatred of prostitutes—is an unorthodox Soviet study of the revolutionary temperament.

Nicknamed the Red Admiral, the real Matiushenko was a wanderer, like the battleship itself. In his wanderings in Europe after the failure of the mutiny, he met Lenin in Geneva as well as Father Gapon, whose protégé he became, but the Red Admiral was not able to settle down and accept the role of revolutionary-in-exile that many of the leading Potemkinites found congenial. In Paris, the hero of the *Potemkin* hoped to start an armed uprising and associated with anarchists. A solitary man of action mistrustful of intellectuals, he could not understand or tolerate party politics and intrigues.

In June 1906, Matiushenko came to the United States where he remained until March 1907. The former machinist on the *Potemkin* worked for the Singer Sewing Machine Company in New York and lived on the Lower East Side, where he made contact with Russian radical circles. On 11 October 1906, Matiushenko met Maxim Gorky, who attempted to help the former sailor get his autobiography published (failed revolutionaries always become authors).

In June 1907, Matiushenko returned to Russia, using a false name and forged passport. There the Red Admiral was soon arrested, still carrying his revolver, probably betrayed by a seeming comrade. He was tried by a military tribunal, sentenced to death, and executed under conditions of high security with several companies of troops standing guard. Even the Red Admiral's lonely death agony was a public spectacle at which he conducted himself with exemplary courage and heroism.

Not long before his return to Russia, Matiushenko wrote from Paris to his friend Zamfir Arbore in Rumania:

> I'm completely fed up with the mugs around here, talking incessantly, screaming about freedom incessantly, while they are nothing

> but slaves themselves, the most despicable slaves of their own lusts. There are many socialists here, but very few real people. They all talk, scream, argue, abuse one another, and are ready to gouge out each other's eyes, without even knowing why. Well, to hell with them, let them argue to their heart's content—the people know what they need without any help. [. . .] I think a lot about the happiness of the people and I shall never cease to do so. But I am now afraid of one thing: will the Russian people, in return for the blood which is now being shed in Russia, achieve what they did in Western Europe and America? If so, I wash my hands of it in advance. I do not need freedom of that sort (1955:147).

The poet Dmitrii Petrovsky (a friend and disciple of the Futurist Velimir Khlebnikov) in his *Black Sea Notebook* (1925)—a collection of poems on the revolt of the *Potemkin,* other naval mutinies, and seascapes—created a documentary poem describing Matiushenko's execution taken directly from an eyewitness account.

> I did not see the execution.
> This is what they said:
> While they read the sentence,
> He paced up and down before the line of soldiers.
> They finished and he said: *Farewell,*
> *Comrades . . .*
> And he stood on the table.
> Akimov started yelling.
> He responded.—"Why are you screaming?"
> And on the table he said:
> — Do your hanging, cowards!
> The professional hangman
> Put the noose over his neck and gave a shove.
> The table flew off.
> They started beating on a drum.
> He hung there for almost fifteen minutes;—
> Then they let him down.
> They took his fetters off:
> *It seemed a waste to bury the iron*
> *In the grave;*
> *They twisted his feet*
> *So as not to have to unlock the chains.*
> *And threw him in his overcoat in his coffin.*
> (1957:40–1)

Such was the lonely death of Matiushenko.

The Potemkin*'s Last Prodigious Adventure: Super-Châtelet and Black Sea Stunt Men*

On the 70th anniversary of the mutiny, The *Potemkin* reached its final destination in Paris at the huge 80,000-seat Palais des Sports. The stage and film actor and director Robert Hossein presented a mass spectacle, *The Prodigious Adventure of the Battleship Potemkin,* recapitulating and synthesizing all the traditions of 19th- and 20th-century historical simulation. Taking part in Hossein's *Prodigious Adventure* were more than 100 professional actors, crews of technicians, special effects people, lighting experts, and the

7. The "Black Sea stunt men" of Robert Hossein's The Prodigious Adventure of the Battleship Potemkin *(1975). (Photo by J.F. Lecocguen)*

recorded Chorus of the Red Army singing Jean Ferrat's popular *Potemkine* in Russian. The replica of the battleship *Potemkin* constructed in the middle of the vast arena of the Palais des Sports—26 meters long, 10 meters wide, and 12 meters high—was an authentic scale model, about one-fourth the length of the actual battleship. It provided a stage on which the crew of extras—more highly disciplined than the Russian sailors—did their daily chores, fell in for roll call, marched, and ran. Called by one critic "Hossein's Black Sea stunt men," the sailors made incredibly high leaps in the air and during the climactic meeting with the squadron jumped from one moving battleship to another.

The Prodigious Adventure dealt in epic fashion with the entire mutiny from joyous exaltation to bitter defeat. Hossein, whose image was projected on a huge screen 14 meters high, served as a filmic chorus throughout, except at the beginning and ending of each performance when the actor himself appeared on stage.

For the leftist French creators of *The Prodigious Adventure,* the *Potemkin* mutiny is a mirror for studying their own failed revolution, the Paris student-worker uprising of 1968. The dominant ideological role is given to the student Feldman (minimized in Eisenstein's film) as the activist-intellectual who attempts to act as a bridge between the armed services and the working classes; the revolt fails in large part because his call for firm and decisive action is not heeded.

The Prodigious Adventure achieves its impact by its striking visual effects, returning to the traditions of the 19th-century military and naval spectacles. The performance opens and closes with a vision of the wanderer-ship, its enchanted crew forever frozen on the deck in a tableau, eternally dreaming the dream of revolution. The title, *The Prodigious Adventure of the Battleship Potemkin,* comes from Gustave Babin's firsthand reporting in 1905 from Constanta for the popular Parisian weekly, *L'Illustration.* But whereas Babin called his account "The True Adventure of the Battleship *Potemkin,*" the Palais des Sports version is prodigious rather than true.

Several French critics with long memories—half-admiringly, half-mockingly—called Hossein's *Potemkin* "super-Châtelet," referring to the 3,600-seat Théâtre du Châtelet which had perfected the traditions of the Cirque Olympique. Nonguet had come to Pathé from the Châtelet, and the filmmaker Robert Hossein is his direct descendent. For the audience in 1975, *The Prodigious Adventure* was a modern live version of the reconstructed newsreel, a grandiose silent film with accompanying musical score and Hossein's recorded spoken subtitles and intertitles superimposed on the action. For both Nonguet and Hossein, the goal is the same: to recreate the historical event so vividly that spectators would have the sense of witnessing what had actually happened. Apart from technological improvements and contemporary ideological viewpoints, the only significant change that has occurred in the 70 years separating the primitive Pathé *Potemkin* from its Palais des Sports grandchild is that the French spectators of *The Prodigious Adventure* knew in advance what they were going to see and realized that they were participating in the ritual celebration of an already sanctified legend.

From Revolutionary Icon to Cardboard Cruiser

What remains for the Battleship *Potemkin*? Can it continue its wanderings and reach new shores? Or has it become a profitable restoration, a reconstruction of an old ship to be visited by tourists?

The repertory of revolutionary imagery and gesture is severely limited; to be effective its signs must be external, public, and instantly recognizable. Crowd emotions are by their very nature large and unsubtle, and therein lies their power. The *Potemkin* tradition would seem to have reached the stage of development where all it can do is repeat itself; newer versions quote earlier versions, sometimes unconsciously, more often deliberately. In several modern films, the famous battleship, canonized by Eisenstein, serves as the occasion for cinematographic jokes and allusions. In Jean-Luc Godard's *Les Carabiniers* (1963), a pretty female revolutionary about to be executed places a kerchief over her head and calls out "Brothers!" while in Dusan Makavejev's *Sweet Movie* (1974) one of the young heroines wears a *Potemkin* sailor hat during much of the action.

The old ship of revolution is starting to mirror its own image, rather than present or future realities. Growing obsolete as a living symbol (sooner or later all symbols become nostalgically cherished and slightly ridiculous fossils), the *Potemkin* has turned into a theatrical prop, and the revolution that failed has proved successful as popular entertainment and icon. Most recently a Polish youth movement, Orange Alternative, marked the 70th anniversary of the Russian Revolution by staging a mock battle between cardboard cruisers named the *Potemkin* and *Aurora* (Taglibue 1988:4).

The journalist Babin—with a bourgeois Frenchman's sharp eye for the centrality of money and theatre in life—reported that from the very start the mutiny became the occasion for a show and a source of profiteering. In Rumania, speculation in *Potemkin* buttons and caps began as soon as the sailors set foot on shore; by the next day, simply the bands from the caps were bringing 15 francs each. Complete uniforms went for the highest prices, since they would be in demand for the *Potemkin* masked balls that would be all the fashion next season.

References

Altick, Richard D.
1978 *The Shows of London.* Cambridge, MA: Harvard University Press.

Babin, Gustave
1905 "Le Véritable Aventure du Kniaz Potemkin." *L'Illustration,* 22 July:55–58.

Barnouw, Erik
1974 *Documentary.* New York: Oxford University Press.
1981 *The Magician and the Cinema.* New York: Oxford University Press.

Benjamin, Walter
1978 *Reflections: Essays, Aphorisms, Autobiographical Writing.* Translated by Edmund Jephcott. New York: Harcourt, Brace, Jovanovich.

Billington, James H.
1980 *Fire in the Minds of Men.* New York: Basic Books.

Booth, Michael R.
1965 *English Melodrama.* London: Herbert Jenkins.

Boucicault, Dionysius
1889 "Leaves from a Dramatist's Diary." *The North American Review* CXIX (August):229–31.

Bratton, J.S.
1980 "Theatre of War: the Crimea on the London Stage 1854–5." In *Performance and Politics in Popular Drama,* edited by David Bradby, Louis James, and Bernard Schratt, 119–37. Cambridge: Cambridge University Press.

Brown, Frederick
1980 *Theater and Revolution.* New York: Viking.

Carlson, Marvin
1966 *The Theatre of the French Revolution.* Ithaca, NY: Cornell University Press.

Cogeval, Gay
1986 *From Courbet to Cézanne: A New 19th Century.* Catalog. Paris: Editions de la Reunion des musees nationaux.

Deslandes, Jacques
1963 *Le Boulevard du cinéma à l'époque de Georges Méliès.* Paris: Cerf.

Eisenstein, Sergei
1969 "Konstantsa. (Kuda ukhodit 'Bronenosets Potemkin')." In *Bronenosets Potemkin,* edited by Naum Kleiman and K. Levina, 290–2. Moscow: Isskustvo.

El Nouty, Hassan
1978 *Théâtre et Pre-cinéma: Essai sur la problématique de spectacle au XIXe siècle.* Paris: A.-G. Nizet.

Hammond, Paul
1975 *Marvelous Méliès.* New York: St. Martin's.

Jeanne, Rene
1965 *Cinema 1900.* Paris: Flammarion.

Kirill [Berezovsky, A.P.]
1934 *Drama v tenderovskoi Bukhtye.* Moscow: Molodaya Gvardiya.

Kleeblatt, Norman L.
1984 *The Dreyfus Affair.* Berkeley: University of California Press.

Kleiman, Naum, and K. Levina, eds.
1969 *Bronenosets Potemkin.* Moscow: Isskustvo.

Laurent, Hughes
1967 "Le décor de cinéma et les décorateurs." *Bulletin de l'Association française des ingenieurs et techniciens de cinéma,* no. 16.

Le Bon, Gustave
1960 *The Crowd.* New York: Viking.

Leslie, Anita, and Pauline Chapman
1978 *Madame Tussaud.* London: Hutchinson.

Matiushenko, Afanasii N.
1955 "K prebyvaniu Potiomkintsev v emigratsii." In *Istoricheskii Arkhiv,* no. 3:134–49.

Meisel, Martin
1983 *Realizations.* Princeton, NJ: Princeton University Press.

Mitry, Jean
1967 *Histoire du cinema.* Vol. 1. Paris: Editions Universitaires.

Nicoll, Allardyce
1962 *A History of English Drama, 1660–1900.* Vols. 3, 5. Cambridge: Cambridge University Press.

Nietzsche, Friedrich
1957 *The Use and Abuse of History.* Translated by Adrian Collins. Indianapolis: Bobbs-Merill.

Osborne, Harold, ed.
1986 *Oxford Companion to Art.* Oxford: Oxford University Press.

Petrovsky, Dmitrii Vasilevich
1957 *Izbrannoe.* With an introduction by Viktor Shklovsky. Moscow: Gosudarstvennoe Izdatel'stvo Khudozhestvennoi literatury.

Piotrovsky, Adrian
1969 *Teatr. Kino. Zhizn'.* Leningrad: Isskustvo.

Rayhill, Frank
1967 *The World of Melodrama.* University Park, PA: University of Pennsylvania Press.

Rearick, Charles
1985 *Pleasures of the Belle Epoque.* New Haven, CT: Yale University Press.

Robertson, Etienne Gaspard
1985 *La Fantasmagorie.* Paris: Café livre.

Rolland, Romain
1913 *Le Théâtre du peuple: Essai d'esthétique d'un théâtre nouveau.* Paris: Albin Michel.

Rostovtsev, Ignatii G.
1962 *Bronenosets Potemkin.* Moscow: Isskustvo.

Sadoul, Georges
1975 *Histoire générale du cinéma.* Vols. 2, 5. Paris: Denoel.

Saxon, Arthur
1968 *Enter Foot and Horse. A History of Hippodrama in England and France.* New Haven, CT: Yale University Press.

Sternberger, Dolf
1977 *Panoramas of the Nineteenth Century.* Translated by Joachim Neugroschel. New York: Urizen.

Taglibue, John
1988 "The Very Young Decide to Form a Cutting Edge." *The New York Times,* 14 June, sec. A:4.

Winter, Marian Hannah
1964 *The Theatre of Marvels.* New York: Benjamin Bloom.

Daniel Gerould *is Distinguished Professor of Theatre and Comparative Literature at the Graduate School of the City University of New York. He has published a number of volumes of translations of the Polish playwright Witkiewicz as well as a critical study of his work. He is now completing a book on the Guillotine.*

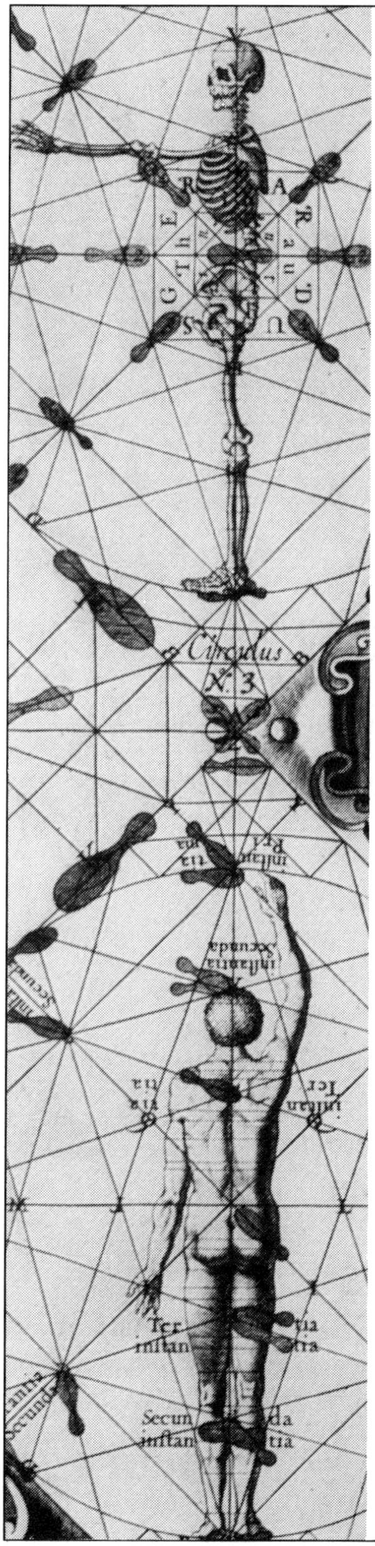

Jean Genet and the Semiotics of Performance

By Laura Oswald

Genet's work can be seen as a struggle of the social outcast to be heard from beyond the borders of the dominant, heterosexual culture. This challenging book tracks the effects of this struggle in Genet's novels, plays, film, and political essays by means of a general semiotics of performance.

Advances in Semiotics

$32.50

Contexts for Early English Drama

Edited by Marianne G. Briscoe and John C. Coldewey

Twelve distinguished scholars appraise old and new contexts, or cultural settings, for early English drama. Divided between sociological and literary approaches, the essays draw on recent research in English social history and culture, especially investigations of local and community life and work relating to dramatic and musical productions and performance.

$27.50

At bookstores or direct from

INDIANA UniversityPress

10th & Morton Streets
Bloomington, Indiana 47405 •812-855-6804

THE ORESTEIA

Aeschylus

A new translation for the theater by David Grene and Wendy Doniger O'Flaherty
Introductions by the translators and Nicholas Rudall

Highly acclaimed translators Grene and O'Flaherty present a new complete translation of the *Oresteia* and, with assistance from director Nicholas Rudall, an abridged acting version. This new version brilliantly creates an effective modern stage play.

"The Court production uses a newly commissioned translation . . . which is streamlined in its storytelling and voluptuous in its use of language."—Hedy Weiss, *Chicago Sun-Times* review of the Court Theater production

Paper $10.95 262 pages
Library cloth edition $32.50

Now in paper

STAGE FRIGHT

Its Role in Acting

Stephen Aaron

An actor and director turned psychotherapist, Aaron uses revealing anecdotes and interviews with many famous actors and actresses to show that stage fright is a necessary part of the process of acting.

"A look at acting that will be fascinating to the general public and challenging to the actor."—James Earl Jones

Paper $9.95 176 pages

THE UNIVERSITY OF CHICAGO PRESS

5801 South Ellis Avenue
Chicago, IL 60637

COMING IN TDR

Nontraditional Casting

Nuoxi and Dixi: Chinese Traditional Theatre

Mnouchkine, Moscoso, and the Théâtre du Soleil

Australian Aborigine Performance

Kabuki Acting in the West

Palestinian Resistance Theatre

Cuban Theatre

Grotowski's Most Recent Experiments

Soviet Theatre Glasnost

Mabou Mines' *Lear*

Circus Midgets

ISTA's *Faust*

Articles by: Laurie Sears, Elizabeth Wichmann, Eugenio Barba, Yu Qiuyu, Zbigniew Osinski, Augusto Boal, Harry Newman, Qu Liuyi, Jill Dolan, Huangpu Cong Qing, Margaret Clunies-Ross, Ed Bullins, Patrice Pavis, Josette Féral, Susan Slyomovics, Randy Martin, *and* K. Scherbakov

ISSN 0012 5962

$7.00

T D R

Non-Traditional Casting
Environmental Theatre Now
Theatre Glasnost
M. Butterfly Speaks
Pavis on Barba's *Faust*
Chinese Nuo Theatre
Dolan Defends Discourse
Schechter's Politics as Theatre
Sears on Javanese Shadow Theatre
and ITItems

blished by MIT Press New York University/Tisch School of the Arts

TDR

The Drama Review *a journal of performance studies*

Katsuko Azuma as Faust (left), Sanjukta Panigrahi as Mephisto (middle), and Kan-Ichi Hanayaghi as Margaret (right) in Eugenio Barba's adaptation of Goethe's Faust *at the 1987 International School of Theatre Anthropology in Italy. See Patrice Pavis' article "Dancing with* Faust*" in this issue. (Photo by Tony D'Urso)*

Front Cover: YOU-The City, *a performance created by poet/performance artist Fiona Templeton, ran by appointment in New York City in May and June of 1988. Performer Greg Arciniega played a "46th Streetperson." See Steve Nelson's article "Redecorating the Fourth Wall: Environmental Theatre Today" in this issue. (Photo by Zoe Beloff)*

Back Cover: *"I was a man in love with a woman created by a man, and now everything falls short." B.D. Wong as Song Liling (above) and David Dukes as Gallimard in David Henry Hwang's* M. Butterfly *at Broadway's Eugene O'Neill Theatre in New York. See John Louis DiGaetani's interview with Hwang in this issue. (Photo by Peter Cunningham)*

TDR

TDR Comment:
Enter, Students 4
Hello, "ITItems" 5
Bullets or Bullshit—or Something Important? 5
Welcome to TDR, Sun Huizhu and Richard Gough 6

Letters, Reports, Etc.

Kirby Sets the Record Straight 7
a letter from Michael Kirby

Missing the Mermaids of Rosmersholm 8
a letter from Per Schelde

XIII Muestra Nacional de Teatro: The New Theatre in Peru 10
MALGORZATA OLESZKIEWICZ

Theatre's Illegitimate Child: The Screen Actor 17
THOMAS W. BABSON

Announcements 20

Holding Back: The Theatre's Resistance to Non-Traditional Casting 22
HARRY NEWMAN

Dancing with *Faust*: A Semiotician's Reflections on Barba's Intercultural Mise-en-Scene 37
PATRICE PAVIS

In Defense of the Discourse: Materialist Feminism, Postmodernism, Poststructuralism . . . and Theory 58
JILL DOLAN

Redecorating the Fourth Wall: Environmental Theatre Today 72
STEVE NELSON

Bananaland: PR, Propaganda, and Infotainment 95
PAUL EVANS

China's Nuo Theatre: Two Views
The Yi: Human Evolution Theatre 103
QU LIUYI

Nuo Theatre in Guizhou Province 113
HUANGPU CHONGQING

Aesthetic Displacement in Javanese Shadow Theatre: Three Contemporary Performance Styles 122
LAURIE LOBELL SEARS

M. Butterfly: An Interview with David Henry Hwang 141
JOHN LOUIS DIGAETANI

Politics as Theatre: Or, How I Too Lost the Election in 1988 154
JOEL SCHECHTER

Plays and Polemics on the Soviet Stage 166
KONSTANTIN SCHERBAKOV

ITItems 175

Volume 33, Number 3 (T123), Fall 1989

The Drama Review *(ISSN 0012 5962) is published quarterly (Spring, Summer, Fall, Winter) by The MIT Press, 55 Hayward St., Cambridge, MA 02142, and London, England, for the Tisch School of the Arts, New York University. Editorial correspondence:* The Drama Review, *NYU, 721 Broadway, 6th fl., New York, NY 10003. Subscription and business correspondence:* The Drama Review, *Journals Dept., The MIT Press, 55 Hayward Street, Cambridge, MA 02142. Subscriptions: $17.00 per year for students; $23.00 per year for individuals; $52.00 per year for institutions. Subscribers outside the U.S. and Canada add $9.00 for surface mail, $17.00 for airmail. Current single copies, $7.00; back copies, $13.00. Back volume rates available. Circulation Dept.: 617-253-2889.* *To be honored free of charge, claims for missing copies must be made immediately upon receipt of the next published issue. Second class postage paid at Boston, MA and additional mailing offices. Postmaster: Send address changes to* The Drama Review, *55 Hayward Street, Cambridge, MA 02142. For advertising information please contact the Advertising Manager, MIT Press Journals (see business correspondence; telephone: 617-253-2866). This publication is made possible, in part, with public funds from the New York State Council on the Arts and the National Endowment for the Arts.*

TDR Comment

Enter, Students

In recent months TDR has been paying a lot of attention to students. By students we mean "young people" whether or not they are at school.

We've been paying attention first by actively seeking more student subscribers. We offer a student rate ($17) plus two free back issues to each new student subscriber. Also we're running a student essay contest (deadline 1 December 1989) with $1,000 in prizes ($500 first prize; two $250 second prizes) plus publication in TDR.

We want to hear more from students. We want your input.

At present, the associate, managing, and assistant editors are graduate students as are three of TDR's contributing editors (albeit ABDs). These people work very closely with editor Schechner and the other contributing editors to shape TDR's policies, what we publish, and what the magazine looks like.

But we want younger students—undergraduates, even high school students—to get involved. This will not mean any lowering of scholarly standards, and it will put new ideas into play.

There are a number of different ways students (and others) can enter the TDR polylog.

Letters: Here we exercise minimal editorial control. "Letters to the editor" are a traditional American means of letting loose the widest range of free expression from manifestos to gossip to debate to complaints about what's been published to you name it.

Reports: Brief accounts of what's going on—especially if it's something new, if it has social or political value, if it can serve as a model for others. Don't forget to send photos.

Announcements: Getting others involved in what you're doing. But remember, TDR goes to bed (in the journalistic sense) six to eight months before it appears on the newsstands so send stuff plenty early.

Etc.: An open category for stuff that doesn't fit in any of the other slots.

How about articles? Of course, but with articles a strict standard of excellence is adhered to and those standards won't be lowered for anybody. About half of TDR's essays are commissioned—we invite people to write, our own editors write, we follow up on stuff, and we publish a lot of interviews. I know from my own experience—and I get around to many places—that some of the strongest thinking about performance is being done by students. But *too often students are shy about submitting their work.*

Don't be.

We accept some articles as is. But more often we read a submission in terms of its potential—and we're not shy about asking for revisions, sometimes more than one. The relationship between editors and writers at TDR is modeled on what goes on during rehearsals. We want to collaborate with writers, not put them through competitive hoops. And we are of course interested in exploring and disseminating a particular program I've been calling the "broad spectrum approach" (see Comment T118 and T122). Actually, I'd like to find a new name for it—right now it sounds more like an antibiotic than a performative manifesto.

Got any ideas?

The best hope for significant renewal in the live performing arts—both in the arts themselves and in the study of arts, sports, rituals, aesthetics of everyday life, and new frontiers hardly yet imagined—are students: younger bodyminds (editor Phillip Zarrilli's coinage) yet to be heard from.

You know our address.

Richard Schechner

Hello, "ITItems"

The International Theatre Institute, ITI, and TDR are natural allies. Both are concerned with performance across, through, around, and in spite of borders and boundaries. ITI's longstanding program has been to promote understanding and exchange among theatre people around the world.

Starting with this issue, TDR will include a section called "ITItems." TDR's editors will not mess with these pages. They will be full of whatever information Martha W. Coigney—director ITI/US and president ITI/worldwide—and her colleagues choose to convey. In giving space to ITItems we further our commitment to a performative polylog: many voices, with many approaches, from many places.

Bullets or Bullshit—or Something Important?

In T112 (Winter 1986) TDR "bit the diacritical bullet" by announcing we would do away with diacritical marks—those dots, slashes, wavy lines that tell readers how to identify sounds and to pronounce words. Exactly one year later, in T116, we spit up the bullet and restored the diacritics. That policy didn't work either because there was much irregularity in authors' practices—some used many marks, some a few, and some none.

The new (and I hope long-lasting) TDR policy is: We will follow each author's practice. This means inconsistency at the journal level, but consistency at the author level. It also allows for a healthy multivocality, giving to individual writers a little more control over how they present their material.

Welcome to TDR, Sun Huizhu and Richard Gough

From time to time, the editors of TDR change. Some editors no longer want to serve; some don't contribute and I ask them to resign. And as editors leave, new ones arrive.

Two new contributing editors have joined TDR.

Sun Huizhu is a Chinese playwright and scholar. In May–June 1989, I directed his *Tomorrow He'll Be Out of the Mountains* at the Shanghai Peoples Art Theatre in China. An account of Sun's *The Old B Hanging on the Wall* appeared in T112. He is a professor at the Shanghai Theatre Academy. Presently he is writing his PhD dissertation (NYU Performance Studies) on an experimental popular theatre in rural China in the 1930s and teaching at York University, Toronto.

Richard Gough heads the Centre for Performance Research in Cardiff, Wales. The CPR—sucessor to the Cardiff Laboratory Theatre Company which Gough also led—is, in his words, "a multifaceted theatre organization that combines pedagogical activities, cultural cooperation, production, and promotion and which pioneers forms and approaches which have a bearing on the rest of the U.K."

Both Sun and Gough, rooted in their own cultures, are committed to intercultural polylog—TDR talk.

Richard Schechner

Letters, Reports, Etc.

Kirby Sets the Record Straight

To the Editor:

PAJ Publications has committed a serious, and probably unprecedented, error that I would like TDR readers to know about. In 1986, they republished my book *Futurist Performance*, indicating on the title page that it was by "Michael Kirby and Victoria Nes Kirby." This is completely false. I am the sole author of *Futurist Performance*.

PAJ has now published a corrected version of *Futurist Performance*. A corrected version, however, does not remove the inaccuracies promulgated by the incorrect version, nor does it necessarily repair the damage that was done.

According to PAJ, the error came about because, in signing a contract with them, I had specified that the name of Victoria Nes Kirby, who was clearly credited in the original E.P. Dutton edition as translator from the Italian of the material in the Appendix, should appear on the cover. PAJ says they took this to mean that "an error had somehow been made in the Dutton version." Let's agree that any reputable publisher understands an author's involvement with their work. Can anyone believe that I or Dutton would have allowed only my name to appear on the original publication if, indeed, there had been coauthors? Could anyone make such a serious "correction" as PAJ did without verification? (It could have been checked with a [local] telephone call to me or to Dutton.) These are people who claim to think about theatre. What kind of thought is involved here?

Another ethical question is presented by the copyright of the PAJ edition of *Futurist Performance*. Although I had specified in the contract that it be copyrighted in my name, it appears as copyrighted by "PAJ Publications"; another copyright is in my name and Victoria Nes Kirby's. One of my handwritten additions to the contract was "misread"; the other was not read at all. These are people who claim to be concerned with the literary aspects of theatre.

No mention is made in the PAJ edition of *Futurist Performance* that the book was previously published. If this is not illegal, it is certainly misleading and disreputable. One infers that they would like to give the impression that they were the first to publish it—even when they were merely shooting from the Dutton pages rather than setting new type. These are people who claim to be concerned with history yet seem to have no qualms about manufacturing their own false "history."

Michael Kirby
New York City

Missing the Mermaids of *Rosmersholm*

To the Editor:

The production of Henrik Ibsen's *Rosmersholm* at La Mama in New York, 8–29 December 1988, as directed by Sarah Pia Anderson, was confusing to say the least. Rebecca West (Suzanne Bertish) wandered around like a feminist Hedda Gabler in disguise: aloof and with an ironic smile playing at the corners of her mouth. From time to time she would descend from her modern feminist heights to belch out key lines and enter the man-to-woman fray with John Rosmer. John Shea's Rosmer was weak to the point of effacement. The actor stood back most of the time watching helplessly as his character skipped across the lines like a pebble on water.

As usual in American productions of Ibsen, the minor characters, played by Carol Morley (Mrs. Helseth), Ted van Griethuysen (Rector Kroll), Gwyllum Evans (Ulrik Brendel), and Peter McRobbie (Peder Mortensgaard), fared better because they wisely settled for the safe: broad comedy characterization.

The production as a whole seemed unfocused, tentative, and full of the wrong kind of respect for a "classic." The actors raced through long stretches of the play to get to the brief passages they had an emotional handle on.

So what is the problem? Is it that Ibsen finally has become obsolete? No, the problem with this as with most other modern Ibsen productions is that it falls victim to a set of preconceived notions about the late plays. The first is that they are "realistic." I shall argue below that this is only a veneer. Another misconception, introduced in the '60s, is that Ibsen was a feminist. This is simply not true. In point of fact, I am not far from claiming that Ibsen was somewhat of a misogynist. He shared with his (male) contemporaries the idea that women are mysterious and dangerous beings.

Ibsen's women derive their strength not from being men's equals but from being precultural, primitive creatures. The struggle between men and women in Ibsen symbolizes the pitting of humanity's primitive but powerful past against its sophisticated and weak present. That women—to Ibsen—represent the primitive, the mythic, the noncultural, has to do with their being linked to and locked into nature because of their natural procreative powers. That is not feminism. *Au contraire*—especially since the attendant claim is that culture, philosophy, ideas, and so on are the property of men.

My contention is that Ibsen in *Rosmersholm* as in all of the late plays (roughly the last seven) is using folklore as an undertext. The characters are the ones from his early, clearly folkloric plays, recycled and dressed in modern garb.

Throughout his career Ibsen was fascinated, as were so many of his contemporaries, with folklore and myth because he believed that a nation's folklore in some kind of mystical way is an artistic expression of "the people's soul." He kept struggling to find a happy solution to the problem of integrating folklore into Literature with a capital *L*. His early plays are quite obviously folkloric in setting, language, and structure. They are also, mostly, unsuccessful.

Beginning (roughly) with *A Doll's House* Ibsen turned to a modern, realistic idiom but he never abandoned folklore. His 19th-century Norwegians retain their folkloric "souls," they are trolls and mermaids/men and *huldres*—a type of indigenous Norwegian wood troll with a long tail and often otherwise very seductive and attractive.

Rosmersholm has three distinct layers of meaning that are woven together into an artistic whole: the first, and obvious, layer involves the "modern" Norwegians. The second layer is one that is always there in Ibsen: an examination of the role of the artist in a bourgeois society. Rosmer is the "artist," the gifted person who wants to ennoble mankind. He needs, as do all Ibsen artists, the help of a woman who combines being virginal with being willing to sacrifice herself for art and the artist. Rosmer has cast Rebecca in this role. But she doesn't fit it—as Ibsen women never do. She has what he lacks—a ruthless will to act—but she is not willing to sacrifice nor to be backgrounded by him.[1] Or, she is willing too late. When she finally throws herself at his feet, all she has to give is her life. The final layer is the "mythic" one where Rebecca the mer creature meets Rosmer the descendant of the Rosmer merman about whom a folk ballad tells that he was fond of seducing young virgins and abducting them to his lair at the bottom of the sea.

Ibsen indicates in a number of ways, some subtle, some not so, that Rebecca West is a mer creature: she is the aboriginal Norwegian, the Viking brought back to life. John Rosmer belongs to a long chain of intensely cultural, socialized humans. His ancestors went ashore way back in the mythic past and since then they have become aboriginal Norwegians only of name.

Ibsen pits these two against each other, leans back in his chair, and watches what happens. Will one of them win? Will the troll in Rosmer come out of hiding and seduce the dangerous but also strangely innocent mermaid? Or will the ruthless strength of the mermaid be the deciding factor?

In the beginning it looks like Rebecca has the victory all but sewn up, but the mermaid has been enculturated. She has been permeated by the spirit of Rosmersholm. She has, like a huldre who marries a Christian man, lost her tail.[2] Her ruthlessness, her strength is gone. She cannot go through with her seduction. The tables have been turned on her. Rosmer, despite centuries of cultural varnish, has the rudiments of his mer/troll instincts intact—*he* has seduced *her*. They have been caught in their mutual web of seductions and there is only one way out for them: the millbrook. They jump together in realization that their game of chess has left them both in checkmate.

There are a number of ways of reintroducing the folkloric and mythic knowledge into performing Ibsen. *Verfremdung* seems obvious: having the actors visibly struggle with folklore characters that strive to break out and take over. Masks are another possibility. But actors and directors will find their own ways to ritualize the plays and to introduce the mythic creatures underlying the modern dress and idiom.

Interestingly, Roger Glossop's handsome set for the La Mama production had some elements that made me, for a brief moment, hope that the director had seen the folklore connection. Unfortunately, the set had to carry the entire symbolic load—an impossible task that ultimately made it look a bit out of place and absurd given what was going on in it.

If we keep seeing Ibsen as the "father" of modern realistic theatre he may become obsolete and boring because the society he describes is so foreign and old-fashioned seen from our vantage point. But if we infuse the late plays with the vibrant undercurrent of myth and folklore the dust will fall off. We have to stop approaching Ibsen with respect and timidity. The plays should be approached as folk tales about universal conflicts. The characters are not just nice and boring and modern, they are mythic creatures, trolls and huldres hiding inside suits, dresses, and polite manners.

For the reader who is interested in a more detailed and substantiated version of my argument, I refer to a book by Barbara Fass Leavy and myself, *Ibsen's Forsaken Merman: Folklore in the Late Plays* (1988).

Notes

1. She is not a virgin either. Freud has pointed out that all the evidence suggests that she had an incestuous relationship with her father (1957). This was made quite clear in the La Mama production.
2. The huldre upon becoming Christian loses her tail which symbolizes her paganism (see Jacobsen and Leavy 1988:106–11).

References

Freud, Sigmund
1957 "Some Character-Types Met With in Psychoanalytical Work." In *Psychological Works*, translated and edited by James Strachey, Volume 14. London: Hogarth Press.

Jacobsen, Per Schelde, and Barbara Fass Leavy
1988 *Ibsen's Forsaken Merman: Folklore in the Late Plays*. New York: New York University Press.

Per Schelde
New York City

XIII Muestra Nacional de Teatro

The New Theatre in Peru

Malgorzata Oleszkiewicz

The XIII Muestra Nacional de Teatro (National Theatre Sampling) took place in the Peruvian town of Andahuaylas from 17 to 24 April 1988. The first Muestra, in Lima, was organized in 1974 by Sara Joffré, a playwright, director, actress, and editor of a series of publications on Peruvian theatre. Joffré saw the need for an exchange of ideas and experiences among the rising number of groups that were part of the "New Theatre."

The New Theatre is comprised of a diversity of styles—from experimental work with no clear political orientation to more political and popular work, as well as peasant theatre. What distinguishes the New Theatre from commercial theatre is its commitment to social change. Its beginnings go back to the first decade of the 20th century and experiments of the workers' theatres in Lima, Santiago, and Buenos Aires. More immediately, the New Latin American Theatre was a response to the political impact of the Cuban Revolution and to the peasant and workers' movements of the '60s, particularly in Peru.

1. The opening parade of the XIII Muestra Nacional de Teatro in Andahuaylas on 17 April 1988. (Photo by Malgorzata Oleszkiewicz)

The New Theatre rejects commercialism; it proposes a redefinition of traditional notions of text and performance and new relationships between author, director, and actor, as well as between actor and spectator. Most of the productions are collective creations.[1] Spectators frequently participate in the performances and subsequent forums. Performances are held in streets, parks, schools, factories, and are directed to audiences which previously had no access to conventional theatre—peasants, workers, children, and inhabitants of shantytowns. These Peruvians have always lived closely with the performance traditions of the indigenous as well as African cultures present in the country. In the Andes, the pre-Columbian ritual and religious forms as well as lighter and humorous theatrical forms (*taquis*) (see Osorio 1983) became syncretized with Spanish medieval religious dramas, processions, and African masking and dance brought by the slaves.

The New Theatre, to a great extent, is bringing these popular traditions back to the people by incorporating them into performances. Music, dance, masks, costumes, myths and legends, as well as the history of the people are an integral part of the work of groups such as Yuyachkani, Barricada, Taller de Teatro del Centro de Comunicación Popular de Villa El Salvador, Septiembre, and others.

The atmosphere for this proliferation of new theatre work was created by General Juan Velasco Alvarado's government in the late 1960s. It introduced a series of sociopolitical changes that brought liberal reforms and revitalized Peruvian cultural life. The popular classes—peasants, workers, and lower echelons of the bourgeoisie—began to play an increasingly important role in society, and artistic activity flourished. Theatrical and musical groups began forming in the early '70s. Among the first theatrical

2. & 3. A demonstration of military force greeted the participants in the XIII Muestra. The marching squadron included an armed, uniformed four-year-old boy. (Photos by Malgorzata Oleszkiewicz)

groups were Yuyachkani and Cuatrotablas, created in 1971. It was in this atmosphere that Joffré initiated the Muestras de Teatro.

The first five Muestras took place in the capital city of Lima, but since the theatre movement has spread throughout the country they have been organized in different departments (states) each year. The site of the 1988 Muestra was Andahuaylas in the department of Apurímac, a rural area in the Andes. It borders Ayacucho, the department which has suffered most from the violence that has spread since 1980 because of the presence of Sendero Luminoso[2] and the Peruvian army. Death and poverty are the daily bread of its inhabitants and migration to Lima is rampant. Andahuaylas, which in the native Quechua means "meadow of varicolored clouds," was until recently part of this emergency zone and is still very militarized. An intimidating military parade takes place every Sunday in the town plaza and the army is always and everywhere present.

On 17 April 1988, a demonstration of this military force greeted actors, directors, critics, and journalists who had come for the Muestra, some of whom had traveled 48 hours by land, unable to afford a ticket on the twice-weekly airplane to Andahuaylas. All had gathered for the parade which traditionally begins each Muestra. The colorful parade was confronted by a marching armed squadron, among them a four-year-old boy, also armed and in uniform. The festive crowd suddenly looked like a group of defenseless kids.

Some 200 people from all over Peru had gathered to spend a week training, demonstrating, performing, evaluating, and discussing. Our day started at 6:00 A.M. with two hours of physical training conducted by selected Muestra participants. The breakfast, served from 8:00 to 9:00, like the other two meals, was donated by the inhabitants of the Andahuaylas province. From 9:00 to 11:00 theatre groups demonstrated their work, followed by two hours of evaluation and discussions about performances seen the previous day and night. Lunch, again prepared by the people of Andahuaylas, was followed by three hours of performances for children and adults, presented outside the theatre in Andahuaylas and in surrounding villages. After dinner, beginning at 8:00 P.M., three or four performances ran as late as midnight. One entire day was also dedicated to *difusión*—performances throughout the region.

All the difusión and afternoon performances were free of charge and each evening of performances cost a token ten *intis* (about five cents). Hospitality is customarily extended to the artists in exchange for entertainment, as it is during all Peruvian popular festivities. Each theatre group is assigned a *cargullo* (caretaker). The same basic system, intrinsic to the Andean culture, supports contemporary popular festivals which, like the New Theatre events, are usually one week long. The Muestra, since its beginning in 1974, has been based on traditional principles of reciprocity and is self-supporting.

Transportation, relatively costly in Peru, is the only expense not provided by the host of the Muestra. Before every theatrical event outside of the home town, each group conducts an arduous search for subsidies from public institutions such as Consejo Nacional de Ciencia y Tecnología (the National Council of Science and Technology), Banco Central de Reserve (a state bank), and the Peruvian airlines, usually obtaining at least part of the money.

But money is always a problem. Several of the more established groups, such as Yuyachkani and Cuatrotablas, own houses where they train, present their work, hold meetings, eat, and sometimes also live. It is a communal existence. The rest of the groups have to train in parks, private homes, or settle for a few hours each week in a rented theatre space. Members of many groups forsake outside jobs in order to concentrate on their theatre work, and they live only on money from performances and classes.

At the 1988 Muestra, 28 groups from all over the country performed. Every night beginning at 6:00 P.M. when the ticket booth opened, peasants who came down from the mountains as well as inhabitants of the town of Andahuaylas crowded in line for a place in the 1,200-seat theatre that had been donated by the Belgian foundation Antoon Spinoy. Performances

4. With songs, instruments, and masks, Taller de Teatro del Centro de Comunicación Popular de Villa El Salvador performed Carnaval por la vida. *(Photo by Malgorzata Oleszkiewicz)*

given daily in the streets, playgrounds, and other public spaces met with the same success. The active interest of the people and their enthusiasm for this art forum where they were represented was apparent. Three of the six theatre groups from Andahuaylas performed. Two of them, Qallari and Javier Heraud, performed entirely in Quechua; the other, Jose María Arguedas, was bilingual (Quechua-Spanish). This marked the first time in the history of the Muestras that plays were presented entirely in a native Indian language.

The military authorities were also present at all performances—to make certain that nothing "subversive" was being shown. Consequently, since the main themes of the New Peruvian Theatre are the search for national identity, settling accounts with history, and the examination of Peru's current reality, constant tension was inevitable. The nervousness was strongest on 20 April when the Taller de Teatro del Centro de Comunicacíon Popular de Villa El Salvador was performing. Their play, *Carnaval por la vida* (*Carnival for Life*) ridicules both the army and the Sendero Luminoso. Actors, organizers, and audience feared arrests might occur, as they had in Lima during the group's performance of another play, *Diálogo entre zorros* (*Dialog Between Foxes*), in 1988. Some in the audience left the theatre but the performances went on uninterrupted.

This theatre group exemplifies the development of the New Theatre in Peru in the social context of the shantytown of the 1980s. Villa El Salvador is a shantytown south of the city of Lima. Ever since it was settled in 1971, it has been a model of cooperation, organization, and development. Villa El Salvador's accomplishments won it a Nobel Peace Prize nomination in 1986.

People from different parts of the country with a variety of cultural backgrounds settled in Villa El Salvador.[3] There was a need for better information and communication among the inhabitants. El Centro de Comunicación Popular (the Popular Communications Center), with its library and workshops in journalism, music and song, film, radio, audiovisuals, and theatre, was created in 1974 by a group of teachers. The lack of mass media as well as the wealth of artistic traditions in Villa El Salvador created a crucial need for live theatre. This first took the form of short sketches dealing with such immediate problems as lack of jobs, housing, water, and electricity.

In 1981 Cesar Escuza became the coordinator[4] of the theatre workshop and, in 1983, founded a permanent theatre group. Under Escuza's direction, the workshop created four long works as well as many *pasacalles*—parades announcing the group's arrival in a new place and expressing their stand on urgent themes and events. The group's premiere work, *La sangre, las velas y la gente* (*Blood, Candles and People*), was a vigil commemorating the death of a popular leader during the 19 July 1977 Paro Nacional (general strike against the military dictatorship) and was presented in roadside grottoes for the dead. In 1985 the members of the group made theatre their full-time occupation, unprecedented for a theatre group in a Peruvian shantytown.

On 20 June 1985 *Diálogo entre zorros* was first performed. It was the group's first collective creation, a process dictated by necessity. In Villa El Salvador there was great demand for a work about the community and its history, but nothing written about it could be found. The group began to improvise based on interviews and observations of daily life. The process took eight months.

Diálogo tells the history of Villa El Salvador while addressing a series of daily problems that plague the population: lack of food, water, electricity, housing, transportation, work, teachers. The actors, all inhabitants of Villa El Salvador, tell the story of their struggles to fulfill these needs. The presentation of the play in Lima's Alliance Française marked the first time a shantytown group had performed in a Lima theatre.

Carnaval por la vida was first presented on 1 October 1987 during the first

5. The New Theatre group Septiembre satirized the Spanish conquest of Peru in Padre, tierra madre *at the Theatre Antoon Spinoy in Andahuaylas. (Photo by Malgorzata Oleszkiewicz)*

regional Muestra in the Lima-Ica-Callao region. *Carnaval* touches on serious issues in a playful manner, using the mockery and punning that is so characteristic of native humor. It portrays the daily struggle of two Villa El Salvador women against unemployment and the high cost of living, and their organization of a communal kitchen. The play's protagonist is Death—starvation, disguised as a member of the army or as a *senderista* (member of the Sendero Luminoso). When Death is buried, a testament expressing the will of the living is read. *Carnaval* makes use of music, song, dance, and masks—all derived from the popular culture and integral to carnivals. Masks are used to create confusion between illusion and reality. A military man about to bury a "disappeared" person takes off his mask and reveals that he is Pablo from the communal kitchen—he says he is only playing a role. The confusion and insecurity of the spectators is that of people in a country harassed by an internal war.

The New Peruvian Theatre, once a marginal and alternative forum, is now an artistic force in Peru. Besides the Muestras, annual national and regional theatre workshops were established in 1987. The first Taller Nacional de Teatro (National Theatre Workshop) took place in March 1987 in Chaclacayo near Lima as an initiative of the Yuyachkani group. The second, in October 1988, was hosted by Villa El Salvador's Popular Communications Center's theatre group. The Cuatrotablas group in Chaclacayo organized an international theatre event, Ayacucho '88, with theatre groups from Europe and Latin America and Eugenio Barba in attendance.

In 1985 MOTIN—Movimiento de Teatro Independiente—was formed to unite about 40 Lima theatre groups. This organization spread to other parts of the country and now publishes the only Peruvian magazine entirely devoted to theatre, *Colectivo*.

The political and economic situation in today's Peru is a very difficult one. Widespread violence on the part of both the army and the Sendero Luminoso, extreme poverty, and escalating inflation are signs of a destabilized country where no one gives credence to the once promising populist government led by president Alan García. The promises of peace, economic growth, and prosperity are still unrealized. The New Theatre movement represents imminent political and socioeconomic change for Peru.

Notes

1. Plays are created as a collective effort of the actors and the coordinator (director), partly because of a lack of appropriate texts and partly because of ideological and artistic convictions.
2. Sendero Luminoso (Shining Path) is a Maoist guerrilla organization.
3. Among the Andean, Selva (jungle), and coastal regions there are at least 59 different languages and cultures (Montoya 1987). The official language of Peru is Spanish, but only part of the population speaks it. The other two widely used languages are the Quechua and Aymara from the Andes.
4. The New Theatre groups use the title "coordinator" instead of "director" because it better reflects the collective reality of the groups.

References

Montoya, Rodrigo
1987 *La cultura quechua hoy*. Lima: hueso húmero ediciones.

Osorio, Betty
1983 "The Dramatic Manifestations of the Incas: Origins and Evolution." PhD diss., University of Illinois at Urbana-Champaign.

Malgorzata Oleszkiewicz *has studied Iberian and Latin American studies at Warsaw University, romance languages at Queens College, and Latin American literature at New York University. She is currently conducting research in Peru on the New Theatre and popular celebrations for her PhD dissertation, and has published articles in* Malandragem *(New York),* La República *(Lima), and* El Público *(Madrid).*

Theatre's Illegitimate Child

The Screen Actor

Thomas W. Babson

MFA graduate actor training programs have historically concerned themselves only with equipping students for life upon the repertory stage. However, these programs now must face the reality that actors have to make a living, and today the career actor's "stage" encompasses a vastly enlarged arena. That arena is dominated by film and television. Because of institutional inertia and the outdated elitist view that the film or TV actor is merely theatre's illegitimate child, graduate acting programs still operate on the tacit assumption that an actor's training is the sole province of the theatre. Therefore, these programs fail to meet a very important need of their students.

The fact is that film and television are where the jobs are. Employment statistics show that in 1985, Screen Actor's Guild (SAG) working members made an average of $10,500, while Actors' Equity Association (AEA) working members earned $9,000 per year. Although the differential is interesting, the more significant element is that there are 48,000 SAG working members, but only 13,000 AEA working members. In other words, almost four out of five working actors are employed in film and television. This is a remarkable statistic, one that cannot be ignored by anyone interested in the development of an actor's career. The graduate training programs that do not offer the tools to permit their graduates to take advantage of these economic and professional opportunities are providing a diminished education.

As part of research for an acting textbook, I designed a survey to determine whether actors trained for the stage wanted to work in film and television, and if so, whether they were being properly prepared for it. The 20-question survey was sent to 25 MFA programs throughout the country. I received 127 responses from 15 programs (60 percent response rate) representing two eastern schools (Yale and Brandeis), six midwestern schools (Wayne State, Purdue, and the Universities of Minnesota, Nebraska, Wisconsin at Milwaukee, and Indiana), four southern schools (Southern Methodist University and the Universities of Miami, Georgia, and Texas at Austin), and three western schools (Universities of California at Los Angeles and San Diego, and University of Southern California). Eighty-three males and 44 females filled out the survey; 44 were first-year students, 41 were second year, and 42 were third year. The average age of the respondent was 26.4.

Not surprisingly, a concept that the survey corroborated was that a career in the arts is a complex thing. Unlike a graduate of business or vocational school, an actor seeks other components of success besides the bottom line; on one hand, stage acting is the most artistically satisfying of all mediums. On a scale of 0 to 10 (10 being the highest rating), the average respondent gave theatre an 8.4 for "artistic fulfillment," but film and television only a 6.8. For "enjoyment of work," the respondent gave an 8.8 for theatre and just a 7.4 for film. When these ratings are combined with the fact that students rated film and television a 5 in terms of their perception of the "quality of acting" compared to a 7 for theatre, the impression that film and television are somehow illegitimate is substantiated.

From this perspective, then, degree programs such as Yale's seem to be doing a fine job fulfilling their students' needs. In the Yale School of Drama's 1987 brochure the institution's objectives were specifically stated: "The goal of the Yale School of Drama is to develop the skills, crafts, and attitudes of its students to prepare them for careers in the professional theatre, in particular for the demand of repertory and ensemble production in permanent theatre companies such as the Yale Repertory Theatre." It is clear from past results that over their 60-year history they have done just that and done it well.

However, economic reality is causing the students at Yale and at schools around the country to reevaluate where their training will take them. For one, they realize all too well where the money is. The average respondent to the survey gave theatre a low 3.9 for "economic potential," as opposed to 7.4 to film and television. Therefore, and most tellingly, when asked to rank career preference, the students surveyed said their first choice was feature film. Further, 70 percent of the actors would choose stage *and* screen as opposed to only 25 percent who preferred just the stage. Theatre and film are two sides of the same economic coin. One third-year student at Yale commented, "By the time the League Auditions[1] are over and I'm on the streets this June, I will have spent three years and be $30,000 in debt from my training. I can't afford to do rep work. I'd like to, I just can't afford it."[2] These young professionals want to achieve a balance between financial security and artistic integrity that will ultimately define their careers.

But their training is quite clearly not balanced. By the time MFA actors have finished their programs, they will have had an average of 35.1 stage roles but only 1.2 screen roles. While they get an average of 6 hours a week in acting classes, 62 percent of the students have had no film training at all and for 26 percent, film technique is not even discussed. An overwhelming majority (70 percent) of student actors throughout the country felt they needed to learn screen technique separately from stage technique. The point was pragmatic for many students: "I came here to be a better actor," one said, "but I also came here because I want to be a professional actor and be able to sustain a career. Style and period training are the same as stage and screen for me; I think I'm capable of both, I want to learn both."

Finally, an astonishing 75 percent of the survey respondents stated that video was never used, even as a teaching tool, in their classes. Why then should one be surprised to hear of the many talented repertory-trained actors who go to New York or Los Angeles for an important audition or screen test, only to lose the part simply because they did not understand the craft? After the League Auditions in June of 1987, one particularly gifted actress admitted that she did very well on her theatre callbacks, but "I blew the first two film auditions. I had to sit in this chair and they videotaped me. I didn't know what the hell was going on. By the third one I started to figure it out. I wish to God I could have those first two over again." The sad truth is that with today's competition, there are seldom any second chances.

Some department chairs are similarly frustrated by the lack of understanding within their academic communities. On the east coast, George White, President of the Eugene O'Neill Theatre Center, finds it difficult to get financial commitment for a transition program that is already in development: "It's a multimedia society we live in," he says, "and even though we're a theatre center, there's a new definition for theatre. Actors have to be versatile, as do directors, writers and technicians" (1987).

At the University of California at Los Angeles (UCLA), in the center of the world's film industry, the theatre department still trains the actors. The department chair, George Scheafer, himself an award-winning director of both stage and screen, finds a lot of resistance: "Even here at UCLA, with our tremendous facilities and reservoir of students, we just don't have acting courses for film. [. . .] It's very hard to convince some of the old guard that we need to integrate film and theatre training. We're not preparing [our directors and actors]" (1987).

To effect this integration, the following tactics should be adopted in our university theatre departments: (1) a screen technique class should be introduced in the third year; (2) video as a screen critiquing tool should be made available and encouraged throughout the program (there is no better way for an actor to understand the realism of Chekhov, than to watch the "truth" of her or his performance on a television close-up); (3) at least one course should be given on the stage and screen "business of acting"; (4) there should be a closer liaison with associated film schools, local TV stations, and similar resources of the community; (5) teachers experienced in both stage and screen should oversee the implementation of such programs to ensure that they meet the highest professional and academic standards and to minimize disruption, reorganization, and undue financial burden.

The accumulation of capital and the unprecedented technological growth which has occurred in the last century and which has accelerated so rapidly in the last 30 years has fundamentally altered the concept of the actor and the stage. It is not surprising that so many have difficulty accepting this; the perception that the theatre is where the "real" actor performs has developed over literally 25 centuries. There is an even stronger intransigence in the academic world, where a sense of history runs deep. But the change is nevertheless undeniable. It is perhaps true that all you need for theatre is "a board and a passion," but for a career in today's multimedia world you need the craft to communicate that passion on screen, tube, tape, film, and disc, as well as board.

Notes

1. The League of Professional Theatre Training Programs (1972–87) was an alliance of professional theatre training institutions joined to assert standards for training,

to encourage public recognition, and to influence public policy in support of the development of theatre artists.

The League developed its annual Actor Presentations, or auditions, to introduce the graduating actors of its member programs to directors, casting directors, and agents representing theatre, film, and television throughout the United States.

2. Unless otherwise indicated, quotations were taken from the author's conversations with students at Yale during the 1985/86 academic year.

References

Scheafer, George
1987 Personal communication, Fall.

White, George
1987 Personal communication, Fall.

Thomas W. Babson *received an MFA from Smith College, taught at Yale, UCLA, and the National Theatre Institute, traveled the country for the Screen Actor's Guild Conservatory Program, and was the Cofounder and Artistic Director of the L.A. Film Actors Lab. He is currently writing a textbook on the actor's transition from stage to screen while continuing his acting career in theatre, film, and television.*

Announcements

Ed. Note: TDR is pleased to print announcements of upcoming conferences, festivals, publications, etc. Please submit all notices at least 6–8 months in advance of the event.

Performance Studies Festival: Call for Papers

Performance Studies International (PSI) will host a festival bringing together both scholars and performers to celebrate the 10th anniversary of New York University's Department of Performance Studies on 3–7 October 1990. The festival will be a forum for the exploration of contemporary performance studies research and experimentation in performance itself. Crossover between these two areas is encouraged. The festival will include panel discussions, workshops, and papers. Those interested in participating please send workshop proposals and papers to Performance Studies International, Department of Performance Studies, New York University, 721 Broadway, 6th floor, New York, NY, 10003.

Young Scholars' Prize

Young scholars who have recently published essays on some aspect of theatre research may be nominated for a $350 prize presented annually by the American Society for Theatre Research (ASTR). To be eligible for the 1990 prize, the essayist must be a student or be presently untenured and within seven years of the awarding of the doctorate degree; the essay must have been published in English in a refereed journal during 1989. Nominations may be submitted by members or nonmembers of ASTR, by editors, by authors themselves (one entry only), or by others. Previous winners are ineligible.

Nominated essays should be sent, together with particulars of publication and evidence of author's eligibility, to Dr. Rosemarie Bank, School of Theatre; Kent State University, Kent, OH, 44242, by 1 May 1990. The winner will be announced and the prize presented at the November 1990 meeting of the ASTR.

Havana Workshop

The International Theatre School of Latin America and the Caribbean (Escuela Internacional de Teatro de la América Latina y el Caribe) is an autonomous organization with pedagogical goals which was born out of the Meeting for Latin American Theatre Workers (Encuentro de Teatristas Latinoamericanos) organized by Casa de las Américas in 1987. The director is the Argentinian playwright Osvaldo Dragún.

The school will have its first workshop in Havana, 15 October–15 November 1989, the subject of which will be "Current Techniques for Theatre Creation in Latin America and the Caribbean." The workshop will be led by eight Latin American theatre workers: Miguel Rubio and Teresa Ralli from the Peruvian group Yuyachkani; Rosa Luisa Márquez and Antonio Martorell from Los Teatreros Ambulantes de Cayey (University of Puerto Rico); Santiago García and Patricia Ariza from La Candelaria (Columbia); and Andrés Pérez and Ignacio Miranda from the Gran Circo Teatro (Chile).

The school headquarters will be: Calle 1ra. Num. 237, esquina A, El Vedado, La Habana, Cuba. Those interested in the school and the workshop can contact Casa de las Américas while the permanent headquarters are being prepared: Calle 3ra. y G, El Vedado, La Habana, Cuba. Phone: 32-3537. Telex: CAMER CU 511019.

Holding Back

The Theatre's Resistance to Non-Traditional Casting

Harry Newman

> *[T]he sloppy and fatuous nature of American good will can never be relied upon to deal with hard problems. These have been dealt with, when they have been dealt with at all, out of necessity—and in political terms, anyway, necessity means concessions made in order to stay on top.*
>
> —*James Baldwin (1963:118)*

> *Hispanic empowerment and Hispanic opportunity and Hispanic education and Hispanic productivity and Hispanic literacy are no longer issues of civil rights; they can no longer be considered in terms of national ideals or Christian compassion. As valid as all of those concerns are, the fundamental question is one of national survival.*
>
> —*Henry Cisneros (1988:70)*

In February 1986 when the Non-Traditional Casting Project (NTCP) began its advocacy work to help forge a truly American performing arts, it was not without a great sense of irony. That an organization had to be formed in the mid-1980s to advocate for the full participation of African-American, Asian-American, Hispanic-American, native American, female, disabled, and other disenfranchised artists in the performing arts was a testimony to our society's failure to acknowledge and accept people of these various groups as individuals and as Americans. This was, after all, over 30 years since the advent of the civil rights movement and more than 20 since the contemporary women's movement began. If these movements, important as they were (and are), had succeeded in re-forming our institutions, rather than merely bending them a little, a Non-Traditional Casting Project would have been superfluous. Unfortunately, although ethnic, female, and disabled persons have been accommodated to an extent in the greater society, their complete acceptance is long in coming. Nowhere is this more apparent than in the performing arts, particularly the theatre.

1. *Embracing creative possibilities: Josie de Guzman as Eliza and Charles Turner as Higgins in a scene from Alan Jay Lerner and Frederic Lowe's* My Fair Lady *at the First National Symposium on Non-Traditional Casting in New York City, 1986. (Photo by Sarah B. Wilkins)*

A four-year study by Actors' Equity Association completed in January 1986 revealed that over 90 percent of all the professional theatre produced in this country—from stock and dinner theatre to the avant-garde to Broadway—was staged with all-Caucasian casts. Without any formal study, the same trends were clear in other media. In addition, when ethnic persons or persons with disabilities did appear, they were often crudely stereotyped. Female characters, who appeared much less frequently than males, were also cast into a handful of common and distasteful stereotypes: the nymphomaniac/prostitute; the alcoholic/drug addict; the good-hearted, misunderstood neurotic; the supportive wife; the undifferentiated mother or grandmother; and the aggressive/ambitious/heartless businesswoman.

Further, if statistics concerning ethnic, female, and disabled writers, directors, designers, choreographers, and other artists were compiled they would reveal even less participation. These disenfranchised nonactors are also stereotyped. Members of these groups are only rarely called upon to work on projects that are not about their specific group. For instance, female directors are most often approached to direct "women's plays," ethnic directors are only sought for ethnic shows, and so on. Since so much of our knowledge, understanding, and compassion for the world is shaped by theatre, film, and television, the absence of full and satisfying roles (in the largest meaning of that word) for these disenfranchised artists has had the insidious effect of reinforcing a view of a homogenous American society that has never been more than a fantasy.

To address the lack of participation of their black, Hispanic, Asian, and native American membership, Actors' Equity conceived of non-traditional casting, which they formally defined as the casting of ethnic and female performers in roles where race, ethnicity, or gender are not germane to the character's or play's development. (The NTCP later expanded this definition to include performers with disabilities.) The definition was formulated by Equity's Ethnic Minorities Committee, which chose the word "ethnic" as a shorthand way of describing its own constituents—the union's African-American, Asian-American, Hispanic, and native American members. When the NTCP came into being, Actors' Equity had successfully negotiated the term "non-traditional casting" into several contracts and had begun to get acceptance for the notion, at least from those on the business side of the theatre.

Although there are drawbacks to the phrase, we at the NTCP adopted it as part of our title because it had already gained a measure of currency in the industry and because it seemed provocative. We called ourselves a "project" because we hoped (and hope) to be short-lived, to act as a catalyst for change, rather than become an institution interested primarily in self-perpetuation. Our organizational goal is obsolescence. As our advocacy work has taken hold and the expression "non-traditional casting" has reached a wider audience, we have met with some criticism about it. But it is essential to stress that we must not waste our energies on endless semantical arguments when we should be working toward creating a truly multicultural, multiethnic performing arts. In time we hope that—like our organization—the phrase itself will disappear, and "non-traditional" casting will become the performing arts' new tradition.

From the outset, the diverse group of people who formed the NTCP took it as their goal to confront directly the assumptions and presumptions that allowed people in the arts to work within these very limited categories. Our challenge was to get our colleagues to recognize that the conventions which guide their choices (or nonchoices) are adopted attitudes, not artistic imperatives. Or, to put it as our central question: How do we get the decision-makers in the arts—our nation's image-makers—to take responsibility for the images they are presenting, or in many cases not presenting? How do we begin to get these people thinking in the broadest terms?

Toward this end, we have launched several programs. In November 1986 we produced the First National Symposium on Non-Traditional Casting at the Shubert Theatre in New York. This two-day event presented 53 actors—from complete unknowns to James Earl Jones—performing in 18 non-traditionally cast scenes from standard plays. There were speeches and panel discussions led by over 40 leaders of the industry including: Tisa Chang, Maria Irene Fornes, Frances Foster, John Houseman, Bernie Jacobs, Raul Julia, Arthur Kopit, Richard Maltby, Bernice Reagon, Ellen Stewart, and Douglas Turner Ward. Nearly 1,000 directors, artistic directors, producers, performers, playwrights, casting directors, educators, and critics from across the country were in attendance. The First National Symposium was followed by symposia on non-traditional casting in Washington, DC (November 1987), San Francisco (April 1988), Boston (June 1988), Los Angeles (October 1988), and Toronto (March 1989). In addition to these symposia, we have produced and distributed *Breaking Tradition*, an educational videotape hosted by Raul Julia, and have published and distributed *Beyond Tradition*, its companion volume (see plate 3). Using the videotape and book, we have held more than 25 forums

2. A panel discusses "the next tradition" at the First National Symposium on Non-Traditional Casting in New York, 1986. From left to right: Hugh Southern, Jeffrey Horowitz, JoAnne Akalaitis, Anna Deavere Smith, Peter Zeisler, Glenda Dickerson, Harold Scott, Samuel P. Barton, Marje Fields, Ruby Dee, Richard Maltby, Jr. (Photo by Sarah B. Wilkins)

and seminars with various industry and educational groups including the Association of Theatre in Higher Education, the Dramatists Guild, the League of Resident Theatres, the League of American Theatres and Producers, the League of Chicago Theatres, the National Theatre Conference, the Ohio Community Theatre Association, and the Society of Stage Directors and Choreographers. Lastly, we have implemented a number of programs to provide the industry with the practical means of achieving non-traditional casting and a culturally diverse performing arts. The most successful practical program has been our Artists Files, files of ethnic, female, and disabled artists, which as of this writing contain over 2,500 actors alone. The files have been consulted regularly for theatre, film, and television productions since they were opened in March 1987. Although exact figures are not available, several hundred actors have been called to audition through the use of these files, and a large number of them have found employment (see plate 3).

Of course, it is a further irony that we have had to go to such lengths in the theatre, where the imagination is supposed to fly free and embrace all creative possibilities. In almost every other segment of American society including the most apparently conservative bastions of the military, the police, banking, government, and civil service, barriers to ethnic, female, and disabled participation have been overcome to a great extent, and not just at the lowest levels. Why are the performing arts, particularly the theatre, so far behind? Hardly anywhere in the country and certainly not in urban settings is it possible to go through one's daily life without encountering people of a variety of ethnicities. At the moment, about 25 percent of our population consists of so-called ethnic minorities—that's nearly 60 million African-Americans, Asian-Americans, Hispanic-Americans, and native Americans. There are 37 million persons with disabilities; 25 million deaf people; more than half a nation of women. By the year 2000, the U.S. Census Bureau (as cited by the Population Crisis Committee [1989]) estimates that the ethnic population will have climbed to almost one-third of our nation's population. Before long, the onerous phrase "ethnic minority" will have to be scrapped entirely. The United States will have become a nation where every group is a minority.

Plate 3.

The Non-Traditional Casting Project

The Non-Traditional Casting Project (NTCP) is a tax-exempt, not-for-profit organization. Its primary funders include: Actors' Equity Association, Capital Cities/ABC, HBO, the Joyce Mertz-Gilmore Foundation, the National Endowment for the Arts, the New York State Council on the Arts, the Ohio Arts Council, and the Shubert Foundation. It has a permanent staff of three, with several volunteers and consultants. Its annual budget is over $150,000.

Breaking Tradition, a half-hour informational videotape hosted by Raul Julia, is available from NTCP for $25 (plus shipping and handling). *Beyond Tradition*, a volume of transcripts from the First National Symposium on Non-Traditional Casting, is available from NTCP for $15 (plus shipping and handling), as well as at theatre and college bookstores in New York, Chicago, Los Angeles, and other major cities.

The NTCP Artists Files can be consulted by appointment free of charge. For those out of the New York metropolitan area, telephone consultations are also available. There is no cost to be in the files. African-American, Asian-American, Hispanic, native American, and disabled actors simply send one copy of a photo and resume. Other artists—ethnic, female, disabled—please send one copy of a resume.

The staff and board of directors are available to conduct seminars and workshops to educational and industry groups throughout the country. These are arranged on an ad hoc basis. To discuss the possibility for holding such a program, contact the executive director. A modest fee may be involved.

For more information or to make a financial contribution, contact the Non-Traditional Casting Project, Box 6443, Grand Central Station, New York, NY, 10163–6021. Or call (212) 682–5790.

The great preponderance of American theatre, film, and television is single-mindedly focused on verisimilitude and realism. Why, then, when it comes to the participation of ethnic, female, and disabled persons, are the decision-makers in these media so reluctant to use our current reality as their touchstone? If it is for "artistic" reasons, what can be gained from excluding thousands of talented artists? If there are other reasons, how can they be brought into the open?

The issues raised by these questions are not new. Hundreds of productions over the decades have incorporated non-traditional casting, long before anyone called it that. But there has never been a systematic effort to make non-traditional casting part of the character of the American performing arts. Up until this time, ethnic, female, and disabled artists have been considered, when they have been considered at all, as little more than exotic flavorings. Or as exceptions, in the cases of those few whose talents have been recognized for a wide variety of roles. We speak of actors and then of ethnic actors, as though they were of different kinds. We speak of writers and then black writers or Hispanic writers or Asian writers. If someone said, "I saw a terrific white play last night," it would sound ludicrous. Why is it acceptable the other way around? It is time to recognize all artists as individual artists *first*, apart from categories that only serve to limit our imaginations. We will not be able to begin to create a truly American performing arts until all the ethnic and cultural elements that are a part of American society are acknowledged as equally valid and essential.

Why don't we have a multiethnic, multicultural performing arts already? If I were describing the NTCP's work to a Brazilian or an Icelander or a person from China it might seem silly. What's the big deal? Why has this change been so long in coming?

Part of the problem, of course, is caused by a fundamental lack of honesty. The notions reviewed above do seem rather straightforward and acceptable—in the abstract. So long as these notions remain generalized concepts of fair play or morality or what-have-you (that is, so long as decision-makers do not have to deal with them as they apply to their own work) they meet with support. Since our founding, it is hard to recall one decision-maker who decried our efforts as foolish or wrongheaded or inappropriate, at least not to us and certainly not in writing. While working to put together the First National Symposium on Non-Traditional Casting, the Broadway producer Manny Azenberg did state at a planning committee meeting that "we won't see non-traditional casting in my lifetime," meaning, of course, that he was (is?) reluctant or disinterested in working to make it happen, but he didn't denounce the concept. In fact, it has been rare for us to hear anyone speak negatively of our goals, especially at the symposia and seminars we have produced. Knowing our position, perhaps few people want to seem old-fashioned or small-minded or—God forbid—prejudiced. Most express support or interest or at least listen attentively as we raise questions. Such indirection, however, only makes it difficult to determine whose professed commitment (or unprofessed non-commitment) is genuine. Whether and how non-traditional casting appears in the work itself is our only gauge of sincerity. Of course, at some point in the history of almost every theatre, an ethnic person was cast non-traditionally or there was an incidence of cross-gender casting or whatnot, and these have been trumpeted to us proudly in many circumstances in order to prove good intentions. The point, however, is not to seek refuge in token examples, but to include these American artists regularly and fully in our performing arts.

"Non-traditional casting—what a great idea," has been a standard public response to our work. But as writers, directors, producers, artistic directors, and others realize that to have our performing arts fully reflect the diversity of our society they would have to change and expand the way they have been working, that more than talk is required, hesitations are often voiced. It is still considered a great idea—for everyone else. Excuses are given: "My audience won't accept it," or "I don't know of any ethnic actors," or "They're not well-trained," or "It's a play about a family." Non-traditional casting becomes a problem, and a difficult one. Though the excuses themselves are easily answered—the programs of the NTCP are specifically designed to meet these various excuses—they only serve to mask a deeper resistance.

How difficult is it to translate even the most genuine concern into action? Fran Weissler's attempt to put together a Broadway production of *Cat on a Hot Tin Roof* starring James Earl Jones provides a good example. After seeing him play Big Daddy in a scene at the First National Symposium on Non-Traditional Casting, Weissler, an established commercial producer, sought to gain permission from the Williams' estate for James Earl Jones to play the role on Broadway. Needless to say, a multiethnic production of *Cat on a Hot Tin Roof* led by this great American actor would be a great victory for non-traditional casting. After a year of courting and negotiating with the trustees of the estate, which included arranging for them to see the play *Fences,* permission was finally granted for the production—so long as James Earl Jones was the only nonwhite actor, as though they couldn't believe that there could be other actors of color equally as capable. Plans for the production have subsequently been put on hold pending the shooting schedule for the film of *Fences.* It may ultimately be produced without him.

Naturally, the deeper resistance to non-traditional casting is a reflection of the racism, sexism, and prejudice operating within our society itself. No matter how much performing artists behave as though they work in a vacuum, we are a part of the greater culture, and affected by it. American culture promotes a myth of individuality, while at the same time demanding uniformity. It is a culture in which differences of any kind are discouraged. Mass marketing, mass media, the blockbuster hit, the runaway bestseller—these have become our ideals. Individuals who are "different" are tolerated only if they can be categorized, or if they can prove that they are in some way "just like the rest of us."

In the so-called mainstream performing arts community, the resistance to non-traditional casting has many sources.[1] Certainly outright prejudice is one factor, whether it is overt or veiled. One of our brochures entitled "What is Non-Traditional Casting?" which we sent out to casting directors, directors, and artistic directors across the country was returned (anonymously) with the answer "the casting of inferior talents, semi-illiterate, and incompetent 'minorities' " scrawled on the back. Other comments written on the brochure included: "the vast majority of black/hisp 'ethnic' actors are ill-educated poor of speech and not intelligent enough to assume featured roles they are unsubtle and can't even speak English properly" [sic]. This was from a theatre professional. And it has not been our only piece of hate mail. We have also received anonymous phone calls, one of which (recorded on the answering machine) consisted of the repeated refrain, "Fuck all the niggers in the ass, fuck them where they breed." Was this a direct response to our efforts? As a final, less personally threatening example, one wonders if *New York Magazine* critic John Simon's repeated attacks on non-traditional casting are fueled purely by artistic considerations.

It is difficult to determine how much unconscious prejudice is at play with decision-makers in the performing arts. This is a question which hounds ethnic or disabled performers at auditions. How much is the recent openness toward non-traditional casting sincere or merely a pro forma reaction to pressure from Actors' Equity and other organizations? Has there been a genuine change in attitude or are the same exclusionary points of view in place while all the talk is hypocrisy?

Since a large number of the artistic directors and producers in the theatre, for instance, are middle-aged or older, it is quite possible that their choices of what is valid, what is good, what is appropriate are guided by attitudes that were shaped during a time when discrimination and racism were the order of the day. Unfortunately, such attitudes are not exclusively held by older persons. At New York's Circle Rep recently one of the few African-American members of the acting company was approached by the young literary manager there in an earnest attempt to expand her horizons. "I wanted to talk to you more about black writers," it was reported to me the manager said, "because I don't know. I mean how do they think? How do they feel? I mean what do they really write about?" The emphasis was on the "they," as though writers of color were a different species. If the attitudes informing such seemingly well-intentioned comments could be brought to the fore, we would be much further ahead in dealing with them.

Parenthetically, it is important to state that as much as possible I try to name the names of persons and organizations that I use as examples. This is not done to embarrass those named, but out of the belief that part of the mechanism that allows these attitudes to be perpetuated is the sly use of confidentiality and euphemism. These are a means of downplaying responsibility for actions or inactions. If we are to make any headway toward affecting a change in the performing arts we must know exactly with whom we are dealing and have the courage to require accountability.

But I don't believe prejudice, whether covert or blatant, underlies most of the reluctance to explore non-traditional casting and the non-traditional participation of all disenfranchised artists. Instead we are faced primarily with ignorance and indifference. Now, ignorance can be eradicated by education and many of our efforts at the NTCP are educational in nature. Our videotape *Breaking Tradition* and its companion volume *Beyond Tradition* were created in order to spread the word to the professional performing arts industry and educational institutions about overcoming self-imposed limitations. Our various seminars and symposia are held for the same purpose. Such efforts can only go so far, however, in the face of indifference.

The past 30 years have brought a supposed flourishing of the performing arts in the United States, especially in the theatre with the development of the not-for-profit institutional theatre movement. There is certainly more professional theatrical activity nationwide now than in the '50s and early '60s. It is even possible to make a living (barely) now in the theatre, and not just a killing. As of the 1986/87 season, for instance, the resident not-for-

4. The First National Symposium on Non-Traditional Casting, held in New York in 1986, included the presentation of scenes from non-traditionally cast plays. Pictured here are (from left) Toshi Toda, Ako, Freda Foh Shen, and Allan Tung in John Briggs' adaptation of Shakespeare's play, Shogun Macbeth. *(Photo by Sarah B. Wilkins)*

profit theatres were responsible for employing more actors than any other kind of theatre. But along with this rise in activity has come the rise of what can only be called an artistic bureaucratism. By this I don't mean the professional artistic management, which adopted a corporate model and much of what comes with it (including bureaucracy) to regulate these new and burgeoning institutions. I am referring instead to the artists themselves, who have allowed their artistic decision-making processes to be shaped by their institutional structures. Every institution has a vested interest in maintaining itself. Such maintenance as a rule precludes change. "Let's continue doing what we do best" is the rallying cry, which translates, of course, to what has been most financially and critically rewarded.

As a result of these factors, plays are now mass-produced, rehearsed in four weeks or less, and marketed to consumer/subscribers. Artistic directors are so busy trying to satisfy these market demands that they no longer have time to be open to new ideas. Much of their time is spent either trying to reduce their workloads or trying to maintain their positions—i.e., their place in the bureaucracy, either personally or institutionally. Although artistic directors have been singled out here, the same forces affect virtually everyone working on the artistic side of these theatres, from literary managers to casting directors.

Such considerations also influence individual artists. Playwrights, for instance, often resist non-traditional casting in the first production of their plays, but are open to it in subsequent productions. At the First National Symposium on Non-Traditional Casting, Arthur Kopit spoke eloquently about his evolution of thought concerning the ethnicity of a character in his play *The End of the World*. He was certain the character had to be Caucasian in the premiere production, but has since realized the actor's ethnicity was unimportant. A.R. Gurney, Jr., has told us that he originally conceived *The Dining Room* for a multiethnic company of actors, since that would have emphasized the essential American quality of the play. For the original production at Playwrights Horizons, however, such a casting choice was dispensed with and it was presented with an all-white cast. What holds these writers back? Is it fear of financial failure? How can this timidity be overcome? These are more than just rhetorical questions. Once a play is produced in a certain way, the casting is usually replicated in subsequent productions. If we can get these and other playwrights to take the "risk" of casting non-traditionally initially, the effect of such choices would be multiplied throughout the industry.

In our present bureaucratized climate it is not hard to see how an indifference or even hostility to non-traditional casting could develop. Hundreds of our industry leaders have made whole careers, often very successful ones, without having to be concerned with these issues. Why should they have to be bothered with them now? Also, many of these leading decision-makers are beleaguered by the pressures to keep their institutions afloat or themselves employed (or both). They view the extra effort it would take to become familiar with black, Hispanic, Asian, native American, or disabled artists as too much to bear. Some managers and artistic directors plainly do not want to work that hard. Non-traditional casting is seen as yet another burden to be taken up, rather than a way of expanding artistic possibilities by opening imaginations to the finest that our various cultures have to offer.

When Zelda Fichandler, Artistic Director of the Arena Stage in Washington, DC, states in a much reprinted article originally written for the Washington symposium on non-traditional casting that she can "imagine" a theatre with a multiethnic company, but doesn't know "how to make it real," one wonders what pressures have served to prevent her from realizing her imaginings (1988:20). (By comparison, John Dillon, Artistic Director of the Milwaukee Repertory, presides over a theatre of comparable size to the Arena and manages to maintain a permanent company of actors that is one-third ethnic.) This example merely demonstrates how far away we have gotten from the essential artistic impulse of experimentation. Yet, whether for artistic or practical reasons, those who make decisions in the theatre must recognize that American society has transformed. It does no good to wish you could continue doing what you have been doing for 15, 20, or even 30 years. There may be a longing for the status quo of one's formative years, but for demographic reasons alone the status quo is changing too. Very shortly, the institutions and artists who refuse to accept our present society for what it is will be bypassed, and very likely made obsolete. Or is racism so deeply entrenched that this won't occur? Are the leaders of the American theatre determined to become artistic Afrikaaners?

Indifference to non-traditional casting manifests itself in two further ways. First, there has been much more interest in talking about non-traditional casting than in doing it. Talking about this issue is a way of not having to actually put it into practice. I have often described our current situation in this regard as the advanced-lip-service phase. With our emphasis on symposia, forums, seminars, and discussions, the NTCP may have become an instrument in preventing what we are seeking to accomplish. Second, there is a resistance to thinking in new ways, or perhaps to thinking at all. This is undoubtedly an outgrowth of the aforementioned artistic bureaucratism and its perverse devotion to the status quo, which delineates the imaginable and the unimaginable. To give an example, when we opened our Artists Files to the use of the industry, we had originally set up two parallel files of actors—one organized according to the categories that exist now (African-American, Hispanic-American, disabled, etc.) and one organized by character (leading man, older character actress, and so on) which contained all the ethnic categories mixed together. Thus, the second file was arranged according to how we ultimately wanted people to think. It was *never* used. Finally, we discontinued that second file, leaving us in a curious situation. In getting decision-makers excited about non-traditional casting, we must call attention to the categories we ultimately wish to transcend.

Resistance to non-traditional casting has also come from members of the disenfranchised communities. Initially, it was difficult to get some artists from those communities to believe our effort was genuine. Hadn't we already gone through this in the late '60s and early '70s with the explosion of ethnic talent that brought Gloria Foster, James Earl Jones, Raul Julia, Ruby Dee, and many others to prominence? What happened in the interim? Why did these performers need to be rediscovered? Why was this suddenly a concern again for the decision-makers who had been happy to let things go for so long? What was to be gained now?

Once the organization made it clear (primarily through our ongoing work) that our project was not a ploy, that it was an earnest effort to affect a true change, we were able to overcome some of the resistance of ethnic and disabled performers. However, a skepticism does remain on the parts of many—including some of those directly involved with the organization—about what kind of effect we ultimately can have. Such skepticism strikes me as healthy. In trying to make change, one is trading on hope.

Our efforts and the efforts of others in having our nation's cultural diversity accepted have created a reservoir of hope among disenfranchised artists, especially those just starting out. A measure of skepticism keeps those hopes from being easily dashed. It also provokes the organization to explore all possible avenues for change, which has led us from speaking purely to the artistic aspects of non-traditional casting to examining its social, political, and legal implications.[2]

Certain objections to non-traditional casting in the disenfranchised communities go much deeper. The leaders of some ethnic theatres and long-established multicultural theatres are concerned that their theatres' roles will be usurped if the more well-endowed mainstream institutions devote their resources to non-traditional casting and full multiethnic participation. It is feared that the mainstream theatres will command more of the already limited support from funding sources to launch programs that will duplicate those in place at existing ethnic and multicultural theatres. These theatres fear being marginalized. In addition, some of them worry that the talent pool they have painstakingly cultivated over the years will be lured away by the bigger money the larger institutions have to offer.

Clearly, these concerns are valid, at least in the short term. Traditionally, mainstream institutions have been substantially better funded than their ethnic counterparts. Their leaders are usually well placed for getting funds because of their past funding records, the size of their organizations, and the fact that many of them are involved with the funding process itself by serving on panels such as those at the National Endowment for the Arts. But as the ethnic population continues to grow, and their economic and political clout gets further acknowledged, this is bound to change. More and more, our currently disenfranchised communities are being seen as part of the United States' new tradition. That this change in attitude is already occurring can be seen in such programs as the Ford Foundation's major support for Hispanic theatres in recent years. By focusing here on the long-term future, I don't want to seem to be minimizing the present intense financial difficulties faced by smaller institutions serving the ethnic, female, and disabled communities, nor seem naive to the possibility of political power-plays by the larger institutions. I am merely trying to emphasize that our whole society is being transformed by the growth of these communities, including the funding sector, and that our postures will not always be determined by circumstances that are becoming outmoded.

Of course, if non-traditional casting did catch on in a big way at *all* theatres there would be a shortage of ethnic, female, and disabled actors. Not only would this make it difficult for smaller theatres, including the ethnic theatres, to attract these actors, it could also quash the enthusiasm in some larger theatres, which, while trying to cast non-traditionally, fail to find the appropriate performers. However, an acceptance widespread enough to create this kind of shortage seems a long way off. In any case, such a paucity of performers would only exist in a tansitional period as non-traditional casting became part of the way the performing arts happened in the United States. After a short time, there would be a much larger pool of these artists—younger ethnic and disabled people would be encouraged to study and take part in the performing arts once it had proven to be a viable career. Besides, using the possibility of a shortage of disenfranchised actors (or any of the possible short-term negative aspects of forming a truly multicultural performing arts) as an excuse for not trying to realize that ideal is like working against arms control because it will lead to unemployment in the military.

5. *Adriane Lenox (left) and Karen Morrow in* Baby, *by Sybille Pearson, David Shire, and Richard Maltby, Jr., performed at the First National Symposium on Non-Traditional Casting in New York, 1986. (Photo by Sarah B. Wilkins)*

It is important to remember that existing ethnic and multicultural theatres have a history of serving a specific and important audience. Non-traditional casting, no matter how widespread, would probably never negate that audience's need. Although these theatres should be regarded as providers of new American plays in the same way that the major off-Broadway theatres have over the years, it is unreasonable to believe that all of their work can or should appeal to a mass audience. In the same sense, the actors who have looked upon these institutions as home will still come back, even when they can work in the mainstream, because they get something in their home theatres that is not available to them anywhere else.

Still, many ethnic theatres and theatres that serve a specific cultural group are in a quandary. Having come into existence partially as a response to being excluded, these theatres must now also face redefining themselves as circumstances change. Although they support their artists' wish to work wherever they deserve to and in the widest range of roles, these theatres don't want to participate in their own demise. Curiously, ethnic institutions are confronting the same questions as those in the mainstream and expressing similar uncertainty. Perhaps this says more about the nature of the bureaucracy inherent in all institutions than about non-traditional casting itself.

There are two other difficulties confronting disenfranchised artists which can only be touched upon here. In the same way that the institutions serving the disenfranchised communities are concerned with losing their hard-won roles, these artists are concerned with the loss of their ethnic or cultural identities; non-traditional casting seems to imply that everyone is more or less interchangeable. One of the main struggles in ethnic, female, and disabled communities during the past 30 years has been for self-definition and identity. Many performing artists from these groups don't want to see that identity manipulated to suit the tastes of those currently making decisions in mainstream institutions. As hard as it is to believe, it is still not uncommon for ethnic performers to be told during auditions "you don't look Hispanic" or "you don't sound black enough," which really means "you don't conform to my expectations"—expectations usually shaped by stereotypes presented in other media. Conversely, actors are also concerned about having to play "white."

This dilemma is particularly difficult for Hispanics. Being Hispanic is a cultural distinction invented originally by the U.S. government. There are black, Caucasian, and Asian Hispanics. If you were an American Indian and lived below the new border after the Mexican-American War, you became Hispanic. In short, there is no way to "look" Hispanic. Yet, in the popular imagination a certain image has taken root, again, primarily through portrayals in the media. This is the source of some consternation in Hispanic communities. To give just one example, a Hispanic actor in California, who happens to have blonde hair, wrote to us last year that she had to buy a black wig to wear to auditions in order to be considered at all. When will we dispense with the need for such monolithic characterizations of whole groups of people?

Tokenism is one last area of concern shared by all disenfranchised artists, and particularly by writers. Under pressure from the funding sector to begin to reflect some cultural diversity (most state arts councils, for example, now explicitly request information regarding the hiring of ethnic, disabled, and other disenfranchised persons in their applications), many institutions are looking for that *one* example—the Asian actor in the bit role, the reading of the Hispanic play—to satisfy those requirements. Rather than make a genuine commitment to exploring the richness of our cultural diversity, these organizations often seem to be more interested in doing just enough to get by. This is not only a great disservice to the artists involved—the actor who never has a chance to cut her or his teeth on a significant part, the writer who is read and workshopped but never receives a full production—but also to these organizations. The fact that the Alabama Shakespeare Festival had not hired an artist of color throughout most of its history and then recently brought in a black actor just to portray Othello, while the other members of its large repertory company were cast in multiple roles, indicates that something is wrong. (Thankfully, through the efforts of several organizations, including the NTCP, the situation at ASF may be improving.)

Yet, even when an organization makes a strong commitment to a certain group, such efforts can result in unanticipated difficulties. For example, South Coast Repertory (SCR) in Costa Mesa, CA, devotes substantial resources to its annual series of play workshops by Hispanic writers, the Hispanic Play Project (HPP). Over the years, the HPP has helped many Hispanic/Latino writers work on and actually see their plays on their feet. Yet, the HPP is distinct from the theatre's usual development process and plays in this program progress much less frequently to full production. After a certain point, wouldn't the theatre be better served if it committed the same resources to including Hispanic plays in its mainstage season? Instead of being developed through segregation, couldn't these plays simply be incorporated into the theatre's body of work? Begun with the best of intentions, a program such as SCR's Hispanic Play Project could lead to perpetuating the divisions it was meant to overcome. The same is true for theatres that present readings of black plays during Black History Month, but none at other times of the year. If conducted in isolation, these undertakings can eventually become seen as patronizing and hypocritical by the very groups they are supposed to "serve." Further, some theatres may have launched programs for disenfranchised artists not with the best of intentions, but as a means of procuring additional funding for other parts of their operations. Such hypocrisy is especially distressing. Still, as

Reuben Cannon, one of the first black casting directors in Hollywood, said at the Los Angeles Symposium on Non-Traditional Casting: "One person's tokenism is another person's breakthrough." There is always a chance that programs created for even the most dubious reasons could provide the opportunity for good work.

Non-traditional casting does not of necessity imply tokenism or loss of identity. It's about having all artists considered as individuals with individual qualities, apart from belonging to groups based on often arbitrary distinctions such as skin color or ethnic origin. To be judged on individual ability is not "playing white" either. It is allowing each artist to bring whatever she is to her work. If a person is very involved with his ethnic or cultural background and it influences his choices, there is nothing wrong with that. In some cases, that background may preclude her from getting a specific role, but that is truly the minority of cases. Nor should we expect that that person must adhere to certain qualities just because he has a specific ethnic or cultural background. In the largest sense, then, non-traditional casting is about thinking through one's choices—what is truly essential for a character—and no longer relying on types, of any sort. It is unfortunate that so valuable a concept can be simplified and compromised so readily, but such trivialization seems inevitable in a society which is obsessed with the easy way out. Will we ever be able to accept an individual for who she is?

We have an opportunity to "re-cast" American performing arts. An opportunity to put aside the assumptions we have accepted unquestioningly for decades. We can create performing arts which uniquely reflect the complexity of American society. Non-traditional casting can be a part of this re-formation. In spite of some negative reaction to non-traditional casting among ethnic, female, and disabled performing artists and organizations, there is general agreement in these communities with our goals. Members of these groups didn't need us to tell them that their capabilities and contributions have been overlooked and undervalued.

In describing the resistance to non-traditional casting, I am drawn to make an analogy. To protect ourselves in winter we bundle up in coats. When the seasons change and summer is upon us we wear as little as possible. It's crazy for someone to walk through Central Park in a cashmere coat in August. The objections to non-traditional casting I've discussed seem very much the same to me. The seasons have changed, summer is here, but far too many people insist on wearing their coats.

Notes

1. In general at the Non-Traditional Casting Project we refrain from using the word "mainstream" because it implies its opposite, a minor stream, one of less importance. Our goal is to get people in the performing arts to realize that there is only one stream. In this context I hope the use of the word will be forgiven for lack of a better term.
2. Just a word about the legal implications. Under the law there are two kinds of illegal discrimination: disparate treatment, where a group is specifically singled out for discrimination, and disparate impact, where although hiring practices may seem neutral on the surface, in practice they exclude entire groups of people. The lack of participation of ethnic persons at some theatres could perhaps constitute discrimination by disparate impact. Such a case would have to be chosen very carefully as it would pit the First Amendment—the defense of artistic freedom—against Title VII of the Civil Rights Act of 1964 or other antidiscrimination legislation. It is far from clear what the outcome would be. This is the

subject of an article I recently completed for the *Journal of Arts Management and Law* (1989). While the Non-Traditional Casting Project has not ruled out the possibility of supporting a court case if such a situation arose, it would only be after we had exhausted all the other possible avenues of change. We choose to focus our energies elsewhere.

References

Baldwin, James
1988 [1963] *The Fire Next Time*. New York: Dell Publishing.

Cisneros, Henry
1988 "A New Day for Hispanics." *The World & I* (September):69–72.

Fichandler, Zelda
1988 "Casting for a Different Truth." *American Theatre* 5, no. 4 (May): 18–23.

Newman, Harry
1989 "Casting a Doubt: The Legal Issues of Non-Traditional Casting." *Journal of Arts Management and Law*, forthcoming.

Population Crisis Committee
1989 Personal communication, January.

Harry Newman *is Executive Director of the Non-Traditional Casting Project. He is also a playwright.*

Dancing with *Faust*

A Semiotician's Reflections on Barba's Intercultural Mise-en-scene

Patrice Pavis

The first week of the 1987 International School of Theatre Anthropology (ISTA) in the Salento region of Italy took place under the sign of *Faust*. Eugenio Barba brought together Eastern performers (Japanese and Indian dancers[1] and musicians) and (Western) spectator-participants in a collective response to *Faust*—especially Goethe's *Faust*, but also Marlowe's as well as the whole Western tradition of the popular character and myth. The work, which lasted five mornings from 6 to 10 A.M., was not supposed to lead to a finished performance nor was it to be presented to an audience outside the group. Was it then an exercise meant to explore a Western director's engagement with Indian and Japanese dancers? Or was it a Western production, however unfinished, which exhibited the characteristics of a mise-en-scene? I tend toward the second hypothesis, although Barba carefully sustained the ambiguity of his work and claimed rather to present a "work in progress" trying out the possibility of a Eurasian theatre.

In what follows, one of the participants—simultaneously judging and taking part and hence forever contaminated by ISTA and deprived of his cherished neutrality—offered the Bari roundtable[2] not so much a description of the "B.A. BA" of BA(r)BA method as a way of imagining how his work on *Faust* might be described with semiotic tools. The anecdotal circumstance of this *relazione* was once again the challenge to semiotics—issued by theatre anthropology—to give an account of the activity of the performers and the mise-en-scene. The (tactical) response to this kind of challenge consists in saying yet again: semiotics has no particular *use*; it is the artist who *makes use* of semiotics: let us merely describe this use by examining the *reelaboration* of Japanese and Indian gestural traditions through Barba's mise-en-scene.

If, as I have suggested elsewhere, every (especially linguistic) translation is an *appropriation* of the source culture by the target culture (Pavis forthcoming), we might say, by analogy, that Barba appropriates oriental performance traditions by transforming and "rewriting" them on the stage for a Western audience. We could then identify a series of appropriations: (1) semiotic, (2) ideological, (3) narratological (in the broad sense). Nonetheless, the term *appropriation* opens the way to an unfortunate misreading if it suggests that the Western director acts like a cultural imperialist *expropriating* (and destroying) oriental traditions, transforming them into Westernized by-products that no longer owe anything to their origins. In fact, the opposite is true: the *reelaboration* of gestural and choreographic materials within a new frame (the plot roughly adapted from *Faust*) by a "stage auteur"—the thoroughly Western notion of the director—for members of an audience accustomed to stage discourse in which meaning is produced especially for them. This neutralized but somewhat insipid term—*reelaboration*—only shows that the cultural and theatrical traditions of the source culture are transformed by the needs of the target culture's theatrical and cultural tradition, that of Barba and his target audience, in this case, the performers, directors, and theorists of ISTA.[3] We will follow the chain of gestural and cultural reelaborations and reinterpretations that punctuate this stage (re)writing of *Faust* with the hope of better understanding the links between cultures, practices, and theatre traditions as well as their confrontation within the mise-en-scene.

Preparation of the Materials

The choice of scenes in ISTA's *Faust* depended on the ISTA participants, who were also the only spectators of this *Faust*. Five or six teams of five or six members were each asked to reread Goethe's play, to summarize the actions, to choose key scenes centered on the kernel of these actions, and finally, to suggest a scenario that would start with simple situations in which the dialog played only an accessory role in the service of clearly defined stage actions. Barba then made selections from these collective written suggestions, without explaining his choice explicitly or implicitly. We can only note that Barba kept the suggestions of actions and concrete situations and rejected philosophical or psychological reflections and literary commentary. He did not seem to be interested in a global dramaturgical analysis or in the text a priori. He did not try to adapt the whole work or remain faithful to the letter or the spirit of the myth or to give it a totalizing, coherent, or consistent reading. He rather treated text and script suggestions as generators of situations and stage actions thematically linked to the plot of *Faust*.

This plot seems in many ways to be a myth that is profoundly and typically Western, and this will be my main hypothesis. As André Dabezies has shown, it has crystallized, from the 15th century legend to Goethe and beyond, the birth of individualism and individual freedom.[4] This evolution of the Faustian myth indicates the emergence of the individual from the familial, social, or national group, the birth of individualism and the aspiration to freedom and knowledge. What is most "Western" about Faust is perhaps not so much this division of being as the active search for knowledge by an individual who feels himself to be sufficiently strong and detached from the group to deal with the devil as an equal (and no longer with a god in his own image), and who sets out alone in search of truth. Confronted with this power of individualism, we would find it hard to imagine how Japanese (buyo) and Indian (odissi) dancers, both coming from national choreographic traditions that are rigidly codified, might particularize and individualize their performances to the point of breaking with their own tradition, of entering into a "gestural and cultural" dialog with each other, and above all, of formally reconstituting this individualist kernel of the Faustian myth. At ISTA, they first follow the instructions and themes of improvisations offered by Barba on the basis of their own traditions, while *incorporating* into their performances certain elements essential to the Faustian themes. Nonetheless, these dancers are well acquainted with Barba, having worked with him on and off for eight years. Their *Faust* improvisations thus take place in the intercultural context of ISTA and represent the continuation of an experiment begun with the first ISTA in Bonn in 1980. The activities of the Salento ISTA session are not new, except for the theme of *Faust*.

The Dancers' Incorporation

The Japanese dancer Katsuko Azuma and the Indian dancer Sanjukta Panigrahi belong to two totally different cultural and theatrical/choreographic worlds. It is difficult to link their arts and to do so would be a very Western simplification based on the facile magic of the term "oriental."[5] Getting these performers to work together is not self-evident, since the contrast in their presence, dynamic, and gestural representation is striking. Moreover, this "Faustian" project, to confront them while imposing the plot of *Faust,* is both perfectly arbitrary and completely legitimate, since it forces the dancers and their director/choreographer to adapt to a third term, to join their efforts in the construction of a story that remains to be invented.

It is difficult to describe the way in which each dancer organizes her improvisation based on the very general instructions given in English by Barba. These instructions are only suggestions for an action/improvisation on the basis of a concrete action, or for a narrative frame within which the

1. Faust (Katsuko Azuma, seated left) and Mephisto (Sanjukta Panigrahi, seated right) listen to the Ages of Human Life read the prolog of Goethe's Faust, *directed by Eugenio Barba, at the 1987 International School of Theatre Anthropology in Italy. (Photo by Tony D'Urso)*

2. *Faust refusing Mephisto's argument. (Photo by Tony D'Urso)*

interpreters can freely improvise. For example, Barba prompts Panigrahi (playing Mephisto) to approach Azuma from a distance, hiding behind trees, while waving her arms as if she wanted to attract Faust's attention. The assimilation of materials derived from *Faust* thus occurs through the dancing body and not through a psychological approach to character or a textual approach to the play. The choreography that develops is not intended to elucidate character or to illustrate various plot situations. The function of the dialog is not to explain character, nor even to be fully comprehensible.[6]

It is not easy to measure the distance between canonical odissi or buyo and the improvisations created by these dancers. Deviation from the codified traditional gestures does not seem to be a threat, but rather a consciously assumed risk.[7] The director's role, closer to Mephisto than to Faust, is essentially to provoke the "fall" of the oriental angel, and to destabilize the dancer, to unbalance her in the sense of imposing a gesture or series of gestures, an attitude foreign to the original codification. For example, Barba puts a glass bottle in Panigrahi's hands and asks her to do drunken—and therefore rhythmically distorted—mudras, to show the character's drunkenness. This process of voluntary *deformation* is immediately followed by *re-formation*, by moving to another type of codification. The dance of the drunken mudras becomes a parody of popular dance in which one dancer imitates the movements of the other, a joyful dance of two drunkards who end up synchronizing their drunkenness. This *de-formation* is not an elimination of the codified traditional form, but its *re-formation* into another kind of gesture, inspired by the tradition and which prepares for the next stages of the reelaboration.

3. Mephisto and Faust, flying in the air. (Photo by Tony D'Urso)

The dancer incorporates into her performance and traditional codification those "foreign bodies," gestures, and rhythms that she had automatically rejected. This appropriation is achieved by way of a sort of "gestural graft," which she must tolerate without rejection. As in the "Eurasian" village which Barba conjures up (1988), the performers (or a single male or female performer) not only analyze a conflict, are guided by the objectivity of the *logos,* telling a story, but also dance *with* and *within* it according to the *bios*, their lived traditions. The two dancers' appropriation/ incorporation of the *Faust* story is the first stage in the process of acculturation, the movement from Eastern encoding to Western decoding,[8] which turns out—as we shall see—to be recoding through the mise-en-scene. The dancers' improvisation constitutes the first shaping of the corporal materials, on the basis of which the mise-en-scene will effect a semiotic, ideological, narratological, and cultural reelaboration.

Concretely, what are the dancers doing? Panigrahi holds a bottle in her hands. She takes a few gulps, becomes drunk immediately. She staggers along, throws the bottle away, and attempts a few mudras which immediately seem uncertain and distorted by her intoxication. Azuma dogs her footsteps, imitating her, trying without much success to synchronize her gestures with Panigrahi's. They improvise a sort of *pas de deux*.

Semiotic Reelaboration: The Gestural Example

Semiotic reelaboration in the strict sense involves the mise-en-scene's manipulation of signs, which can be described and itself constitutes a set of pure semiotic operations. This claim will be tested briefly here.

1. MONTAGE

Barba juxtaposes two choreographic traditions in the idiosyncrasies of the two dancers. He does not impose continuity in the "gestural interaction." He does not try to give the illusion of a transition, sequence, or even a "dialogic interaction" (question/answer). As in film montage, each dancer's gestural sequence maintains its autonomy; it unfolds and is perceived at the same time as her partner's, without the continuity, coherence, or order that "speaking in turn" in speech or gesture would produce. According to Barba, a performer's gestures can be compared to film montage, which is itself "material for subsequent editing." The director edits the heterogeneous materials the performers have provided: "it is usually the director's work to combine the actions of several performers, whether in succession as though in response to each other, or in simultaneous presentation in which the meaning of both arises directly from their juxtaposition" (1985a:179). Linking these gestural moments to establish coherence and continuity is up to the spectators, who are obviously guided by the mise-en-scene.

This technique can be seen in the sequence in which Azuma (Faust) briefly recapitulates the entire Faustian problem of origins ("In the beginning was . . ."): (1) she digs up a book; (2) leafs through it without understanding; (3) mechanically reads aloud the author and title; (4) throws it away and moves to a completely different action. These actions are run together to give the impression of an accelerated film.

2. JUXTAPOSITION OF EMOTIONAL TONALITIES

The mise-en-scene not only juxtaposes the dancers and their sequences of gestures in montage, but also treats their gestural and emotional tonality in counterpoint, opening the gap and clearly differentiating their emotional worlds, displaying the absence of communication. In an extremely powerful scene, for example, we have Faust and Mephisto downstage, squatting face to face, unearthing the remains of a child, while behind them Margaret (played by the onnagata Kan-Ichi Hanayaghi) goes through a series of emotions and states of mind, which she (he) demonstrates by showing each

4. Faust and Mephisto dig up the remains of Margaret's murdered child. Margaret (Kan-Ichi Hanayaghi, seated behind) demonstrates a series of emotions through posture. (Photo by Tony D'Urso)

posture and its range of expressions (see plate 4). Three gestural keys, corresponding to three clearly distinct emotional tonalities, are thus presented "in the same shot." Plates 5 and 6, taken during an improvisation on madness, illustrate this spatial, temporal, and emotional juxtaposition.

The solitude of each character, the difference and originality of each, but also the similarities within the differences can be seen. The Danish actress Iben Nagel Rasmussen plays a Margaret who represents a consuming murderous madness, Azuma and Panigrahi repeat the same gestures (carrying and observing the child, perhaps) with finger positions and tensions both similar and different (plate 5). Individual improvisation sometimes leads to interaction and correlation: Kan-Ichi Hanayaghi's Margaret (plate 6) turns her back on Faust, but remains in earshot, while Faust directs her gaze to the child that Mephisto is carrying. The juxtaposition is sustained at particularly meaningful moments by its opposite, the interaction and the synchronization of emotion and gesture. The two dancers use little speech, but

5. & 6. During an improvisation on madness, performers illustrate distinct spatial, temporal, and emotional "language-body" responses. (Photo courtesy of Patrice Pavis)

incorporate memory in a long series of gestures. The language-body (*verbo-corps*)[9] of each dancer and each language-culture is very different. Japanese language-body gives the impression of meticulously stitching together restrained and internalized cries, while Indian language-body is fairly externalized ("audible lips," gesture underlining speech, stressing paralinguistic facial signs).

3. Focalization

Juxtaposing and coordinating gesture clearly reveals the mobility and fragility of the performers' relationship. Furthermore, the body is never exposed as the body of an individual (i.e., as an indivisible whole), but remains a mobile montage of its separate parts. Each dancer has the power to focus the spectator's gaze on the part of the body judged pertinent at any moment. This technique of foregrounding a meaning or a part of the work, a method much praised by the Russian formalists, leads to focalization, to the enlargement of a detail, to lengthening certain moments, to holding certain poses. Continual changes in focalization set up a narrative of the body, guiding reception by creating narrative continuity—despite the fragmentation of the foregrounded shots—cut off from the overall structure.

Focalization magnifies or underlines a detail, eliminates signs judged secondary or irrelevant at a given moment, expands or concentrates time at will, "dilates" or "contracts" the performer's body, ensures the hierarchical arrangement of signs in performance. This montage of gestural microactions makes sense only if it anticipates how spectators will *receive* the sequence (in the sense of receiving blows or caresses). We can see this focalization in Panigrahi's use of her hands. Her gaze, like that of her partner, is fixed on them. She uses her hands to distill the most obvious gestural variations, encouraging the spectator to make sense of these sequences.

4. Confrontation of Gestural Moments

The polarization of the roles of Mephisto and Faust and the clearly legible system of oppositions establish a hierarchy of signs. The casting is certainly not an accident, but Barba has not to my knowledge explained it, assuming perhaps that it is self-evident. The casting inscribes oppositions for the spectator:

***Mephisto* (Panigrahi)**	***Faust* (Azuma)**
large	small
mobile	hieratic
comes from outside	already there
ease	obstruction
openness	closure
expressive face and arms	expressive bust and poses
activity	passivity
Western masculine principle	Western feminine principle

Comparing these two kinds of gestures and codifications can be done only by way of a third point of view that borrows from neither one nor the other, or from a referential system that seeks universality, a Western obsession. In this search for transcultural categories, can we locate ourselves in what Barba calls the "pre-expressive" (see Barba 1985b)?

We might rather say that we are faced with a narrative model, thoroughly influenced by a Western ideological and cultural model. The opposition and the heterogeneity of gestural moments take on a dramaturgical significance that corresponds more or less to the traditional Western image of the Faustian myth (from Marlowe and Goethe to Murnau and Valéry). Mephisto appears as the foreign element, disturbing and tempting, dominant and seductive, whereas Faust is linked to immobility and the hearth, to the passivity of a seduced victim: a stereotypical Western opposition between masculinity and femininity, which makes of this couple of men (in the traditional *Faust*), or women (in this mise-en-scene), a homo-, a-, or pansexual couple (whose sexuality is bracketed or elevated to the level of a universal principle). Thus it is possible to "tell" this gestural dichotomy and gestural dialog by bringing them together in a plot or anecdote, by projecting onto the plot the oppositions perceived on the level of formal and gestural rhythm. But isn't this a Western view? Indeed, but of course we judge Barba's experiment according to our narrative habits that encourage us to "translate" the performers into dramatic characters, then to compare and contrast these characters according to sex, age, activity, and individual traits. The theatrical and choreographic codification here shifts to another much more subtle and implicit codification, that of culture, in which ideology is one component among many.

It is certainly artificial to set up an opposition between East and West and yet separate the Japanese from the Indian tradition. Let us note simply that, in Panigrahi's performance, due to its expressiveness in mime and attitude and its emotional externalization, the Indian tradition seems closer to the West than does the Japanese, and thus appears more "legible" to a Western audience. In other words, Mephisto is the Western face of Faust, the one who questions and provokes the entirely Eastern interiority of his consenting victim.[10]

5. Cultural Dichotomy of Gestural Moments

This differentiation between Japanese and Indian cultures is nonetheless reduced as soon as we contrast them with the tradition of Faust. Faust is an archetypal Western Christian character, the fundamental figure of *streben*, "striving towards," of elevation and the torturous quest, the original principle of dialog and conflict and of the division of the soul. The conflict in Faust's character, induced by the devil himself, is difficult to transpose into a Japanese theatrical tradition which does not recognize Western categories of psychology and does not represent inner conflict choreographically by elevation, the rising movement of humanity and the soul toward God. As Moriaki Watanabe notes, the Japanese tradition is rooted in the ground, in the earth: it is a kind of celestial power which descends to earth and stays there for a while, whose energy human beings would like to capture (1982).

ISTA's *Faust* offers us a perfect illustration of the principle mentioned by Watanabe. Azuma "plays" a Faust who is barely mobile and whose only gestural ventures are revolts that are quickly suppressed. On the contrary, Panigrahi never stops moving, advancing or retreating, constantly changing her center of gravity, directing her piercing gaze at the other. In this sense, the inversion of signs produced by Azuma, tied to the ground by the powerful forces of the earth and by a rising, airborne Mephisto, is as remarkable as the global inversion of the Western myth of *Faust* in a choreography rooted in the earth by Japanese buyo. Paradoxically, the Indian tradition and Barba's mise-en-scene are allied in restoring to *Faust* some of its Westernness.

Which Semiotics?

Semiotics has some difficulty in describing this fragment of *Faust* since it has not really decided whether to judge by the results of this acculturation-recodification that Barba and the dancers propose or the dynamic process of appearance and disappearance of these same codifications. In other words, it has to choose between a Western semiotics following St. Thomas, which believes only what it sees, or an "energetic" semiotics (as Jean-Francois Lyotard would say) that attempts to "produce the greatest intensity (by excess or default) of what is there without intention" (1973:104), that is, to imagine the direction of choreographic and cultural reinterpretation of the signs which are themselves only the superficial traces, the discarded skin of a vanished snake. We ought to imagine this energetic semiotics that Barba and Lyotard dream of, a semiotics that would concern itself not with results and visible signs, but with the cultural reinterpretation in which we can still see the old under the new, like the "rough sketching which indicates traces of other movements and features all around the fully worked-out figure" (Brecht 1964:191). Like the traces in which one sees both what has just been expropriated and what is appropriated, deculturation as well as acculturation. In order to read this kind of semiotics, one would have to be an "ideal" spectator, who should be, according to Barba, capable of following or accompanying the performer in the dance of "thinking in action": a moving subject par excellence who has to describe an evolving object. This is perhaps the new challenge to semiotics: to shift perspective on an object itself in motion without giving up the notion of sign and pertinence but allowing sufficient play and fluctuation.

Western semiotics is naturally aware of this principle of concatenation, of the syntagmatic and metonymic organization of signs. But it ought to become a little "oriental" and try to understand the simultaneous actions, their paradigmatic and metaphorical organization. Ideally, semiotics ought to follow this "thinking in action," and the theorist, like Barba's ideal spectator, ought to be able to "follow or accompany the performer in the dance of thinking in action" (Barba 1988:129). Semiotics ought to be able not only to pin down the already perceived meaning, but also to anticipate its *direction*, to imagine what Indian theatre theory calls the spectator's *nritya*, what Panigrahi herself calls "the combination of dance and emotional expression accompanied by meaningful gestures, modes of speech or a lyric poem. It is so carefully wrought, so perfect, that it is enough to keep the spectators alert and able to follow all the unexpressed thoughts and the conception of a character" (1983:87).

This "energetic semiotics" would no longer have to recognize and describe the pertinent features of a sign—as is still the case in Western semiotics—but rather would hide and reveal signs in the same moment and the same movement of denegation.

7. Barba watching Panigrahi and Azuma enact the scene with the knife "in the cathartic register of a theatre of cruelty." (Photo courtesy of Patrice Pavis)

Ideological Reelaboration

The semiotic control and reelaboration of gestural moments by the mise-en-scene are so clear only because they correspond to certain familiar ideological-emotional categories of the Western audience—namely that human action, motivation, and comprehension must be easily understood, identified, and accepted. The action of Barba's *Faust* conforms to the spectators' horizon of expectation. This often leads to a universalizing of values and gestures, which translates sometimes into a humanist universalizing of diverse cultures and sometimes into a uniformity induced by the combined effect of simplification and the influence of technology and mass media.[11]

1. Pathos

Certain situations are particularly apt to generate pity and terror, the good old categories of Aristotelian tragedy. For instance, exhuming all that remains of the child, the swaddling clothes that Mephisto slowly unearths with malicious pleasure. Barba prolongs this scene by slowing down its rhythm and accompanying it with melodramatic music composed by Jan Ferslev for guitar, flute, and four female voices situated behind the performance area. In the background, Margaret's emotional reaction. Barba creates pathos that must deeply touch every spectator. In the same spirit, the scene with the knife (plate 7) is played in the cathartic register of a theatre of cruelty, which clearly appears, even in Artaud's rebellion, as the culmination of the entire Western tradition.

2. Melodrama

The systematic and insistent expression of universal feelings (fear, despair, suffering, sense of injustice, etc.) relates to the technique of emotional manipulation characteristic of melodrama. This is reminiscent of Friedrich Murnau's magnificent silent film of *Faust* which also makes abundant use of universal feelings, pauses, and poses of joy and despair, playing on all the nuances of melodrama. Barba uses Western music to underline the melodramatic atmosphere of the text, which highlights in an altogether different way a text as crude and grotesque as the ballad of Margarethe (*"Meine Mutter, die Hur, die mich umgebracht hat!"* ["My mother, the whore, who killed me!"]). To the extent that melodrama was a typical form of Western theatre in the 18th and 19th centuries, it is not surprising that it works especially well for the re-Westernization of the Faustian myth.

3. Burlesque

On the other hand, several scenes employ burlesque: Faust's and Mephisto's drunkenness for example. The pact with the Devil is celebrated in an unconventional and sympathetic way—by getting the signatories roaring drunk. This turn of the drunken lurching actor is one seen a hundred times in popular comedy or silent film. It gives the immediate and sensual pleasure of recognizing a dramatic type. It is also the pleasure, almost relief, of seeing the drunken and suddenly uncontrolled bodies of the dancers, freed of constraints, codification, and prohibitions, very similar to those of Western spectators; these bodies are provisionally at the mercy of physiology, since alcohol has no bounds. But the bodies remain full of culture, since one lurches differently if one has received the gestural education of odissi or buyo.

Ideological adaptation in this *Faust* does not occur by neutralizing formal or philosophical options of theatre traditions, nor through praising some virtue of the Western soul, but rather through fine-tuning some great universal feelings, by appealing to fundamental categories of reception (pity, terror, comedy, melodrama). The function of this adaptation is to erode codified theatrical or choreographic forms that are too specifically honed to single cultures and performance traditions, the better to adapt to the audience's universalizing demands. Thus, the human and dramatic situation becomes immediately comprehensible, without the mediation of the artistic codes of specific theatrical forms. This flattening is the price paid for the spectator's comfortable reception of what Barba calls the pre-expressive, what we could also call a psychologizing ideology of the universal.

The semiotic and ideological reinterpretation of this *Faust* improvised by Azuma and Panigrahi can be particularly clearly seen in the way Barba chooses to *tell* the story, and one can see the gestural and rhythmic narrative as the backbone of the mise-en-scene and thus speak of a complete narratological restructuring.

Narratological Reelaboration

This narratological restructuring takes place in the wings, as it were, since there are two significant absences at ISTA: the erotic body and structural narratology (and if you had seen our long, undivided dormitory, you would understand that we had no desire to practice structural narratology). Barba does not appear to pose the question of narrative in his writings: is there a universal, transcultural way of telling stories or are there on the contrary narrative techniques peculiar to each cultural tradition? There is furthermore a danger, which neither Barba nor Grotowski escape, of limiting narrative to logos, instead of seeing narrative as a structural principle, which manifests itself in several substances (verbal language, gestural moments, painting, cinema, etc.). For example, Grotowski opposes *logos* to *bios*, instead of envisaging them as parallel ways of telling (*lexis*), whether verbal or gestural:

> We have *logos* and *bios; logos* is linked to descriptive and analytical discourse. In a different way, the problem of *logos* even arises in the case of the Eastern performer. In that tradition, the Eastern performer uses his or her body to express words, sentences, discourses, i.e., logos. But it is as if this *logos* has, because of the performer's strong tradition, retained certain principles of *bios;* for this reason, the Eastern performer seems alive to us (Grotowski 1982:56).[12]

It is questionable to assert, as does Grotowski, that the body of the Eastern performer expresses words, i.e., logos, even if the performers, especially in kathakali, do indeed have at their disposal a repertory of signs—mudras—referring to objects in the real world and if they tell their story according to an implicit sentence, which specialists can practically "hear" as they follow the performers' hand movements. The kathakali actor offers a gestural narration, a story told not with words (logos), but with gestural narrative units, which can certainly be identified or described with words, but are not themselves words (logos).

In Barba's professional, Eurasian "village," it often occurs that:

> [. . .] the actors (or a single actor) not only analyze a conflict, let themselves be guided by the objectivity of the logos, and tell a story, but dance *in* it and *with* it according to the growth of the bios. This is not a metaphor: concretely, it means that the actor does not remain yoked to the plot, does not interpret a text, but *creates a context*, moves around and within the events (Barba 1988:129).

Barba also takes up the opposition between logos and bios, mistakenly limiting the story told to verbal language (logos), but at the same time he attempts to overcome this opposition. The dance *with* and *within* the story redefines the relationship between the "physical" performer and the spoken text. One is not reduced to the other, but they form the "dance," an interaction between what the performer does with gesture and what the text says. The performer should not reduce or interpret the text, but rather invent (together with the director and the mise-en-scene as a whole) a situation within which the text makes sense.

Once this model has been established, it is easier to understand how Barba reappropriates the (Western) myth of *Faust* using the improvised material that the dancers provide. He transposes the original microstructures of buyo and odissi into a gestural and narrative macrostructure. This narratological retotalization is not, however, an adaptation in the Western sense. Barba does not feel obliged to restore the proportions and complexity of Goethe's text. He does not start from a global outline of the play or a preconceived idea or Brechtian dramaturgical analysis. He treats *Faust* rather like an argument for a ballet or a possible story.

1. From Micro- to Macrostructures

Buyo and odissi use gestures to tell stories. The gestural narrative is made up of a very large number of microsequences, each of which corresponds to an episode or a detail of the story. Only specialists can analyze, identify, and paraphrase these codified microsequences. We do not need to

8. Mephisto tempting Faust. Barba treats Faust *"rather like an argument for a ballet." (Photo by Tony D'Urso)*

recognize them, however, in order to appreciate the dances. As director and reorganizer of these microsequences, Barba has to take the ignorance of his Western audience into account.

On the other hand, in the Western tradition, meaning is not established analytically from myriad gestures and codified episodes, but from a narrative macrosequence which sums up a whole scene or even the whole play. Brecht, for example, bases his mise-en-scene on a search for the fundamental *gestus* of key scenes, "extracting" the story of the play, i.e., "the theatre's great operation, the complete fitting together of all the gestic incidents, embracing the communications and impulses that must now go to make up the audience's entertainment" (Brecht 1964:200). The gestus is a synthetic narrative macrostructure that includes a long series of episodes, but can be divided up only a posteriori, once one examines the actions in detail.

In his reelaboration of *Faust*, Barba indeed uses materials available to him through the dancers' improvisations, but he edits and integrates them into a larger structure: a situation, a scene, or a gest. He had advised the "scenario writers" not to enslave themselves to the letter of Goethe's text, but rather to suggest global actantial narrative situations, broad frames in which action and situation would be clearly readable. Once Barba had selected and defined the general narrative framework, the dancers could concentrate on inventing and fixing the details of plot and text. Due to this synthetic procedure, in the adaptation as in the performance options, the dancers and then the spectators can normally and easily identify the overall situations and the unfolding of the narrative as the dancers inscribe the detail of their improvisation within the broad and firm framework of the narrative macrosequences. Barba's narratological appropriation thus involves restructuring the analytical, gestural codification into a narrative macrostructure with large units dissociating, in the mise-en-scene as well as in the spectator's mind, the analytic and coded reading of word and gesture from the global reading of the story. Because the adaptation and the mise-en-scene propose large units of situation and action, the spectator succeeds in locating and *linking* (as well as *reading*) [*lier/lire*] the episodes of *Faust*'s story. Inevitably, this process involves some simplification, since each tradition must adapt to the other and can only enter into dialog with the other if it simplifies its narrative arguments.

2. A Classical Narratology

This dissociation of narrative macrostructure and gestural microsequences is reinforced by Barba's narratological model. His model is binary, transitive, active, and thus classical in its simplicity. It is of the type: Subject + Verb + Direct Object.

Paul eats an apple
Faust sells his soul
Faust loves Margaret
Barba likes ISTA

The actants can be easily identified and are engaged in a simple action in which the one influences the other actively and directly. Modeling (which influences action) or metatextual reflections are avoided or postponed or reduced to some microsequences, without losing overall legibility. Everything abstract, intellectualized, or diluted by philosophical commentary is eliminated in the interests of concrete and univocal action. The suggestion of our group to adapt the passage in Goethe in which the issue is knowing what came first—the word, meaning, power, or action—a key passage for the philosophy of the work—is concentrated in a few seconds and "translated" into a visible and explicit action: Azuma holds a copy of *Faust*, mechanically reads everything written on the cover, and then throws the book away—a very explicit way to get rid of the text's philological subtleties and to translate Goethe's lucubrations by a series of actions.

Exit the Book!

3. From Epic to Dramatic

The Western macrostructural narrative logic efficiently compensates for the partial unreadability of the traditional Eastern microstructures. Dancing according to their traditions, Azuma and Panigrahi speak with their bodies: *the story is told in an epic fashion by the dancers' actual bodies.* They do so by focusing on the details of their facial expressions or postures.

On the contrary, classical Western narrative logic, which Barba imposes through the improvisations, infiltrates and restructures the material according to an encompassing dramatic action conveyed by the two actants: *the story is acted out in a dramatic fashion by the characters' fictional bodies.*

4. Labeling Meaning

The narratological transfer brought about by Barba is possible only to the extent that spectators are in a position to identify and differentiate the units of the narrative. The choice of the title *Faust* immediately suggests to a knowing spectator certain themes, actions, and characters, which are more or less recognized and confirmed. Western culture functions by labeling, naming, appraising.

5. Western Subtitles

Labeling would still not be enough to guarantee an approximate deciphering of the story of *Faust*. What is necessary is some kind of subtitling, as in a silent or foreign film. The words pronounced in Italian (by Cesare Brie) clarify the Sanskrit or classical Japanese. The German choir or the cries of "Heinrich" function as intermediaries, "fixing" meaning as indices open to the intelligence and the culture of ISTA's Western audience. The subtitles complete the narratological reelaboration and Western adaptation of the choreography inspired by *Faust*.

Cultural Reelaboration

Does the conjunction of semiotic, ideological, and narratological reelaboration suffice to describe and explain the genesis as well as the reading of this *Faust* montage? An analysis would not be complete without examining the overall view of the director who takes up and synthesizes a certain number of typical cultural practices of Western mise-en-scene (see Pavis 1988).

1. The Unifying Subject

It is the director's responsibility to select and edit the improvisations. As the stage *auteur* "signing" the production, Barba does not have to justify his choices other than by way of a subjective search for expressiveness, coherence, and formal clarification, a search which never completely reveals its own logic. The mise-en-scene is the site on which bricolage becomes structural. Western mise-en-scene—and thus the appearance of a third party, the director, alongside author and actor—is linked to the historical development of Western culture: the decline of classical performance traditions, the disappearance of a strong form, the culmination of a bourgeois individualistic tradition, the formation of a theory of the subject and the author, in this instance the stage subject (a theory which, barely constituted, explodes under the pressure of Marxist and psychoanalytical deconstruction).

The director's cultural reelaboration of these Faustian fragments is indispensable if this Italian-German-Indian-Japanese encounter is not to produce the most volatile mix. Here Barba is both a conflicting subject (preserving the diversity of forms proposed by the dancers) and a unifying subject (bringing all these centripetal forces back to the Western story of *Faust*). His *Faust* returns finally to its point of departure: a Western vision conveyed by Eastern traditions reworked by a Western director ending up with a sketch which bears all the distinguishing features of Western mise-en-scene.

2. A Metacultural Vision

This unification is realized also by the neutralization of one theatrical and cultural tradition by another, by the discovery of transcultural values, by "the constant factor in cultural variation" (Grotowski 1982:56). These transcultural values are very general: quest (Faust), temptation (Mephisto), fall (Margaret), melodramatic sentiments. The neutralization is also achieved by frequent parodies of one codification by another—for example, when Azuma/Faust drunkenly attempts mudras imitating Panigrahi/Mephisto. The parody of one form by another implies the ability to imitate, but above all to quote, rewrite, in short, to appropriate. This parody can easily become metatextual, since it implies a reflection on forms and the means of surpassing them. As Juri Lotman remarks, the "twentieth century has produced not only scientific metalanguages, but also metaliterature and metapainting, and is now apparently creating metaculture, a metalinguistic system to the second degree that encompasses everything" (Lotman and Uspensky 1978:229). For this kind of activity we need a *meta*cultural (and not simply *trans*cultural) vision that could confront forms and dramaturgies. Parody does not exclude interaction between the parodist and her/his object; it reveals their mutual influence. In the above mentioned example (see plate 7) of the semantic opposition between Panigrahi/Mephisto's externalized and aggressive and Azuma/Faust's internalized and passive gestures, for instance, we can observe the interaction between each dancer's gaze. The more Panigrahi is present in her gaze, the more Azuma internalizes her gaze, her suffering, her body, the more she reduces her movements, giving way to the demon tempter.

Their interaction and the "montage by attraction" that Barba establishes do not amount to a simple semiotic or narratological operation. They engage an entire ideology and culture as a montage of antagonistic forces. They also bear witness to Barba's refusal to completely *expropriate* "foreign" theatre codification and his determination to maintain cultural "transparency," i.e., to let cultures be seen through cultures. There is always a double displacement of the Japanese or Indian source culture. Barba's Western spectator must see, on the one hand, that these cultures are foreign (easy enough), but on the other hand that these cultures diverge from their usual codification and norms as a result of the work of the mise-en-scene. The codes of oriental theatre appear both as foreign and as displaced in our direction. Awareness of *difference* remains intact. This confrontation never results in ideological or transcultural uniformity, but is rather a relativizing practice conducted by the actual spectators discussed by Barba, who, East or West, are few in number, but "for whom theatre may become a necessity." For such spectators, Barba adds:

> [T]heatre is a relationship, which neither establishes a union, nor creates a communion, but ritualizes the reciprocal strangeness and the laceration of the social body hidden beneath the uniform skin of dead myth and values (1988:130).

Does Barba get to a "Eurasian theatre" at the end of this *Faust?* The term is not without ambiguity and contradiction. That is in fact its raison d'être. But can we go beyond Barba's observation that "In the meeting between East and West, seduction, imitation, and exchange are reciprocal" (1988:127)? It is almost impossible to think the "inter" in the "intercultural," except in terms of concentric metaphors—exchange, sharing, contact, barter, revitalization, appropriation—a stealthy imperialism that has swapped the gun for theatre interculturalism? The danger certainly exists, but isn't there something a little ridiculous and demogogical in the concern of someone like Rastom Bharucha (1984) who warns intercultural directors not to exploit "donor" countries by appropriating their substance like cunning Western vampires, when these artists make the effort not to reduce one culture to another, while assembling the theoretical and metacultural bridges that allow us to observe a give-and-take between them, when Japanese and Indian cultures have abundantly drawn from the Western technology for better or worse? How can we reproach Barba, for example, for having reelaborated a Western vision and mise-en-scene of *Faust* when we easily accept the idea that the dancers help themselves without reservation to the argument and the materiality, the letter and the spirit, of "our" *Faust?* Doesn't the value of this intercultural mise-en-scene lie in the way it confronts oriental codification and choreography and the typically Western organization of mise-en-scene? The conflict is still intact.

"Zwei Seelen wohnen, ach! in meiner Brust" (Two souls, alas, are housed within my breast) lamented old Faust. But if he had known that his breast would one day be a theatre of interculturalism, God knows whether he would have agreed to sign a contract with the Devil!

—*Translated by Loren Kruger*

9. Faust and Margaret. The codes of oriental theatre appear both as foreign and as intact. (Photo by Tony D'Urso)

Notes

1. I will not discuss the question of defining the performers here as actors or dancers. The distinction is far from being as distinct in Japan or India as it is in Europe: I prefer the term "dancer" as a way of focusing on the very gestural codification of the performers. Deciding whether this is a theatrical dance (using speech) or a theatre codified like choreography is not very important. *[Translator's Note: The English term "performer" provides the semantic suppleness that the French chases after here; I have therefore translated* "acteur" *and* "actrice" *as "performer."]*
2. "Primo Incontro Internazionale fra Semiologia e Antropologia Teatrale" [First International Convention of Semiotics and Theatre Anthropology], Bari, Italy, 12 September 1987. The Odin Teatret has a video of the rehearsals, made by Italian television.
3. Barba likes to speak of a "new elaboration," borrowing Richard Schechner's term, "restored behavior": restored behavior is a living action treated as a filmmaker treats a sequence on film. Each sequence has to be edited and reconstructed. It is independent of the set of causes (social, psychological, technological), which have given it birth. It is behavior in its own right *[un comportement propre]*. The original truth or intention of this action may be lost, unknown, or hidden, engendered or deformed by the myth constituting the initial materials of a process, used in the course of rehearsals to get a new elaboration, the performance itself; these visual sequences of the action are no longer processes, but rather objects, materials" (Barba 1985a:179; see Schechner 1985:35–116).
4. Dabezies identifies three stages and variants of the Faustian myth. (1) "The Christian myth of sin and the risks of freedom"; (2) "the risks of greatness and freedom," of the "quasi-metaphysical aspiration to the infinite and the ideal"; (3) "triumphal freedom," which culminates in the view that Oswald Spengler offers of Faustian man, "the mythic figure of the West as a whole" in *The Decline of the West* (Dabezies 1972:312–16).
5. "The popular slogans about individualism and realism in the West opposed to the mass mentality and mysticism in the East reveal their absurdity as soon as we analyze them seriously" (Goetz 1960:3). Likewise, to speak of "oriental theatre" (as Artaud does in his essay "Occidental and Oriental Theatre" [1958]) can be a source of simplification.
6. To quote Artaud: "Furthermore, I am well aware that the language of gestures and postures, dance and music, is less capable of analyzing a character, revealing thoughts, or elucidating states of consciousness clearly and precisely than is verbal language, but whoever said that the theatre was created to analyze a character, to resolve the conflicts of love and duty, to wrestle with all the problems of a topical and psychological nature that monopolize the contemporary stage?" (1958:41 [translation modified]).
7. Panigrahi created her dances from the songs written in another language in her native region, Orissa. Her work at ISTA gave her the opportunity to expand her repertory: "I asked Barba if I might work with him to discover new possibilities. I do not believe that this work could threaten my traditions. If that were the case, I would stop at once" (1982:68).
8. Barba describes his "good advice" for Western and Eastern actors in the following way: "Contemporary Western actors have no organic repertory of advice on which they can rely and on the basis of which they orient themselves. In general, their point of departure is a text or the director's instructions. They lack these rules governing action, which would aid them without constraining their artistic freedom. Traditional Eastern actors, on the other hand, base their work on an organic and tested body of 'absolute advice,' that is, rules similar to the laws of a code. They codify a self-enclosed style of action to which every actor of that genre must conform" (Barba and Savarese 1985:4).
9. For the notion of "language-body" see my essay "On the Specificity of Theatre Translation" (forthcoming).
10. The Japanese director, Moriaki Watanabe, notes that Sanjukta Panigrahi's dance appears close to Western art: "If Sanjukta's demonstration seems strange to you

Westerners, from the Japanese perspective, there are many things in her performance that are closer to Western art, based on her way of codifying the performance, similar to your ballet. In the four traditions of Eastern theatre [Indian, Japanese, Balinese, and Chinese], there are common elements, but also great differences. Indian dance's proximity to Western dance, for example, can be seen in Béjart's ballets, such as *Le Sacre du Printemps* that makes good use of Indian techniques (the Tribhanga, for example); but when Béjart imitates Japanese dance, the result is catastrophic" (Watanabe and Ruffini 1982:59).

11. Marcel Mauss, in his presentation at the Première Semaine Internationale de Synthèses, *Civilisation, le mot et l'idée,* identified progress as a "general acquisition by societies and civilizations" (1930:478) and an "increasing uniformity of civilizations" (481).

> Just as, at the national level, science, industry, art, even "distinction," are no longer the exclusive patrimony of a minority and become, in the major nations, a sort of common privilege, the best features of these civilizations will become the common property of more and more social groups" (478).

> It certainly seems that we are heading towards increasing uniformity in civilization. Cinema is one of the instruments: from one end of the world to the other, filmic mimicry and scenes exercise a suggestive power, encouraging imitation (481).

Mauss wrote this in 1929 during the era of silent film, which tended to emphasize mimic expression and which had not yet invaded and Westernized the world. Thus he observed that this growing tendency to uniformity had not yet reached Japan: "Nonetheless, Japan appears immune to our Western films and vice versa. For Japanese laugh at scenes that make us cry and conversely" (1930:481).

12. For a thorough discussion of the relationship between body and language in Grotowski see Michel Bernard (1976).

References

Artaud, Antonin
1958 *The Theater and Its Double.* Translated by Mary Collin Richards. New York: Grove Press.

Barba, Eugenio
1985a "Montage." In *Anatomie de l'acteur* by Eugenio Barba and Nicola Savarese, 177–85. Cazilhac: Bouffonneries Contrastes.
1985b *Beyond the Floating Islands.* New York: PAJ Publications.
1988 "Eurasian Theatre." Translated by Richard Fowler. *The Drama Review* 32, no. 3 (T119):126–30.

Barba, Eugenio, and Nicola Savarese
1985 *Anatomie de l'acteur.* Cazilhac: Bouffonneries Contrastes.

Bernard, Michel
1976 *L'Expressivité du corps.* Paris: J-P Delarge.

Bharucha, Rastom
1984 "A Collision of Cultures: Some Western Interpretations of the Indian Theatre." *Asian Theatre Journal* 1, no. 1 (Spring):1–20.

Brecht, Bertolt
1977 [1964] "A Short Organum for the Theatre." In *Brecht on Theatre,* translated by John Willet, 179–205. New York: Hill and Wang.

Dabezies, André
1972 *Le Mythe de Faust.* Paris: Armand Colin.

Goetz, Herman
1960 *Inde—Cinq Millénaires d'art.* Paris: Albin Michel.

Grotowski, Jerzy
1982 "Lois pragmatiques: Entretien avec Jerzy Grotowski par Franco Ruffini." *Bouffonneries* 4:53–56.

Lotman, Juri, and Boris Uspensky
1978 "On the Semiotic Mechanism of Culture." *New Literary History* 9 (no. 2).

Lyotard, Jean-François
1973 "La dent, la paume." In *Des Dispositifs pulsionnels,* 95–104. Paris: UGE.

Mauss, Marcel
1930 *Civilisation, le mot et l'idée*. Paris: La Renaissance du livre. Reprinted as "Representations collectives et diversite des civilisations" in *Oeuvres,* vol. II. Paris: Editions de Minuit. 1969.

Panigrahi, Sanjukta
1982 "Interview with Sanjukta Panigrahi." *Bouffonneries* 4.
1983 "La danse Odissi." *Bouffonneries* 9:83–94.

Pavis, Patrice
1988 "Du texte à la scène, un enfantement difficile." *Théâtre public* 79:27–35.
forthcoming "On the Specificity of Theatre Translation." In *The Play out of Context,* edited by Hanna Scolnikov and Peter Holland, translated by Loren Kruger. Cambridge: Cambridge University Press.

Schechner, Richard
1985 *Between Theater and Anthropology*. Philadelphia: University of Pennsylvania Press.

Watanabe, Moriaki, and Franco Ruffini
1982 "Entre l'Orient et l'Occident. Entretien avec Moriaki Watanabe et Franco Ruffini." *Bouffonneries* 4:57–61.

***Patrice Pavis** is Head of the Drama Department at the University of Paris VIII. He is author of* Languages of the Stage, Dictionnaire du théâtre, Le théâtre au coroisement des cultures *(forthcoming).*

In Defense of the Discourse

Materialist Feminism, Postmodernism, Poststructuralism . . . and Theory

Jill Dolan

Ten years ago feminist theatre and performance criticism was something of an oxymoron. Like most avowedly political criticism, feminist work in the late 1970s and early '80s seemed caught in conflicting demands of aesthetics and ideology. Feminist critics of feminist work teetered uneasily among the desires to support women's production efforts, to investigate the ramifications of an unprecedented switch in gender perspective, and to compare women's theatre and performance with an aesthetic standard that had not yet been formulated. Critics writing for feminist presses usually chose to validate what they saw; those writing in academic venues generally took a sociological approach to theatre's reflection of women's social roles. The bulk of the critical effort was aimed toward redressing the historical invisibility of women in the field.[1]

When French theory began to find its way across the Atlantic it changed the contours of feminist criticism in the academy. Isabelle de Courtivron and Elaine Marks published their landmark anthology *New French Feminisms* in 1981, and suddenly gave American feminist criticism a whole new vocabulary and new territories to cover. Heléne Cixous, Luce Irigaray, and Julia Kristeva, among others, seemed powerful and poetic in their descriptions of female sexuality as a subversive, antipatriarchal textuality. If women could write with their bodies, as *l'écriture féminine*'s florid manifestos proposed, could the body also be a site of a new theatre practice and textual analysis? Could the French feminist pantheon's borrowings from Jacques Derrida and Jacques Lacan give feminist theatre and performance critics new tools for describing the field?

American feminist criticism in the '80s has also been shaped by the field of cultural studies. The influx of British materialism, with its focus on ideology formation in representation, has allowed critics to dig deeper, farther, and wider in the investigation of representation as an ideological apparatus with an active role in preserving social arrangements. The materialist approach has moved academic feminist criticism away from sociological analysis based on assumptions that theatre serves a mimetic function for the culture, into an analysis of representation as a site for the production of cultural meanings that perpetuate conservative gender roles. Where sociological criticism considers theatre as a mirror of positive or negative social images, the materialist emphasis on representation as a producer of meaning also takes into account the reception and interpretation of cultural signs by spectators differentiated by gender, race, class, and sexual preference.

Deconstruction, poststructuralism, psychoanalysis, and materialism often appear to be unlikely traveling companions along the critical terrain, but if nothing else, they have prompted an increased focus on theory over sociology. Feminist theatre and performance criticism, as a result, has arrived at the end of the decade with its contours shaped roughly by three different analytical methods based in divergent ideologies: (1) a liberal feminist insistence on traditional criticism that supports the play as the basis of the dramatic experience; (2) a radical (sometimes called "cultural") feminist reification of theatre as a mimesis that can validate women's identities; and (3) a materialist feminist approach to theatre and performance as ideologically marked representation, an approach which borrows variously from psychoanalysis, poststructuralism, and Marxist criticism.

These three approaches to feminist theatre and performance criticism have recently been at odds. At the Women and Theatre Program's (WTP) annual preconferences, liberal and radical feminist critics and practitioners have butted against materialist theorists' methods and ideologies. Poststructuralism, especially, seems to challenge many long-held theatrical assumptions that some liberal and radical feminists aren't eager to release. The heralded "death of the author" (Barthes 1977) displaces the playwright's primacy and locates the responsibility for producing meaning in the hermeneutic sphere. The traditional triumvirate of playwright-director-actor has been disrupted by the spectator's insertion into the paradigm as an active participant in the production of meaning.

Author's intent has become suspect or irrelevant; the director's authority challenged; and the actor's position as manipulable object traded for one of resistance. Poststructuralism's sacrilege, according to those who deplore its theory, is its unwillingness to idolize the text and its insistence on the shifting, historical nature of the meanings representation produces.

Poststructuralist theory threatens what some see as feminist criticism's role in validating women's identities in performance. The issue of identity is particularly vital in theatre, which has historically solicited its responses based on empathetic identification techniques. The larger struggle in feminism over how to reconcile its conflicting theories of identity and the self, then, is particularly urgent in theatre and performance.

Poststructuralism Versus Identity Politics

Over the last several years, the popularity of poststructuralism and the prevalence of identity politics in feminism has prompted the development of opposing feminist theories of the self. Identity politics claims to define women's subjectivity by their positions within race, class, or sexuality, positions which the dominant culture—and often, the dominating voices in feminism—have effectively squelched. Poststructuralist practice suggests that any such coherent conceptions of identity are specious since even race, class, and sexuality, as well as gender, are constructed within discursive fields and changeable within the flux of history. According to poststructuralism, subjectivity is never monolithic or fixed, but decentered, and constantly thrown into process by the very competing discourses through which identity might be claimed.

These opposing feminist camps base their arguments on definitions of experience, as the old slogan "the personal is political" comes back to haunt in unexpected ways. Feminism at this historical moment seems caught between reifying experience as truth, and proclaiming that although experience does dictate a certain material reality, it's a reality necessarily constructed in relation to social ideology and cannot be the basis of any fixed objective truth.

The two camps split on the issue of identity. Radical feminists propose that female identity is coherent and whole, and defined in opposition to male identity. The politics that stem from this position carve out a place in gender, race, and class that is solipsistically unified and that elides the differences within and between women. Radical feminist performance texts, as Elin Diamond has written, tend to romanticize female identity by assuming that a transcendent female self can be mirrored in "woman-identified" theatre (1985).

Asserting a ground of experience from which to theorize feminism is not romanticized or totalized under materialist feminist analysis, which borrows some of its tenets from poststructuralism. Teresa de Lauretis, for instance, cautions that the assertion of identity is not the goal, as it is in feminist identity politics, but a point of departure for a multivalent, shifting ground of subjectivity, a "self-contradictory identity, [. . .] made up of heterogeneous and heteronomous representations of gender, race, and class" (1986:9). Identity becomes a site of struggle, at which the subject organizes and reorganizes competing discourses as they fight for supremacy.

Materialist feminist performance criticism uses poststructuralism to deconstruct both traditional, male-identified realism and alternative, woman-identified ritual drama and performance art for their belief in coherent, unified identities. If feminist poststructuralism is the tool of this critique, postmodernism is the style that offers potential performance applications. Logically, a postmodernist performance style that breaks with realist narrative strategies, heralds the death of unified characters, decenters the subject, and foregrounds conventions of perception is conducive to materialist feminist analyses of representation.

The intent of the growing, diversifying field of feminist postmodern performance theory is to develop theatre and performance strategies that will create new meanings at the site of representation, which has historically outlawed or silenced women within its frame. Feminist postmodernist performance theories intervene in representation to encourage spectators to think differently about their positions within culture, differently than the comfortable conventions of realism ever persuade them to think. Feminist performance theories give critics a language that unmasks the seeming transparency of performance texts and that potentially articulates the insidious ideology of any representation that presents experience as truth.

Continually watchdogging themselves and their bedfellows, feminist performance theorists have also chastised the commodified brands of postmodernist performance that devolve into an endless plurality of meaning; a chic, politically apathetic ennui; or a retrograde nostalgia for master narratives (see Dolan 1987; Case and Forte 1985). The project of feminist theory is unflaggingly political, as it studies not simply the superficial structure of performance, but its affect on the culture and the search for modes of effective social change.

A wealth of invigorating thinking and criticism has come from pondering the alliance of feminist criticism and postmodern style. But concurrently, feminist criticism's struggle between poststructuralism and identity politics has provoked a metadebate over theory in feminism. Theorists who subscribe to poststructuralist analysis are accused of oppressing radical feminist identity politicians with the privileges of an elite language. Accusations of silencing are hurled about, since this argument takes place in discourse and is very much about the power of language.

Struggles in Discourse: Recent Writings and (Mis)Readings

Tensions between these opposing camps have been exacerbated by the increasing visibility of critical and theoretical work in feminist theatre and performance. Feminist panels sponsored by WTP at the annual Association for Theatre in Higher Education conferences, as well as at the Modern Language Association conventions, have been very well attended over the last several years, and publishers are beginning to seek out feminist books in the field. Helen Krich Chinoy and Linda Walsh Jenkins' anthology *Women in American Theatre*, originally published by Crown in 1981, was revised and reissued by Theatre Communications Group in 1987; Karen Malpede's collection *Women in Theatre: Compassion and Hope* was published in 1983 (Drama Book Specialists); Helene Keyssar's *Feminist Theatre* was published in 1985 (Grove Press); and Kathleen Betsko and Rachel Koenig's anthology *Interviews with Contemporary Women Playwrights* appeared in 1987 (Beechtree Books).

These four editions essentially reflect the sociological approach to feminist criticism and theatre history. The Chinoy/Jenkins anthology is a valuable sourcebook of information on women playwrights, producers, directors, and actors that provides a solid introduction to the wealth of women's work overlooked in distant and present theatre history. The collection is marked, however, by its early-'80s perspective on feminist theatre criticism as an ill-defined plurality of approaches. The reissued volume surveys more recent critical methodologies in the field, such as semiotics, materialism, and poststructuralism, but shies away from a rigorous investigation of the ideological meanings of different feminist analytical styles.

The Betsko/Koenig collection of interviews is grounded in the liberal feminist assertion of the text's primacy. The book succeeds in providing women playwrights an important, public forum in which to speak for themselves about their politics, their creative processes, and their projects. Like the Chinoy/Jenkins anthology, *Interviews* does not provide an overarching, specific framework for feminism, aesthetics, or ideology. The editors intentionally avoid such distinctions.

Three books published in 1988 take on the task of sorting through feminist ideologies and their various critical perspectives: my own book, *The Feminist Spectator as Critic* (UMI); Sue-Ellen Case's *Feminism and Theatre* (Routledge); and *Making a Spectacle: Feminist Essays on Contemporary Women's Theatre*, edited by Lynda Hart (University of Michigan Press). My book applies critical theory in an effort to investigate the feminist spectator's position vis-à-vis the representational frame and favors a materialist feminist approach. Through case studies of work by Marsha Norman, Richard Foreman, At the Foot of the Mountain, the Women's Experimental Theatre, Spiderwoman, and other performance groups, I attempt to specify the ideological underpinnings of various performance theories and practices.

Case's *Feminism and Theatre* is a handbook that introduces feminist critical theory in theatre and performance. Case rejects the assumption of theatre as mimesis, and argues that theatre history and dramatic literature cannot be read for information about actual women's lives. The book begins with an attack on the Aristotelian, Greek, and Elizabethan theatre traditions as forums for patriarchal ideology that repressed actual historical women. Case suggests that the feminist reader studying *The Poetics* and other canonical texts that gird the Western theatre tradition can "discover the methodology and assumptions of patriarchal production" on which they are based (1988:19).

Hart's anthology mixes liberal, radical, and materialist perspectives under sections that address women playwrights' metaphors, their use of aesthetics and history, and their disruptions of the patriarchal ideology Case describes. Hart characterizes the articles in her collection as documenting the "shift in feminist perspective from discovering and creating positive images of women in the content of drama to analyzing and disrupting the ideological codes embedded in the inherited structures of dramatic representation" (1988:4). The book serves as a focal point for applications of diverging feminist critical thought on contemporary theatre.

The published responses to these books have been somewhat illuminating regarding the debate between poststructuralism and identity politics, and relevant to the dissension among varying feminist perspectives. The anthologies of the early or mid-'80s were generally applauded when they appeared, and were seen as correctives to women's invisibility in theatre history. Keyssar's *Feminist Theatre* (1985) also garnered favorable reviews; her book analyzes plays by women through a more or less traditional critical approach.

Case's book, on the contrary, is a historical/critical/theoretical study with a polemical force that has made it subject to two aggressively unfavorable reviews. Gabrielle Cody, writing in *Performing Arts Journal,* chastises Case for a "lack of intellectual rigor," and an "inability to rise above [her] rhetoric" (1988:117). This attack on her scholarship in fact seems to mask Cody's discomfort with Case's politics. Cody particularly lambastes Case's work on Greek and Elizabethan stage conventions, criticizing her for reducing "thoughts to ideology, literature to sociology" (117).

Cody misreads Case's thesis by attempting to locate her work within the sociological criticism from which Case points away. For example, Cody challenges Case to investigate Sophocles' and Euripides' women for their strength as characters. In her chapter on the Greeks, Case states explicitly that the feminist critic or historian, reading Greek theatre history through its production practice rather than its texts alone, can no longer view these representations as in any way linked to the lives of real women (1988:25).

Similarly, Cody accuses Case of insulting women by "avoiding the images in Shakespeare (often the only representations of female power in Elizabethan England) by emphasizing his techniques of production" (1988:117). But production is exactly Case's point. She insists these texts be read through living cultural history rather than detaching them into a transcendent sphere. Case's poststructuralist approach does not focus on ahistorical content or images, but analyzes the representational apparatus and the ideology that it enforces through theatre history.

In her parting shot, Cody writes that Case's book "posits that women have been robbed of their own representations throughout theatre history, but a more inclusive mimesis is possible through the creation of a feminist-identified culture" (1988:118). This statement directly contradicts Case's final assertion that "the production of signs creates the sense of what a person is rather than reflecting it (in the traditional mimetic order)" (1988:132). Case's approach is, in fact, antimimesis, and Cody does her a disservice by consigning her work to a radical feminist ghetto of feminist-identified culture in which theatre is a validating mirror.

Joyce van Dyke's lead article in the *Women's Review of Books* contrasts Case's book with the Betsko/Koenig interview collection and Hart's *Making a Spectacle* anthology. Van Dyke applauds the collection of interviews as "energetic, lithe, funny, vivid" (1989:1), then goes on to deplore the "considerable gap between feminist critics and feminist playwrights" (3). She calls Case's story a "lopsided one," and implies that she is more of a semiotician than she is a feminist (3). Van Dyke suggests that Case's work is selectively exclusionary and "does not admit the existence of what it leaves out" (3), such as the women who did perform on the continent during Shakespeare's era, and the wealth of women's theatre work that happened after Hrotsvit and Aphra Behn, on whom Case focuses in an early chapter.

Van Dyke feels Hart's anthology is more "balanced" in its view of contemporary women's theatre and engages her critique particularly with Yolanda Broyles Gonzalez' essay on the women of El Teatro Campesino. Van Dyke's article takes its most ideological turn when she begins to summarize the ramifications of the three books she reviews. She feels that feminist critics place themselves at a remove from work by living writers to focus on their own arena of "critical combat." Suddenly, references to critical militarism ground her review:

> There are a number of governing metaphors that shape literary criticism today [. . .] [b]ut the prevailing metaphor is the militarist one, and feminists seem to have adopted it as enthusiastically as other critics. In this climate, the critical vocabulary of attacks, defenses, tactics and strategies seems natural and inevitable. Critics are praised as "brave" and "daring"; "discipline" (with its implications of hierarchy and punishment) and critical "rigor" (not just phallic but suggestive of military bearing, and other life-threatening or lifeless forms) are frequently equated with intellectual respectability. [. . .] There are other metaphors available to criticism that would be more in keeping with feminism: for instance, the theatrical metaphor [. . .]. It suggests a collectivist enterprise, one that is at least potentially nonhierarchical. It proposes a life-giving and pleasure-giving activity in an arena of liberation from gender and other prescribed roles. It welcomes [. . .] a multiplicity of styles and personal voices (1989:3).

Van Dyke's equation of feminist criticism with life-threatening militarism is extremely disturbing. Her suggestion that criticism is male-like unless it's nurturing, "life-giving and pleasure-giving" implies that unless the feminist critic once again places herself fully in the service of the playwright—the ultimate creator, the idealized mother of the dramatic text—she is participating in an imperialistic, nihilistic act that's merely an exercise in power.

As feminist performance critics and theorists move farther into the project of distinguishing the feminisms and their criticisms from the amorphous mass of pluralism, a peculiar backlash has begun to operate. Liberal feminists such as Cody get uneasy when the canon is attacked; radical feminists such as van Dyke refuse to take responsibility for their own positions as critics, since they regard criticism and theory as male-like; and materialist critics get trashed for their willingness to be "daring" and "brave," for attempting to chart new pathways in performance theory's territory. Although my sympathies are clearly with materialist feminist theorists and therefore cloud my so-called "objectivity," it seems to me that the critical attacks on Case's book in particular (despite radical feminist claims to be antiaggressive) are part of feminism's general backlash against theory.

A Personal Defense of Theory in Discourse

Because poststructuralist theory questions the authenticity of experience as truth, many feminist theorists have been attacked as jargon-wielding elitists who have no political project and who trivialize years of political action organized around radical feminist epistemology. This is not the intent, as I know it, of theory. Poststructuralism simply questions the liberal humanist notion that men or women are free individuals capable of mastering the universe, and points out the way in which ideology is masked as common-sensical truth (see Weedon 1987). Poststructuralist performance criticism looks at the power structures underlying representation, and the means by which subjectivity is shaped and withheld through discourse. These are intensely political projects.

But rather than arguing the implications of such a poststructuralist perspective, some feminist academicians and activists attack the project of theory. Black feminist critic Barbara Christian, for instance, in her article "The Race for Theory," reasserts the accusation that theory silences (1988). She believes that theory became popular when marginalized minority writers were successfully clamoring to be heard in academia.

Christian criticizes theorists for ignoring black women writers in their drive to immerse themselves in the verbal gymnastics of famous white men. She implicitly charges that because feminist poststructuralism acquiesces to the death of the author, it's complicit with a reactionary silencing of women authors. Christian is not the only woman to voice these concerns, and from a certain perspective, the point she raises is valid. In theatre, much of the recent dissension over theory comes from a similar unwillingness to unsettle playwrighting as one of women's primary activities. If we agree that the author is dead, how can we continue talking about women playwrights? Feminist poststructuralist theories, however, don't intend to kill off women authors a priori, but to simply enlarge the consideration of texts to take into account the meanings that are constructed in performance as well as on the page.[2]

Christian angles her argument through a racial perspective, insisting that her race theorizes from the basis of its experience as a minority. Other women attack theory by insisting that their experiences of oppression keep them from using its language. How can I, as a feminist theorist, respond to these concerns? How can I negotiate the differences between Christian and myself? Christian says she works in literary criticism to save her own life. I work in theory to save mine. Theory allows me to articulate my differences from a feminism I first learned as monolithic. Theory enables me to see that there is no tenable position for me in the totalizing strategies of radical feminism, and that I can align myself profitably elsewhere.

Through theory, I can articulate the roots of my own identity in the conflicting discourses of lesbianism and Judaism, and know that there is no comfortable place for me within any single discourse. Theory enables me to describe the differences within me and around me without forcing me to rank my allegiances or my oppressions. As feminist critic Gayle Austin would say, theory enables the divided subject to fall into the cracks of difference and to theorize productively from there, knowing that truth is changeable, permeable, and finally, irrelevant (1988).

The irony of articulating my own experience as a defense of feminist poststructuralist performance criticism is not lost on me. The pervasive glorification of experience, and the testimonial strategies used to enforce it as truth, require that I, too, throw myself back on positions that theory otherwise allows me to detach from.

Struggles for Identity in Discourse: A Final Example

The antitheory stance of feminists who posit experience as truth and who want to enter representation on the basis of authentic female experience was illustrated at the 1988 WTP preconference in San Diego, for which I served as coordinator. The following account is a testimony to my experience of the event.

The conference was devoted to the intersection of theory and practice. Poststructuralism and postmodernism were employed and discussed. Some participants talked about the contamination of narrative, the subject's decenteredness, and the impossibility of getting outside of ideology. Other participants felt alienated by this language, by words and phrases that appeared impenetrable. Alongside the discourse of theory swelled a nostalgia for a lost female narrative that would nurture, support, and rock women at the bosom of gender.

Despite the intense confrontations that the preconference generated between these conflicting perspectives, three performances were presented that productively illustrated the potential of feminist postmodernism and provided opportunities to examine theory in action. The first was by Anna Deavere Smith—the only black woman of the 100 women attending—who performed an oral history of the WTP. She used the words of black women and white women she had interviewed to editorialize about her subjects and to create versions of their identities and their programs through her perceptions of them as a black woman. The spectators could identify the subjects of Smith's performance—many of whom were in the audience—but were encouraged to see her performing them, to hear her choose their words, and to grapple with the foregrounding of race and ideas.

But some spectators expected mimesis, and railed against their absence from Smith's opaque mirror. Because they didn't see the radical implications of Smith's performance, and because they didn't hear her critique, they proceeded to attack the history of the program instead. Lost in the ensuing struggle among white women was a confrontation with the ideas about race and representation in the performance text Smith constructed. By searching for an "authentic" representation of their own experience, and focusing on their dissatisfaction with its absence, the spectators erased the residue of Smith's commentary on her experience.

At the second performance, Kate Bornstein, a male-to-female transsexual, performed her experiences of gender identity. Bornstein delivered a male character's monolog as she once played him as a male actor, aware of her imprisonment in her theatrical and social role. She then performed a female character as she once did as a male actor, protected by the theatrical

1. Kate (Al) Bornstein as King Lear at Brown University in 1969—a male character as she once played him as a male actor. (Photo by Glenn Jonnesen)

convention of gender impersonation while her body enacted this impersonation in everyday life.

Bornstein performed a noncoincidence of body and language, a Brechtian, postmodern dissociation of presence and discourse. Her monologs traded among shifting, constructed identities, layered on a body that has experienced all of these constructions. Bornstein hired a surgical knife to allow her to play the gender role she desired in a body that would look the part. Confined by gender construction, Bornstein opted to reconstruct her body to fit herself into gendered discourse. Or did she subvert gendered discourse by her choice to tamper with biology? Watching her perform, I was unsettled by my awareness that Bornstein has no neutral body, that even her biology is not immutable but constructed. Is this the death of character? Where is the truth in this experience?

2. Kate (Al) Bornstein performing a female character as she once did as a male actor in Brecht and Weill's Happy End *at The Wilma Theater in Philadelphia, PA, 1985. (Photo courtesy of The Wilma Theater)*

3. Kate Bornstein as she appeared on the Geraldo Rivera Show in 1989. (Photo by Ingrid Wilhite)

4. Marianne Goldberg in "Ballerinas and Ball Passing" in Women and Performance Journal *(1987/88:18)—a literarization of the body. (Photo by Babette Mangolte)*

The third preconference performance was by Marianne Goldberg, a performer/theorist who refuses the traditional and feminist dichotomies that split those terms.[3] She stood behind a lectern and used her body to form words. Her performance was a literarization of the body *à la* Brecht, not an incidence of *l'écriture féminine*—in fact, Goldberg insists, "We can claim our bodies only if we stop claiming that they give us truth." Her body became a text written in space, and she played reflexively with the meanings it created.

Goldberg positions herself as the unmasked performer, as a lecturer and demonstrator, as a colleague who refuses the position of "naive art object." Her body, she says, is "in motion and at risk" (see Diamond 1988a), present in a discourse in which she is engaged and competent. She speaks to spectators, and points out that she is exchanging the gaze with them. She is an author who refuses authority, a subject intent on shifting her identity even as she speaks.

These performances illustrated the potential of a feminist postmodern style to concretize the poststructuralist problematics of meaning and experience. Smith performed the spectator, literally blackening Snow White's theatrical mirror. Goldberg performed theory, inviting spectators to theorize with her as they looked at her. Bornstein performed permutations of gender on a body that can't help but editorialize its constructedness, thwarting any attempt to arrive at biological or ideological truth.

These postmodernist experiments happened in the context of feminism, in which the political stakes were very material and quite high. After the conference, Anna Deavere Smith left for a famous regional theatre to perform as a whore in a play by a famous white man. Kate Bornstein returned to a city where she has no job working in theatre. Marianne Goldberg went home to rewrite her performance, since her text is continually in process. An instance of theory had occurred.

Feminist postmodernism happens in theory. Our experiments are conducted at conferences and in universities, and most often on paper rather

5. Behind a lectern, Marianne Goldberg uses her body to form words, underscoring rather than ignoring the body's readability and placing it provocatively "at risk." (Photo by Robert Tobey)

than on big stages sodden with spectacle. Feminist postmodernism does not play indulgently with meaninglessness or plurality, charges that might be leveled against some postmodern performance auteurs. Feminist postmodernism is committed to meaning, to sifting through the referents of material reality and drawing blueprints of their construction that can be historically revised and changed.[4]

Positions of identity are equally historical. Elin Diamond, on a panel about feminist criticism at the same preconference, remarked that positioning is utterly provisional, that once you have a position, you inherit issues of identity that you want to put into crisis (1988b). My challenge as a materialist feminist performance theorist, then, is to reposition myself constantly, to keep changing my seat in the theatre, and to continually ask: How does it look from over here? To ask myself, how would Barbara Christian see this, and how might she and I prod each other to look differently? Working in theory allows such fluidity, since the only productive position for the theorist is balancing precariously on the edge of the differences between, among, and within women, who are the site of conflicting discourses in which there is no immutable truth.

Notes

1. This article expands on papers presented at the New Languages for Stage Conference in Lawrence, KS, October 1988, and at the Modern Language Association convention in New Orleans, LA, December 1988.
2. When I gave a version of this article as a talk at Brown University in May 1989, playwright Paula Vogel, who teaches at Brown, pointed out that many women playwrights are still struggling to live, literally, in the mainstream theatre context, which makes the metaphorical death of the author something of a moot issue for them. Poststructuralist theory, she implied, which describes a moment in which authorship is dispersed across various reception strategies, seems premature for women playwrights who have not yet gained access to the author's position.
3. A performance-for-print version of Goldberg's preconference presentation appears as "Ballerinas and Ball Passing" in *Women and Performance* (1987/88).
4. Because of its concentration in theory, feminist postmodernism has been vulnerable to assimilation by academic critics. The implosion of what might be called "apolitical" postmodernism and the feminist variety poses a very real problem for feminist critics determined to employ theory for political ends. The question resides, once again, in discourse—even publishing an article such as this one in TDR makes the movement's issues available to a readership outside its purview. Yet for feminist theory to become familiar and useful to those inside the movement, who have political investments in its utility, it seems important to speak through the public forum journals such as TDR provide.

References

Austin, Gayle
1988 Comments made on "Elucidating Terms and Issues" panel, Women and Theatre Program Preconference. Horton Grand Hotel, San Diego, CA, 1 August.

Barthes, Roland
1977 "Death of the Author." In *Image-Music-Text*, 142–48. Translated by Stephen Heath. New York: The Noonday Press.

Betsko, Kathleen, and Rachel Koenig, eds.
1987 *Interviews with Contemporary Women Playwrights*. New York: Beechtree Books.

Case, Sue-Ellen
1988 *Feminism and Theatre*. New York: Routledge.

Case, Sue-Ellen, and Jeanie Forte
1985 "From Formalism to Feminism." *Theater* 16, no. 2 (Spring):62–65.

Chinoy, Helen Krich, and Linda Walsh Jenkins, eds.
1987 [1981] *Women in American Theatre*. New York: Theatre Communications Group.

Christian, Barbara
1988 "The Race for Theory." *Feminist Studies* 14, no. 1 (Spring):67–80.

Cody, Gabrielle
1988 Book review. *Performing Arts Journal* 11, no. 2 (PAJ32):117–18.

de Courtivron, Isabelle, and Elaine Marks
1981 *New French Feminisms*. New York: Schocken.

Diamond, Elin
1985 "Refusing the Romanticism of Identity: Narrative Interventions in Churchill, Benmussa, Duras." *Theatre Journal* 38, no. 3 (October): 273–86.
1988a "Brechtian Theory/Feminist Theory: Toward a Gestic Feminist Criticism." *The Drama Review* 32, no. 1 (T117):82–94.
1988b Comments made on "Feminist Criticism" panel, Women and Theatre Program Preconference. Horton Grand Hotel, San Diego, 2 August.

Dolan, Jill
1987 "Is the Postmodern Aesthetic Feminist?" *Art & Cinema* 1, no. 3 (Fall):5–6.
1988 *The Feminist Spectator as Critic*. Ann Arbor, MI: UMI Research Press.

van Dyke, Joyce
1989 "Performance Anxiety," *Women's Review of Books* 6, no. 4 (January):1,3.

Goldberg, Marianne
1987/88 "Ballerinas and Ball Passing." *Women & Performance* 3, no. 2 (#6): 7–31.

Hart, Lynda, ed.
1988 *Making a Spectacle: Feminist Essays on Contemporary Women's Theatre*. Ann Arbor: University of Michigan Press.

Keyssar, Helene
1985 *Feminist Theatre*. New York: Grove Press.

de Lauretis, Teresa
1986 "Issues, Terms, and Contexts." In *Feminist Studies/Critical Studies*, edited by Teresa de Lauretis, 1–19. Bloomington: Indiana University Press.

Malpede, Karen, ed.
1983 *Women in Theatre: Compassion and Hope*. New York: Drama Book Specialists.

Weedon, Chris
1987 *Feminist Practice and Post-structuralist Theory*. New York: Basil Blackwell.

***Jill Dolan** is Assistant Professor of Theatre and Drama and Women's Studies at the University of Wisconsin-Madison. Her book,* The Feminist Spectator as Critic *(1988), is available from UMI press. Her article "Desire Cloaked in a Trenchcoat" appeared in T121. She has also published feminist performance criticism with* Theatre Journal *and* Modern Drama, *among others. She is contributing editor to* Women & Performance *and Vice-president of the ATHE's Women and Theatre Program.*

Redecorating the Fourth Wall

Environmental Theatre Today

Steve Nelson

It has been 20 years since the term "environmental theatre" first entered the critical and practical performance vocabulary. The intervening years have brought about a different audience sensibility. Performers and techniques once considered part of the theatrical fringe have become decidedly mainstream. Philip Glass now makes scotch ads while Robert Wilson and Spalding Gray have become fixtures of public television (Gray is even available on home video). The stylistic and methodological innovations wrought by these practitioners are also becoming more familiar. Actor/audience relationships that were daring and novel in 1968 are now commonplace. The growth of performance art during the past decade, and its steady emergence into the mainstream of aesthetic consciousness, has served to make environmental theatre a more complex and less straightforwardly theatrical enterprise.

This article will explore the evolving nature of environmental performance in the theatre by examining four contemporary environmental productions, their relationships to one another, and their connection to the larger tradition of environmental performance. The shows discussed by no means represent a comprehensive survey of productions utilizing environmental staging, but they do provide a representative sample of the directions taken by contemporary artists.

Environmental theatre has meant many things to many people since Richard Schechner first applied the term to the experiments of the late 1960s (see plate 1). At the very least, it implies nonfrontal staging and a flexible approach to the actor/audience relationship (see Aronson 1977). The concept has also been largely associated with the avant-garde, although the past decade has seen the increasing use of environmental techniques in the commercial theatre. Today's environmental productions lack the urgent political and artistic agendas that typified such efforts in the '60s. They are also more reliant on the eclectic, smorgasbord-style blending of techniques and traditions that typifies much postmodern performance.

There is also a very definite shift in focus from engagement to entertainment in the pieces themselves. Terms such as "theme park," "carnival,"

6 Axioms for Environmental Theatre

Richard Schechner
From TDR 12, no. 3 (T39), Spring 1968

1. The theatrical event is a set of related transactions.
2. All the space is used for performance; all the space is used for audience.
3. The theatrical event can take place either in a totally transformed space or in "found space."
4. Focus is flexible and variable.
5. All production elements speak in their own language.
6. The text need be neither the starting point nor the goal of a production. There may be no text at all.

and "fun house" appear often in descriptions of these shows and in their own publicity jargon. One of the most remarkable things about today's environmental theatre is its ability to draw not just on the aesthetic tradition of earlier avant-garde practitioners (Artaud, Cage, Kaprow, Grotowski, Schechner), but on the older and more varied traditions of popular environmental staging.

Tamara, an elaborate environmental mystery/melodrama with food and drink now playing in New York and Los Angeles,[1] is a perfect example of this kind of assimilation. The audience selects different actors to follow and moves with the performance through ten different rooms on three floors of the Seventh Regiment Armory in Manhattan, which has been decorated to resemble an Italian villa in 1927. I recently overheard a conversation in the ticket line at *Tamara* which reveals how much the environmental revolution has seeped into the consciousness of the average theatregoer:

WOMAN: I hope this isn't some '60s shit. They don't actually make you *do* anything, do they?

MAN: It's a kind of *Nickelby* thing where they walk around during intermission and talk to the audience.

WOMAN: Oh.

MAN: I think it's sort of like *Edwin Drood* where you figure the ending out for yourself.[2]

This exchange points up two very important differences between today's environmental theatre and the experiments of previous decades. One obviously relates to the complex set of expectations, preconceptions, and contemporary cultural baggage that an audience brings to the performance. Today's patron seems equally interested in a novel experience, but without the participatory demands or political agendas that characterized much of the late-'60s avant-garde. Theatre is viewed very much in the apolitical materialist terms that characterize the culture consumption habits of Yuppies and other well-to-do types who make up the bulk of theatre audiences.

The second aspect relates to the different thrust and style of the performance itself, which may be viewed as an attempt to cater to a more withdrawn and voyeuristically inclined audience. *Tamara,* for example, is more akin to Broadway's *Nicholas Nickelby* and *The Mystery of Edwin Drood* than to its largely noncommercial environmental predecessors of the '60s and '70s. *Tamara, Nickelby,* and *Drood* are each enormously successful period spectacles that make judicious use of environmental staging and audience involvement techniques explored in the '60s. From the strolling actors and carefully orchestrated food-fight that begins *Nicholas Nickelby* to the audience-as-jury outcome of *The Mystery of Edwin Drood,* each show seeks to temper its innovative aspects with a judicious awareness of the audience's capacity for the unusual. In any event, there is a conscious effort to move away from the frequently confrontational style of earlier avant-garde environmental productions. "I'm embarrassed by that kind of thing, and I think most people are too," explained *Tamara* director Richard Rose. "When an audience feels uncomfortable or put upon, they tune out" (1988).

Tamara

Very much like a complex amusement park environment or Disney-style ride, the audience at *Tamara* is carefully coddled and prepped for its journey. The Seventh Regiment Armory is a magnificent high-ceilinged affair that appears to have survived untouched (and undusted) from the turn of the century. One enters the space from Park Avenue up a long, awning-covered double stairway and through two imposingly ponderous oak doors into a grand 40-foot high foyer. Regimental banners, ornately framed paintings, and assorted military paraphernalia festoon the halls. Patrons are greeted by attractive young performers in black, miniskirted serving-maid costumes who proffer "Tamara Cocktails," a sweet alcoholic drink featuring liquor donated by a sponsor. They also speak in carefully subdued Italian accents as they welcome you to Il Vittoriale, the opulent villa-like setting for the performance. Producer Moses Znaimer even went so far as to hire speech coaches for the support staff so that their ersatz Italian would have an authentic lilt.

Waiting in line for tickets, I was struck by an atmosphere more appropriate to a gallery opening or large cocktail party. One of the performers plays soft, languid piano music as background to the buzz of lobby conversation. Upon arriving at the reception area (which resembles the check-in ambience of a small European hotel), one receives a "passport" from a gentleman and lady in formal evening dress. Very much in the manner of Disneyland, the concern with the totality of the illusion is scrupulous. Audience members are referred to as "guests" and are constantly welcomed and admonished to enjoy their stay by the roving maids and other appropriately attired support staff. After obtaining a passport (covered in heavy textured blue paper to resemble the real thing), the audience stands in another line to have the document stamped by one of the show's main characters, a fascismo policeman in black jackboots who stares coolly at patrons and advises them to "obey our laws or face deportation." He also sternly suggests that one remember the date on the front of the passport and (most importantly) NEVER lose the thing.

The passport contains the usual cast and production credits as well as the aforementioned laws, "The Ten Commandments":

The Ten Commandments

1. Read your Passport. Know its contents. Get caught without it and you will be deported.

2. For greater comprehension, previous guests have observed that following only one or two characters yields greater order. But, if variety is the spice of your life, it's OK to follow your impulses.

3. Ten people live in this house. Always follow one of them. If you wander about on your own you break the law. Worse, you will lose the thread of the story you are creating.

4. Be brave. Act on your choices with conviction.

5. Be bold. Go directly to an opposite side of the room. Chances are you will see more.

6. If you are here with friends, split up. Several sources of information are better than one. Interrogate those around you. Compare notes during "Intermezzo" or later over coffee and dessert.

7. Watch the stories or watch the watchers. One way or another, get involved.

8. If you become tired, you will be comforted to know there is always a story on the main floor.

9. For your own safety, do not stand in a doorway. Do not open a closed door. Do not follow someone who deliberately closes a door in your face.

10. Move quickly. Move quietly. Speak only when spoken to.

The last commandment is largely irrelevant, since the audience is almost never addressed directly, except during intermission and after the show when certain cast members mingle with the crowd. Once during a scene I was asked by a performer to comment on the personality of a particular character. I was later informed by the stage manager that the actress had been told that I was a reviewer. Of the eight times I visited the production, this never recurred, nor was any other spectator I spoke with ever confronted directly by an actor during the performance.

The parameters of acceptable audience behavior are also dealt with in the show's introductory segment, which is spoken by the actor playing the valet. A large ship's bell is rung in the foyer to end the pre-show music and gather the audience together. The crowd is addressed from the stairway with a hearty "*buon giorno,*" to which they are asked to respond in kind. The valet is accompanied in his introductory remarks by the fascist cop Aldo Finzi who stamped the passports. Gabrielle d'Annunzio, the enigmatic proprietor of the villa appears along with his coquettish maid/whore Emilia and several of the other principal players. We learn that Finzi has suspicions about Mario the new chauffeur and that d'Annunzio has designs on Tamara de Lempicka, the woman who is coming to paint his portrait.

The valet also reiterates the passport "commandments" in a joking but serious tone reminiscent of the "keep your hands and feet inside the car at all times" warnings issued at amusement park rides. Although the audience is strongly encouraged to follow one person, anarchic choices are not prohibited, provided one agrees to remain in a room for the duration of a

2. The valet, Dante Fenzo (Leland Murray), greets Tamara *guests with a hearty* "buon giorno" *from the stairway. (Photo by Steve Nelson)*

3. Louisa Baccara (Laura Esterman) with the fascist cop Aldo Finzi (Thom Christofer): "The bad guys are almost cartoonish in their sneering obsequiousness." (Photo by Steve Nelson)

scene. This tight but relatively unobtrusive means of crowd control is one of the keys to the success of *Tamara*'s elaborate actor/audience choreography. Wandering is permitted, provided you don't amble about the halls in the middle of a scene. Those who stray are quickly directed to the room of their choice by the support staff, who know the moment to moment location of each performer.

At the end of the introductory session, the audience is divided by the valet into three groups and packed off to three different parts of the environment. After brief expository sessions in which they learn more of the villa and its inhabitants, the groups reconvene briefly in the foyer, at which point one may follow the same performer or choose another.

Given the great distances the performers cover dashing from room to room, the pace of the show remains remarkably crisp. Advertisements suggest that the audience wear "sensible shoes." It is sound advice, as some of the more frenetic characters often cover 50 yards or more over stairs and hard stone floors on their sprints around the space.

The meat of the plot centers on the efforts of Mario the chauffeur, a secret Communist agent, to induce d'Annunzio to challenge Mussolini openly and on the subsequent attempts by Finzi to uncover the plot. The title character Tamara is primarily window dressing for the intrigues that result from Mario's presence at the villa. Ostensibly, the play comments on the rise of fascism and how the decadent apathy of those at the villa contributes to its success. But despite the sinister doings of Finzi and his slimy rival DeSpiga, the fascism of *Tamara* is largely backdrop for a sexy soap opera cum mystery, rather than a sustaining political commentary. The bad guys are almost cartoonish in their sneering obsequiousness and the dilettantes of the Villa seem to have emerged from a European remake of *The Man Who Came to Dinner*.

Nothing is allowed to intrude on the melodramatic energy of the evening, which is generated by getting extremely close to talented actors and watching them simulate sex, violence, and gut-wrenching emotion. The show adheres closely to Harold Clurman's oft-quoted observation that, "once you fake the truth, you've got it." *Tamara* is certainly an enjoyable environmental piece, taken on its own terms. Its pretensions to any substantive "content," however, are not to be taken seriously.

The show has a definite "upstairs/downstairs" structure, both in terms of plot and in the physical division of the space. The play takes place in ten different rooms spread over three levels. The servants are downstairs and the masters up, with each sharing the action on the main level. The servants, who get most of the steamy sex and violence scenes, tend to draw the biggest crowds, although d'Annunzio's efforts to bed Tamara are also popular.

Taken purely as voyeurism, *Tamara* is indeed a great deal of fun. The action, though by necessity somewhat complex, is nicely suited to the follow-it-from-room-to-room approach. The Armory's stuffy Victorian atmosphere and marvelous period fixtures have been used to great effect. One gets the feeling of actually being in a functional villa, down to the working kitchen in which D'Annunzio cooks and eats an omelet. One spectator remarked to her companion that Tamara was obviously the guest since her bedroom was the only one with air conditioning. In many respects the show is a logical extension of the hyperrealism advocated by Belasco and Antoine. But rather than hanging meat before an audience, *Tamara* serves it to them.

Tamara may well be the first show in which a chef receives equal billing with the author and director in the advertisements. The production's lavish promotions trumpet the culinary efforts of Daniel Boulud (chef at LeCirque, currently one of New York's premier French restaurants) and the availability of "free-flowing" champagne, courtesy of Perrier Jouet. The sumptuous buffet is indeed delicious, given the limitations of intermission fare, but one pays for it. *Tamara* ticket prices range from $60 for Wednesday matinees to more than $100 on weekends.

The show's advertisements also seem aware of the problem created by $100 ticket prices. Conscious of the danger of being labeled upscale dinner theatre, producer Znaimer has distributed ad copy that compares the *Tamara* price to a typical Broadway evening, with food, drink, and other attendant costs thrown in. It is a familiar ploy of pop forms when taking on cultural icons: i.e., we're the better value.

While the audience dines (they are allowed to eat anywhere in the performance space), Dante the valet mingles in character to answer questions and chat with the audience. The other performers are not seen. The bell is sounded to end intermission and the audience is herded to the foyer. Dante addresses them as before and reiterates some of the caveats about not entering closed doors and moving to the back of a room. Finzi then speaks and summons a hapless patron who has "misplaced" his or her passport. This person is questioned and then led off by Finzi amidst much audience snickering. The *Tamara* staff insure the presence of a sucker at each per-

4. The spectator as voyeur—the steamy sex scenes draw the biggest crowds at Tamara. *Aldo Finzi (Thom Christofer) with the maid/whore Emilia Pavise (Roma Downey). (Photo by Steve Nelson)*

formance by snatching someone's passport at intermission. At the end of the performance, which concludes in the foyer with a flurry of gunfire and sprawling bodies, the audience gathers for dessert and coffee with the cast.

Tamara is a fun show in both the best and worst senses of the word. It is slick, well acted, and deftly staged; an eminently enjoyable production that is easy to like. It also makes no more demands on its audience than the physical stamina required to sprint from room to room. In terms of brain drain, it's about on the level of a PBS mystery series. Had the intellectual content of the material been as challenging as the movement and decor, the show would have some claim to being a genuinely arresting experience.

Bananaland: A Central America Theme Park

A more political use of familiar popular forms is employed by Seven Stages Theatre of Atlanta in its environmental piece *Bananaland: A Central America Theme Park,* which, as its name implies, attempts to appropriate

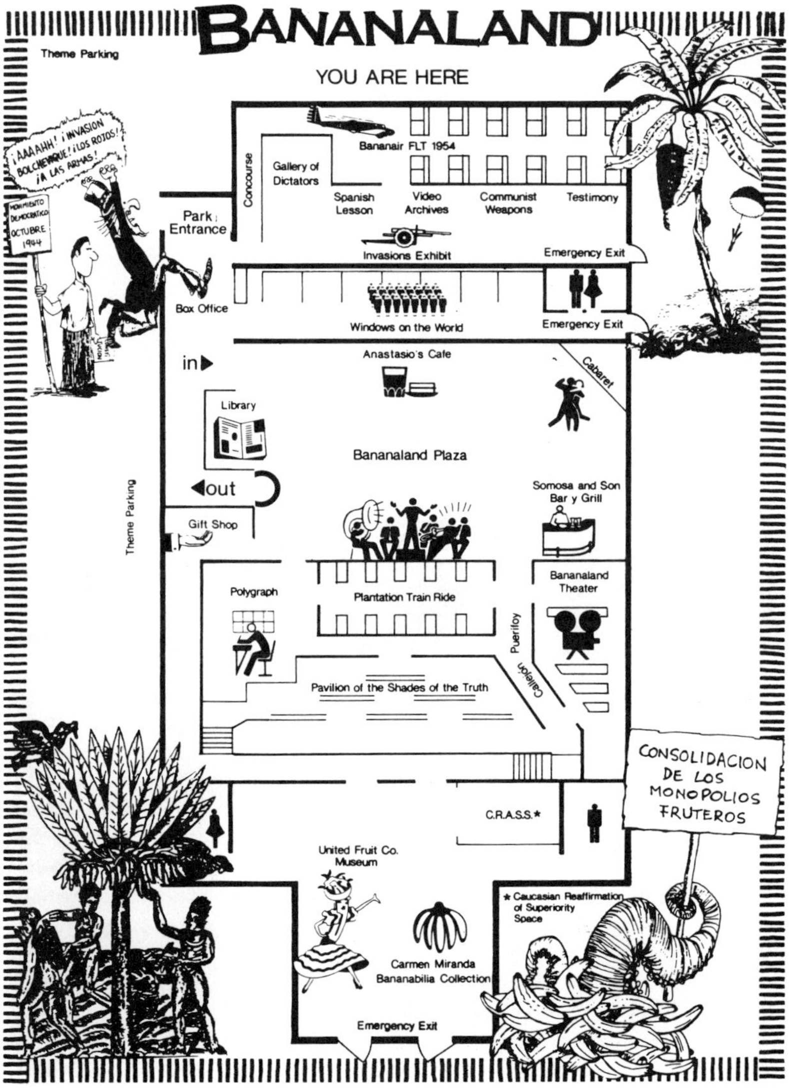

5. *Map of* Bananaland *performance space.*

6. The "Mrs. Somoza Memorial Library" on Bananaland*'s central plaza. (Photo by George King)*

the features and techniques of theme parks and world's fairs to a theatrical setting [see also Paul Evans' article in this issue]. Essentially a walk-through environment (see plate 5), *Bananaland* takes visitors on a tour of the more repugnantly colonial aspects of U.S./Central American relations during the past century. With the feel of a Brechtian-flavored "Saturday Night Live," *Bananaland* alternates between the silly and the serious, mixing archival film footage with live performances, puppet shows, dioramas, and such standard theme park fare as a gift shop, train and plane rides, and guided tours of a banana museum.

The show was developed by writer/director Ruby Lerner and visual artist and documentary filmmaker George King out of their realization that most Americans know very little about Central America or the history of U.S. involvement there. "We felt that if we didn't understand, our friends probably didn't either," Lerner told me (1988). They began by extensively researching the recent history of the region at Tulane University's Middle American Library, a collection endowed appropriately enough by the United Fruit Company, a principal villain in the exploitation of Central American resources. What Lerner and King found was the bizarre and chilling story of how the United Fruit Company, frightened by the prospect of land reform in Guatemala (where it was the largest landowner), engineered a major PR and lobbying campaign that resulted in the CIA-orchestrated overthrow of the legitimate Guatemalan government in 1954. The surreal quality of this and other low points in U.S./Central American relations prompted Lerner and King to search for an equally surreal means of realizing the story theatrically. "We decided the way into that story for us would be through bananas," remarked Lerner, wryly referring to the main reason why the United Fruit Company bothered to topple a regime. The problem was making the performance work as entertainment as well as politically charged history. Wishing to avoid a traditional approach, they turned to popular entertainment.

The format that most suited King and Lerner's mix of seriousness and absurdity was a combination of world's fair and theme park. They felt an expansive multifocus environment would allow them to play with the wealth of historical information in a more free-form and nonlinear fashion. They then embarked on a second round of research, visiting theme parks (from EPCOT to the Tupperware Museum in Florida) and researching the history of world's fairs (including my article on EPCOT in T112, Nelson 1986) as performative cultural advertisements. According to Lerner, "we wondered whether it was possible to take a form—the theme park—which seems to promote fantasy and passivity, and twist it around so that it explores reality and encourages engagement" (1988).

The performance itself is a comic-book mix of vaudeville routines, museum exhibits, puppet shows, newsreel footage, and audience sing-alongs. Audience members have ample opportunity to participate as well as to observe in such segments as the "Polygraph" in which the park's "trained psychiatrist, Dr. Mengele" interrogates audience members who are strapped into a chair and adorned with wires. There is the Caucasian Reaffirmation of Superiority Space (C.R.A.S.S.) and what appears to be a Disney-style automated "founding father" of the United Fruit Company (in actuality, a live actor). The heavily satirical and slapstick tone of the show is reinforced by what Lerner calls "a high-tech cardboard aesthetic," referring to the intentionally sly but cheesy feel of a sideshow funhouse that permeates the environment's design (1988).

The audience enters the theatre (a 40 × 100 foot black-box space subdivided into different areas) to a central plaza which includes the Somoza and Son Bar and Grill, Anastasio's Cafe, and the Mrs. Somoza Memorial Library, all of which peddle food, drink, and souvenirs. Patrons are greeted by a performer playing General Somoza, who speaks from a balcony and explains some of the evening's activities. The plaza also features strolling vendors, cabaret acts, and a Carmen Miranda send-up named Juanita Marimba.

From the plaza, the audience is taken on tours of the "museum" and "Guatemala." These activities include a plane flight to Guatemala and a train ride through a banana plantation. The plane and train "rides" are intentionally slapdash assemblages of canvas with stationary wooden benches and are designed to mock the pristine sleekness of Disney's environmental rides. After the tours, the audience is free to move through the

7. The Dole Pineapple display has the "intentionally sly but cheesy feel of a sideshow funhouse." (Photo by George King)

space and select what parts to view at will. Throughout the environment there is a mix of factual materials (displays, slides, and videos) and campy performance that parodies museums, documentaries, and theme parks while simultaneously utilizing their most potent techniques to good effect. There is a videotape of the 1954 Guatemalan coup d'état and film footage of U.S. Secretary of State Dulles congratulating the people of Guatemala for "liberating" themselves.

One of the most fascinating components of the show is the use of the character Edward Bernays, the insidious public relations godfather who helped mastermind the United Fruit Company's PR campaign. The actor playing Bernays bases his address on Bernays' writings and the various accounts of his work for the United Fruit Company. The company's exploits are also celebrated in the lyrics of one of the show's many satirical jingles:

> United Fruit, United Fruit
> Bananas made us lots of loot.
> We took the peasants' land away
> Avoided taxes we should pay
> With good PR and lobbying
> You can get away with anything (King and Lerner 1988).

The *Bananaland* environment has a rambling homemade look reminiscent of the Bread and Puppet Theater or England's Welfare State, although its content is less overtly "political" and more historical. The $10.50 ticket price, and the show's appearance during the 1988 Democratic National Convention, assured a broader audience than might normally attend an avant-garde show in Atlanta. Lerner and King were careful not to let the information side of their "infotainment" overwhelm the entertainment side. Part of the goal of the show was to be political without being dogmatic; to provide information and let the audience draw its own conclusions about the correct course of action. This is where the theme park

8. The Bananaland *environment is a mix of documentary displays and campy performance. Here, the audience views the "History of U.S. Invasions" exhibit. (Photo by George King)*

environment comes into play, and also where the show takes its greatest risks. This safe and familiar popular format is indeed ripe for political and social satire, but it also lets people off the hook by allowing them the comfort of light and easily digested humor. The sale of food and souvenirs makes for a more effective theatrical realization of the theme park atmosphere, but it also occasionally dilutes the impact of the satire.

But then again, its creators are not out to change the world. "This is not an attempt to spread the word universally," notes King. "We're after a theatre audience that is arguably somewhat apolitical, which we attribute in part to the fact that they're uninformed" (in Murray 1988:5). Perhaps, but the larger issue (at least as far as the performances discussed in this article are concerned) is that environmental theatre today is more concerned with a good time than with any specific content. Just as *Tamara* used the evils of fascism as a backdrop for melodrama, so *Bananaland* gives us postmodern environmental satire packaged as historical commentary.

YOU - The City

Where *Tamara* and *Bananaland* draw heavily on the popular entertainment side of the environmental tradition, *YOU - The City* by Scottish poet/performance artist Fiona Templeton is more firmly rooted in the aesthetics of Allan Kaprow, John Cage, and other seminal contributors to the genre. But unlike the primarily visual and aural orientations of Kaprow and Cage, Templeton's medium is language.

YOU - The City—which ran from 18 May to 5 June 1988 in New York City—is presented for an audience of one. To see the show, one makes an "appointment" and is assigned a time to appear at a prescribed location—in this production of the piece, a midtown Manhattan office building. The prospective audience of one (referred to as a "client") arrives at the building and is directed to a waiting room where s/he is asked by a receptionist to complete the following questionnaire:

YOU - The City
CLIENT QUESTIONNAIRE

A. Your name ....
Your address ....

B. Why you? ....

C. Are you now or have you ever been? ....

D. Isn't that exactly why you're here? ....

E. What is this making of you? ....

F. If you can't know if you mustn't ask, why look? ....

G. Do you know where you're going? ....

H. You see enough of yourself, don't you? ....

I. Do you believe you can act? ....

Will you yield anyway? ....

Should I be sorry that I could not satisfy you in person? ....

J. Are you to end there? ....

K. Does it help? ....

THANK YOU

9. A receptionist (Kachin Kobayashi) greets the "client" who has made an "appointment" for YOU - The City. *(Photo by Zoe Beloff)*

10. A "YOU executive" (Barbara McKechnie) escorts the client from the office building. (Photo by Zoe Beloff)

After receiving the completed questionnaire, the receptionist introduces the spectator to a second performer who, while delivering a vague but pointedly inquiring monolog to her audience, leads the client down to the street to be whisked away in a car by a third performer. The following speech is delivered to the client while waiting with the performer for the elevator to the street:

> Why you? Why you? The exclusive everything makes you impossible. Bite with your heart the only in two. [. . .] Did you see what I saw? Oh you missed yourself, sister/brother. But you mustn't know. And I tell you. Because does it matter if I tell you the truth when I'll only speak to you in the smile of the game? You must invent the truth, and you must choose the lie.

During the next two hours, the client is passed from performer to performer for a total of 14 scripted encounters in 12 different locations throughout the Times Square area. These include a subway station, a variety of outdoor locales, a sleazy club, a church, and a particularly arresting encounter in a peepshow booth. In this sequence performer and client sit in adjacent sections of a booth where the performer can see the client through a two-way mirror. The client sees only his/her reflection while listening to the performer:

> You . . .
> What do you mean?
> Of course you were what was intended, but I've had to take your place, because . . . I mean you.
> How would you like me to be for you? Would you like me to surprise you more?

Twenty-two individuals can be accommodated during a single day's performing, with each client beginning the journey at ten-minute intervals from 3 P.M. to 8:20 P.M. Since clients also encounter one another as well as performers during the course of the event, the first and last clients to begin the performance are augmented by "fake" clients to maintain the consistency of the experience. The complex shuttling of clients between performers and locales—in a beat-up clunker with fake leopard-skin seat covers and numerous empty beer bottles littering the floor—both blurs and contrasts with the tightly scripted poetry. It is difficult to know who might be a performer and when—or where—the next encounter may occur. In a scene that takes place in a shabby 46th Street club called the Harlequin, one is never certain who is who: Is everyone in the place part of the performance or are the performer and client just "blending in"? One of the interesting by-products of performing on the streets of New York is the tendency of even the most overtly theatrical performance to become subsumed in the chaos of Manhattan life. The uncertainty generated by performing in the "real" world proved troublesome for the disguised actors in other ways, as many of them were confronted by the area's street people. One actor claimed to have been propositioned on the street by a stranger during the course of the performance.

The script of *YOU - The City* is oblique, elliptical, and frequently cryptic, resembling Beckett, Pinter, or Heiner Müller, although in performance it has a more direct and pointed effect. The tone is often probing, but never really threatening. The client is frequently accused of various indiscretions and there is always the sense that the performers mean both more and less than they say. The lines are always addressed directly to the client or occasionally to a second performer about the client. And always they orbit about the personal pronoun "you":

> How can you be dumb when only you make me speak? You think you don't understand but you do. Do you know what I'm talking about? Then you understand as much as I do. I'm the one who doesn't understand the meanings you've agreed on, which are not meanings but where to stop. I'm the one who believes you when you think I know it's not true. I don't want to stop with you. There are words I want to say to you because you might recognize them and think you do understand, but I'm afraid to because you might recognize them and stop. How can you know yet what I mean by

> them and not only what someone else meant, or what you meant before. So I say all these other words meaning that because they mean themselves and don't stop. If I surround myself with strange words between us it is because I don't know how to speak to you. Things are things and change and words do, all while there is something that I want to say, that is, all I know is that I mean to tell you what you mean to me. And if you want to hear, you make me mean something, because then you understand. Only because of you can I not be dumb.

The neatly ordered but enigmatic poetry both nettles and shields the client. So although the experience of being led around town by actors speaking strangely is often confusing, it's never really scary. This is art and no effort is made to make one think otherwise or to completely submerge the piece in its surroundings. As Templeton notes, "There is no [. . .]

11. It's difficult to tell who is a performer or when the next encounter will occur. Performer Greg Arciniega is a "46th Streetperson." (Photo by Zoe Beloff)

expectation that the client participate verbally in the encounter, and the texts are basically conceived as monologues pretending to be dialogues" (1988). Like *Tamara, YOU - The City* relies on the detachment and passivity of the spectator. While there are ample opportunities to respond to the performers' questions, the replies seldom crack the wall of words, although, according to Templeton, some clients did make attempts at outperforming the performers. Anticipating a certain degree of audience befuddlement, Templeton wisely provided for an after-performance session in which clients and performers could meet to discuss the show at the private club that was the final scene of the performance.

The words of *YOU - The City* serve to insulate performer and client from the real world at the same time they play against the grain of the piece's environment—the edgy, threatening world of New York City's streets. Reference is seldom made by the performers to an actual place, rather they seem to be trying to construct a counterpoint to the ongoing random cacophony of street action. Although a variety of places are visited, there is little in the way of conventionally performed action. The performers spend most of the time talking to or about the clients. The performance is a protracted interrogation of the audience in which they are not obligated to respond; one is both isolated and surrounded, alone and intimately "with" another.

The frequently numbing circularity of the words washes over the client and provides a strange but familiar reassurance: You can relax. This is art, and therefore safe. We may speak oddly and take you to places that might otherwise be menacing, but we won't *do* anything to you. The postmodern craze for voyeurism and simulated experience is well served here. You observe and are observed; you are spoken to and about; you are at the center of things but at the same time invisible, safe, unchallenged and unchanged. The show is a house of mirrors in which the image reflected is different for each participant. Like a good thrill ride, *YOU - The City* succeeds in providing the sensation of risk without the consequence of it.

A film version of the show is currently in the works, and a book version is being published by Segue Books, with full script, directions, photos, and notes on the New York City production. Templeton produced the piece again in London in July 1989, and has made tentative arrangements for additional performances in Amsterdam, Glasgow, and San Francisco. Recognizing that the performance is largely defined by the character of the city in which it takes place, she plans script revisions for each new locale.

Description of a Picture/Explosion of a Memory

An interesting environmental attempt to bring together the "high" art tradition of the European avant-garde and the political agendas of various new and Third World cultures was made recently at the Castillo Center in New York City. The first staging in this country of Heiner Müller's *Description of a Picture/Explosion of a Memory* (1985) ran at the center from 22 May–6 June 1987. The Castillo Center was created in 1983 to bring together various traditions—feminist, gay, Latino, black—that its founders felt were not being accommodated by existing cultural institutions. At the time of this performance, the Center was housed in a loft space that was formerly a sweatshop for the manufacture of police uniforms.

Director Eva Brenner decided that the Center needed to look at the work of European contemporary theatre artists. "I wanted to bring in the European avant-garde theatre tradition and say 'you need to look at this.' I think progressive culture has to be international, and there is a lot to learn from

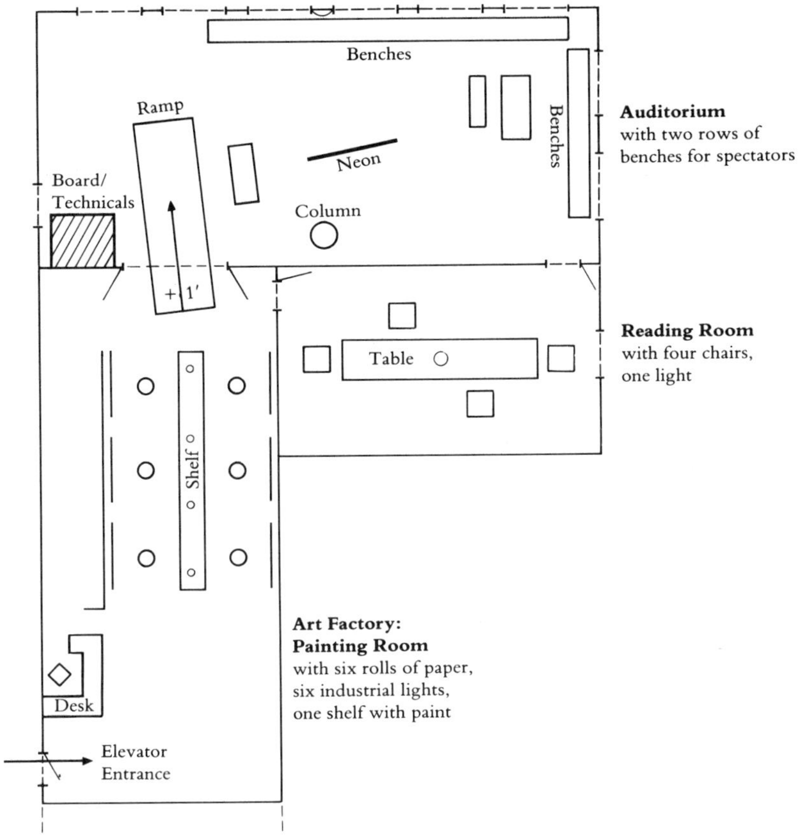

12. Floorplan by Eva Brenner for Description of a Picture/Explosion of a Memory *by Heiner Müller, performed at the Castillo Theatre in New York City. (Graphic by Caroline J. Kavanagh)*

Müller. I wanted to see the clash, to see how people responded to this."[3] Although Müller is a Communist, and very much a political being, his work does not often contain an obvious or easily discernible partisan content. *Description of a Picture/Explosion of a Memory* is perhaps the least overtly political of his plays.

At the first reading, the Center's patrons were less than enthralled. One woman, a black stand-up comedian said, "This is bullshit. I don't know what this is, what this guy believes, how he's going to change things. This may be for you, but it's not written for me." Nonetheless, Brenner persisted. "At first I thought people would follow me. I had credentials, I'd done a lot of plays, but they said, 'No, if I don't know what this does for me and my community, I don't want to do it.' "

In the process of trying to convince the Center's constituents to go along with the project, Brenner brought in a variety of community leaders to join the discussion. She began to see, after so many people reacted to the piece as detached, white, and arrogant, that maybe the European historical avant-garde was out of touch with the Third World and needed to deal with it. An eight-page monolog that talks about a painting isn't easy to sell as political theatre. "But I still felt that we needed to go beyond the existing forms, beyond agitprop, social realism and all that," Brenner noted. "Müller asked me why I wanted to do *this* play; why not pick another of his works that does make a statement? I told him I wanted the line of greatest resistance and most potential conflict."

Brenner feels that Müller touches on the tragic side of the European political dilemma by illuminating the stagnation, the stalemate between

East and West. His work poses the question, "What happens to a country where the revolution was imported and imposed by an outside power?" Brenner notes that Müller's work always comes back to the deadly fixedness of European society, the killing of possibilities. "The picture in this play is a picture of stasis; it's why I left Europe," she observed.

Müller's densely packed description seeks literally to explode the picture, an image appropriate to the conflict that arose around the piece at the Castillo Center. And indeed, this became the raison d'etre of the performance—the depiction of the clash between slick, finished, European "high" art and the volatile, impulsive input of the Center's diverse constituency. The tension, though seemingly insoluble, did have a potentially useful energy. "We finally decided that staging the conflict rather than the play itself was the only way that all of us could remain in the same building. The environmental design of the piece came up because we didn't know how to resolve the conflicts that broke out." Brenner found that the normally autocratic process of directing ran head on with the egalitarian aims of the Center's political agenda. "Now here's this big loud guy talking about the revolution and the people and I think 'Oh my God.' But who am I to tell him what's more important or to say 'you don't fit our aesthetic, go read your poem outside'?"

Out of a desire to accommodate everyone involved, Brenner and codirector Josef Szeiler of Vienna's Angelus Novus Theater, devised what they call "the art factory." Basically a participatory option for the audience, it consisted of three rolls of paper suspended from the ceiling of the first room the audience entered. The paper and a variety of writing and drawing materials were offered to those who wished them by a "shop steward," who also told people of their option to move around the space. Throughout the performance, the sound of the text being read in the main space was piped to the art factory.

The play text is literally a description of a painting, and it was from that basic premise that the work began. The actors in the main space first played with the idea of museum visitors stepping into the Müller picture. The focus later shifted to the performers' selecting pieces of the text that they wished to explore through movement and vocalization. Brenner began to function as a conductor (in the fashion of Tadeuz Kantor)—intervening, stopping, shaping, and restarting the process at different points during the performance. The movements were slow and deliberate, emphasizing grouping and regrouping, the formation and dissipation of tableaux.

The text itself was read in the main room by a performer seated at a table with a glass of water and a stopwatch. She began reading precisely at eight o'clock and read for one hour, taking one-minute breaks every three minutes. The music for the piece followed a similar pattern of sound/silence, playing for five minutes followed by a minute of silence.

In addition to the art factory and the main space where the Müller play was performed, there was a third area called the reading room. Here was a long table with chairs, texts of the play, pencils, and paper. The performer stationed in the room was a Harlem high school principal named Barbara Taylor who wrote poetry and read from the text. She also encouraged others to join her, write, or take the texts into another room and read on their own or with the actors.

The space accommodated close to a hundred people, with crowds ranging from a dozen to near capacity during the two-week run of the show. The rooms were gray and dimly lit with a minimum of properties and

13. The actors in the Castillo Center's main space group and regroup, their movements slow and deliberate. (Photo by Ricky Flores)

14. Barbara Taylor presides over the "Reading Room," reading poetry and the text of Description of a Picture/Explosion of a Memory. *(From the video by Elena Bernstein)*

seating for only 30, which forced the audience to circulate through the space. The actors wore white and black and gray. The sounds and movements of the performers were augmented by the sounds and sights of the city, as all of the windows in the space remained open throughout the evening.

"The place had a feel like a mausoleum which was heightened by all the life outside," Brenner observed. "We wanted to show our struggle and failure to communicate inside the mausoleum, like the characters in Müller's painting." The clash between the highbrow art and the chaos outside was further reinforced by the tension between those performing the Müller text and those doing their own thing in conjunction with the play. Many of the actors felt resentful and threatened by the activities in the art factory and the reading room, which many viewed as peripheral. Turf battles erupted during rehearsal as to whether those reading a poem by Rene Castillo outside the theatre should be permitted to do so inside the space.

Many of those attending the performance were unsure of whether they could move from room to room or to what degree their participation was required. As Brenner noted, "Some felt that they had paid their ten dollars and should be left alone in their seat," a reaction hardly new to those who stage environmental theatre. Several spectators thought that the comments of the shop steward were an imposition; they did not wish to be told to paint or where to go. Brenner said that the audience seemed to react positively to the playground/sandbox qualities of the environment (one reviewer called it a "postmodern kindergarten" [Massa 1987:97]). Most people moved through the initial art factory space, perceiving it to be a lobby, into the main space, which, with benches along opposite walls, bore the greatest resemblance to a performance space. It was also the darkest room in the space, heightening its status as the most "theatrelike" and "important" of the three rooms.

The question arises as to whether *Description of a Picture/Explosion of a Memory* is "political" in the usual sense of the word or if it simply represented the Castillo Center's internal conflict over this play. While the conflict between aesthetics and action is always interesting, it is not in itself good theatre, political or otherwise. Political theatre may or may not be prescriptive, but it must on some level engage its audience and reveal its own values and attitudes. Many people attending the show seemed more intrigued by the cleverness of the staging than by anything that might be construed as political content. After attending the performance, John Cage referred to it as "restful," an adjective not usually applied to political theatre.

As was the case with *Bananaland,* the environment took on a life of its own and often upstaged the written text. In many respects there were two performances: one that revolved around the Müller play and one that developed as a reaction to it. The performers who read a Rene Castillo poem, entitled "Apolitical Intellectuals," outside the theatre during the show seemed almost to be protesting against the piece rather than participating in it. Audience engagement, as such, tended to be more with the postmodern funhouse quality of the space and its gimmicks than with any message the piece might have conveyed.

There is a misconception on the part of many critics that environmental theatre is an intrinsically participatory experience. Writing in the *New York Times,* Stephen Holden described audiences at *Tamara* and other current environmental offerings as "not just passive spectators but active participants" (1988:1). Nothing could be further from the truth. All of these productions employ specific rules and boundaries that rely as much on spectator passivity as do conventional proscenium shows. Movement of actors and spectators in a space does not necessarily eradicate boundaries or require participation. The use of elements from popular environmental entertainments (theme parks, carnivals) serves to emphasize the shows' status as "party worlds" (Holden's phrase) in which amusement is more central than engagement or participation. Most of the audience members I spoke to at these shows talked about the novelty of the staging or the proximity of the performers. The content and purpose of the work seemed to get lost in the shuffle.

Environmental theatre is no longer a novelty, but neither is it currently possessed by the urgency to find new forms or effect social and artistic change that characterized many environmental works in the '60s and early '70s. The issue of audience participation is critical here because "environmental" implies not just a different physical relationship between actor and audience, but a different understanding of the performer/spectator contract—of what is expected and delivered by each party.

Participation was not simply an option in the 1960s—to many it was a necessity, the raison d'etre of the performance itself. Schechner once wrote of the audience's "responsibility" to respond in an active way (1973:19), an idea that seems a long way from the relatively passive (intellectually if not physically) audiences at many contemporary performances. Radically altering the audience/performer contract is no longer the concern. People walk about and get close physically, but the barrier between actor and spectator remains intact. Today's environmental theatre may move the fourth wall around a bit, but no one is put up against or through it. The actors say their lines and go through their routines without being unduly affected by what the audience does or does not do. "Confrontation," a term so endemic to the social/political/aesthetic discourse of the '60s, is alien to the new environmentalism. The need to change, provoke, alter, or transform spectators no longer seems central to the aims of many practitioners.

The interesting link between the pieces coming from an "art" background *(YOU - The City* and *Description of a Picture/Explosion of a Memory)* and those drawing on popular environmental forms *(Tamara* and *Bananaland),* is that each is more concerned with the illusion of intimacy than with communicating a specific message to the audience. In this sense, these works are truly indicative of their times. To paraphrase Marshall McLuhan: the package *is* the product; the means of staging have become the ends. The point could be made that form *is* content; that the manner in which something is done is inseparable from what it is saying. But this falls back on the art-for-art's-sake argument used to justify the self-absorption typical of much postmodernist performance. Even *YOU - The City,* the most provocative piece conceptually, uses the same voyeuristic hook as its contemporaries, it simply reverses the equation: rather than observing, you are observed. People may opt to respond, but it is hardly required. The show still maintains the essentially passive role of the spectator and the carefully wrought barriers between audience and performer.

But perhaps it is unfair to castigate the current crop of environmental productions for failing to challenge or engage audiences in the manner of their more activist predecessors. Formalism and detachment remain, after more than a decade, the preeminent aesthetic values in contemporary performance. The irony of environmental theatre today is that its very success has prevented it from functioning as a viable catalyst for new directions in performance. The alluring potential of an infinitely malleable form has pushed the question of *what* the theatre ought to be saying into the background. This is not just a problem for the avant-garde; *Cats* continues to pack them in and the settings frequently receive more applause than singers at the Met. Spectacle is in the ascendancy as theatre tries to hook a public weaned on MTV and Steven Spielberg. As long as audiences and artists are more beguiled by appearances than content, little will change.

Notes

1. *Tamara* opened in Toronto on 5 May 1981 and in New York City on 2 December 1987. It is currently on an open run in New York.
2. Conversation taped by the author at *Tamara* performance, 10 July 1988.
3. All quotes from Eva Brenner are from an interview with the author, 22 October 1988.

References

Aronson, Arnold
1977 *The History and Theory of Environmental Scenography*. Ann Arbor, MI: UMI Press.

Brenner, Eva
1988 Interview with author. New York, 22 October.

Holden, Stephen
1988 "It May Be Fun, but Is It Good Theater?" *The New York Times*, 7 August, sec. 2:1, 14–15.

King, George, and Ruby Lerner
1988 *Bananaland* program.

Lerner, Ruby
1988 Telephone interview with author, 17 August.

Massa, Robert
1987 "Means of Production." *The Village Voice*, 24 June:97.

Murray, Steve
1988 "Banana Picking and Foreign Policy." *American Theatre* 5, nos. 4–5 (July/August):4–5.

Nelson, Steve
1986 "Walt Disney's EPCOT and the World's Fair Performance Tradition." *The Drama Review* 30, no. 4 (T112):106–46.

Rose, Richard
1988 Interview with author. New York, 22 July.

Schechner, Richard
1968 "Six Axioms for Environmental Theatre." *The Drama Review* 12, no. 3 (T39):41–64.
1973 *Environmental Theater*. New York: Hawthorn Books.

Templeton, Fiona
1988 Introduction to *YOU - The City*, unpublished manuscript.

Steve Nelson *is an Assistant Professor in the Theatre and Film Department at Hunter College. His article on EPCOT and World's Fair performance appeared in T112.*

Bananaland

PR, Propaganda, and Infotainment

Paul Evans

Bananaland: A Central American Theme Park is vaudeville propaganda, a guerrilla exercise of schtick engaged in sabotage. Conceived as a theme park, the work deploys surprise tactics to attack consumerism-as-imperialism. But salesmanship is just one of the targets hit by the piece co-authored by Ruby Lerner, former executive director of the Southeastern arts coalition Alternate ROOTS, and documentary filmmaker George King.

Wryly coopting the media ploy of "infotainment"—reportage tricked out as show biz—*Bananaland* dismantles the myth-making machinery of the U.S. empire. Cabaret, video, installation pieces, pirated texts, and puppetry tipsily coalesce into a "mockumentary" that undercuts the doctored objectivity, coy sobriety, and contrived reassurances that characterize news-bite history. Besides exposing specific political iniquities, the work reveals how the manufactured mix-up of news and advertising aggravates a blithe obliviousness, a "bananality" of evil.

The show's run, 7–24 July 1988 at Seven Stages Theatre in Atlanta, was set to parallel the larger circus of the Democratic Convention where presidential candidate Michael Dukakis would charm a demographic with snippety Spanish. It began fortuitously the week *Time* magazine, flourishing the headline "¡Magnifico!," played fast and Luce with Hispanic chic. Here we found an epithalamium honoring the season's tempestuous marriage (or marketing-brainstorm link-up) of Latino *sensibilidad* and gringo pop. Celebrated with equal zest were Nancy Reagan's big-ticket Adolfo gowns, Ruben Blades' emancipatory crossover dreams, and the reactionary funk of Miami Sound Machine. Although quavering with proper indignation about barrio poverty and waxing dramatic about this ripest ethnic "identity crisis," the general tone remained appropriately apologetic for the conqueror. Doting and conciliatory, ladling all manner of edge and diversity into the melting pot, *Time*'s was a quintessential mainstream "feature" story—authoritative, affirmative, conclusive. And a quick and painless read.

Countering not only that message but its method, *Bananaland* marshals a "journalism from below"—subjective, fragmentary, personal, open to question. Against the summarizing "photograph" of gloss-reportage, the work presents an "action collage" of crossreferential moods and genres that resists closure, pat scanning, or comfy ingestion. And for the illusion

1. Juanita Marimba (Nita Hardy) and her lackey accordionist Lenny Bellows (Rodger French) stroll among the fake palm trees of the Bananaland *plaza. (Photo by Joe Lesterlove)*

of inevitability and solution inherent in quotidian journalism (and Aristotelian theatre), *Bananaland* exchanges a plotless ranging that arrests the implied "march of progress" of narrative form. A theatre of random epiphanies, *Bananaland* "hops more than it marches," as Voltaire said of an essay of Montesquieu's. And, suiting its assault on unbordered ambition, it does its work more spatially than temporally.

Certainly *Bananaland* invades its performance space. Taking advantage of Seven Stages' high ceiling and unobstructed floor, as well as the lobby and capacious auditorium, carpenters have put up partitions, booths, and tunnels to create a carnival maze [see *Bananaland* map, plate 5 in Steve Nelson's article, this issue]. The riotous Caribbean color scheme (yellow, red, green) and slapdash construction spoofs the manicured attractions of Disney World. Dimly lit passageways add tension and dread, a feeling of EPCOT becoming Inferno.

In a parody of imperialist appetite, the theatre is transformed into bananarama—the immense yellow fruit atop the marquee; George King, on the sidelines, in a T-shirt sporting Andy Warhol's banana artwork for the Velvet Underground's debut LP; a Gift Shop peddling Juicy Fruit kitsch, condoms, and *Bananaland*wear (Panama hats, touristy garb airbrushed with banana designs). A TV screen flashes the logo for Woody Allen's *Bananas;* banana smoothies are sold at a bar; a Carmen Miranda Bananabilia Collection displays an acre of ads for Dole, Chiquita, and United Fruit Company (or, as rendered Joycean by the firm's own PR, "Unifruitco").

2. From his balcony, General Anastasio Somoza (George Nikas) greets Bananaland *patrons. (Photo by George King)*

To the taped strains of one of the show's spunkier original tunes ("[H]ere at Bananaland / The jokes are cheap / The laughter's canned / It's more fun than Disney / Or Graceland"), the audience enters a Bananaland Plaza of fake palms and cabaña dreck. Banana-hatted Juanita Marimba and lackey accordionist Lenny Bellows (Nita Hardy, Rodger French) parlay nightclub rhumba and cocktail banter. From the balcony perch so dear to dictators, a lounge-act version of General Anastasio Somoza (George Nikas) toasts himself, pumped up by boombox applause, as "Senator for Life," "Promoter of Rural Electrification," "Ridiculous Parody of a National Leader," "The Main Enchilada," "Close Personal Friend of Richard Nixon." Sharkishly sportive in the kind of Ruritanian uniform Hermann Göring affected, Somoza, the evening's MC, drops names (Charro, Juan Valdez, Wayne Newton) and barks orders, dividing the audience into tour groups.

On a staggered schedule, the crowd takes alternately the Guatemala Tour and the Museum Tour, stopping for refreshment at Anastasio's Cafe (*el comandante* dices bananas with his machete) or Somoza e Hijos Bar Y Grill, before ending up at The Shades of Truth Pavilion. They can pause at the Library, which, as counterpoint to the crassly commercial gift shop, distributes tracts from such groups as the Atlanta Committee on Latin America, No Business As Usual Action Network, and the Committee in Solidarity with the People of El Salvador.

First up on the Guatemala Tour is a ride on Bananair, Flight 1954. The audience gathers in a narrow space, its plyboard walls painted to suggest

3. Passengers on the Guatemala Tour take Bananair, Flight 1954. The slapdash constructions spoof the manicured attractions of Disney World. (Photo by George King)

the interior of a cut-rate airliner. Passengers hear an announcement that rosaries will drop toward the seats in case of emergency, that prayer cards are provided, and that "iguana-on-a-stick" is available for snacks. Then "Operation Success," an "In-Flight Thriller Puppet Show," commences. Written by King, Lerner, and Jon Ludwig (of Atlanta's Center for Puppetry Arts), "Operation Success" is performed by airline crewmen (Jim Brooks, Neill Bogan) and a cast of golf trophies, *Ghostbusters* toys, and G.I. Joe figurines. It relates the rape of hope in the country whose per capita income stands at $1,198. New Year's Day, 1954, a rare time of land reform and democracy, gives way to May of that year, when Ike's CIA and the United Fruit Company, Guatemala's largest landowner, conspire to nix popularly elected President Jacobo Arbenz.

After offering the role to Adolf and Benito (the two stooges of evil chirp "Nein!" and "Ciao!"), Big Business picks an indigenous puppet, the monstrous Carlos Castillo Armas, to lead a faked revolution. Its outcome is predictable: the abolition of unions, the brutal "questioning" of suspects, book burning, and a return to vengeful private ownership. As they caterwaul doggerel political lyrics to Sam the Sham's "Woolly Bully" and hurl props and dolls, the flight attendants come to resemble demonic Cub Scouts, the undeclared war a sort of *Boy's Life* farce.

The flight concluded, next comes a trek through a darkened hall lit with exhibits by an ad hoc collective of visual artists—a warped Smithsonian of pillage and hidden persuasion. From a TV monitor, faded newsreel footage flickers: Secretary of State John Foster Dulles is rehearsing sincerity for a press conference to boost "benign" interference down South. A wall chart of the House Committee on Foreign Affairs chronicles a history of dubious intervention. An artwork, somewhat recalling the photo collages of David Hockney, makes of the banana a totem, numinous and detached. A blowup of a dictionary page lists, with deadpan overkill, words with the prefix "super." There's a Gallery of Dictators, garish busts of the Latino Neros painted metallic, their heads, as in the paintings of Arcimboldi, constructed of jumbles of found objects—toy soldiers, menacing bric-a-brac. Idols, Golden Calves, the pieces have a brassiness that sassily mimics the busts in *Playboy*'s annually published pop star Hall of Fame.

Among the most effective pieces is *The Spanish Lesson,* an instructional chart bordered by corporate logos (AT&T, IBM, Gulf & Western) that dilutes the language of Juan de la Cruz, Miguel de Cervantes, and Pablo Neruda to Orwellian pablum *("Me gusto Madonna y Michael Jackson," "Yo estudio a Marx").* Also powerful is a cage, nearly hidden in darkness, from which the gestural eloquence of a wire figure crumpled in a pose of torture articulates anonymous suffering.

Turning the corner, there's Windows on the World, boxed tableaux of miniatures; logos with explanatory texts that reiterate the theme of corporate conquest, of ITT, Castle & Cook, and Firestone as a transnational, meddling brain trust.

The Museum Tour first takes the audience on a Plantation Train Ride. Mirroring Bananair's addled flight attendants, docents Helen and Betty (Taylor St. Clair, Kim Dixon) are neurotic Barbies. Brandishing beauty-queen grins, they're relentlessly fulsome ("Our most sanitary fruit comes carefully wrapped in its own sanitary container!"). Regaling the riders with banana trivia and conducting pop quizzes in "banana math," they shimmy at the marvel of "the money tree, the shekel shrub" and then usher the crowd into the Banana Theatre. There, a 1922 silent film from the Ford Educational Library shows Yanqui traders business-suited astride burros, and back-broken laborers as "men of the soil." It's creaky, Kiplingesque, and campy-scary.

Helen and Betty lead finally to the United Fruit Co. Museum, a shrine to the backhanded terrorism of big-league Capital. Company propaganda and photos of the founders line the wall, providing accompaniment to the docents' doubletalk delivery of Unifruitco history. Theirs is a cotton-headed account of robber-baron land grabbing, tax-bracket shystering, and high-stakes Monopoly (aside from its hold on Central American banana production, UFC so controlled transport centers and communication lines that it earned the nickname "the Octopus"). Supplementing the homily is a video show 'n' tell: Alistair Cooke loftily recounts the company's romance (courtesy of a substitute voice-over), a crummy "How-I-Spent-My-Vacation" film clip reduces an epic of corporate bravado to a yuck-fest of the sort coaxed by the "home movies" of early "Saturday Night Live." All polyester and errantly emphatic enunciation, a TV preacher (Levi Lee) lauds God's own fruit; a pair of pedants (Joe Feldman, James Taylor) dignify company lore with academic chat.

Sporadically, the boosterism gets undercut from within, as one docent can't help divulging the ghastly suicide of UFC bigwig Eli Black (who threw himself out a window), and a waxwork effigy of grizzled founder Capt. Alonzo D. Baker (Kent Whipple) springs to life to bellow blood and thunder.

Meanwhile, back at the Plaza, two labcoated imps (James Brooks, Neill Bogan), leering Groucho-like, lure audience members into a polygraph station bordering *Bananaland*'s last stop: The Shades of Truth Pavilion. The mad scientists are The Doctors Mengele, and their polygraph a Rube Goldberg contraption. As the clinicians interrogate, the machine judges each victim by a skewed standard ("Lies Without Knowing" . . . "A Pack of Lies" . . . "A Relative Personal Truth").

Such casuistry is a mugged version of the Machiavellianism hyped by Edward Bernays (Kent Whipple). Bernays, a genius carnival barker of global hoodwink, was PR counsel to an astonishing range of clients—the Bank of America, GE, GM, Procter & Gamble, the U.S. Armed Forces, *and* Actors' Equity and the NAACP. Freud's nephew and author of two

4. The Doctors Mengele (James Brooks, Neill Bogan) administer a polygraph test to General Somoza (George Nikas) at the Shades of Truth Pavilion. (Photo by Joe Lesterlove)

portentous how-to's, *Propaganda* and *Public Relations,* he evolved his strategies from a central question: "If we understand the mechanisms of the group mind, is it not possible to regiment the masses according to our will without their knowing it?" Here Bernays delivers a lecture about the "engineering of consent" that reveals him as a master of deceit—Dale Carnegie turns out to be Satan. The character of Bernays is, in the context of the whole performance, underlit, unobtrusive. But as he talks, his voice inflected with icy professionalism and suppressed threat, he betrays himself as the sly Wizard of *Bananaland*'s psychotic Oz.

And the work of Bernays' mindset forms the final exhibit—the Propaganda Maze. Dark walls make up a blackboard labyrinth wherein the wandering audience is confronted with signs posing mockingly provocative questions, absurdist brainteasers: "Are people in small communities more susceptible to propaganda than residents of large cities?"; "Is there a difference between advertising that provides information and advertising that is designed only to sell a product?"

Not only does the abrupt severity of the silent black maze jolt the audience, but the spare, meditative construct is so open-ended a symbol that it

5. *Edward Bernays (Kent Whipple) lectures on the "engineering of consent." (Photo by George King)*

prompts a heady allusiveness (the "black box" retrieved from crashed jets; a Western Ka'bah; a test for human rats; the Vietnam war memorial; an alarming circus sideshow). It functions as a profane tabernacle of language—words in dramatic isolation contend toward unimaginable meaning; bouncing off walls, they provoke a dizzy, puzzled, desperate response.

It's precisely that engineered confusion—stirred up by the entire assaultive circus of *Bananaland*—that sets the stage for catharses which, if any take place, will probably happen outside the theatre. For so busy and thumping is the piece that it encourages a thirst for clarity, for a stillness within which to think the work out. *Bananaland* seems predicated on a kind of metaphysical, specifically existentialist trust: the performance not only leaves the ultimate hermeneutical discovery to the individual viewer, but its noise and brio seem primed for self-combustion—the most effective examination of the ideas it conveys is possible only after its packed static has been cleared away.

The apparent danger of this approach is either that the confusion will linger, or that any of a number of interpretations, not necessarily false, might compromise the work's density by sacrificing the whole to a part. For instance, reading *Bananaland* as a farce—which can almost be done, as its Barnum sometimes overwhelms its Brecht—can reduce the work to shaky comedy, its jokes inhibited by a straining toward consciousness-raising. On the other hand, any exclusive expectation of, say, a policy statement against colonialist intervention or a mourning for the corpses of conquest, will not be satisfied, either because the gags could seem to obscure the politics, or because the work, while obviously empathetic with their struggle, refuses the hubris of coopting the suffering of the Central Americans.

Bananaland eludes a reductive or "clean" reading exactly because its method *and* message are about confusion: the confusion of good intentions and perverse payoffs, progress and domination, truth and PR, art and propaganda, seriousness and humor, information and entertainment—even, theatre and theme park. In its critical function, the work attacks the evils of deliberate confusion—the hypocrisy and deceit that engender victimization, alienation, detachment, inertia, compliance. And yet the work's creative tension also acknowledges confusion as a state of possibility and expansiveness. Not only does *Bananaland* offer the stylistic pleasures of a jumble of genres and approaches, but it finds in its refusal of "certainty," in its insistence on polyphony, an ideology of openness. It seems to work not so sharply toward dialectic as toward a pregnant coalescence.

Such an ideology may find its source in the democratic ideal. And while we can read in it the somewhat touching, effusive desire to offer "something for everyone" (which *Bananaland,* remarkably, accomplishes), we can see further, in its very tentativeness, its critique of the ways power forecloses options. Cautioning against the Ugly Americanism of missionary manipulation and the disingenuous coercion of the melting pot, the work posits as corrective an ideal of mani*fold* destiny.

That such an ideal remains a very (North) American dream seems only to underscore the honesty of *Bananaland*'s creators. Resisting, as a subtle imperialism, the romantic agony of an artificial identification with Hispanic strife and culture, they yet realize their implication in both the American Promise and the American Machine. And it's from that insider's position of privileged knowledge that their sabotage draws its accuracy, confidence, and force.

Involving more than 20 visual, media, and performing artists, *Bananaland* took King and Lerner over two years to research. After poring over source material at the Tulane University Middle American Library and gamely taking junkets to Gator World, Citrus World, and the Tupperware museum, they managed to recapture the ambiences of both library/news room and theme park/circus. The near collision of these contradictory moods—brow-furrowing/side-splitting—keeps the audience intrigued and on edge. And since both library and theme park are places of control (the library a vault of "irrefutable facts," the theme park a mechanical funhouse), the juxtaposition builds tension. The Bergsonian release of tension through comedy is instantaneous. And yet, properly, the tension prompted by the information *Bananaland* uncovers and disseminates seems intended to continue beyond the theatre.

Bananaland emerges finally as a theatre of vigilance. By keeping its audience off kilter and on guard, it performs its sleight of hand—intellectual challenges spring out from behind its vaudeville screen. This is theatre that forces the eyes open, initially to the trickery of the performance itself, and then to the trickery of a larger theatre—the forces of the "real" propaganda, the disinformation networks of reductive analysis and "objective" news.

Paul Evans *was, until recently, editor of* Southline, *a weekly journal of politics, art, and ideas.*

China's Nuo Theatre

Two Views

Qu Liuyi *Huangpu Chongqing*

Ed. Note: What follows are two articles on nuo theatre in China. To some degree the articles overlap since they deal with some of the same materials. But their takes are entirely different. Qu Liuyi is interested mainly in the historical descent of nuo while Huangpu Chongqing details certain actual performances. We are printing both accounts to begin to familiarize TDR *readers with the variety in contemporary Chinese performance scholarship. In future issues there will be more material from China (including other articles by Qu and Huangpu) exhibiting different styles of Chinese scholarship. The articles below were written before the events in China of May and June 1989.*

The Yi Human Evolution Theatre

Qu Liuyi

Theatre in many regions of China originated in rituals aimed at driving away evil and welcoming happiness in the form of an abundant harvest. These performances are called "nuo," a term that appears very early in Chinese. In the eighth century BCE the *Analects of Confucius* record that the great philosopher saw "nuo in the countryside" near his home in what is now Shangdong province. Over the course of its long development, nuo absorbed into its practice elements of Taoism and Buddhism.

This "sacrificial ritual" was led by a "wizard"—a priest or shaman—and was usually done at the end of the year (January-February). During his performance, the wizard wore different masks made from leather, wood, or papier-mâché. These masks showed that the wizard represented different deities, that he was not himself but the god. When, at some point, the wizard also enacted different folk stories or historical events, he clearly became an actor.

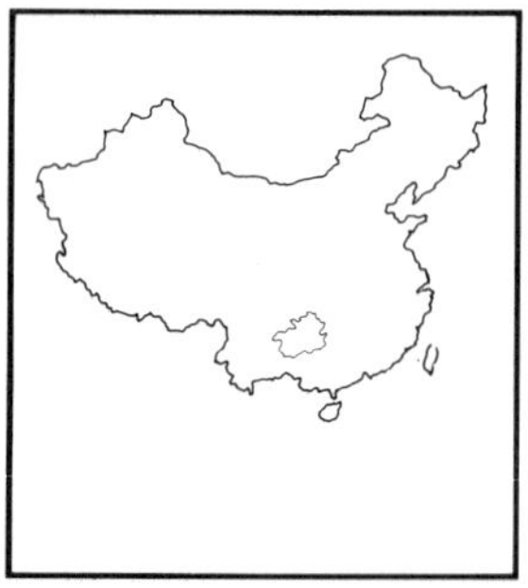

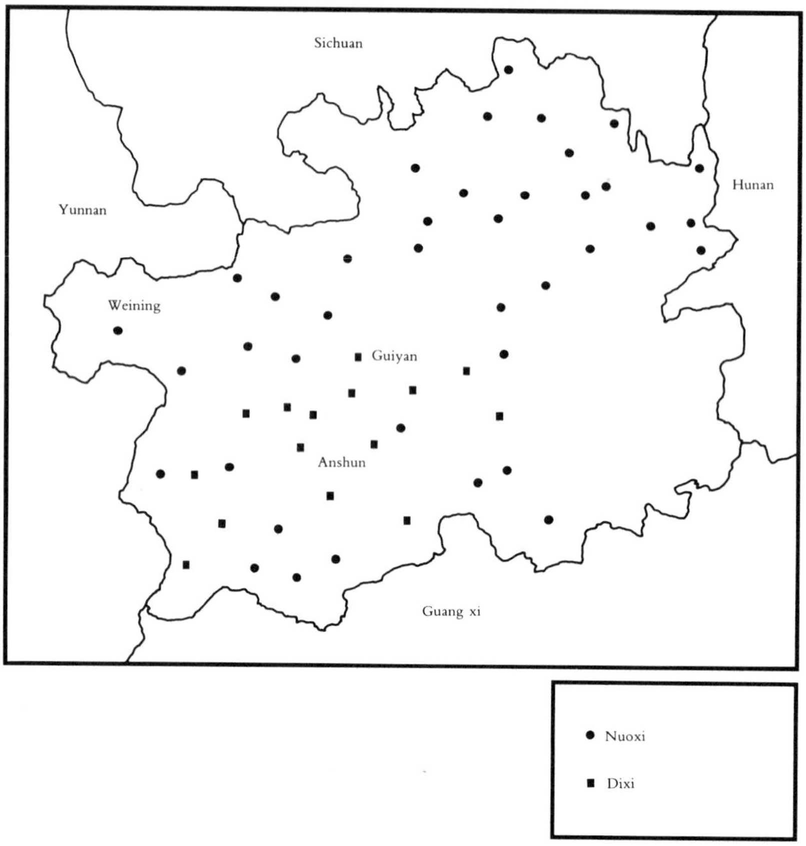

1. A map of China locating Guizhou province. The detail of Guizhou shows the location of nuoxi and dixi throughout the province. (Graphics by Caroline J. Kavanagh)

Nuo is not found all over China, but only in specific areas. China can be divided into different culture belts:

1. The shamanic in the northeast including Inner Mongolia. The Hezhe, Man, Dawoer, Elunchun, Weiwuer, and Mongolian nationalities live in this area. The shamanism practiced here is continuous with the shamanic practices of Siberia. Although shamanic activity is less pervasive today than previously, we can still find shamanic rituals in the rural areas of Lia Ning and Ji Lin provinces. The deities worshiped are nature gods like Mountain, Stone, Water, Fire; and animal gods like Bear, Tiger, Snake, Eagle; and the gods of the Ancestors. Most of the shamanic peoples are nomadic, engaged in fishing and hunting. There is no nuo theatre among these people even though they have rich traditions of song, dance, and folk art.
2. The Islamic in Xinjian and Ningxia provinces in the northwest. Uygur and Kazakhstani peoples moved into these areas and converted to Islam. Because of the Islamic prohibition against idolatry and mimetic representation, no nuo exists in this area.
3. The Buddhist, found in almost all of China. Buddhists use artistic forms to propagate and maintain their doctrines. Sakyamuni and other deities are represented by statues, paintings, and other means. Buddhism first entered China during the Eastern Han dynasty (25–220 AD) and developed great influence rapidly—but with the exception of Tibet, where it established itself by the seventh century, Buddhism did not become universal in China until later. In Tibet Buddhism absorbed the

rituals, songs, and dances of Benism (a kind of shamanism) leading to the development of Qiangmu, the "dancing god." Tibetan theatre is an advanced form of nuo. Many Mongols of Inner Mongolia were highly influenced by the Huang Jiao (Yellow sect) of Tibetan Buddhism, giving up shamanism and accepting the Qiangmu rituals.

4. The central plains of the Huanghe (Yellow) River valley where nuo theatre originated. For more than 2,000 years, in the ancient capitals of Chang'an (now Xi'an), Luoyang, Kaifeng, and in the countryside, there have been large-scale nuo performances. Today in the rural areas of Shanxi province we can find performances of saixi, duixi, lungyan zaju, heyang, duangong, and qu fan and drum theatre. The fan and drum theatre still obviously retains the vestiges of third-century Han dynasty ritual. These nuo theatres use chanting rather than singing which may be related to the Dunhuang narrative literature of the seventh-century Tang dynasty.
5. The Baiyue of the Yangtze River valley and the large area to its south. Many non-Chinese nationalities once lived here. In Quanzhou in Fujian province there appeared the drama *Breaking Into Hell (Da Cheng)* which describes how heros broke into hell to save the damned. Other kinds of nuo appear in Jiangsu, Anhui, and Jiangxi provinces. The Mulian theatre, originating probably 1,000 years ago, was once very popular in this region. The hero of this drama—which takes about one week to perform—is Mulian, a pious disciple of Sakyamuni, who saves his mother from hell.
6. The Bashu and Jingchu, mainly referring to Sichuan and Guizhou provinces in the upper reaches of the Yangtze, and to Hubei, Hunan, Guangxi, and Yunnan provinces in the middle reaches. As early as 2,000 years ago, sacrificial rituals were very popular here. Qu Yuan, the earliest great poet of China (340 BCE–278 BCE), was exiled to this region by the king of the Chu. Qu's *Nine Songs (Jiu Ge)* drew most of its materials from local "witch songs." Textual research on *Nine Songs* indicates that the nuo rituals of that time involved many theatrical elements such as song, music, dance, and perhaps the narration of some legends. This kind of nuo is considered the earliest, although still in an embryonic form. Guizhou is the province where the Bashu and Jingchu cultures met. And the nationalities living in this area—Han, Yi, Miao, Dong, Buyi, and Gelao—all have their own styles of nuo.

Nuo theatre can be divided into four types: palace, folk, temple, and army. Palace nuo was mainly performed in ancient capitals like Chang'an, Luoyang, and Kaifeng in the Huanghe River valley and ancient Hangzhou in the Baiyue culture belt. Temple nuo was active in Tibetan areas like Gansu, Qinghai, Sichuan, and Yunnan and in Mongolia. Beijing's famous Yong He Temple had "dancing spirit" *(tiao gui)* exorcism rituals performed by lamas into the 1950s. Folk nuo was very popular and could be found all over the country except in the Islamic areas. Army nuo refers to rituals performed by expeditionary forces and the military stationed on the frontiers. One thousand years ago there were professional actors, *zhujun,* in the frontier station of Guilin, Guangxi province. The large-scale army nuo influenced the local nuo dramas of the Han and Zhuang nationalities. At that time a set of 800 masks was sent to the capital, Kaifeng.

Folk nuo is the basis of the other types. The folk nuo of the Yi of Guizhou is the most "primitive"—perhaps the oldest—of any that have been found by researchers so far in the whole country. At present only two

2. A set for the nuo theatre of the Buyi people in Guizhou province. (Photo by Huangpu Chongqing)

other kinds of nuo are still performed: the dixi of Guizhou and the Guansuo xi of Yunnan. These dramas tell war stories, praising patriotism and bravery. A peasants' dixi company of the village of Anshun, Guizhou, was invited in 1986 to perform at festivals in France and Spain where they were enthusiastically received.[1]

Cuo Tai Ji

Luojia is a tiny community of not more than 50 households in Weining county where Guizhou, Sichuan, and Yunnan provinces meet. There the Yi still perform nuo, called *cuo tai ji*. Cuo means "man" or "human"; tai means "evolve" or "change"; and ji means "game" or "theatre." So cuo tai ji means "the drama of how human beings evolved" or, as I call it, the "human evolution theatre."

This drama involves ten actors and two musicians.[2] Six of the actors play men, two perform lions, and two oxen. The cast may be further specified as follows:

Nuogabu (also called Rejia'arbu)—the old man of the forest, a character without a mask but with a black paper beard, white hair, and dressed in the ordinary long gown of the Yi.
Abumo (or Arbumo)—the old Yi grandfather, aged 1,700 years, masked, with a white beard.
Adamu (or Ardamu)—the old Yi grandmother, aged 1,500 years, masked and carrying a baby on her back.
Aga, or Aran—a young boy, masked.
Mahongmo—literally an old man of the Miao, aged 1,200 years, masked.
Hengbu (or Heibu)—literally an old man of the Han, aged 1,000 years, wearing a mask with a harelip.
The animals—all masked.
Two musicians playing drums and cymbals.

The performing area is a cleared grassy space with the audience on all sides; lanterns burn at four corners. When the drum arrives, the made-up actors, both human and animal, are led by Nuogabu into the performing area to form a circle. With sticks in their hands and their legs stiffly ex-

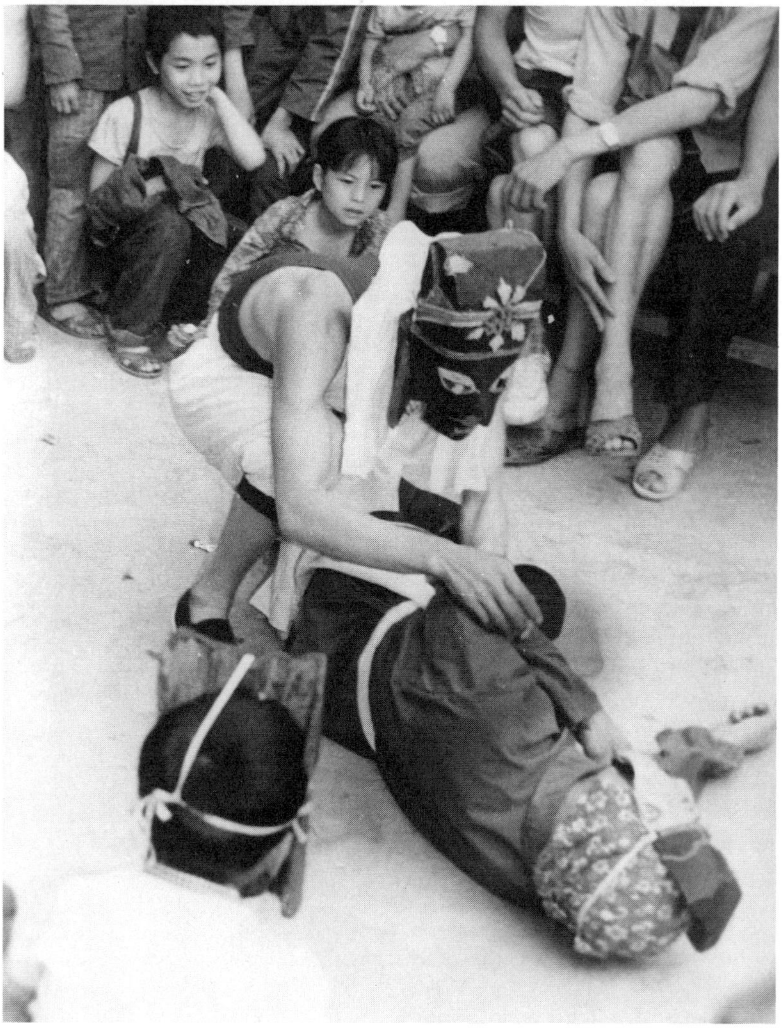

3. & 4. Two nuo performances of the Buyi people. (Photos by Huangpu Chongqing)

5. *The masks of* cuo tai ji, *the nuo theatre of the Yi people of Guizhou province. (Photo by Huangpu Chongqing)*

tended they look like they have come from far away, deep in the forest. Their voices sound apelike—in fact, the Yi believe that humans evolved from creatures with monkey faces and mice teeth who ate wild fruits and wore leaves instead of clothes. The performers line up and prostrate themselves to the sky, the earth, the god of the mountain, the god of rice, and the ancestor in the west. They drink wine.

Then Abumo tells Nuogabu and the audience that they have brought seeds from Yunnan in order to save the hungry people. They then begin to cultivate the land. Nuogabu tries to persuade the others to buy oxen with Adamu's private savings so that they can better make use of the land. After the harvest, they make buckwheat. When they rest, Aga comes and sucks Adamu's breast and then plays with her. At this moment, Hengbu teases Adamu and has sex with her from behind. Abumo chases Hengbu away and has sex from behind with Adamu himself. After Nuogabu finishes weighing the buckwheat, he tells the others they have 12,000 dans (about 600,000 kilos). They all happily encircle the buckwheat, walking and praying, and telling the story of how they came from Yunnan. Nuogabu tells them to speak after him:

> Let's propose a toast
> to Father of the Sky
> to Mother of the Earth
> to 99 gods of the Sky
> to 66 gods of the Mountain
> to the grain, the bitter buckwheat
> to the Bride, the sweet buckwheat.

Afterwards, they toast grain, rice, potatoes, and so on. Then to the accompaniment of the drum they dance the lion dance.

6. Abumo, the 1,700-year-old Yi grandfather—a character in the cuo tai ji. *(Photo by Huangpu Chongqing)*

This drama is part of a larger New Year's celebration, *Driving Away Sparks (Sao huoxing),* celebrated between the third and fifteenth days of the first lunar month. Immediately after the cuo tai ji the driving away of sparks begins. Nuogabu leads the others to the village, giving his best wishes to all:

> May all adversity and calamities go away with the old man. May only good things remain. May the domestic animals thrive. May everyone be rich all year round, with an abundant harvest providing ample food.

Every householder welcomes them with meat and wine. If the owner of the house and the actor playing Nuogabu are of the same generation, the actor will sing an old love song. If a couple cannot have children, the actors will show them how to have sexual intercourse. When they leave a house Nuogabu speaks again:

> We want eggs and flax
> And wine to use in worship.
> All disease goes away,
> All children grow like phoenixes,
> All hardship goes away,
> Only happiness remains.
> All calamities and disease
> Go away, go away!

Before leaving, the old men will take some cogon grass (thatch) from four corners of the house and go just outside the village or to the foot of the mountain near the village. There they bury three eggs and set up a stick frame over the burial spot. Then they burn the cogon grass, cooking the remaining eggs and eating them as they shout: "Sparks fly away, the sparks fly away!"

The men then take off their masks and return to the village. The masks are carefully kept in one actor's house as if they were the spirits of gods. When the season to perform comes around the next year, the old men will dig up the eggs. If they are still there and unbroken, it means the coming year will be good with a full harvest. But if the eggs are missing or broken, bad times are forecast.

As I said earlier, nuo theatre originated from nuo rituals. But if we want to know what nuo is today we must research mainly the artistic form and the characters as they are presently played, as well as the rituals still attached to the performance. The cuo tai ji is linked to *Driving Away Sparks*. The whole is a single ritual package performed just after the start of the new year. The drama is actually the prelude to the *Driving Away Sparks* ritual. At its start and again at its conclusion the cuo tai ji involves actions related to driving away disease and paying tribute to the gods.[3]

The Yi of western Guizhou and northeastern Yunnan accepted Han ways earlier than the Yi of Sichuan. The Guizhou and Yunnan Yi gave up the 10-month year and used the Han 12-month calendar. The proof is in the cuo tai ji where they say that "dog year is a famine year, pig year is a frosty year, in tiger year the oats will go bad, in rabbit year the buckwheat will not fruit." These Yi also accepted Buddhism and Taoism from the Han. And at the start of the 20th century, this area was greatly influenced by Christianity. In 1904 when an English missionary set up churches, many Yi and Miao gave up their old customs and accepted Jesus. But despite all this we can't find any influence of Buddhism, Taoism, or Christianity in the cuo tai ji or *Driving Away Sparks*. The only deities in these performances are gods of nature, grain, or ancestors. This indicates that these ritual performances, which arose in the transitional period from clan society to agricultural society, are still performed without having been influenced by any religious practice later introduced into the area.

Today over 30 different local styles of nuo theatre are performed in China. I believe these ritual performances have persisted for about 2,000 years. The leading figure of nuo in southwestern China is always a wizard and so are many of the actors. Only in the Yi theatre under consideration are all the performers ordinary people, including four old men. I take a great interest in these four men's costumes, voices, their way of walking, and their performance of sex from behind. They wear long cloth hats wound in such a way as to make their heads appear tapered. This indicates that their ancestors favored tapered hairstyles. Their bodies and limbs are tightly bound with white cloth, indicating that their ancestors were naked. Their strange vocalization means that their ancestors had not learned how to speak like human beings. (During the rituals, Nuogabu says a sentence in Yi and the others respond in a strange voice.) Their way of walking is also odd, with their legs stiffly outstretched. This implies that their ancestors had just learned to walk on two legs. As for having sex from behind, the local people say, "This is how we've performed it in cuo tai ji for a long time." Sexual intercourse from behind is the common practice of four-legged animals. When apes evolved into humans, they changed to face-to-face intercourse. This great change early in human evolution fills sex with love and so lays the foundation for the change from group marriage to polygyny and then to monogamy. The sexual intercourse shown in the cuo tai ji indicates that the Yi ancestors were still in a transitional period of social evolution.

Someone may ask, "How can the Yi, who live in this out-of-the-way region and who weren't exposed to modern science until after Liberation in 1949, represent a view of their evolution in their theatre? How could the ancestors of the Yi know about sexual intercourse from behind and other developments from animal to human behavior?"

It is not easy to answer this. But several nationalities, including the Tibetans and the Yi, have stories of human evolution from anthropoid apes. Among the Yi there are three classics: *Ancestors of Axi (Axi de Xianji),* the oldest; *Genesis (Chuangshi Ji);* and *Human Studies of the Universe (Yuzhou Renwen Lun).* These works all emphasize that water is the origin of everything in the world. As for the origin of the human species, *Ancestors of Axi* says it is the god Are and the goddess Awei that created men and women out of white and yellow muds. *Genesis* from Sichuan says the god tried all kinds of ways to create humans but failed. Later there appeared a Chinese parasol tree that produced a fog which rose to the sky and descended as red snow. The red snow melted nine days later becoming water. The water changed into bones, the snow into muscles, the wind into breath, the rain into blood, and the stars into eyes. Thus a snow clan came into being. This snow clan consisted of twelve beings—six with blood and six without. Those without blood became plants like grass, trees, sugarcane, and so on. Those with blood became six animals: frog, snake, eagle, bear, monkey, and human.

The mythology of cuo tai ji is based on the view that all life originates from nature, from water. Snow is crystallized water. *Genesis* says that the monkey divided into three families, while in cuo tai ji the three nationalities of Yi, Miao, and Han are referred to. There is the belief that these three are brothers—Miao is the eldest, Yi the second, and Han the youngest. As for depicting sexual intercourse from behind, the Yi cannot give a scientific explanation. But simple observation confirms that animals perform sex one way, humans another. Since the ancestors of the Yi believed that humans evolved from monkeys, they would naturally compare human sexual intercourse with what they see monkeys do.

Genesis, written late in the Zhou dynasty (ca. 800 BCE) and known in Sichuan, proposed the theory of human evolution from anthropoid apes. But the *Ancestors of Axi,* circulated in Yunnan, and *Human Studies of the Universe,* circulated in Guizhou, did not include this theory. In the cuo tai ji the old man of the Yi says his people came from Gou Cou Fa which, according to the people of Luojia, is in Yunnan. However, researchers have not been able to locate Gou Cou Fa in Yunnan. I believe that Gou Cou Fa is in Sichuan, not Yunnan, because the theory of evolution performed in cuo tai ji accords with what is told in *Genesis.* The three old men of the drama came from Sichuan, passed through Yunnan, and ended in Guizhou.

This can be corroborated. According to historical records in both Chinese and Yi languages, the Yi were very closely connected to the ancient Di and Qiang peoples who lived in the west of China. As early as the second century BCE the ancestors of the Yi were active in southeastern Xichang, Sichuan. After the third century AD they spread to northeastern Yunnan, northwestern Guangxi, and western Guizhou. And, according to historical legend, the ancestors of the Yi originally lived in Qiong Zhi Lu which might be in northwestern Xichang. It is said that Qiong Zhi Lu was at the foot of a Great Snow Mountain; that is why the Yi consider snow as the origin of life, the material from which humans were created.

We can conclude that the cuo tai ji is a very old form of nuo. It and the *Driving Away Sparks* ritual indicate a very early combination of religion and theatre.

Translated by Xu Anxiang
Translation edited by Richard Schechner

Notes

1. This is the same troupe that Richard Schechner saw perform in Anshun in February 1988. For his account see Schechner (1989).
2. For another account of this same nuo performance see Tuo Xiuming (1988).
3. According to Tuo, "For the sacrificial offerings, four lighted lanterns are placed at each corner of the area of ground which serves as an arena. The Old Man of the Forest issues a command, then the performers circle the arena and take their places. After that, Arumo leads several other old men who stagger into the arena, sticks in hand and shouting like ape men just out of the forest. They each pour out a cup of wine and offer it in sacrifice to Heaven, their ancestors, the Mountain God, and the Grain God. [. . .] The Bell Dance is also performed at the sacrificial ceremony, usually by eight young men. They move to the rhythm of the bell, recreating scenes of the ancestors' journey over mountains and across streams on their way to Lujia village. The main opera follows the sacrificial ceremony" (1988:30–31).

References

Schechner, Richard
1989 "Notes from Abroad: Nuoxi, Dixi and Today's Chinese Experimental Theatre." *American Theatre* 5, no. 12 (March):52–54.

Tuo Xiuming
1988 "The 'Nou' Opera of the Yi Nationality." *China Reconstructs* 37, no. 7 (July):29–31.

Qu Liuyi *is the director of the Research Institute of the Chinese Theatre Association in Beijing, Editor-in-Chief of the* Chinese Theatre Yearbook, *Vice-Chairperson of the Association of Chinese Minority Nationality Theatres, Chair of the Association of Chinese Nuoxi Studies, and has published several books on nuo theatre and minority theatres throughout China.*

Nuo Theatre in Guizhou Province

Huangpu Chongqing

In 1988, just after the beginning of the Chinese new year, in a village high on the plateau of Guizhou in southwestern China, people gather in the center room of a farmer's house. The room is about seven-foot square and is illuminated by candles, the air misty and fragrant with smoking incense sticks. The crash of gongs and drums hurts the ears, the rhythm insistent, pierced by the sharp call of an ox horn. In the middle of the room a nuo wizard chants and dances in trance as if drunk and crazy. The room—crowded with people, noise, music, smoke, chanting, dancing—is a special, magical place.

In front of the wall facing the door is a shrine dominated by two wood sculptures of the god and goddess of nuo: Nuo Gong (the God of the East Mountain) and Nuo Po (the Goddess of the South Mountain). Incense sticks and candles burn in front of them and money and food offerings are piled high. Near the god and goddess are items of religious practice: a *shi dao* (knife), *pai dai* (belt), and *gua zi* (divining instrument). Under the shrine—which actually sits atop a table—are the consecrated masks of the nuo gods. Behind the shrine are paintings (usually three to seven) of nuo gods, each about two-feet by four-feet. Plastered on the wall next to the paintings are exorcistic charms and couplets which tell of good luck. The musicians (usually three to five men) sit next to the shrine.

In different parts of Guizhou the wizard is called by different names—Zhang Tan Shi, Duan Gong Shi, Xian Sheng, Ming Jing, and so on. He wears a flower crown and a special robe—clearly the main performer. The wizard is an envoy linking humans to heaven and hell and the officiant of the nuo altar—as well as being the stage director of the nuo performance and the principal performer skilled in singing and dancing. Sometimes he practices divination using special incantations and movement-language; sometimes he ignites the incense sticks and burns money to appease the gods of hell; sometimes he kowtows and prays to the souls of past wizards in heaven asking them to bless his ritual so it will succeed; sometimes he waves the knife, the belt, and a tablet on which inscriptions are written as he drinks wine; sometimes he fills his mouth with wine and then spews it around the room and burns magic paper in order to exorcise the ghosts who want to disrupt the ritual; sometimes he blows the ox horn to shake heaven and earth, to report to the kings of the "three worlds" why the farmer who owns this house is sponsoring the ritual. The wizard is speaking to Yu Huang Da Di, god of heaven, to the emperor of the human world, and to Yama, ruler of hell, the lower world. The wizard prays that these rulers will send deities to the nuo altar to help the sponsor avoid calamity (or to get through one already plaguing him) and receive happiness instead.

Legend says that all the implements of the nuo altar come from an ox with golden horns ridden by Tai Shag Lao Jun, the legendary founder of Taoism: the divination instrument was the ox's hoof, the oblong wooden tablet his tongue, the fan his ear, the knife his nose ring, the horn his horn.

Thus the various gods from different places are called to the nuo altar one after another. All the deities are played by masked wizards who have

1. Nuo Gong, the God of the East Mountain, and Nuo Po, the Goddess of the South Mountain—the nuo God and Goddess. (Photo by Huangpu Chongqing)

2. A nuo sacrificial altar. (Photo by Huangpu Chongqing)

3. A nuo wizard waves his shi dao *(knife) and* pai dai *(belt). (Photo by Huangpu Chongqing)*

washed their hands and lit incense sticks. Every god enters from outside through the crowd. They perform an introductory sequence determined by nuo: first they tell the origin of the particular god and the reason she or he has come to the altar; then they greet the sponsor. They also may improvise depending on the specific circumstances of the performance and the mood of the audience. They make jokes in slang or sing folk songs popular in the area. Or they mime sexual intercourse which usually is forbidden on the stage—their sex acts are very open and exaggerated, apparently expressing their dissatisfaction with pervasive Chinese puritanism. Finally, they perform a nuo drama enjoyed by both gods and humans.

The above constitutes a nuo ritual in Guizhou. Sometimes the lengthy activities are done in a devout and serious manner, filled with the mysterious air of religion and superstition; sometimes the performance is enthusiastically loaded with wit and humor, full of secular delight. Always the performers—gods—mix with the spectators—humans. The room is crowded with people, deities, and ghosts gathered in a common devotion, expressing a collective wish which, accomplished, results in general happiness. A very particular world is created, a world which is elusive but real, disorderly but clear, devout but blasphemous, full of conflict but unified.

Nuo ritual and nuo theatre originate from ancient exorcism ceremonies arising from shamanism. According to records from the period, there were nuo activities in the Shang dynasty (16th–11th centuries BCE). And if these records actually refer to nuo, then the practice has been developing for several thousand years. Over time its content has become more rich. First it was an exorcism ceremony directed against ghosts, later it developed the capacities for driving out epidemic diseases and calamities, avoiding danger, suppressing evil, practicing divination, treating a specific illness, and gaining happiness, wealth, or good luck. Nuo combines aspects of Confucianism, Buddhism, and Taoism with folk customs and practices of everyday life. There are various schools of nuo—such as the Mao Shan, Shi Niang, Lao Jun, and He Nan sects; and various kinds of altars such as the Wu Xian, Shi Deng, Bai Hu, Dou Dou, Niang Niang, Qing She, Zi Tong, and so on. There are also different types of nuo: court, temple, army, patriarchal, and popular. Nuo evolved from a performance designed to entertain the gods to one that entertains humans, from religious observance to popular culture; it has developed into an event that permeates many aspects of social life.

Guizhou is located in the Yungui highlands of southwestern China. Because of its poor transportation systems and its economic underdevelopment as well as various historical, political, and military reasons, Guizhou is isolated and so preserves many practices (nuo among them) that have been extinguished in other parts of China. Nuo remains popular in the villages of Guizhou.

Two kinds of ritual nuo have survived—*chong nuo* and *huan yuan*. In chong nuo, deities are invited to exorcise ghosts; this form is practiced both on behalf of individuals and whole communities. Chong nuo is relatively simple and can be performed in one day. It retains much of the earliest practice of nuo. If after a chong nuo the sponsor's wish has been fulfilled, the sponsor promises a huan yuan. "Huan" means "return" and "yuan" means "wish." Thus a huan yuan is a thank you to the deities for their blessings and for good fortune received. Because the sponsor is thanking the gods, he can't be stingy. In addition to offering them incense sticks, candles, hell money, and food, he must also offer songs, dances, and dramas—entertaining the gods as they eat and drink. If the sponsor is rich, a huan yuan can last seven days and nights. Some poorer people have spent their entire fortunes sponsoring a week-long huan yuan.

Because nuo arose from folk customs, it secularizes the gods and humanizes their feelings. If someone wants to invite a god s/he first must ask the "leader" of the gods—Yu Huang Da Di—for instructions. For example, a person might say, "It has been told to me that there, in such-and-such county in Guizhou, believer so-and-so has nightmares. S/he has been depressed for many years and has no peace of mind. S/he asks for long life." This is an example of a *shen wen*—a kind of "invitation to the gods" often used in nuo. Messengers from the three worlds come to earth to receive the invitation. They go to heaven and give it to Yu Huang Da Di who accepts the invitation, and so forth. It's easy to see how this set of rituals was created by past wizards who secularized, standardized, rationalized, and humanized nuo life according to the prevailing customs of the Guizhou villagers. But the wizards didn't foresee two consequences of these four changes. First, the scary atmosphere of the nuo altar is relaxed—the gods and ghosts who are played by wizard-actors in masks become kind and familiar, losing their earlier function of frightening humans. Nuo thus becomes an event at which villagers gather comfortably instead of in fear. Second, nuo no longer entertains the gods so much as it entertains the people. The food offerings become delicious treats for the invited relatives and friends of the sponsor. The nuo theatre which is supposed to be an entertainment for the gods becomes spiritual food for the villagers' enjoyment and education. Although nuo ritual has different names in different areas—nuo tan, nuo tang, nuo yuan, duan gong, yuan, ging tan, huan yuan, zi tong, yang, yin, shen, etc.—the people call all these "theatre," which it has become even as it is also ritual and a social occasion.

Up to 100 spectators gather at the sponsor's home. Many are relatives and friends; the others are neighbors and villagers who simply want to watch the performance. To make the event more accessible, the sponsor removes the door to the house as well as the wooden front wall. The place is very crowded because people want to see the wizard's magical acts such as "climbing the knife ladder" (barefoot, he climbs a ladder whose rungs are knives) or "crossing the sea of fire" (he walks barefoot on fire) or "opening red mountain" (he is stabbed in the head). They also want to hear

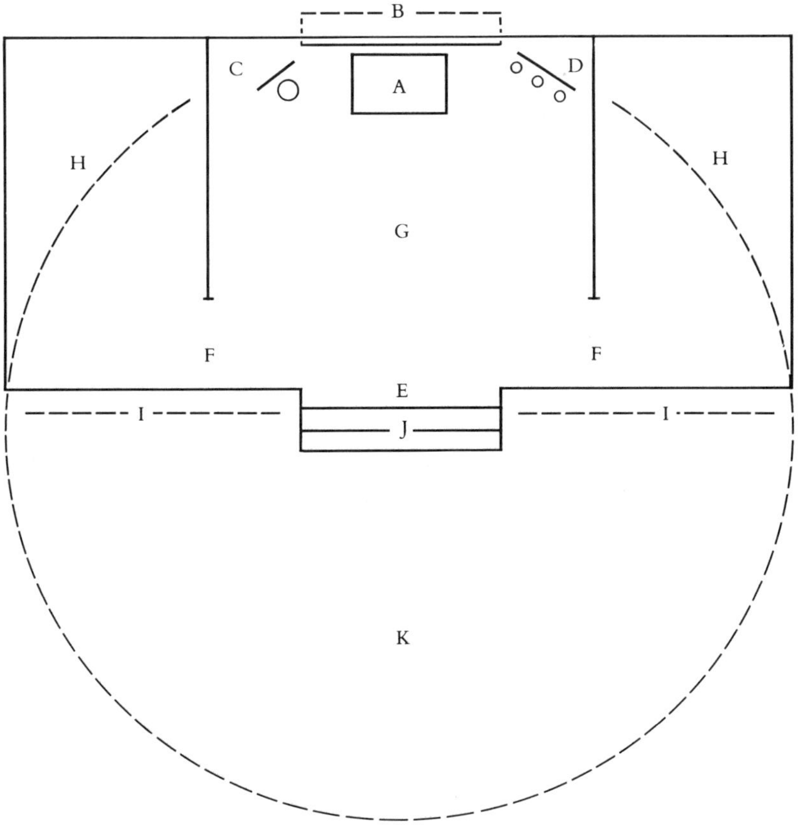

A. Shrine
B. Colorful deity paintings
C. Wizard's seat
D. Musicians' seat
E. Door
F. Door to the bedroom
G. Center room
H. Bedroom
I. Moveable wooden wall
J. Steps
K. Audience area

4. A groundplan of nuo performances in Guizhou. (Graphic by Caroline J. Kavanagh)

the songs and see the dances about the gods Kai Shan, Zhong Kui, Shan Wang, and others who chase ghosts away; and comic skits such as "Gan Sheng goes to the capital to take the imperial examination," "An An delivers rice," "Ride the dragon who jumps in the sea," "Tudi of Liang Shan Mountain," or "Guo Laoyao takes his wife back to his hometown"—and many others. Just listening to these titles makes it clear why the people experience nuo not only as ritual but as drama and theatre.

According to historical records mostly from the Ming and Qing dynasties (1368–1911 AD) and my own investigations in 1986–88, nuo exists all over Guizhou—although it has disappeared in some places during the past 40 years for obvious reasons. Differing conditions of life have resulted in an uneven development of nuo making it possible to distinguish four types:

1. *Nuo ceremony*. Since nuo began several thousand years ago it has undergone many changes. It is not possible to maintain that it is a "fossil" preserving what was done in the past. However, nuo ceremony does seem closer to the older forms than either nuo dance or nuo theatre. The

5. The nuo ritual is performed at a farmer's home in Guizhou province. (Photo by Huangpu Chongqing)

character 倛 (qi) in the ancient *jia gu wen* writing style (inscriptions on bones or tortoise shells from the Shang dynasty, 17th–16th century BCE) stands for an exorcist who wears a mask. In the *Zhou Li, Xia Guan* (historical records of the Zhou dynasty, mid-11th century to 77 BCE) it is written that "Fang Xiang Shi wears a bear fur and a mask which has four golden eyes, he holds a spear and a shield in each hand, and leads 100 slaves in the practice of nuo ritual." Then a nuo ceremony of the Zhou court is described—a performance relatively close to some of today's nuo where the wizard stands for Fang Xiang Shi and the masks of Kai Shan, Shan Wang, and Er Lang replace the mask with "four golden eyes." As in the Zhou period, the masked ceremony is an exorcism. The actions of today's nuo ceremonies are close to that of the Zhou period, although in chong nuo the deities have been secularized and there are some comic songs, dances, and dialogs. Ceremonial nuo is mostly religious ritual (what many modern people call superstition) with only a little entertainment added. This kind of nuo is still practiced in the remote mountain villages of southwestern Guizhou and in some minority areas.

2. *Nuo dance.* This kind of nuo contains many dances and songs. Its ceremony is very simple, with only traces of the ancient nuo. For example, the Miao "Dance of Beating Lei Gong" (thunder god) in the Yun Wu district of Guiding county has a ritual in which the wizard invites the gods down to earth. This ritual is supported by a Miao legend: A new daughter-in-law has not been obedient to her parents-in-law so she is

6. Spectators crowd around the wizard at a nuo performance. (Photo by Huangpu Chongqing)

struck by lightning, an act of Lei Gong, and goes mad. Her husband asks a wizard to heal her. The wizard performs his craft, generals and soldiers are invited to descend from heaven to defeat Lei Gong. The woman recovers.

In the ritual, the wizard makes a scarecrow symbolizing Lei Gong as villagers blow the *lu sheng* (a reed wind instrument) and dance in celebration of the victory. These activities show traces of an ancient rain ritual added to the nuo exorcism and healing ceremony. Over the years, the nuo has had added to it the rain ritual, songs, dances, and simple stories. Just as in the Miao nuo, other nuo includes such performances as the "dance of seeking the soul," the "dance of the monkey drum," the "dance of the tall man and the dance of the short man," and the "dumb actor"—all played by the Bu Yi people of southwest Guizhou. In fact, most of the surviving nuo dance performances are in minority nationality areas.

3. *Nuo that includes or mingles with drama.* Here nuo ritual mingles with dramatic episodes, some of which are relevant and others irrelevant to the ritual being performed. The long nuo rituals bore people, so performers include entertainments to attract and amuse spectators. During an interval in the ritual, one or two wizards enter and perform dialogs, songs, and dances. The main wizard takes a rest and the audience enjoys some variation. The form is open and free, the content simple and comic. Legends about gods and ghosts, and stories from real life are performed. The actors improvise, the audience laughs. The villagers very much appreciate these intervals. Some of the most popular short plays are: "the strict judge grants the wish of the believer," "Mulian visits the court," "An An delivers rice," "Gan Sheng goes to the capital to take the imperial examination," "Mao Ji forges iron," "the rebel leader catches a pioneer," and so on. This kind of nuo is popular all over Guizhou.
4. *Nuo theatre.* Although people call this kind of theatre "nuo," they do not mean either the original nuo or the nuo ceremony still practiced in remote areas. In the case of nuo theatre, "nuo" indicates an inherited descent, an acknowledgment of origins. Nuo theatre, with its own integral and independent dramatic shape, is wholly separate from nuo

7. A nuo mask for the character Kai Shan. (Photo by Huangpu Chongqing)

8. A wizard performs the character Tu Di, his phallus hanging between his legs. (Photo by Huangpu Chongqing)

ritual. Although nuo theatre is often performed in public with the huan yuan ritual, it has absolutely no connection with the gods of the nuo altar. Because the center room of the sponsor's house can contain only a relatively few people, nuo theatre is performed in the open—on the ground or on a makeshift stage. This kind of theatre is called "Nuo Tan" or "Nuo Tang," or "Yang" theatre and it is very popular in the east, north, and south of Guizhou. Nuo theatre includes many well-known traditional plays such as *Woman Named Meng Jiang (Meng Jiang Nü), Woman Named Pang (Pang Shi Nü),* and *Daughter of Dragon King (Long Wang Nü).* There are also some plays taken from other kinds of theatre.

In addition to all this, there is *dixi* which originated in the ancient army nuo and which is popular in Anshun, Puding, Pingba, and other places. What all these kinds of nuo theatre share is their common descent from nuo ritual. But today they are separate. These performances have left the realm of ritual and proudly entered the world of theatre.

Translated by Cao Lusheng
Translation edited by Richard Schechner

Huangpu Chongqing, *a graduate of the Department of Dramatic Literature of Shanghai Theatre Academy, is a researcher for the Guizhou Arts Research Institute.*

Aesthetic Displacement in Javanese Shadow Theatre

Three Contemporary Performance Styles

Laurie Lobell Sears

In Java today, *dhalang* (shadow puppeteers) are manipulating the oral and written texts which have mingled in the oral tradition of the shadow theatre for centuries. The domain in which the shadow theatre operates as an oral tradition passing on meaningful information to future generations has narrowed in the late 20th century. One can, however, find both traditional and modern styles of shadow play performance in Java today. In the traditional domains, Javanese aesthetic authority is dominant—coincidence, embellishment, and the subversion of linearity continue to generate meaning in traditional ways. But modern ideas are penetrating traditional domains, and village styles of shadow theatre performance are absorbing new ideas and technologies. While these new ideas and technologies enter the shadow theatre, they enter in traditional ways, through the flexible workings of the oral tradition. Yet in new urban styles, Western aesthetics which have developed out of the Aristotelian unities of time, place, and causality (see Becker 1979:216–19) seem to be gaining in authority and visibility. The clash of old and new authorities, and old and new aesthetics, is particularly visible in the Javanese shadow theatre tradition as it responds to modern and Western influences.

In this essay I discuss three contemporary types of Javanese shadow play performances, one very traditional and two among the more modern performance styles. In *ruwatan,* traditional exorcistic performances, the voice of the puppeteer is the sole authority and this authority derives from the puppeteer's command of magical and mystical knowledge. The text used during these performances, which exists in both oral and written forms, is non-Indic and very sacred; pregnant women are asked to leave the room before the text is recited, so powerful are the words believed to be. The text is usually available in written form but is most often recited from memory. Yet the written text has come to symbolize and enhance the puppeteer's authority. It is the correct performance of the various sacred texts that is important; the texts are in this sense oral, and their association with a written text reflects the increasing importance of written texts in Javanese society.

The second performance style to be discussed here is a modern phenomenon which takes place once every Javanese month (35 days) in the home of Ki Anom Surata, a famous Solonese puppeteer. These *rebo legi* (sweet Wednesday) performances are only loosely connected with a ritual occasion and are held for the benefit of the community of puppeteers. The host invites various puppeteers from all over Java to perform at his monthly celebrations. Because the host has made the pilgrimage to Mecca and is a member of Golkar (Golongan Karya, the political vehicle of the present government), the unspoken authorities at these performances are strict Islam and the Indonesian government. The performances are unconventional in many ways. The boundaries of the oral texts have been stretched to allow new words and phrases into the tradition. New styles are tried, there are no shadows, and many performance rules are broken, but the performances still begin at nine in the evening and end at five in the morning. The innovations seen at these performances are changes in the oral tradition, changes in what is appropriate for certain scenes, changes in the characters who are allowed to fight together, or changes in the puppeteer's behavior during the performance. The clash of traditional and modern authorities is striking in rebo legi performances and perhaps that is why they are so thoroughly enjoyed by the audiences of puppeteers who attend them. Village puppeteers are breaking the rules that were codified by the Dutch-influenced central Javanese courts in the early 20th century.

The last modern performance style discussed in this essay is the *padat* or condensed performance, which has developed at the Academy of Fine Arts in Solo (Akademi Seni Karawitan Indonesia [ASKI]) over the past ten years. These are shortened performances, generally an hour or so, and the puppeteer must follow a fixed written text, a task often difficult for performers accustomed to manipulating remembered oral texts. The authority in these performances is Western. Humardani, the late director of ASKI, helped to create this style, and he was familiar with Western performances and Western dramatic theory. The oral texts in these performances are controlled, limited, and standardized. The flow of the oral tradition is limited also and performance scripts are carefully thought out, values are changed, and the texts are written down. The scripts are published and copyright laws are discussed. The interaction among text, authority, and performance is carefully controlled in padat plays, both by Western models and influences and by the Indonesian government, which supports the academy.

Trained in Western academic traditions, some Javanese scholars at ASKI have written scholarly essays which interpret and analyze the tradition in self-conscious ways (see Humardani 1983; Murtiyasa 1984). These Javanese artists-turned-academics (or, in Humardani's case, doctor-turned-art critic) were and are seeking to preserve and upgrade the tradition, as the Dutch scholars tried to preserve and upgrade the shadow theatre tradition in the early part of this century. The scholars at ASKI want to make the tradition relevant to the urban, modernizing sectors of the Javanese population who no longer value all-night performances nor the rituals that such performances celebrate. The scholars seek to harmonize the older stories with modern values and lifestyles.

In the villages, performance styles from the academy have less influence than the rebo legi performances. Puppeteers who attend the rebo legi performances bring the innovations they see back to the villages. These

1. Setting up the stage and building a temporary roof for spectators before a traditional village performance in Kebumen, Central Java, in November 1983. (All photos in this article are courtesy of Laurie Lobell Sears)

2. Kasar *puppets are set up for a traditional performance in the village of Ngawi in May 1984.*

innovations are easier to absorb because in rebo legi performances the oral tradition still operates in familiar ways. In the villages the tradition changes and thrives as it responds to the current wave of modernization overtaking Javanese life. Motorcycle puppets, colored lights, Western-style drums, and English expressions are increasingly woven into all-night performances. The clowns make fun of the respected heros, materialistic values replace those of village solidarity, and female characters demand new rights and new visibility. Restraints on format and characterization are loosening in the villages, and this mirrors the loosening of those restraints in modern Javanese life.

Traditional Shadow Play Aesthetics and Exorcistic Performances

In 19th-century Javanese poetry, embellishment was a crucial feature which made the poetry meaningful to Javanese audiences of the day. In the

3. A puppeteer as she performs in Kartasura, April 1984.

shadow theatre tradition, texture, embellishment, and "density of context" mark the aesthetic concerns of the Javanese puppeteer. While in Javanese classical poetry embellishment was used to develop the *rasa* or mood on a poetic level, in Javanese shadow theatre embellishment is a generative device for text production. In the aesthetic world of the shadow theatre, mood development is achieved through embellishment and the building of texture—the interplay of music, recitation, tapping, and the clashing of metal plates, in addition to the activity of the puppets on the screen and the story line, which often seems extraneous to the performance. In a nine-hour performance that ends at the beginning or begins at the ending with a plot that often seems to go nowhere, it is the sheer texture of the performance, moving in toward the puppeteer and out toward the audience, that appears to motivate its action. The linearity, in the simple sense of genealogy, which the Indian epics brought to the thought-world of the Javanese, has been mediated by the Javanese concern with texture and density of context.

Ruwatan, or exorcistic performances, have been part of the shadow theatre repertory since at least the 17th century (see Brandon 1970:5). Today in central Java there is generally one story used, *Murwakala (The Birth of Kala).* In this story the gods descend to the earth to perform in a *wayang* (shadow theatre) play in order to halt the murderous assault of the ogre-god Kala (son of the high god Siwa) who symbolically pursues the child or adult being exorcised. The represented victim then hides in one of the instruments being used in the play within the ruwatan performance and, as the puppeteer reads the powerful mantra, Kala is appeased, the victim is exorcised, and order returns for a time to the world.

One performance which I attended in Spring 1984, in a village outside the city of Solo, was a *sadranan,* a special type of ruwatan which combines an offering made at the graves of the ancestors with a ruwatan shadow play—a common practice in modern Java. Ruwatan performances usually take place in the daytime, beginning at around 10:00 A.M. and ending at around 4:00 P.M. Since it is a daytime performance, the invited audience generally sits behind the puppeteer watching the puppets on the screen rather than inside the house watching the shadows as in most village performances. Generally only older puppeteers from puppeteering families stretching back many generations, whose fathers have already died, are considered to be strong enough to handle the magical forces that surface in ruwatan performances.

It is when the gods descend to the earth to take part in the wayang performance in the *Murwakala* play that the ruwatan becomes texturally rich and dense. The gods must disguise themselves and take on the forms of other characters, *malihan* in Javanese. Wisnu, a high god, becomes the puppeteer but takes on the form of Arjuna, the noble warrior; Brama, another god, becomes the gender player and takes the form of Arjuna's wife Sumbadra; and Narada, a funny misshapen god, takes the form of Semar, clown-servant to the hero Arjuna and older brother of the high god Siwa, and becomes the *pengendang*, or drummer. In this way, two wayang performances intersect—the one that is being held and the play within the performance.

Because the performance I am describing was an offering to the ancestors as well as an attempt to address the problems of the family holding the ritual, the ancestors appeared in the story. Coincidentally, this particular family happened to be a family of puppeteers and musicians. After the ancestors had been on the screen for a while, fiercely pursued by Kala, the present living family members, who were holding the performance, appeared as puppets on the screen.

Then a few twists were added to the ceremony. The puppeteer performing the play belonged to the family which was holding the performance, and he was familiar with the characters on his screen. The puppeteer happened to be the father of Anom Surata, the famous Solonese dhalang. By coincidence, I happened to know the woman who was holding the performance and who was being represented by a puppet on the screen. I did not realize when I came to the performance that she was the one who had organized it, but I had once visited her home and had bought some puppets from her. She was pleased to have Westerners at her performance, especially one whom she knew—it raised her status in the eyes of the neighbors—and she came over and sat down next to me. As she was being represented by a puppet on the screen, I felt as though I too was being drawn into the performance and soon might be face-to-face with Kala himself.

On the screen the living family members met their ancestors, and they asked for permission to hold the ceremony that was currently being held. This was enacted in a very humorous way revolving around the Javanese concept of *pangling*. Pangling means to meet people you know very well without recognizing them. When one meets good friends in Java they often say *"Kok, pangling,"* the implicit meaning being "I didn't recognize you because you look better (or worse) than I remember." To apply this concept to one's ancestors who have been dead for generations is at once funny and familiar.

The living relations confronted and threatened Kala. One of the living relatives happened to be a musician in the performance and was struggling to play his instrument while watching his own antics on the screen—accompanying, on his instrument, the movements of the puppet representing him. As he was being portrayed by the puppeteer in a very buffoonish manner, this all caused much hilarity. A Yudistira puppet appeared next depicting a member of the living family whose daughter could not get along with her husband. As the group of puppets representing living family members met the group of ancestor puppets, the puppeteer enacted a clever bit of family therapy. They all decided to hold the ceremony that was being held, and they then met the puppeteer who, as we remember, was a disguised character, a malihan for the high god Wisnu.

I have described enough to indicate the nature of this event and the density of texture that is so meaningful in Javanese wayang. All the puppets in a ruwatan performance are disconnected from their usual roles—all the associations are displaced. Any linearity in plot development has been totally circumvented and the meanings of the performance multiply and resonate in unpredictable ways. Ruwatan performances are the most Javanese of shadow play performances in their disconnection from the action of the Indian epics. The stress on malihan is another common phenomenon in many traditional performances. Ogre characters or gods disguised as heros motivate the action of many *lakon* (plays) and further subvert the linearity of plot development.

This ruwatan performance reached out and drew the audience in, and reached out further as the puppeteer was the father of Anom Surata, a national figure, who was present at the performance and became the butt of many of his father's jokes. The performance reached back across time to the world of the gods and the ancestors and brought them face-to-face with members of the audience. The ancient connections between aesthetics and mysticism are emphasized in ruwatan performances as it is the mystical power of the shadow puppeteer expressed through his art that enables him to heal the psychic imbalances that prompt families to hold performances. The authority in these performances belongs to the puppeteer and he represents the forces of pre-Indic animist Javanese culture despite his use of Hindu gods. The gods are displaced and disconnected from their usual roles in the performance. In a sense their power is tapped and tamed. The ruwatan performance represents the way in which the Javanese have tapped the power of foreign authorities and then used these powers for their own purposes.

The interaction between written text and oral performance is also unique in ruwatan plays. While traditionally the use of written texts in all wayang performances was frowned upon, the reading of a particular written text containing the sacred mantra recited at the end of the ruwatan performance is nowadays part of ruwatan performances. The recording of these sacred mantra in written form may be due to the influence of the Solonese scholar R. Tanaya, who in the 1930s published a version of the *Murwakala* text—a sign of fear, perhaps, that the sacred text might be lost if it was not written down (see Tanaya 1954). Since only older dhalang respected for their command of mystical knowledge are allowed, or are brave enough, to perform ruwatan plays, it is the power of the dhalang rather than the power of the text which is important in these plays. The puppeteer must be strong enough to handle the sacred mantra, or the power of the mantra could harm him. In the *Murwakala* story, the mantra which must be recited to ward off the rapacious Kala are supposedly written on Kala's body. Although even the victim could technically read the mantra and thus send Kala away, it is Wisnu pretending to be a dhalang who must recite the mantra out loud in order to activate their power. In traditional wayang performances, the power of the puppeteer controls the power of the written or oral texts. While the importance of shadow theatre plays may be diminishing for the modernizing elites who have moved to Jakarta from the villages of central Java, ruwatan performances are surprisingly popular in today's Java. Several puppeteers whom I knew in Solo were invited to Jakarta to perform ruwatan plays for family members who had moved to the big city. Ruwatan performances may not be the most representative

4. The shadows on the screen are emphasized in traditional performances such as this one at ASKI, April 1984.

shadow play performances, but they are the most Javanese in their disconnection from the action of the Indian epics and their subversion of linearity.

Rebo Legi Performances

Rebo legi (sweet Wednesday) performances are held every 35 days (the intersection of the five and seven day Javanese weeks) to celebrate the Javanese birthday of the Solonese puppeteer Surata. Surata invites puppeteers from all over Java to perform in his home for payment or exchange.[1] It is mostly other puppeteers and wayang enthusiasts who are invited to these performances. Many students from the fine arts academies also attend, as well as some stray foreign tourists.

These performances differ from other wayang performances as they gather a number of puppeteers from different areas in one place. In older times, puppeteers were wary of performing outside their own villages because of the possibility of running into heavy black magic, which their mantra and other charms might not be strong enough to counter. Since so many well-known puppeteers attend these events, performers are often thrust into a position of wanting to amuse their friends and make fun of their host through friendly but pointed humor. Thus a style of flashy puppet movements, suggestive humor, and the breaking of conventions has become dominant in these performances.

Other customs are displaced in the rebo legi performances. To begin with there are no shadows.[2] Since the main emphasis is on the puppeteer and there is no ritual ceremony connected with the event other than Surata's Javanese birthday, a certain foreshortening of the tradition takes place, both in the texture of the unseen dimensions of the performance—

5. A puppeteer seen from the back with a gamelan orchestra in the foreground. Though this picture is of a rehearsal at ASKI, it illustrates the "no shadow" perspective of rebo legi *performances, where the emphasis is on the puppeteer rather than the shadows.*

the ritual and mystical side—and in the texture of physical possibilities. One can only sit in back of the puppeteer, as the screen is most commonly placed against a wall.[3] At these performances, the audience is displaced and invited and uninvited guests share the same space. At village wayang performances, the invited guests sit watching the shadows inside or near the home of the host of the performance, while uninvited people from the neighborhood gather in back of the puppeteer and musicians.

Many other conventions are broken during these performances. There is often interaction between the audience and the puppeteer and on occasion the puppeteer will turn around and say something to the host or to a heckler. Many modern and even English words have worked their way into a tradition that formerly frowned upon the entry of Indonesian into inappropriate parts of the plays. The puppet movements are very innovative and often puppets are thrown off the screen or onto the screen in unconventional and abrupt ways. Fights take place between characters who would never fight in more traditional performances—I once saw a fight between the Pandawa hero Bima and his trusted clown-servant Petruk—and the jokes often begin in the first audience hall scene, a place where all humor is traditionally banned.

On one particular night, the young puppeteer Bambang Widjojo whom I often followed was scheduled to perform. Bambang was considered to be one of the best up-and-coming puppeteers and was also a good friend of Surata. He had been studying with a serious older puppeteer who was attempting to impart the deeper teachings of the tradition to him. The story that Bambang was preparing was a trunk story close to the main story line of the Javanese *Mahabharata* epic. I stayed at the performance until quite late (3:00 A.M.). Bambang was doing well for a while. His audience hall scene was very serious and he can be a very moving puppeteer when he is serious. But after a while the environment began to get the better of him and he began to respond to the crowd. He often turned and looked at the audience and replied to his hecklers with quick humor. By the middle of the performance, all restraint was thrown to the wind and Bambang enacted a lewd clown scene, using a very phallic-looking weapon for a clown battle. To the insistent beat of the strong-style *gamelan* (gong-chime ensemble) pieces that accompany battle scenes, the weapon became the clown's giant penis battering opponents with well-positioned jabs. Needless to say, the crowd loved this, but Bambang's older teacher did not talk to him for days and refused to watch him perform at the radio station several days later.

The point here, I believe, is not merely Victorian—village performances have a history of coarse humor. Bambang's teacher was disappointed because the younger puppeteer had lost his composure and dignity and pandered to the whims of the crowd. This episode clearly illustrates the clash between the refined wayang tradition of the Solonese courts and the village tradition. In the accepted code of behavior for village wayang performances, the puppeteer is supposed to cater to the tastes of the audience. But in the tradition that was nurtured in the courts under Dutch influence in the 1920s and '30s, wayang was supposed to be refined and elegant, not earthy and coarse. The younger puppeteer's mentor had been raised by a Dutch woman whom his father—a well-known puppeteer—had married; the older puppeteer shared the vision of wayang that he believed would have been acceptable in the Solonese courts.

Rebo legi performances, while not typical performance events, are certainly significant performance events in the world of Solonese wayang. Innovative styles from one area of central Java are seen at these performances and then carried away to other areas of Java. Students from the fine arts academies see a side of the tradition they do not often encounter in their formal schooling. From a political point of view the puppeteers are gathered together and thus easier for the government to keep an eye on. Some puppeteers stay away from rebo legi performances as they dislike the close connections of the host with both Golkar, the ruling party in Indonesia, and the strict interpretation of Islam.

In the flattening or foreshortening of the wayang tradition in the rebo legi performances, older aesthetic patterns are being displaced and deep texture is giving way to flatter styles of generating meaning. By emphasizing the play of humor and fancy puppet movements, the mystical power of the tradition is being channeled into more predictable grooves. Characters who once wielded authority and power are now ridiculed and the clown characters, representative of the Javanese folk, assume greater and more important roles. This shift in emphasis reflects the changing tastes of Javanese society as Western values of equality and individualism become more prominent in Javanese life. Rebo legi performances are dynamic and the audiences love them. It is through the innovations seen at these performances that one knows that the wayang tradition is still alive and vital, and the interactions between the puppeteers, the host, the audience, and instructors from ASKI may lend new types of texture to these performance events.

The changes evident in rebo legi performances are changes within the oral tradition. While some of the puppeteers who perform use unobtrusive notes or written materials, these performances are still primarily oral. New techniques or styles are *seen* and *heard;* when I once asked a famous older puppeteer how she learned the tradition she responded, "With my eyes and ears." There are changes in puppet movements, changes in the characters who fight with one another, and humor has free reign, but the order of scenes, the stories, the use of music, and the performance length are all intact.

The rebo legi puppeteers are innovative from a position of total mastery over the tradition. If they break the rules, it is because they know the rules so well. The rules that the puppeteers are breaking at these performances are the rules that were enforced upon the village dhalang in the 1920s and '30s when court elites, responding to Dutch influences, attempted to upgrade and refine the wayang tradition. Thus the puppeteers seem to be defying the once great power of the Solonese courts when they handle the puppets in new and irreverent ways. The styles of the popular village puppeteers who perform for rebo legi may even be more Javanese than the Dutch-influenced court styles of the late colonial era. Rebo legi performances are modern in that they appeal to modernizing audiences and they incorporate modern dialogs into the performances. But nothing about these performances is Western. Occasionally performers from ASKI will be invited to perform. These puppeteers will try out the new styles being generated at the academy, but the hall will empty out before midnight and the usual hilarity will not prevail.

Rebo legi puppeteers wield increasing power over the tradition and yet, at these performances, one feels a subtle struggle between the unspoken authorities at the performance—Islam and the Jakarta government—and the visible authority of the individual puppeteers. The aftermath of the turbulent '60s lingers at these performances and the lines drawn at that time still seem to have meaning. Puppeteers are careful to direct their humor in innocuous ways so as not to upset the government authorities who also attend on occasion. When these same dhalang perform in the villages, the crowds they draw are impressive. One night in Sragen, a village outside the city of Solo, there may have been close to 1,000 people surrounding the home of a famous dhalang who had asked one of the popular, modernizing dhalang to perform. These rebo legi puppeteers insure that the wayang tradition continues to have meaning for contemporary audiences.

Padat Performances

The third and last contemporary performance style to be discussed is the wayang padat, or compressed wayang, developing in the milieu of the Academy of Fine Arts.[4] One cannot speak of wayang padat without evoking the spirit of "Gendon" Humardani, the late director of ASKI, and brother of a deceased general in the Jakarta government. While wayang performances of less than nine hours have been around for a long time, and any puppeteer is able to shorten a performance as the needs of the occasion demand, Humardani and the well-known author Sri Mulyono, who were students together at Gadjah Mada, are credited with visualizing the metaphor of the shadow puppet theatre as an empty bucket with a thin layer of water on the bottom. They believed that the size of the bucket needed to be in proportion to its contents and said that the essence *(isi)* of wayang needed to be separated out and worked over *(digarap lagi)* to produce a style of performance more in keeping with the times. Trained as a medical doctor, Humardani spent several years in Europe and paid a few visits to America where he encountered Western performing arts and performance styles.

6. A performance in Klaten in March 1984 by the light of the traditional blencong *oil lamp.*

An earlier criticism of the length, language, and backwardness of the shadow theatre (see J.K. [J. Kats] 1923) had been promoted by the arts organization LEKRA (the Institute of People's Culture) in the 1950s and '60s. The technical changes desired by the members of LEKRA included shortening the wayang night, employing an electric lightbulb rather than the flickering oil lamp (which distorted the shadows), using a stage without a screen, incorporating more than one puppeteer (which could then represent the mass line), and abandoning the dress requirement for puppeteer and musicians (see McVey 1986:30–31). More general changes promoted by LEKRA included making Javanese wayang more accessible to other non-Javanese cultural groups within Indonesia, reforming the interpretation so it could fulfill the needs of the revolution and development, creating new lakon to enhance political messages, and expanding the role of the clowns. While some of this agenda—using electric lightbulbs, reforming the interpretation to fulfill the needs of government messages, and expanding the role of the clowns—has come into general use in many traditional wayang performances, the ASKI creators of wayang padat also see a need for a radical revision of the tradition. The ASKI use of more than one puppeteer and the abandonment of the dress code for padat performances have received sharp criticism from more traditional puppeteers. The padat plays developed at ASKI promulgate new ideas and values that often conflict with the interpretations of puppeteers of earlier generations.

One of the major differences that sets the ASKI padat plays apart from the LEKRA agenda is ASKI's use of only the most traditional wayang stories for development into padat plays. These were the stories most often criticized as feudal by the members of LEKRA. The ASKI interpretations also reject feudal values by upsetting the traditional hierarchical placement of the puppets on the screen *(tanceban)*. Today in Java, ASKI rejects any association with LEKRA and the Communist movement of the '50s and '60s. As an organization firmly associated with and supported by the New Order, ASKI staunchly promotes the values and programs of the current government. These values permeate the padat plays as well.

Padat performances employ written playscripts, which are either memorized for or read in performances. The scripts generally run between an

7. The electric lamp, one of the changes promoted by the Institute of People's Culture, can be seen suspended behind this tanceban, *or puppet placement, for the opening scene in a performance in Kartasura, April 1984.*

hour and an hour-and-a-half (although I did see one that was 12 minutes long). Although padat performances may have the same author and performer, often one person writes the script, another performs the script, a third person organizes the musical accompaniment (a crucial part of any wayang performance), and a fourth directs the whole show.

If we said that the audience was displaced in rebo legi performances, we can say that the audience is effaced in padat: Between 1982 and '84 there were no audiences for wayang padat in Java outside of the fine arts academies and the activities they generated.[5] Padat performances are often created to be performed in Europe when ASKI goes on its annual tours, and all the students in the puppeteering section of the academy are required to write and perform a wayang padat in their final semester. Padat performances are also brought to the annual festivals in which the various fine arts academies sponsored by the Indonesian government participate.

The stories most often chosen for wayang padat are the *Bratayuda,* the stories recounting the great war of the *Mahabharata* epic. These are the stories most avoided in traditional wayang because they are felt to be too "heavy" to handle—catastrophes tend to happen in their wake, or so the belief goes. *Bratayuda* are also the most linear of all the stories associated with the shadow theatre. I believe that these stories are chosen to lend weight to the padat performances, a weight that cannot be achieved in any other way. The concept of weight is highly valued in wayang and the Javanese word used, *bobot,* resonates with the American slang "heavy."

As mentioned above, Humardani, the founder of wayang padat, was familiar with Western performance styles. He read English fluently and knew Western dramatic criticism and aesthetic theory. Humardani disapproved of humor in padat performances and the clown scenes are generally brief and scarce. But what wayang padat lacks in the way of humor, it more than makes up in the way of noise. The music is loud, fast, and dramatic. The mood-setting songs of traditional wayang are shorter and more romantic (in the courts this mood was not considered appropriate for wayang performances). The strictures against abrupt mood changes have been abandoned for wayang padat.

Other interesting innovations in padat performances include changing the story line to admit more modern values. Thus in *Srikandi Maguru Manah* (Suwarno 1980), where Srikandi (the second wife of the refined hero Arjuna) learns to shoot a bow and arrow, she is actually the one who kills Jangkungmardea, rather than Arjuna as in the traditional version. The puppeteer Bambang Suwarno even created a new puppet for this performance—a woman character who wears pants. Humardani also asked his students to have the characters take responsibility for their own actions—no longer are the gods allowed to incarnate in humans and be the cause of their ignoble actions.[6]

An example of the innovations that can arise in padat performances is illustrated by the story *Karno Tinandhing* which was created by various members of the puppeteering section of ASKI in the spring of 1983 for the IKI (Institute of Indonesian Arts) Festival held in Solo at that time. Humardani was still alive then and his intense energy and spirit filled the ASKI performances. The students were encouraged to innovate. Rehearsals were frequent and frantic. Compositions were criticized by the other students and instructors, and changes were made. The whole process was exciting and exhilarating, as though Humardani was forcing creativity out of his students.

Karno Tinandhing (Karno Meets His Match), one of the most famous stories of the *Mahabharata* cycle, is a *Bratayuda* story telling of the battle between half brothers Karno and Arjuna, so equally matched that it is hard to tell the difference between them. The puppeteering section of ASKI was allowed 20 minutes for its performance. The gimmick of their interpretation was to use a very large screen so as to permit the different puppets each to be handled by separate students who would also say their own lines. The lamp was moved further back from the screen so that the shadows were greatly enlarged. The shadows were all that was offered to the audience as the activity backstage was rough and lively—many people running around with puppets in their hands.

The effects produced in the performance fell somewhere between shadow puppetry and cinema (an image suggested to me by Roger Vetter [1983]). There were special combinations of horses and chariots and riders used for the very impressive battle scenes. There were also creative effects achieved in the final battle between Karno and Arjuna when three representations of the battle went on at the same time—one large image and two smaller images, using six puppets in all. The music for the performance was innovative, suggesting the dignity and sobriety of Gregorian chant, with no female singers. The first audience hall scene also broke conventions as the characters just floated around, displaced from their usual hierarchical positions on the screen. Several *gunungan,* or "tree of life" puppets as they are sometimes called, were used to create shadows and spaces and to fill the large screen. Lastly, the script was in Indonesian so that it would be understood by students from the fine arts academies in Bali and Sumatra.

The performance was well received by the audience of students and faculty from the various government-sponsored fine arts academies, as well as by the members of the educated and artistic elites of Solo. It was a successful example of the isi (content) of a traditional story undergoing digarap lagi (reworking) and being presented in a fitting container. For the Javanese who saw it, *Karno Tinandhing* was still a part of the wayang tradition. The basic realities of wayang—screen, shadows, and well-known characters—were all there although the language, the music, the puppet movements, the duration, and the puppeteer were all displaced.

The audience was offered little texture—they were denied access to the activities behind the screen. The plot of the story was totally linear, ending in the death of a major epic hero—the plot actually went somewhere. The mood of the performance was serious from beginning to end, and I for one felt moved at the end of the performance; I knew a great hero had fallen.

Karno Tinandhing was the best padat performance I encountered during my two years in Java.[7] Students and instructors at the academy are not yet satisfied with their efforts to refine the padat style. Padat plays, in general, have been released from the structural constraints of the tradition as well as from the content of the traditional stories. If one of the rules of a traditional wayang says that all wayang stories must begin and end in a court, wayang padat no longer feels the need to abide by this rule. The tanceban (puppet arrangements on the screen) have also been the targets of innovation, and puppets do things that make older puppeteers cringe. According to Alan Feinstein (1984), in one padat performance a young ASKI puppeteer substituted the puppet of another character altogether to represent a well-known character in his story. "Who is speaking" in padat wayang performances no longer has the weight of tradition and consensus—it now arises from an individuated author.

A.L. Becker, writing about a dozen years ago, said of Javanese shadow theatre: "Deep change [. . .] would be change in the plot, change in the constraints on selecting and ordering characters and motifs. Deep change would be change in the Javanese conception of time and event, change of epistemology" (1979:230). I see wayang padat as deep change. While one may say that the effects of the padat versions are confined to the fine arts academies, the young men and women who study at ASKI all come from the villages and they bring ASKI ideas back to the villages. My puppeteer friend Bambang from the rebo legi performances, who has very little education, uses ideas from ASKI in the creation of his performances.

In a discussion that I attended at ASKI in July 1983, one of the advanced students asked, "Are we supposed to perform in order to earn a living or to raise *(membangunkan)* the standards of wayang?" Then Sumanta, head of the puppeteering section of ASKI, asked, *"Anda mau menjadi perjuang?"* ("Do you want to become a fighter?"). In other words, he was asking the students if they were brave enough to introduce new ideas to the populace—ideas that might be rejected.[8] Rather than the bearers of an oral tradition that flows through them, the ASKI faculty and students (and there is no hard line between these two groups—students become faculty and the faculty are often still students) are aware of being caught between worlds. In the words of Bambang Murtiyasa who teaches at ASKI:

> The collision with development *(pembangunan)*—which today is clearly oriented toward material things—is greatly influencing society. We cannot avoid our society becoming a society of consumers, a society of imitators of Western culture which is considered to be modern. This is causing confusion within the society and among the artists, the critics, and the officials. Because, one side of us wants to be modern while the other side of us does not want to be robbed of its identity (1984:1).[9]

In padat performances, the textured signification of the older performance styles is being displaced by linearity,[10] the spontaneity of the oral tradition is being displaced by a fixed text, and the unlimited play of signification is being channeled in certain acceptable directions. The introduction of authors into the wayang tradition is a new phenomenon accelerating the production of fixed texts. What governments have not been able to do for generations—control the voices of the puppeteers—seems to be happening through the spread of technologies which bring greater skill in the storing and handling of knowledge.[11]

In contemporary Javanese wayang we are seeing the proliferation of signed authors in a tradition that previously worked with anonymous authors or authors who merely retold and reinterpreted traditional stories. Young puppeteers in Java today are starting to think about copyright laws. I attended a panel at a shadow puppeteering conference held at the academy in 1983 devoted to such problems. Questions of copyright led into questions more fundamental to the development of the shadow puppet tradition. Ki Caritawijaya, a well-known village puppeteer who attended the panel, asked, "What are the limits of change in [shadow puppet] performances?" (1983).[12] There was discussion as to whether puppeteers were offended when others used their stories. The problem of using other puppeteers' *naskah,* or written texts, is complicated. In earlier times if a puppeteer borrowed another puppeteer's story, he had to rework and reinterpret the story in order to make it his own. Now puppeteers can memorize and deliver someone else's text, often with little understanding of the issues that the text deals with. Puppeteers can be asked to deliver texts with which they do not agree.

Today at ASKI students who have not yet mastered the basics of the tradition are taught new styles. Those students are losing touch with the old oral texts that have been handed down for generations. Traditionally puppeteers could choose one oral text from their remembered repertory to use in many different situations. By freezing the oral texts and limiting stylistic possibilities, students learn to get along with fewer ways of doing things. They become dependent on their texts.

The power of the individual puppeteer is fading at ASKI. By using different people to write, perform, and direct padat plays, the puppeteer's power is diffused. In the fine arts academies, the written texts are becoming more important than the puppeteers who perform them. The individual puppeteer's voice cannot be heard in padat performances—her/his voice blends into the academy's voice. The ever-present authority in academy performances is the Indonesian government, and Western attitudes and ways of thinking make the government's voice stronger.

Padat texts signal a change from oral performance and oral transmission to a system dependent on written texts. Written texts are easier to standardize, easier to control. In padat plays, sex, knowledge, and power are seen in more individualistic terms than in the past. An individual, rather than gods or parents, can control her/his own destiny. It is interesting that this attitude of individualism should arise at a time when the Indonesian government's control over sex, knowledge, and power is more pervasive than at any time in the past. Today in Indonesia, the government has launched an intense and successful birth control program which has drawn the puppeteers into supporting its message (see Clara van Groenendael 1986). The government has greater control over the shadow puppet tradition than ever before, through monitoring what stories are performed, channeling the tradition into the government-sponsored fine arts academies, and having the academies take an increasing role in the development of the tradition outside of the academies. Wayang competitions *(lomba)* are frequently sponsored by city and village government organizations—the judges for these events are inevitably drawn from the fine arts academy. The government also oversees the stories that are chosen for the monthly performances broadcast on the national radio station. The protection that the shadow theatre receives from the government may, in fact, be retarding the pace of change and mediating the influences that modern education and proliferating technology could be having upon the tradition.[13]

Conclusion

In this essay I have looked at the edges of the wayang tradition in contemporary Java.[14] The ruwatan performance is representative of older performance styles and signification strategies—it is the most quintessentially Javanese. The rebo legi and the wayang padat are among the most modern performance styles. The effects of these new styles are being felt throughout Indonesia. Creation of mood through embellishment, the intertwining of the mystical and the aesthetic experience, sheer density of context—all seem to be giving way to more Western modes of signification, as the Indian-inspired Javanese aesthetics give way to Aristotelian-based aesthetics. One-and-a-half to two-hour play formats, linear plots, directors, scripts, and rehearsals, have all been derived from Western theatre. The new style is felt to be modern, more in tune with contemporary Javanese life.

Today in Java the boundaries of the written and oral texts are shifting quickly. At ASKI written and oral texts are becoming fixed and standardized. Certain oral texts are accepted; others are rejected. This is not new. What is new is that the teachers at ASKI are dictating this process in more rigid ways than in the past. When the 19th-century courts held their "upgrading" courses, the puppeteers went home after a few days having absorbed as much as they desired. In their own villages no one knew what they had learned at the courts. But today, students are graded on how well they perform the texts which they are given, and the "best" students are kept on at the academy. They become *pegawai negeri,* or government workers, with guaranteed lifelong salaries.

In the public domain, on the other hand, the boundaries of the texts are widening. New written and oral texts are entering the tradition. Puppeteers are just now becoming acquainted with 19th-century texts which previously were hidden inside palace libraries. At the same time these puppeteers incorporate stories which they see on TV into wayang. New words, new texts, and new technologies are all welcomed. Rather than becoming scholars or government workers, popular puppeteers are becoming celebrities, sometimes on a national level. While puppeteers in days past tended to live outside accepted social norms, today puppeteers are acceptable. Parents who wielded mystical power in the past want their children to be integrated into modern society. Puppeteers now seek formal education.

The three performance styles described here are representative of the types of performances that coexist in Java today. Traditional, modern, and Western styles intertwine as the boundaries separating them grow increasingly difficult to discern. Students from ASKI bring Western ideas to the villages which are incorporated into village performances. Rebo legi puppeteers mingle with puppeteers from the academy and are invited to the academy to take part in the series of conferences and workshops that form part of ASKI's curriculum. The academy employs respected traditional puppeteers to teach the first years of courses and innovative puppeteers at the academy are often the children of famous traditional puppeteers. The existence of all this activity argues for the continued popularity of wayang projecting its rich and complex legacy into succeeding generations.

Notes

1. Puppeteers often exchange performances for their family or friends. It is a good idea to exchange with Anom Surata—a performance by him in 1984 could cost up to $2,000.
2. When I was in Java between 1982 and '84, the positioning of the screen against the wall at these performances rarely enabled the audience to see the shadows. When there were shadows, they were often seen only by the crowds outside, the opposite of traditional performances where the invited guests see the shadows and the uninvited onlookers see the puppeteer. It is interesting that at radio station RRI performances, held once a month in Solo in a Western-style theatre, audiences are denied access to the puppeteer rather than to the shadows.
3. Kent Devereaux, who was in Solo in 1986 and '87, informed me that Surata reintegrated the shadows back into these performances in 1987 (Devereaux 1988). When Devereaux arrived in 1986, the shadows were still deleted. The emphasizing of the puppets over the shadows reflects the increasing importance of the puppeteer at the expense of the tradition at these performances. Surata himself is somewhat of a "superstar" in the world of Javanese shadow theatre. In Solo, people say that the constant building that goes on at Surata's house in the center of the city of Solo is a mystical exercise *(laku)* that he performs to augment his powers.
4. There is a distinction made at ASKI between wayang padat and wayang *ringkas*. Wayang ringkas (shortened wayang) may be performed in three or four hours, but the basic structure and content of the performance remains very similar to the regular performance format. In padat performances, rules are broken, stories are changed, puppet movements are innovative and the musical accompaniment can be very radical. At ASKI, first and second year students study traditional performance styles; in the third year they study wayang ringkas taught by a traditional older puppeteer; in their final two years they study wayang padat taught by the younger and more innovative instructors.
5. Bambang Murtiyasa, an instructor at ASKI, wrote in a recent paper: "At Sasanamulya [the place where ASKI was then located] we often have performances for various reasons—to honor guests, receptions, exam presentations, competitions, festivals, experimental performances, etc.—the audience is overflowing and yet it is limited to our own closed circle or to a specific group" (1984:2, translated by author).
6. An interesting example of this arises in the two versions of the story *Alap-alapan Sukeksi (The Marriage of Sukeksi)* published by ASKI. In the traditional version written by Ki Naryacarito (1980), Sukeksi and the ascetic Wisrawa, who has come to ask Sukeksi to marry his son, marry one another because they have been entered by the spirits of the gods Siwa and Durga. In the version by Soemanto (1980), Naryacarito's nephew and head of the puppeteering department of ASKI, Sukeksi and Wisrawa marry because they fall in love. As the height of character development in traditional Javanese culture is the person in control of his or her passions, a holy man who goes to secure a wife for his son and then falls in love with her and marries her himself seems out of tune with older values.
7. Devereaux notes that the ASKI performers have turned the performance style of *Karno Tinandhing* into a new performance genre called *sandosa* (a convoluted acronym for Wayang Bahasa Indonesia, wayang in the Indonesian language). One or two new stories have been added and are performed in the manner described above, with Indonesian text and a group of puppeteers (Devereaux 1988; see also Devereaux forthcoming).
8. This is in tune with the government program which is trying to reify the slogans of the revolution for the purpose of *membangunkan desa* or building up the villages, and promoting *Pancasila,* the five guiding principles of the present government.
9. *"Dampak pembangunan—yang sekarang secara nyata lebih berpusat pada materi—sangat berpengaruh pada masarakat. Kita tidak bisa mengingkari masarakat kita menjadi masarakat konsumen, masarakat tiru-tiru budaya Barat yang dianggap modern. Men-*

yebabkan masarakat sekarang menjadi bingung termasuk didalamnya: senimannya, kritikusnya, dan penjabatnya. Karna, satu pihak kita ingin modern pada pihak lain kita tidak ingin kehilangan identitas." It is interesting to look at the Western words in this bit of Indonesian: *materi* (material), *konsumen* (consumer), *modern, kritikus* (critic), *identitas* (identity)—words particularly representative of a Western mode of discourse.

10. Benedict Anderson commented 20 years ago on the declining aesthetic complexity in wayang theatre and on the tendencies of performances to be purely entertaining and not edifying (1965:29–30). I suggest this declining complexity may be a return to village performance styles and a move away from the reconstructed tradition of the Solonese courts. See also Victor Turner (1982:54–55) whose discussion of "liminal" and "liminoid" phenomena explores the transition from ritual to theatre in contemporary societies.
11. Michel Foucault has said: "[. . .] the author does not precede the works, he is a certain functional principle by which, in our culture, one limits, excludes, and chooses; in short, by which one impedes the free circulation, the free manipulation, the free composition, decomposition, and recomposition of fiction. [. . .] The author is therefore the ideological figure by which one marks the manner in which we fear the proliferation of meaning" (1979:159). These ideas seem appropriate in regard to the appearance of "authors" in the wayang tradition.
12. A.L. Becker discusses traditional versus modern artistic expression: "One of the most important differences between traditional artistic expression and modern individualistic artistic expression is that in a traditional medium the artist is consciously expanding a prior text, an open corpus of literature, art, or music, whereas an artist whose intent is self-expression creates and develops his own text, his own mythology, so far as he can and still communicate" (1979:228).
13. Amin Sweeney (forthcoming) describes recent changes in the world of Malay shadow theatre. The pace of change seems to be faster in Malaysia where the government does not oversee the development of the shadow theatre tradition as closely as the Indonesian government does.
14. See Keeler (1987:3–14) for an excellent description of a traditional village shadow theatre performance.

References

Anderson, Benedict R. O'G.
1965 *Mythology and the Tolerance of the Javanese.* Ithaca, NY: Modern Indonesia Project, Cornell University.

Becker, A.L.
1979 "Text-Building, Epistemology and Aesthetics in Javanese Shadow Theatre." In *The Imagination of Reality,* edited by A.L. Becker and Aram A. Yengoyan, 211–44. Norwood, NJ: Ablex.

Brandon, James R.
1970 *On Thrones of Gold.* Cambridge, MA: Harvard University Press.

Caritawijaya, Ki
1983 Comments on panel at Akademi Seni Karawitan Indonesia in Solo, Indonesia. 28 February.

Clara van Groenendael, V.M.
1986 *The Dalang Behind the Wayang.* Dordrecht, Holland: Foris Publications.

Devereaux, Kent
1988 Personal communication, April.
forthcoming "Contemporary Trends in Javanese Wayang Kulit." *Asian Theatre Journal.*

Feinstein, Alan
1984 Personal communication, 25 December.

Foucault, Michel
1979 "What is an Author?" In *Textual Strategies: Perspectives in Post-Structuralist Criticism,* edited by J.V. Harari, 141–60. Ithaca, NY: Cornell University Press.

Humardani, S.D.
1983 *Kumpulan Kertas tentang Kesenian.* Solo, Indonesia: Akademi Seni Karawitan Indonesia.

J.K. (J. Kats)
1923 "Verkorting van den duur der Wayang-Koelit-Vorstelling." ("Shortening the Length of the Wayang Kulit Performance.") *Djawa* 3:43–45.

Keeler, W.
1987 *Javanese Puppets, Javanese Selves.* Princeton, NJ: Princeton University Press.

McVey, R.
1986 "The Wayang Controversy in Indonesian Communism." In *Context, Meaning, and Power in Southeast Asia,* edited by M. Hobart and R. Taylor, 21–52. Ithaca, NY: Cornell Studies on Southeast Asia.

Murtiyasa, Bambang
1984 "Kegelisahan kehidupan seni yang menggelisahkan." ("A Worrisome Restlessness in the World of the Arts.") Paper presented at the Diskusi Teater, PKJT Sasanamulya. 10 April.

Naryacarito, Ki
1980 *Alap-alapan Sukeksi.* Surakarta, Indonesia: Sub Bagian Proyek ASKI.

Soemanto
1980 *Alap-alapan Sukeksi.* Surakarta, Indonesia: Sub Bagian Proyek ASKI.

Suwarno, Bambang
1980 *Srikandi Maguru Manah.* Surakarta, Indonesia: Sub Bagian Proyek ASKI.

Sweeney, Amin
forthcoming "Literacy and the Epic in the Malay World." In *The Boundaries of the Text: Epic Performances in South and Southeast Asia,* edited by J.B. Fleuckiger and L.J. Sears. Ann Arbor: University of Michigan Center for South and Southeast Asian Studies.

Tanaya, R.
1954 *Cariyos Padhalangan Lampahan Dhalang Kandhabuwana Murwakala (Wayang Story of the Puppeteer Kandhabuwana and the Play Murwakala).* Kediri, Indonesia: Tan Khoen Swie.

Turner, Victor
1982 *From Ritual to Theatre.* New York: Performing Arts Journal Publications.

Vetter, Roger
1983 Personal communication.

Laurie Lobell Sears *is Assistant Professor of Southeast Asian History at the University of Washington. She spent four years in Java studying the interaction between oral and written traditions in Indonesian history.*

M. Butterfly

An Interview with David Henry Hwang

John Louis DiGaetani

David Henry Hwang's *M. Butterfly* went into rehearsal during the first week of January 1988 and into preview on 6 February at the National Theater in Washington, DC. On 10 February the play opened and played to excellent reviews until the first week in March. On 20 March 1988 the play opened on Broadway at the Eugene O'Neill Theatre, where it has been successfully running ever since.

M. Butterfly takes place today in a Paris prison, and, in recall, the years 1960–1985 in Beijing and Paris. The events of the play were suggested by recent newspaper accounts of an actual international spy scandal. A French diplomat by the name of Bouriscot (Gallimard in the play) was stationed in Beijing, China, during the period of the American war in Vietnam. During Bouriscot's stay, he started a long-term affair with someone he thought was a female star of the Beijing Opera. When the lovers tried to enter France, they were both charged with espionage. Only then did the diplomat discover that his mistress was a spy for the Chinese government—and also a man. M. Bouriscot was tried, found guilty of espionage, and sentenced to prison. He was released from prison in 1988.

I spoke with Mr. Hwang in New York City in September 1988.

HWANG: I wrote *M. Butterfly* as an attempt to deal with some aspects of orientalism. I assumed that many in the audience would be coming to the theatre because they hoped to see something exotic and mysterious, but what exactly is behind the desire to see the "exotic East"?

DIGAETANI: One of the things I found interesting is that your play suggested the Western naivete about the East. Many Westerners tend to think of the East as a pretty little Madame Butterfly rather than seeing what is actually there in the orient. It's a kind a racism combined with sexism.

HWANG: Yes, that's true. The play has been taken as a commentary or a criticism of Western attitudes toward the East, and I think that's accurate. But I would like to think that the play is fairly even-handed in saying that the East also misperceives the West. The East is guilty or complicit in this dual form of cultural stereotyping. The West, having had the advantage of

1. B.D. Wong as Song Liling and David Dukes as Gallimard in M. Butterfly *at the Eugene O'Neill Theatre on Broadway in New York, 1989. (Photo by Peter Cunningham)*

being the colonial power and of being the more powerful of the two over the past couple of hundred years, has an attitude of condescension toward the East. But the East has played up to that to its short-term advantage without thinking of the long-term ill effects that reinforcing those racial stereotypes causes. I think both parties are equally guilty.

In terms of Western misperceptions, there is Edward Said's term, "orientalism." I read Said's book after I wrote the play. John Dexter, the play's director, recommended it. It was one of the reasons he was interested in doing the play. This notion that the East is mysterious, inscrutable, and therefore ultimately inferior, is something that definitely is consistent with themes in Puccini's *Madame Butterfly*.

DIGAETANI: Well, an aspect of the Puccini opera that I think is often overlooked is its attack on that Western view. Pinkerton is one of the great heels in all opera. Puccini presents the West as oafish and insensitive.

HWANG: Puccini presents that view at the same time that he presents a view of the East as helpless to resist. I think that the East has played into that stereotype by saying, "Oh, yes, we are helpless" and therefore trying to manipulate the situation to its own advantage.

DIGAETANI: Naivete can be used as a ploy. One of the interesting things about the Puccini opera is that it presents the East as a place in the early stages of its victimization by an imperialist power. In other words, in the beginning people think that the changes are all wonderful and mean progress and the modern way. They don't realize that they are being used. Of course Madame Butterfly does eventually realize the horrible consequences of being colonized. Are you an opera fan?

HWANG: I was trained as a musician, so I'm a music fan in general. Opera is actually something that I've only become interested in during the past couple of years, and to some degree because of *M. Butterfly*. Ironically, when I decided I wanted to incorporate the plot of Puccini's *Madame Butterfly* into the play, I actually didn't know much about opera. So I started listening to a lot more of it, and particularly during the rehearsals for the play I started listening to the Puccini opera and I really learned to appreciate it. My play, which sets out to lampoon opera, has made me an opera buff.

DIGAETANI: Your play brings up lots of interesting questions, one of which is: Can we love a person as a person if we are unsure of that person's gender?

HWANG: The play is to some degree about the nature of seduction—in the sense that we seduce ourselves. Sometimes when you have the desire to fall in love or you desire to have someone to be some kind of ideal, you can make that person ideal in your own mind whether or not the actual facts correspond to the reality. I think that it's often true in a smaller, less extreme sense that we get involved with people and decide to blind ourselves to their faults so that they can be the perfect love that we've always wanted. And on some level we're aware that that is not the case. But we prefer the fantasy over the reality. The play presents an obviously more extreme and less common situation, where the reality is so radically different from fantasy that at the core, even the simple, fundamental fact that it's a man instead of a woman is something that the person in love chooses to block out. But it's not actually that different qualitatively from everyday types of deceptions that people make in order to convince themselves they're in love.

DIGAETANI: I remember when I first read the story in the newspaper. I thought, how could this have happened? What was your reaction?

HWANG: Of course, I had the same reactions as everybody else—how could it have happened? But then on some level it seemed natural to me that it should have happened, that given the degree of misperception generally between East and West and between men and women, it seemed inevitable that a mistake of this magnitude would one day take place. As a metaphor, the story made perfect sense in the context of the general misunderstanding that I have always perceived takes place between these different groups. In retrospect, it seems to me that that was what really piqued my imagination. I felt the impossibility of the situation and the inevitability of it, both at the same time.

DIGAETANI: Men playing women is of course very much a part of Western theatre. But one of the ways I interpret your play, and I'd like

2. & 3. B.D. Wong and David Dukes as Song Liling and Gallimard—creating and maintaining the "mirage." (Photo by Peter Cunningham)

your comments about this, is that Gallimard was really a homosexual from day one. He was living in a much more homophobic period than today, and the thing about his affair with Song Liling, the thing about the mirage that he and Song Liling created, was that he never had to face his own homosexuality. In other words, he had an affair with a man and never told anyone, not even himself.

HWANG: The lines between gay and straight become very blurred in this play, but I think he knows he's having an affair with a man. Therefore, on some level he is gay. Our director John Dexter told me that he never found the situation to be that unbelievable because of an experience he once had. Dexter once shot a movie for Columbia called *Virgin Soldiers*. He hired macho Englishmen and brought them to Singapore where they went to Boogie Street, the transvestite street. A few of these men picked up these guys, I mean these women who were really men, and the next day Dexter overheard them talking and they said, "No, it was a girl. I know men and I know women, and that was a woman." If you want to believe it's a woman, that's fine. I mean, the fact is you're sleeping with a man, but if you choose to believe you're heterosexual, then that's your prerogative, to live in that fantasy. I think this would apply today to people in Chinese, Italian, Spanish, and some of the other Latin cultures. People in these cultures believe that if you have sex with a man and you do the screwing, you are not gay, but if you're screwed, you're gay. I mean, that sort of distinction has existed since time immemorial.

DIGAETANI: Oh, the Chinese believe this is true?

HWANG: So what does gay mean at that point? I don't know.

DIGAETANI: In what you're saying, gay means being a passive homosexual. If you're not passive, you're not gay.

HWANG: Correct. So, the situation in *M. Butterfly* is not so far-fetched. Gallimard chooses to believe he is heterosexual.

DIGAETANI: Is Gallimard still in jail?

HWANG: The name of the real Gallimard is Bouriscot and he just got out of jail.

DIGAETANI: Have you tried to contact him?

HWANG: No. I think we may want to have some kind of legal arrangement with him, but we'll see what happens.

DIGAETANI: He might want a cut of the royalties.

HWANG: Probably.

DIGAETANI: And he deserves it?

HWANG: I wouldn't mind giving him a little.

DIGAETANI: Not a lot?

HWANG: No, since the play is not literally based on him. I don't know that it's his story. But on the other hand, I think the guy's been in jail, he's suffered a lot of indignity, so since it's him, why not?

DIGAETANI: Have you tried to incorporate many elements of Oriental opera or theatre into this play? Or was it primarily Dexter who wanted to do this?

HWANG: The main reason we ended up using Chinese opera was because it was relevant. In reality, Song Liling was a practitioner of Chinese opera. But I also wanted to explore why it is that in Asian theatre and also in Shakespearean theatre men play women's role. It's just touched on briefly. Song Liling says, "Why are women's roles played by men?" And the answer is: "Because only a man knows how a woman should act." Let's look at that in kabuki terms because in kabuki it's expressed much more clearly. In kabuki they say that a woman can only be a woman whereas a man can be the idealization of a woman. This is obscene, and it's inherently sexist. What it's saying is that only a man can be a man's idealization of a woman.

DIGAETANI: Not a woman's.

HWANG: Right. Song Liling is able to be such an effective fantasy for Gallimard because, as a man, she knows how a man wants to see women, and therefore can become a man's woman—which is why Gallimard says toward the end of the play: "I was a man in love with a woman created by a man, and now everything else simply falls short." I thought the play was a very interesting way to deal with the concept of the onnagata in the context of a Western play.

DIGAETANI: Another interesting conflict I saw in the play was between Japanese and Chinese cultures. They're really different.

HWANG: One of the things I wanted to do was to indicate both the differences between cultures as perceived by Asians and the similarities as perceived by Westerners. In other words, the West looks at the "East" as sort of a monolith. Whether we've been at war against Japan or Korea or Vietnam or in a Cold War with China, it's all "Oriental." But of course the Asians see themselves as very different. I also have to say, again, that the reverse is true, that Asians tend to see the West as very monolithic. Perhaps from each point of view, it's a legitimate position to take because there are probably more similarities between the Asian cultures as opposed to the West than differences, and vice versa. But from the point of view of the West, America does not consider itself to be the same as France. And Japan does not consider itself to be China.

I think one of the more simple things the play's trying to say is that eventually one must look past all the cultural stereotyping we do of each other, West to East and East to West, and deal with each other just as humans if we're really to reach any point of true understanding.

DIGAETANI: In the play, when the truth is finally out, Song Liling offers to continue the relationship as a man but Gallimard absolutely cannot deal with that. In part, he realizes he's been abused, and he's very angry. Another reason why is that this would force him to deal honestly with his own homosexuality, and he's never had to do this because he's been able to live a fantasy, even though he's known deep down that Song Liling was a man.

HWANG: Such a fundamental component of the relationship is the fantasy. Without that, it is no longer the same relationship. Gallimard is in love with a butterfly, he's not in love with this Asian man.

DIGAETANI: Do you mean that fantasy is necessary for all love? That strict realism will destroy love?

HWANG: Gosh, am I saying that?

4. *"I was a man in love with a woman created by a man, and now everything falls short." (Photo by Peter Cunningham)*

DIGAETANI: I'm just bringing it up as a possibility.

HWANG: I'm asking because the answer doesn't roll off my tongue immediately. I would hate to be so cynical or so rigid as to say that we can only fall in love with a fantasy. It is possible, I think, to fall in love with someone in reality, and it's also possible to fall in love with a fantasy that's completely disassociated from the real person. They're both equally possible, but the latter is more dangerous because then someday your bubble may burst and leave you with nothing.

DIGAETANI: And there are some people who perceive that you want a fantasy and are very, very willing to create it.

HWANG: Yes, that's true.

DIGAETANI: As with Song Liling.

HWANG: Yes. I think one of the things that I tried to do, though I was not quite successful and would like to work on more in future productions of the play—or in a movie version—

DIGAETANI: There's going to be a movie?

HWANG: I think so . . . is this whole idea of the diplomat's wife. The diplomat's wife has a fantasy which is more commonplace, but which is, again, not qualitatively far from Gallimard's fantasy. She has the fantasy of being the diplomat's wife and playing that role and believing that she has a completely faithful husband. But on some level she knows that the whole thing is a sham. And I think she does something not that different from what Gallimard is doing. While Gallimard plays the role of the macho Western male, she plays the role of the diplomat's wife.

DIGAETANI: One of the things I liked about the play was its use of various styles. There seemed to be a TV sitcom style, for example, when Suzuki/Comrade Chin says, "He's a loser. Dump him!" I like the fact that you wove that into the play. Some critics didn't like it. What's your feeling about this?

HWANG: Well, I'm very interested in the butting up of unlikes. You can take the crassest type of sitcom and butt it up against high culture like opera, and find a relationship between the two. That creates variety for the audience, it keeps them on their toes, it is inherently theatrical. The other reason I like it is because it allows us to cut through what I consider to be a line of misconceptions of what the piece is about. So many times when you deal with characters from the East as they are portrayed in the West, they seem very distant, "wise" and "inscrutable." But in fact Asians can be just as crass as people are here.

So it was fun to take an Eastern character like Comrade Chin and have her talk like the crassest person on television because in reality that probably would be how she would talk if she were speaking English. To me there's a certain emotional truth about it which is more interesting than something which might seem more seamless to a critic.

DIGAETANI: I thought you were also emphasizing the difference between Japan and China. She is not a meek little Japanese woman but a Chinese party member.

HWANG: Yes, I think that applies as well.

DIGAETANI: We have this concept of the little Plum Blossom as an ideal of Japanese culture, and Chinese women don't fall into that category.

HWANG: To some degree this is also a function of class. Since many of the party cadres came from the Chinese working classes, they would have a certain realistic way of expressing themselves. This image we have of the Plum Blossom is to some degree a Japanese upper-class image. The Japanese peasant woman has a different quality. And the same occurs in China. Wealthy Mandarin women, in part because their feet were broken, moved very slowly and gracefully, but again, that's a class difference.

DIGAETANI: I had an argument with a friend about the scene with the nude Danish student. My friend insisted that the scene was trashy. But I argued that the scene showed Gallimard's discomfort with liberated women.

HWANG: The scene had two purposes for me. One was the point you mentioned. As Gallimard says: "It is possible for a woman to be too open, so as to seem almost too masculine." That concept of femininity is false to the core. The fact that you have a real woman who acts "masculine," and a man who acts "feminine," is the ultimate irony. So that was one purpose for the scene, to show the difference in what we perceive to be the Western woman and what we perceive to be the Eastern woman. The other reason is a plot point. I wondered whether at some point in the relationship—after a couple of years when the initial lust waned—something would have happened to provide the impetus for the relationship to continue over the next 15 or so years?

DIGAETANI: Well, there is a child, for one thing.

HWANG: Right. But I thought it would be interesting plotwise if he did go out and now, feeling his oats as a macho male, have an affair with another woman. But having had that relationship, Gallimard goes back to Song Liling, causing lust to evolve into some sort of real love, and this child could come out of that. The Danish student, Renee, serves, then, as the trigger or the transition from Gallimard's growth as a macho male to someone who falls in love in some deeper sense with his Madame Butterfly.

DIGAETANI: Why was the only frontal nudity in the play that of a female? Song Liling never appeared frontally nude. I was surprised at that because the audience is, of course, curious.

5. Kathryn Layng (who took over the role from Lindsey Frost) as the Danish student with whom Gallimard has an affair. (Photo by Peter Cunningham)

6. Song Liling, Gallimard, and the baby. (Photo by Peter Cunningham)

HWANG: Well, that was kind of an interesting little aesthetic debate we had. What John Dexter said one day was that he'd done male frontal nudity with actors and he found that you had to deal with the fact that it was extremely distracting. He said if you have a penis here and you have Sir Laurence Olivier there, everybody looks at the penis. At that point in the play it's very important to focus on Gallimard's reaction rather than to focus on Song Liling's penis. So we decided to stage the scene the way we did, with Song Liling downstage and Gallimard upstage where we were basically seeing his reaction, because that really is the important thing at that moment.

DIGAETANI: Were the actors willing to do frontal nudity?

7. When the deception crumbles, both characters realize what they've lost. Hwang's use of comedy underscores a situation that's "essentially tragic." (Photo by Peter Cunningham)

HWANG: Yes. There are some actors who feel comfortable with nudity on stage and others who don't. I think Lindsey Frost, who plays the Danish student, does not feel totally comfortable with her nudity on stage, and Brad Wong [Song Liling] seems to be the opposite—he seems to grow into his nudity on stage.

DIGAETANI: He wants to do it all the time?

HWANG: Yes, such that I find now he is angling himself to the audience more and more.

DIGAETANI: I guess some people can really get into nudity.

HWANG: John Lithgow was nude in his first Broadway play, *The Changing Room,* for which he won a Tony Award. He said that after getting over the initial shock of doing it, it became extremely liberating. So maybe that's how Brad Wong is taking it.

DIGAETANI: I was interested as well in your choice of language in the play.

HWANG: We decided to use the American convention in language. It's such an international play in the sense that there are French, Chinese, Chinese playing Japanese, Japanese playing Chinese, even Danish people. If we had everybody in accents, I think it would actually be rather confusing and pointless. One of the advantages of the stage is that, since you are working in metaphor in general, you can make a decision like that. You might as well just face the fact that we're all Americans, so let's speak American and make that the convention of the play. So I made a very conscious choice to be American and use a lot of American slang. In particular in the male bonding scenes between Gallimard and Marc, the way they talk about sex is very American. That's something that some critics have problems with, but it's a very conscious choice, a reflection of the fact that I perceive this as being a very American play, in spite of the fact that it's about a number of intercultural topics.

DIGAETANI: If this play were done in England, would you insist on the cast speaking American English?

HWANG: Well, that's a whole other question. I'm not sure about that. We are in fact planning a London production, and I may not be quite so rigorous about the choice of slang in London. I talked earlier about the butting up of unlikes, to have this American slang and then also sometimes to have a more classical type of English, and to see the relationship between those two types of languages and the way that they can attract.

DIGAETANI: I also liked your play's mixture of comedy and tragedy because the story itself is tragic. Gallimard winds up in jail, and I'm glad to find out he's finally out. But I found myself laughing a lot in the play. Do you want to comment on how you tried to combine tragedy and comedy—or maybe you didn't see the play as essentially tragic.

HWANG: I do see the situation as essentially tragic. I think it's a tragedy for both of the characters because to some degree even the Song Liling character, like Pinkerton at the end of *Madame Butterfly,* realizes what it is that he's lost. The Song Liling character has enjoyed to some degree being able to perpetrate this deception, and being able to continue to stay adored by someone in spite of his sexual confusion. When Song Liling loses that, he realizes his narcissism is not as great as his need for the adoration which he has built over the last 20 years, so he realizes what he's lost in the same way that Pinkerton realizes too late at the end of the opera.

But, as for the use of comedy, first of all I think that comedy is very theatrical. I am generally interested in ways to create total theatre, theatre which utilizes whatever the medium has to offer to create an effect—just to keep an audience interested—whether that's dance or music or opera or comedy. All these things are very theatrical, even makeup changes and costumes—possibly because I grew up in a generation which isn't that acquainted with theatre. For theatre to hold my interest, it needs to pull out all its stops and take advantage of everything it has—what it can do better than film and television. So, it's very important for me to exploit all those elements, and comedy is one of them. I think that, secondly, there's the fact that in this particular play, since we're dealing with a number of important issues, it's necessary to leaven those issues with some comedy in order for the play to be palatable even to me, let alone to an audience. I would not be comfortable with a play of mine which very stridently or humorlessly hammered home a particular message.

DIGAETANI: You're not a Brechtian, it sounds like.

HWANG: Brecht uses humor. But, while I admire some of Brecht's principles, I personally don't feel comfortable with my own work taking a strident tone, and so I think that these messages need to be delivered in a humorous context. I then feel more comfortable with the material and I think the audience feels more comfortable with it.

Also, many of the situations in *M. Butterfly* are inherently comic. The comedy helps the audience to suspend its disbelief, particularly in the face of this seemingly impossible plot. If we dealt with some of these situations humorlessly, doubt and sarcasm would start to pop up in the minds of the audience. If instead we take those doubts and sarcasms and put them on the stage and let the audience laugh at them and then address them, we're much more able to help the audience suspend its disbelief and get into the head of the character who's in this impossible situation. So I think the comedy actually becomes an essential element, particularly when you're dealing with a seemingly impossible plot.

The cocktail party scene at the beginning of the play is at the beginning to get over a lot of things that would be in the audience's mind anyway. So let's laugh at it now, get it all out in the open, and then let's go in and really look at this thing.

DIGAETANI: You're saying that while the situation is essentially tragic, it is also essentially comic.

HWANG: Definitely. There is certainly a dimension of personal tragedy which is inherent in the situation. But anyone who steps outside and looks at that situation, just at the bare bones of the plot, would have to say that it's comic as well.

DIGAETANI: What plans do you have for future plays?

HWANG: I have a couple of ideas for my next play, but they are not anything I can really talk about right now. I've gone through phases in my life when I've said I was only writing plays which in some way relate to Asia. And I've gone through phases when I've said that I wasn't going to do anything more that had to do with Asia. And now I think that I'd have to say honestly that I don't know.

John Louis DiGaetani, *PhD, is Associate Professor of English at Hofstra University in Hempstead, NY. His most recent books include:* Carlo Gozzi: Translations of "The Love of Three Oranges," "Turandot," and "The Snake Lady" *(Westport, CT: Greenwood Press);* Puccini the Thinker *(New York: Peter Lang); and* An Invitation to the Opera *(New York: Facts on File). He is currently editing an anthology of essays on Luigi Pirandello for Greenwood Press, to be titled* The Companion to Pirandello Studies.

Politics as Theatre

Or, How I Too Lost the Election in 1988

Joel Schechter

From 1980 to 1988, while a former Hollywood actor served as president of the United States, it became increasingly difficult for me to discuss theatre without referring to the Actor in Chief. Ronald Reagan's progress from Hollywood films to White House press conferences attested to a theatricalized society which has praised politicians and office-seekers for gifts previously appreciated in actors.

Reagan's rehearsals for press conferences and his reliance on media advisers called attention to the inherent theatricality of political events. He was hardly the first political leader to win public support through oratory and performance skills; Aristophanes suggested in *The Knights* that ancient Athens, too, had leaders only as good as their rhetorical sleights-of-tongue (1985 [424 BCE]:78). In that play the tyrant Cleon lost a debate to a sausage seller more adept than him at public deception. Perhaps Aristotle had Aristophanic comedies in mind when he wrote in *The Poetics* that "the older dramatists made their speakers talk like statesmen" (1962 [330 BCE]:78).

With these examples and others to inspire me, I became a consciously theatrical political candidate in 1985, and taught seminars on politics as theatre at Yale and in New York University's Department of Performance Studies.

An interest in political satire, theatre, and local politics first led me to campaign for elected office in 1985, as a candidate for the New Haven Board of Alders; in 1986, I ran for the Connecticut State House of Representatives; and in 1988, for the state senate. Each time I ran as a third party candidate, representing the New Haven Green party, and each time I lost to an incumbent Democrat, in a city controlled by a Democratic party machine.

The campaigns let me practice theories about theatre, satire, and politics developed in my book, *Durov's Pig* (1985). In one chapter I had examined the German Green party's transfer of street theatre tactics and political humor to parliament in Bonn (1985:191–211). In 1985, after visiting Greens in Germany, I learned that New Haven residents were forming a

NEW HAVEN GREEN PARTY

JOEL SCHECHTER
For State Senate
11th District

Joel Schechter is a community activist, teacher, founder of the satiric Developers for DiLieto, and columnist for the New Haven Independent.

As State Senator, he wants to:

- Save the Coliseum - repair it with State funds.
- Create an elected Board of Education by law.
- Create recycling plants, not incinerators
- Improve childcare and education with state funding
- Build more affordable housing.
- Phase out nuclear power and the nuclear war industry in Connecticut and create alternative employment.
- Reduce property and sales taxes, by taxing the wealthy.
- Protect the environment from pollution and developers .
- Keep drunken drivers off the road.

The New Haven Green Party offers you a choice. You no longer have to vote for Democrats who give tax breaks to wealthy developers while your taxes get higher. You no longer have to vote for Democrats who are developers. The New Haven Green Party was founded in 1985 to help give New Haven residents a voice in deciding the priorities of their city. We want communities to decide their future rather than those who want to build malls,condos and high rises in our neighborhoods.

VOTE GREEN PARTY - NOVEMBER 8

Paid for by the New Haven Green Party, Frank Annunziato, Treasurer

1. A consciously theatrical political candidate. (Graphics courtesy of New Haven Green party)

local Green party, and I joined them. Only a few of the New Haven Greens had an interest in political theatre; most were seeking social change through electoral politics and activism. A half-dozen of the hundred founding members started a theatre group to perform skits at public hearings and meetings.

New Haven's Green party, like Germany's, was founded to oppose nuclear weapons and nuclear power, and protect the environment. The Green slogan—"Think globally, act locally"—led New Haven Greens to develop specific urban American programs: plans for massive recycling (not toxic incineration) of solid waste, for more affordable housing, and for an elected (rather than mayorally appointed) board of education.

The New Haven Green party remains a largely serious alternative to local Democratic and Republican parties, which have failed to address the city's worst problems. Like other urban centers, New Haven lacks funds for public housing, education, parks, and health care. It has a high unemployment rate among black youths. The city government and Mayor Ben DiLieto promote development of luxury condominiums and new offices. Residents who cannot afford such real estate subsidize it through local government tax abatements to developers.

In case one of the Democrats I campaign against in the future is reading this article, I should add that none of my electoral efforts were purely field research or experiments in satiric theatre; if I had been elected in 1988, I would be serving in the state senate today, and calling for the legislation advocated during my candidacy. In fact, I continue to call for it at public hearings.

Developers for DiLieto Drink Champagne

To underscore Mayor DiLieto's favoritism of developers, Green party members Jack McKivigan, John Willoughby, and I formed a satiric group called Developers for DiLieto early in 1987. Our fictitious association was modeled to some extent on the Berkeley theatre group, Ladies Against Women, whose performers mimic antifeminists and Moral Majority leaders to comic effect. Developers for DiLieto issued satiric press releases and appeared in public as developers to praise the mayor whenever he offered other developers another tax break or sold them city property at a bargain price. We performed our roles as any professional impersonators might, with serious demeanor, elaborate costumes, and the city's buildings for our stage set.

Admittedly, our costumes could provoke some doubts about the seriousness of the organization. The official evening wear of Developers for DiLieto consisted of black tie, tuxedo (or other luxurious attire), and a bright yellow hard hat topped by a champagne glass. The hat was designed for those who want to drink champagne while standing under the girders of an unfinished, city-subsidized building, and it has proven to be quite popular among local photographers. One television cameraperson spent at least a full minute filming my hat the night I stood outside the New Haven Coliseum toasting the mayor's plans to tear down the arena.

That particular event, in February of 1988, turned out to be one of the most widely publicized our group ever held. Earlier in the evening the mayor delivered his annual "State of the City" address to the board of alders, praising his own development plans and renewing his vow to replace the Coliseum with a shopping mall. As Green party members we shared the objections of many area residents to DiLieto's plan at a time when low-income housing, job training, and education funds deserved to be higher priorities than a new (second) mall.

As Developers for DiLieto, we celebrated the prospect of a new mall, which would benefit the developers who built it. "Action News Eight" and channel three's "Eyewitness News" filmed our champagne toast to the mayor outside the Coliseum. I told the anchor persons that "New Haven is becoming a city of, by, and for developers. The public is consulted only second or third." Whether TV viewers took the champagne toast seriously or as satire, I doubt many of them found it flattering to developers. The newscaster gave me air time equal to the mayor's, and I began to regard our satiric group as the city's alternative government; if developers were not already running the city, perhaps Developers for DiLieto could take over the bulldozers for them, and drive toward city hall.

Endorsed by a 350-Pound Pig

Fear of too much media coverage led the National Organization of Women (NOW) to ask me not to appear at another event. In March of 1988, Developers for DiLieto announced it would bring two guests to the city's annual Knights of St. Patrick dinner—a 350-pound pig named Rooter and his veterinarian friend, Dr. George Whitney. The all-male dinner, attended by the state's leading politicians, including the mayor and the governor, had provoked protests against its sexism two years in a row. The Green party and NOW were among the sponsors of the 1988 protest, which Rooter, Whitney, and I planned to join. We would carry signs objecting to "Male Chauvinist Humans"—those men who were giving pigs a bad name by excluding women from the banquet.

Much to my surprise, a NOW organizer called me three days before the protest to ask that the pig not appear. The media would focus on the pig and ignore the other demonstrators, I was told. Furthermore, NOW did not want to insult men by implying they were pigs. I told the organizer that pigs were admirable animals: they were peaceful vegetarians for the most part, and they didn't discriminate against women. But after some debate, I agreed to NOW's request, and, in solidarity with Rooter, I too stayed away from the demonstration.

2. Joel Schechter models the Developers for DiLieto uniform. The hat was designed for people who want to drink champagne while standing under the girders of an unfinished, city-subsidized building. (Photo by Diana Scott)

The night I stayed home, two local papers phoned me to ask why the pig had not appeared. New Haven theatre critic Margaret Spillane wrote a lengthy, wry column on the canceled "performance" (1988a). It was entitled "The Pig Who (Almost) Came to Dinner," and it elicited numerous letters to the *New Haven Independent*'s editors. Some of the letters attacked me for cruelty to animals—as if I had forced Rooter to march in an angry mob, and not stayed home. George Whitney published a letter stating that Rooter, the pig, spoke to him, saying "Joel did not give me anything to eat last time he visited [but] people should listen to my friend Joel. I think highly of Joel's position on the issues" (1988). And that is how I received a political endorsement from a 350-pound talking pig. The Democrats in town could soon find themselves repeating the question Will Rogers asked about agricultural policies in 1928: "Will the cows and chickens cooperate?" (1982:62).

In Praise of the Press

Television and print coverage of Developers for DiLieto and Rooter prepared the public for my state senate campaign. At least it prepared the press, which heralded me as the founder of a satiric group when I announced my candidacy in August 1988. I should add that I am a member of the press, too. I wrote and still write a monthly column of political satire for one of the city's three papers, the *Independent*. As a result, many reporters writing about my 1988 campaign were acquaintances, colleagues even. One or two were my editors. When I invited the press to a Developers for DiLieto event in October, reporters from the three city papers and two radio stations showed up on less than two hours' notice. They came to be amused, out of friendship, or perhaps to cover a speech by a state senate candidate, though this strikes me as the least likely.

Judging from my 1988 race, it appears that reliance on print media and door-to-door campaigning may no longer be effective in the age of television. My chief opponent, the incumbent Senator Anthony Avallone spent his campaign funds on billboards, mass mailings, radio ads, and a few newspaper ads, and hardly ever met the public outside of benefit dinners and breakfasts. The fact that two local newspapers endorsed his opponents (including me) and attacked him for a conflict of interest deterred some voters from supporting him, but not enough—he received over 60 percent of the vote. After the election, I met with Paul Bass, editor of the *Indepen-*

dent, and asked whether his paper's endorsement of me and attacks against the incumbent had made any difference. He guessed that the *Independent*'s campaign coverage had an impact on 15 percent of the readers. We agreed that television coverage is far more influential.

But media coverage did not determine the outcome of my race. My Democratic opponent benefited most from his party machine's support, which brought out thousands of voters who would not consider voting for a second party, let alone a third, whoever the newcomer was. His machine, and the money that came with it (about 100 times what I spent), made the difference.

Shakespeare and Christ Turn Green

But it is not necessary to win an election to win small victories and effect some local change through theatre and activism. I attribute one of these victories to a protest Developers for DiLieto led against city hall. The battle began when Mayor DiLieto let it be known, as already noted, that he wanted to tear down the Coliseum and replace it with a mall rather than repair the arena's crumbling garage. To secure space for the mall, DiLieto vigorously opposed the opening of a discount store, Ceasar's [sic], in an abandoned building near the Coliseum. Ceasar's low prices would not bring wealthy patrons into the city, so the mayor harassed the store's developer, Mordecai Lipkis, who refused to apply for permits the city told him to seek.

Developers for DiLieto sided with Lipkis against the mayor in this most peculiar contest. I publicly commended Lipkis for his efforts to reopen an abandoned building and offer merchandise affordable to most city residents. I also announced a rally to support Ceasar's. Lipkis called me two days before the rally and agreed to join me at a press conference. Our imaginary association of developers found an ally who actually was a developer: reality conformed to our theatrical illusion!

The city's largest circulation newspaper, the *New Haven Register,* offered the following review of our protest, in a page-one story:

> NEW HAVEN—Lawyers for Ceasar's Department Store and the city Tuesday tried to resolve conflicts that have stopped the store from opening in the former Edw. Malley Co. building, but the compromise fell apart.
>
> Meanwhile, a local group demonstrated its support for the discount store outside Superior Court on Church Street. Demonstrators carried signs reading "Render unto Ceasar's that which is Ceasar's" and "Praise Ceasar's, Don't Bury Him." [. . .] Lipkis left the court building Tuesday only to walk into the waiting arms of "Developers for DiLieto," a political group holding a sidewalk demonstration supporting him.
>
> [. . .] Joel Schechter, a founder of the group, said, "We are here at the courthouse today to show support for Ceasar's department store owner Mordecai Lipkis [. . .] for trying to revitalize downtown New Haven without destroying the Veterans' Memorial Coliseum" (Hamm et al. 1988).

I was especially pleased that our slogans parodying Christ and Shakespeare appeared on page one of the *Register.* Bruce Shapiro of the *Independent* also reported on Ceasar's receiving support "from an unexpected quarter Tuesday: the satirical group, Developers for DiLieto" (1988:12). Shapiro quoted my tongue-in-cheek speculation that the mayor probably only "opposed the store to give it more publicity and promote its grand opening," since he favors developers more than anyone. The most comic line in the *Independent* came later in the story: "Lipkis admitted he had never before heard of Developers for DiLieto. 'But we appreciate the fact that this organization came forth,' [he said]." Once he realized we were satirizing developers, it was too late for Lipkis to disavow us completely.

Shortly after our demonstration, some of Mayor DiLieto's most prominent opponents, including black Democratic Senator John Daniels, who has decided to seek the mayoral position himself in 1989, announced formation of a new consumer's protection association and joined Lipkis in his fight against city hall. The mayor's opponents within his own party would not let Green party satirists enjoy a monopoly on growing support for Ceasar's. Here as elsewhere in my campaign, I found politicians from other parties following the Green party's lead.

As public support for Ceasar's increased, the mayor's aides stopped their harassment of the department store. It opened a few days before the November 8th election. I was there among the first shoppers, passing out campaign leaflets and shaking hands with Lipkis, the friendly developer.

A Clown Saves the Coliseum

A greater preelection victory, for which I also take some credit, occurred when the mayor withdrew his plan to tear down the Coliseum, something I had called for throughout my campaign. While I thought other issues (affordable housing, recycling, an end to nuclear power) were more important, I knew the Coliseum's rescue was of great concern to the public. A newspaper poll indicated 70 percent of area residents favored its preservation. No doubt the mayor dropped his plan in order to appease that 70 percent, but my campaign probably hastened his decision.

The Coliseum's need for repairs, due to city hall's negligence, inspired one of Developers for DiLieto's finest events. Prior to the opening of the Moscow Circus, I announced that an extraordinary clown, Mikhail Trautmansky, would comment on the Coliseum's state of disrepair. On opening night several reporters and a TV camera crew met me and professional

3. Developers for DiLieto and friends parody Shakespeare and Christ. From left to right: Joan Whitney, Mordecai Lipkis, Joel Schechter, Chris Gray. (Photo by Diana Scott)

Plate 4.

Commie Clown Critiques Coliseum*

SOVIET CLOWN MIKHAIL TRAUTMANSKY LIVE AT THE COLISEUM.
Directed by Developers for DiLieto. Closed.

Margaret Spillane

Before the Moscow Circus came to town, some people were hazarding guesses about just what kind of protest pickets the Soviet presence would draw. Surely the animal rights people would be there, as they are for every circus regardless of its national origin. Perhaps we'd see other groups making ideological statements: for instance, any of the numerous captive nations or ethnic minorities to whom Moscow means something considerably more baleful than dancing bears. Or maybe a loony, solitary freedom fighter, wearing a red-white-and-blue top hat and handing out smeary fliers announcing "Jesus Hates Commies."

Well, no such collection of armies clashed on the corners of Orange and George streets on the circus's opening night. The animal rights people were the only protesters there, distributing fact sheets on cruel techniques of animal training and filling the air with many bullhorn-enhanced voices urging people not to attend the Moscow Circus. Unfortunately, this high-tech advantage all but drowned out the earnest, unmiked voice of a most extraordinary sidewalk performer: the "renowned Soviet Clown" Mikhail Trautmansky, in town to offer not only entertainment but emergency assistance.

Unlike the outfits of his American counterparts, which resemble outsize children's pajamas, Trautmansky's attire reflected the far more respectful position accorded circus artists in the Soviet Union. Trautmansky looked smart in his European-cut tuxedo; only a bulbous red-plastic nose made clear his solidarity with the oppressed clowns of Ringling's.

Could the tuxedo also have been a concession to Trautmansky's sponsors, Developers for DiLieto, who only remove their dinner jackets to put on yachting gear? Or was it a comradely salute to those American clowns who perform as senators, bankers and judges? In any case, Trautmansky's performance was introduced by DFD chairperson Joel Schechter (also looking elegant in evening

---

clown Michael Trautman outside the Coliseum. Forty animal-rights activists were also there, protesting against circus exploitation of trained animals. Their presence received more attention than our small theatre event, and many circus patrons must have thought that Trautman and I were animal-rights supporters as we performed our routine in the midst of picketers. Trautman in his red clown nose was also mistaken for a Soviet clown by more than one spectator. The event was reviewed by Margaret Spillane (1988b). I reprint her description in full, because it led thousands of readers to wonder if the Soviet Union had tried to take over New Haven's Coliseum. Abetting our prank, Spillane never revealed that "Trautmansky" was an American posing as a Soviet (see plate 4). Several days after Trautmansky's act, the mayor announced he would not tear down the Coliseum after all. Had the "Commie Clown" led DiLieto to realize that his demolition plans were as ridiculous as ours?

Impersonating the Next Vice-President

I staged one other theatre event at the end of my senate campaign. The July 14th Housing Action Committee, of which I am a member, planned a demonstration against warehousing which keeps apartment units vacant wear and his signature accessory, a yellow hard hat topped with a champagne glass).

But wait—Trautmansky was wearing a hard hat, too! How ironic! A citizen of a nation that once told America "We will bury you," Comrade Trautmansky expressed his own immediate fear of being buried in New Haven. This remarkable comic artist claimed that he was forced to wear a hard hat in order to "perform in an arena (Veterans Memorial Coliseum) which could fall down on our heads at any moment."

But in the true collectivist spirit of his homeland, Trautmansky's concerns extend far beyond just saving his own skull. He worries as well about the concert-going, hockey-loving citizens of New Haven who should not have to risk being maimed or buried by their own coliseum every time they go to a music or sports event, since "they have enough danger in their lives already. On behalf of his new American fans, Comrade T would like to offer a most useful gift."

Though he comes from the land where the Five Year Plan is the rule, Trautmansky opted for an initial short-term solution to the Coliseum crisis. He presented Schechter with some good solid workers' tools to get the job started immediately—a hammer and a sickle. The hammer, no doubt, will help strike the necessary blows against the bureaucratic empire that's neglected the Coliseum's structural problems for so long now. The sickle will come in handy for hacking the thicket of red tape around the Coliseum (or is it tape that's holding the Coliseum together?).

On the other hand, was this gestureof help merely intended to soften up New Haveners, so we'd be more comfortable about compromising our pride and our fierce independence for Trautmansky's next proposal? "If you cannot secure repair money from your government," spoke Comrade T, "perhaps you should try ours. We give to underdeveloped countries, and maybe we will try to give to city developers too. *If* you give us a tax break."

Did this guy really expect the patriotic working people of New Haven to bear an even bigger tax burden just so some superpower can sit on a prime piece of New Haven real estate and never put a penny into the municipal coffers? Just what does the Soviet Union think it is, Yale University?** Go back where you belong, Commie Clown.

**Reprinted from* The New Haven Independent, *3 November 1988:13.*
***Yale is tax exempt and rarely pays for the city services it receives.—Schechter*

until they can be sold at a huge profit. We prepared to commit civil disobedience by placing a banner demanding affordable housing over a warehoused building's exterior. The chances of being arrested for this were small, but real.

I was asked to write a short play for the protest. The performance featured labor historian Jeremy Brecher adorned by a large bird feather as Senator Dan Quayle, the Republican vice-presidential candidate. He paraphrased a speech in which Quayle questioned whether there *was* a lack of affordable housing in America. "I can afford any home for sale," he said in our skit. Other speakers, representing evicted tenants, explained that their fathers were less wealthy than Quayle's. On 4 November the skit was broadcast by radio station WELI, at which time I was also asked to explain the play.

Post-Yippie Politics

Cultural historians familiar with street theatre of the late '60s may recall similar or bolder electoral theatre and satire from that era. In 1968 Yippies conducted a national campaign for Pigasus (a pig) who was the first "black and white female Presidential candidate." Yippie cofounder Paul Krassner justified such electoral campaigns by saying that "the real elections are a prank" (in Juno 1987:91).

Yippie humor inspired me, but I saw my own campaign as more than a prank or protest against the electoral choices offered by the Democratic and Republican parties. I offered voters the Green party platform as a constructive alternative for local social change. My associates and I won public attention through street theatre antics; but we also issued serious legislative proposals in the name of a party that had won more than 10 percent of the vote citywide in 1985 and 1987. I campaigned for a nuclear-free Connecticut, a ban on toxic waste incineration, and state tax reform that would ease the burden on lower income taxpayers.

I suspect that many activists of the '60s have moved in a similar direction—toward alternative, third party political platforms. Wavy Gravy and Abbie Hoffman both endorsed my state senate candidacy in 1988. Wavy Gravy, in case you don't know him, was a Merry Prankster whose group, the Hog Farm, provided medical care at numerous rock concerts including Woodstock. More recently he has conducted a national campaign to elect "Nobody for President," because "Nobody's perfect and Nobody cares." He endorsed me by saying, "Joel is better than Nobody" (1988). My opponents were endorsed by a member of congress and a senator from their respective parties—but I preferred Abbie Hoffman's public compliment: "Schechter's my kinda guy" (1988). I also secured an endorsement from TDR editor Richard Schechner, who noted that "We need more theatre people in politics, despite the miserable record of the Great Communicator" (1988).

Wavy Gravy predicts that a third party composed of Greens and the Rainbow coalition will surface in time for the 1992 presidential race. Of course, he is a stand-up comedian these days, and he could be joking. But it is possible that more third party activists will create Green and other alternative zones of progressive representation, by playing the role of candidate in elections, and validating their role through ballot returns and preelectoral victories like those I won.

Jean Baudrillard has argued in *Simulations* that our age is one of simulated political power, where "power, too, produces nothing but signs of its resemblance [. . .] power is no longer present except to conceal that there is none" (1983:46). Electoral contests are simulations, in which prior to the vote count, signs of power and the theatre that produces such signs may be mistaken for power itself. I found evidence of this in my state senate campaign when the Republican party asked me to withdraw from the race.

Just Saying No to the Republicans

There was always a chance that I would win in New Haven. That prospect was one sign—or superplot if you will—central to my electoral theatre. The threat of winning, the possibility of winning, invested my endeavor with signs of power. I realized this most fully a few weeks before the election, when I received a phone call from the press coordinator for my Republican opponent, Sandra Astarita. She wanted me to withdraw from the race, thinking my share of the votes as third party candidate would make the difference between a Republican win and loss. In this race, incidentally, the Republican was generally regarded as less conservative than the incumbent Democrat. Later, the chair of the New Haven Republican party phoned to make the same request. Twice I just said no. It turned

5. Staging an electable alternative: Joel Schechter (in overcoat) and Green party members perform for a New Haven TV news team. (Photo by Diana Scott)

out that the Republican lost by a two-to-one margin anyway. But the preelection prospect that I might determine the outcome of the race, even if I did not win it, made the Green party candidacy significant to Republicans as well as Greens. That I could make a difference, that my position on nuclear power or recycling might change the outcome of the state senate race, was a political and theatrical illusion I welcomed.

I lost the election in November, but almost no one knows the percentage by which I lost. For weeks after the election, friends and strangers would approach me and say: "I voted for you. How many votes did you get?" I won't answer that question in print, because I now know that the percentage was far less important than the fact that I ran at all. What people remember are the names of the parties, the candidates, a street theatre scene or two. During the campaign, the *Register*'s Elizabeth Bodine called the three-way race I entered "the city's most interesting," and devoted more space to it than any other state campaign (1988). But when it was over, the same paper reported almost nothing about the race aside from its winner's name. The other two papers in town wrote more about the race's losers than its winner. If my campaign was theatre, it was more process than product—signs of power, not power itself, mattered most to its reviewers.

Power itself in the form of the Democratic party machinery, money, and patronage ultimately triumphed. I have reservations about Baudrillard's thesis that the signs of power are all power now produces. Homelessness, unemployment, hunger are also the products of the ruling powers in New Haven. Democratic party campaign expenses are paid by construction companies and developers, who later find compensation in city subsidies for their new buildings which replace low-income housing with more profitable dwellings. The homeless are displaced by more than free-floating signifiers of power.

Electoral theatre by itself will hardly change this constitution of power, although it provides the illusion that an electable alternative exists, and in the case of developer Lipkis joining Developers for DiLieto, reality conformed to illusion for a while.[1] Until Green coalitions grow to the size and strength of the anti-Vietnam war movement or the civil rights movement, the existing power structure may not take our alternative programs seriously. Satire offers its creators the advantage of not needing to be taken seriously.

For the present, I console myself by quoting another third party candidate, Will Rogers, who campaigned as the Anti-Bunk party nominee for president in 1928. Rogers used to say, "Things are looking better for us [in the third party] every day, for those other [two] parties have just about done their worst" (1982:29). Unfortunately, the other two parties had not and have not yet done their worst. Voters gave them another chance last November.

I plan to continue teaching my seminar "Theatre for Prospective Politicians." There is always the chance that one of my students will become Connecticut's next senator or America's president by the year 2008. But if we never see another actor elected president, that too would be fine with me.

Note

1. In March 1989, Ben DiLieto announced that he would not be seeking reelection this year. This could be the beginning of the end for Developers for DiLieto.

References

Aristophanes
1985 [424 BCE] *"The Knights."* In *The Birds and Other Plays,* translated by Alan Sommerstein, 29–89. New York: Penguin.

Aristotle
1962 [330 BCE] "The Poetics." In *Literary Criticism,* edited by Allan H. Gilbert, 69–115. Detroit, MI: Wayne State University Press.

Baudrillard, Jean
1983 *Simulations.* New York: Semiotext(e).

Bodine, Elizabeth
1988 "3-Way Race in City Spotlight." *The New Haven Register,* 10 October:10.

Gravy, Wavy
1988 Interview with author. New Haven, CT, November.

Hamm, Steve, Nick Povinelli, and Elizabeth Bodine
1988 "Compromise Fails Between City, Ceasar's on Opening." *The New Haven Register,* 7 September:1.

Hoffman, Abbie
1988 Personal correspondence, October.

Juno, Andrea
1987 "Paul Krassner" [interview]. *Re Search:* 81–91.

Rogers, Will
1982 *He Chews to Run.* Stillwater: Oklahoma University Press.

Schechner, Richard
1988 Personal correspondence, October.

Schechter, Joel
1985 *Durov's Pig: Clowns, Politics and Theatre.* New York: Theatre Communications Group.

Shapiro, Bruce
1988 "Praise for Ceasar's, Criticism for DiLieto." *The New Haven Independent,* 8 September:12.

Spillane, Margaret
1988a "The Pig Who (Almost) Came to Dinner." *The New Haven Independent,* 24 March:11.
1988b "Commie Clown Critiques Coliseum." *The New Haven Independent,* 3 November:13.

Whitney, George
1988 "Pet Gripes" [letter to the editor]. *The New Haven Independent,* 7 April:21.

Joel Schechter *is Editor of* Theater *magazine and Associate Professor of Dramatic Criticism at the Yale School of Drama.*

Plays and Polemics on the Soviet Stage

1987/88 Premieres

Konstantin Scherbakov

Ed. Note: We received the following article from VAAP-Inform—the informational wing of the All-Soviet Agency for Author's Rights. It may help readers formulate a picture of theatre in Moscow since glasnost. *From 1985, Soviet theatres have been working under new conditions of relative freedom. The article begins with an interview with Mikhail Ulyanov, an actor and chair of the board of the Theatre Union of the Russian Federation—whose establishment marked the beginning of* perestroika *(restructuring) in the Soviet theatre.*

ULYANOV: It was our theatrical environment that paved the way for the decisions taken by the congress of theatre people of the Russian Federation and, subsequently, the National Congress. Who artistically expressed the need for and the essence of the favorable social changes taking place in the country? The theatre did and it did it before, and more vigorously, than anyone else. One needs only recall such productions as *The Silver Wedding* (1986), *The Dictatorship of Conscience* (1986), *Speak Out!* (1986), and others to realize this. Today these names have become standard references in article after article. That they have become so familiar in such a brief period is due to the fact that time is becoming so compressed, so filled with amazing new developments. Eighteen months ago no one could even imagine theatrical productions presenting such acute civic and social issues. Still, even then the best minds in the theatre were preparing for a time when they could express themselves freely; they were accumulating a spiritual charge, so when the moment arrived they were all set to confront the issues posed by the new times. The congresses only helped us to become aware of what had been ripening in us anyway. And the indivisibility of the creative (artistic) and the civic (social) elements is also the salient feature of this moment.

SCHERBAKOV: It seems to me that the most important message of those theatrical congresses is that they revealed the readiness of the creative artists to take into their own hands the leadership of the theatrical process.

ULYANOV: Yes, we got tired of the state cultural agencies' patronage, of having a large pyramid of controllers and supervisors towering over each theatre and each production, of people who earnestly believed they knew "what the people want" though they took no part in the creative process themselves. It was not even so much our tiredness. It was just that the bureaucratic management gradually, but inevitably, was leading the theatre to a dead end.

SCHERBAKOV: Were many productions banned in the past few years?

ULYANOV: No, to be fair, not many. But a number of good, truthful plays several theatres have wanted to produce for years are only now finding their way to the audiences. I recall the arduous passage toward the stage of Georgi Tovstonogov's 1974 production of *Three Sacks of Wheat and Weeds* (based on a story by Vladimir Tendryakov) or Mikhail Shatrov's *We Are Bound to Win!* (1982) at the Moscow Art Theatre, both recognized now as major theatrical achievements. Why should artists waste their nervous and physical energy on "pushing" what they have created instead of doing creative work? But the saddest thing was that as a result, fewer and fewer people were going to the theatre, and those who did go were becoming less and less eager to participate in a serious and sincere dialog. The audience saw one thing in reality and something entirely different on the stage. As a result, two parallel scales of values sprang up—one genuine, one mythical, invented for someone's comfort. But the Soviet theatre has always been a rostrum and was never meant to shun social issues. We could no longer tolerate that division.

SCHERBAKOV: And as a result of the free democratic process, the delegates to the congresses established the Theatre Union of the Russian Federation and of the USSR. But can they influence the state of the theatre?

ULYANOV: These Unions have sufficient creative and social authority including the right to suspend, in some instances, the implementation of administrative decisions. They now have the final say in evaluating the theatrical process and, alongside governmental cultural agencies, bear full responsibility for progress in this art.

A new atmosphere, new possibilities. A theatrical experiment, initiated by the USSR Ministry of Culture on 1 January 1987, gave theatre companies a greater economic and creative independence than they ever had before. Seven new theatres were set up in Moscow alone. But was the past season rich in interesting premieres? Unfortunately not. There were only a few significant new productions in tune with the new times, while the number of mediocre productions was as high as in the past. However, I will not dwell on the latter. It is more rewarding to examine those plays which reflect, albeit to a varying degree, the hopeful trends.

The undisputed leader of the season was Mikhail Shatrov's *The Brest Peace Treaty,* produced at the Vakhtangov Theatre in Moscow by the Georgian director Robert Sturua, distinguished for his interpretations of Shakespeare. The full impact of the play is felt as soon as it begins: a group of Bolsheviks with stern, powerful, rhythmic strides cross the stage until they come face to face with a woman, clutching her child, bending over the coffin of her dead husband.

We see the Bolsheviks, who have blasted away the old lifestyle, facing an overturned country full of people who believed in them and waited for them to bring peace, truth, and justice. The Bolsheviks, who must explain to the widow why her husband had to die, are not some kind of a mono-

1. *Mikhail Ulyanov as Lenin and Vasily Lanovoy as Trotsky in Mikhail Shatrov's* The Brest Peace Treaty. *Shatrov drew the legendary Russian leaders not as symbolic figures, but as "living human beings." (Photo courtesy of VAAP-Inform)*

lith; instead, they are a group of individuals each with his own personality, hard-won convictions, and ambitions. The production is one of the first attempts by a Moscow theatre to recreate historical reality.

Among the group are Nikolai Bukharin, an impetuous, hot-blooded knight of the revolution whose devotion to it is totally uncompromising; the forceful and persuasive Leon Trotsky, who vacillates between sincerity and artistry; and the smiling, ingratiating, conflict-free Josef Stalin, in whom one senses the as yet barely perceptible air of the horrible future to come.

Only a few months ago, newspapers mentioning the name or publishing a photograph of Bukharin, even in a most neutral context, were snapped up from the newsstands. But now no one seems very impressed by the mention of a once-banned name or issue. How, then, do these characters appear to today's audience? I would say that their presence in the political, moral, and social reality portrayed in *The Brest Peace Treaty* seems perfectly natural. Bukharin, Trotsky, Stalin, Georgii Lomov, and Inessa Armand are not political theses marked with a plus or minus brought to life through the efforts of the director and actors—not even the most updated, just and true theses. They are living human beings capable of love and suffering, insight and mistakes.

We see their relationships with Vladimir Lenin, who is interpreted by Mikhail Ulyanov without the traditional fast-moving gestures, burred speech, or even makeup. Basing his character on the competent and thoroughly organized material presented by Shatrov, the actor has created a version of Lenin which is inseparable from his own thoughts and emotions. This Lenin has a stern, harsh face and the manner of an exhausted man. Each line he utters pulsates with thought which virtually electrifies both his interlocutors and the audience. This Lenin does not see anyone as an opponent, only as a comrade whom he must persuade. And the issue which calls for this persuasion is pivotal to the destiny of the revolution, the country, and millions of people—such as the woman in the opening scene who cast such a demanding and inquiring look at Lenin and his comrades.

The debate over whether the Brest Peace Treaty had to be concluded or not is presented as a drama of ideas embodied in living and incongruous personalities. Lenin's place among them is one of loneliness among one's own people. The internal spring, the nerve of the action is the work of Lenin's intellect and will, which ultimately helps him overcome his isolation. His opponents in the debate offer arguments gained after much suffering, not the proverbial "patently false" ones, and Lenin's victory in the finale is due not only to the political foresight on which he built his arguments, but also to the golden assets of his personality.

One detail that detracts from the performance's strong overall impression is that in key scenes Ulyanov clearly outperforms the rest of the cast. It is tempting to think that if the director had moved still further and given Lenin's opponents more scope and equal status, the scale of the confrontation (resolved by the casting of votes and the conclusion of the Brest Peace Treaty) would have been greater, and the emotional impact on the audience witnessing the laborious birth of truth more profound.

In the finale, Lenin exits through the same backstage door through which he entered in the beginning; thus he leaves his comrades alone with the country for which they are responsible.

No matter how significant a theme is, a confrontation of ideas and principles on the stage is bound to fail unless it touches people's hearts. I hate to admit it, but even today I can clearly foresee some dull production playing up the repressions of 1937. Once the taboo has been removed, the subject loses much of its attractiveness. Since it speculates on an already open theme, I was apprehensive at the beginning of Arkady Stavitsky's *Four Interrogations,* staged by Alexander Tovstonogov at the Moscow Stanislavsky Drama Theatre. Based on factual material, the play depicts a moral duel between the old-guard Bolshevik Gronina, arrested on the strength of a slander, and the young Stalinist investigator Korolkov. It seemed improbable that this play could add anything to such recently widely read material as the actor Georgi Zhzhenov's memoirs of his days in the prison camp published in *Ogonyok* magazine (1988) or to an account of the similar period in the life of the wife of one of the most popular Soviet leaders, Mikhail Kalinin—both staggering human documents. But it did.

As the heroine Gronina goes over her life she realizes that, although unwillingly, she played her part in molding thousands of Korolkov lookalikes in all walks of life in the USSR. It is frightening when the nation is divided into executioners and victims; it is even more so when their lives become so inseparably intertwined. Gronina's sense of dignity overpowers Korolkov's mechanical heartlessness, and as a result the young investigator, accustomed to carrying out his orders unquestioningly, suddenly becomes aware of the abyss around him.

Is it not juggling with facts when, out of thousands of unthinking and unrepentant monsters, the author selects one whose awakened conscience compelled him to act responsibly despite his instinct for self-preservation? No, in so far as art is concerned, it is a deviation from the current "norm" that helps to gain a more precise understanding of the norm, and in art that has always been important.

Alexander Chervinsky's *The Leningrader,* produced at the Soviet Army Theatre in Moscow by director Yuri Yeryomin, is set in the early 1950s.

Although we see no interrogations or prisoners on stage, the play stresses the ties between that period and the grim late 1930s.

This story about a family of shipbuilders begins with the funeral of its head, a leading engineer. After the funeral, the main characters go to their countryside home, behind a high fence topped with barbed wire and watched by plainclothesmen: the owner of the house is privy to state secrets which have to be guarded.

The director is very specific about everyday details, but what is baffling is that his heroes appear as clockwork dummies. Moreover, they are painted with one stroke of the brush, as it were, in an unusually vague manner for both Yeryomin and Chervinsky. Further on, an imbalance in the acting becomes apparent: the older characters are drawn sketchily, while one of the younger characters, Stepan (played by Vadim Ledogorov), is portrayed more fully. Stepan follows a different tempo in life, which induces him to act and speak differently as well.

Finally, one realizes that this rhythmic disparity and the two-dimensionality of most of the characters does not result from negligence; it is a deliberate interpretation by the director who sensed the absurd in the play. The outcome is an image of a clockwork, stiffly programed world whose victims are chained to unalterable orbits. Abandoning one's part in this game is costly, as Stepan finds out. Having married and chosen a profession without the approval of the "system," he is doomed to an in-between, neither-friend-nor-foe existence—disowned by the old system, he is still shackled by its spiritual dogmatism which passes itself off as respectable family tradition.

The play's protagonist, Fyodor (played by Andrei Tashkov), also attempts to break out from his orbit. As the son of the head of the family he is bound more by tradition than others, but in Tashkov's interpretation he also emerges as more diverse in character. On the one hand, he cannot even think of shifting from his predetermined orbit, but, on the other, his young and healthy nature misses no chance to assert itself. Therefore, he may fit the "approved" pattern, but then again he may become something quite different.

But here we must mention yet another character—Victor (played by Fyodor Funtikov). He seems the most benevolent, obliging, charming, dynamic, and understanding of all. He does not fuss or get in anyone's way; he seems not to be there at all—unless he is needed. Victor is a confidential friend, the bodyguard and protector of both state secrets and family traditions. He is part of the soul of this family, poisoned as it is by its defense mania, spacial restrictiveness, and predetermination. Without being aware of it, perhaps, Fyodor fights Victor for the mastery of his soul, his indivisible self.

Having started out in life with both himself and Victor in his soul at the same time, Fyodor, deceiving his soul's guardian for a while, finds love and happiness. One more step and he attains an opportunity for an unfettered realization of his personality. But at that moment, Victor, leaping out from Fyodor's own soul, it seems, manages to snatch him back to where he "belongs."

Yes, the "Victor" is in hiding in all of us. He barely let us feel his presence as we lived through the late 1950s and '60s, but he straightened out again in the '70s. New times are here but can one vouch that the mistakes committed 30 years ago, when we conceitedly claimed we had been rid of the previous fears and inner insecurity, will not come back?

Only openness and collective vigilance can provide such a guarantee. (It is not accidental, one is led to suppose, that growing opposition to perestroika and the creation of guarantees against its dismantling are among the principal topics discussed in the press.)

Alongside journalists, creators of fiction, films, and theatre are also working to establish such guarantees. Although no one needs simulated efforts on the theme of perestroika now, just as such time-serving efforts never enjoyed much respect before. Neither literature nor stage and screen arts can exist today unless they reflect what is going on.

One proof of this is the premiere of the new play by Roman Solntsev, *Celestial Brakes,* directed by Pavel Khomsky at the Mossovet Drama Theatre in Moscow. The very first look at the stage is dazzling: huge white-on-red streamers proclaim "Perestroika, Democracy, Glasnost," "Restructuring, Not Adaptation," "Let Us Mark the Visit to Our Region of the General Secretary of the Communist Party's Central Committee with New Achievements at Work!" and so on. Two TV monitors set at either side of the stage show sequences of Gorbachev's visit to a major Trans-Ural city. Standing in the center of the stage is a table at which the bosses of the region share their impressions after the meeting between the general secretary and the prominent men in the local party, government, and industrial establishment. Left alone, this inner circle attempts to find ways to deflate the healthy critical mood that arose in the audience during the meeting, and ways to preserve the status quo which they have pledged to change. The conference behind closed doors proceeds apace, but what its participants ignore in the heat of the discussion is that one of the television cameras is rolling. They become aware of it when the cassette with the compromising material is already on a flight to Moscow.

What follows is close to a detective thriller as the "bosses," fearing exposure, disgrace, and loss of power, go out of their way to intercept the film.

Used to passing all decisions in the privacy of their soundproof offices, where they say altogether different things from what they proclaim from the platform, they stoop to anything to restore their crumbling world. In fact, they fear change even more than exposure, for then they will be recognized for what most of them have become: cogs and wheels of the bankrupt self-reproducing bureaucratic mechanism which is being scrapped.

No one hopes that the change that the bureaucratic mechanism of management must undergo to become a democratic one will be gradual. The mechanism must be broken and the breaking is bound to hurt. One has to admit here that many more people were found to be involved in the bureaucracy than was previously thought. Solntsev shows us how and why more and more new people become involved in the chase for the compromising film, driven by the complicated interaction of mutual interests. One begins to wonder how things would have worked out were it not for that extraordinary event. What if the confidential conference proceedings were not recorded?

The part of the regional party secretary in the play, Makhonin, is played at the Mossovet Drama by Georgi Zhzhenov, an actor whose striking individuality fit his character. Makhonin despises his entourage, all those he has broken in and depersonalized but cannot do without. He is attracted to people who have preserved their independence and dignity, but he does not speak their language. Authoritarian, unbridled power has corrupted not only the "cogs" and "wheels," but their boss as well. There seems to be no way out of this trap for Zhzhenov's character.

While the best production of the season under review *(The Brest Peace Treaty)* was about Lenin and the kind of human relationships to which we must return today, the other notable premieres were about the distortion of these norms of behavior, about the legacy which hampers our effort to live in freedom and with dignity. That legacy resembles Victor in *The Leningrader* who, working from the inside, dictates the laws and principles of everyday existence, builds a hierarchy of moral and social values, and creates his own elite and outcasts.

A dreary looking, narrow, dirty room, a row of stark rusty steel beds: you are forced to stare at a blank wall—placed by the set designer almost at the footlights, so there is barely any living space for the room's inhabitants. For all that starkness, the women who live there put on a nonchalant look, exchange stories, even joke. The opening scene of *The Stars on the Morning Sky* by Alexander Galin is obviously comical.

The play was directed by Lev Dodin and Tatiana Shestakova at the Leningrad Drama Theatre, which took it to the 1988 New York theatre festival. It presents one aspect of life that has been practically untouched by Soviet art in the past. The time of action is stated with utmost precision—the summer of 1980, the days when long-distance runners were carrying the Olympic torch to Moscow. For the festive occasion, the city fathers decided to remove all prostitutes from the capital in an attempt to forestall possible complications with visiting foreigners and insure a general picture of Moscovite radiance. We see four such women brought together to this gloomy room in a barrack outside Moscow.

News that Alexander Galin was writing a play about Moscow prostitutes deprived of their share of Olympic festivities but eager to get at least one glimpse of the magnificent runners approaching their city spread several years ago. Most reacted by shrugging their shoulders—some in irritation, others in regret that the play would never be allowed to go on the stage. In other words, both parties accepted as inevitable the logic by which the city's establishment sought to "cleanse" the Olympic capital in 1980.

But even as fresh winds began to blow, the dam developed a crack and "unedited" reality started finding its way onto the stage. The warnings and admonishings were heard again: Sure you can admit it, but there is no call to lay it on so thick. But what about Dostoyevsky, Tolstoi, Kuprin? Did they whisper about what was tearing their hearts apart?

The Leningrad Drama Theatre is not seeking gratitude for its presentation of a formerly banned subject. Passionately devoted to getting at the essence of things, these artists do not look back. What would life be like if people who are eager to state their grievances and know how to do it were constantly looking back?

Stars is a traditional Galin play, its drama tempered with humor and sincerity and told in a quiet voice. And just as sincere and unaffected is the playwright's sympathy for his heroines. But the directors, Dodin and Shestakova, choose not to follow Galin's lead to the end. At one point they shift the play abruptly into a different gear: one cruel scene follows another, the voices of the heroines grow shrill, hysterical, desperate. And instead of quiet, understanding sympathy the women demand from the audience an ardent compassion, a compassion that can help, that can find the answer to the question: Whose fault is it that these women are what they are? Who is responsible for their suffering?

But, suffering aside, what about these women? Didn't they choose their fates? The answer is yes, of course, they did have a choice, a way out, once. But both the playwright and the directors have sufficient humanity not to

2. *Alexander Galin's* The Stars on the Morning Sky: *a play about the desecration of human dignity. Pictured are Serghei Kozyrev, Natalia Akimova, and Vera Bykova. (Photo courtesy of VAAP-Inform)*

reproach the heroines for their failure to make the right choice. This performance does not pass judgment on those who no longer stand on their feet, it does not give a moral sermon to human beings who, perhaps, have never known what pity is about. Their anger, their moral and social protest is directed at those who sit in their brand new cars packed with expensive liquor and food, waiting for these meek "girlfriends" to give them pleasure and then to be treated as dirt. And not only at them, but also at those who are behind, and above, them.

So whose fault is it that we are faced today with such social evils? *The Stars on the Morning Sky* invites us to look for the answer. Its other message is: Do not comfort yourselves by thinking that you have nothing to do with the underside of life. For in an essential way this is a story about disregard for and desecration of human dignity, about the withering away of fundamental moral notions without which everything is senseless and futile. Should we not make it our top priority to work for the resurrection of human dignity befitting the citizens of a great country where we, all of us, have tolerated so many iniquities?

On the eve of their graduation ceremony, four nice young people, three boys and a girl, pay a visit to their favorite teacher. They bring her flowers and champagne, but it soon transpires that the intent of their visit is far from benign. These "nice" kids want their examination papers replaced so they can get better grades. The only way they can do it is through their "dear Elena Sergeyevna." At first, they all sweetly ask her for her key, then they demand it. But faced with her refusal, they go mad and brutally search their "dear, beloved" teacher.

One could say many things about these children of their times as they are encountered in Lyudmila Razumovskaya's *Dear Elena Sergeyevna* (directed by Svetlana Vragova at the Moscow Drama Studio on Spartakovskaya Square). But their principle trait is their lack of dignity and honesty. These young souls are clearly an offspring of the social atmosphere which promoted dual morality—one for home consumption, another for use in public. And one of those who helped nurture these double standards, albeit unwittingly, was none other than Elena Sergeyevna. It seems to me that no one play can properly reveal the measure of blame and responsibility that belongs to either the older or the younger generations. But this play raises this important issue.

Vragova offers an interesting interpretation of *Dear Elena Sergeyevna,* which, if treated as a traditional psychological drama, tends to drag and stop now and again (as does its screen adaptation by director Eldar Ryazanov). To overcome such snags, the director drastically changes the styling of the action in the middle of the play. The "nice" children are suddenly replaced with gaudily painted monsters with mechanical movements and strident voices who proceed to torture their victim. Reality turns into the theatre of the absurd which actually accentuates reality and graphically reveals its hidden essence. The image of a trial without dignity or mercy created by Vragova captures the attention and, moreover, evokes all sorts of associations from distant and not so distant reality.

How are we to rid ourselves from monsters, phantoms of fear, spiritual slavery, and aggressive heartlessness? How are we to return to our roots, to retrieve the original values of the new society after they have sustained such a prolonged abuse? In a few of the best productions of the recent season, Soviet theatre sought the answers to these questions, and called on audiences to do the same.

Reference

Zhzhenov, Georgi
1988 "The Sled." *Ogonyok* 15 (April):26–31.

Konstantin Scherbakov *is a theatre critic for VAAP-Inform in Moscow.*

ITItems

Richard Schechner has offered the International Theatre Institute of the U.S. a place in TDR!!! In each issue of TDR there will be news, background information, arguments, howls of joy and rage, announcements of ITI events, past and future, and a wonderful opportunity for us to be better known to you.

Martha W. Coigney
Director, ITI/US
President, ITI/Worldwide

The International Theatre Institute, founded in 1948, is a worldwide communications network serving the professional needs of theatre people and institutions. When the founders, including Rosamond Gilder, gathered in Prague 40 years ago, they still breathed the ashes of World War II and their governments had just invented the Cold War. The founders of ITI set themselves an impossible job. They decided to create a network of exchange, protection, and information among theatre artists. To promote peace and mutual understanding. All around the world. Regardless of hostilities, barriers, and bureaucracies.

Their job was impossible, but . . . nobody told them, so they did it!

ITI started with eight countries. Forty years later ITI/US is one of 76 national centers established to promote and facilitate the international exchange of people, information, and practices in the theatre arts. Included in the ITI/US program are the Visitor Service, International Exchange Service, Consultation Service, and the Library and Information Service.

In this, our first appearance in TDR, our Library will be the featured attraction. Recognizing a need for the systematic collection and dissemination of information on contemporary theatre abroad, ITI/US established a reference Library devoted to international theatre since 1945. Opened to the public in 1970, the Library (located at 220 W. 42nd St., NYC) now houses, in addition to the play collection, 5,100 volumes; 11,000 programs/playbills; and 250 periodicals on the performing arts around the world. The theatre of 145 countries on 5 continents is documented not only by plays, books, and periodicals, but also by directories, newsletters, press releases, production schedules, monographs, pamphlets, yearbooks, reviews, and clippings.

We are extremely proud to announce the availability of our recent acquisition: Theatre of Latin America Collection. The TOLA Collection consists of 2,650 items documenting modern theatre in 20 countries of Latin America and the Caribbean.

A grant from the Ford Foundation supported the six-month process of cataloging and housing 466 books; 1,277 plays (including 455 manuscripts); 153 issues of a wide range of periodicals; 307 programs or playbills; 147 photographs; 300 clippings, pamphlets, monographs, and brochures.

Many of the volumes and manuscripts are one-of-a-kind; some are no longer in print even in the country of publication. This valuable material, most of which is not accessible anywhere else in this country, was collected by Joanne Pottlitzer while she was director of Theatre of Latin America, Inc. (TOLA), from 1966–1980. The collection was donated to ITI/US by the Americas Society, Inc. where it was housed and augmented until 1986.

With the acquisition of the TOLA Collection, the ITI/US Library has greatly expanded its holdings on Latin American theatre. In the Library's international play section (11,000 plays from 92 countries), the number of scripts from Latin America and the Caribbean has quadrupled, reaching a total of 1,774 plays from 25 countries. The books and other materials in the TOLA Collection (cataloged and housed by country of origin in a second section of the Library) cover theory and criticism, history, dramaturgy, theatrical forms, popular entertainment, and productions. Photographs, playbills, brochures, and reviews document the work of 245 performing arts companies.

We look forward to sharing this valuable resource with our professional colleagues. The Library is the collective result of the network of ITI centers, the ceaseless travels of Rosamond Gilder during her years of dedication to ITI, and the generosity of theatre friends who travel and bequeath us their programs. To put it bluntly, however, the Library would not exist if it were not for the singleminded and ferocious work of Elizabeth Burdick. It was Elizabeth Burdick who got the collection from boxes to shelves and who has overseen and caused its growth in both size and quality. Elizabeth Burdick has made good her threat to retire and lead a normal life. One of the many compliments to her work is that the Library attracted Louis Rachow as her successor.

In the next issue, more about other aspects of our work in the U.S. and around the world. We are immensely grateful to Richard Schechner and TDR for this welcome to our work and our ideas.

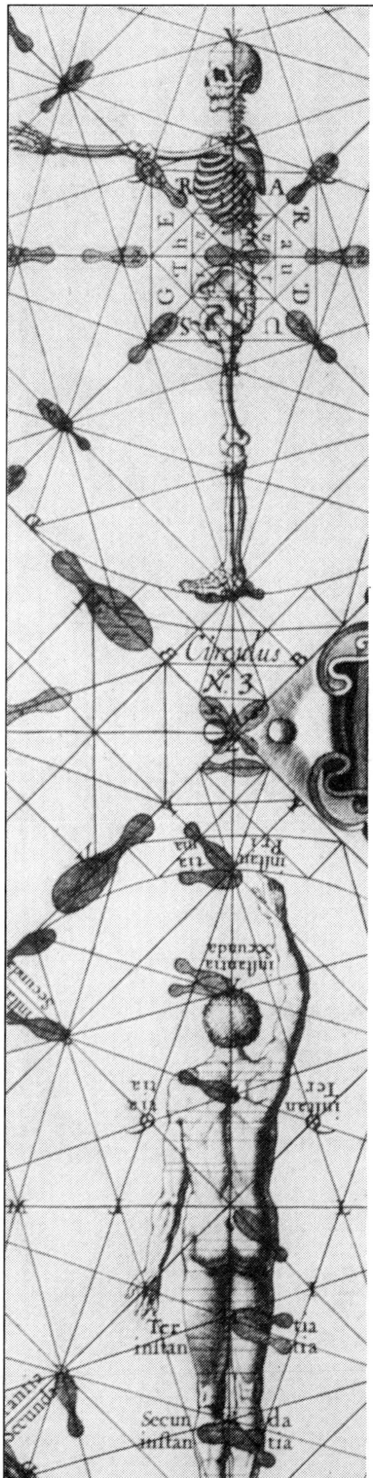
Circulus
N. 3

COMING IN TDR

Josette Féral
Mnouchkine, Moscoso, and the Théâtre du Soleil

Suresh Awasthi
Theatre of Roots

Eugène van Erven
Killed in Action: New Delhi Street Theatre

Margaret Clunies Ross
Australian Aboriginal Performance

Yoram S. Carmeli
Circus Dwarfs

Douglas Anderson
East End Poverty Theatre

Also: Cuban Theatre; Boal in New York/Boal in Brazil; Roundtable on Contemporary Indian Theatre; Grotowski's Most Recent Experiments

Other articles by: Elizabeth Wichmann, Zbigniew Osinski, Eugenio Barba, Ed Bullins, Randy Martin, Catherine Schuler, Deborah Hay, Robert Bethune

ISSN 0012 5962

T D R

Articles by:
Féral Awasthi Hay
Carmeli Bethune
van Erven Clunies Ross

Letters and Reports from:
Case Hughes Banes
Overn Fuchs Daly
Fuegi Renzi

Play of a Circus Dwarf
Safdar Hashmi's Street Theatre
Arnhem Land Ritual
Théâtre du Soleil
Computerized Aristotle
Theatre of Roots
Kabuki Training
and the Western Actor

Published by MIT Press
New York University/Tisch School of the Arts

PSI
PSI is a conference / festival addressing the cultural import of performance and the critical methods appropriate to its study. PSI will consist of performances, workshops and panels designed to explore recent developments in both the practice and study of performance.
October 4-7, 1990
Dept. of Performance Studies
New York University
Tisch
NEW YORK UNIVERSITY
A PRIVATE UNIVERSITY IN THE PUBLIC SERVICE
PRACTICE
THEORY
HISTORY
CRITICISM
PERFORMANCES
PANELS
WORKSHOPS
For more info, write Performance Studies, Dept. of Performance Studies, New York University, 721 Broadway, NY, NY 10003, or call (212) 998-1623

TDR

The Drama Review *a journal of performance studies*

Safdar Hashmi narrates his political street theatre piece Machine *for workers at the Thumbs-Up bottling plant in New Delhi on 1 May 1988. See Eugéne van Erven's article "Plays, Applause, and Bullets: Safdar Hashmi's Street Theatre" in this issue. (Photo by Eugéne van Erven)*

Front Cover: *Circus midget Wee Pea in a 1975 performance of the musical entree with the Brown Circus of Britain. See "The Total Play of the Dwarf in the Circus" by Yoram S. Carmeli in this issue. (Photo by Yoram S. Carmeli)*

Back Cover: *An old* Larreija *(Sawfish) hollow-log coffin standing at Mardangajirra, east of the Blyth River in Arnhem Land, Australia. See "Aesthetics and Politics of an Arnhem Land Ritual" by Margaret Clunies Ross in this issue. (Photo by Les Hiatt)*

TDR

The Drama Review

TDR Comment:
Public Demonstrations and Secret Politics in China 4
THE EDITORS

Letters, Reports, Etc.
Finley Facts or Fictions? 8
letters from Michael Overn and Elinor Fuchs

A Case Concerning Hughes 10
letters from Sue-Ellen Case and Holly Hughes

Terpsichore Combat Continued 17
a letter from Sally Banes

Pedagogy and Performance: Teaching the *Poetics* with Computers 18
a review of *Aristotle's Greek Tragedy Construction Kit*
VINCENT R. RENZI

To Dance Is "Female" 23
a review of *Dance, Sex and Gender*
ANN DALY

Willett on Weimar 28
a review of *The Theatre of the Weimar Republic*
JOHN FUEGI

Announcements 30

Plays, Applause, and Bullets: Safdar Hashmi's Street Theatre 32
EUGÈNE VAN ERVEN

"Theatre of Roots": Encounter with Tradition 48
SURESH AWASTHI

Playing Awake: Letters to My Daughter 70
DEBORAH HAY

Théâtre du Soleil
Mnouchkine's Workshop at the Soleil: A Lesson in Theatre 77
JOSETTE FÉRAL

Building Up the Muscle: An Interview with Ariane Mnouchkine 88
JOSETTE FÉRAL

Théâtre du Soleil—A Second Glance: An Interview with Sophie Moscoso 98
JOSETTE FÉRAL

The Aesthetics and Politics of an Arnhem Land Ritual 107
MARGARET CLUNIES ROSS

Wee Pea: The Total Play of the Dwarf in the Circus 128
YORAM S. CARMELI

Describing Performance in the Theatre: Kabuki Training and the Western Acting Student 146
ROBERT BETHUNE

ITItems: The Weather for the '90s 167
MARTHA COIGNEY

TDR Volume 33 Index 169

Volume 33, Number 4 (T124), Winter 1989

The Drama Review *(ISSN 0012 5962) is published quarterly (Spring, Summer, Fall, Winter) by The MIT Press, 55 Hayward St., Cambridge, MA 02142, and London, England, for the Tisch School of the Arts, New York University. Editorial correspondence:* The Drama Review, *NYU, 721 Broadway, 6th fl., New York, NY 10003. Subscription and business correspondence:* The Drama Review, *Journals Dept., The MIT Press, 55 Hayward Street, Cambridge, MA 02142. Subscriptions: $19.00 per year for students; $25.00 per year for individuals; $55.00 per year for institutions. Subscribers outside the U.S. and Canada add $12.00 for surface mail, $18.00 for airmail. Current single copies, $7.00; back copies, $14.00. Back volume rates available. Circulation Dept.: 617-253-2889.* *To be honored free of charge, claims for missing copies must be made immediately upon receipt of the next published issue. Second class postage paid at Boston, MA and additional mailing offices. Postmaster: Send address changes to* The Drama Review, *55 Hayward Street, Cambridge, MA 02142. For advertising information please contact the Advertising Manager, MIT Press Journals (see business correspondence; telephone: 617-253-2866). This publication is made possible, in part, with public funds from the New York State Council on the Arts and the National Endowment for the Arts.*

Public Demonstrations and Secret Politics in China

For a few weeks in May and June 1989, the Chinese people told the world what they wanted in the most open way imaginable. The Chinese "leadership" (who are they leading? who do they represent?) operated in such a clandestine way that, except for a few very core people, nobody in the world knew who was in charge or how they made their decisions. And nobody could see or locate or even identify these few core people. Rumors like "Deng Xiaoping is dead" and "Premier Li Peng has been shot" were broadcast by even the most prestigious Western media. President George Bush tried unsuccessfully for a week to reach his "old friend" Deng—or any other Chinese leader.

Such deep secrecy was a shock to many Westerners who were excited by the magnitude of the Chinese people's open political activities—parades, speeches, sit-ins, hunger strikes. Westerners could contrast the public activities of the Chinese people with the power of China's secret political operation—palace intrigue, family ties that matter more than anything else, behind-the-scenes maneuvers, and finally the abrupt and bloody crushing (literally) of the people's prodemocracy demonstrations in Tiananmen Square. All this followed up by arrests, executions, purges, and repression. To Westerners, the story is a shocking setback to the world trend toward democracy and open politics.

In the West, with the power of the media behind them, journalists routinely investigate and expose politicians' private lives while politicians, with the power of the media at their service, make insincere and banal public displays of themselves and their policies. In China, on the other hand, political maneuvering is too secret with too little public monitoring. The bloody crackdown and merciless purge which began in June 1989, for example, was determined in secret meetings by mostly "retired" old guards headed by Deng. Weeks after the Beijing massacre, the government still refused to say who was responsible for the military action. This lack of transparency is in fact only one extreme example of China's conventional secret politics inherited from numerous emperors and their court advisors. Because of its incompatibility with modern political institutions and any kind of democracy, secret politics was precisely the target of the prodemocracy movement from the beginning.

What the Chinese want is openness, or as they say, "transparency." The Communist Party promised such openness when the Beijing students began their demonstrations after the death of the ousted CP general secretary Hu Yaobang. At first the students asked the party to give a full account of Hu's ousting; his official elegy praised him highly but didn't mention the dismissal at all. The leaders disregarded the students' demand—they even planned to keep the students out of Tiananmen Square, away from Hu's funeral. Next the students called for a free press that would tell the true story of the demonstrations. And they demanded an end to "official profiteering," which the government had promised to eliminate but never did.

But what was most important to the students was their demand that the leaders come out of their heavily guarded compound and engage in dialog. To make this dialog open to the greatest number of people, the students insisted it be televised live on China's national network. The students saw in such public dialog the basic element of democracy. For this very reason, dialog is precisely what the leadership fears and avoids.

On several occasions, a million or more Beijing citizens came into the streets in support of the students. There were many other demonstrations as well all over the country. For the first time the Chinese were dedicated to open politics, aware of the public nature of their demonstrations and of the media that transmitted these displays to the world. Demonstrators carried banners in both Chinese and English and thousands raised the "V" sign to the cameras. These demonstrators seemed to have forgotten the caution and fear Chinese used to have in front of foreigners, even those without cameras or tape recorders. During May–June 1989 untold numbers of Chinese were proud to publicly demonstrate for their ideals—not only in Tiananmen Square but in many places throughout China.

Most high government leaders were afraid of being seen in public. They tried to defer and ignore the students' demands, disregarding petitions, sending out lower ranking officials who could answer no crucial questions, selecting which students could participate in so-called "dialogs." The top leaders even prevented party secretary Zhao Ziyang, a reformist who advocated transparency, from meeting with thousands of hunger-striking students. When he finally went to the Square on his own initiative, he had only the students' own megaphone to speak with. Zhao's decision to talk with the students led to his being dismissed from office and purged from the Communist Party. Typically, Zhao has not been seen in public since those days. That's the way the Chinese do it—disappear the "guilty" until they are displayed at some staged trial.

When hardliner Premier Li Peng finally met the students in the Great Hall of the People, there was no dialog. Li delivered a lecture, an ultimatum; later, the secret police used this assembly to identify the student leaders, all of whom are now in jail or on the most-wanted list. By the time they met with Li, the fate of the demonstrators was sealed; it was only a matter of strategy as to when the troops would move in. All this while Western leaders were blindly "appreciating" the Chinese government's "restraint." In fact, the leaders never wanted to solve the problems through dialog with the people because the leaders only believe in behind-the-scenes manipulation of power.

But, of course, even China's aging leaders live in the late 20th century. No matter how much they hate public presentations, they are vaguely aware of how indispensable the image is in modern life—at least the young leader, 60-year-old Li Peng knows. He could claim to be the first Chinese leader to give long speeches on TV—though his wooden style makes him the worst performer among the world's top politicians. His televised declaration of martial law on 19 May—intended to threaten people and keep them indoors—actually provoked tens of thousands of Beijing residents into the streets to block army convoys. Shanghai's biggest demonstration took place on 20 May. Besides the content of his speech, Li's resentful facial expressions, his harsh, closed-fisted gestures, and his flat voice angered people. Nevertheless, Li is the winner of the power struggle and for the time being remains premier because of his overt and covert connections with the old guards.

Before the crackdown, Beijing's streets were filled with demonstrators; the first weeks after the massacre saw little if any public show. For a few days even the faces of the news announcers disappeared from TV. "Viewers" only heard voices repeating lies about the "glorious crackdown against the counterrevolutionary rebellion." In this way, the authorities prevented announcers from conveying countermessages with their lowered heads, sad facial expressions, and mourning clothes. After several days, when those in charge were sure that the announcers would not betray the official message by means of the medium, faces reappeared. But still there was little visual news, just spoken lines. When Li Peng first showed up on TV after a week during which no Chinese leader had appeared, he positioned himself far away from the military brass he was supposedly meeting with and spoke only briefly. High-ranking officials supposedly spoke out in favor of the military action, but few faces were seen on the screen or even in the newspapers. This lack of public image made people doubt the truthfulness of the reports they were being given. It seemed that those in "support" of the official line couldn't be trusted to perform their roles. To see them might throw the sincerity of their support into question.

After secret politics (and secret police) secured the hardliners' power, the propaganda campaign began to use visual images to justify the government's bloody repression. But what the propagandists were good at were tricks that could not bear the light of day. When spokesperson Yuan Mu answered NBC's Tom Brokaw's question about the incredible discrepancy between the official Chinese death toll and the Western videos shot at the scene, Yuan said that modern technology made it possible to construct any desired images. As a matter of fact, this is exactly what the Chinese leaders have done to hoodwink the rural Chinese who have no access to the Voice of America, the BBC, phone calls, or fax messages from overseas or Hong Kong. Using editing tricks—a new technology in service of the old secrecy—the official China Central TV put together all the shots of civilians attacking armed soldiers and showed them over and over to "prove" their lie that "hooligans" had killed many soldiers. In fact, they could name only ten dead "Guards of the Republic," only one of whom was actually shot in Tiananmen Square by unidentified "thugs." The official TV featured shots of relatives mourning for soldiers and of wounded soldiers in hospitals. There were, of course, no shots of the thousands of wounded civilians, no interviews with relatives of dead students. When official TV broadcast a student leader eating at a restaurant after he had ended his hunger strike (a scene videotaped by hidden camera), the voice-over said that "during the so-called hunger strike" the student had secretly feasted at an expensive restaurant, that he was a hypocritical, insidious instigator.

The full meeting of the CP's Central Committee on 24 June offers another example of China's secret politics and distorted official public image. This presumably crucial meeting was supposed to debate the crackdown and elect a new party leader to replace Zhao. At the meeting the vote to dismiss Zhao was not unanimous, but TV showed a scene of people raising their hands unanimously, a scene grafted from another vote but distorted by the voice-over. It took just one day to rubberstamp all the decisions Deng and other non–Central Committee members had made in secret over the previous weeks. This meeting was held suddenly—superceding the postponed-without-explanation 20 June convening of the legislative People's Congress—because the top leaders had to make sure no disagreements were aired in public. Could such actions repair the party's public image—even with a new "leader," former Shanghai mayor Jiang Zemin, who is well-educated and speaks several foreign languages?

The only scenes the authorities were proud to show the people were of the public humiliation of the dissidents arrested and sentenced to death by gunshot. The way these people looked—heads bent, faces empty or terrified, arms held behind their backs—reminded people of the Cultural Revolution when such "red horror" scenes were often made public. But unlike the Cultural Revolution, when many fanatics spontaneously took such "revolutionary actions" against others, the current crackdown is solely the work of a totalitarian government acting against the Chinese people. During the Cultural Revolution many naive people enjoyed watching "criticism scenes," but today most resent such inhuman public humiliations. Having realized the negative effects these horrible images were having on the public, including the foreign public, the authorities soon changed their strategy, returning to secret arrests and persecution. Deng and other hardliners accuse the students of causing turmoil like that seen during the Cultural Revolution, but it's the other way round. It is Deng and his followers who call again for "class struggle" and "unified ideology." As for the students, their peaceful and disciplined demonstrations over a period of weeks showed the world that they do not resemble Red Guards. The students are idealists who consciously used public demonstrations to fight China's secret politics. They are so idealistic they did not get involved with the secret politics within the party—and thus their failure this time was inevitable.

The Editors

Letters, Reports, Etc.

Finley Facts or Fictions?

To the Editor:

Karen Finley and I just returned to New York from Europe and we were made aware of Elinor Fuchs' "Staging the Obscene Body" (33, no. 1 [T121]:33–58). Upon reading the section pertaining to Karen, we became very upset due to the numerous errors by Ms. Fuchs concerning certain facts of Karen's career and performances.

Obviously, everyone has the right to their own opinion and observations about Karen's work (we sometimes call Karen a "human Rorschach test"), but misrepresenting her work with false facts in a journal such as TDR hurts Karen in terms of the historical viewpoint and in terms of her career. We were just getting over the myths and falsehoods concerning "the yams" (see #7 below) and the sensationalistic press that fueled this controversy. We felt that it was publications like TDR that helped to bring Karen out of that and enlighten readers as to the motivation for her work and its validity in the art world. Now it seems like we are seeing it all over again due to the fact that this article was written without a call to us for fact-checking.

For the record, I will list the wrong facts below and correct them:

1. **Page 47, paragraph 2—"[. . .] we don't see her abuse her body anymore [. . .]"**—She has never "abused" her body in any performance.
2. **Page 47, paragraph 2—"She caused riots in Rotterdam, was closed down in London [. . .]"**—There were never any riots in Rotterdam. I believe what she was referring to was once, in Rotterdam, a woman came up on Karen's stage and knocked over her prop table. It turned out that this had nothing to do with the performance but that the woman was crazy. Also, she was not closed down in London; she elected not to perform due to their sexist laws concerning women performers.
3. **Page 47, paragraph 4—"[. . .] performances on the East Village club circuit in 1979"**—She moved to NYC and started performing in 1984.
4. **Page 47, paragraph 5—"[. . .] along with stories that have a ring of truth—an abortion perhaps, or the known suicide of her father"**—This statement is simply not true and it is an assumption on Ms. Fuchs' part that she shouldn't make. Does anyone feel that Truman Capote is a mass-murderer because he wrote *In Cold Blood?*
5. **Page 47, paragraph 5—"[. . .] smear garbage over herself [. . .]"**—She has never done this.

6. **Page 48, paragraph 1—"[. . .] she poured dog food, cream [. . .]"**—She has never done this.
7. **Page 48, paragraph 1—"[. . .] she actually put yams up her ass on stage [. . .]"**—Once and for all: *SHE HAS NEVER DONE THIS!!!* She smeared tinned (whipped) yams on her buttocks but she has never, repeat, never put a yam up anywhere. It may seem like a petty mistake but you wouldn't believe the problems this mistake has caused Karen over the years.
8. **Page 48, paragraph 1—"[. . .] emptying her diarrhetic guts into an onstage bucket"**—This is not true. Karen was sick while performing and did this into a bucket offstage—there's a big difference.
9. **Page 49, paragraph 2—"Carr reports near-riots during Finley's club performances in which excited men threw lighted cigarettes at her, dropped their pants or yelled 'Whore' "**—This might be my opinion, rather than falsehoods, but these were isolated incidents that I feel were sensationalized from the beginning in the *Village Voice* and when they're grouped together and discussed in this "near-riot" mentality, this makes it seem like this happens all the time. It doesn't. These were three separate isolated incidents by people who were certainly the exceptions in the audience and definitely not the norm.

Aside from the facts being wrong, we also have a problem with the photos of Karen published with this article. As far as we know, Ms. McAdams was never consulted as to her photos being used for this issue, and a release form was never signed by anyone. Karen feels that photos of her performances are part of her artwork and for that reason we like to have a say in the publication of any photos. We have a special and exclusive relationship with Dona Ann McAdams for exactly this reason.

Anyway, these are our complaints and we wanted to set the facts straight. We are especially concerned about this since we understand that you will be publishing another article in which Karen is discussed by Catherine Schuler. [Schuler's article, "Spectator Response and Comprehension: The Problem of Karen Finley's *A Constant State of Desire*," will appear in the next issue of TDR.] Many times what people read about Karen is based more on myth than truth and I'm sure that TDR does not want to be one of those publications. Thank you for hearing me out.

Michael Overn
Manager for Karen Finley

Elinor Fuchs replies:

Though I am puzzled by the vehemence with which Mr. Overn protects the image of a performer whose career was initially built on transgression, I sincerely regret any factual errors I may have made in translating the early Karen Finley through published newspaper accounts and videotapes. He is right: I should have consulted Ms. Finley directly. At the same time, a number of Mr. Overn's objections seem to turn less on fact than on issues of interpretation. And finally, to put this exchange in perspective, I hope Mr. Overn is aware that my article was not primarily concerned with individual performers, but with a theme or gestalt running through certain women's theatre work of the past decade.

That being said, I can't resist adding that Mr. Overn should check his own facts. For instance, in TDR 32, no. 1 (T117), Karen Finley herself says she was banned by the Westminster Council and Scotland Yard in the summer of 1987 (152).

Ed. Note: All photos of Karen Finley were received from and published with the permission of the photographer, Dona Ann McAdams.

A Case Concerning Hughes

To the Editor:

Although I am not certain that a debate among feminists (worse, lesbians) should appear outside of journals specifically allied with the movement and the critique (such as *Signs* or *Women and Performance*), I cannot help but respond to the Spring 1989 issue of TDR (33, no. 1 [T121]). I both applaud Richard Schechner for repeatedly publishing such cutting-edge material that other journals do not and worry that in publishing articles on pornography, he cannot help but play the man Dolan referred to in that issue as "cloaked in a trenchcoat."

At any rate, in the TDR issue on/of pornography, Rebecca Schneider refers to my remarks after the Ann Arbor production of *Dress Suits to Hire* (though she admits she was not present [172, 182]) and Kate Davy refers to my butch-femme aesthetic article (though she admits it was not available to her at the time [167]). I do not object to either Schneider's or Davy's work—in fact I admire their rigor in remaining with the contradictions in the reception of such material and I respect their writing within the tradition of feminist scholarship, carefully cited and interestingly applied.

However, in the context of some remarks by Holly Hughes in her interview in TDR, and my own desire not to be misrepresented, I would like to clarify my own position. In the Schneider interview with Holly Hughes, I seem to be one of what Hughes calls "chicks [. . .] having trouble with the show" who "want a lesbian utopia" which Hughes conflates with a "lesbian Disneyland." While I might prefer a lesbian Disneyland, I have never objected to a work because it was not tendentious. In fact, my unease around the *Dress Suits* production was something quite different. Although, at the time, my objection had strictly to do with the context of reception of the piece, there was also something in the text itself that disturbed me and foregrounded the conditions of reception.

First, to clarify the reception situation. In Ann Arbor, I remember a discussion in which (thanks to some insights from Vicki Patraka) Hughes' play was described as a kind of Sam Shepard piece with its nostalgia for earlier American geography and its lifestyle, a tendency toward monologs combining pop language with a sentimental set of memories of the family unit, and settings like service stations in the desert, etc. Certainly, Hughes' style seems more like Shepard's than Hélène Cixous' notion of *l'ecriture feminine*, Monique Wittig's fictional style in *The Lesbian Body*, Gertrude

Stein's "landscapes," the monolog/narrative structure in plays by Peggy Shaw, Lois Weaver, and Deborah Margolin, etc. In other words, *Dress Suits* does not seem to grow out of a feminist, or lesbian tradition of writing. In fact, it may be this Shepard-like style that makes Hughes' work accessible in a way that these other works are not. Thus, perhaps, her own assessment of herself as "the preeminent lesbian playwright of our day" has something to do with her revisionary writing within the dominant tradition. I am reminded of the preeminence of Marsha Norman and Beth Henley, whose alignment with other dominant forms of theatre have rendered them accessible/successful. The difference between Norman/Henley and Hughes is presumably the adjective "lesbian."

Because of the heterogeneity within the position, the term "lesbian," like "feminism," should become "lesbianS" as the latter term has become "feminismS." Nevertheless, amid such contradictions, and without a tradition of lesbian scholarship and theory, I would still like to explore the difference between what seems lesbian to me and the way it is represented by Hughes. In Hughes' interview in TDR she situates the word "lesbian" as proximate to "bisexual," "polymorphous perversity," "scientist," "gazing," a "stagnant glass-bottom boat," and "women sexually vis-a-vis men." Whereas we "chicks" want a lesbian utopia in Disneyland, it seems Hughes' sense of the lesbian playwright is a kind of Captain Nemo–type dominatrix in the dark workshop of a bisexual (lesbian) production of *True (mid) West*. Postmodern slippage is one thing and lesbian sexuality on a banana peel is another. For me, Hughes' interview and play beg the questions of what is a lesbian play and how that is determined.

In Ann Arbor, the Michigan mimesis in the play certainly seemed as vibrant as the exotic lesbian Lower East Side remnants the university drama department had imported. Also imported, I must add, were Elin Diamond and myself as "feminist critics." The issue I wanted to raise at the time, which implied my own situation there as well, was the issue of appropriation/assimilation—an issue increasingly acute in the late '80s. Schneider, Davy, Dolan, and Elinor Fuchs all wrestle with this in their articles and of course, the TDR issue itself, with its "pornographic" photos raises the issue again. Times have changed. Works by feminists and lesbian feminists are no longer restricted to the ghetto. Shaw and Weaver, who have struggled and starved for years, got paid, got invited to a university campus, got a good reception. Shaw rightly and fervently told me that during the post-show discussion. Elin Diamond and I got paid. Holly Hughes got her play published. So why did I spoil a perfectly lovely evening by bringing up assimilation?

The first night, I was sitting at the back of the house, quite far from the production (a distance Davy interprets) looking through a large number of students who were either on dates, or at least appeared to be sitting in gender pairs, watching actors I had always admired generally accompanied by lesbian hoots and whistles. Although there seemed to be some lesbians in the audience and some others who, I am certain, responded to the camp irony and other ghetto techniques, I wondered what some young male students saw when Weaver and Shaw came on in feathered boas, high heels, and garter belts. What was the men's frame of reference for these images—situated, as I have noted, among Michigan memorabilia monologs, the not unfamiliar stories of eccentric family members, and images that resonate with hetero Shepard-like culture, but not with lesbian subcultural history? That is, if the writing chooses not to mark itself by the lesbian tradition, with lesbian code words and the subculture, doesn't its proximity to the heterosexist tropes of Shepard make it available to the young male within his own frame of reference? This play played during feminist night in Ann Arbor (a place with a strong feminist history) where no women faculty members were prominent; Elin and I were escorted and introduced by men, etc. How, exactly were we or it feminist? How could "lesbian" appear in that context and what did it mean? What use was it and whom did it serve? What was transgressive in its sexual identity? If one does not secure the context of reception, how does a play, or a critic, resist such institutional cooptation?

In such a context, I could not, like Hughes, imagine my actions to reside in a kind of recess-at-school period called art. Nor did I, as an older butch materialist feminist, want to be caught with my pants down in the role of a dominatrix who entertains, hurts, teases, denies, and SCOLDS men until they . . . and I'm firmly convinced that I can slowly discover that I am in their play, cast by them in that role they love, performing for the price they have set. Nor did Elin Diamond want to be the heterosexual feminist expostulating on a lesbian production. Nor did I want a lesbian production to be reconfigured within heterosexual tropes of desire, nor any of us to become titillation/pornography. I went to watch Weaver and Shaw, whose work had come to mean for me the cutting edge of feminist performance—I did not really expect to see their disruptive strategies in tension with the reception of them. Tardily, I became aware of the contradictions there in my own institutional affiliations, as well as that of the performance. I was dismayed at the glee of the audience, who seemed challenged by nothing and entertained by much.

Feminists in the United States have not, perhaps, been as sensitive to issues of cooptation and assimilation as German feminists (informed by the history of fascism) or postcolonial, colonial, and Third World feminists. We're inured, to some extent, to the role of dominatrix by our national history, as Kathy Acker, Annie Sprinkle, and others illustrate. I'm not surprised that our World Bank of neopornography demands a lot of interest, nor that we are naive about how the investment of our life savings can garner interest for men. One factor the patriarchy now has in its favor is the speed to which it has accelerated assimilation: we've barely begun to write or perform lesbian sexuality among/for/by ourselves when presses, ivy league schools, and regional theatres are already bedecking themselves with lesbian/gay themes and studies like wearing Liz Taylor's diamond (which Andy Warhol said he wanted to be in his next incarnation)—forget it, Andy, you can become jewelry in this life.

Meanwhile, back to Holly Hughes, who has gone from Little Peter to top banana at lightning assimilative speed. Davy puts her finger on part of the problem in her article, never disengaging the play from its reception. Noting that it could have been fetishized in Ann Arbor because of the spectatorial position, and noting, in her conclusion, both sides of what she perceives as the debate: "the importance of *Dress Suits* as an instance of lesbian discourse outside of lesbian performance contexts, and the importance of segregating pieces like *Dress Suits* in spaces where lesbians and women are the only spectators" (167). Davy knows her stuff—that's one debate. Yet another point in this particular case might be that there is something in the text that makes it too dependent upon its spectatorial context—that it can lose its lesbian identity in certain circumstances. I mean, Jane Chambers' plays are lesbian even when awkwardly played by hets and watched by them. Why? Because their language, their issues, their character types, their narratives are drawn from that subculture and refer back to it. Alas, is this, then, a question of mimesis? Perhaps a bit. But more, what about Judy Grahn's notion in *The Highest Apple,* of a lesbian writing tradition? Can lesbians coopt male images, styles, voices and not be playing the dominatrix? Not opening their work to a male, heterosexual "reading"? Isn't there a crucial resonating difference in reclaiming Chevys and service stations which do not resonate with lesbian lives or subculture and reclaiming, as in the play *Split Britches,* women's images from earlier, rural times?

I think so. But there's something else, too—the way the text moves. One place in the text that illustrates the way in which the movement doesn't feel lesbian to me is in the following: Deeluxe says, "[. . .] he'd go off and leave me trying whether to decide whether to be a lesbian today or put it off till tomorrow." Of course, the problem she states itself is on the bisexual line. Some pop lines about malls and references to some guy and a Sam Shepard Chevy line follow. Next, when we get to Michigan's breasts they're inscribed in a moon metaphor, then Deeluxe resists "temptation" and gets wrapped in pearls, then Michigan gives a monolog about desire which comes to nothing except her singing in a peignoir—her desire ensconced in metaphors of peaches, palominos, and collapsing centers, isolated and left unfulfilled. Then Deeluxe puts on a dinner jacket and delivers one of those geography (Ohio, this time), eccentric-family monologs.

Perhaps it's because the Lacanian metonymically moving desire has become so fashionable that this sort of slippage seems like lesbian desire. Unfortunately, that very metonymic displacement is based on Lack, the Phallus-veiled-in-a-trenchcoat, and impossibility. For women in a heterosexual/phallic/patriarchal economy of desire, this slippage seems better than nothing. I think this avant-garde form is perhaps somewhat liberating in that sense. For lesbians, who do not belong to that economy (as Dolan notes in her article), it seems like slippage away from desire. Deeluxe acts out that flight. The two characters are isolated, and discourse, as Lacan suggests, replaces pre-oedipal *jouissance.* However, the lesbian need not sacrifice her phallus and she might reclaim that mother's body—that jouissance. Instead, Deeluxe acts out the loss, the sacrifice, the substitution in her several flights from Michigan and finally, in her embodiment of Little Peter. Because of this, Hughes' text makes me feel that it moves away from lesbian desire, tempted by it, incarnating it in Michigan's unfulfilled yearnings, but ultimately situating it, as Hughes did in her interview, in proximity to the phallus, leaving only the potential of bisexuality as fecund; the most water Freud could imagine in his patriarchal desert of desire. The lesbian did not get the girl.

This slippage, compounded with the Sam Shepard tropes made, for this spectator, the lesbian text reside in the performances of Shaw and Weaver, dependent, as Davy suggested, on how they as performers related to the audience. Thus, when the audience did not provide a lesbian context, the play seemed assimilated, or coopted by the dominant culture that imported it. Perhaps I should not have made these observations public in Ann Arbor, nor here. Solidarity, after all, is a reality of politics. On the other hand, in the late Bush '80s, I think assimilation and cooptation must be understood, and resistive strategies invented. If not lesbian mimesis, then a textual movement back to the mother's body, or forget the mother and get the girl. Leave the impossibilities to those (others) who choose them and as for the penis, or the phallus in a trenchcoat, or bisexuality . . . it reminds me of the Gay Pride Parade in San Francisco a few years ago. Many groups passed by, to the cheers, hoots, applause of those standing on the street. When the bisexuals passed by, the spectators were silent.

Sue-Ellen Case
University of Washington

Holly Hughes replies:

Dear TDR,

Thank you so much for allowing me to respond to Sue-Ellen Case's letter. If you hadn't personally sent it to me, I don't think I'd have been able to wade all the way through it. Not even for the sake of my girlfriend, Donna, who was very concerned about lesbian slippage. At first she thought it sounded nice. We like lubricants. No such thing as too wet, I always say. Imagine her horror when she discovered that lesbian slippage is a horrible, possibly contagious disease, and that I've got it bad, complicated, as Sue-Ellen Case points out, with a touch of heterosexual tropes. Good God almighty, said Donna. And then the really bad news. I'm not a lesbian, I don't meet the entrance requirements as established by Sue-Ellen Case. What a shock to my girlfriend. And what a way to get the news—from the highest authority on true Orthodox Lesbianism, Ms. Case.

I hope Donna and I can still be friends.

And dear TDR, thank you for sending me a copy of Ms. Case's letter. I do relish a bad review as much as any artist. An artist likes to know they've moved someone. But I must admit, even my attention wandered a bit. Such long sentences, dear TDR. And Ms. Case is fond, as are other writers in the Spring TDR, of forcing nouns like "foreground" to do the hard and dirty work of verbs. While I protest that this is not usage (this is slippage) I do recognize that such slippages do have some merit. They make the sentences longer. Perhaps Ms. Case gets paid by the word. Ms. Case is not assimilated, she says she is far outside "the male economy of desire" and she needs to have as many words as she can possibly stuff into a paragraph. I guess the University of Washington, where last I heard she was a tenured professor, must not pay very well. Ms. Case needs her cluttered, wordy prose, every penny of it. Wouldn't it be tragic if Ms. Case got paid by the idea, especially the original idea. She might starve to death.

Let's give Ms. Case a big hand for practicing what she preaches. She knows that accessibility is the root of all bad art. She is quick to point out that it's one of my sins against the Lesbian Nation. And she's right there, my work is accessible. But I do admire her, I do, for taking the higher road of inaccessibility.

I was so happy when Ms. Case cut, as it were, to the car chase to tell me why *Dress Suits to Hire* sucks. Of course, it's not the main concern of the letter. Her main concern, her passion, is this: "How can you determine a lesbian play? How can you tell the faux feminists, the cheap dimestore, chevy-driving bisexuals in lesbian drag, from the real McCoy?" Certainly, these are burning questions of the day. And I'll respond to them a bit later on. But first, let's dish the text. Ms. Case gives a pretty good synopsis of what little plot there is. When the time comes I'll hire her to write the Cliff Notes. O, it's not far off, dear TDR, as Ms. Case has hinted, I either have or am about to sell out. I don't know where she gets her information, and she doesn't waste any valuable time by presenting a shred of evidence that I've sold out, but you can tell by her tone, she knows.

Hurray—I've sold out! The check must be in the mail. Soon I'll be able to quit my temp job and earn a living as a playwright. Of course if it doesn't pan out, if I flop as a playwright, I guess I can get a job like Ms. Case's. In a university, trashing other people's plays. That's a beautiful idea—I could get paid to rip up the work of artists who never get paid!

If I survive my lesbian slippage, that is.

Ms. Case says that what's wrong with the plot of *Dress Suits to Hire* is that the lesbian doesn't get the girl. Of course I thought she did. I mean, the girls live together, and have for years. They never go out and no one comes in. If getting the girl is that important to Ms. Case I have to say: "How much more gotten can a girl get?" But I digress. Ms. Case has shown the formula for a successful 100% USDA approved *LESBIAN* play. Forget about the gritty slippage of lesbian desire in the real world, not to mention in the lesbian subculture, just make sure the lesbian gets the girl in the end. I once took a writing class with the lesbian playwright, Maria Irene Fornes. Stingy woman, she wouldn't give us her secrets. She claimed there were no rules. I felt cheated. Why didn't I study the rules of theatre with Ms. Case. She makes theatre so simple and easy, so much like TV.

As for her other critical remarks on my play, I must say she's got an original mind there. The common garden variety of critic or scholar chides a writer for being derivative. But Ms. Case takes me to task for being derivative of the wrong writers! Apparently Sam Shepard owns the copyright on any play that mentions Chevys or gas stations. But here's the good news: images of an earlier, rural South are in the public domain! I can reclaim them without poaching on Flannery O'Connor's, Carson McCullers', or Tennessee Williams', back forty as long as I stay within "a lesbian writing tradition." O, I wish you'd explained a bit more at this point, Ms. Case. How does one know which part of the country, which appliances, are acceptable as subject matter? She doesn't say. Darn. And how does one know which writers one should make reference to and which ones are off limits? No help from Ms. Case there, either. It must be obvious to those not suffering from lesbian slippage.

In fact I'm slipping so bad I'm about to slip out of the clubhouse all together. Ms. Case is very clear about this: lesbianism is a club. Ms. Case points out we've got a subculture, an approved reading list, and even—get ready for this—code words! O, Ms. Case, send me the kit right away. And don't forget the decoder ring. And all the rules, Ms. Case. I bet you wrote the book. Thank you for showing us that lesbianism is a tree house looking down on the dominant culture's backyard, that patriarchal desert. Everybody wants in, you know how it is these days, everyone wants in to our club. We've got to keep the entrance requirements stiff to keep out the bad element. This is familiar to me. My family belonged to a country club that was supposedly open to anyone, but we knew better. There was no way any people of color would ever get in. Once they slipped up and let a few Jews in, well you can bet they lived to regret that. O please, Ms. Case, let me into the club! I know I'm a naughty, naughty bisexual and a professional dominatrix to boot and you should spank me but good, but have some mercy on these hands that have touched a dick or two, on this heart that's looked at love from both sides now. Ms. Case, you know what it's like to get kicked out of the lesbian clubhouse. Didn't you identify yourself as a butch? But my dear Ms. Case. Ten years ago that was taboo in the clubhouse, remember? Back then it was: "Knock-knock, who's there? Androgyny!" Remember?

Ms. Case is right to say that *Dress Suits to Hire* doesn't dovetail with the notion of lesbianism as a clubhouse. She may have inadvertently stumbled upon the heart of the play: I wrote about the impossibility of withdrawing from the world. The world has a way of creeping in through the cracks of any separate reality. I maybe have even been a wee bit critical of this isolationist desire. So *Dress Suits* is not clubhouse material. I was surprised it was so popular with lesbians across the country. I guess slippage is epidemic. Ms. Case must be worried.

She is a woman with a mission: she is a born again lesbian, a Shiite lesbian. Her calling—to protect the fragile flower of true lesbian art. Ms. Case sees lesbian art as the fruit of one system of beliefs all lesbians agree upon, the lesbian pledge of allegiance. All those heathens that don't repeat the pledge—they must never gaze upon the tender blossom. They will surely trample it into assimilation. Or cultivate it for their own evil purposes. Apparently this is happening all over the country: mainstream producers are clamoring for lesbian art, says Ms. Case. I'm waiting for that call from the Actor's Theatre of Louisville, the Public. When I was young and foolish I used to sit around with other faux feminists, chatting about the need to see more work by women and non-white artists in Janson's *History of Art,* and in the important anthologies. And I used to think it was dandy to have my work presented in a variety of venues, as long as I had artistic free rein. I used to think this was more radical than preaching to the converted, as Ms. Case would have us do. I guess that I was suffering from slippage even then. I guess it's OK that my play was produced by a lesbian producer in a women's theatre and I was never paid, because I secured the context of reception. Far better to not get paid by a lesbian, than misinterpreted by a man. I now see the value of insulating art. Let August Wilson and Alice Walker restrict their audiences to only blacks! Prevent assimilation, guard against the dangers of misinterpretation before it's too late! Forgive those days of slippage, of backsliding, when I believed there was no one correct reading of a work of art. Gone are the days when I saw theatre as a public art form, when you invited the public and were not too picky about who came. Even if the godless heterosexuals came in accursed gender pairs, like animals loading into the ark, I was compassionate and let them in.

O I see the error of my ways Ms. Case. I see that the foundation of feminism—self-determination—is another heterosexual trope. Ms. Case speaks highly of tradition. I think she means the tradition of defining women by others' terms. It used to be the job of the Church and the State to separate the good girls from the bad. But Ms. Case has taken over. She's herding us all, weeding out the Satanic Kathy Ackers, the dominatrixes, the Beth Henley clones, the Shepard impersonators, and anyone who dares to disagree with her. O she makes a brief reference to plurality, but it's quite clear that's not where her heart lies.

O—Donna's back. I think we'll whip up a cool pitcher of Michigan mimesis and invite over a trope of my friends. They'll be certainly happy to hear the word of the Ayatollah, I mean, Ms. Case. Of course some of my proselytizing has fallen flat. People always ask: "Who is Sue-Ellen Case and why should I care what she thinks?" I am embarrassed because I just don't know those answers.

Nightie-night.

Terpsichore Combat Continued

Ed. Note: The following is the final round: Sally Banes' response to Susan Manning's response to Sally Banes' response to Susan Manning's response to Sally Banes' book, Terpsichore in Sneakers. *See "Modernist Dogma and Post-modern Rhetoric" (32, no. 4 [T120]) and "Terpsichore in Combat Boots" (33, no. 1 [T121]).*

To the Editor:

I'm glad to see that Susan Manning is no longer claiming to be a theorist. So let's talk about dance history.

Manning says she uses so-called "modernism" in the conventional way (obviously there are at least a score of these conventional ways). That is an historical error which she seems incapable of understanding. *Terpsichore in Sneakers* uses what I claim, on historical grounds, is the operative concept of modernism in the dance-historical context I wrote about. That is, I wrote in terms of the notion that had historical influence and causal efficacy. This, unlike Manning's peculiar claims about reconstructing dances, *is* one of the basic concerns of historical understanding.

Manning prefers to offer loose analogies—in the manner of the type of critic she disdains—and declares Nijinsky a modernist (in one of her "conventional" senses), whereas I focus on the influence of a specific notion of modernism in a dance-historical context. But analogy is an ahistorical mode of interpretation—suited to the kind of "critical apology" Manning is invested in making for Mary Wigman (the subject of her unpublished dissertation). Until dance historians can distinguish between relations underpinned by causality—such as (among others) artistic influence—and fledgling analogies (after all, everything is like anything else in some respect), dance history will stagnate, no matter how many dance reconstructions people like Manning undertake. I have worked on dance reconstructions, too, and find them valuable enterprises. But I don't mistake them for basic historical research; on the contrary, they rely on antecedent scholarship. Indeed, I don't see how dance reconstructions can be historically accurate if the reconstructor can't tell the difference between analogies and causal determinants. A bright idea like the importation of Judsonian modernism to a piece of Nijinsky's on the basis of some glancing analogy would be a historical fantasy, not a historical reconstruction.

As is well known, Manning is a specialist in German dance. Given this, I wonder who is the critical apologist here. She is apparently trying to tie Wigman's fortunes to the coattails of the historical (and historically bounded) achievement that I documented in *Terpsichore in Sneakers*. And though there is nothing wrong with criticism, I fail to see why she thinks she ought to valorize this transparent and commonly used maneuver as dance history (somehow backed up by unnamed reconstructions). Dedicated to her German subject matter, she also wants to use the American dance I wrote about to lend part of its luster to Pina Bausch. Within limits, this may be historically acceptable. Bausch has certainly been influenced by the American postmodern dance, as I state in the new introduction to *Terpsichore in Sneakers*. However, she is not a central member of that company, as a simple matter of fact; she is just not part of the modernist generation that I wrote about. This is not at all to denigrate Bausch or to minimize her current impact on much European dance, as Manning seems to take it.

Descartes wrote a ballet libretto and, in conventional usage, he is the first modern philosopher. He is not part of the modernist movement documented in *Terpsichore in Sneakers;* neither is Wigman, though she was a modern choreographer who influenced much American modern dance. Manning is confusing the terms modern and modernist. Obviously, you can define both terms as broadly as you want, and the more broadly you go, the more people you can include. But without respect to historical practice, that will result in neither sound history nor sound criticism.

Sally Banes
Associate Professor of Dance History
Cornell University

Pedagogy and Performance

Teaching the *Poetics* with Computers

Vincent R. Renzi

Aristotle's Greek Tragedy Construction Kit, Beta Ver. 2.0. By James Bierman. Santa Barbara, CA: Kinko's Academic Software Exchange, 1988. System requirements: Apple Computer Macintosh Plus, SE, or II; minimum one megabyte RAM; running Apple Computer. $17.

James Bierman, professor of theatre arts at the University of California, Santa Cruz, has recently written a new piece of instructional software titled *Aristotle's Greek Tragedy Construction Kit* (1988). These days, computer-aided instruction has become widespread; but in the theatre, computers were first used as technical devices—for example, to control lighting and manage productions—or they were to be found in the business and box offices. More recently, following the use of computers in design, film and video editing, and animation, computers have also been used by artists either to help simulate ideas for blocking and mise-en-scene in general or they have appeared on stage as an active part of the mise-en-scene. Bierman's package is the first I have encountered among those that move the use of computers into the study of theatre, and his package is well executed. But since the use of computers in teaching about theatre is new, and because *Aristotle's Greek Tragedy Construction Kit* is an attractive piece of software, Bierman's package also highlights some concerns about computer-aided instruction. Specifically: inasmuch as theatre is essentially a performative medium, and inasmuch as teaching is also essentially an activity—something which must be performed, its purpose not being exhausted by the knowledge imparted—the use of computer-aided instruction in the study of theatre leads us to consider pedagogical problems faced by computer-aided instruction in general. Let me first review Bierman's effort before going on to these general concerns.

Aristotle's Greek Tragedy Construction Kit is not, as its title might suggest, a software package for writing tragedies of the style Aristotle recommends; rather, it is a "hypertext" exploration of Aristotle's *Poetics*. The package is a "stack" written in Apple Computer's *HyperCard,* which it describes as a "software construction kit": in short a user-friendly programming language. "Hypertext" is a notion Bierman's package trades on, and it is a notion which informs and predates *HyperCard*. Simply put, it is the literary idea of intertext virtually realized; but it is perhaps best explained within a discussion of *HyperCard*. The paradigm of *HyperCard* is a "stack" of file cards, each of which may contain text, graphics, functions, and so on, and which may be related to other cards via "buttons." By clicking the mouse on buttons of various types, new cards or further information will appear. In this way, in the hands of a good programmer, the content of each card can be linked in a nonlinear, associative sequence to other cards.

Bierman uses such features to good effect, interrelating scattered discussions of the *Poetics,* and relating those discussions in turn to others both in Aristotle's own works (e.g., the *Rhetoric* and the *Nicomachean Ethics*) and to other historical sources. Bierman also makes full use of other *HyperCard* features; for instance, allowing the student to switch between the English translation and Greek text of the *Poetics*. He uses the program's graphics capabilities both to illustrate cards with images from Greek vases and to animate cards—to memorable effect. The package also includes a lexicon of major terms, from which, by selecting a term, the user is brought to the card showing the passage in the *Poetics* or in Bierman's commentary where the term occurs. Finally, a note facility is included (so the student can make running reading notes for her/himself), and there is also an analysis feature in which the student responds in short essays to questions on the reading, the application of the *Poetics* to playscripts, or to any other questions the user may write and install in the program. There are a few technical shortcomings of which I'm sure Bierman is all too aware (it being the nature of computer software to be continually revised—indeed, before I even began writing the present essay I was provided with an update, which is the version I am concerned with here). The package is of limited scope—it does not include the full text of the *Poetics* or a complete index—but it is not intended as a research tool: *Aristotle's Greek Tragedy Construction Kit* is an introduction to the *Poetics,* an electronic textbook for the beginning student. It may serve well as such an introduction, for Bierman's scholarship is careful and his programming good. Within its scope as an introduction, *Aristotle's Greek Tragedy Construction Kit* renders the perhaps somewhat intimidating *Poetics* "user-friendly" without compromise of scholarship.

Precisely because Bierman's package delivers on a scholarly level and is yet so "user-friendly" we must be careful not to overestimate its pedagog-

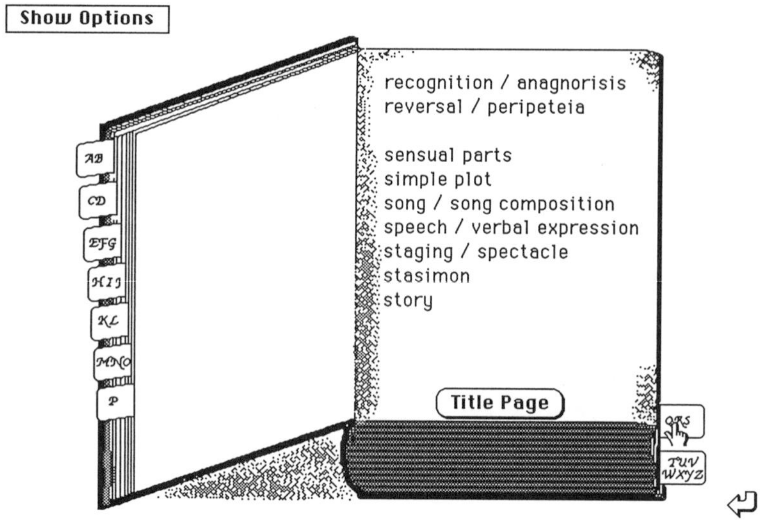

1. *A screen from the "lexicon" feature of* Aristotle's Greek Tragedy Construction Kit. *Selecting a word on the page advances the user to the screen on which the word is discussed. Pages are "flipped" by selecting the index tabs (as the cursor hand is about to do). Clicking on the "Title Page" button returns the user to the first-page screen of the lexicon. Selecting "Show Options" pulls down a command menu. (Graphic courtesy of Vincent R. Renzi)*

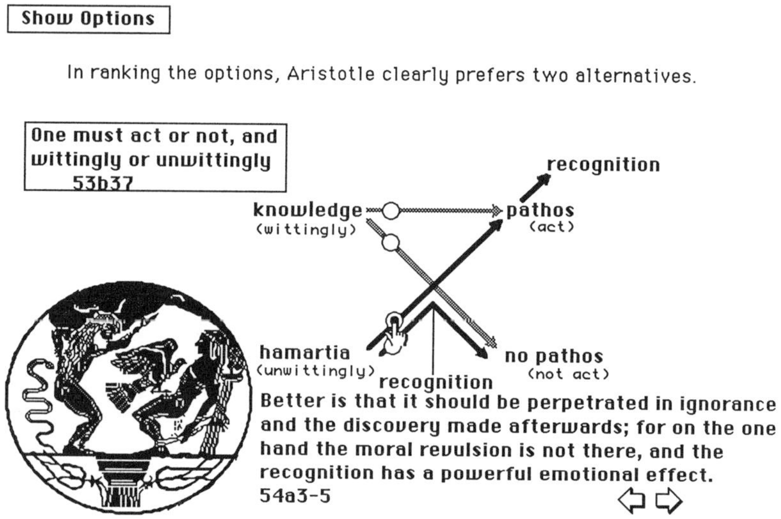

2. *The cursor hand has just clicked the button to select "hamartia." The program is now displaying the relevant citation from the* Poetics. *(Graphic courtesy of Vincent R. Renzi)*

ical value. Recent research has shown that micro-computer based computer-aided instruction is most effective in mathematics and the sciences (see Roblyer 1988). But it has been my own experience even with a package such as *Valid* (1984)—written at Stanford University for instruction in formal logic—that even when computers are used in fields most related to their own functioning, they miss fundamental aspects of teaching. The pedagogical ineffectiveness of instructional software seems to me to be due to two factors. First, instructional software is heir to all the problems of a book, most obviously the book's or the software's inability either to discipline the student (that is, provide an occasion for the student to learn) or to teach her to think critically (that is, to provide the condition for her to learn). As these are weaknesses of both books and software, we can hardly indict software on these grounds; it is enough to point out that instructional software isn't immune to these problems.

But second, and specific to software, is that computer-aided instruction misleads us into thinking that it does actively teach. While the untutored

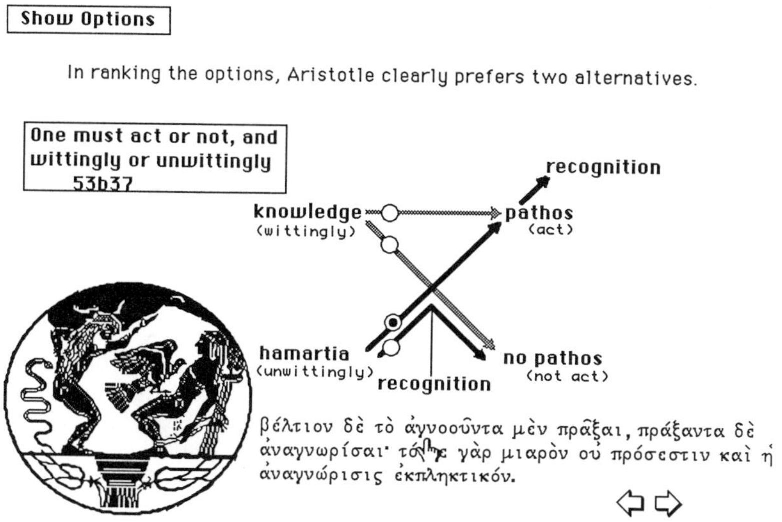

3. The cursor hand has just clicked on the text citation which the program now displays in Greek. (Graphic courtesy of Vincent R. Renzi)

reading of books can be instructive to a student, though a student may not get as much out of them as he would have had the books been read in conjunction with a class, there is never any question of ascribing intelligence to a book. No one is doing research in artificial intelligence for books. Certainly the best authors adopt strategies to guide their readers (e.g., the dialog form) but this is precisely because these authors realize the limitations of their medium. Perhaps the clearest example of such a realization is Plato's denunciation of writing in the *Phaedrus,* a book that seeks to both consider and overcome in some small way the limitation of books as teachers to their readers. In contrast to such efforts, in the case of *Valid,* students have to solve logical problems before they are allowed to advance in the computer lesson; while the computer is able to check the student's work, it cannot do the problems itself. Moreover, for exactly the reason that it can only check the problems, it is also incapable of recognizing innovative but correct solutions that fall outside its necessarily finite answer key. Nonetheless, because the computer interacts with the student and, indeed, prevents the student from advancing until a "correct" solution is entered (or until the programmer gave up hope of the student finding one—say after four of five attempts—and has the program volunteer a solution), it seems the computer is an active teacher, providing the occasion for learning. So, too, in *Aristotle's Greek Tragedy Construction Kit,* the student, clicking buttons to advance the lesson, seems to have a personal tutor (the computer) who advances the lesson at the speed appropriate to the individual. Furthermore, the program seems to provide the condition for knowledge because, in fact, Bierman has succeeded in connecting up the scattered themes of the *Poetics* and because he provides background information in his commentary. In both these cases the computer provides only the appearance of real teaching, and I suspect by the time the student gets back into the classroom, the damage has been done. The student has fallen for the appearance of personalized and user-friendly instruction and has also internalized the limited creativity the computer demands. Far from aiding instruction, the computer seems to menace it.

It may be that alert teachers will recognize these shortcomings of computer-aided instruction and structure their curricula to make full use of it while avoiding such problems. But the problem in the study of theatre is something else again. We may want to say that plays and texts about theatre can only be known truly if students are working in the practice of theatre. But even if we had completely accurate recreations of Attic theatrical performances, those recreated performances would still not have the same relationship to students of Aristotle today as the originals had to Greek audiences of 2,500 years ago. It could only be from extant plays and texts and from the physical traces of archaeological discovery that we could ever have knowledge of the ephemera of a culture. On the other hand, unlike the study of mathematics or of literature, study of theatre and visual arts in general crosses media. In studying mathematics, one learns to do mathematics; with literature one at least shares the use of language, though not the form, with the object of one's study. The study of performance and computer-aided instruction are alike in this crossing of media. Both face the problem that their object is so unlike them. Further, computer-aided instruction about the theatre is not helped by the visual aspects of computer presentations, for the problem here is the real yet fleeting nature of the object of study, the practice of the art. Theatre and teaching are things that must be done. It may be interesting or important to teach the *Poetics,* but that will be teaching a text, not knowledge of theatre or of the *Poetics'* original relation to the theatre of its time. In the same way, it may be helpful to use computers to aid teaching, but they could never substitute for the actual performance of teaching; they could never provide discipline to the student or encourage her creative efforts. But whereas the experience of Greek theatre is lost to us, except in its traces in texts and ruins, actual theatre and real teaching are performances we can and must continue to mount if indeed we want to impart real knowledge.

It may well be that instructional software will come to be written with strategies as subtle as Plato's, so as to avoid or at least acknowledge and alert us to the problems raised by the limitations of its medium. I suspect such an understanding will be some time in coming, but I'll hazard a guess that it will come first from computer games, since they have an immediate stake in exploiting the possibilities and recognizing the limitations of their medium. (Perhaps this will prove a Dionysian origin analogous to that ascribed to theatre.)

To return to *Aristotle's Greek Tragedy Construction Kit*: I hope what I have said will dispel any notion that such a package could replace teaching just as a made-for-TV movie could not substitute for the performance of a play—they are simply different things. As to whether Bierman's package, good as it is, can *aid* instruction—that is a question I leave to the creative efforts of teachers.

References

Roblyer, M.D.

1988 "The Effectiveness of Microcomputers in Education: A Review of the Research from 1980–1987." *Technological Horizons in Education Journal* 16, no. 2 (September):85–89.

Valid

1984 Stanford, CA: Department of Philosophy and Institute for Mathematical Studies in the Social Sciences, Stanford University. (Modified for Columbia University.)

Vincent R. Renzi *holds an MA in Performance Studies from New York University. He is currently pursuing a PhD in Philosophy at Columbia University.*

To Dance Is "Female"

Ann Daly

Dance, Sex and Gender: Signs of Identity, Dominance, Defiance, and Desire. By Judith Lynne Hanna. Chicago: The University of Chicago Press, 1988; xx + 311 pp. $39.95 cloth, $15.95 paper.

I learned a disconcerting lesson recently at a symposium called "Reclaiming or Effacing? How Women Artists Handle Sexist Images in Performance"[1]: there is very little understanding—even amidst the interested, intelligent people who attended this event—of the vigorous and extensive feminist inquiry that has been going on in the arts for the past decade. It finally hit home why practically no choreographers are investigating the issues of women and representation, compared to their colleagues in film and the visual arts: the issues involved in the study of gender in dance are still generally misunderstood, if they are in circulation at all.

The panel's moderator, Peggy Shaw of the Split Britches Company, was most interested in exploring whether women performers' use of gender stereotypes serve to subvert or to reinforce those representations. This was an excellent and timely question, given the popularity of pastiche these days; but the discussion suffered from a naive concept of "sexism" that ended up scapegoating women in the process of mythologizing individual free choice, and from a general confusion about the complexity of the issues at hand.

Despite its comprehensive title, Judith Lynne Hanna's *Dance, Sex and Gender: Signs of Identity, Dominance, Defiance, and Desire* is no antidote to the confusion.

Addressing the whole of Western theatrical dance as well as selected dance around the globe, Hanna's stated goal is "to enrich the discourse on male/female body images and social change by spotlighting and clarifying how gender is socially and culturally constructed and transformed in a critical medium of human communication—the dance" (241). This is an unquestionably important aim, shared by a modest but growing number of dance scholars. Dance is an ideal laboratory for the study of gender, because its essential medium—the body—is where sex and gender are said to originate; it is where the discourses of the "natural" and the "cultural" thrash it out. Dance is a significant clue to the management of the female body in any given time and place. Furthermore, the politics of dance as an institution, sometimes dominated by women, more often dominated by men, demands its own inquiry.

Hanna's reach, however, far exceeds her grasp. Though she has identified the area of investigation, she fails to develop a coherent framework for analysis and neglects to ask fundamental questions. She calls her work a synthesis, but synthesis depends upon meaningful organization and insightful connections. On both counts, *Dance, Sex and Gender* fails. Hanna is uncritically dependent on the work of other anthropologists and critics—she uses citations as substitutes for analysis. Hanna darts, often tediously, from quote to quote (some so long as to be teetering at the edge of impropriety), without any apparent purpose other than to feign rhetorical legitimacy. Though the format of the book is much like a textbook's, with an introductory chapter defining key words in italics and chapter summaries, *Dance, Sex and Gender* is muddled, beginning with her definition of terms.

Hanna's constant bobbing and weaving appears to stem from her determination to avoid becoming politically embroiled. In a footnote leading off her chapter entitled "Patterns of Dominance: Men, Women, and Homosexuality,"[2] Hanna writes that:

> After my 1984 presentation, a male colleague said he was disturbed that it was not clear where I stood; I sounded like a feminist who did not deliver. However, my intent is to present facts, issues, and perspectives of participants involved in a process, not to advocate (119n).

Gender, however, is not a matter of fact. It is a matter of ideology and its constantly evolving discourse.

For someone who insists on the historical and cultural nature of dance, Hanna's book is curiously ahistorical and acultural. It consists of an endless series of examples. She plucks out a few superficial aspects of a given dance to make a point, to fit it into a category, without setting any dance into its larger context. Thus specific dances are rendered meaningless. In the quest for "synthesis," Hanna resorts to strange lists (nine words that identify sexuality and sex roles in criticism: androgynous, erotic, gender, heterosexual, homosexual, sensual, sexual, sexy, and suggestive) and absurd compressions ("Nijinsky danced superbly, had an affair with the famous impresario Diaghilev, eventually married, and suffered from mental illness" [185]). Her fondness for tidy cause-and-effect leads to facile assertions, like "Women created new fields such as modern dance, social work, kindergarten teaching, and librarianship rather than compete in male professions" (131) or "Gay men identify with the effeminate yearnings, feelings, and romantic idealizations of the ballet, which is not marked by sexual preference so much as by sexual grace for both sexes" (137).

Hanna pays lip service to the methods of Erving Goffman and Ray Birdwhistell, but the body of the book bears no resemblance to their brand of astute observation, rigorous analysis, and provocative theory. Hanna's perspective is a quaint hybrid of Darwinian functionalism, the sociologist's impulse to categorize types, and a kind of primitive communications theory predicated on a simplistic sender-receiver model. None of which gets us closer to understanding the ways gender and sexuality are constructed in dance. And because of her aversion to politics, the author never thinks to ask *why* gender is constructed the way it is. Though claiming to take a semiotic approach, she never gets to questions of meaning. And she commits the fatal error that gives semiotics such a bad reputation in dance: movement is treated as a series of static things rather than as an ongoing process.

The book's most serious flaw is its hazy use of such basic terms as: sex, sexuality, gender, sexual identity, and sex role (which she uses as a synonym for gender). The terms tend to slip, even when Hanna appears to be neatly defining them. For example, at first "sexual identity" is said to "depend[s] on biological criteria of genetic, anatomical, and physiological characteristics" (7). Not a few lines later, it is said to "refer[s] to sexual interaction: heterosexual, homosexual (gay, lesbian), or bisexual" (8). Certainly if sexual orientation is tied to biological sex, then all women would have the same orientation and so would all men. Hanna's definitions only make sense within her Darwinian paradigm, where sex is said to dictate sexuality and gender. There is no room in this scheme for the fundamental distinction that gender studies makes between biology and behavior. Hanna disregards the historical, cultural, and ideological factors that help to construct our notions of sex, sexuality, and the body.

Hanna sees not only sex—but also sexuality, which is really a separate matter—as the function of the survival of the species. This is an untenable position when analyzing dance in cultures where sexuality and reproduction have been wedged apart. In those cases, one's sexuality does not derive necessarily from the drive to procreate. Within Hanna's functionalist scheme, homosexuality and lesbianism are completely marginalized.

Although she rightly emphasizes the intertwined relationship between sexuality and gender in the dancing body, she leaves it at that, never attempting to untangle the vines. Because she identifies sex with sexuality and sexuality with gender,[3] she therefore links sex and gender, implicitly affirming that "biology is destiny." Hanna starts and ends with the assumption of difference, so she will never "enrich the discourse on [. . .] social change" (241), for it is the insistence on difference that leads inevitably to dominance.

Like the "Reclaiming or Effacing?" symposium, Hanna operates on the superficial level of "sexism," as if the problem were simply a matter of a bad attitude. For all its rhetoric about anthropology and the cultural construction of gender, *Dance, Sex and Gender* is naive concerning the dissemination of culture, reducing the process to simplistic notions of modeling and "vicarious learning" (11). Hanna sees this as a conscious, cognitive process. Actually, gender is a much more complex, culturally entrenched process of representation, which encompasses the spectator and her process of interpretation as well. Looking at "images," the way Hanna does, only deals with half the phenomenon, which in recent feminist scholarship has been dubbed the "male gaze" (see Mulvey 1975; Kaplan 1983). As tiresome as this term has become to some, it remains a fundamental concept: that, in modern Western culture, the one who sees and the one who is seen are gendered positions. The possessive gaze is "male," while the passive object of the gaze is "female"—regardless of the dancer's or spectator's sex.

Gender studies is not yet widely accepted among dance scholars, and Hanna's book will do nothing to recommend what is, to my mind, the field's most intellectually compelling frontier.[4] For to scrutinize the construction of gender in the dancing body requires the most subtle of analyses. Indeed, what is so fascinating about this project is its greatest challenge: to figure out, and then to verbalize, the ineffable experience of the dance spectator—to find the clear, accurate, and necessarily poetic language to express how it is that a dancer's focus, or the way she activates her skin, or the palpable feeling of the spatial environment, signifies a particular way of seeing and being seen.

In the effort to theorize alternatives to the male gaze, we need to think a lot more about performative presence. Presence is the silent yet screeching excitement of physical vibrancy, of "being there." It is one of the thrills of watching dance, to see someone radiate pure energy, whether it is in stillness or in flight. Questions abound: What constitutes presence? How do we know it when we see it? Is it pan-cultural, or is it highly coded? How is it related to the structure of spectacle? Why is it so seductive? Does that seductiveness demand possession? Can that seductiveness be derailed? There appears to be an affinity between presence and the male gaze. At one end of a continuum, ballet strives for presence and, concomitantly, is a highly coded spectacle that reifies the male gaze. At the other end, performance art in its early, most radical moments aimed to undercut traditional conventions of performing and presence, opting instead to try to confound the usual audience-performer relationship. Deborah Hay straddles both ends of that continuum. She is striving toward a kind of movement-in-stillness that she calls pure "consciousness" at the same time she insists on inviting the audience to share in her performance rather than consuming it from afar [see Hay's article in this issue].

The concept of the male gaze comes from feminist film theory. In film, the woman performer is literally a celluloid object. She has no presence in the movie theatre; she cannot look back at the spectator and is thus rendered passive. In dance the situation is not as clear-cut. The dancer does have a literal, if not always effective, presence. S/he can participate in a give-and-take with the audience. A highly accomplished technician looks anything but passive. Nevertheless, the dancer becomes more than just a technician within the stage frame. S/he becomes part of a dense thicket of completely familiar codes and conventions that conspire to position her/him as the willing object of our desire. We need to face squarely the risk factor in trying to jam those conventions: much of the beauty and pleasure of dance as we know them are tied up with the erotics of display and spectatorship.

There are times and places, however, when the conventions are in such flux that it seems possible for the gaze to be unfixed and for the performer to elude possession. I don't happen to think we're living in that time and place. Our existence is too overcoded. But very early modern dance, or early postmodern dance, for example, may have been such a time-and-place. In order to find out, we need to examine those dances and dancemakers both in the minute details of their performance and in the full context of their culture. The late '20s and early '30s as well as the '60s were a time of great change—old rules were being discarded and new ones were being invented at an alarming speed. In that space of radical cultural change, the confounding of the gaze in dance may have reinvented gender, too—until the new conventions became entrenched. Modern and postmodern dance today are as much a spectacle as ballet.

It is ironic that, when feminist literary theorists come to a point where words no longer suffice, they often invoke dancing as a metaphor. And yet dance is too infrequently the subject of feminist inquiry. I still think Jacques Derrida's words, in a published interview called "Choreographies," are ones to look and think and write by:

> [W]hat if we were to approach here [. . .] the area of a relationship to the other where the code of sexual marks would no longer be discriminating? [. . .] As I dream of saving the chance that this question offers I would like to believe in the multiplicity of sexually marked voices. I would like to believe in the masses, this indeterminable number of blended voices, this mobile of non-identified sexual marks whose choreography can carry, divide, multiply the body of each "individual," whether he be classified as "man" or as "woman" according to the criteria of usage. [. . .] Then too, I ask you, what kind of a dance would there be, or would there be one at all, if the sexes were not exchanged according to rhythms that vary considerably? (Derrida and McDonald 1982:76)

I admire Hanna's attempt to tackle the analysis of gender in dance across cultures. At a time when everything in our own culture seems to lead unrelentingly to the difference between "man" and "woman," cross-cultural study holds the promise of freeing up our imaginations. What is gender in a culture that is not bound to bipolar opposites: to the mutual exclusivity of here and there, of you and me, of male and female? And what is its dance?

Notes

1. This symposium, part of Movement Research Inc.'s Studies Project, was held 19 December 1988 at the Ethnic Folk Arts Center in New York City.
2. This chapter was originally published as an article in TDR 31, no. 1 (T113). My response to that article and Hanna's subsequent reply were published in the following issue, TDR 31, no. 2 (T114).
3. Hanna explicitly states her reasons "why gender is coterminous with sexuality in dance" (46):

> In contemporary Western society the separation of sex and gender becomes significant when we attempt to make political and economic opportunity relevant to qualifications for positions instead of physical markers with which an individual is born.
>
> However, because a gender role for most people is sexual reproduction, a perceived body in dance, especially when performers appear nude, in anatomically revealing dress, or in stereotypic male or female costume, conflates biological thought and behavior (arousal and sexual identity), gender, and the historical relationship of dance and sex. Of course, people express gender signs in situations unrelated to sexual activity, but in adolescent and adult interaction the manifestation that refers to everyday stereotypes and violations of them is most dramatic (13).

Apparently Hanna believes that dance representation is irrelevant in the culture-at-large. And apparently homosexuals and lesbians do not figure into the picture, because, unlike "most people," their gender role does not follow from sexual reproduction. And apparently all dance is sexually arousing to Hanna.

4. For the past several years many of my ideas have been sparked, challenged, and encouraged by participants in a study group in feminist theory and dance: Ann Cooper Albright, Judy Burns, Marianne Goldberg, Ellen Graff, Carol Martin, and Leslie Satin.

References

Derrida, Jacques, and Christie V. McDonald
1982 "Choreographies." *Diacritics* 12 (Summer):66–76.

Kaplan, E. Ann
1983 *Women and Film: Both Sides of the Camera*. New York: Methuen.

Mulvey, Laura
1975 "Visual Pleasure and Narrative Cinema." *Screen* 16, no. 3 (Autumn):6–18.

Ann Daly, *a contributing editor to* TDR, *writes dance criticism for* TDR, High Performance, Ballett International, *and* Women and Performance. *She is Assistant Professor of Dance History/Criticism at the University of Texas at Austin.*

Willett on Weimar

John Fuegi

The Theatre of the Weimar Republic. By John Willett. New York: Holmes and Meier, 1988; 350 pp. $79.50.

The combination of this particular writer and this particular publisher bodes well. John Willett is known as a leading authority not only on the modern theatre of the German-speaking world but on the international and interdisciplinary context of the Weimar period. He was here given a mandate to produce a large and handsomely illustrated volume on the Weimar Theatre, to be published by the distinguished and progressive house established and now run by the European emigré, Max Holmes.

Noting the absence of a comprehensive volume, in any language, on the Weimar theatre as a whole, John Willett sets out to fill this gap. In fact, the title of the book actually vastly understates the range of the project. Not only does he provide a wealth of factual information on theatres within the physical boundaries of the German state of Weimar per se, but he also casts his net wide enough to include the German language theatres of Switzerland, Czechoslovakia, Austria, and even Poland. This largesse with regard to the physical space of "Weimar Theatre" is then also applied to time. Whereas the Weimar state, of course, had but a short life, being created hard on the heels of World War I and being technically wiped out with Hitler's rise to supreme power in early 1933, Willett traces the prehistory of the Weimar theatre at considerable length and then devotes a large section of the volume to what he calls "Weimar and After." As a result, what we have here is a compendium of facts, radiating out from the Weimar theatre and Weimar period per se, to include a huge range of extremely valuable materials on German language theatre in the late 19th and much of the 20th centuries.

Encyclopedic in scope, yet organized in its first sections in chronological narrative form, the book contains an extraordinary amount of sheer factual information on German-language theatre of this century. Beyond the narrative early chapters, the appendices alone run from page 215 to page 350. These pages, taken together with the 75 or so pictures contained in the volume, add up to virtually half the book. For those seeking information on the theatres themselves (some 180 of them are covered in detail), or on who played in what, when, and for how many performances, this book will serve as a standard reference work. Though there are a very few obvious omissions (for example, the listing of only some of the Cambridge University Press Directors in Perspective volumes devoted to German figures), in general the book is factually comprehensive and reliable. While not presented as an encyclopedia of its subject, the book has, in my view, this specific character and it is this which constitutes what I feel will be its enduring strength.

In filling his book to the brimming-over point with detailed lists of purely theatrical data, Willett himself is aware of what sacrifices of context he has been required to make. At one point he notes (just a bit plaintively perhaps): "In Appendix 2, which is the main chronology, political or parallel events have not been included" (216). Yet he notes also a few sentences further on, "It is of course essential to see all the information given here in the light of larger historical events." In teasing out the thread of *theatre* from the general fabric of Weimar, and the times in which Weimar was both created and destroyed, much is gained in depth of knowledge of the facts of theatre history, but much is lost in placing those facts in an essential historical/political context.

What I find is that my appetite is whetted by Willett's theatrical compendium. I would now like him (or somebody of comparable range and concern) to build upon this base of collected facts to create a companion volume on some of the nagging and enduring issues that these facts will raise for many contemporary readers. Some further areas that could now be explored immediately suggest themselves. A strong interdisciplinary feminist analysis of the data Willett has here compiled is a most obvious need. An in-depth look at the often neglected playwrights Elisabeth Hauptmann, Marieluise Fleißer, and Margarete Steffin would be a splendid place to start, together with an examination of the phenomenon of the cabaret often led or supported by women such as Rosa Valetti and Trude Hesterberg in Berlin and by the incomparable partner of Karl Valentin in Munich, Liesl Karlstadt. And, very importantly, we need to take a close look at the mechanization of women's bodies on the Weimar stage as on so many other stages in the Western world. Work along the research lines of Klaus Theweleit's recent examinations of Weimar could be extended with great profit, so I feel, to the theatre.

Similarly, more thorough work needs to be done on the comparative merits of the theatre of Weimar. That theatre, as we know from other work by Willett (*Art and Politics in the Weimar Period: The New Sobriety, 1913–1917,* for example), was deeply interwoven with Soviet and French stage experiments. It is worth remembering that when Hallie Flanagan toured Europe (both West and East) on a Guggenheim Grant in 1926/7, she saw less of merit on Berlin's stages than on Moscow's (see Flanagan 1928). Just how good and how genuinely innovative was the Weimar theatre when compared to that of Moscow in the same period, before Hitler crushed German experimentation and Stalin drove the Russian avant-garde to its untimely death?

A volume addressing questions growing out of an assembly of facts would need to examine one absolutely basic question. Why, despite the obvious loss of a number of key figures through murder or immigration in the Third Reich years, did so much that was distinguished in Weimar carry over into the Nazi theatre and then continue in the postwar years? After all, not only did key members of the Brecht circle (Caspar Neher and Herbert Ihering being two particularly obvious examples) stay on in Nazi Germany hardly missing a step in their work, but we also know that Goebbels actually made attempts to have at least Piscator and possibly Brecht also return to work in the Third Reich.

To carry such a question a step further, could it be argued perhaps (as Eric Bentley has sometimes suggested) that dictatorship per se was part of the fabric of the working practices of the German stage during and after Weimar and indeed after Hitler had left the stage? Could a serious analysis now be done on a question as fundamental as: Was the key, and continuous theatrical event of Weimar not the Volksbühne or Piscator's or Brecht's relatively small stages, but Hitler's theatre of the street, the court, the Zirkus Krone, and of the then newly developed German radio? David Bowie, for instance, has wondered whether Hitler should not be seen as the first major rock star. We might remember also that Brecht and Bronnen themselves noted in Munich in the very early '20s the clear theatrical and circus orientation of the then still tiny Nazi apparatus.

Building on the extremely valuable facts contained between the covers of *The Theatre of the Weimar Republic,* what I would now like to see is a second book, one which weaves the thread of Weimar theatre (or in this case German language theatre of various countries) back into the fabric of Weimar society and the international conditions in which that society played out its short, fruitful, and murderous life. I would strongly suggest that Max Holmes and John Willett get back together again to build on the base of this first volume and to plan a second volume on the political and historical context of the Weimar theatre.

References

Flanagan, Hallie
1928 *Shifting Scenes of the Modern European Theatre.* New York: Coward McCann.

Willett, John
1978 *Art and Politics in the Weimar Period: The New Sobriety, 1913–1917.* New York: Pantheon.

John Fuegi *is the author of* The Essential Brecht *(1972);* Chaos, According to Plan *(1987); and* Nothing Immoral *(1989). He has edited 14 volumes of the proceedings of the International Brecht Society, and was the Associate Director of the TV series "Beckett Directs Beckett."*

Announcements

Ed. Note: TDR is pleased to print announcements of upcoming conferences, festivals, publications, etc. Please submit all notices at least 6–8 months in advance of the event.

ACT Now

The ACT, an internationally distributed journal of performance, is seeking material for publication. *The ACT* presents new performance activity from around the world, historical research, and critical discourse on performance, representation, and critical methods. Both internationally known artists and writers and lesser-known artists are presented. Contact editor Jeffrey Greenberg, Performance Project, POB 3192 Church Street Station, New York, NY, 10008–3192.

Performance Studies Festival: Call for Papers

Performance Studies International (PSI) will host a festival bringing together both scholars and performers to celebrate the 10th anniversary of New York University's Department of Performance Studies on 3–7 October 1990. The festival will be a forum for the exploration of contemporary performance studies research and experimentation in performance itself. Crossover between these two areas is encouraged. The festival will include panel discussions, workshops, and papers. Those interested in participating, please send workshop proposals and papers to PSI, Department of Performance Studies, New York University, 721 Broadway, 6th floor, New York, NY, 10003.

Schneider Conference: Call for Papers

A national conference devoted to the study and celebration of Alan Schneider's multifaceted career as a theatre director, educator, and administrator will be held on 8–11 March 1990, and papers are invited. Topics may include any subject related to Schneider's work, or to work in which he took an interest, and may involve a wide range of methodologies and perspectives. At least some of the selected participants will be paid for their contributions. The conference will include productions, workshops, exhibits, etc., and is open to the public. It is recommended that abstracts of 250–300 words be submitted by 15 November 1989. For more information, write to the Alan Schneider Conference, Department of Theatre and Drama, 821 University Avenue, University of Wisconsin, Madison, WI, 53706.

Women Wrighters in *Studies in American Drama*

Studies in American Drama, 1945–Present will publish a special issue on women playwrights in March 1990. This volume will contain original work by Megan Terry (her one-act play, *Amtrak*) as well as excerpts from Ntozake Shange and Emily Mann's *Betsey Brown*. Five original interviews—with Megan Terry, Tina Howe, Adrienne Kennedy, Constance Congdon, and Joan Schenkar—are slated, as well as critical essays on the work of Shange, Maria Irene Fornes, Alice Walker, and Beth Henley. *Studies in American Drama* is edited by Philip C. Kolin and Colby H. Kullman; subscription information can be obtained from J. Madison Davis of Behrend College, Erie, PA, 16563.

Sun Son

Editor's Addition: TDR contributing editor William Huizhu Sun and Faye Chunfang Fei are pleased to announce the birth of their son, Kevin Fei Sun, on 20 July 1989.

Plays, Applause, and Bullets

Safdar Hashmi's Street Theatre

Eugène van Erven

The sun was setting hazily on Delhi's enigmatic skyline of red brick and junk slum as the express train from Bangalore slowly completed the final minutes of its 40-hour journey. Dust constructions in pale red, dilapidated multicolored vehicles, and masses of brown people pasted themselves to my weary retina in vague orange blots. New Delhi would be my last stop before returning to the Netherlands after a three-year quest for genuinely effective political theatre, a quest that had taken me to the remotest parts of rural and urban Asian jungles. I was exhausted but somehow managed to muster the energy to search for Safdar Hashmi who, according to friends in Pakistan, Calcutta, and Bombay, I absolutely had to meet. He was one of India's most effective street theatre artists. Now, months later in the northern European winter, I am glad that after a day's search I found his modest two-room apartment tucked away in an endless row of tenement houses near Jawaharia Nehru Stadium. He opened the door with an inviting smile. I apologized for disturbing him at home. Not at all and would I please step in. He was lean and tall and wore slippers under a white tunic and trousers. An unmanageable forelock of black hair hung down about his spectacles. An Indian version of Danny Kaye, I thought. "You must be Eugène van Erven," he said in fluent English. "Come in. I have been expecting you." I had written to him several times without receiving a reply. Later I realized it may have been his idiosyncratic way of testing foreigners; if they really wanted to speak to him they should prove their determination by tracking him down—the hard way. My effort had apparently been satisfactory and during the ensuing five days Safdar took me in rickshaws and on scooters to several performances of his legendary street theatre group, Janam, and shared with me his wealth of knowledge and his original insights into Indian politics and culture.

The Politics of Indian Traditional Theatre

Safdar Hashmi is a respected columnist for *The Economic Times*, a Sunday paper. He has also made documentaries and written scripts for television. But for the past 15 years his main concern has been to develop a kind of political theatre that would effectively express the emotions and concerns of India's working class and peasantry. Peter Brook's *Mahabharata*

1. Safdar Hashmi introduces Machine *to New Delhi workers at the Thumbs-Up bottling plant on 1 May 1988. (Photo by Eugène van Erven)*

and tours by Indian musicians and kathakali ensembles have confirmed a growing Western interest in Indian performing arts, but to the committed Indian artist the traditional cultural heritage remains problematic. Says Safdar Hashmi, "We feel the need to liberate ourselves from the stranglehold of colonial and imperialist culture which has swept over our entire country and which has destroyed our traditional culture also. Of course, all of us feel the need to work in the forms which are familiar to our people and which our people have been using in expressing their own hopes for centuries. But the problem is that if you work with the traditional form, along comes the traditional content with its superstition, backwardness, obscurantism, and its promotion of feudal structures."[1]

Safdar Hashmi sees a complex collaboration between Indian upper-class bureaucrats and Western development agencies behind the upsurge in promoting traditional Indian performing arts. Despite the surface democratic structure, he claims, India is still actually ruled by an alliance of capitalists and feudal lords. One of the most potent weapons for perpetuating their power is to keep the common people backward: "Against the backdrop of the rising people's discontent all over the country and the growing organized expression of this discontent in trade unions, peasant, student, youth, and women movements, and the people's culture movement, I think the ruling classes have formulated their own strategy for countering it at the level of consciousness by propagating and strengthening all that is backward, obscurantist, and superstitious. One of the ways they have chosen is to promote the traditional arts in the name of promoting an 'Indianness' to our theatre."

The history of modern theatre in India is very short. Its urban manifestations do not go back for much more than 100 years in cities like Bombay, Calcutta, and Delhi. Elsewhere it is even younger than that. But a much older folk theatre continues to flourish in the countryside. The champions of traditional theatre argue that pure Indian theatre can only achieve genuine "Indianness" if it isolates itself from the contemporary concerns of the people. These bourgeois intellectuals, as Safdar Hashmi calls them, look at theatre merely in shallow decorative terms. "They think 'Indianness' is the image of a Hindu God, the image of fire and tree worshipping, the soul dance," he explains disapprovingly. "Of course, looked at from an aesthetic point of view, this theatre looks very different from Western theatre. It looks 'Indian' in terms of richness of costume, dance, the rhythms. But I feel that instead of imparting a unique 'Indianness' to theatre, these things are actually imparting a unique backwardness."

Safdar Hashmi does not reject traditional performing arts outright. He and his colleagues consider them very rich and potentially very useful for their own kind of theatre, but they want to be careful not to vulgarize and thereby exploit them. "Let us say there is a tribal hunting dance. Some dancer becomes a bear or a lion or a buffalo and others become the hunters and they go around and around doing their ritualistic movements until they zero in for the kill. This dance is still reenacted although it is no longer a part of their everyday life. Now suppose I wanted to use this form to depict, for example, the Indian people rising up to defeat Indira Ghandi's semifascist government in 1977. If I reduce her Congress(I) Party and all that it stands for to that buffalo, I will be practicing mere reductionism. I will not be enriching the understanding of the people toward the complexity of the contemporary political phenomena. It is too convenient, you see. I can't just go and sit at the feet of a kathakali guru for six months and then come back and do a play in the kathakali style." Yet Safdar believes that a different kind of tradition lives in him and finds expression in his work. Over the years he has become widely known for his songs which, he admits, are often based on the traditional folksongs he learned as a child. "There is a kind of song called the *Alhay* which is still popular in the states of Uttar Pradesh, Haryana, Madhya Pradesh, and Rajistan. It tells the story of two brothers, Alhay and Udel, who are very brave. The narrative song has a particular rhythm. Now the tune, the rhythm, and the narrative function are totally part of me. So when I sit down to write a song about the history of May Day then my pen automatically begins to move in the Alhay meter."

The History of Janam

Safdar Hashmi's group is called Janam, which is Sanskrit for "New Birth." Janam is also an acronym for *Jan Natya Manch,* meaning "People's Theatre Front." Since its birth in 1973 it has performed at least 4,000 times and has produced more than 20 plays, most of them written by Safdar Hashmi. Eleven of their plays have been translated into practically every major Indian language. Janam's original plays always relate to a specific social or political issue and therefore the troup's curriculum vitae reads like an alternative cultural history of India's past 15 years. Not surprisingly, it reveals a radically different picture from the one presented by the international media and the official records: no smiling, motherly Indira or charming, chubby Rajiv married to an Italian hotel owner's daughter, but a ruthless dynasty of powermongers keeping their mass of 800 million starving people in a stranglehold.

Safdar Hashmi first became involved in theatre as a newly recruited member of the Student Federation of India's cultural unit. The unit performed songs from the independence movement and a short play on Vietnam at rallies. Soon the group wanted to expand its activities beyond the student movement and began calling itself IPTA after the nationwide Indian People's Theatre Association that had been active from 1943 until approximately 1958. Since then, IPTA has only been able to reorganize itself in West Bengal. But apart from the historical significance associated with the name, Safdar Hashmi's group had another, very pragmatic reason for calling itself IPTA. Chuckling, Hashmi explains that IPTA had gone into decline in Delhi as well and that from 1958 it had become a club where people gathered once a year. "They had their own office in Connaught Place, the big roundabout in the middle of Delhi's business district. In 1966 the then-Secretary of IPTA saw to it that the association became totally defunct. He captured the office and established an import-export business in it. We heard about this and went to him to tell him that we were IPTA now and that we wanted to use the office. Of course he refused but we were young and quite numerous so we physically pushed him out and threw his things down from the first floor." The reborn IPTA became a regular theatre troupe and began interacting directly with the organized left, performing full-length plays on makeshift wooden stages in working-class areas. The group also operated a song squad which performed for striking workers at factory gates. Their plays were extremely popular, often attracting 6–7,000 spectators. Having little or no theatre training, the group at first performed simplistically interpreted didactic plays like Brecht's *Exception and the Rule*. "We would begin at ten o'clock in the

2. Janam, Safdar Hashmi's street theatre group, performs Machine *for workers at 6:00* AM *on 1 May 1988. (Photo by Eugène van Erven)*

evening and end around midnight. Then at one in the morning the second shift would come out of the factory and they would watch until 4:00 AM."

In 1973 the new IPTA was kicked out of its Connaught Place premises as unceremoniously as it had entered. The reason for it had to do with the rather complex relation that exists between India's two competing Communist Parties, CPI and CPI(M), which split in 1964 over the issue of whether to collaborate with Nehru's Congress Party. The CPI-Marxist faction—hence the "M"—was opposed to what they regarded as an unholy alliance with the capitalist bourgeoisie and the feudal landlords. During the State of Emergency in the mid-'70s, CPI supported Indira Ghandi's repressive regime, which cost them their mass following. Today, CPI(M) is India's largest Communist Party. In West Bengal and Kerala it runs the state government and in Uttar Pradesh, Tamil Nadu, and Maharashtra it has a very strong mass base as well. Safdar Hashmi's IPTA had not yet taken any sides in the early '70s and performed for the trade union, youth, and student platforms of both parties. But in March 1973 IPTA refused to perform at a big CPI demonstration: "That's when they came and threw us out of the office," states Hashmi laconically. "Most of our members got scared and we were unable to regroup them. With four of the remaining students we then founded Janam."

Desperately needing funds, Janam decided to enter a Bengali-language version of Irwin Shaw's *Bury the Dead* in the annual Durga Pudjah festival organized by Delhi's Bengali communities. "During this event big circus tents are erected all over the place. Originally it was a religious festival dedicated to the goddess Burda. So on some sites you see people worshipping. But anywhere else it has become a cultural festival. In Delhi alone it is celebrated in 65 different places. Every neighborhood has its own Durga Pudjah committee which raises lots of funds for the occasion. They pay up to 1,000 rupees [US $75] for a performance. The festival lasts five days and we went racing around, performing sometimes up to three times a night." Janam's first production was received with great enthusiasm everywhere they went and quickly the group's membership grew to about 50. Some highly respected theatre people also decided to join Janam. "One very talented singer came who has now become a famous television and film star. Bunod Natpal was his name. His wife also. She was a well-known critic and theatre director. A young playwright wrote a special play for us called *The Architect of India's Destiny*. The title is drawn from our national anthem. It was an ironic title and dealt with elections. We produced it in September. A famous music director and legendary singer called Mohuno Pritti composed the music. It was a three-hour play. It was written as a well-made play, but Mrs. Natpal, who was the director, brought in the characters of the narrator and the counter-narrator. Her husband was the narrator and I was the counter-narrator. It was a kind of Brechtian device used for comments on the action and through songs we also announced what was going to happen next.

"The play became extremely popular and was very well received by the critics. We started taking it to colleges and working-class areas. We also performed it in parks. In January and February 1974 we did a tour of western Uttar Pradesh during a state election campaign. In some places we had massive audiences. There is a town in western Uttar Pradesh called Amroha. We had gone to perform there only one night and the first night we had an audience of 15,000. We weren't prepared for such a huge crowd. The stage wasn't all that high, you see. People insisted we stay one more night and perform again the next day. So we decided to stay one more day and build a higher stage. Now something very interesting happened. We advertised our play by putting a loudspeaker and a microphone in a rickshaw going around the city announcing that tonight at such and such a time and place a play would be performed. It was a town of around 100,000 and we had sent three rickshaws around. Now it so happened that an extreme rightwing political party had also put their rickshaws out into the streets to tell people not to go see the play because it was obscene and was sponsored by these Communists who had brought prostitutes from Delhi to dance. When we heard that we told our rickshaws not to bother anymore because we knew the people were going to come anyway. We ended up having about 35,000 people watching the show. It was impossible. Although we had raised the stage, people couldn't watch it from that far away. People would push from the rear trying to come to the front and waves of people would be pushed against the stage. Suddenly 200 of them would be pushed onto the platform. It was an intolerable situation. At that moment something unique happened.

"Bunod Natpal, the singer, used to be quite fond of a few drinks and every night he would get slightly tipsy. We were traveling in a bus and the driver would buy country liquor every once in a while. He would add salt to it so it would get more potent. That night Bunod must have consumed at least half a bottle. He was totally pissed out. So with all this commotion we couldn't start the play and Bunod was lying in the bus. He had said that he was not in a position to perform. He is a very tall man, about six foot two. Very handsome. Very strongly built. So I went to him and woke him up inside the bus, which was parked right behind the stage. I said, 'You have to go on stage now.' He entered wearing a traditional Indian dress, you know, those loose tunics and trousers. He also wore a big shawl round him. I told him to sing whatever he wanted to sing. He started humming something classical which usually is not appreciated by the people. He took a very heroic posture and we pressed the chords for him on the harmonium. Then, to that classical tune, he started singing lyrics by Fez, the revolutionary poet.

"There is a classical way of singing in India which requires you to just sing the notes before you come to the actual words. This is called *alak*. He sang those notes for about 15 minutes. Just abstract sounds. It was as if a spell had been cast on these 35,000 people, many of them women and children. There had been total pandemonium before and now total silence. When he saw that, he couldn't stop the notes. He was an artist you know and he could sense the magic of his song. So he sang for 35 minutes standing in the middle of the stage and swaying from side to side because he was still tipsy. There was a pin-drop silence. When he finished singing the audience went on clapping for a long time. Then we started our play and it went on uninterrupted until well into the morning."

The play in question is set in a small rural constituency where two people, representing two different parties, are pitted against each other in the election. One of them is a capitalist, the other a big landlord. They wage a cut-throat election campaign. The ordinary people do not know whom to vote for because both of the candidates are exploiters. Eventually they decide to enter a candidate of their own, an ordinary cobbler. He represents the lowest of the casts, the *harijans* or untouchables. People start responding to his candidacy and flock to his meetings. This development jeopardizes the candidacy of the two others who, fearing they may lose, resolve to join forces behind the people's backs. They hire assassins who murder the cobbler. The play ends on a note of defeat with the two narrators singing a song about how the struggle continues and how the play was intended to expose who the real enemies are.

Street Theatre During the Emergency

Since the Uttar Pradesh elections of 1974, Janam has been punctuating landmark political events with new theatrical creations. The events preceding the declaration of the State of Emergency in June 1975 propelled the group into street theatre. On 12 June of that year the High Court in Alahabad proclaimed that Indira Ghandi had used unfair means to win her election, that she should vacate her seat in parliament, and that, consequently, she also should resign as Prime Minister. She refused and appealed to the Supreme Court which, 13 days later, overruled the Alahabad judgment. The next day, Ghandi declared the State of Emergency and arrested all her political opponents. India was turned into a virtual police state for the 18 months that followed. "When she refused to resign," recalls Safdar Hashmi, "we got the idea to write a small skit called *Kursi, Kursi, Kursi* [*Chair, Chair, Chair*]. It's about this elected king who is sitting on a chair when a new king is elected. He gets up from his chair but the chair rises with him and no matter how hard they try to separate the king from his chair, it is impossible. We had built some dialog around this simple gag. We performed it outside on the Boat Club Lawns, which was the hub of all political activity at that time. All the political parties would hold their rallies there during lunch hour. It is the area where all government employees work, about 150,000 of them. We would go under the shade of a tree and start playing our skit. Within seconds, thousands of people would gather. The skit grew every day. We would add new things. And after the performance people would come to us and say, 'You could do this and talk about that also.' We performed it for about a week. That was our real initiation to street theatre."

During the Emergency, Janam was forced into inactivity. Safdar Hashmi left New Delhi to teach English at Kashmir University. He returned in the fall of 1978 and reactivated the troupe. But their traditional outlet, the trade unions, had been totally destroyed by the Emergency. They had no funds to pay for even a modest production. Lacking the confidence to write their own texts, the troupe was at a loss as to how to continue. An older leader of CPI(M) inspired the solution, explains Safdar. "He told me about an incident that had just happened outside Delhi in an industrial town. There is a chemical factory there called Herig-India where the workers didn't have a union. They had two very ordinary demands, which you can't even call economic demands, really. Workers came from 15–20 kilometers away to work. They wanted a place where they could park their bicycles and a canteen where they could get a cup of tea and heat up their food during recess. The management wasn't willing even to grant these basic demands. So the workers went on strike.

"The Janatha Party had just come to power and people were still very uptight about police brutality against striking workers during the Emergency. So the new Janatha government was not yet willing to resort to such actions, although later they proved to be just as antiworker and antipeasant as the Indira Ghandi government. The industrialist, unable to count on the police, hired gangs of antisocial elements from the area, gave them arms and uniforms, and made them into guards. So when the workers went on strike, the guards opened fire, killing six workers. When I heard this story I decided to write a play about it."

Machine

"A friend and I sat down one night to write and practically on its own something started to emerge. We created the dialogs almost naturally. Both of us had some talent in writing rhyming dialog. Soon the image of a machine was born. We wanted to use it as a metaphor for the system. The different components of the machine would be the worker, the guard, and the owner. Each one of them would talk about their relationship to the machine. We would then show how together they made the machine work and how this collaboration was experienced differently by the worker, the guard, and the owner."

I saw *Machine* three times. The first time was at six in the morning on May Day 1988 before a large gathering of night-shift workers from a small steel factory in an industrial area of Delhi. The second time was at eleven in the morning of that same day in front of a soft drink bottling plant downtown. The third time I saw the play, at ten in the evening of 2 May, it was rudely interrupted by a well-organized gang of right-wing hooligans who created so much noise and commotion that the actors could not make themselves heard. Hashmi told me afterwards that harassments of this kind happened regularly and that they had also been violently assaulted on occasion.

The short play starts when five people dressed in black enter the circular space left open by the audience seated on the ground. The five actors represent three workers, a guard, and the owner. Together they form a machine in motion, making all kinds of hissing and peeping sounds. Then the narrator (Hashmi) comes in and addresses the audience for a few minutes. When he is finished, the sounds of the machine become audible again. Suddenly the machine comes to a stop. The narrator says, "What has happened? The machine has stopped. This is a first-rate crisis! Why has it

3. The factory owner explains his position in Machine, *Janam's legendary piece that was first performed in 1978. (Photo by Eugène van Erven)*

stopped? Can someone tell me?" One of the machine's components liberates himself and says, "I have stopped it. I could not tolerate it any longer." He is a worker. He talks about how he feels exploited by the machine. He works for the machine, for the owner, and is oppressed by the guard but gets nothing in return. After he returns to his place in the machine, the owner steps forward, and then the guard. The machine starts up again as arms and legs begin to rotate. The narrator starts to speak but is suddenly interrupted by an explosion in the machine. The components fall to the ground. The three workers get up and start making demands. They want a cycle stand and a canteen. They also explain that the owner has refused their simple demands and that the guard has threatened them. They decide to go on strike and shout *"Inkalab Indawat"*, which means, "Long live the Revolution!" This time the guard fires on them and kills the workers. As they lie on the floor the narrator pronounces a final speech: "No matter how many bullets you pump into us, the workers are not going to be defeated. They will rise again." On this cue the workers rise and surround the terrified owner and guard in slow motion. The narrator continues: "The workers have always advanced. No one can stop them." The end comes with the workers, the guard, the owner, and the narrator forming a back-to-back circle, singing a revolutionary song.

Over the years *Machine* has become legendary in India's working-class circles. During the performances that I witnessed some of the workers in the audience apparently knew the text so well that they whispered along with the dialog, adding a ritualistic quality to the event. The 1978 premiere of the play coincided with the announcement of a new industrial relations bill that allowed local governments to apply preventive arrests of labor leaders during looming strikes. To coordinate the protests, on 19 Novem-

4. The final song of Machine *as performed on 1 May 1988. After the 1978 premiere at a trade union rally, union members jumped the rails and lifted the performers to their shoulders. (Photo by Eugène van Erven)*

ber 1978 an All-India trade union meeting was held in New Delhi's Talkatora stadium and more than 7,000 trade union delegates attended. The next day a mass rally of 200,000 workers was scheduled to take place at the Boat Club. This was, of course, a golden opportunity for Janam to premiere *Machine*. "We went to the stadium early in the morning and we pleaded and pleaded with the organizers to allow us to present our play to them," Hashmi grins. "But they couldn't see what a play had to do with a serious trade union session. We kept on pestering them. They didn't even know us. We stayed until evening. Finally they got sick and tired of us and told us we could perform it after the final resolutions and slogans had been passed. 'We are not even going to make an announcement. If you can do it on your own you can go ahead,' they said.

"The way the stadium was built helped us. It's an arena. There is a big basketball court in the center with seats all around. The delegates were all sitting on one side and the leaders were speaking from a rostrum on the other side. We were all wearing black tunics and blue trousers. We were five men and one woman, my wife. The moment the final slogans had died down and people were beginning to file out of the stadium, imagine these six strange people in black running to the middle of the court and quickly mounting a human machine with loud hissing, rhythmic sounds. People turned around to watch what the hell was happening. Normally we run the machine for 20 seconds at the most but since there was a lot of noise in the hall we went on running it for two minutes. We had to do it at a very high pitch so we were exhausted after that. You see, the nearest person in the audience was at least 60 feet away from us. Then they finally became silent. I gave a signal to stop the machine and started speaking.

"It was an incredible success. After we sang the final song, the trade union delegates jumped over the rails. The leaders were like kids. They lifted us on their shoulders. We became the heros. People took our autographs on cigarette packets. And they invited us to come and perform during the rally the next day."

The next day Janam performed *Machine* at the Boat Club for an estimated 160,000 workers. "A month after the rally we started getting reports from all around the country that people were performing *Machine* there. Many people who had been at the rally had taken tape recordings of the play back to their people and had reconstructed it in their own languages. All the leaders of the leftist movement in Delhi were also at the rally. They saw that this was something that really inspired workers. Immediately we were flooded with invitations. We started going to the working-class areas and we received a tremendous response wherever we went. The workers absolutely love this play."

Since 1978 Janam has made approximately 20 other street plays on a variety of political topics. *Gaon Se Shahar Tak* (*From Village to City,* 1978) deals with a small-time farmer who loses his plot of land and is forced to become an industrial worker in the city. *Hatyare* (*Killers,* 1979) tackles the problem of communalism, the Indian term for religiously based, violent clashes between Hindus, Muslims, and Sikhs. *DTC Ki Dhandhli* (*The Strategems of DTC,* 1979) was specifically designed to mobilize a mass protest against a 100-percent price hike by the Delhi Transport Corporation (DTC) in February 1979. The agitprop play succeeded in attracting large crowds which moved with the actors from one performing site to another. *Aurat* (*Woman,* 1979) is one of the first plays to deal openly with issues like bride burning, dowry, and wife battery. *Tin Crore* (*30 Million,* 1979) is about the ever-increasing army of the unemployed in India.

Apharan Bhaichare Ka (*Wake Up Oh Brave,* October 1986) is about the complex problem of the Punjab and the Sikh extremists. Safdar Hashmi has his own historical reading of it. "In 1978 there was a parliamentary by-election in Punjab. Mrs. Binder, the wife of a hated police commissioner, was the Congress(I) candidate. At that time an unknown holy man of the Sikhs, Bindranwale Singh, was inducted into the Congress(I) to be the election agent of Mrs. Binder. He was a nonentity in Sikh politics at that time.

"The Akali Party has been dominating Punjabi politics since the 1920s. At that time they had waged a glorious struggle against the British imperialists. The party is very strongly entrenched amongst the Punjabi peasantry, which is largely Sikh. It played a very healthy role during the struggle for independence. During the Emergency, it fought very bravely against Indira Ghandi. But the party is based on religion and from the very beginning it has harbored seeds of communalism. They talk in terms of Sikh nationhood based on religious ideas, not on Punjabi cultural identity.

"Congress(I) has been trying to break Akali's hold on Punjab since time immemorial. In 1978 the Congress(I) started playing a very dirty trick. They built up Bindranwale as an alternative leader of the Sikhs. They started playing the communal card. Bindranwale took a very militant communal Sikh posture against Hindus and Akalis. He built a private army of his own. He carried arms and killed people. He even came to Delhi and moved around with armed bandits. Once he was arrested for alleged involvement in a murder but within hours he was released through intervention of the central government. Now the imperialists don't sleep, you see. They saw their chance to penetrate Bindranwale's following and once he started receiving aid from the States via Pakistan he began to get free from Indira Ghandi. The paper tiger that Congress(I) had created started roaring for real and thus became a danger to Indira Ghandi. By this time a schism had already been created in Punjab and the whole social fabric had been communalized. Indiscriminate killings of the Hindus had already started by then. And Hindu fundamentalists started retaliating down here in Delhi by first building up a hate-campaign against Sikhs followed by sporadic attacks. Then came the Indira Ghandi assassination on 31 October 1984.

"We see the assassination as the handiwork of the Americans. Afterwards there was organized and orchestrated violence against the Sikhs. Within three days more than 8,000 Sikhs were killed—3,000 in Delhi alone. We saw it with our own eyes. People were dragged out of buses and thrown into fires, lynched, torn apart. The police stood by and even participated in the killing, the looting, and the burning. The army was brought out in the afternoon of 1 November and for three days curfew was declared but never enforced. The army moved around and stood by, watching the killings. Rajiv Ghandi allowed all this to happen. And later, during a mass rally in Delhi, he even justified it by saying, 'If a big tree falls, some of the earth will always be unsettled as well.' "

Operation Blue Star, the attack on Amritsar's Golden Temple complex on 5 June 1984, resulted in an enormous bloodbath in which Bindranwale was killed along with several hundreds of his followers. But Rajiv Ghandi's Congress(I) Party has not learned from their previous mistakes, claims Hashmi. "They're still playing the communal card and hobnobbing with the extremists. They have recently released five top extremists. At the ground level in Punjab, each of the Congress(I) leaders is involved either with a Hindu communal organization or with the Sikh extremists. They are playing lethal games with our country, you see. The extremists are very well entrenched with the people and that's why they are able to escape from the police. In many places they are running their own parallel government. They are getting arms by the thousands from across the Pakistani border, which in turn come from the Afghan Mujahidin, who get them from the United States. Now that the Afghan settlement has come, these arms are going to come in a much bigger way."

According to Safdar Hashmi, similar trouble is in store for Kashmir and other border regions. "The Afghan arms are also surfacing in Darjeeling, in the Gurkaland agitation. Through Sikkim and Nepal all these things are going on. It's a great danger to our country. Today the unity and integrity of our country is the most important problem which we have to address. The Communists are the only people in Punjab who are fighting the extremists. Many of them have already given their lives."

Apharan Bhaichare Ka uses the device of a magician's street show. A boy lies down in the middle of the acting area. A black cloth is placed over his head and the magician tests the boy's ability by making him identify objects in the magician's hand. The first thing he takes is a pigeon. The boy guesses correctly and the magician continues: "Good, but what is the pigeon holding in his beak?"

BOY: A bulletproof jacket.

MAGICIAN: Why would he be holding a bulletproof jacket?

BOY: Well, because the government cannot protect the life and property of the ordinary people, everyone has to make his own arrangements.

MAGICIAN: So why don't you have one?

BOY: Poor people like me, our lives wouldn't be safe with bulletproof vests. We die of hunger in any case. We need hungerproof jackets. (*He points to the crowd.*) But what are all those people doing here anyway?

MAGICIAN: They have come to file an F.I.R. [*F.I.R. is a so-called "First Instance Report." When something is stolen, one goes and files an F.I.R. at the police station.*]

BOY: What for?

MAGICIAN: Well, you see, their Brotherhood has been abducted. Can you go look for it?

The boy goes in search of Brotherhood and meets a person dressed half as a circus ringmaster and half as Uncle Sam. Uncle Sam introduces himself as the executive president of the World Wildlife Fund and manager of the Great American Circus. The boy asks him what he wants from India. Uncle Sam answers that he is looking for "Sam Prodi Acta," which he pronounces with a heavy American accent. The boy gets scared and responds: "I hope you don't mean *samprodayacta?*"—the Hindi word for communalism. Uncle Sam: "Yes I am, son." The boy then replies that the government has just proclaimed samprodayacta as India's national animal and has placed it in a sanctuary. Uncle Sam states he wants to catch it anyway in order to introduce some World Wildlife Fund measures for its protection. He leaves to get the permission of the Home Minister. As he exits, a Sikh extremist, a Muslim fundamentalist, and a Hindu communalist enter. They are spewing their poison as Brotherhood comes onstage. He wants to stop them. Brotherhood sings about unity but in the middle of his song the three fanatics attack him and throw him on the floor.

Meanwhile the magician has become worried about his boy and he goes looking for him. When he finds him he asks if he has found what he was looking for. The boy, thinking he is referring to Uncle Sam, answers that he has gone to see the minister. The magician gets angry and tells him, "I never told you to help the bloody Americans! Go look for Brotherhood!" So he goes off again and eventually finds the injured Brotherhood lying on the floor. He wakes him up and asks him who he is and what has happened to him. In reply, Brotherhood yells at the boy, who becomes a symbol of the people: "I am ashamed of you. Don't you even recognize your own Brotherhood? I am the one whom you people fought for against the Britishers. You don't recognize me? Who has made you so blind?" "They have," the boy replies, pointing to the three fanatics. He wants to attack them but he is easily defeated. The three extremists capture Brotherhood and take him away.

As the three fanatics take Brotherhood away through the audience, the injured boy reenters the circle. Weeping, he tells the magician that Brotherhood has been captured by the three extremists and the Great American Circus. Then the magician addresses the audience: "So, now you know where your Brotherhood is. Let us go and liberate him. Come on!" But of course the people do not move. The boy and the magician leave. During the final scene of the play, Brotherhood enters. He is held captive by the four villains and sings an appeal to the people: "You better come and liberate me, otherwise this will be the end of this country." The play ends on a very despondent note, exhorting the people to fight for the integrity and unity of their nation.

Janam has been playing for the Indian working class for over 15 years now. Its oldest member is 48, the others are well into their thirties. Apart from Safdar Hashmi who makes a living as a freelance writer, there is an office clerk, a printer, and a schoolteacher. But the pressure of livelihood and family is beginning to tell on the actors. "Ten years ago when we started none of us were married. Now all of us are married. Many of us have children who are growing up. Our parents have retired. We have become the only earning members in the family. All these domestic pressures are there. Take Manish. He is one of our finest actors. Both his parents are over 75. His wife is always ill. He has two little children. He is running a small printing press which is not doing well. He is surrounded by 1,001 problems. He wants to give time to Janam but he can't and there is this constant sense of guilt." Some of Janam's actors are among the finest in the capital. There have been offers from television and cinema. So far they have refused. But Hashmi realizes that his group must become professional or perish and he has been thinking of establishing a workers' cultural center of which Janam would become the resident repertory company.

The People's Theatre Institute

To realize this dream many hundreds of thousands of rupees will be needed. Hashmi calculates that it will cost between 25 and 30,000 rupees just to pay minimum salaries to ten actors. He has been thinking of writing for the cinema for a few years to save money with which to start a trust fund. "With that trust fund," he explains enthusiastically, "I could set up a video production business or something that could generate 40 or 50,000 rupees a month. We have built in certain safeguards, of course. The trust will be set up even before a penny comes in. No money will come in my name but only in the name of the trust. Seven people are going to have control over the money in the trust. I will become an employee of the trust and I will receive a salary of 2,500 rupees a month provided I earn at least twice as much for the trust. If I don't, then I don't get anything. I come from a very poor background. If I see 200,000 rupees I may just lose my balance. The idea is that we buy a plot of land with that money in a working-class district of Delhi and construct a simple building there without a fixed stage or anything but where we could have proscenium or theatre in the round or whatever we wanted and which could also serve as a studio so that it could go on generating money. There we could have a repertory of 10 or 12 professional actors who would do nothing but theatre, training ourselves. You see, we have become rusty. We have been performing so much that we have not been able to learn. Some of us were talented 10 years ago. To some extent we have been able to develop that. But theatre has advanced a great deal since then. We are feeling the need to learn so many new things."

Hashmi wants to establish the institute and the repertory in an area with about 200,000 workers. His idea is to perform two or three nights a week in the institute, offering other things besides the agitprop theatre Janam is doing now. He dreams of producing Shakespeare, Gorky, Chekhov, and Tolstoy for the workers to compensate for the third-rate Bombay films and television programs that constitute their regular cultural fare. But he is also aware that Janam needs to expand into some kind of a people's theatre movement. "I dream of making our future institute into a training center for groups like ours who could come to us from different parts of the country. We could arrange for their board and lodging and organize a 15-day workshop. During three months of the year we could also tour the country. But right now it seems a farfetched dream. To start it we would need about 2,000,000 rupees. The whole thing would cost about 4,000,000 rupees. I don't know where we are going to get hold of this money but we are going to try. The members of Janam have given me three years to try and raise it. If I can raise half a million rupees through work in cinema and television, even if I will have to give up working in theatre for a year-and-a-half, I will still do it. But only if I am confident the group can run without me."

Dusty Delhi had become a much more pleasant place with the knowledge that such friendly, smiling, gentle people as Hashmi lived there. Suddenly I was also much more hopeful about the future of India's divided art movement. Young, energetic, bright, and charming, Hashmi seemed to possess the qualities and the vision to pull it all together. But then, in the second week of January 1989, an ominous missive arrived from Moloyashree Hashmi, Safdar's wife.

In the early afternoon of 1 January 1989, Janam was performing Safdar Hashmi's latest play *Halla Bol* (*Attack!*) for workers in Jhandapur, an industrial town east of Delhi. The play dealt with government repression of the labor movement. Janam had been performing *Halla Bol* to support CPI(M) in its local election campaign. In the middle of the performance Mukesh Sharma, a right-wing political candidate backed by the Congress(I) Party, arrived on the scene. He was surrounded by nearly 100 hired goons armed with heavy bamboo sticks and guns. They ordered the performance to be stopped. When Janam refused and the audience started protesting, Sharma's gang launched a violent attack. An eyewitness saw Sharma shoot dead a Nepali migrant worker at point blank range. The crowd dispersed in a panic. Janam, including three recently recruited young women, ran for its life to the nearby Trade Union Office where

5. *Safdar Hashmi narrates in* Machine. *He was beaten to death at a performance of* Halla Bol (Attack!) *on 1 January 1989 by right-wing political candidate Mukesh Sharma and his gang. (Photo by Eugène van Erven)*

they barricaded themselves behind an iron gate. "In order to give us time to escape over the back wall," writes Moloyashree, "Safdar held the door closed as long as he could. It was inevitable that Safdar bore the entire brunt of the attack. The goons dragged his body through the streets back to the performance site and killed him there with innumerable blows to the head. It was obvious that the thugs wanted to kill—there was not a scratch on the rest of Safdar's body." According to newspaper and magazine reports Hashmi folded his hands in humble greeting when the murderers broke through the gate. Despite his peaceful surrender they beat his head—the source of all his versatile creativity—to pulp with bricks and bamboo sticks. The police never showed.

On 4 January Janam, including Safdar's widow, returned to the scene of the crime to complete their performance of *Halla Bol,* the title now laden with added emotional and symbolic significance. Thousands upon thousands had come from Delhi to mourn the deaths of Safdar Hashmi and Ram Bahadur, the slain worker. On 9 January Safdar's songs and plays were performed all over India during a massive National Day of Protest which, for the first time in recent history, united all progressive artists behind one single issue. In a statement read at the opening ceremony of the Bombay International Film Festival, famous film star Shabana Azmi directly implicated Rajiv Ghandi's Congress(I) in Safdar Hashmi's murder. Artists all over the country canceled their shows and joined protest rallies. In Calcutta, film and theatre personalities like Utpal Dutt and Arun Mukherjee joined a large gathering at Chowringhee. Safdar Hashmi's violent death provides ample evidence that, despite India's claim that it is the world's largest democracy, freedom of expression continues to be a questionable right. Even though Janam may not have been ready for Safdar Hashmi's untimely departure, the troupe has vowed to go on without him. Meanwhile there are signs that his death may rally other progressive Indian artists, which could well lead to the realization of Hashmi's vision—a truly people-oriented Indian cultural movement.

Note

1. All quotes attributed to Safdar Hashmi are from interviews with the author conducted in New Delhi on 29 April and 3 May 1988.

Eugène van Erven *is a University Lecturer in American Studies at the University of Utrecht. He is the author of* Radical People's Theatre *(Indiana University Press, 1988) and is a frequent contributor to* New Theatre Quarterly, Minnesota Review, *and* TDR *(T114 and T119). His current book-in-progress is* The Playful Revolution: Theatre and Liberation in Asia and the South Pacific. *He was the European producer of* Cry of Asia!, *a multimedia theatre show involving 17 artists from 13 different Asian countries that had its premiere at the Avignon Theatre Festival in July 1989 and then toured through Great Britain, West Germany, Austria, and the Netherlands.*

"Theatre of Roots"

Encounter with Tradition

Suresh Awasthi

I am taking the risk of giving a label—"theatre of roots"—to the unconventional theatre which has been evolving for some two decades in India as a result of modern theatre's encounter with tradition. Theatre of roots has finally made its presence felt. It has compelling power, it thrills audiences, and it is receiving institutional recognition. It is deeply rooted in regional theatrical culture, but cuts across linguistic barriers, and has an all-India character in design. Never before during the past century and more has theatre been practiced in such diversified form, and at the same time with such unity in essential theatrical values.

Apart from giving a label, I would also like to admit my "guilt" (my friend, director Shyamanand Jalan, talking about this new theatre, calls me the "guilty" man) for raising the question of relevance of traditional performance for contemporary theatre in a national seminar in 1961 which I organized as the general secretary of the Indian Center of the International Theatre Institute (ITI).

As part of the great cultural renaissance of the post-Independence period, there has been a most meaningful encounter with tradition in various fields of creative activity. The return to and discovery of tradition is inspired by a search for roots and a quest for identity. This is part of the whole process of decolonization of lifestyle, social institutions, creative forms, and cultural modes.

The modern Indian theatre, a product of colonial culture, felt an intense need to search for roots to counteract its violent dislocation from tradition. Directors like B.V. Karanth, K.N. Panikkar, and Ratan Thiyam have had meaningful encounters with tradition and, with their work, have reversed the colonial course of contemporary theatre, putting it back on the track of the great *Natyasastra* tradition.[1] It sounds paradoxical, but their theatre is both avant-garde in the context of conventional realistic theatre, and part of the 2,000-year-old *Natyasastra* tradition. *Natyasastra*'s survival is strikingly marked in the art of the actor, in the use of music and dance in realizing the performance text, in a whole set of conventions for treating time and space, and in the overall design and structure of a performance.

In this context it is of interest to note that the search for roots, the liberation from Western realistic theatre, and the emergence of a new thea-

1. Theatre of roots: liberation from Western realistic theatre. Pictured is director Balwant Thakur's production of Baba Jittoo. *(Photo courtesy of Sangeet Natak Akademi)*

tre is an Asian phenomenon. Also, the processes of this phenomenon and artistic features of the new theatre have a common pan-Asian character. It is regrettable that this newly emergent Asian theatre remains largely unnoticed in the Western world except for the work of a few Japanese directors, such as the late Terayama and Suzuki Tadashi. Roughly during the same period many directors in Sri Lanka, Indonesia, South Korea, Japan, and more recently China, discarded the realistic mode of theatre, and by utilizing the rich theatrical heritage of their respective countries, evolved a style in tune with indigenous values and aesthetics. It is also significant that the theatre of roots in Asia has emerged at a time when the avant-garde theatre in the West inspired by Asian theatrical traditions and values has declined.

In the mid-'50s the noted director Habib Tanvir broke away from realistic theatre and started on a journey in search of roots. With his two productions—*Mitti Ki Gadi* (1954), a popular operatic version of the Sanskrit classic *Mrichchhakatikam* (*The Toy Cart*) and *Agra Bazar* (1954), his own unconventional play on the life and poetic works of the popular 19th-century Urdu poet Nazir of Agra—Tanvir brought music and poetry back to the theatre, and a traditional sense of gaiety and celebration. He continues to work with a group of brilliant folk performers, synthesizing folk and modern theatrical traditions. Girish Karnad's famous *Hayavadana,* inspired by the yakshagana of Karnataka, begins with the prayer "Jai Gajavadane"—"Victory to Ganesha," the elephant-headed god—and its innovative and improvisatory production in 1972 by B.V. Karanth with music, mime, and movements heralded the return of Lord Ganesha, the presiding deity of traditional theatre. With this event, we might say, contemporary theatre began its encounter with tradition.

Working as general secretary with the Sangeet Natak Akademi, the national academy of music, dance, and drama (1965–75), I launched a program sponsoring traditional performances, festivals, and exhibitions in Delhi and other cities all over the country. Initially, there were whispering voices of disapproval from cultural elitists and an attitude of indifference from theatre artists. But gradually the program acquired the character of a movement. A whole generation of theatre artists was exposed to the richness and vitality of traditional theatre. By the early '70s, many started changing their attitudes and got creatively involved.

I remained concerned with this question, and in 1971, while still working with the Akademi, I organized the National Roundtable on Contemporary Relevance of Traditional Theatre. In the very formulation of the theme for the roundtable, the question of contemporary relevance was emphasized. Directors, playwrights, actors, and theatre critics from all over the country attended. It provided them with a forum for exchanging ideas and experiences, and discussing the nature and process of the new theatre. It also served as reassurance, and the new theatre moved ahead with greater confidence and vigor. In any discussion of the encounter with tradition and the resultant theatre of roots, two events—the national seminar of 1961 and the roundtable of 1971—will always remain points of reference.

Aesthetically, the theatre of roots must be seen against the backdrop of the past century of Western realistic theatre as practiced in India. The models and conventions of realistic theatre were borrowed, and always remained alien to Indian theatre. The inherent conflict between the two could never be resolved. A creative visionary like Rabindramath Tagore understood the nature of this conflict. He tried to resolve it in his lyric plays by synthesizing the two opposed dramatic traditions. But he failed to evolve an indigenous nonrealistic style of production. The theatrical power of Tagore's plays could be revealed only in the mid-'50s by Sombhu Mitra in his productions of such plays as *Rakta-Karabi* (*Red Oleanders*) and *Raja* (*King of the Dark Chamber*).

Of the several factors important for an understanding of the aesthetics of the theatre of roots, none supersedes the rejection of the proscenium theatre by most of the directors and their use of a variety of performance spaces. This innovation allows the dramatic text to find and create an environment appropriate to it, brings about a closer relationship between the actor and spectator, and affords a new perception of the performance by the spectators. The first feeble efforts to liberate the actor from the inhibiting influence of proscenium theatres were made by violating their conventions even while performing in them. Actors entered and exited through the auditorium, sat in the auditorium and spoke their lines, or enacted entire scenes there, such as processional and crowd scenes.

It is paradoxical that in a theatrical tradition which provides a great variety of spaces—temple precincts, fields, streets, and market squares—the modern theatre that arose during the mid-19th century chose for itself the proscenium theatre. The first proscenium theatres were built in Bombay and Calcutta in the 1860s, nearly 300 years after England's first proscenium theatre (1576). So it took three centuries and colonialism for the proscenium to find a place in India. But when it came, it totally changed the traditional concept and character of theatrical space, from the points of view of both actor and spectator. It brought about separation between the two, critically affecting their traditional intimate relationship. It also forced spectators to view performances frontally from a fixed seat and a fixed angle. Traditionally Indian audiences have watched performances from different angles and levels, having a constantly changing perception of the performance. Even temple sculpture is designed to be seen while moving, a practice conventionalized by the rite of *pradakshina,* circumambulation of the temple.

Some 40 years ago directors started using both closed and open spaces in preference to the proscenium theatre. E. Alkazi used his terrace in Bombay as a performance space in the late '50s. In the early '60s after moving to Delhi as director of the National School of Drama, he used a variety of spaces—from the school's small closed Studio Theatre to the open-air Meghdoot Theatre, and also unusual environmental spaces with ramparts, gates, and multilevel platforms at the sites of historical monuments, such as Firozshah Kotala and Purana Qila, Delhi's Old Fort. This also, perhaps, happened because the school never had a proscenium theatre. Badal Sircar has now been using ordinary halls and public parks for nearly 15 years, manipulating spaces to create a variety of spatial relationships between the actors and spectators. In recent years, a number of other directors have used a variety of open spaces to suit their production designs. They fully realize the importance of space in shaping a performance, and the role the spectators play in such neutral and informal spaces.

Theatre does not simply occur in available space. It creates its own space, and alters what is already there. Performers and spectators separately and also jointly contribute to the transformation of space, creating a variety of spatial configurations during the course of the performance. The character of the performance, the physical setting, and the placing of the spectators in relation to the performance space all have a role to play in shaping and determining theatrical space. But the main determinant is the presence of the actor. A given space acquires new forms and changes dimensions according to how the actors use space. In the traditional environmental theatre of the Ramlila, the entire space is animated and transformed in endless ways by the performers moving through it, and by the spectators occupying their own and the performers' spaces.[2] In such a situation, the border between the two spaces is constantly blurred, and this has a magical effect on theatrical communication.

Stylization is the essence of the theatre of roots. After breaking away from the realistic mode in its search for roots, the new theatre embraced stylization—the hallmark of Indian traditional theatre for centuries. The stylized approach to theatre brought about a revolutionary change in the art and techniques of the actor, and in the entire process of transforming the dramatic text into performance text. So the theatre of roots developed its aesthetics by using informal performance spaces, providing a new perception of the performance, and evolving a whole scheme of stylization covering various aspects and elements of performance.

It is ironic that although the director of the theatre of roots is mainly concerned with treating the text in theatrical terms and transforming it into performance text, s/he is often accused of infidelity to and suppression of the text. True, the treatment of text and its transformation into performance in the new theatre is totally different from that in realistic theatre. Theatre of roots uses music, chants, verbal sounds, and rhythmic syllables (*bols*) to multiply the staging signs and maximize their impact. In realistic theatre, the number of staging signs is kept low, their impact minimized. This is intended to preserve the integrity of the verbal signs, and is taken as fidelity to text. Because of the multiplication of staging signs, plays such as Bhasa's *Urubhangam* (*Broken Thigh*), *Madhyama Vyayoga* (*The Play of the Middle One*), and *Karna-Bhar* (*Karna's Burden*) take four times longer to perform than to read. The difference in the reading-time/performing-time ratio between realistic theatre and the theatre of roots is obvious.

In the theatre of roots the approach to and treatment of dramatic text is the primary factor in the conception and design of productions. All materi-

2. Stylization is the essence of the theatre of roots, as demonstrated by performers in Mudrarakshasam, *directed by Jos Chiramel. (Photo courtesy of Sangeet Natak Akademi)*

als and tools used are chosen to realize the dramatic text. It is this concern which brings into use the elements and conventions of a variety of traditional performance forms. It is not the other way round. The observation that directors of the theatre of roots use certain "elements" from traditional forms is both superficial and misleading.

The transformation of dramatic text into performance text has been the primary concern of Indian performance theory. Even the *rasa* theory in its essence as formulated by Bharata in the *Natyasastra* has a strong performance orientation. It takes into account the performer-spectator interaction and their reciprocal relationship. Performance aesthetics even provides a separate word for it. Drama as text is *drishya-kavya,* "visual poetry," and as performance it is *prayoga,* meaning "skillfully arranged." Each performance text is a new avatar of the dramatic text. It has its own laws and its own semantic world. Theatrical practice has also been concerned with this same problem—how to fashion the performance text. The factors involved in realizing the performance text are the highly evolved and codified art of the actor, theatrical space and its conventions, the scheme of stylization, and a whole set of stage conventions.

Because of the stylized character of the productions and the developed art of the actor, it is often said that directors of the theatre of roots are obsessed with form, that form dominates and suppresses the content of their plays. Having practiced realistic, nonstylized theatre for over a century, we seem to forget that the Indian theatrical tradition, both in theory and practice, has been greatly concerned with form: but form which is integral to content, not imposed on it; form that is primarily concerned with the art of the actor; and form which illuminates the dramatic text, transforming it into a performance text of plastic, visual images. Kathakali, kutiyattam, and yakshagana show this concern for form and, by implication, for the highly developed art of the actor. It is the same with the theatre of roots. In productions of *Chakravyuha* (*Army Formation*) and *Urubhangam* by Ratan Thiyam, of *Madhyama Vyayoga* and *Karna-Bhar* by K.N. Panikkar, *Barnam Ban* (*Macbeth* in Hindi), and Kalidasa's play *Mala-*

vikagnimitram by B.V. Karanth, the forms that emerge are not oppressive and dominating; they are light, harmonizing with content and illuminating their dramatic texts.

Another charge that is leveled against the theatre of roots is that it encourages the "tyranny of the director." But to the contrary, overemphasis on direction is a product of Western realistic theatre. Directors have acquired greater importance over the years with the elaboration of stagecraft. In the new theatre, various conventional elements of stagecraft have become secondary and their character and function have changed. The director's role has also changed. His or her primary concern is with those elements of a theatical performance which are related to the actor's art. Therefore, in the new theatre the actor has acquired greater importance. The director's task is to bring out the full potential of the actor and thereby realize her or his conception of a production. So rather than the tyranny of the director, it is more the return of the actor after a century of ineffectuality. Some of these productions are so highly stylized and codified that the actor decodes the performance score conceived by the director. This is similar to what happens in traditional performance forms such as kathakali, in which the actor decodes a performance score evolved by the performing tradition.

For these directors, actors' training and preparatory workshops have become more important than conventional rehearsals. Several directors have developed their own methods utilizing warm-up exercises and movement patterns from regional systems of the martial arts, gymnasium, acrobatics, theatrical forms, ritual performances, and oral forms of recitation and chant for training in body, voice, and speech. This again is in line with indigenous theatrical traditions. For kathakali and yakshagana actors there is no such thing as a rehearsal; what they go through is long and rigorous training, and then a preparation before each performance. It is amazing that while in the other performing arts there are fully developed systems of training which we expect musicians and dancers to go through, we have not until recently designed a system for training the modern actor. With the emergence of the new theatre and its trained actors, the amateur untrained actor is fast becoming obsolete. By the year 2000, there will be no place for an untrained actor in Indian theatre.

3. Plays such as Madhyama Vyayoga (The Play of the Middle One), *take four times longer to perform than to read because of the use of music, chants, and stylized movement. The production pictured here was directed by K.N. Panikkar at the 1989 national theatre festival in Delhi. (Photo courtesy of Sangeet Natak Akademi)*

4. A moment in a performance can be frozen into a pose—crystallizing an emotion. Performers in director B. Jayshree's production of Lakshapathi Rajane Kathe *strike a tableau with swords and steeds. (Photo courtesy of Sangeet Natak Akademi)*

An important feature of the new theatre is a sense of physicality which has always been a concern in the Indian theatrical tradition. The *Natyasastra* gives great attention to the discussion of *angikabhinaya,* bodily movements. In forms like kutiyattam, kathakali, and yakshagana, the physicality of the performance and the actor's body language play a vital role. But the text—sung or spoken—is not negated. There is constant tension generated between the actor's body and the dramatic text. A kutiyattam actor speaks 40 to 50 words and then his/her body "speaks" for 40 to 50 minutes, transforming the multiple semantic layers of the verbal text into visual images.

Stylized performance invested with plasticity was the essential feature of classical Sanskrit theatre which developed parallel to the traditions of painting and sculpture. In India there is a long history of mutual exchange between the performing and pictorial traditions. Theatrical forms never ceased to integrate a variety of visual and plastic modes, and the pictorial traditions took from the performing tradition conventions of treating space and organizing narrative. The actor's body attitudes, stylized movements, and the static poses of Sanskrit theatre can be seen not only in theatrical forms like kutiyattam and kathakali, but also in the Ajanta murals and many temple sculptures. The dynamics of carved figures in sculpture reflect a frozen moment in a mobile plastic pageant. In the same way, a given moment in a performance can be frozen into a pose, crystallizing an emotion.

These qualities of the Sanskrit theatrical tradition drew Panikkar, Thiyam, and Karanth to the classics. All of them have made highly stylized and theatrically satisfying productions of Sanskrit plays. During the very first phase of modern theatre in the mid-19th century, interest was awakened in the classics. Kalidasa's renowned *Shakuntala* was produced in translation or adaptation in most of the major Indian languages. This interest in the classics, however, was not inspired by a creative urge or a search for roots. It was more a matter of nationalistic pride and orientalism in reverse gear. *Shakuntala* was received in India with great enthusiasm after its translation into English by William Jones and its glorification as part of the strong wave of orientalism in Europe. It was with the same feelings of romanticism and nostalgia that in 1954 the Sangeet Natak Akademi organized its first Natya Samaroh (national drama festival), inaugurated with a production of *Shakuntala*. That production was in a most decadent Western realistic style totally against the nature and spirit of Sanskrit drama. For all these decades, Sanskrit plays have been produced, both in the original and in translation, in an inappropriate realistic style. Such a "classic" could never become a meaningful part of contemporary theatre activity. It is only during the last ten years or so that productions of some Sanskrit plays have given spectators an authentic and deep theatrical experience. It is also interesting to note that the most significant productions by Panikkar and Thiyam are of plays not by Kalidasa but by Bhasa, discovered only in 1912.

The return to Sanskrit classics has given a sense of tradition to the new theatre and strengthened its values. It is of great interest to note that, in a way, both Panikkar and Thiyam discovered their distinctive production designs by doing Bhasa: Panikkar in the original and Thiyam in Manipuri. These classics preserve the utterances and behavior of a whole era. Their words and images strike many Indians as overwhelmingly pertinent. Their interpretations in these productions give them contemporaneity and relevance; but the pressure to be relevant does not wipe out or annul the sense of history that they preserve. There can be no such thing as relevance of classics objectively determined. Relevance is subjective; it emerges from a particular director's theatrical vision. These productions, however, have been greeted with suspicion by purists, literary scholars, and historians of theatre who often raise the question of "authenticity" in regard to the classics. But authenticity of style is a self-defeating objective. It negates the very purpose of doing a classic, which by its very nature lends itself to different interpretations and approaches in accordance with contemporary tastes and values of theatre practice.

In light of the preliminary aesthetics of the theatre of roots, we will have a quick look at the work of three major directors, noting the distinctive qualities of their styles. B.V. Karanth uses a great variety and range of source material, both for his repertoire of movement and of musical modes. His approach to creating the performance text is to add many staging signs to the written text. He places great emphasis on theatricality in his productions, and his actors perform as if fully conscious of their audience, very much like folk performers do. They are most demonstrative, and also show a strong sense of playfulness. In his *Andher Nagari* (*Unjust Town*), a 19th-century Hindi farce by Bhartendu Harishchandra produced in 1979, the actors not only play *Andher Nagari,* they play at playing *Andher Nagari*. This playfulness is a special trait of most of Karanth's productions. In his version of Kalidasa's *Malavikagnimitram,* a harem comedy, he has two *vidushakas* (participating stage managers) in place of one as in the play. One duplicates the words and gestures of the other in a highly exaggerated manner. Karanth's use of this and other similar devices to achieve a certain degree of exaggeration and distortion of lifelike reality is the key to the aesthetics of his productions.

Karanth's approach to performance is very Brechtian. He seems to have arrived at it because of his childhood theatrical experience in yakshagana, a traditional theatrical form of Karnataka. The yakshagana actor enters the performance arena and the *bhagavata* (reciter of dramatic text) sings his entrance in the third person. Then there follows a brief question-answer sequence between the bhagavata and the actor about the identity of the actor's character. It is only after this that the actor reveals an identity and starts speaking in the first person. The actor maintains this duality throughout the performance, and performs as if "outside the radius of the character," to use an expression of Brecht's. Also, the actor never erases her/his face as a performer to assume the face of the character. Again using Brecht's expression, "he keeps the two faces overlapping."

Karanth uses music in a variety of ways to sustain and enhance the theatricality of a performance. The nature and function of music in Karanth's productions, as in Panikkar's and Thiyam's, are totally different from conventional theatre. Music has acquired the character of theatrical language, and become an autonomous channel of communication along with the dramatic text and movement patterns. In some of their productions, as in Thiyam's *Chakravyuha,* music acquires the character of an independent text with its own semantic world. Musicians use a variety of instruments (often unconventional ones), chants, and *swara* (note) and *tala* (time cycle) patterns integrated with *vachika* (verbal acting) and *angika* (bodily movements).

Music has also become integral to the actors' gait, movements, and physical acting. It accentuates actors' entrances and exits, highlights their gestures, and provides a frame for visual images. Panikkar's actors in his productions of Sanskrit plays make entrances in highly stylized gaits set to a tala; the same tala is taken over and played on drums—*mridangam* and *chenda*. This greatly increases the impact of actors' entrances and their stage presence. In *Madhyama Vyayoga,* the entrances of Bhima and Ghatotkacha to the accompaniment of drums have a tremendous impact and are unique in contemporary theatre. Here also Panikkar follows traditional theatre and *Natyasastra* prescription. In kathakali, the entrances of ferocious and brave characters like Ravana and Hanuman are dramatized and prolonged with the use of a half curtain. The "curtain entrance" as executed by a famous actor in the role of Ravana or Hanuman becomes almost an autonomous unit of performance. Actors' entrances, exits, and movements are so fixed for different types of characters that one can recognize a role-type just by seeing the leg movements, as by seeing the make-up or headdress. It is no wonder that all these directors use a variety of drums. Drums are used all over the country in operatic folk performances as well as in highly developed, codified forms. In many traditional forms, such as ankia nat of Assam or Purulia chhau, elaborate drumming is part of the preliminaries of a performance. It is interesting to note that *nandi* (auspicious verse) according to some scholars also means drum. Nandi is an important element in the preliminaries of Sanskrit theatre.

Panikkar's productions of Sanskrit plays are marked for their sculptural, visual images based on poetic images of the text. Most Sanskrit plays are rich in poetic images meant to be transformed into visual images by the art of the actor. To create visual images Panikkar uses movement patterns from kutiyattam, kathakali, and the Kerala martial art, kalarippayatt. Panikkar achieves a plastic, sculptural quality by extended gestures and freezes. He uses the singsong delivery of kutiyattam, a 1,000-year-old form and the only survivor of the tradition of Sanskrit drama. It is this careful interlocking of vachika and angika which is the most distinctive feature of Panikkar's productions; its roots are in the theatrical traditions of Kerala.

Panikkar explains his production process using classical terminology. He writes the performance score of his productions in the manner of the *attaprakaras* (directors' manuals) of the plays in the repertoire of kutiyattam. These attaprakaras are kept in manuscripts by the families of traditional kutiyattam performers and have been used for centuries in creating performances. Panikkar has brought the *Natyasastra* and its whole tradition up to date.

With his ability to transform the poetic images of a text into visual images infused with great dramatic power, Panikkar has made a unique contribution to the production of Sanskrit plays. One can see how he dramatizes the descriptive verses of Sanskrit plays and converts them into visual images in his *Madhyama Vyayoga* in the confrontation scene between Bhima and Ghatotkacha. In one of the verses, as Ghatotkacha vividly describes Bhima's appearance, Bhima dramatizes it and translates it into visual forms, image by image. Similarly, when Bhima delivers the verse describing Ghatotkacha, the latter transforms it into visual images. Such treatment of vachika and its relationship to angika is a strong Indian theatrical tradition. It is amazing that for decades Sanskrit plays were considered unfit for theatre because of these descriptive verses. Panikkar has revealed the theatricality inherent in them.

Ratan Thiyam often writes his own plays based on Manipuri myths and legends, or constructs a playscript—such as *Chakravyuha*—with his actors. Like Kerala, Manipur has a varied and rich theatrical tradition which provides Thiyam with his source material. Depending on the production design, he uses elements from a great variety of performance forms—minor oral forms of recitation and storytelling, the martial art thang-ta, ceremonial and ritualistic performances, and the complex and composite forms of natasankirtana, which involves recitation, chant, drumming, cymbal-playing, and intricate movement patterns. Thiyam's productions powerfully echo his regional theatrical culture, which is pronounced even when he does epic themes and Sanskrit plays.

Thiyam's treatment of speech utilizing the techniques of the oral form of recitation of the two epics is his primary source of theatrical power. Strong speech delivery supported by strong body movements of actors has such a compelling power that the Manipuri language, totally unintelligible to audiences outside Manipur, is not a barrier to theatrical communication. In his production of Bhasa's *Urubhangam,* the soldiers' description and mimed account of the devastation caused by the Great Kurukshetra War is unique in contemporary theatre. Nearly one-third of the play is this description, but the delivery of speech carries such a power that in spite of our Western notion of dramatic action we are greatly moved. In treating speech, Thiyam's concern, like Panikkar's, is with the transformation of poetic images and action into visual and plastic form.

Thiyam too lays great emphasis on actors' entrances and exits with stylized gaits and a developed sense of rhythm. In *Chakravyuha* the characters enter with colorful shawls loosely hanging from their shoulders and move sideways along with their hand movements in the manner of Javanese dancer/actors. Their actions acquire an amazing sense of solidity and mass appropriate to heroic characters. Some enter holding banners and umbrellas, and in the stage formations these create fantastic visual images. Thiyam seems to conceive his productions frame by frame, like a film. He also makes very effective use of montage in regard to image, sound, form, and color. His productions are a delight to watch. Visual images, movements, gaits, and speech are all reinforced musically, mostly by the beat of drums. In *Chakravyuha,* Thiyam uses drums, gongs, bells, conch shells, recitation, and chant to create a most expressive acoustic communication channel.

I have briefly talked about the work of three directors, and also tried to formulate an aesthetic basis of the theatre of roots. However, there are several other directors who have significantly contributed to this movement, and each has discovered and related to the theatrical heritage in his or her own way. Also, a new wave of young directors is appearing on the

5. & 6. Two views of Ratan Thiyam's production of Antigone, 1988. *(Photo courtesy of Sangeet Natak Akademi)*

scene to strengthen the movement and take it further. The statements by some of them published along with this piece show both the vigor and the variety of the new theatre. These directors participated in the fourth national theatre festival organized in 1988 by the Sangeet Natak Akademi, which sponsors a number of programs to support the new theatre. The three previous national festivals and four regional festivals, each held annually, have produced a substantial body of new theatre work, and today we can talk of "parallel," or alternative, theatre as we have been talking of parallel cinema for over a decade. With one major difference: while the parallel, new cinema is waning and losing ground, parallel theatre is growing stronger and showing signs of becoming an alternative to the conventional, and—as Peter Brook says—deadly modern theatre.

Theatre of Roots Roundtable

The following roundtable, convened by Richard Schechner, took place in New Delhi during the 1988 national drama festival organized by the Sangeet Natak Akademi. Attending were (in order of speaking):

K.S. Kothari, general secretary of the Sangeet Natak Akademi.

N.C. Jain, theatre critic, former instructor at the National School of Drama (NSD), editor and publisher of the quarterly Hindi journal *Nataranga*.

Waman Kendre, director (Bombay), former student of the NSD.

Suresh Awasthi, teacher, theatre scholar, former chair of the NSD, former general secretary of the Sangeet Natak Akademi.

Bharat Dave, director (Ahmedabad, Gujarat), former student of the NSD.

Chandrakant Jambe, director (Karnataka), former student of the NSD.

Neelam Mansingh Chaudhry, director (Chandigarh), former student of the NSD.

B.R. Bhargava, assistant secretary (drama) of the Sangeet Natak Akademi.

B.V. Karanth, senior director and former director of the NSD.

K.N. Panikkar, senior director, poet, and playwright.

KOTHARI: I conceived this idea of encouraging young directors to have an encounter with tradition and formulated a draft scheme in 1980 while working with the Akademi as drama officer. This was in realization of both the need and search for that indefinable quality called "Indianness" in Indian theatre. Also, by 1980 considerable theatre work was already there to justify such a scheme and support this new theatre. But I could not pursue the scheme because for nearly three years I was assigned another job in the Akademi. I revived the idea in 1983 when I started functioning as secretary of the Akademi. The scheme is now in its fourth year of operation. My colleague, Mr. B.R. Bhargava, drama officer, is looking after its implementation.

Our primary objective is to encourage younger directors whose talent often remains unrecognized and unsupported. This focus on younger directors is also because of the fact that some senior directors, a number of whom are here with us today, had already done significant work in this area, and some were being adequately supported.

One important aspect of the scheme is that we have a built-in provision for monitoring the quality of new productions. During these four years some 60 productions have been prepared. Each year festivals are held in four different zones: north, south, east, and west. The cities, sometimes towns, selected for the festival in each zone are changed every year. The number of productions at each zone's festival varies from four to six. From each festival one and sometimes two productions are selected for the national festival, always held in Delhi.

To make the scheme broad-based and participatory, we have involved the State Akademies and sometimes an important theatre institution, both administratively and financially. We also have both national and regional advisory committees of experts who help us select groups and directors, and attend the festivals in the zones to select the best groups for the national festival. This widespread network helps us locate and encourage often unknown directors working in small towns. They have the opportunity to get to the national forum once selected. The collaborative character of the scheme is important because during the last few years we have tried to decentralize our activities—so much so that now our annual awards ceremony and the accompanying one-week festival are held in different cities.

One of the most important features of the scheme is its multilingual character. Plays are done every year in several languages, often as many as 10–12 languages. The scheme also provides for interaction between directors. For the national festival we invite a large number of directors from all over the country as observers, especially those who have earlier participated in the scheme. This gives them the opportunity to see one another's work. We also organize informal discussions. Senior directors, especially those who are members of various advisory committees, are also invited to the national festival. Thus, the scheme truly acquires a national character not only geographically but also linguistically and theatrically.

Some other features of the scheme are:

1. Each selected group/director is offered a production subsidy of 12,500 rupees (about $1,560 U.S. dollars at time of writing). A group selected for participation in the national festival is entitled to a further subsidy of 3,500 rupees toward performance expenses.
2. Only new productions of original plays in Indian languages and translations of such plays are acceptable.

JAIN: Modern Indian theatre, as we all know, as it originated and developed was totally cut off from the folk and traditional theatres, and for all these decades there has been no contact between the two theatrical streams. This became a matter of concern for me and some of my other colleagues, such as Suresh Awasthi, who have been writing on contemporary theatre. It also seemed to me that with the new cultural impulses of the postindependence era, there was a definite possibility for forging links between the two theatrical traditions. So when the Akademi launched this scheme in 1983, I welcomed it and readily agreed to be closely associated with its implementation.

The basic problem in such a scheme is that contemporary theatre activity is mostly concentrated in cities and in large towns, and that directors and actors working in these centers have no awareness of folk theatrical traditions, even of their own regions. During the last 150 years, folk forms have been pushed to the rural areas and there has been no interaction with urban theatre work. In such a situation, encouraging any meaningful interaction and building bridges between contemporary urban theatre and folk theatrical traditions was very difficult. However, there were a few directors who realized the importance of such an encounter, and some younger directors, such as Ratan Thiyam and Bansi Kaul, had even done some directorial work involving the use of performing elements from traditional theatre. They came forward and eagerly participated in the scheme. There were several other much younger directors who also took advantage of the scheme out of a creative urge and artistic need. In four years it has acquired the character of a movement.

Another factor which contributed to this movement was a renewed interest in our Sanskrit classics. It is only in the traditional theatre—in forms like kutiyattam, the 1,000-year-old temple Sanskrit theatre of Kerala, that the directors could get some ideas and materials for doing Sanskrit plays satisfactorily. After doing the classics for nearly half a century we know that doing them in a realistic style kills their spirit.

I would now like to refer to one serious problem facing this movement of new theatre inspired by tradition: a shortage of playscripts suited for such directorial treatment. When I talk of the lack of such scripts, I am not in any way undermining the importance of some plays written during the last 15 years or so which have proved to be ideal for the new theatre. The need for suitable scripts has been met in several ways. Some directors chose Sanskrit plays, some adapted and deconstructed available realistic plays, while others prepared their own performance-oriented scripts to suit a particular theatrical form. There were, of course, already some plays like Vijay Tendulkar's *Ghasiram Kotwal* and Girish Karnad's *Hayavadana,* written and ideally suited for such a treatment. The 60-odd plays that have been done in four years under this scheme represent all the various approaches to the problem of playscripts.

If one looks at the entire theatrical scene, one finds that some of the memorable productions of the last 20 years are the product of this new theatre movement. These productions and their directors include Karanth's *Hayavadana* and *Barnam Ban* (*Macbeth* in Hindi), Jabbar Patel's *Ghasiram Kotwal,* Panikkar's *Maddhyama Vyayoga* and *Karna-Bhara,* and Thiyam's *Chakravyuha.* The movement has acquired a definite character and is pervasive. This year a young director from the small town of Jammu did some innovative work inspired by a lesser-known form of the region. Last year, another young director from a village near Srinagar did an inventive production using the *maskharas* (clowns) of the Kashmiri folk form, bhand pathar.

KENDRE: As a child I had a great deal of exposure to the folk forms of my region in Maharashtra. My father was a folk performer in Bharuda in a form involving the recitation of traditional devotional poetry and enactment of poetic allusions. I have childhood memories of visits to my village by a variety of folk performers. They came throughout the year following the agricultural cycle. From morning to evening they sang devotional songs, recited philosophical poetry, danced, mimed, performed acrobatics, entertained. This daily performance cycle is an integral part of village life. Villages serve both as audience and as patrons to these performances. This is the general pattern of art activity all over the country where arts remain integrated with society. These folk performances of storytelling and recitation left deep impressions on me. When I started directing in the new theatre these impressions became a source of inspiration and strength for me. Also, after graduating from the NSD, I spent two years in Kerala seeing and studying traditional performances.

When I did my first production in this style with the first-year students of the NSD I made many mistakes. It was more a matter of using elements of traditional forms than conceiving a production design which incorporated such elements by necessity. When I returned to Bombay, I was forced to work for the commercial theatre. I felt very unhappy with this situation; my Kerala experience was making me restless. I started looking for a script which could lend itself to a stylized treatment, where I could use movements and music, and exploit the full potential of the actor. I also felt very strongly that to be able to use the elements of folk forms in plays

7. Director Waman Kendre: "Live theatre can survive only by doing nonrealistic theatre which has a composite character like our traditional theatre." Shown is Kendre's Zulva. *(Photo courtesy of Sangeet Natak Akademi)*

dealing with myths and legends was not enough. It should also be possible to use these folk forms and their performance elements in plays dealing with contemporary social problems. Only then would they have relevance for us. It was with this belief that I chose to do *Zulva* in Marathi for the festival. Doing this production I learned that the nature and degree of stylization and use of folk elements in plays dealing with social themes must be different from that in plays of myths and legends. I firmly believe that folk forms such as tamasha of Maharashtra can easily take on new social content. In doing *Zulva* I also realized that I, as a modern city-based director, have no right to take a folk form and debase it. I know I cannot do justice to it. I have to, therefore, choose some of the values, concepts, and elements of a folk form and use them creatively. To my mind, that can be the only creative process—one may succeed or fail. My own problem in staging such productions is that in Bombay the commercial and realistic spoken theatre has a stronghold. It is very difficult for someone like me to make a place and build up an audience. But I am optimistic. I have done eight performances of this production and all had a very good audience. We can certainly win over the audience. Also it is my belief that in a film-dominated milieu, live theatre can survive only by doing nonrealistic theatre which has a composite character like our traditional theatre.

AWASTHI: Tell us something about the dramatization of Uttam Bandhu Tupe's novel *Zulva*; how did you develop the play text and the performance text?

KENDRE: I am glad you have asked this question. It was at this point that my problems began. I asked a playwright to give me a dramatic version of Tupe's novel. What he gave was a conventional realistic play. It was of no use to me. Finally, I decided to improvise the script with my actors and my music composer, who wrote the songs. Some of the melodies he took directly from traditional forms, the rest had a strong traditional flavor. I introduced a chorus to enrich the musical content of my production.

SCHECHNER: I have a question at this point. Is there any provision in the plan to take performances back to village audiences? Wouldn't this complete the circle and vitalize the movement?

KOTHARI: There is such a provision, though a limited one that has not operated effectively. Under one of the conditions of the scheme, the participating theatre group is required to do at least three shows in the group's home state; there is a small (12,000 rupees) subsidy for these shows.

JAIN: Schechner's question is very important. There is total separation between theatre activity in the cities and villages. Even in a state like Maharashtra, where we have a strong theatre movement and a large audience, it is only commercial companies which visit mid-size towns, not even large villages. The logistics have to be worked out for new theatre groups to be able to go to villages and perform for village audiences. I agree that a circle has to be built, but many arcs of the circle are just not there.

SCHECHNER: But no one is living outside history. If the theatre is changing in cities and urban centers, it cannot remain unchanged in rural areas. They are not living in mythological time. Historical forces are bound to create a circle.

DAVE: I have been doing theatre in Gujarat for 12 years. I do not have any experience of or exposure to the folk theatre of Gujarat. Also, until 1984 I did not have any knowledge of this new theatre movement. I had done many full-length plays, from *Waiting for Godot* to Lorca's *Yerma* to Girish Karnad's *Hayavadama*. My work, in a way, was a part of the commercial realistic theatre in Gujarat. After having done plays in my own way for such a long time, I suddenly realized that as a director I was not making any creative contribution, functioning only as a kind of manager for the playwright, a mere link between the writer and the actors. I then started looking for creativity in my work as a director.

In 1984, I participated in the Akademi's regional festival held in Panaji, Goa, with my production of Brecht's *Good Woman of Szechuan*. I was not quite clear in my objectives and approach. In the festival, I saw some productions which used elements of traditional performances. Also in the seminar sessions I learned something of the approach of the directors, and got some ideas about this new theatre movement. But I was not clear how to begin. Also, there was a problem. In Gujarat, the only living folk form with some interesting elements and conventions of performance is bhavai. First, living and working in Ahmedabad, I have a very superficial understanding of bhavai techniques; second, my city-based actors had neither any knowledge nor sensitivity to the folk idiom. But the festival made deep impressions on me, and led me to think about this problem.

When I thought of doing a production for the Bhopal festival, I felt that I must have a play suitable for such treatment, a play with a flexible structure. I discussed my ideas with a young playwright, Chetan Datar, and he developed a script. I worked on it, and felt a kind of freshness in my directorial work. Also, I realized that in doing plays like *Waiting for Godot,* I was far from my own reality, my own experience. I began to see that the text, the words, are not everything in a theatrical performance, that the director has to add and organize other elements. After seeing Thiyam's *Chakravyuha,* based on the Abhimanyu episode from the *Mahabharata,* I was convinced that this was the direction in which theatre has to move. But right now the situation in regard to this new theatre is like that of tourists: interest in our crafts. This kind of theatre work in my view has to acquire a deeper level of creativity and experience. Also it should not remain the work of directors only, but involve playwrights, actors, technicians, and audiences.

In Gujarat I have another problem. The Western-oriented and club-culture people are the ones who go to theatre, and their interest in this new theatre is as superficial as their newly found interest in traditional decorative crafts. A craft piece in their drawing room merely gives an ethnic feeling to the decor. Also, I am convinced that with the growing popularity of television drama and soap operas live theatre can only survive in the form of this new theatre, which shuns realism and emphasizes stylization, conforming to the nature and genius of our theatrical traditions. So I, and most of us, are drawn to this kind of theatre for artistic reasons. I respect tradition, but have no interest in its revival. What I am interested in is its renewal, its updating. I also firmly believe that this new mode of theatre will in the course of time attract audiences. Their response so far is very encouraging.

JAMBE: I have been doing "drama" for many years, but I have been doing "theatre" now for only four years, since my graduation from the NSD. In regard to my theatre work and discovery of my roots, I would like to submit at the very beginning that for me it was not a question of moving from the city to the villages in search of folk forms. I was already there. I retain childhood impressions of folk performances. My training in Delhi helped me to cultivate a sense of theatre with modern sensibilities. There is a dedicated and unique institution in a village in Karnataka with a repertory company. I am working as the head of the company. We perform for village audiences all over Karnataka. In view of my background in folk theatre, it was easy for me to make a production under the Akademi's scheme. I have imbibed the elements of traditional theatre as part of my life in the villages. I also undertook training in yakshagana movement for one year. In my directorial work my primary concern is to construct a production design and communicate it. As part of this concern I use elements of traditional theatre. For me these elements have the same character and importance as the dramatic text. Music and movement for me are theatre languages.

SCHECHNER: Once again I would like to raise the question of authorship. Who is the final authority: playwright, actor, or director? Even if a performance is the result of a collaboration, who has the final say? When you print the publicity poster whose name is given first or biggest billing? In the case of film, the director or star actors are commonly credited most prominently. You have to search for the name of the screenwriter in the poster.

SEVERAL DIRECTORS: It is the director's name that is given prominence in the new theatre. The director's role has become the most important and decisive.

AWASTHI: In this situation, some people feel unhappy, believing that the director is ignoring the dramatic text in the pursuit of an interpretive production design. The question of the treatment of dramatic text by the director is a big debate in the new theatre movement.

JAIN: I really do not think that the director should be given overriding authority in creating a performance. Director, actor, playwright—all must contribute. Perhaps a new combination will emerge. Also, this movement is sure to nurture new playwrights who will create playscripts suited for such treatment, and then dramatic texts will not require this kind of strong intervention by the director.

CHAUDHRY: For the past few years while working in Chandigarh, I concerned myself with the rich folkloric theatrical traditions of the Punjab. I found immense possibilities in lively forms of recitation, ballad singing, and storytelling. The great love legends of the Punjab—*Heera Ranjha, Sassi Punu,* and *Mirza Saihiba*—products of Sufi religious and cultural ethos, have been dramatically sung and danced for centuries by the Dadhis, a community of Muslim Sufi singers. Utilizing this folkloric material, I produced *Heera Ranjha,* one of the first tradition-inspired productions in my theatre work. My production of *Raja Bharthari* (*King Bharthari*) for this festival represents a second phase of my work. For this production I used naqal, a comparatively more developed form with narrative, storytelling, music, dance, and mime. I also used traditional performers of the form, called *naqqals* (imitators). Currently, the form is in a most degenerate condition, and their repertoire contains a series of smutty jokes and vulgar songs. The female impersonators use names such as Miss Hurricane and Miss Thunder. They also perform crude dances such as *hijaras* (hermaphrodite) on auspicious occasions, weddings or births.

Working with a group of traditional performers, I reconstructed authentic traditional movements, melodies, and stage conventions by talking to the elderly naqqals and studying the regional pictorial tradition. Thus, my production is in a way both a revival and a rejuvenation of a traditional form and an experiment in new theatre.

I also used the very popular traditional story of King Bharthari, who renounced worldly pleasures, left home, and became an ascetic. His story of renunciation is sung all over the Punjab in songs and ballads with soul-stirring music. It gives me great satisfaction and a sense of fulfillment to see that the naqqals are currently performing *Raja Bharthari* in some 25 villages in the Punjab, constantly improvising and enriching the performance.

AWASTHI: I would like you to tell us something about your experiments with space, especially the open-air theatre you designed with Nek Chand, famous designer and builder of the Rock Garden in Chandigarh, who also created a similar garden a few years back in Washington, DC.

CHAUDHRY: I have always felt uncomfortable working in a proscenium theatre—especially in productions utilizing folk performers and conventions of folk theatre. It just doesn't suit my production design, and doesn't allow the use of some of the most vital and primary conventions of folk theatre. The actor-audience relationship, the source of the magic of the folk theatre, is fully destroyed in the proscenium theatre. Nek Chand and I

8. Neelam Mansingh Chaudhry's production of Raja Bharthari (King Bharthari): *"a revival and rejuvenation of a traditional form and an experiment in new theatre." (Photo courtesy of Sangeet Natak Akademi)*

designed and built a most imaginative open-air theatre in Chandigarh in order to meet the demand of a special kind of space for my productions. It has ravines, rocks, waterfalls, flowing streams, terraces, staggered levels, trees, and the glorious sky above. Seating is in tiers. The theatre lends itself to a variety of approaches and treatments. The rocks make for perfect acoustics.

Transcribed and translated by Suresh Awasthi
Translation edited by Richard Schechner

Postscript

In January 1989, the scheme completed its first five-year cycle. In the first week of January the fifth national theatre festival was held along with a seminar to evaluate the achievements of the scheme, and also to discuss the nature and the processes of experimental work done under the scheme. Other related topics such as the new audience for theatre, the problem of sustaining theatre activity generated under the scheme, and the question of supporting the newly discovered directors with potential for long-term financial support were also discussed. The achievements of the scheme were shown through charts supported with factual data. A large photograph exhibit covering all the regional and national festivals of the last four years was also mounted. The number of directors, actors, and groups participating in the scheme and its attendant festivals was astonishing.

A cursory review of the data showed that a total of 25 festivals (of which 20 were held at the regional level and 5 at the national) are estimated to have attracted an audience of approximately 200,000 with a total of 134 performances (regional: 98; national: 36). The scheme has made it possible for people of one region to get to know the work being done in other regions of the country. The regional festivals have been held in towns and cities, some of which may never have had the opportunity to see the theatre from other parts of the country before. Besides the regional festivals directly sponsored by the Akademi, the plays selected have also been staged in different towns in their respective states, as stipulated in the scheme. Plays in 21 Indian languages have been produced under the scheme; this figure includes several plays in dialects which have never before been used for full-length works.

The scheme has made it possible to promote interaction among a large number of theatre workers and experts from different language-areas of the country. The seminars held at the festivals numbered over 98. As many as 248 observers, 90 theatre directors, 60 members of expert committees, 2,500 actors, stage technicians, and so on have taken part in the seminars. The scheme has created, on an unprecedented scale, multilingual forums for the exchange of ideas among theatre practitioners from the different language-areas of the country. Ninety young directors have explored the traditional theatre of India in their quest for an indigenous idiom. Practitioners of traditional forms have also benefited from this interaction. Productions by 30 young directors have been seen in the national festivals in Delhi.

Young theatre workers and their groups (90 directors and an equal number of groups) have received 2 million rupees in financial support as direct subsidy for new experimental productions, and further support of about 1.6 million rupees for staging these productions all over the country. By implementing this centrally sponsored scheme the Akademi has been able to extend its collaboration with state-level organizations. Twelve state Akademis, five departments of culture, and one regional cultural center have cooperated with the Akademi in organizing the regional festivals.

No formal and methodical study has been conducted on the scheme's overall impact in different regions in terms of generating, supporting, and accentuating local theatre activity and creating and enlarging theatre audiences in regions and towns over the last five years. But, after talking to some of the experts and observers who attended various theatre festivals and seminars, it has become obvious to me that the scheme has made significant contributions to all areas of theatre activity, especially in those regions and small towns which have been theatrically barren. Another significant achievement of the scheme has been that local publications have reported theatrical events for the first time, both in English and local languages. Performances and seminars were widely covered, and also interviews with some of the directors and experts were published.

Young directors greatly benefited from their interactions with experts, observers, and local theatre artists in lively discussion sessions on mornings following performances. Directors explained both the theatrical forms and elements of their particular region and their methods of using them in their productions. These creative decisions were often questioned and led to heated and lively debates. Directors of previous years and those of other regional festivals expressed their doubts and questions and participated actively in these discussions. Never before have artistic problems in theatre practice been discussed on such a scale and with such passion in India. While focusing on personal artistic choices and decisions, these discussions always had a larger framework—looking at such basic questions as the relevance of traditional theatre, tradition, and modernity in the context of creative activity.

The scheme also encouraged theatre in several dialects which so far had not had any modern theatre activity. This brought about a most meaningful interaction between contemporary theatre activity and the rich oral traditions and cultures of the regions. Several directors, using local performance conventions and local legends and folk tales as thematic material, rightly decided to use local dialects which proved to be powerful linguistic media for the new theatre. Modern Indian theatre, being the product of colonialism, urban culture, and literary traditions, could never spread to smaller towns, and always felt shy of using dialects and other non-urban material.

The new theatre movement has generated an unusual widening of the frontiers of theatre, bridging gaps between the urban and rural theatrical cultures. What is of even greater importance in this context is that local poets and writers who had been writing in a literary language, are now using dialects, expressing themselves with great sensitivity and power in idioms which are their mother tongues. This phenomenon has greatly enriched the dialects and also proved their vitality. It is the result of this phenomenon that the repertory company attached to Bharat-Bhavan, the prestigious art complex at Bhopal, Madhya Pradesh, has used several dialects in the translation and adaptation of even great classics, both ancient and modern. They have done classical Sanskrit plays, Shakespeare, and Brecht in dialect.

In this theatrical phenomenon of using traditional elements in experimental productions, it is not only the contemporary theatre that has benefited. The advantages, both organizational and artistic, of this interaction between the theatrical traditions have also gone to the traditional theatre. It gained acceptance and respectability, and its performing techniques have acquired sophistication. Traditional performers were also often involved in these experimental ventures, and they enjoyed working with their urban counterparts and brought a sense of celebration to a theatrical event. Several directors used traditional performers during rehearsals to train city-based actors in movement, music, and speech. Some directors used them in their productions along with the city-based actors. Some chose to do productions exclusively with folk performers. Senior director Habib Tanvir has been working for over 30 years with a group of folk performers from his rural region in Madhya Pradesh. This process of creative interaction with the traditional theatre has been strengthened by the fact that the festivals of folk and traditional theatre organized by the academies, newly established regional culture centers, and two Apnautsavas—national festivals of folk arts—held in Delhi in '85 and in Bombay in '89, have greatly popularized a wide range of traditional performances.

The scheme also aroused controversy and received opposition which has become more vocal since the completion of the first five-year cycle. The second five-year cycle has been announced with modifications in the scheme. The controversy has been there from the very beginning. It is really part of the larger, more fundamental historical situation of the contemporary Indian theatre. During the past two decades, ever since this new trend of the creative utilization of traditional theatrical modes, materials, and elements began as part of the process of cultural decolonization of theatre, those directors and theatre artists who continue to practice deadly colonial theatre and want to preserve the status quo have been opposed to this new theatre of roots which has now acquired the character of a strong movement. These theatre artists, some of whom are now members of the Akademi's governing body, raised the objection that the Akademi as a government-funded institution should not promote a particular type of theatre. To meet their objections, the objective of the scheme has been partially modified. While earlier the policy statement of the scheme said that it was to encourage those theatre artists who are interested in experimental work inspired by indigenous artistic traditions, it has been changed to say that it is to support the endeavors of young theatre workers engaged in the production of new exciting works which promise to enlarge the frontiers of theatre both in terms of production values and thematic content.

Suresh Awasthi

Notes

1. The *Natyasastra* (2nd century BCE–2nd century CE) is the Sanskrit manual of performance attributed to the sage Bharata. Combining myth with very detailed instructions to performers, directors, and choreographers, the *Natyasastra* has been, and continues to be, extremely influential among scholars and performers.
2. Ramlila is a cycle play telling the story of one of Vishnu's avatars, Rama. Ramlilas are staged environmentally in the Hindi-speaking belt of north India every year. Some Ramlilas last only a few days, others for 20 or more. The Ramlila of Ramnagar, the most elaborate of all, takes 31 days to complete.

Suresh Awasthi, *director and proponent of India's theatre of roots, is the former general secretary of the Sangeet Natak Akademi and former chair of the National School of Drama. He has taught at New York University, Columbia University, Brown University, and Tokyo University, and has written extensively on Indian theatre in Hindi and English. He is the author of* Drama: The Gift of Gods, *a book on traditional Indian theatre.*

Playing Awake

Letters to My Daughter

Deborah Hay

Ed. Note: Performing artist Deborah Hay wrote the following letters to her daughter, Savannah, earlier this year.[1] *They describe both the process of performing for 22 evenings straight in January-February 1989 and the evolution of her newest work,* The Aviator. *The piece completes a trilogy, which Hay began in 1986 in collaboration with new-music composer Ellen Fullman, titled* The Man Who Grew Common in Wisdom. *Parts I and II,* The Navigator *and* The Gardener, *premiered in New York City in 1987 and Amsterdam in 1988, respectively. At presstime, the completed trilogy was scheduled to premiere in Austin at the University of Texas Opera Lab Theatre in September 1989.*

February 10, 1989

Dear Savannah,

I am home alone, the first night after 22 consecutive performances in the studio of our house. Some nights only two people came. Two nights no one came. Last night there were 24 people, about 18 were art students from the university. They had interesting things to say and they asked challenging questions. I felt genuinely optimistic in their presence.

People behaved differently on these nights. They took time to look at the paintings, the objects, the fabrics everywhere. Many sweet compliments. Permission to "look" came with buying the ticket to a performance in an artist's studio. Actually, some evenings people didn't look. Some came to be encouraged to eat and drink. We served wine, cheese, crackers, chips, and hot sauce. Harry* prepared a beautiful table each night—with candles, flowers, and incense. A group would hug the table until the performance began. Then they would hug the table from the time we left the studio until the time they left the house.

Everyone who came, however, tried to be open to having an unusual experience in the studio. Some couldn't make it. I have to credit them with trying. I did everything possible to demystify the traditional separation

**Ed. Note: Harry Porter assisted Hay in her 22-night run.*

1. Deborah Hay in her studio in 1988. (Photo by Phyllis Liedeker)

between audience and performer, from Harry's jovial greeting to sitting in our living room, with drinks from our kitchen glasses, space to study the family photos pasted on the bathroom cabinets, time to check our plants.

The next thing we know we are sitting on the floor of my studio in stocking feet with perhaps three or four other people. I am only two feet away speaking, urging them to be comfortable amidst these unusual performing conditions, and that they use this opportunity to release themselves from centuries of intimidation. I advocated a more powerful and dignified role for audience. "My intention is not to seduce but rather invite you to play attention. Attention is a gorgeous feeling. It is freeing, mercurial, and constant at the same time. I support you in *playing audience* more dynamically. Our old ways are outmoded and stale. It is up to the audience to create new roles to play for itself. Most performers will just nail you right where you've already been."

The forum afterwards became an opportunity to hear about the experience of the audience members. Some people had an absolutely marvelous time from start to finish and I would say they were the least informed beforehand about my work.

The Aviator goes like this:

1. I imagine every cell in my body invites being seen playing *The Aviator*. To "invite being seen" is itself a verb. It is made up of three verbs at once: to invite, to be, to see. Inviting being seen spontaneously creates relationship between the player/performer and audience who may otherwise go unrealized. I thereby replace my separation from the audience with a field of positive action that invites audience to engage attentionally.
2. *The Aviator* perceives the idea of the fixed three-dimensional body as a sleight of hand because, in fact, it is changing every moment. One may think one sees an identifiable figure but, in fact, that figure is never the same. This paradoxical reality—that one looks like one is here but here is always in flux—is of crucial importance to the person playing *The Aviator*. The key is the ability to access the imaginative chemistry of inviting being seen not being identifiable in one's fabulously unique three-dimensional body. The physical experience of this paradox releases the player from fixity of mind, body, and spirit. *The Aviator*'s physical experience of intuiting the three-dimensional body as a sleight of hand becomes elevating and joyous.

I wanted to explore *The Aviator* without structural limitations. *The Aviator*'s perception *is* the dance. To support my attention to playing *The*

2. & 3. Deborah Hay in The Navigator, *part I of the trilogy* The Man Who Grew Common in Wisdom *(Austin, TX 1987). "To 'invite to be seen' is a verb." (Photos by Phyllis Liedeker)*

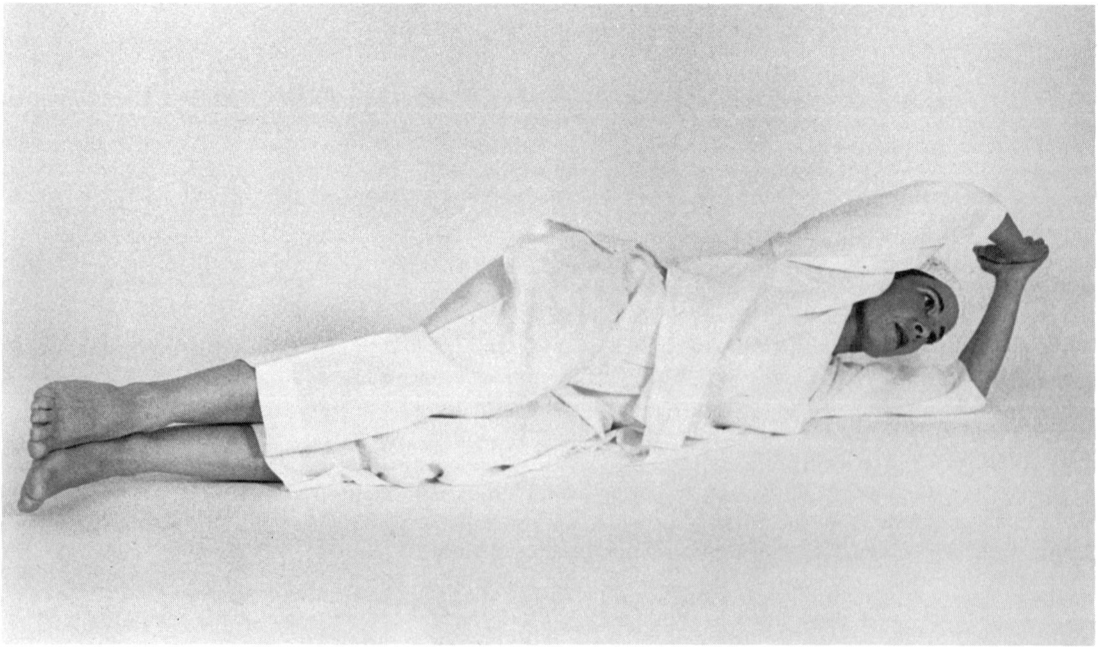

Aviator without choreography, I deliberately avoided performing riveting moments, the kind we, as audience and performer, love to grasp during performance. Sensually, it was a great delight to engage in nondefinitive action for 35 minutes. I felt like a child. This added to an already existing sense of freedom and joy—not drawing attention to myself through the performance of captivating moments, and still inviting being seen.

About halfway through the run I began to describe myself as an artist-in-relationship-to-the-world. This followed on the heels of a Merce Cunningham residency here [at the University of Texas]. It was already understood that I would not perform on the same two nights as the Cunningham Company because of my own interest in seeing Merce's work again. Sitting on a couch with him at a reception following his last performance, I asked how long, once a piece of his is choreographed, before the performance of it is realized? (This really should have been addressed to one of the performers.) Merce responded by saying that a dance is completed once all the parameters of time and space are taken into account. He simply did not relate to the experience of performance as material. His response caused me to more clearly recognize how the resources for my choreography are not and have not been movement, space, and time. The performer is the material for my dances:

1. the vessel, the whole infinitely changing and vital human who is performing the movement, and
2. that same performer's relationship to the world, practiced as the willingness to be seen whole and changing.

No other tangible outside stimulation is being used (to date). I manage every last bit of imagined cellular intelligence to support playing awake. I invite being seen as a performer in this process because when it is shared

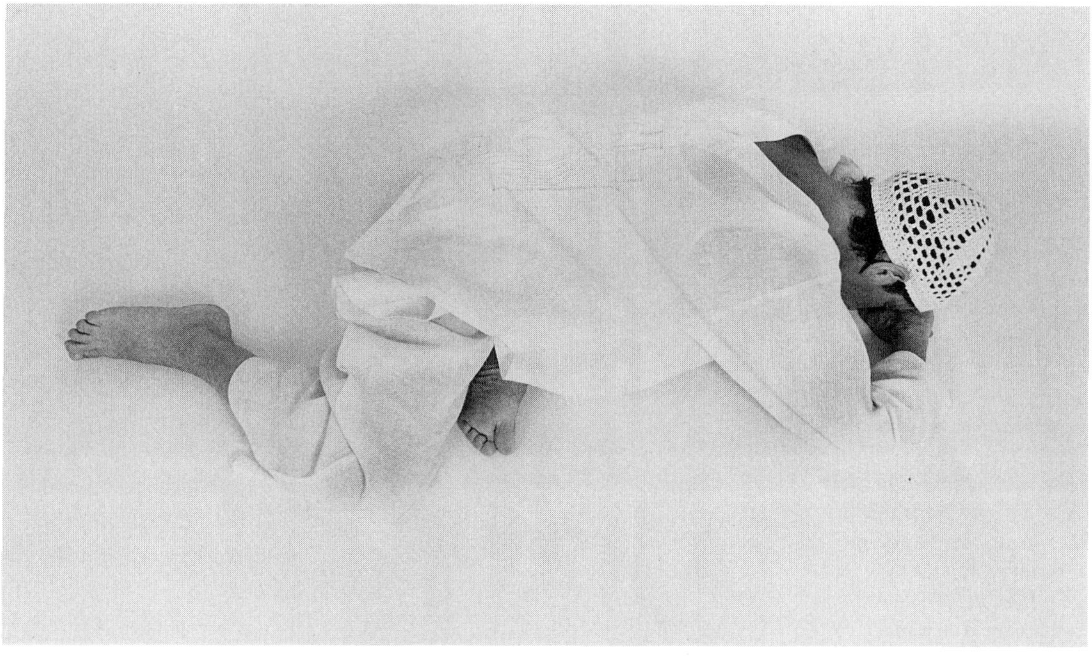

the experience of playing is much greater. Performing is practicing relationship to the world as rigorously as practicing being awake.

The most radical shift in understanding by the player of *The Aviator* came three nights before the last performance. I had a terrible day, feeling very sorry for myself, feeling untapped and unnecessary, wanting recognition sorely. Several hours later I stepped into the studio practically swaggering with the strength of my faith in this process. I played my resources flagrantly. I so completely addressed my practice of relationship with the audience, playing this outrageously liberating dance, that they could not help but be alert, just as I was equally compelled to be. One member of the audience said I looked like an idiot savant. I was finally happy.

The Aviator is the fool.

June 5, 1989

Dear Savannah,

. . . So, I set out to write a graduation message for you. I would like to give you a trick to take with you on your travels during the next six

4. & 5. Performing is practicing relationship to the world. Here, Hay is pictured in Part II of The Man Who Grew Common in Wisdom: The Gardener *(Austin, TX 1988). (Photo 4 by John Leatherwood; photo 5 by Ave Bonar)*

months. Tricks help me short-circuit negative or outmoded patterns of thought and/or action. Tricks wake me up to "playing awake." The only hard part is remembering to play. So here's one for you now.

When you are walking down the boulevard in Paris, or anywhere else in the world, and you feel lost and wonder where you are and why, play "Whatever I see reminds me of my wholeness changing." Use your seeing to instantaneously remind you of your actual physical reality, as a whole, all at once.

At the same moment, remember that this corporeal reality is in fact changing every single instant. It is. It may not look like it but all of those cells are actually in a different relationship to each other every instant of your life. To play this is not to necessarily believe it or act it out. It is a way to remind yourself of how rich it is to simply be awake, whole, and alive in this world. Remember, the work is to remember to play!

Playing is also an exercise in developing your consciousness to include more than one practice at a time. You will be seeing, reminded of your great wholeness, and in the same moment how that wholeness is always changing. Then, play at suspending that moment as long as you can.

Note

1. I'd like to thank my brother, Barry Goldensohn, for his help in preparing these letters for publication.

Deborah Hay *was born in Brooklyn and grew up watching Balanchine and the Rockettes. She was a founding member of the Judson Dance Theater in New York in the early '60s and a member of the Merce Cunningham Dance Company in 1964. Her interest in movement lies in discovering ways to practice the most impeccable performance, no matter what its shape or form. Her work with large groups of trained and untrained dancers, along with her devoted solo performance practice constitute the wealth of her days.*

Mnouchkine's Workshop at the Soleil

A Lesson in Theatre

Josette Féral

Of all types of professional training, theatre training is the most difficult to assume and follow. After schools and conservatories—the classical route for artistic training, even if the teaching is periodically put into question—come the universities. For the past ten years, universities have developed their own programs of practical training. (This is more true for American and Canadian universities which have budgets permitting real training programs than for the always terribly underequipped French universities.)

Yet there are routes to follow besides these two types of training. There are the training programs and workshops offered by theatre companies to their members (such as those by Peter Brook and Ariane Mnouchkine). These training programs are sometimes, but too rarely, open to others, all of whom—with or without talent, with or without prestigious affiliation—have a real desire for learning and perfecting their skills. For these artists in search of improvement there is a great shortage of such workshops. Many training programs are offered on the market, but none of them have the value of those offered by theatre companies, nor are they as interesting.

Some popular training programs are unannounced, their dates passed on among friends. Ariane Mnouchkine's annual workshop at the Théâtre du Soleil's Cartoucherie in the suburbs of Paris is one of these. People wait a long time to get into this renowned program. Many candidates apply from all over the world, over 1,000 in 1988. Mnouchkine sets up a preliminary interview with each applicant to determine who can stay. Nothing fundamental is said during the few minutes of interview—just the reasons why each applicant wants to take part in the workshop. Undoubtedly Mnouchkine detects a certain sincerity, sensitivity, or expectation that tips the scales. The candidates themselves are often incapable of saying what might have determined the final decision.

We were 220 at the end of this stage, from 42 countries. More than 200 for a workshop lasting seven days, perhaps ten—we overheard the trainees say that sometimes Mnouchkine extends the training and everyone began to hope she might do it this time also. . . . When we asked, Mnouchkine

1. Ariane Mnouchkine. (Photo by Martine Franck)

answered that she didn't know yet, that it depended on a lot of things, especially on us trainees.

The Rules are Given

We arrive at 9:10 AM the first day. Because of the large number of people, the hall of the Cartoucherie seem to be waiting for a show. With the help of Sophie Moscoso, Mnouchkine reads off our names and hands everyone an attendance card. At the end of the call, Mnouchkine retains the late ones and berates them vehemently. The first rule of the actor is punctuality. Latecomers in the future will be crossed off the list. Advice to those interested.

Other rules are imposed very quickly: absolute respect for masks and costumes, absolute silence in the hall, attentive observation of everything that happens on stage (apprenticeship involves looking as much as acting, Mnouchkine sharply reminds us at various moments). Also, the hall must be cleaned at the end of the day. However, despite these strict rules, actors keep going in and out during improvisations, costumes always end up in a heap on the floor at the end of the day, trainees sitting on the bleachers aren't always as attentive as they should be. The cleaning is reduced to a team of a few volunteers who put the hall back in order every night. Only the masks hold everyone's respect. The initiation to an ethics is difficult! Mnouchkine is outraged.

Overcome and discouraged by so much laxity and lack of good will, she ended the third day of work by announcing that she would interrupt the training and everyone could go home: The training really started off very badly; the level was too low this year; there had been no effort toward real collaboration. Also, she felt a general animosity toward the stage which did not help stimulate work.

Mnouchkine's dictum was like a cold shower. Confronted with this unexpected blow, we woke up and tried to make Mnouchkine change her mind, but she resisted. After two hours of discussion, the workshop was allowed to start up again. But this time everyone understood that we would not be given the three extra days we'd all secretly hoped for.

Never did Mnouchkine say that she offered this free workshop out of generosity, out of love for theatre and for actors. (Of all the workshops she gives, this one is the only one that costs nothing.) She does it because she is very worried about the future of theatre acting, a practice that is waning and must be saved. Besides, from the beginning she was very clear: "There are perhaps 20 actors among you; if such is the case, this would be very good. We will try to do theatre together then, and if we are able to have a few minutes of theatre during these few days, only a few minutes, then it would be fantastic."

It turned out that Mnouchkine was right: during those seven days, where everyone improvised an average of two scenes in groups, you could count at most one short half-hour of intense and exceptional theatre. This half-hour was not delivered in one block of time but in fragments of a few seconds or sometimes a few minutes when spectators witnessed the emergence of a story and the exceptional osmosis of a character and an actor.

"Masks that Travel Very Well"

"I would like to remind everyone that this is a workshop. Seven days we will share together. It is not an audition. If you come to the carpet to show yourself, or to show *me,* you will not be showing anything. It is not a training to prove yourself. It is a training for theatre." The warning that Mnouchkine begins with is important. The actors, some of them present for their second or even their third workshop, know that this is where Mnouchkine recruits her actors. It happened that way for the *Indiade* and before that for the *Sihanouk*. That is why some are hoping, while others attend simply for the pleasure of participating and learning under Mnouchkine's merciless eye.

2. Théâtre du Soleil's Cartoucherie in the suburbs of Paris. (Photo by Josette Féral)

3. Mnouchkine, front right, with a group of actors inside the Cartoucherie. (Photo by Martine Franck)

Sitting in the first row, she follows all of the improvisations—even the most pitiful ones—with total attention and a great listening power, searching with determination for a sparkle of theatre. If the improvisations go on without genius, Mnouchkine does not show any less respect for an actor's work as long as that actor brings a true desire for creation to the stage.

She can sometimes be strict, or even ferocious, which paralyzes even the bravest beginnings. "There is not even a minimum amount of sound needed," she says before an actor can leave the stage. But her judgment is always right, without complacency. Her look is precise, her attention intense. She is in search of theatre in all of the bits of improvisation which are presented to her during the course of the day (from 9:00 to 5:00 interrupted by two brief coffee breaks and a lunch hour). She also looks at all gestures and even behind the masks. She may abruptly interrupt an improvisation after a few seconds, or have the actors leave the carpet, or forbid an actor to enter the stage because his appearance shows a lack of respect for the costume and for the mask. Everyone ends up accepting these moments—they are never arbitrary and are compensated by remarkable times when direct dialog and interaction emerge before everyone's eyes without mediation between Mnouchkine and a character. And so, during the most productive moments of the workshop, Mnouchkine singles out one group of actors or an isolated actor with whom she works to almost give birth to a character. She assigns a trajectory, which opens a vast imaginary world, animating the actor with a certain wind, giving her depth and projecting her forward.

As is her custom, Mnouchkine makes her actors work with masks. It appeared during the course of improvisations that masks from commedia dell'arte and from Bali marry well and adhere to the same theatrical laws. We made our acquaintance with Pandeba, Rajissan, Pucci (baptized during the workshop). "I will not give you the characteristics of a mask, otherwise I would reduce them," Mnouchkine said to begin with. "Some have names, others not. This one is Rajissan, for example. They all have greatness. They have a complete soul. Do not look down on them. Do not caricature them even if they are uncultured. Contrary to the masks of the noh theatre that we embalm so well that we cannot find them, these are human. But they are sacred, too. We called this one Punta. This other one has eyes, it dances. It is very difficult, it doesn't have a name. This one is Pandeba. The mask is heavy, but be careful, he is light, very light. This one also: do not make him out to be more of a simpleton than he is. This one is complete. He has buttocks and a hole in the butt. It's obvious that the best thing that can happen to you is to love one of these. To love it means to recognize it, to have known it. You will see, they travel very well. They are surprised but they adapt themselves very well. It is the opposite for the commedia dell'arte. They are run over by character traits, they die under characteristics. They are human beings.

"These masks are made of leather and wood. They are very fragile. Erhard Stiefel made them. You can imagine what would happen to you if you break one." We laugh.

4. Mnouchkine's actors work with masks. She warns, "They are human beings. You can imagine what would happen if you break one." (Photo by Josette Féral)

"In Order for There to be Theatre, You Only Have One Second's Time"

After presenting masks and using them for the first time, we proceeded to teamwork: the choice of a character, the development of a scenario, the preparation of a costume.

Mnouchkine proposed a theme—occupation. Last year, the subject was invasion. Improvisations centered this time around collaboration, resistance, black market, fear, rivalry, cowardice, denunciation. All Théâtre du Soleil costumes are at the actors' disposal: the clothes from *The Shakespeare Cycle,* from *Sihanouk,* and even those from *l'Age d'Or* and *1789*. Mnouchkine has a special taste for costumes. She likes them to be lively, rich, exact, finished. These preoccupations produced the splendor of the Shakespeare costumes, their extreme sensuality, the warmth of the *1789* costumes, the opulence of the velvet and lamés, still shining from the various shows. During the workshop, dressing became an important phase of the preparation, the phase that allows an actor to enter into her character.

Actors got together by affinity to develop scenarios together for improvisation. One quarter-hour, one half-hour, sometimes three quarters of an hour of dialog for improvisations that often only lasted several minutes. "It's too long," Mnouchkine would sometimes say. The actors have the tendency to lose themselves in the maze of a convoluted intrigue to the detriment of work on details of events and states of being. "In order for there to be theatre, you only have one second's time. When you enter the stage, the story is already being told. I want to see a character right away.

5. Georges Bigot and Cyril Bosc (kneeling) in Mnouchkine's 1981–82 production of Richard II *at the Cartoucherie. "Mnouchkine has a special taste for costumes." (Photo by Martine Franck)*

6. Costumes hanging in the Cartoucherie are at the actors' disposal. (Photo by Josette Féral)

Where is he? Why does he arrive? Why is he there? The spectators have paid, you cannot tell them: wait until I get settled.

"We, the public, are there, and they, the characters, know that we are there. I know that you know that we are there. And you know that I know that you know that . . . we are there. And we are there for them. That is the most difficult thing."

Mnouchkine Directs an Improvisation

Punta enters pulling a donkey, Rajissan pushes. Both of them make great efforts and the donkey seems to resist. They both stop and get on the donkey.

MNOUCHKINE: Daniel! Be calm! Be calm! You are out of breath before entering. You break the slightest image. Calmly continue, both of you. Show the distinction between apoplexy and dynamism. If it is apoplectic before you have left the curtain, what have you invented?

The actors begin again. After several minutes, Mnouchkine interrupts them.

MNOUCHKINE: What is your theme?

ACTORS: It's exodus, we have escaped. Over there is a bridge, but the donkey is reluctant. It will not be easy to get across.

MNOUCHKINE: And what if the donkey is not reluctant? What would you do? You do not let this donkey improvise. He will go across the bridge and wait for you at the other side. You will be the ones to lose your balance. Do this over with a donkey who is not reluctant. He knows the escape. Everytime there is an escape, someone comes to fetch him.

The actors repeat, the donkey passes. But the change in the scenario leaves them unprepared.

MNOUCHKINE: You are going to do something with the donkey grazing, and at the same time, you want it to go to the other side!

The actors start the skit over and talk to the donkey.

MNOUCHKINE: The only thing you got from the donkey was the fact that it has to leave. When you speak to it, it looks fake.

End of improvisation.

Some Basic Rules for the Actor

Mnouchkine repeats incessantly the same advice—it's simple, but always turns out to be difficult to put into practice:

For Preparatory Work and the Scenario[1]

Do not make confabulations as though you are staging *Les Misérables*. Content yourself with three good lines of preface. The goal is not to get to the end of the story. Work together. What can you do all alone at home? Nothing. You have to learn together. Listen to yourselves. Take yourselves in. You must accept things from others. If that person proposes something to you, take it. To imitate does not mean to plagiarize, it means to recognize. They have been imitating for generations in the East. It is not a question of imitating from the exterior but from the interior. Not to imitate what the other has done but what he was. If it is impossible to imitate in this sense, then it is impossible to imitate someone else, a character. You have to have the humility to put your feet where others have left traces.

You also have to have imagination and secrets. Do you have secrets? [*Laughter.*] Could it be that in this workshop there are no secrets? You must learn the patience and humility of mystery. Do not try to be original at any price. I do not care about originality. Learn from others. When someone does something good, do it yourself a second time and bring it further.

Avoid falling into an idea, search for the true, not the realistic. The true is not realistic. To enter onto a stage is to enter into a symbolic place where everything is musical and poetic.

For the Mask and the Character

The masks make terrible and unyielding demands. The costume is chosen on the basis of the mask and the character. The mask is not makeup. It is not a nonentity. Everything is at its service. If you use it wrong it will denounce you right away. You are the one to yield to the mask, it will never yield. So you have to respect it, love it. If not, it is as though you don't recognize that these masks have a history, a past, a divinity. Instead of wishing to rise toward them, you bring the masks down toward you, you make them banal. You have to make a journey toward them. You do not use a mask in any which way. You do not use just any mask, either. Our relationship to the mask is one of magnanimity. These masks come from far away, from another continent. The theatre is another continent. It seems as though you would like the theatre to come here. No! Theatre is not comfortable here. When you call a character, it comes with its world. It is complete. It is not a group of functions. Keep the autonomy of each character. Keep some air around them. No prettiness, no coquetterie. I want to see a character. I feel as though you are expecting instructions behind the mask. No!

For the Costume

Finish your costumes well. They can be your friends. They are your enemies if they are badly made, if they don't hold together. The brains themselves have to be made, covered, without hair. Bare skin is difficult to

7. Mnouchkine adjusting Falstaff's costume during a rehearsal of d'Henri IV *of* The Shakespeare Cycle *in December 1983. (Photo by Martine Franck)*

use with masks. Hands, feet: it all makes it too realistic. Do not become bizarre and ugly creatures. It is a sin to not believe that in every creature there is beauty.

For the Acting

Look for your little interior music that gives rhythm to your actions. Let your imagination come to you. The difficult thing is to let yourself do while doing. You are either *in doing* which blocks you or *in the letting yourself do* where you do nothing.

Use your imagination. The imagination is a muscle. It can be built up, enriched, nourished, by looking at others with mischievousness but without meanness. The actor is an active receptacle: this is not a contradiction but a difficulty. He must be concave and convex. Concave to take in and convex to project.

Avoid moving around all the time. If you move constantly, I don't see you. You must find your stops and your rhythm. The stops give movement, the states of being give life. In order for me to see you, you must stop. Only do one thing at a time. If you jump for joy, good. So jump, then speak, but do not do both at the same time. Sometimes you have acted out two things: your despair and your mistrust. You have not been able to act one thing at a time. So we haven't seen anything. Complete your gestures. Take the time to finish everything. Do not stammer with your gestures. Complete your stops. Also, avoid slowness that tries to be profound. It's often too slow to be honest. Do not fall into true slowness. You have to act out this slowness, but at a quicker pace. Slowness is an enemy. After several seconds there is nothing left of the previous illumination.

Avoid overacting and being idea-filled. Verbiage is as gestural as it is verbal. Avoid decorating. Some people do not realize the physical exertion this demands. Do not adorn your acting when you haven't got the essential down. There are people who arrive and who don't have anything in their bag. And others who arrive with many things in their bag and it is worse. It's fake. Proceed in a simple way.

You are so rushed that you explain yourself to us instead of living. Do not comment on your gestures constantly. The public is not stupid, it understands. You do not take the time to act out your desires and your anger. You are not in the *present*. You are here already and I do not see your desires. I want to know what you want before you get here.

One of your only weapons is action. But while you are in the doing alone, nothing can happen to you. You need states of being, presence. It is the state of being that justifies actions. The most important thing is to find your state of being. You need a *pure state of being,* a series of pure states of being. Is it enough to work on the state of being? Are we sure that if we work on a state of being, the state of being will follow? No!—a lot comes from what you believe or do not believe. But to *believe* is most important. You believe that space is outside of you. This is wrong, it is in you. I can only take in space if I see you take it in. I only see this distance by your look. We are the ones who see you seeing. You must be visionaries. It is essential. As long as we have illustrative entrances, figurative ones, you cannot fly off. If you illustrate space, there is no stage, there is no theatre. You have to see to believe. You want to create by intelligence, no. Give yourself time. The problem is a rapport between the interior and the exterior. If you are not able to translate this rapport, you do little things, instead of daring to tell us, instead of making signs. Signs ask the question. If you haven't at a given moment felt both the emotion and the externalization by the sign, you haven't found it. Do not hide yourself, reveal yourself. You have to dare to discover. You are being figurative instead of metaphorical, instead of finding the sign.

Your problem will be to translate your state of being. Dramatic acting is a translation. Translate something immaterial, an emotion in a body. It is through the body that this emotion operates. The actor is a double translator, because his own translation must be translated also.

"The Mask Is Essential for Training the Actor"

During the course of the workshop it was shown that the mask is essential for training the actor because it does not allow lies and it uncovers all the weaknesses of the actor: lack of imagination, knowing how to act more than how to be, lack of presence, lack of listening power, etc. By its very nature, the mask uncovers all complacencies, all weaknesses. It goes against the actor who doesn't enter it and uses it to hide herself. Inversely, it can become sublime and bring forth theatrical moments of rare intensity.

Behind the mask, thanks to it and its support, characters emerge and are led into extraordinary adventures.

It is true that the use of the mask imposes a certain form of acting which other less typed theatrical forms do not. But it is evident that the rules of theatre which apply themselves to the mask are valid everywhere.

During the course of the classes, certain simple principles came back again and again although it was always difficult to apply them: The distinction between easy and simple, decorative and necessary, fakeness and trust, big and little, solitude and listening, displacement and action, illustrativeness and state of being, exteriority and externalization.

Some of the advice Mnouchkine gave to the actors ended up having the strength of maxims: Finding the true and precise little detail; looking for the little to find the big; not mixing up displacement and expression, apoplexy and dynamism, slowness and depth; refusing moves for the sake of moves in theatre; not acting counter to the mask; not accepting a versatility during the improvisation; and knowing when to give up what we had planned on and accept what might present itself. But more than anything Mnouchkine untiringly stressed the importance of the vision we bring to things, the vision that teaches, listens, and recalls. The necessity of apprenticeship by observation.

Despite the numerous failures, the rare successes, this workshop was a deep lesson in theatre. Mnouchkine reminded us at the end that the laws of theatre undoubtedly exist but during the night they hide and the next day no one knows where they have gone.

—Translated by Anna Husemoller

Note

1. The following advice is compiled from statements delivered by Mnouchkine during the 1988 workshop. Sometimes she was speaking directly to an actor and sometimes her comments were general. They have been edited together here.

Josette Féral *is Professor at the Drama Department at the University of Quebec in Montreal. She specializes in drama theory and criticism and has written several articles on theatre in Canadian, French, and American journals. Féral is editor of two books:* Theatre in France: Ten Years of Research *(Madison: Substance, 1978) and* Théâtralité, écriture et mise en scène *(Montreal: HMH, 1981).*

Building Up the Muscle

An Interview with Ariane Mnouchkine

Josette Féral

Ariane Mnouchkine is one of the best-known directors in France. She founded Théâtre du Soleil in 1964 and has been its director for 25 years, becoming a leading figure in today's theatre. The following interview took place in March 1988 at the Cartoucherie, home to Théâtre du Soleil, during a performance of Mnouchkine's production of *Indiade* by Hélène Cixous. As we talked, we could hear drums, gongs . . . the whole music of the *Indiade* emanating from the background.

Are There Theories About Acting?

FÉRAL: Ariane Mnouchkine, I know right away that you are going to answer my first question by saying that there are no theories about acting.

MNOUCHKINE: I do not know if I would say that. I know that I myself do not have any, maybe because I am not in the position to develop a theory on acting. I may not ever be capable of developing a theory about acting. Because in fact the idea of a theory of acting involves a written development of the theory of acting and a practice of acting. That is to say that we, directors and actors, put into practice the practice—we don't practice the theory. I think that if there is no theory of acting, at least there are theoretical laws that we may find, curiously enough, in all traditions of acting. It is true that the term "theory of acting" does not seem fundamentally wrong, but it seems always somewhat imperialistic and pretentious. I prefer to use *fundamental laws* which we sometimes know but then sometimes lose and forget. It is only practice that all of a sudden can make law or tradition rise to the surface. I will not say then that there is no theory of acting; on the contrary, there have been many of them. Of course, what interests me in these multiple theories are the essential laws that are common to all of them.

FÉRAL: In the '60s there were several theories of acting that everyone referred to: Bertolt Brecht, Antonin Artaud, Jerzy Grotowski, for example, represented a very important historical moment together in the evolution of theatre. They were theoreticians, some of them being practitioners, and others not. Artaud, for example, was not a practitioner in the same sense as Brecht. On the other hand, what he said about theatre had enough weight to influence a whole epoch. Actors today, beginning actors in the formative stages, are quite unequipped because these masters are not masters for us today.

MNOUCHKINE: They were not the only ones. There were people like Stanislavski of course, and Meyerhold. But there were also people in France who wrote absolutely essential things: Jacques Copeau, Charles Dullin, Louis Jouvet. If you were to read them again, you would notice that there are things in Copeau that you find in Zeami, and that is what is interesting, moving, not so much reassuring but comforting. You can then see that Zeami wrote in 15th-century Japan what Copeau wrote in 20th-century Europe. And Brecht, as original and ideological as he may be, fully rediscovers in his least logical moments traditional elements of Oriental theatre. You are right, I will not differentiate between master-of-thought-practitioner and master-of-thought-nonpractitioner because from what we know even Artaud, for example, failed in practice. He failed probably because he did not have the physical or the mental strength to produce what he wanted. But what he wrote was so close to practice, so lucid on the practice he discovered—on the practice of Balinese theatre—and makes such a strong translation into theory that his work ends up being quasi-practice.

1. Ariane Mnouchkine watches a rehearsal of Mephisto *in 1978. (Photo by Martine Franck)*

FÉRAL: Would you say that Stanislavski, Brecht, and Artaud have one thing in common, and that is that the laws they attempt to uncover rest upon a vision of a theatrical act in its essence?

MNOUCHKINE: I would not put Artaud and Brecht on the same scale. Artaud is closer to the foundations than Brecht. Brecht gave laws of a certain type of theatre, sometimes of course with fundamental laws that can be found in all types of theatre. I believe that Artaud had a much deeper conception of the function and mission of the actor, less political and more metaphysical.

FÉRAL: Nowadays, we seldom refer to Artaud, just as we seldom refer to Brecht. Is it because we have surpassed them or is it because we have assimilated them?

MNOUCHKINE: Neither! No! I think it is because they are for now—[*the phone rings and we break off*].

Such Mysterious Fundamental Laws!

FÉRAL: Can we turn back to these fundamental laws which govern theatre throughout the world? It seems that theatre practices, in the East and West, are universal. Even if techniques vary from one place to another, they are governed by fundamental laws. What are these laws?

2. Théâtre du Soleil actors in the film Moliere, *written and directed by Mnouchkine in 1977. (Photo by Michèle Laurent)*

MNOUCHKINE: Do you want me to make an inventory of them? [*We laugh.*] How shall I tell you? They are so mysterious and so volatile. Sometimes we have the impression that a rehearsal goes by and we've forgotten laws we thought we knew perfectly the day before. All of a sudden during a rehearsal there is no more theatre. An actor cannot act, a director cannot help an actor anymore. We ask ourselves why and we cannot understand. We have the impression we are respecting the laws and actually all of a sudden we realize that we have lost the essentials, for example, *being in the present*. I believe that theatre is the art of the present for the actor. There is no past, no future. There is the present, the present act. When I see young students work on what they call the "Stanislavski method," I am surprised to find how much they go back to the past all the time. Of course Stanislavski talks about the character's past: Where does he come from, what is he doing? But the students are not able to simply find the present action. So they go back and I always tell them, "You enter leaning backwards, weighted by all this past, while in the theatre only the moment exists."

I think that the greatest law is probably the one that governs the mystery between inside and outside, between the state of being (or the feeling as Jouvet would say) and the form. How do you give a form to a passion? How do you exteriorize without falling into exteriority?

How can the autopsy of the body—I mean the heart—be performed by the body? My slip of the tongue is revealing because the autopsy of the heart must be performed by the body. An actor or actress worthy of the name is a kind of autopsy-er. His or her role is to show the inside.

Yesterday was beautiful. There was a short debate with high schoolers who were theatre majors and all very young. They did not stop asking me the same question, "Why is there so much emotion?" They were talking about the moment in *Indiade* when Nehru says "I am afraid." A small young woman hardly 15 years old asked me this question, then a boy did the same. So we asked ourselves the question together. Why? How could a young Frenchwoman of 15 be moved all of a sudden by a particular scene of Nehru's? And we said that this was something specific to theatre: the memory of the unlived. That is, a young Frenchwoman who has not lived is capable, by the grace of theatre and the actor, to understand and recognize what she has in common with a 60-year-old man who is from a country that has 400 million inhabitants and to understand his fear. We were happy about this discovery. And we said this is what theatre is all about. That is: when an actor succeeds in making the unknown familiar and making the familiar enchanting and moving (and not the day-to-day, because the day-to-day is precisely what is worn out in advance). You ask me, "What are the laws?" If I knew them all the time, I would not have to ask myself what I say everyday in rehearsal, "Okay, now, what is theatre? Are we going to succeed in producing a moment of theatre today?"

Emotion Comes from Recognition

FÉRAL: You talk about emotion from the actor's point of view, but doesn't emotion exist for the spectator as well?

MNOUCHKINE: The emotion is different in the two cases. For example, Indian theatre offers something very beautiful from this point of view. There are big theoretical books on the subject. There is Zeami, of course, but there is also an Indian book [the *Natyasastra*], an enormous work that gives the theory of the whole Indian theatre. There we can find some laws

3. Simon Abkarian as Abdul Ghaffar Khan and Andres Perez Araya as Mahatma Ghandi in Mnouchkine's 1987 production of L'Indiade ou l'Inde de leurs rêves *by Hélène Cixous. (Photo by Martine Franck)*

that I find extraordinary. For example, there are different words to define the emotion of the actor and the character [*bhava*] and the emotion of the spectator looking at the actor [*rasa*]. I find in Western theatre, in the acting style of certain actors, an ability to bring together what should be their emotion, which should be a part of the action, and what the emotion of the spectator should be. These are the good moments. The good moments are when all of a sudden a spectator has tears in his eyes while what the actor acts out is a moment of enthusiasm, happiness, and laughter. Why do you all of a sudden start crying with joy or recognition?

FÉRAL: Because you perceive at this very moment the exactitude of what is happening. It is the truth of the moment we experience, independently from what is expressed.

MNOUCHKINE: Exactly, the emotion comes from recognition. From the fact that it is true.

FÉRAL: This recognition is not solely that of the subject matter, of that which is said, or the life that is acted out, but it is recognizing the exactitude of what goes on on stage, grasped in the actor's performance. What is astonishing about the Théâtre du Soleil is that so often the actors hit it right. There is something in their gestures that recalls the necessity or urgency of the moment. They are so efficient, we recognize theirs as the only gesture that could have been performed at that very moment with that much precision. This brings us back to one of the laws that you talked about earlier. You said that the actor must be present.

MNOUCHKINE: Wait, I did not say "be present" but be *in the present.* The theatrical act occurs in the moment and once this happens, something else happens.

FÉRAL: We talk a lot about a concept we borrowed from the East which people like Eugenio Barba use in their work with the actor: the actor's presence. It is a very difficult notion to grasp but as a spectator I can identify an actor who has presence and one who hasn't.

MNOUCHKINE: Presence is something you state, but I myself have never worked with this idea. I would not be able to tell an actor to "be present." On the other hand, what I do know, what I try to tell the actor, is that he should be in his present, in his action, in his emotion, in his state of being, and in the versatility of life as well. These are the lessons Shakespeare gives. With him we can begin a verse in a murderous rage, have a moment of forgetfulness of this rage to simply be happy about something in the text, then fall back into a strong desire for vengeance, and all of this in two verses—in a few seconds, therefore in the present. The actor truly playing such a verse is "hyperpresent." Present to the second.

As for the actual concept of the actor's presence . . . There are actors who are present, and others less. It comes with talent. There are no bad actors who have presence, unless it's bad presence, and presence increases with the capacity of the actor to be naked.

FÉRAL: How do you help an actor to be in the present? Do you use a technique? Do you have a method? Is your method a form of listening?

MNOUCHKINE: I believe that there are no techniques. There are methods and I believe every director has one, maybe an unconscious one. I believe I have one, but I do not know it.

The last word you said is very important: "listening." I believe that I know how to do that well. There, that is the only thing that I can say. I think I know—no—I would not even say that I know, but I love, I love to listen, and I love to look at the actors. That I love with a passion. I think that is already a way to assist them. They know that I never tire of listening to them, of watching them, but how do I help them? I do not know.

FÉRAL: In one of your texts you wrote, "You must build up the muscle of the actor's imagination." This nourishment you feed the imagination is a form of assistance.

MNOUCHKINE: I encourage the expression "building up the muscle." When I work with very young actors one of the first questions I ask is, "What do you think is the actor's most important muscle?" Of course no one thinks of it, and so I tell them it is the imagination. And it can be conditioned, worked on.

FÉRAL: How do you proceed?

MNOUCHKINE: With sincerity, with emotion. By acting, really by acting. Not by the memory, I don't believe in that. You have to be able to have visions little by little, to be a visionary, to see what they talk about, to see where they are going, where they are, to see the sky above them, the rain, to take in the emotion of another and to believe in it.

We are trying to talk very seriously and very severely about theories of theatre, but really *the* essential theory is that you have to believe in it: believe in what we act, what we are, what we incarnate; and believe in what another incarnates, believe in the emotional trouble, in one's strength, one's anger, one's joy, one's sensuality, one's love, one's hatred, whatever you want . . . but you have to believe in it.

The common misinterpretation of Brecht is that we thought he said you shouldn't believe in it. Brecht never said that. He said you should not deceive.

I think there is something in the actor's work that obliges him or her not to fall back into childhood but enter childhood. He must divest himself of all made-up images which go against the work of the imagination. These made-up images are clichés or crutches where there is no emotion.

FÉRAL: But this imagination must nourish itself somewhere. It is not enough for the actor to say to himself, "I will believe in it" to believe in it.

MNOUCHKINE: There has to be a true situation to start from. I will not say a pretext because we know that it is possible to improvise from this. But there has to be a theatrical situation and a desire to create a character. There has to be invention, discovery.

We Must Have Theatre the First Day

FÉRAL: Does work on character happen alone? In a group? In discussions?

MNOUCHKINE: Nothing ever happens alone. The work happens from the beginning by acting. For us, there is never, never any work at a desk.

4. "We must have theatre the first day." (Photo by Martine Franck)

We read the play once and the next day we are already on the stage. The actors can decide to try all the characters they want for several weeks, even several months. They have old bits of costume at their disposal to disguise themselves and they begin. And we act right away. We must have theatre the first day.

FÉRAL: Are there any points of reference that can be used to start off with? Do actors keep the memory of what they have done on stage so that the good things they have found during improvisation are retained? Or is it simply a period of exploration?

MNOUCHKINE: There is a period of exploration but the good things remain when they are really good. This is what you were saying about the precision of gesture, the evidence of gesture. The gesture is not what remains because things are fixed much later. But we will know that such and such a character has this type of gesture, that he is a little like this. Then we will discover something else. Because one of our most important laws is to keep it firmly in our mind that all the characters, *all* of them, have a complete soul. We realize it is a little dogmatic to say that each character in a play contains all the others. There is a little of Prince Hal in Falstaff, a little of the father in the son, a little of the fiancée in the fiancé, a little of Juliet in the nurse, a little of the nurse in Juliet . . . Everyone is complete. Because otherwise we do not progress. This happens to us sometimes. There were times when I realized that the concept of work on a character, the concept of character itself, could be very limiting, that we could often translate a character by limiting it instead of creating someone without limits who always is a surprise. There are character types of course but you always have to be able to go beyond the type.

FÉRAL: Do you make a psychological study of the characters? I am asking you this because in the *Indiade* we don't have the impression that the characters have a psychology. We have the impression instead that the characters are from the theatre, presented as theatrical constructions, with a complexity, but without day-to-day psychology. They are emblems. They are motivated by signs rather than by psychology.

MNOUCHKINE: We flee daily life. We do not talk of psychology but rather of the characters' souls. Not of their psychology. But they have emotions, sensations. They are cold, they are hungry, they are proud, they want power, they don't want it, they are stubborn. Each one of them has their way of being, their own world. Nicolas Boileau said "the truth is not always verisimilitude" and verisimilitude is not necessarily true. This can be precisely understood in a historical play. That is, what happens, happens. These characters experienced it, oriented it, or made it happen. It was with their "psychology," as you say, that the events took place. But there is no question about it, the theatre is not supposed to represent psychology but passions, which is totally different. Its role is to represent the soul's different emotional states, and those of the mind, the world, history. In the Théâtre du Soleil, psychology has negative meaning. When I say to the actors, "Watch out, that is psychological," it's a criticism. They know very well what I am saying—I mean their performance does not reach truth, it is slow, complicated, and narcissistic. Contrary to what we believe, psychology does not pull toward the interior, but toward the interior mask.

Theatre is Eastern

FÉRAL: There is no tradition of gesture in the West. Many directors must look for this tradition in the East. You yourself in the Théâtre du Soleil have to find inspiration from Asian theatres. What are you looking for?

MNOUCHKINE: Theories that have marked all people of theatre. They have marked Artaud, Brecht, and all people of theatre because it is the source of theatre. I think that we go East to look for theatre. Artaud said: "Theatre is Eastern." This thought goes very far. He does not say, "There are Eastern theories that are interesting for theatre." He says, "Theatre is Eastern." I believe Artaud is right. So I tell the actor to go look for everything in the East. Both myth and reality, interiority and the exteriorization, and the famous autopsy of the heart by the body we talked about. We also go to look for the nonrealism or theatricality. The West has only given birth to the commedia dell'arte—and even this comes from Asia—and to a certain type of realism which great actors escape from. It is true that a great actor, even when he is in a realistic theatre, succeeds, I do not quite know how, in not being realistic himself. But it is difficult.

FÉRAL: Theatre is in need of traditions?

MNOUCHKINE: It needs sources and memory. It needs to be worked on in order to allow the depths and origins to come to the surface. You can't easily say that we need traditions. We have them. Lineages exist and they belong to us completely, even beyond national borders.

FÉRAL: How do you choose your actors?

MNOUCHKINE: I meet with a lot of young actors in person. There is a lot of opportunity to select. The workshop is one of the times when selection takes place, although not the only one, because I do not do it from that perspective. I do not know how I choose the actors. First, I choose people that make an impression on me. People who make an impression on me in a human way before an artistic way. I choose people who move me, like ones where I sense a strength, innocence, fantasy, gaity, and also rigor from the beginning.

FÉRAL: Do you sometimes make a mistake?

MNOUCHKINE: Yes! But not very often. My mistakes are bad ones because it is very bad to make a mistake in a group. When I notice it in time, it's easy to patch up. But sometimes this provokes moments of crisis. Still, I would say that in 24 years, my major errors have not been more than the fingers of one hand. There were plenty of little mistakes, but minor ones. There were people whose place turned out not to be at the Soleil, but that was harmless. People who attempted to upset the group, and thereby did upset the group, were very rare.

FÉRAL: You have said that the duty of every director is to make workshops for actors. Is this because actor training in school is not sufficient?

MNOUCHKINE: Yes, there is schooling but it is insufficient when you consider the demand. There are one or two good schools [in France] which take 30 to 40 students each year. And then even the students who have gone through the schooling need to continue to work. When they do not act, they lose their adaptability.

5. *Georges Bigot as Sihanouk and Guy Freize as de roi Suramarèt in Mnouchkine's 1985 production of Hélène Cixous's* L'Histoire terrible mais inachevée de Norodom Sihanouk, Roi du Cambodge. *(Photo by Martine Franck)*

We Do Not Invent Theories of Acting Anymore

FÉRAL: Why don't you put your theories about acting in writing?

MNOUCHKINE: First of all, my area is not writing. Also I sincerely think that everything has been said already and in an extraordinary fashion. A little like Jean-Jacques Lemêtre, our musician at the Théâtre du Soleil, who replied when someone asked him if he invented instruments: "You do not invent instruments anymore, you transform them, you rediscover more, but you do not invent them anymore. They have all been invented." I, too, reply that you do not invent theories of acting anymore. The problem is that theories exist but they have been buried at the same rate as they have been pronounced. Let the young students read Zeami, Artaud, Copeau, Dullin, Jouvet, also Brecht . . . Everything is there. And let them do theatre. We do not need to say more.

—*Translated by Anna Husemoller*

Théâtre du Soleil—A Second Glance

An Interview with Sophie Moscoso

Josette Féral

FÉRAL: We are here at the Cartoucherie and it is May 1988. You have been Ariane Mnouchkine's assistant and have worked closely with her for almost 20 years. The company has changed a lot over the years. How many members are there now? How many nationalities? How do you operate? Is your budget sufficient?

MOSCOSO: At present we are 60 in the group, from 21 countries. We receive an annual subsidy of five million francs [$800,000] from the government. We are about 60 employees with an equal salary for everyone at 7,500 francs per month [about $1,200 dollars]. If you add social benefit charges, everyone's monthly salary costs the Théâtre du Soleil 13,000 francs—calculate that for 12 months, multiply by 60! Plus, the costs of producing a show (scenery, costumes), the perpetual upkeep of the Cartoucherie, and the fact that we take the time we need to rehearse for the play.

In general, we rehearse six months and perform about one year or more including tours. In performance periods 50 percent of our operating costs are covered by our box office successes which I think is quite rare. We have been carrying a debt for some time which keeps increasing because of the interest we have to pay. All of this together means that the subsidy, which has not changed since 1984 (it was doubled in '81 by the socialist government), is insufficient. This means we have to stop operating for a few months after one project before we are able to work on the next project.

The nature of our group work necessitates a long rehearsal period which is indispensable: we need the time for the actors to research, discover, learn, apprentice, and blossom. The rehearsal time is compensated by the fact that we perform for a long time, of course, but also because we are organized in such a way that we don't each do just one job at the Théâtre du Soleil: we all do a whole series of tasks which otherwise would call for specialists. This way of working has to do with a certain ethics of the troupe—but also saves money! It is a way to function, and for those who

1. 1789, a collective creation of the Théâtre du Soleil directed by Ariane Mnouchkine, was attended by 281,370 spectators in 1970–71. (Photo by Martine Franck)

are comfortable with the Théâtre du Soleil, it is an evidence, a richness, the individual responsibility of the medium which is collectively owned.

The troupe oscillates between 50 and 60 people in general. It consists of an office crew or administrative staff, the team that is responsible for public and community relations, and the technical team which is competent with various materials according to what is needed at the time—for example, the space of the *Indiade* called for a big construction job. Then there is the couture team, three of them, who design and make the costumes. And the musician—

FÉRAL:—who makes up an orchestra by himself—

MOSCOSO: And the kitchen crew and . . . the actors. There are presently 31 of them for the *Indiade*. There were a lot of new actors who joined the group in 1981—we needed to hire them with *The Shakespeare Cycle*. A troupe is like a little planet, a little country: certain people, thinking they have finished learning, go off to travel elsewhere, others come to put up their tent and work on fulfilling their dreams, both individual and collective. This is also what life is about.

So, a certain number of actors joined in '81, and most of them are still here in '88. We met some of them in a workshop during the production of *Mephisto*, in '77–'78. It was the first workshop that lasted a long time, thanks to both the availability of Ariane and the appetite of the participants. The work concentrated on commedia dell'arte and the mask. It did not necessarily mean that participants would be accepted into the Théâtre du Soleil, like other workshops up until then, but certain encounters were made.

2. Georges Bigot as Richard II and some of the other "Shakespeares" who joined Théâtre du Soleil after the successful 1981 workshop. (Photo by Martine Franck)

So, for the Shakespeares in '81 we made a kind of workshop-audition which extended itself over one month, and more for specific people. It was at that time that Georges Bigot, Maurice Durozier, Clementine Yelnik, Myriam Azencot joined . . . and then others during the Shakespeare adventure, Jean-Francois Dusigne, Serge Poncelet, Andres Perez.

It's actually always a question of encounter, passion, mutual desire—fate does the rest. In any case, you do not join the Théâtre du Soleil solely to act out a role or participate in a show. You join to create, make a troupe live, look for theatre, learn, and try to create it—life, that is, all the colors of life: the obscure and the luminous, the pitfalls, the exaltation, the day-to-day and the exceptional . . .

The actors who joined the Théâtre du Soleil during this period of revival in 1981 knew the troupe and knew what they wanted to find there. They were nourished by the apprenticeship from the older ones, seized what was offered to them and appropriated it. Their arrival in the troupe reaffirmed the rules of operation which had perhaps become dormant, forgotten, or rejected.

FÉRAL: When you say that it "reaffirmed," did it reorient the Théâtre du Soleil?

MOSCOSO: The group was renewed. I don't want to go back too much in time but . . . the production of *L'Age d'Or* (1975) was difficult. The film *Molière* (1977) allowed an interruption. *Mephisto* was a kind of rite of passage toward the return to the text, and it's true that the apprenticeship by the Shakespeares inaugurated a new step forward for the troupe.

FÉRAL: Does it ever happen that the actors only stay for one show?

MOSCOSO: They do not come to just work on one play. You join the Théâtre du Soleil. When someone comes to the Théâtre du Soleil it is not only for an apprenticeship or to learn the profession, it is also to build up the troupe. So the human qualities are as important as what are called the professional qualities. Or, as Louis Jouvet would say, *"Tel homme, tel comedien"* ["The person and the actor are one and the same"]. The moral and ethical qualities, that is, the ethics of the Théâtre du Soleil, are essential.

FÉRAL: It's also the ethics of theatre in general. This lesson came out very clearly in the workshop Mnouchkine gave this year. For many, this workshop was not only a lesson in theatre, but also a lesson in life.

MOSCOSO: Yes, and that has been verified in our history . . . by things that were either difficult or exalting to live through. There is necessarily a very strong link between the capacity to create and the capacity to learn, to work with others (which is essential to theatre), which means having the capacity to be curious about others, to open oneself to the public, to imagine and invent, because to be an actor is to "play another." It is to be in direct contact with human qualities. You cannot lie.

FÉRAL: And these qualities vary, individuals evolve.

MOSCOSO: Their expression varies, but I imagine that truly human qualities must show a strange persistence! And also the Théâtre du Soleil is very heterogenous. The individuals are very different. You ask me how many nationalities there are. There are now 21. There is a Chilean, an Argentine, some Brazilians, a Spanish woman, some Portuguese, an Iranian, a Tunisian, some Algerians, two Indians, a German, some Belgians, a Guatemalan, an Armenian, a Turk, some Italians, two Cambodians, and several French people. It is very, very rich because everyone brings her or his own tradition and culture, the shape of his or her imagination. Through all of this, we put into practice the search for the expression of feelings that are common to everyone, or as we say, universal.

FÉRAL: Are these people who ended up in France before they came to the Théâtre du Soleil or did they come directly?

MOSCOSO: It varies. Everyone has their own adventure.

FÉRAL: Were there any that were recruited during some of the trips?

MOSCOSO: Yes, Simon Abkarian who has been with us since *Sihanouk* was brought in by Bigot who met him during the Los Angeles tour. After the performance and tours of the Shakespeares, the Théâtre du Soleil was not operating for four months, and Bigot directed a mask workshop in L.A. Abkarian worked with him. And Georges took Simon in his suitcase!! This is just one example. Nirupana Nityandran and Asil Rais were discovered during the trips to India. Otherwise, we got to know certain actors by way of workshops: Liliana Andreone, for example, who is in charge of public relations, is an Argentine political refugee who got to know the Théâtre du Soleil during the shooting of *Molière* and then little by little . . . The trajectories were very different. It is actually a matter of meeting each other.

FÉRAL: Once you have entered the Théâtre du Soleil, you share your life with everyone?

MOSCOSO: It depends on what you mean by this! We share a lot, just by the amount of time we spend together, often 13 to 14 hours a day. Then by organizing our work: the division of tasks. We do not only work at the Théâtre du Soleil, we live there. But we each have what you call a private life, a house, children . . .

FÉRAL: You talked about different crews. You have basic crews in each area but the actors serve as supplementary assistance to the basic crews?

MOSCOSO: Of course, absolutely. During the rehearsal period the time is divided up and there are different work areas. In performance periods, the reception of the public, the bar, the preparation of meals, the cleaning and maintenance of the space is divided among us. Every morning, we have a meeting for the purpose of dividing up the work.

FÉRAL: And when the Théâtre du Soleil is rehearsing, what is a normal day like?

MOSCOSO: First of all, exactitude is of primary concern. We begin at nine in the morning. At first the day lasts until six o'clock, then very soon after it goes on longer. After a coffee together, we make up teams. The actors go to the rehearsal hall and after some physical training, they choose scenes they will work on, and characters they would like to try.

There is no established cast. Then everyone puts on costumes, makes themselves up. Finally, the groups get back together, "concoct" their teams, and the adventure begins. We explore . . . We don't work on the play in order—be it Shakespeare or *Sihanouk* or the *Indiade* of Hélène Cixous. This only happens much later . . .

Little by little, not before two or three months of rehearsal have gone by, evidences of casting appear, the form becomes more elaborate. Simultaneously, among Ariane, Guy-Claude François, and the technical team, the work of the imagination brings the stage, the space, into being.

FÉRAL: Is the method of working similar to what happens during the actors' workshops? That is, the actors improvise and propose something? Mnouchkine seizes "theatrical moments" and helps the actor to follow her or his own ideas, own imagination.

3. Mnouchkine fanning the "little flame at the corner of a character's soul." (Photo by Martine Franck)

MOSCOSO: Of course. But the actors' workshops are indeed workshops. The objective is different. Building a show, telling a story, putting on scenes, forces you to go further. One thing for sure is that in both cases what we are looking for is theatre! When we begin rehearsals we don't know anything anymore. Ariane and the actors begin all over again, from the bare beginning, from zero. And we say to each other: "We are not working from experience!"

FÉRAL: Do all the actors play all the characters? Do they choose them? Who makes the selections?

MOSCOSO: At the beginning, everything is open to everyone, no casting is done. Everyone chooses the characters he feels like exploring and discovering, but of course a young trainee who has just joined will not try Gandhi! Everyone works at his own apprenticeship. An actor or apprentice actor who knows that he is not yet capable either to open himself up and reveal aspects of a character, or to make a scene go forward, will not do it.

FÉRAL: So the actors propose something. There are other actors who are in the Hall. Do they show their reactions and give their opinions? Do they comment on the acting?

MOSCOSO: Comment on the acting . . . no. How shall I say? . . . It's like during training: the observation of others is essential if it is positive, desirous, truly open; if each person is not trying to think of what she would do afterwards, but is actively attentive to the work being done on the carpet.

When a minute of theatre is born, that is a moment of truth, life, in a form that everyone sees. Benches tremble! And Ariane formulates what happens from this speck, this little flame at the corner of a character's soul,

4. Performers in Mnouchkine's production of L'Indiade ou l'Inde de leurs rêves, *by Hélène Cixous, at the Cartoucherie in 1987. (Photo by Martine Franck)*

this truth of a stage moment which begins to be drawn. She guides, she brings it further. So we make progress in the forest. Or else, when it doesn't work, we try to understand why, which law of theatre we forgot, what the essential thing we do not see is, and we begin over again.

Generally, we don't talk very much during rehearsals, we talk afterwards. The work happens on stage, that is where we have to look for theatre, not by chatting and making comments, but by looking, desiring, helping another, then retrying, stumbling and falling on our faces.

FÉRAL: We learn that looking is an operating force. By habit one settles into looking and doesn't notice anything. What the workshops teach, especially Mnouchkine's, is to keep moving, looking at the same time, taking a step, even though everything leads us to think the contrary.

MOSCOSO: We learn a lot by looking, if we have learned to receive. One of the essential rules that we have discovered with the *Indiade,* and what Ariane says over and over again to the actors as they act, is: "Listen to yourself *truly,* look at yourself *truly,* answer yourself *truly.*" It is apparently as simple as that. And it works in action more than in commentary.

To come back to your question: "Are there commentaries?" No! Not about the work of others. Sometimes we talk together at the end of a day or a morning, like that, before leaving each other. We have a little "briefing" to recount, recollect what we have discovered that day or what we should remember—and have a tendency to forget—as a law of theatre.

FÉRAL: So, to come back to the actors, they work on stage . . . and Ariane is always there to look at them.

MOSCOSO: Of course.

FÉRAL: So at a certain time, I assume she says: "OK, let's stop, because it is not going anywhere." Or else, "It is not exact anymore." Or even, "The actor wandered away from his character."

MOSCOSO: Or, "There is not even the minimum amount of sound needed!"

FÉRAL: Is there any work around the table or a read-through of a play?

MOSCOSO: We read a play together once. We read the text to listen to it in its complete and unabridged version together and that's all. It is not by the "reading" of a scene or by the intellectual analysis that we will understand it, but by the exploration of the characters' passions. This is how sparks of scenes are born, which gradually become more and more numerous. At the end, all the elements of the story are expressed.

FÉRAL: One thing that struck me in the workshop is the importance attributed to costumes and disguises.

MOSCOSO: Of course, because to act is to transform oneself. So it's already the beginning of a trip, because the essential muscle that the actor has to put to action when he begins to work is the imagination. How are you supposed to have imagination if you stay in the jeans that you wore in the metro when you came? The Théâtre du Soleil has always worked with costumes.

FÉRAL: There are theatre groups that have worked without costumes, that divested themselves of costumes and looked for other means. I am thinking about what Jerzy Grotowski did during his "poor theatre" pe-

5. Mnouchkine at her théâtre. "There is not even the minimum amount of sound needed." (Photo by Martine Franck)

riod, where the actor did not disguise himself, did not put on a physical, palpable, concrete costume, but divested himself of all daily "masks."

MOSCOSO: Yes. This is not contradictory to our way. The costume unveils the character. That is, it is the beginning of the search; she mustn't cover, she must unveil. She makes the character appear.

FÉRAL: Mnouchkine speaks of the "beauty of the costume." The expression does not refer necessarily to something aesthetic but to something harmonious?

MOSCOSO: I do not believe it is a question of harmony. I believe it is a question of truth. It is like the evidence of theatre: either there is theatre or there is not. You have the curtain, either someone comes in or he doesn't.

As for the costume, it is beautiful if it is true, when it is exact in relation to a character. Each detail is important, everything is important. And, among the actors of the Soleil, there are some who know more, some less. There are some who are completely obsessional and precise in their vision and others more sketchy. In these cases, also, the observation of others allows for progress.

FÉRAL: What is the role of improvisation at the Théâtre du Soleil?

MOSCOSO: There are two ways of using the term "improvisation": either in the sense of "collective creations" or of "improvisational work." Collective creation is a theatre without text—little groups of actors create scenes, invent their text. That is total improvisation, if you like . . . Improvisational work is a work of research. In this case, even if you have a text, there is improvisational work. That is, you improvise with the text. The text asks, invites us to incarnate it, and the improvisational work of the actors and Ariane's watchful eye—not the reading but the call for life, toward incarnation—are what allow the text to be consummated in life, in flesh. If not, the text waits, lifeless.

FÉRAL: So this is a fundamental law in theatre.

MOSCOSO: Yes, in this second form of improvisation you have to be able to discover what provoked the words. Not to act with words, because the words exist by themselves, but discover what is at the origin of the text. This is total exploration and discovery. But you cannot distort the text, force or make things happen which aren't in the text. It is better to not talk of "improvisations" in this case. I would talk about the search for states of being, passions, that is all. That is what is essential.

I think that this notion of the "search for states of being" is more exact than the term improvisation. What is truly essential is the search for states of being. This allows us to explore the human heart. And when the actor takes on a scene, when he acts it out, there, every night, the essential thing he has to find in the present, every night, is a state of being and its truth.

—*Translated by Anna Husemoller*

The Aesthetics and Politics of an Arnhem Land Ritual

Margaret Clunies Ross

Setting the Scene

From June to August 1978 I was a member of a small party who were guests at a funeral ceremony held by the Anbarra Aboriginal community. Their homelands lie around the estuary of the Blyth River, which flows into the Arafura Sea on the north coast of Arnhem Land in the Northern Territory of Australia. The visitors were anthropologist Les Hiatt, myself and our two children, and Kim McKenzie, a filmmaker from the Australian Institute of Aboriginal Studies in Canberra, together with his sound recordist, Peter Barker. Les had known and worked closely with the Anbarra since 1958, I had known them since 1975, but Peter and Kim had never met them before. Betty Meehan, Les's former wife, was also visiting the Anbarra at this time, in order to investigate aspects of their material culture.

We had all come to a place named Junawunya to participate in the final rites for an Anbarra man named Angabarraparra and to make a film of the ceremony. This man died in 1972 and was buried in the Christian cemetery at a nearby government settlement called Maningrida. His bones were now to be given a final ritual disposal in a hollow-log coffin painted with clan emblems. Angabarraparra had been a famous singer and ritual leader in his day. Furthermore, he was the older classificatory brother of Les's main instructor in Anbarra culture, a man then in his fifties named Frank Gurrmanamana. Frank and Les had been planning Angabarraparra's final rites for several years and had often discussed the possibility of filming them. Now Kim and Peter had come up from Canberra at Frank's request and the ceremony and filming that followed were very much a collaborative venture on the part of the Aborigines, the film crew, and the scholars involved. Twenty hours of film and sound tape were recorded and out of it emerged a 57-minute film, *Waiting for Harry* (McKenzie 1980).[1]

I have chosen to illustrate the nature of the aesthetics and politics of Arnhem Land ritual from the camera rolls that formed the filmmaker's raw material for *Waiting for Harry*. These are accessible in the archives of the Australian Institute of Aboriginal Studies, together with the sound tapes, the transcriptions of the Anbarra's discourse in the Aboriginal language Gijingarli and an English translation of these. The transcriptions and trans-

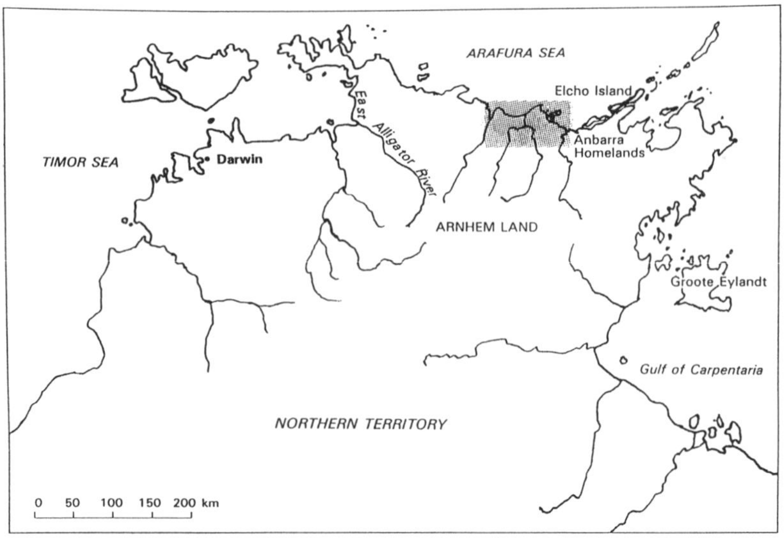

1. *Map of Northern Territory, Australia.*

lations were the product of about two months' collaborative work by four of the Anbarra men who took part in the ceremony, Les Hiatt, and myself. I use some of the translations in this paper to exemplify Anbarra aesthetic and political concepts but I realize that, in doing so, I offer my own contextualization and interpretation of them. That is inevitable, and it is also unavoidable that some aspects of the subject of this paper are not discussed on the *Harry* footage, especially some aspects of what I shall argue are dominant aesthetic principles of Arnhem Land ritual, for the reason that these matters are rarely discussed in the abstract by Aboriginal people.

There are, however, other ways of approaching the immanent but unarticulated principles of an oral culture like that of the Anbarra. In this study I have drawn on several kinds of data: what Anbarra people have said to each other and to me, particularly in ritual contexts, which is discourse that I and others have recorded and can contextualize; texts and recorded performances of songs and dances and what people have told me of their meanings; what I know of the technical vocabulary of Anbarra performance styles in song, dance, and the visual arts; and inferences that I and other scholars have drawn from repeated observations of Arnhem Land ritual.

There is no doubt that *Waiting for Harry* as an artistic entity was shaped by non-Aboriginal aesthetic principles and notions of cohesion. It is equally true, however, that it incorporates and expresses Aboriginal notions of what is important in ritual performance. Because of this, the film has a dual focus. The senior Aboriginal participants in the ritual explain to their Aboriginal guests at Junawunya significant aspects of Anbarra life and rites. They also direct themselves from time to time to Kim the filmmaker or to a general European audience in order to explain their worldview to people outside their culture. The film records Aboriginal people interacting among themselves at a funeral rite while at the same time offering a privileged outsider's view of the nature of Anbarra ritual politics, focusing on the problems a ceremonial leader faces in organizing a complex ritual in contemporary Aboriginal Australia. The outsider's viewpoint is overtly

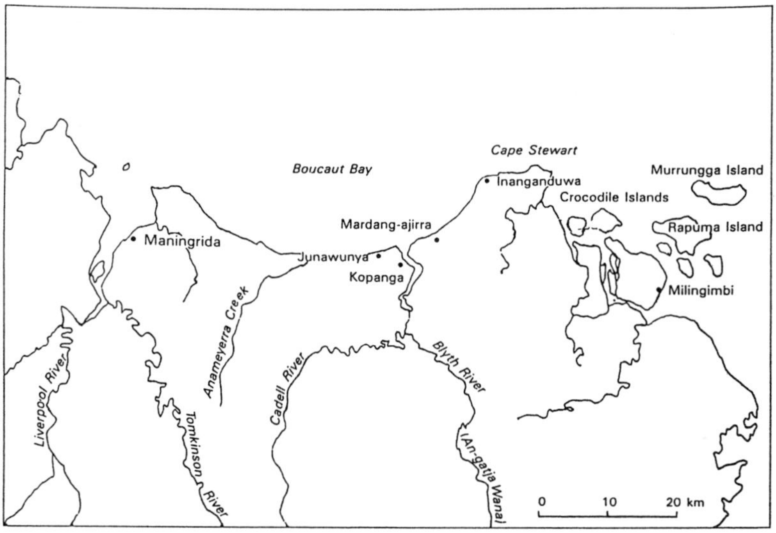

2. Map of the Anbarra homelands.

that of Les Hiatt, who speaks the commentary, but his voice often gives way to the edited sound track of Aboriginal discourse (the conversation and singing being largely in Gijingarli). In the last analysis it is the filmmaker who has chosen what footage to keep and what to throw away, what scenes to juxtapose, and whether to observe the chronological sequence of events as they happened in real time or to occasionally cut and splice chronologically disparate footage.

Anbarra Society and Belief

The Anbarra, whose name means "river mouth [people]," speak a language they call Gijingarli and others call Burarra. They number over 200 people and include members of 6 clans, each of which owns a separate area of land near the Blyth River mouth. In earlier times they ranged over the lands of the constituent clans. Men hunted animals and speared or trapped fish while women gathered shellfish, plant foods, and reptiles. In 1957 the Northern Territory Administration established a trading post at Maningrida, a place to the west of Anbarra territory on the eastern bank of the Liverpool River. Anbarra, as well as other neighboring groups, moved from their homelands to this new settlement and some of them have lived there ever since. However, since the mid-1970s increasing numbers of people have returned to their homelands to live for all or part of each year (see Hiatt 1965:8–13; 1986a:3–8).

Like all Aborigines, the Anbarra believe that the universe comprises two coextensive but disparate domains. The first is the world of the here-and-now, which is perceptible to the human senses. The second is the world of the spirits, a transcendental world assumed to lie beyond the realm of the senses, but from time to time realized in this world. Individuals may sometimes perceive the eternal realities of the Dreamtime world, as it is often called in English, both through dreams and in ritual performance.

The Dreamtime was a period of creativity. Anbarra people believe that in the Dreamtime various deities, called *wangarr,* created the land and shaped the landscape as we now know it. Some of them are particularly associated with specific clan lands, where they are thought to now lie quiescent in focal points of the landscape. Before these deities retreated, they left behind tokens of their being in the form of designs—drawn on human bodies, bark or wood, or on the ground—songs, dances, and carved stone or wooden objects. These palpable signs of the wangarr are owned by specific clans and may be reproduced under certain circumstances, usually of a ritual nature. Other wangarr, who were not necessarily creators, are associated with specific clans and their estates and are celebrated in the clan songs, dances, and designs the clan members own.

Anbarra thought is dualistic. People believe that in the Dreamtime the whole world was divided into two categories or moieties called *jowanga* and *yirrchinga* and has remained so ever since. All living beings, including humans and the observable world of nature, belong to one or the other of the moieties. Thus all barramundi fish are yirrchinga, while eels are jowanga. Humans, however, are divided between the moieties in accordance with a principle of patrilineal descent, so that an individual belongs to the same moiety as his or her father. Land is also either jowanga or yirrchinga and so are the wangarr associated with it and the clan songs that celebrate them.

These clan songs, called *manikay,* are owned and sung by groups of clans who feel a strong corporate link as a result of their joint ownership, even though their estates may not be contiguous and they often speak more than one language. The Anbarra have direct links with three song series, called Djambidj, Goyulan, and Bugala. The first two, which concern us in this paper, are jowanga and the third belongs to the yirrchinga moiety. Manikay song series comprise between 20 and 40 song subjects, each made up of a number of verses. Each manikay celebrates a separate set of wangarr spirits, which usually includes natural species, for example, Shark, Bittern, Bandicoot, and King Brown Snake; natural phenomena like Morning Star and North-West Monsoon; important artifacts such as Canoe and Boomerang; natural resources like Wild Honey and Red Ochre; and groups of humanlike spirit people.

Although manikay songs are owned by all members of relevant clans, including women, they are sung by a small number of mature men. These men sing and beat out a rhythmic accompaniment for themselves on pairs of hardwood clapsticks. Another man provides a low drone on a *didjeridu* or wooden trumpet, which also at times erupts into a series of hoot patterns on a higher tone (see Clunies Ross and Wild 1984:214–46). Women may dance to one side of the singers and other men may beat time with sticks or sing softly. A full-scale performance of manikay songs requires men's as well as women's dancing. This normally happens in ritual performance.

Manikay songs are sung for several different kinds of rite, but their most serious and formal purpose is to ritualize death. They also personalize death, for, as Hiatt has put it, "an individual's song series is sung on his or her deathbed. A verse or two announces the death in neighbouring communities. And prolonged singing accompanies each stage in the mortuary procedures, beginning with burial or tree-platform disposal, followed by purification of the bereaved with fire and water, retrieval and cleaning of the bones some months later, and ending after years have elapsed with the disposal of the bones in a hollow-log coffin" (1986a:9–10). The ritual filmed in *Waiting for Harry* was an example of the last stage in these mortuary procedures.

3. Mardadupa (background) prepares a hollow log for painting while Gurrmanamana sings Wild Honey. His son Gumugun plays the didjeridu. Kopanga, Blyth River, 1975. (Photo by Les Hiatt)

Ritual Aesthetics

The important objects of Arnhem Land ritual discourse are two—the spirits (wangarr) and human society. These two objects provide the inspiration for creativity in ritual performance and ensure that each ritual enactment is unique, even though it follows observably consistent procedures common to all performances of a particular type of rite. Uniqueness, in the case of funeral rites, stems from the fact that the relationship between an individual, the involved clans, and the particular set of powers with whom these people claim a special attachment is unable to be duplicated. Within such often repeated rites there is a foundation of common structures that permit them to function as group celebrations, yet the unique arrangement of the component parts also allows them to act as the eulogy of the individual for whom the rite is enacted and to express the connections that individual established over the course of her/his life with the world of the spirits (see Morphy 1989). Such connections are typically made through participation in ritual, so there is a sense in which the final goodbye for any individual refers consciously to all the ritual texts s/he participated in throughout life and so to that person's most significant encounters with the wangarr. Mortuary rites are a kind of performed epitaph for the dead.

At several significant points in the *Waiting for Harry* rite, people paused to give due praise to the dead man, Angabarraparra. One particularly sacred moment came when one of his personal belongings, a paperbark bundle representing the wangarr Mulanda, a sea bird, was burnt in a ritual font. This action both celebrated and brought to an end the dead man's role as a ritual leader, for the bundle is of a kind that leading dancers and cantors carry when performing their ritual roles. The bundle in a sense represented Angabarraparra as a ritual leader.

During his funeral people were reminded of him as they discussed the importance of the spirit beings they were representing in visual, song, or dance form together with the estates these beings moved in during the Dreamtime. In the course of a painting session on the coffin, Andrew Mardadupa, whose mother belonged to the dead man's clan, remarked:

> This cross-hatching I'm painting and Marrawal [a spirit man] there, belong to the country of my mother's clan—here where we are now. It's the clan of the dead man who lies up there on the platform [pointing to a covered suitcase containing Angabarraparra's bones] (camera roll 59).

Later, Harry Diyama, nephew of the deceased, reminisced about the great age of the sand sculpture design of an ancestral stringybark tree that the men were making for the funeral, and recalled that this design had an interesting history. Although it had been conventional to draw it for Junawunya clan members before World War II, the dead man's political maneuvering with other clans brought about a change in practice which could, apparently, only be modified after his death:

> LES HIATT: Did you make Stringybark after the war?
>
> HARRY DIYAMA: No, we didn't. When people died, we made sand sculptures, but your brother, the dead man, said that as he'd been given the Fish Trap sand sculpture, we should make that. There was a lot of trouble over that (camera roll 66).

So it happened that Angabarraparra's own funeral was the occasion for the revival of the old emblem and the continuance of the practice he had instituted himself. Stringybark was the major sand sculpture at the men's ground, but Fish Trap was selected as the ground pattern within which the finished coffin was erected.

The aesthetic principles in play during the enactment of a particular mortuary ritual have to do with the most effective, the most complete, and the most appropriate entry of the powers into the domain of mortals that is possible through human effort. There is an assumption among Aborigines that, in spite of the discontinuities between divine and human worlds, certain kinds of ritual representations of the powers, executed in certain ways by appropriate performers, can create a feeling that the powers are present to the human senses. There is, indeed, an assumption that the powers *are* actually present in ritual performance if they are correctly represented. Thus the aesthetics of performance are designed to maximize the impact of the powers, not as objects of worship, obeisance, sacrifice, or invocation, but as entities and essences. Characteristically, Aboriginal ritual texts do not inscribe a particular position for the human agent vis-á-vis the divine powers (see Maddock 1982:105–7; Clunies Ross 1983).

The individual components of ritual performance—the songs, dances, and paintings, for example—are expressive epitomes of the spirit beings they represent. In song, unique and particular details of the power's being are seen as manifestations of an archetypal or ideal form in a manner similar to the forms of Platonism and these archetypes are credited with an independent existence (see Hiatt and Jones 1988:10–19; Clunies Ross 1986:65; Clunies Ross and Mundrugmundrug 1988:14–15; Merlan 1987:149–50). So, for example, the metonymic epithet "fatty-necked one" applied to the Djambidj spirit-being Turtle both typefies and idealizes it. Ritual performance transforms this essentially contemplative mode of songs and painting into dramatic display, so that the songs, dances, and designs assume a kinetic power and brilliance which increases the intensity of their manifestation of ancestral power. Howard Morphy (1989) has suggested, writing particularly of the painting of the Yolngu, eastern neighbors of the Anbarra, that the paramount aesthetic objective of Arnhem Land art is to realize the presence of the ancestral powers in the most brilliant possible way.

The desire to represent the powers with intensity affects the performance style of Aboriginal people. To represent the powers enhances an individual's own reputation in human society because it demonstrates that person's rights in and closeness to ancestral events. Performers act with vigor and intensity but they do not allow themselves to be possessed by the powers. They are self-conscious, frequently evaluating their own and others' performances. Anbarra performances are characterized by fine control and split-second timing. Undoubtedly one of the most highly valued attributes of a performer is the ability to time a dance, song, or invocation with precision and to transfer from one kind of movement to another or from one kind of song style to another easily and without apparent effort. Criticisms are often made of men who forget their lines and break down under the stress of having to produce invocations of strings of clan names under pressure. Good cantors are said to "have a big head," that is, to be able to remember and reproduce names in correct order in ritual performance. So, in the *Waiting for Harry* rite, a couple of men complained that one of the cantors, Roy Riwa, kept forgetting the clan names. Riwa's excuse was that he was so overcome with grief on behalf of the dead man's clan that it interfered with his recall (camera roll 96).

Precision and good timing coupled with vigor are the hallmarks of a good performer and it can be readily understood that these qualities enhance the *éclat* of the wangarr's instantiation. Good dancing men are admired for their crisp and vigorous leg and thigh movements. High leaps called *jangalk* are a spectacular and much-valued part of leading dancers' routines. A dramatic, finely timed finish to a dance is most important. Outstanding didjeridu players are the ones who can produce clearly defined, contrasting hoot patterns on the overtone above the fundamental sustained drone. Singers are praised for vigorous and carrying voices that allow them to sustain the momentum of ceremony for days, weeks, and even sometimes months. Their virtuosity in improvising strings of verses to form the liturgy of ritual is also much admired and given special scope in unaccompanied vocal codas that form the terminating section of each verse.

Both the formal structures of Anbarra ritual and their semantic components work together to produce a dramatic contemplation of the powers. The building blocks of the ritual are short song verses, whose average duration is a little over a minute, together with short invocations of clan names and the names of spirit beings. These elements assume different strophic forms depending on the nature of the ceremony of which they form a part and on the context of their use in that ceremony. They are therefore plastic and context-sensitive (see Clunies Ross and Wild 1984; Clunies Ross 1986:48–51). At the same time they are the foundation of a kind of ritual that uses the common oral technique of variation and repetition in an iterative mode to produce performances of concentrated intensity.

Variation and repetition occur within each song verse as the singers repeat varied combinations of conventional phrases describing the wangarr subjects. Major themes to do with each subject are repeated and developed from verse to verse, and one subject leads to another with which it has a thematic association in the mythology that underpins each clan's emblems. So, for instance, a Djambidj singer might follow a sequence of Wild Honey verses with verses from the song Marsupial Mouse, a being who feeds on

4. Maragulbiana, a widely respected dancer, executes jangalk *(high leaps) in the Cockatoo dance from Djambidj. Kopanga, Blyth River, 1975. (Photo by Les Hiatt)*

nectar and honey. The fact that these rituals are multimedia events, with song, dance, and visual display all representing the same wangarr subject, further reinforces the intense quality of performances.

I indicated earlier that an Anbarra mortuary rite is reflexive in respect to each individual whose life it celebrates. There is also another dimension to reflexivity in Arnhem Land ritual and that is to be found encoded in the song texts that form its liturgy. Often these texts are about spirit beings in whose honor the whole ritual was instituted in the Dreamtime, or they may be about a spirit being that is an agent of human ritual practice. In the Anbarra song series Goyulan (Morning Star), Fire is one of its subjects. Fire is a powerful cleansing agent in Arnhem Land ritual and this is the central focus of the song, which is not concerned with the multifarious functions of fire in the human and natural world. Rather, the song's exclusive concern is with fire's ceremonial significance, especially in the *darda* rite in which a dead person's possessions are burned and those who have touched the dead body are brushed with smouldering bunches of green leaves to remove death's pollution. The fire song also alludes to the belief that the precedent for this rite was established in the ancestral past when a spirit man first made a darda sand sculpture and danced beside it in sorrow for the departure of the morning star from the skies every dawn. It is the Morning Star spirit who gives her name to the Goyulan song series and is also the subject of another ritually reflexive song (see Clunies Ross and Mundrugmundrug 1988).

Concentration of meaning in ritual comes about in another way too. The thematic elements from which it is constructed each have a number of potential meanings, some generated within the ritual in hand, others generated contextually or associatively. This is because both formal and thematic components can be used in several different types of rite in combination with other components so that they reflect the central themes of a particular ceremony. For instance, Wild Honey imagery occurs both in funerary rites for Djambidj-owning clans and in another ceremony called Rom, which is a ritual of diplomacy (see Hiatt 1986a:10–13). In mortuary ceremonies, Wild Honey is associated with the spirit being Hollow Log (presumably because in nature wild bees often make their nests in hollow trees) and hence with dead bones. A painted hollow-log ossuary in fact receives the crushed bones of the dead in these rituals. In the Rom ceremony a decorated wooden pole is also the main ritual artifact, but it is not hollow. Hence the emphasis of Wild Honey in this rite is on its energizing and life-giving qualities in the context of a ceremony devoted to cordiality and goodwill (Clunies Ross 1986:52–53).

5. *An old* Larreija *(Sawfish) hollow-log coffin standing at Mardang-ajirra, east of the Blyth River, 1960. (Photo by Les Hiatt)*

6. Relatives of Harry Diyama obliterate a sand sculpture at a darda *ceremony for him. Maningrida, 1986. (Photo by Les Hiatt)*

Because components of Arnhem Land ritual take on a variety of meanings in the different ritual contexts in which they appear, they tend to be polysemous (see Keen 1977). Polysemy is a powerful instrument in the construction of a particularly important aesthetic quality in Arnhem Land, and indeed all, Aboriginal ritual. This is the quality of exclusiveness whose value depends on the notion that only certain classes of society, usually among Aborigines initiated men, can have access to full knowledge of the spirit world. The dichotomy between inclusion and exclusion is an underlying preoccupation of most Aboriginal ritual, even in those which, like mortuary rites, are not absolutely exclusive of women (see Maddock 1982:132–36). In the *Waiting for Harry* funeral ceremony there is a physical separation of the men's ground and bough shade, where preparation of the coffin takes place, from the camp where women and childen carry on their daily lives. This distance is only mediated twice in such a ceremony, in both cases by revelatory dances. The first is the dance of the Mulanda bird and the second is the final procession in which the filled coffin is brought out into public view. Even this bold gesture is often qualified by the desire to withhold the full power and revealed presence of the wangarr from the laity. In 1975 I was present at a similar funeral in which men painted an elaborate coffin called *dupun* (see Clunies Ross and Hiatt 1977). Only the men ever saw the elegantly painted emblems. They decided, after a lot of debate, that the fine cross-hatched lines that covered the log's surface made the coffin "too dear" for women and children to look at. This is because cross-hatching, above all other elements of a painted surface, represents the power of the wangarr most fully. Morphy (1989) indicates that Yolngu people have a similar view. The result, in the 1975 case, was that when the hollow-log coffin was brought out to the public camp and dance ground it was swathed in cotton bandages. It remained so during all the public dances and invocations and when it was finally buried in a grave the next morning. This instance, one among many that could be adduced, indicates that considerations of sacredness and the control of the sacred always take precedence over the uninhibited aesthetic appreciation of the visual impact of sacred designs.

I suspect that this concern with control of the sacred is also the basis for an apparent inconsistency in the execution of Arnhem Land ritual. People show a concern for permanency and stability in the representation of the wangarr, to the extent that an oral medium allows. On the other hand, they have a habit of erasing or blurring sacred designs immediately after they have served their ritual purpose, as if to leave them might allow their power to work in uncontrolled ways after the ceremony had finished. Sand sculptures are often erased after they have served as the locus for ritual events. In darda purification rites people cleanse themselves from the pollution of death by washing and brushing themselves with burning leaves in a font within a sand sculpture. Immediately afterwards the sculpture is destroyed, often by kinsmen of the dead who crawl through it to obliterate its outlines. Similarly, the hollow-log coffin filmed in *Waiting for Harry* did not remain erect at Junawunya displaying its clan emblems, as Frank Gurrmanamana so proudly announced it would on the film. A year after it had been put up, there was a consensus that it should be taken down and buried, ostensibly so the log would not split and allow the bones to spill out, but probably also because the tension between the desire to flaunt clan emblems and the desire to conceal and so control them became too strong. The fact that this coffin, like the 1975 dupun, was also wrapped in cloth before burial, gives support to my surmise.

7. *At the end of the* Waiting for Harry *rite the painted hollow-log coffin stands inside a sand sculpture of Fish Trap at Junawunya. (Photo by Peter Barker)*

8. *One year after the* Waiting for Harry *ceremony, people decide to cover up the hollow-log coffin and bury it. Junawunya, 1979. (Photo by Betty Meehan)*

The Politics of Ritual

If the aesthetics of performance are designed to maximize the impact of the powers in human society, the politics of ritual performance are based upon notions of clan and individual rights in and responsibilities for the powers. There is an assumption among Aboriginal people that the ancestral powers of the Dreamtime entrusted tokens of their being to particular groups of people in the form of songs, dances, and designs. In the case of mortuary ritual, the relevant groups are land-owning corporations of people related to each other by descent in the male line. Hiatt has argued that the memorabilia that the wangarr entrust to these patrilineal clans function as badges of allegiance as well as serving as a palpable bond with the dead of the clan, who are the link between living members and the transcendental world of the spirits (Hiatt and Jones 1988:10–11). It follows that each clan, and individuals within clans, have both a right and a duty to reproduce the ancestral designs that were imparted to their forebears. The production of clan songs, dances, and designs is a living demonstration of an individual's or a group's engagement with the transcendental world.

Although land ownership and ancestral designs are inherited through the male line, men have significant privileges and responsibilities in respect to their mothers' land and their mothers' clan emblems. This also applies to men in respect to their mothers' mothers' lands. Hence, in a mortuary rite, performance roles are shared between men of the deceased's own clan, between men whose mothers were from the deceased's clan (*ngamonbeninga*), and men whose mothers' mothers came from the clan (*aburramari*) (see Hiatt 1965:54). People performing these roles assume certain expected responsibilities and behavior patterns.

Men who belong to the clan of the deceased and are the owners of the ritual songs and emblems to be deployed are expected to take primary responsibility for assembling and hosting visiting participants and for making sure that the ritual procedures run smoothly. They are also expected to present the leading performers with gifts at the conclusion of the rite. These days the gifts usually include *damper*—flat unleavened bread, supplanting the cycad palm nut bread of the past—tobacco, and lengths of cotton cloth. Any blame for a ritual that goes wrong is laid at the door of the senior men from the deceased's clan, which is why Frank Gurrmanamana expresses such frequent anxiety in *Waiting for Harry* that the funeral might not be well attended by sufficient numbers of important people and, in particular, that Harry Diyama, the senior ngamonbeninga, might not be present during critical stages of the ritual.

Although the owning group has the sole right to decide when its designs should be employed and which designs these should be, they are expected to make a formal request to the ngamonbeninga group to draw the designs for them. Thus the ngamonbeninga are the custodians of the owners' sacred emblems by virtue of their mothers' clan membership in the dead person's land-owning unit. It is their prerogative to produce the clan designs and to ensure that all preparations are correct. Diyama expresses this responsibility clearly on camera roll 62:

> We who were born of women from your clan will work and see all is done well.[. . .] It must be correct.

Gurrmanamana endorses Diyama's authority over him in this regard, explaining to Kim McKenzie, the filmmaker:

9. Some of the clan emblems on the hollow-log coffin prepared for the Waiting for Harry *ritual. There are two Turtles and a Fish species. The cross-hatching represents Junawunya, estate of the dead man. (Photo by Peter Barker)*

> I've been waiting for Harry and yesterday he came. Today I'll start painting [the bones]. The dead man was his uncle on his mother's side. His blood uncle. That's why I waited. As the dead man's nephew, Harry's my boss (camera roll 60).

It was the inherent tension between the owner and ngamonbeninga roles, and the way they were played by the individuals concerned, that provided the dramatic framework and cohesion for the film of this ritual. The title *Waiting for Harry* epitomizes what the filmmaker and his anthropological advisors saw as the dominant political issue of the ceremony, but this is not at odds with the expressed concerns of the protagonists.

To some extent the ngamonbeninga role involves criticism and admonition of the owners for the way ceremonial procedure is being carried out, though this is shared by the aburramari, men whose mothers' mothers came from the dead person's clan. Their special role is to inspect the work at the completion of the preparatory phase of the ceremony and to confirm that it is correct and well done so that the final phase of breaking up the bones of the dead and placing them in the hollow-log coffin can proceed. These responsibilities are taken seriously to the point where, if permission to proceed is withheld by the aburramari, the whole ceremony is endangered and cannot be continued until they have given their approval. This happened, as Hiatt tells *Waiting for Harry* viewers in the voice-over commentary, in a similar mortuary rite in 1975, when the same group of aburramari who attended the filmed ceremony inspected a hollow log at Kopanga, a settlement at the Blyth River mouth. They had traveled by boat from Milingimbi mission further to the east, took one look at the art work on the coffin and announced that it was no good. They then returned to Milingimbi and eventually came back to Kopanga a fortnight later.

Toward the end of *Waiting for Harry* one of them, Leo Wujal, remembers that event and reminds the owning clans of the aburramari's responsibilities and their importance, while at the same time suggesting that they might not have come to such a lowly event if they had not been acting out their role as mothers' mothers' kin:

> The white men wanted to make a film of the ceremony. Whenever Gurrmanamana and his younger brother Malkorda put on a ceremony, I am there. You remember a few years ago they buried two of their kin at Kopanga. Hardly anyone bothered to turn up. But we were there—my brothers and I from Milingimbi. We came, didn't we? We came to pay our respects to the dead from Junawunya.
>
> We are always the first to come to your ceremonies. Again and again we've come. We've come to your funeral and your Rom ceremonies, and we're here now for this one. And we'll come again.
>
> The symbols on this coffin belong to the clan of my mother's mother's brother and I am responsible for them.
>
> Whoever you are, and wherever you are, don't dare to steal them from me! Don't try to tell me what to do! (camera roll 99).

It is clear from this speech and many others like it on the *Waiting for Harry* footage that the spirit of cooperation and helpfulness between aburramari and the owning clans points to an only thinly veiled underlying rivalry. Rivalry between owners and ngamonbeninga is also evident, and in both cases alternates with statements of concern and threat against anyone who would dare to steal and use their clan designs without permission. Diyama articulates this nexus on camera roll 67:

> This sand sculpture represents a tree called Biyarriyarri or Galupanda. Only we whose mothers come from this country are allowed to make it. That is the law. You say in English "allowed." Our word is *joborr*. It means that we have the right to do this, and no one can interfere.
>
> So only we are allowed to make it. We've got to hold on to this emblem. It was put here for us by the gods. When we make it, we must do it very carefully. We mustn't rush it, or we might leave something out. And we've got to keep our eyes open to make sure that others don't steal it. If someone tried to steal this sand sculpture, we would say: 'Get out! Where are your emblems?' That's the way it

> is for sand sculptures, sacred emblems, ceremonies, and so on. We can't share this sand sculpture with anyone else. It belongs to us. No one else has a right to this sand sculpture. It has always been ours. It's the same with our totems. No one can take Seagull from us, or Eel, or Brown Snake, and so on.

Arnhem Land ritual politics and their ceremonial realization are products of a tension between the desire of the parties involved to cooperate and the desire to be exclusive. The latter is expressed on many levels and involves both structural and semantic elements of performance, as we shall see, as well as clan and individual rivalries. Thus the complementarity of the owners' role vis-á-vis those of the ngamonbeninga and aburramari can easily be transformed into an assertion of fitness of the latter to take over clan emblems and clan lands, should the owning clan's numbers dwindle. So what is normally an assertion of support can become a takeover bid; what is theoretically a complementary role may become a vehicle for personal aggrandizement at the expense of a kinsperson, even if this is often only half serious (see Hiatt 1986b, especially 12–15).

In this context, it is interesting to see how individuals realize their conventionally determined performance roles in ceremonies like the one represented in *Waiting for Harry* and make the most of the opportunities they offer for personal advancement. The examples of Harry Diyama and Frank Gurrmanamana are instructive. While both men play conventional ritual roles, their performances are also expressions of their own personalities and the opportunities they derived from the occasion of a filmed ritual for self-promotion and the display of their clan emblems to a wider audience than the Aboriginal world of Northern Arnhem Land.

Diyama exploited his custodial and executive role as ngamonbeninga with considerable panache and vanity. He made the most of the ready availability of motor transport to ration his appearances at the ceremonial ground, thereby signaling the importance of his presence. Undoubtedly, modern technology makes life both easier and harder for ritual organizers like Gurrmanamana. It is easier to use a steel axe and a four-wheel-drive vehicle to cut down a large log and transport it to where it is to be painted, easier to use trucks to transport loads of performers to the ceremonial ground. But it is also easier for key participants to come and go away again just at the crucial moment. And that is what Harry Diyama did. The relative mobility conferred on important men by access to trucks, boats, and planes makes the possibility that a ceremony may not be brought to a satisfactory conclusion rather more likely than in traditional times. Diyama was keen to indicate that he was in demand all over the countryside, not just locally at Junawunya:

> I'm needed for another ceremony at Mewunba. I must take people to that one as well (camera roll 28).

When at last he deigns to attend the climax of the Junawunya rite, his arrival is celebrated by two Morning Star singers giving a spirited performance of their Brolga song, upon which he comments petulantly:

> I thought the singer would really bang those clapsticks in honor of my recent arrival, but he just sat there tapping them (camera roll 91).

Diyama was also critical of things that were really exceptionally well done.

Men had cut and hauled a very large log to Junawunya for the coffin. When Harry inspected it, he criticized it because it was too short:

HARRY DIYAMA: The log is too short. The hollow is not big enough for the bones. You should have cut a bigger one.

JOHNNY MUNDRUGMUNDRUG: It's a small one to paint [i.e., if it were bigger we'd have even more to paint].

HARRY DIYAMA: I don't want to come back some day and see that the coffin has fallen down and spilled the bones out! (camera roll 62).

Gurrmanamana's performance of the owner role is even more interesting and highly innovative in its exploitation of the medium of film. Although most people were conscious that they were performing for the camera most of the time—and often engaged in running jokes centering on the camera as phallus—only Gurrmanamana was able to utilize the film in an extension of his traditional role in the ritual. There is no doubt that he conceived of the film as an arena where he, as owner of his clan's symbols, could display them to a wider audience, even though he ran the risk, as he saw it, that some unscrupulous outsider might steal them. He saw his part in organizing a team of anthropologists and filmmakers as a proper one for a ceremonial host and owner of clan designs:

> This film is mine. It is an important thing. I am standing here to speak. The patterns on this coffin belong to me. They were laid down by the gods, and I have always followed them. Now people everywhere will see them, just as in the past I have seen theirs. I have been to many places and seen much. Now others will see the sacred designs that belong to me.
>
> This is a great victory. The sacred symbols that I hold so dear are now on a film. For that reason the film is also precious to me.
>
> I told these cameramen that I wanted them to come. I brought them here from Canberra to make this film. It is now done and I am filled with pride (camera roll 99).

Gurrmanamana's role in exploiting the potentialities of the double performance event—the ritual that took place in real time and the film of the ritual—goes far beyond a conventional understanding of the owner's part to an exploration of the opportunities film offers him and his culture for self-examination and freedom from the evanescence of oral performance. He recognizes the possibility that film holds for aesthetic enhancement of the visual effect of ancestral designs. At one point (camera roll 41) he instructs one of the painters to paint a whole variety of fish on the coffin, not just one, as "it will look good on the film." He instructs someone else to take away a large fish he's brought home for dinner, because "it's had its picture taken." He also recognizes the comic potential of the film to juxtapose the formal and the everyday aspects of ritual:

> This film is ours. It will be taken to Canberra and then returned. You'll look at it and laugh. There'll be me eating cockles [. . .] (camera roll 77).

He is aware of what seems to him to be the essential narcissism of Western film in relation to its audience:

> This film is ours. These filmmakers are working for us. They will go away and return the film to us. The picture will stay here. We'll look at ourselves, just like white people look at themselves and applaud. We'll clap at ourselves and sit talking (camera roll 30).

The Anbarra are by no means unusual in Arnhem Land society in taking ritual politics seriously. Traditionally ritual business has been, and often still is, that area of human activity in which the highest political power could be won. It is not for nothing that Arnhem Landers refer in English to ritual as "business" and to ritual experts as "businessmen." Ritual is business in several of its Standard English senses: it is serious, professional work; it is action on stage—in the theatrical sense; and it is trade, trade in emblems other than one's own and in the rights to perform other peoples' songs and dances (see Thomson 1949; Berndt 1951; Hiatt 1965:68–70, 1986). Finally ritual business is the management of people and affairs that, if done well, brings immense prestige to the entrepreneur. Other benefits outside the ritual sphere quite often follow prominence in ritual as a consequence of the network of personal relationships that ritual experts build up through attendance at many ceremonies and the resulting exchange of songs and emblems. Often, for example, connections with ritual trading partners could lead to offers of marriage (see Hiatt 1986a:12). Furthermore, political power and executive ability in the performing arts go hand in hand. There are few if any ritual businessmen in Arnhem Land who are not virtuoso performers in one or more of the major art forms. So the ability to achieve technical brilliance in performance and the power to give aesthetic and emotional pleasure go with the power to manage ritual and to make executive decisions about when, how, and with whom a ritual performance should be enacted.

I have mentioned the complementarity of performance roles in Arnhem Land ritual on the level of the kin-determined contrastive behaviors of owners and the two executive and managerial groups, the ngamonbeninga and aburramari. This complementarity of owners and managers, as anthropologists term them, is widespread in Aboriginal Australia and by no means unique to the Anbarra (see Maddock 1982:47–55). There are other levels of complementarity apparent in Anbarra ritual which depend upon the fundamental dualism of Arnhem Land thought that divides the whole world, including human society, into moieties. We have seen that areas of land, the powers associated with them, and the owning human clans belong to one or the other of the two moieties, jowanga and yirrchinga. As marriage within the moiety is prohibited (though sometimes irregularities occur), an individual and her or his mother normally belong to opposite moieties. So, in view of the fact that men whose mothers belonged to a particular clan are required to participate in every funeral, a full-scale mortuary rite must be carried out by performers from several clans of opposite moiety. This means that songs, dances, and designs from both moieties are usually executed, with the dominant moiety being that of the deceased person. Often singers from the same moiety as the owners' group but with distinct song series will assist the owning clan to provide the main liturgical accompaniment to the funeral.

People place high value on the participation of other clans of the same moiety whose songs have themes that link up with those of the owning group. So, for instance, all the "Sugar Bag" (Wild Honey) clans assist one another at ceremonies and thus enrich the aesthetic and emotional effect of mortuary ritual. The participation of several groups of singers also leads to structural complexity of performances, so that there is frequently regular alternation between performing groups, each taking turns to sing a thematically appropriate and complementary song. Such practices have been recorded in many parts of Aboriginal Australia (see Howitt 1904:524) and are probably an important characteristic of Aboriginal performances generally.

The thematic cohesion produced by these complex performances is made possible by the existence of rhetorical conventions common to both jowanga and yirrchinga song series of the region and corresponding similarities in the repertoire of dance movements that accompany the songs. For instance, the two jowanga moiety song series Djambidj and Goyulan each have a song and accompanying dance about a species of bird associated with the open sea and rocky coastal islets. Brown booby (Mulanda) is the Djambidj bird, while white-breasted sea eagle (Damalkurra) belongs to Goyulan. Not only does each song present its subject using comparable topoi, but the ritual uses of the two songs are similar. Each is strongly associated with the ritual invocation of the names of the clans who own the song series and related emblems. There is also a similarity between the associated dances and iconic representations of these two spirit beings. Further, the Mulanda of Djambidj is closely related to the subject of another song from a different jowanga song series named Gamalangga, which is owned and sung by the mothers' mothers' brothers of Djambidj owners. At the *Waiting for Harry* rite, Djambidj and Gamalangga singers took turns to explore the thematic interrelatedness of their two songs (see Clunies Ross 1983). Such structural and conceptual similarities across songs and dances allow the general sequence of mortuary ritual to remain constant while at the same time permitting all kinds of variation within sequences and the juxtaposition of comparable but not exactly similar elements of performance. Politically, the effect is one of cooperation and integration; aesthetically and emotionally, the performance becomes more intense.

For the Aboriginal performers, the invocation of strings of clan names is probably the most emotive part of mortuary ritual. These clan names belong to the song owners, both living and dead, whose clan estates may lie scattered over the landscape for quite a distance. The invocations, which occur at climactic points of the ritual, are undertaken by a specialist cantor whose performance is judged by the criteria of correctness in the enumeration of clans (moving from east to west), comprehensiveness in enumeration (not leaving any clan out), and an ability to maintain the rhythmic and melodic pattern of the invocation over a long period of time. We have already seen that participants can be highly critical of failure on any of these scores and also most admiring of success. Yet at the same time that they insist on correctness and completeness, they become impatient with the long roll-call of names as the invocation runs on. One can often detect a to-ing and fro-ing between the desire to conclude and the desire to include, often expressed by the same individual. We find this well evidenced in dialog between the performers toward the end of the *Waiting for Harry* ritual:

ROY RIWA: Where are the cantors?

FRANK GURRMANAMANA: Call some more clan names.

JOHNNY GUIYABAKA: Again, again!

10. Men sort and clean the bones of a deceased brother and sister in part of a sand sculpture, while two Goyulan singers (left, at the suitcase) perform their Red Ochre song. Kopanga, Blyth River, 1975. (Photo by Les Hiatt)

SOMEONE: Call the clan names. Again, again!

LEO WUJAL: Call the clan names.

FRANK GURRMANAMANA: Don't make it too long.

[*Cantor calls some names.*]

SOMEONE ELSE: They're close to the end.

HARRY DIYAMA: Call out!

SOMEONE ELSE: Hurry, please!

WILLIE JOLPA: Leave that out.

[*Cantor calls more names.*]

JOHNNY GUIYABAKA: Stamp your feet when the clan names are called.

FRANK GURRMANAMANA: Bring it to an end. [*To cantor*] Call the western clan names (camera roll 98).

There is no doubt that the reason why the invocations are the most emotive parts of mortuary ritual is because the broad sweep of clan names reminds each individual that he or she is a participant in the process of actualizing the transcendental powers within the human world. Each person is also part of the process of ensuring the safe passage of the dead from the world of the living to the realm of the dead, which the Anbarra believe lies under the sea near their clan lands. The calling of all the owning clans, both existing and extinct but still remembered, places each participating individual in a comprehensive social and spiritual universe and at the same time structures a frequently performed rite anew to focus uniquely on the individual for whose death the ritual is enacted.

This all-embracing quality of mortuary ritual is symbolized in the *Waiting for Harry* performance by the Booby bird spirit named Mulanda: Leo Wujal expounds on a painting of Booby and his homes:

> This is Booby and this . . . is his home. From this hole . . . to this, this is his track. He flies to this rocky island. He flies away. His track links our coastal clans: Nuchiturro, Mananjara, and Gunal . . . these, and more: Wordeiya, Bingurrama, Kalamagondia [the dead man's clan]. Then home to Cape Stewart. That's his track. Here on our chests we paint Booby's wings. These enable him to hunt for fish . . . and to come back once again to his home (camera roll 87).

The politics and aesthetics of Anbarra mortuary ritual come together in the Mulanda symbol, which bears a political message of clan solidarity within the Anbarra universe. As this bird spirit links the owning clans in its flight path, so its emotional and aesthetic value for every participant is enhanced. Wearing the Mulanda body paintings, each clan member can be like the Mulanda bird. But Wujal stops short of saying that dancers with Mulanda body paintings can become one with the spirits. Closeness does not imply identification but maintains to the end the discontinuity between the human and transcendental worlds.

Note

1. Obviously, this essay would make more sense if the reader were able to view *Waiting for Harry*. In North America, the film is available from the Extension Media Center, University of California at Berkeley. It may also be obtained on video cassette from the Australian Institute of Aboriginal Studies. The Institute's address is G.P.O. Box 553, Canberra, A.C.T. 2601, Australia.

References

Berndt, Ronald M.
1951 "Ceremonial Exchange in Western Arnhem Land." *Southwestern Journal of Anthropology* 7:156–76.

Clunies Ross, Margaret
1983 "Two Aboriginal Oral Texts from Arnhem Land, North Australia, and Their Cultural Context." In *Words and Worlds: European and Asian Essays in Society and Culture,* edited by S.T. Knight and S. Mukherjee, 3–30. Sydney: Sydney Association for Studies in Society and Culture.
1986 "Rom in Canberra" and "Rom: The Ritual Objects and Bark Paintings." In *Rom: An Aboriginal Ritual of Diplomacy,* edited by Stephen A. Wild, 33–53; 55–99. Canberra: Australian Institute of Aboriginal Studies.

Clunies Ross, Margaret, and L.R. Hiatt
1977 "Sand Sculptures at a Gidjingali Burial Rite." In *Form in Indigenous Art,* edited by Peter J. Ucko, 131–46. Canberra: Australian Institute of Aboriginal Studies.

Clunies Ross, Margaret, and Johnny Mundrugmundrug
1988 *Goyulan the Morning Star.* Canberra: Aboriginal Studies Press.

Clunies Ross, Margaret, and Stephen A. Wild
1984 "Formal Performance: The Relations of Music, Text and Dance in Arnhem Land Clan Songs." *Ethnomusicology* 28 (no. 2):209–35.

Hiatt, L.R.
1965 *Kinship and Conflict.* Canberra: Australian National University Press.
1986a "Rom in Arnhem Land." In *Rom: An Aboriginal Ritual of Diplomacy,* edited by Stephen A. Wild, 3–13. Canberra: Australian Institute of Aboriginal Studies.

1986b *Aboriginal Political Life*. The Wentworth Lecture 1984. Canberra: Australian Institute of Aboriginal Studies.

Hiatt, L.R., and Rhys Jones
1988 "Aboriginal Conceptions of the Workings of Nature." In *Australian Science in the Making*, edited by R.W. Home, 1–22. New York: Cambridge University Press.

Howitt, A.W.
1904 *The Native Tribes of South-East Australia*. London: Macmillan.

Keen, Ian
1977 "Ambiguity in Yolngu Religious Language." *Canberra Anthropology* 1 (October):33–50.

Maddock, Kenneth
1982 *The Australian Aborigines: A Portrait of Their Society*. 2nd. ed. Ringwood, etc.: Penguin Books Australia.

McKenzie, Kim, director
1980 *Waiting for Harry*. Film: 16 mm., 57 mins. Canberra: Australian Institute of Aboriginal Studies.

Merlan, Francesca
1987 "Catfish and Alligator: Totemic Songs of the Western Roper River, Northern Territory." In *Songs of Aboriginal Australia*, edited by Margaret Clunies Ross, Tamsin Donaldson, and Stephen A. Wild, 142–67. Sydney: Oceania Monograph 32.

Morphy, Howard
1989 "From Dull to Brilliant—The Aesthetics of Spiritual Power Among the Yolngu." *Man* 24 (no. 1): forthcoming.

Thomson, Donald F.
1949 *Economic Structure and the Ceremonial Exchange Cycle in Arnhem Land*. London: Macmillan.

Margaret Clunies Ross *is Associate Professor in the Department of English, University of Sydney, where she teaches Old English and Old Icelandic as well as Aboriginal Studies. Her research interests are in early Scandinavian literature and myth and Aboriginal oral literature, especially Arnhem Land songs and dances.*

Wee Pea

The Total Play of the Dwarf in the Circus

Yoram S. Carmeli

The discourse on what is considered "unusual" and "extraordinary" has long been recognized by anthropologists as an important clue for understanding society's main cultural assumptions and classifications (see Douglas 1966; Turner 1969). In this context, attitudes toward human freaks—those abnormal in form, such as a three-legged person, or in size, such as giants and midgets—and the beliefs concerning their coming into existence, make an interesting test case.[1]

For early 16th-century Christians, human freaks were considered prodigies, a sign (*monstrum*) of God's will. This conception changed toward the latter part of the 16th and into the 17th century. Freaks were explained as jokes or whims (*lusus*) of a personified nature, natural "wonders," and were often exhibited in fairs (see Park and Daston 1981; Fiedler 1978).

During the 18th century, with the growing influence of bourgeois culture, a growing rationalization of the concept of nature emerged. Nature was studied by various scientific disciplines and freaks and natural wonders became objects for scientific observation (Park and Daston 1981:51–54).

Changed concepts of nature and human freaks also evolved in the sphere of popular culture. Freaks were still popular in the 19th-century fair, exhibited as nature's wonders, "Real," "All Alive!" curiosities. They gradually became marginal, however, with the introduction of mechanized games and rides (see Frost 1844; Sanger 1940; Tyrwhitt-Drake 1946; Cunningham 1977; Judd 1983). It was out of the dwindling fairground that the traveling circus developed in the first quarter of the 19th century (Frost 1875; Cunningham 1980).

The traveling circus represented the new experience of nature and of social and cosmic order which had become dominant within the rising industrial order. Freaks and animals were not only exhibited but gathered in a ring, under a tent, playing and being played by rules of performance. The circus turned the marginal vagabond lifestyle of traveling acrobats, clowns, and trainers into a display, a show for the public (see Carmeli 1987a). As nature's marginal characters and specimens of its main categories are, thus, played, and as people turn their real lives into a display, they traditionally constitute an experience of enigma and anxiety for the public: real but played, they are desemanticized, emptied of their real nature, their nature as subjects who share in social time and relations, and epitomize a realm of timelessness and nonrelations (see Bouissac 1976; Carmeli 1987a, 1988a, forthcoming). A comment is thus constituted on the ontological bases of the social and cosmic order. Through being played, the everyday taken-for-granted order is experienced in the circus as secularized, rationalized, controlled and yet, because of these very features, deprived of its nature-like givenness.

Traveling circus performers make their living by playing and exposing the order's ontological bases and manipulating the public's existential anxieties. Though human freaks are usually eliminated from this play and are now deplored by most circus performers as "oddities" belonging in the "dirty fairground," circus owners do occasionally include a "midget" (or a strongman) in the circus program to attract public interest.

In this paper, I study closely the participation of a midget and the conceptualization of human dwarfism within the context of the traveling circus.[2]

JS and Circus Midgets in Britain

JS was 32 years old when I first met him in 1975 at Brown Circus. He was two-foot-five-inches tall. He traveled with the Brown circus alone (without a family) and participated in the clowning acts as a midget. He was referred to in the ring as well as among circus people by his circus name, Wee Pea.

JS was born in Manchester to a family of six normal-sized sisters and brothers. When he was three, he became ill and stopped growing. He was sent by his parents to a boarding school ("because I was different") where he loved geography and history and was good at English but did not like math. When he was 17 years old he fell in love but was rejected: "I realized I should never fall in love again." JS later lived with his parents and for a time worked with one of his brothers. He did not want to be supported by his family but could not face the world around him. A few years later he applied to a circus tender for "a circus midget." JS was over 20 when he started to work in circuses and worked many years for Robert Brothers' Circus, one of the big traveling shows in Britain.

When a human dwarf is incorporated into a circus show as a midget, he[3] is staged to be conceived of by the public as a "really small (grownup) person." Firstly, the smallness has to be experienced as unequivocal and unambiguous, according to the public's everyday criteria. Secondly, authenticity of the midget freakishness has to be confirmed and dramatized. As for the first, although a dwarf is medically defined as anyone under four-feet-ten-inches (Ablon 1984:4), not any dwarf will be accepted as a circus midget. When a man as tall as a ten-year-old boy came to Brown's circus, he was first employed on the lights and other general tasks with the intention of transferring him to the ring. However, he was never admitted to the ring as he was not small enough to be accepted by the public as a midget. As for the second, a midget's appearance must not be perceived by the public as involving any trickery, fakery, or acting. The public should never suspect the midget of being presented by a child. The dramatization of this smallness and "realness" will be analyzed later. At this stage, suffice it to say that they exercise constraints on the casting and on being accepted as a circus midget.

JS's working conditions in the Roberts' show were very poor and improved only a little when he joined Brown's. At £25 per week in 1975, the midget was the lowest paid performer in the circus.[4] Although salaries were a secret in the circus, everyone knew JS's salary.

To supplement his low income, JS sold balloons during the show interval. This concession, which he shared with others, though adding two or three pounds a week to his salary was to a certain extent imposed on him as 90 percent of the profits were taken by the owner.

JS was not related to Brown, nor had he any "house-performer" privileges. In winter, unless work was found, he was forced to go back to his family. As he could never afford a caravan and vehicle for traveling with the circus, he was provided some space in the double-decker bus which had been converted into a living wagon and accommodated five tentworkers. As JS's body was small, he was given the driver's compartment as lodging. This compartment, however, was not really his own. When Duddy, a circus clown cum technician, drove the double decker from town to town he was, in fact, occupying JS's room.

Although JS had to change several times during the show, he did not have a dressing room (all other performers could use the backs of their lorries for this purpose). JS changed in a corner behind the bandstand, which necessarily involved exposing his body to people standing at the doors. Circus animals were all around and people working the tent during the daytime used the corner for pissing.

According to his agreement with the owner, JS had to take part—together with the clowns—in the various publicity stunts and street parades which were, for him, most difficult to accomplish. In spite of his small body, he also had to take part in the work of building-up and pulling-down the big top when the circus moved from town to town. His work consisted of laying down the seating boards on their heavy metal frames, a job performed mostly by the tentworkers aided by local casual workers. JS had to find his way among the big boards and the sometimes inexperienced casual workers. He often had to be picked up by someone and placed on the higher rows where the height was dangerous for him. While this was being done, he would bitterly utter his sarcastic, nonsensical, private words: "barrastak, marrukas, karaawwka, babawwa, majawwan."

Clowns and the Midget in the British Circuses

In the circus program the midget is included in the clowning acts and clowning provides a general paradigm for the conceptualization of dwarfism in the British circus tradition.

Clowning itself is included, in one form or another, in all British circus productions. Although clowns constitute a traditional emblem of circus and often appear as a central theme on circus posters, the situation for clowning and clowns themselves in Britain is poor. In the small and mid-sized British family shows, clowning, like many other acts, is usually performed by members of the family that runs the show even though it is often considered an unwanted task. (It is commonly held among circus people that clowning, although the most demanding art in circus, is very seldom really successful with the British public.) Clowning is usually undertaken by family members whose main jobs are in administration or transport, or by those who have tried acrobatics unsuccessfully, or by performers who have had accidents and lost their skills. Clowns, when not from the family of ownership (as was the case in Brown's circus), are the most openly criticized and mocked performers in the circus. They are the lowest paid and the most dispensable performers because, as people often remark, "nearly everyone here was, at sometime, a clown."

A number of stock characters provide the traditional models for clowns in Britain. The main acknowledged types among Brown's performers were the white-faced clown (wise, arrogant, serious) and the auguste clown (funny, grotesque, stupid), the contrast between these types implying strong hierarchic and conflictual relations (see Bouissac 1976:164–165). However, in the British circuses of the mid-'70s, the clever white-faced clown was a rare figure. Clowns tried to attract their public mainly by trickery and slapstick, behavior characteristic of the auguste clown.

An important feature of auguste clowns is that they are, in a sense, more communicative and closer to the public than other characters in the show. Clowns use mimicry, their faces and bodies, to express themselves. They talk. Unlike other characters who appear in one act only, clowns appear in the ring time and again, establishing for the public the identity of a (human) performer.

However, these humanlike, communicative figures are portrayed as lacking self-awareness. As subjects, they do not distinguish themselves as objects, this component being realized through excessive "unaware" self-reference. In their talk routines (loud, impersonal, repetitive), clowns exchange comments on one another's follies, later performing these same follies themselves. They get hit by their own props, trip over their own shoes.

In many clowning acts in Brown's, these aspects of the clown's characterization—humanlike and communicative as well as nonreflexive and objectlike—are emphasized in the dialectical relations between the clown and the midget. JS did not participate in all the clowning acts and had very little say concerning the incorporation of various tricks into the acts or his participation in them. Within the paradigm of circus performance and the more specific taxonomy of clowns, JS, as Wee Pea, gradually assumed certain features similar to the auguste clown. In the ring, Pea's hat was small and flat. His suit was made of orange and yellow plaid. His makeup consisted of a white circle around his mouth and a red spot on his nose. However, his participation in the clowning acts, which were directed by Brown himself (with some help from the ringmaster and advice from the chief clown), often required other costumes: a monkey, a little girl, a sheriff, or a policeman.

The following description of some clowning acts in Brown's only partially describes the clowns' performances, concentrating on JS's participation.

JS's Participation in Clowning

The Opening Charivari

The ringmaster announces, "Here come the clowns!" And the clowns call out "Hello" to the public. JS is also there, dressed in his stock costume. He enters the ring last—as an attraction, a surprise. Often the children are astounded, the parents giggle. The clowns then perform comical acrobatic and slapstick routines, falling over and bumping into one another, ending up with leap-frog. The midget is the last to jump, but instead of jumping like the others, he pushes them over and makes them all stumble—teasing not only the clowns but also the public by showing off his clever, malicious nature.

A Musical Entree

A white-faced clown is playing a sopranino recorder in the ring. The public applauds. From the audience, the white-face is heckled by the other clowns (the midget among them) who carry on applauding and raucously calling out "Bravo! Bravo!" The white-faced clown calls them into the ring: "Come in here! This is the place for fools!" They enter. The white-faced clown teaches them tricks. He throws an egg in the air and catches it—unbroken—on a plate. He balances a plate on his arm, lets it drop, and catches it before it falls and breaks. A comedy evolves based on their failure to copy him, and ends with their playing two saxophones and a clarinet, with an organist accompanying them from the bandstand. Pea, relatively passive up to now, does a headstand, his buttocks turning into a music stand. The entree ends with a musical parade. Pea, last in line, carries the big drum in front of him, nearly hidden by it. At the ring doors, Big-Brian, the ring boy, is waiting. He makes fun of the midget by saluting him. (In a later version of this musical entree a clown plays music and Pea,

1. JS as Wee Pea in a 1975 performance of the musical entree. (Photo by Yoram S. Carmeli)

dressed in a blue ballerina skirt, a big ribbon on his forehead, enters the ring dancing and repeatedly stealing the clown's music.)

The "Ghosty" Entree

This routine is performed by Pea with two other clowns and a ring boy who plays the ghost. The three clowns are sitting on a bench. One clown makes fun of the others by spitefully upsetting the balance of the bench, causing them to fall. Pea takes revenge by making him fall the same way—he is the clever one, the last to laugh. Eventually, the clowns all sit on the bench and sing a song together. "Ghosty," a humanlike figure wrapped in a sheet, sneaks up behind them, kidnaps Pea, and carries him away. (Children at this stage do not know who or what the Ghosty is. Some are afraid or pretend fear.) Baffled, the two clowns turn to the public: "Where is he, children?" The children shout: "Ghosty!" The clowns do not hear. The question and answer sequence is repeated. The clowns turn to each other: "Do you see any ghosty?" "No, I don't see any ghosty, I don't care!" Dismissing the shouts, the clowns sit down and continue singing. Ghosty comes up from behind. The children scream: "Ghosty! Ghosty!" The clowns continue their hilarious singing. Ghosty tickles one from behind, then surprises and beckons him. The clown runs away, chased by Ghosty to the back of the ring. The other clown keeps on singing but suddenly realizes he is singing alone. He wonders out loud: "Where is he, children?" ("Ghosty! Ghosty!" etc.) Ghosty then reappears from behind the clown followed by another Ghosty, and yet another little ghosty. This last is Pea, for sure. Now the identity of the first and second ghosts is clear, too. (Pea reveals it all, but is now charged with trickery and the fear and tension which are finally released.) The three ghosts surprise the big clown who runs away, chased out by the others.

Short Gags and Cover-ups

The Safe Gag

A clown is dressed in his usual costume with his eyes masked by a black burglar's mask. The ring is unlit, with the exception of spotlights focusing on the clown and on a gray box in the rear part of the ring—the safe. The clown approaches the safe, tries to open it, fails, and decides to explode it. A comic thief. The children are on his side. He places the explosives at the safe's door, lights the fuse, and draws away, watching in anticipation. Explosion. Pea pops out of the box, dressed as a policeman and blowing on a whistle. He chases the clown out of the ring.

The Cowboy

A clown wearing big cowboy trousers and a hat enters the ring with a large toy rifle, boasting. The clown shoots in all directions. Pea enters from the ring door, riding a pony. He has his clown makeup on but is dressed as a sheriff with a star on his shirt. Pea orders the clown to stop. They confront each other. Pea shoots. The clown's trousers fall down. The clown raises his hands in embarrassment.

The Monkey Gag

This is presented while the lion cage is being dismantled. A clown approaches the ringmaster.

2. Wee Pea (left) and two clowns in the "Ghosty" routine, as performed in 1975. (Photo by Yoram S. Carmeli)

RINGMASTER: What are you doing here?

CLOWN: I'm looking for a friend of mine.

RINGMASTER: Where is he?

CLOWN: Oh, I don't know. Somewhere in the public.

RINGMASTER: What do you mean "in the public"? What does he look like?

CLOWN: Well, he is . . . a monkey.

RINGMASTER: A monkey?!! Here?!! Take it away immediately!!

The spotlight focuses on Pea in the upper rows, dressed as a monkey but clearly identifiable as the midget. The people nearby are somewhat surprised. Sometimes someone is a bit frightened, too. The children shout and direct the clown: "Here! He's here!!!" The clown, also in a spotlight, ignores their shouts and does not notice him. He searches the darkened parts of the audience. Finally, he approaches the gangway where Pea is sitting and discovers the monkey. The clown chases the monkey. The monkey outwits the clown and runs away, finally disappearing and ending the act behind the ring. (In another version the monkey is performed by a person of normal height, an acrobat, who instead of running off behind the ring, climbs a swinging pole, like a monkey, but then takes off his monkey costume and performs acrobatics on the pole.)

The Chair Gag

A clown dressed as Charlie Chaplin comes into the ring with a chair. Pea follows behind, watching him. The clown performs a handstand on the chair. He turns to the public, demanding applause. He sits on the chair, rolls forward onto the ground and backwards onto the chair, again demanding applause. He turns to Pea, boasting.

CLOWN: I bet you I can do it again!

PEA: Oh, no, you can't!

CLOWN: *(Halfway turned toward the public, both arguing and calling for support.)* Oh, yes I can!!

Both contenders try to make the public participate but are only partially successful. The public is sometimes on the side of Pea, who talks to them though he faces the clown.

PEA: Oh, no, he can't.

CLOWN: *(Challenging Pea and the public.)* I bet you one pound I'll do it again.

He sits on the chair, rolls forward onto the ground, stands up and rolls backwards. Meanwhile, little Pea smartly removes the chair before the clown lands. The clown falls on his buttocks. Pea leaves hastily, carrying the chair with him.

Finale Parade

To end the circus show, all performers march into the ring, take positions at the ring fence, and wave to the public, holding flags. The strongman is in a chariot pulled by circus horses, two high-wire walkers sit in an open carriage, and a circus child rides on top of an elephant's head. The midget, dressed as a monkey, stands in a cage drawn by two ponies.

Analysis

JS the dwarf chose performing a midget as a way of making his living in an attempt to overcome the predicaments of life outside the circus. However, the midget character itself as well as the dwarf's condition in the circus are primarily shaped in the context of the semiotic constraints of circus and clowning performance, along with the social, cultural, and situational conditions in which the performance takes place.

In the following analysis I concentrate on the features of the midget characters as constituted within the context of clowning.

The Ostensibility of the Midget's Smallness

In the circus the dwarf, as a midget, appears in a built-up ring within a program. JS, the dwarf, together with the other performers in the ring, shares with the townsfolk the separation and exclusion of the circus event from everyday time and place. Throughout the clowning performance the dwarf and the other participants portray traditional characters and relations familiar to the public. They communicate the discommunication among them to the public, often turning directly to them. The public is expected to participate and react during the act and applaud at its end.

The display of humanlike characteristics (talk, etc.) by the performers, the sharing of expectations and conventions with the public, the intersubjectivity shared with the public in constituting the entire encounter—all frame the clowning act as a human performance. The character of the circus midget is then experienced as constituted in a kind of play, by a performing-playing human being.

Several constraints of his human performance may then be noted. An important rule observed is that JS never performed the midget Pea by himself but always together with other clowns—not only alongside them but interacting with them. In this copresence and interaction a certain characteristic of the midget is constantly reinforced and dramatized—the smallness of his body. The midget's smallness is made distinctive and his measure dramatized by the juxtaposition with the other clowns. By the common-sense standards of the public, other clowns are in the range of average-size human beings. In the ring there are no intermediary measures between the midget and the others. Pea is the only one of his kind. Not only is he distinctively small, but his smallness is thus introduced as an exception.

This oddity, as a constituent property of the midget, is also revealed to the public by the nature of the midget's interaction with the clowns throughout the performance. Generally speaking, the midget character in circus performance is rooted in the confrontation or antagonism between him and the others. Pea is the small policeman running after the big man, the small sheriff threatening the big guy, or the small guy who mocks the others in the ghosty entree or chair gag—seeming to outwit the others by his trickery. Entrees and gags are created so as to facilitate the performance of the midget's smallness, exceptionality, and antagonistic confrontation with the other characters. As the clowning texts change, the midget character is reproduced. When the midget is dressed as a sheriff or a British policeman, he is miming stereotypical figures manipulatd to communicate the characteristics of the midget.

The uniqueness of the midget character is not exhausted by his smallness, exceptionality, and antagonistic confrontations with the clowns. Rather, this uniqueness also concerns the very relationships between the onstage persona and the offstage performer's self, the nature of the performer's offstage human self as revealed and defined through the staged character.

The clown character in Brown's is performed as a performer playing his own offstage self and self-awareness. The performer plays the fool, but performs and comments on his own foolishness. This play, then, eventually discloses the performer as a reflexive human being.

The nature of the midget performer is unfolded differently. Like the performers of clowning, the midget's human nature is communicated to the public through his onstage antics: his use of human talk, comic dancing, drumming in the music parade, and whistling-miming the policeman. On the other hand, unlike the clowns, the midget character is not performed by the playing of this human self, playing the performer's own human awareness. The midget does not cause himself to fail or fall; he does not wear big shoes and make himself trip over his own apparel in order to comment about it. Rather, through his interaction with the others, the midget character is experienced by the public as a display of cleverness, maybe maliciousness, characteristics not commonly attributed to a living human dwarf. While the clowns' natures are disclosed in their capacity for playing their own selves, the nature of the midget performer in Brown's is revealed in his human capacity for display and in the significance this capacity confers on other components staged as his real offstage nature. In clowning the performer's self-awareness—his human reflexive nature—is at stake, constantly problematized and then reassumed, while the midget's character is compounded both by the performer's capacity for display and the constant redefinition of his genuine, offstage oddity through this display. At stake, then, is his real smallness.

Reversals

Considering the clowning acts in general and more specifically the midget's performances, one notices that except for the musical act, the monkey gag, and the finale, the midget ends up on the winning side, seemingly outwitting the others. These victories are, however, dubious. The public identifies with his rivals—the fool, the thief, the bandit. Although the midget has the upper hand in the chair gag, the Charivari, and even in the Ghosty act, he ends up somehow defeated by his victories, creating antagonism and mockery among the public.

Some "reversal" is communicated throughout the clowning act as the small one is on top—the small one renders the others (e.g., the acrobat in the Charivari or the chair gag) funny and foolish. This reversal can be initially approached through a certain comparison. The little one on top in a performance or play situation is not unique to circus. As accounted for by various anthropological descriptions, playful reversals are evident in daily face-to-face interactions, as well as in more formally organized situations (Sutton-Smith 1972; Turner 1969, 1974). These reversals generally take place in ritually secluded times and places, and involve social relations between people of known categories (sex, age, position in hierarchy). The ritually framed reversal play clarifies and confirms the categories and relations in the real, out-of-play, social world.

Although seemingly similar structurally to this type of play, the circus play is different. Though small, the midget, as staged, is not a child. Though the little one is on top, neither social hierarchy nor authority are reversed. The midget has no authority, his power is awarded no legitimacy by the clowns in the performance. Rather, the midget is staged as gaining his victories in scenes of relations without communication—scenes of discommunication and trickery staged for the public. In the various acts the midget and clowns make use of known images as well as of familiar reversal structures—small equals weak, big equals strong are seemingly reversed. However, they are sharing a play (or metaplay) with the public here as these familiar reversal motives are only seemingly confirmed. The real play being performed in the clowning is a play of intersubjectivity, of communicability, a kind of a play of playing itself.

The mimetic gags (the safe gag, the sheriff gag) seem to contradict this hypothesis as, in addition to the midget and clowns, social roles and social hierarchy are clearly represented, reversed, and manipulated here. This reversal and manipulation is, however, not of the social order. It is clearly through trickery rather than authority that order is maintained, and it is not a child but a midget who stands for order. Although the little one is on top, social order is confirmed. The policeman wins and so does the sheriff; authority is present, hierarchy is maintained. It seems that rather than being the object of reversal and reordering, the social order provides the scenery or prop: through manipulation of established images and stereotypical social relations, primordial bases of human association and the constituents of human nature are explored, brought up as an issue.

The nature of this reversal play can be examined through more detailed observation of the participating characters—the clown and the midget—and their confrontations.

The Clown: The Midget's Counterpart

Not all British circuses employ midgets. The clowns, however, constitute an essential part of every circus show, and it is their self-referential nature that crystallizes the clowns' character. A clown's play as a subject unaware of his objectness is a play which conjures the constituents and syntax of the human self in the public's experience. On the one hand, the clown is human and communicative. On the other, this human nature is played with. The clown-performer is experienced as transcending his own individuality to constitute a general comment on human nature. The clown, therefore, transcends and comments on the human self from the "outside" as if embodying a realm prior to human time and relations, prior to history and meaning. Generally, in the context of circus play, and the context of the enigma and existential anxiety embedded in the performance, the clowns take an interpretive and cathartic role. As their self-referentiality is accomplished in the context of imitating and parodying other circus acts, they both explicate the circus and mediate its various performances to the public (see Bouissac 1976, 1981, 1982; Peacock 1978; Handelman and Kapferer 1980; Handelman 1981; Carmeli forthcoming).

The entry of the midget serves to shift the significance of the clowns' character. In order to understand the effect of the midget on the clowns we need to observe the framing of the midget's participation within the clowns' performance.

As dwarves have traditionally been conceptualized as mythical and wondrous figures, various images and mystifications of the dwarf are invoked by JS's performances as a circus midget alongside the clowns: the dwarf as a kind of demon (living somewhere under the surface of the earth); the dwarf as a wonder of nature (as presented in the old traditional fair); the dwarf as a child who did not grow up; the dwarf as a wise old man who did not die but shrunk (living in a mythological world, beyond human reality, beyond the changing time) (see Bettelheim 1976; Fiedler 1978:39–90; Park and Daston 1981).

However, by the admission of a dwarf into circus clowning, myths concerning dwarves undergo reframing and transformation. Because circus clowning is a human performance, myths about the dwarf are textualized, their narratives turned into rules of performance. The clown is human—the dwarf must be human, too.

In this process the bodily dimension of the clown and human bodily height become ostensible and dramatically significant. So does the clown's communicative nature. The clown's liminality is now redefined: in relation to a midget, the clowns seem more like ordinary grown-ups. When the midget is in the ring the clowns are the human beings whose bodies grew up in time but who have not socially matured (so as to discern themselves as objects). The clown's character is not only the embodiment of a presocial time in which human meanings and relations are yet to be constituted. He also embodies the margins of time in which ordinary people grow old, although he does not. Through the maturity, yet objectness of his body (often dramatized by his hurting his body and thus emphasizing its objectness even more), the clown now embodies margins of social space, where meaning and sense are accomplished, although he does not take part.

In Brown's circus the clowns are made to confront the midget in a play of "big and little" seemingly familiar to the public. However, rather than dealing with characteristics of social identities and positions, the "reversal" now is of big-equals-foolish vs. small-equals-clever, and through these characteristics the play defines problems of human identity and human existence. The particular manipulation of the dwarf which is included in Brown's clowning concretizes the concept of human self played by the clown. As the midget's human smallness and exceptionality are emphasized the clown is redefined as ontologically within the realm of the social. The midget is presented as clever, while the clown's self-referencing becomes comic—less an expression of spirituality or sublime innocence than of human senselessness. The clown performer himself, that is, the particular traveling circus performer whose own self is being played and abstracted, combines human nature, social marginality, and a kind of ontological inferiority in his grotesque physical character. Historically emerging and sustained within the context of the social and political dominance of bourgeois culture, this clown character is shaped through the performers' manipulation, their playing of their own marginality. While rationalizing and secularizing the order, they also represent dominant cultural notions of social boundaries and social hierarchy (see Cunningham 1980; Carmeli 1988b).

The Midget

Our initial points of reference in analyzing the circus midget are his dual components as the mythic dwarf and the real living dwarf.

Unlike the clown, whose ordinary, human reflexive nature is part of his character, disclosed while being played, the dwarf character involves myths concerned with a phenomenon categorically and epistemologically problematic. While the clown's play transcends everyday reality the myth of the dwarf is a concept of exclusion, ritualizing the boundaries of reality rather than playing and deconstructing its constituents. It is a concept defining reality from the outside, excluding that which threatens its comprehension and coherence. Unlike the clown character, who is established through dissociation and paradox, the mythical dwarf, who is defined as an entity outside the ordinary human world, contains no immanent incongruency. His small body and his wisdom or wickedness are both parts of his mythical nature.

By incorporating the mythical dwarf into the clowning, his smallness, rather than being confined to the realm of myths, is socialized, measured by human measure and, as such, its exceptionality is constituted and ostended. Also, the dwarf does not remain a separate mythic figure endowed, according to folk beliefs, with mythic wisdom but engages in confrontations and relations of nonrelations: the midget's victories are accomplished through the clown's misunderstandings and by the tricky use of the smallness of his body. The midget is unexpectedly hiding, waiting to surprise. The clowns, the big ones, do not notice little Pea who is cleverly using his smallness to outwit them. While the clown becomes "big" in comparison to the midget and, thus, more of a human (and a foolish one), the midget, through the play of the clown, is less human, exceptionally small but seemingly omnipotent. The circus midget character is not experienced by the public as either a "realization" of the mythic dwarf or a "representation" of the mythic dwarf. The latter is not transformed into "a role" "played" by a performer. The midget character is, rather, constituted through the display of the mythical dwarf's characteristics—a display performed by a human dwarf whose unequivocal authentic dwarfism provides the ground for his casting and whose display is highlighted through his copresence and confrontations with the clowns.

A dialectical process between the transformed mythical dwarf and the performing real dwarf emerges in the midget character and a new concept of dwarfism, the circus concept of dwarfism, is thereby dramatized for the public.

As the wisdom and the power of the mythical dwarf are transformed into a human performance, the freakish real dwarf is human, voided of mythical power—he is only performing. The myth is "only a play" (hence, some of the public's relief and laughter). This, however, is but one dimension of the transformation occurring to the mythical dwarf in the midget's character. Through the clowning acts the myths are also dramatically refuted, proven false, and it is at this point that the performance of the midget mostly affects the real human dwarf.

The root of the refutation lies in the contradictory and reversed implications of playing "big and little" for the clown performer and the dwarf. The clown plays, but the dwarf displays. Though experienced by the public as human because of his capacity for displaying, the dwarf's performance is not a play of the syntax of (his) human nature (like the clown's is). Rather, his performance is ruled by the syntax of that which he displays—the syntax of the big and the little. While exposing the myths and turning them into performance, the displaying dwarf is deprived of his human nature as he is reduced to the "little" through the clown's play and his own display.

The performance of a midget turns the condition of dwarfism into a new exposure and constitutes a redefinition of nature's incongruence for the real performing dwarf and his public. Stripped of the mythical shelter, his body's ostended freakishness becomes his tool of communication. The more he is in the ring, the more his human self is defined by circus text. As he manipulates his smallness in outwitting the clowns, he newly realizes for the public the totality of his smallness—the reduction, the impossibility of his human nature. As a freak he is human, but as a human he is only the little one.

The midget's victories (by which clowns are tricked and rendered human), are turned in the public's experience into the means of excluding the dwarf from human intersubjectivity. Compared to the clowns' play of discommunication, the midget's performance is a play of excommunication and reification. It reduces JS the dwarf, in the public's experience, to the various realizations and significances which the smallness of his body takes on through his acts. For the public, the dwarf's exceptional and epistemologically problematic smallness is, thus, abstracted, deprived of its human substance.

While the mythical dwarf's smallness is an accepted part of his nature, an index to what he really is, the dwarf's rationalized smallness in the circus engulfs his human and social identity. In the world which Brown's circus performed for, the dwarf performing the midget is not really presented as a clown character. In the parody played by the clowns and the midget, the midget—"the winner"—is no partner. He is the parody's object and its tool.

The "little," as a concept, focuses and directs the public's perception, overpowering the dwarf's human nature, caging him in his play. Every new realization, every new significance of this smallness, as demonstrated by his cleverness, is one more accomplishment, one more proof of the reduction of his human nature to his size: the midget is perceived as the small man with the drum bigger than himself, propelled forward by it, dwarfed by its largeness; he is the one who is kidnapped and carried off by the others in the Ghosty act; the one who is put in a box in order to pop out of it (like a "Jack-in-the-box"). A creature abstracted from any meaning, he is rendered a sign for whatever is little—a man, a woman (dancer), a monkey, a music stand—an empty, reified signifier. By the rationale of the circus performance, JS, the human dwarf, is conceptually mutilated, rendered a human axis around which the clowns build their comic situations.

This, so the public discovers, is the *real* nature of the dwarf. It is this realization (rather than merely the rationalization of the dwarf) which is turned into every gag's punch line—the public's laughter is relief, solution, and rejection. It is not that the mythical dwarf is not frightening because he only plays, it is that the playing dwarf is not really a person—he is only a midget, just a Wee Pea.

In circus clowning, as carried on in Britain in the late '70s, the fool and the midget performed together. Though similar in many respects they embody, through their dialectical relations, two ontologically different states. While the auguste clown communicates with the public, the midget who outwits the clown is existentially positioned outside society. In the world played by the clowns, the midget's part is that of a category's distortion.

Both the fool and the midget embody a rationalized, secular society's anxieties. In the circus, a genre which emerged with the rise of the industrial order, "nature" is played; consequently, the power of nature metaphors to validate and ritualize the boundaries of human identity has been eroded. In the circus the real dwarf plays as if he is as ordinary as anyone else, as ordinary as the public. The human self is experienced as being invaded—the freak is human and the human is (possibly) a freak!

Circus drama seems not only to invoke the existential anxieties of a rationalized, played reality, but also directs them. The very play which articulates anxiety experienced seems to confine it as rationally controlled.

The public's notions of self and of human nature seem to rebound through the midget's exclusion from the clown's play. The pretended upside-down play is disclosed as a new inside-out definition. The pretended social reversal is disclosed as a play of existential and cosmic exclusion.

But the existential threat, the anxieties which the circus midget gives form to are not eliminated, they are rather both distanced and redefined. While the dwarf is excluded from a rationalized social order the mode of his exclusion—his reification, the abuse and dissociation of his human (rather than mythical) nature—represents the existential problematics of living in the realm from which he is excluded. And, in the circus acts, as the dwarf stands more than ever before inside the realm from which he is excluded, participating in his own exclusion, communicating to the public his own discommunication, the public is not only threatened by being similar to the freak but shares through the midget their own fear of exposure and loss of self. The dwarf, no longer secluded as a freak is, perhaps more totally than before, turned into a scapegoat.

Some earlier observations brought up concerning the staging of a midget in the circus may now be interpreted. A midget must clearly be a real dwarf; a child (or, for that matter anybody) cannot "act" the midget. Not only can a child not act a midget but the midget cannot still be a child. A child, though small, is growing. A child is not a freak and thus cannot meaningfully suggest the clown's play concerning the human self. In the antagonistic confrontations with the clowns a child would turn the whole event into merely a play of (social) reversal, thereby making the midget just as human as the others. This constraint is not only "cognitive" but is anchored in morality, too. A child cannot, must not, become a source of public fear to be released by his rejection and exclusion—a child ought not even playfully be abused.

The Discourse of Dwarfism in the Everyday Life of the Circus

It is not only within the performance of the circus show that the discourse of dwarfism in circus is taking place but also in the performers' own offstage lives, their encounters with the public outside the ring, and in daily life in town. Brown's total control of JS's performance and JS's situation in the circus—as earlier described—are important dimensions here, as the dwarf's marginality within circus and the circus' marginality in British life are made clear.

While the play in the ring is conceptually brutal, it also provides JS with a certain protection. As far as he is concerned, he is trying to cultivate a source of pride and a shelter played out within the rules and standards of the performance. JS tried to develop his character into a full auguste so that he would be presented in the least degrading manner. His Pea was dressed "elegantly," so he would say—his hat flat in keeping with the human proportions of his body, his makeup minimal because "as I am small, heavy makeup would be ridiculous." According to JS, he was trying to dramatize a young, carefree fellow. This character allowed him, perhaps, to take part in the clowning comedy as (only) a joke played on himself by himself.

JS did not like his monkey roles, especially that of the monkey in the cage during the parade. On the other hand, JS was reluctant when he had to perform most distinctly as a human, that is, while talking, as this disclosed his human nature most and therefore—in the circus context—his deformity.

In the various clowning acts JS often turned to physical feats in an attempt to display skill. Talking about his performances in the past he remarked on being at the top of the pyramid in clowning acts at the Robert Brothers' Circus. In the Charivari act at Brown's he demanded that in the last gag he jump over all the clowns bending in a row (instead of viciously pushing them). This change was eventually approved by Brown. Apparently, it was still in accordance with the concept of the midget.

At the ring doors ("behind the curtain"), like other veteran performers, JS, claiming a performer's identity, would initiate the repetitive daily complaints about the circus going downhill. He, like the others, explained this as a result of the lack of devotion to and love of circus by present day performers. Like the other performers he also used to complain about the public's lack of understanding of the circus. It was particularly important for him to make the public laugh during his gags and win their applause at the end, as this sustained both the frame of play and his identity as a human performer. However, this proved difficult as the public very often barely laughed or did not laugh at all, and because the clowning was often explicitly ridiculed by other circus performers.

Though there were some people with whom he had fairly close personal relationships, JS as the midget Pea posed a problem for most circus performers. For the clowns, who were rated low by other performers and sustained only a precarious boundary between their performance and offstage selves, the midget provided some relief. In the presence of the midget, a clown more clearly assumed his human identity in his play. Yet, in the British circus the clowns' situation is not that different from the midget's; thus, it was not only the low social and economic position, but also the inferior and marginal nature of the auguste that prompted clown performers to maintain boundaries between themselves and JS.

Circus acrobats in Britain consider themselves to be doing something "real," something which "they [the public] cannot do." A lot of the drama of their performance is expected to emerge from the enigmatic nature of this play of real life and the challenge it presents to the public. The manipulation of JS's deformity and the exploitation of his exposure was considered by circus professionals not only degrading for JS himself but, to some extent, a threat to other performers too. What they were trying to dramatize and sell as enigmatic play was turned by the midget into a "cheap" solution of displayed freakishness (see Carmeli 1988a). While some pitied his exposure or his status as nothing more than "just a good prop," in fact Wee Pea presented a pitfall, hinting at the potential for degrading interpretations relating to them all.

While the performers were not happy with the Wee Pea character and the nuances he had added to the show, JS was a focal point in the daily routine of circus life: he was a medium through which the circus people could comment on the predicaments of their everyday lives (see Carmeli 1987b). In the ring doors, JS commented on the absurdity of his own life, approaching the others with his nonsense dialect, malicious mockery, and little games of aggressive trickery. The others would often cooperate, following and sharing in his game.

More difficult, however, were JS's direct confrontations with the world outside. As circus is a play of the real, every social confrontation with the outside world is, traditionally, turned by circus- and townsfolk into a display and play of the travelers' real lives. The more JS was made to expose his real deformity, the more he was reduced as a human being to just being his small size. Midgetness became a total performance for the dwarf, constituting both his show and his central existential condition. When JS in costume stood in the big-top doors during the show's interval selling balloons, people would watch him closely. Children would approach him to pay, asking their mothers if he was a "real man." Mothers would sometimes allow their children to draw nearer and touch the circus midget and JS could only murmur to a circus man standing nearby: "Get them little bastards away from me."

In the pub, where JS was sometimes seen with a circus friend, the deformity of a circus midget was often turned into an object of "friendly" joking—joking which often went beyond what he could take.

On the way to one morning performance at a local school, circus folks formed a small publicity parade. The circus midget and other clowns, some llamas, and a camel walked through the streets. People stopped for a minute, stared and giggled. JS, hinting at the public's indifference during the performances of his clowning acts, bitterly remarked, "You see, *now* they laugh!" Even though the comedy often fails in the ring, its play frame protects JS. The circus parade provides a more porous protection. As long as he marches in the parade JS is exposed but also protected within the precarious play frame of the parade. As long as he performs a circus midget, JS, the dwarf, is partially sheltered. But, as long as he *is* a circus midget, he must go on.

Notes

1. This article is based on 15 months of fieldwork conducted in Jimmy Brown's circus, Britain, between March 1975 and October 1979. All quotes are taken from material collected during the fieldwork. I am grateful to Daphna Birnbaum-Carmeli for her comments and assistance throughout the preparation of the article.
2. Following the traditional circus terminology, the word "midget" is reserved in this article for the character presented in the circus. "Dwarf" is used to denote an exceptionally small person.
3. A circus midget is never performed by a woman. Also, there is only one woman clown in England and, as this fieldwork was done with only male clowns, male pronouns are used throughout.
4. The average weekly wage of a manual worker (male) in Britain in 1975 was £59.58 (Central Statistical Office, *Annual Abstract of Statistics,* 1977, no. 114, table 6.19, p. 173, London, Her Majesty's Stationary Office). In the circus, the lowest paid were the tentworkers who earned £18 a week. Most family and house performers earned £35–50 a week. Some top performers earned £70–100 a week.

References

Ablon, Judith
1984 *The Little People of America.* New York: Praeger.

Bettelheim, Bruno
1976 *The Uses of Enchantment: The Meaning and Importance of Fairytales.* New York: A.A. Knopf.

Bouissac, Paul
1976 *Circus and Culture.* Bloomington: Indiana University Press.
1981 "The Timeless Tool of Time: Circus Performance Revisited." *Communication and Cognition* 14 (nos. 2/3):133–52.
1982 "The Meaning of Nonsense (Structural Analysis of Clown Performances and Limericks)." In *The Logic of Culture,* edited by I. Rossi, 199–213. South Hadley, MA: J.F. Bergin.

Carmeli, Yoram S.
1987a "Why Does the Jimmy Brown's Circus Travel? A Semiotic Approach to Circus Ecology." *Poetics Today* 8 (no. 2):219–44.
1987b "Played by Their Own Play: Fission and Fusion in British Circuses." *The Sociological Review* 35 (no. 4):744–74.
1988a "The Travelling Circus: An Interpretation." *European Journal of Sociology* 24 (no. 2):258–82.
1988b "Billy's Wig: Playing Versus the Performance of the Real in a British Circus." *Assaph—Studies in the Theatre* 4:93–110.
forthcoming "Performing the 'Real' and the 'Impossible': Paradoxes and Reification in the Performance of British Circuses." *Semiotica.*

Cunningham, Hugh
1977 "The Metropolitan Fair: A Case Study in the Social Control of Leisure." In *Social Control in Nineteenth Century Britain,* edited by A.P. Donaygrodzki, 163–84. London: Croom Helm.
1980 *Leisure in the Industrial Revolution.* New York: St. Martin's Press.

Douglas, Mary
1966 *Purity and Danger*. London: Routledge and Kegan Paul.

Fiedler, Leslie A.
1978 *Freaks: Myths and Images of the Secret Self.* New York: Simon and Schuster.

Frost, Thomas
1844 *The Old Showman and the Old London Fairs*. London.
1970 [1875] *Circus Life and Circus Celebrities*. Detroit: Singing Tree Press.

Handelman, Don
1981 "The Ritual Clown: Attributes and Affinities." *Anthropos* 76:321–70.

Handelman, Don, and Bruce Kapferer
1980 "Symbolic Types, Mediation and Transformation of Ritual Context: Sinhalese Demons and Tewa Clowns." *Semiotica* 30 (nos. 1–2):41–71.

Judd, Mark
1983 "The Oldest Combination of Town and Country: Popular Culture and the London Fairs 1800–60." In *Leisure in Britain 1780–1939*, edited by Y.K. Walton and Y. Walvin, 11–30. Manchester: Manchester University Press.

Park, Katherine, and Lorraine J. Daston
1981 "Unnatural Conceptions: The Study of Monsters in Sixteenth and Seventeenth Century France and England." *Past and Present* 92:20–54.

Peacock, James
1978 "Symbolic Reversals and Social History: Transvestites and Clowns in Java." In *The Reversible World: Symbolic Inversion in Art and Society*, edited by Barbara Babcock, 209–24. Ithaca, NY: Cornell University Press.

Sanger, George
1940 *Seventy Years a Showman*. London: J.M. Dent & Sons.

Sutton-Smith, Brian
1972 "Games of Order and Disorder." Paper presented at the annual meeting of the American Anthropological Association, December, Toronto, Canada.

Turner, Victor
1969 *The Ritual Process: Structure and Antistructure*. Chicago: Aldine.
1974 "Liminal to Liminoid in Play, Flow and Ritual: An Essay in Comparative Symbology." In *The Anthropological Study of Human Play*, vol. 60, edited by E. Norbeck, 53–92. Rice University Studies.

Tyrwhitt-Drake, G.
1946 *The English Circus and Fairground*. London: Methuen.

Yoram S. Carmeli *is an anthropologist at the University of Haifa, Israel. During his fieldwork he participated in circus performance as a musical white-faced clown as well as a tentman, ringboy, and a teacher for circus children. His current areas of research are the anthropology of art, performance, and religion.*

Describing Performance in the Theatre

Kabuki Training and the Western Acting Student

Robert W. Bethune

From September 1978 to April 1979, the University of Hawaii at Manoa conducted a special program in kabuki theatre known as "Kabuki-Hawaii 1978–1979." Either Nakamura Matagoro II, Chief Instructor in kabuki at the National Theatre of Japan, or his assistant, Nakamura Matashiro, was in residence from September to March to teach kabuki acting techniques. Other well-known Japanese artists came to Hawaii for varying lengths of time to teach kabuki music and to assist in technical theatre. Nakamura Matagoro directed an adaptation in English of the kabuki classic *Kanadehon Chushingura*. The production played during March and April under the title *The Forty-Seven Samurai* (Brandon 1982) and toured the mainland United States, playing at colleges and universities in California, Utah, Kansas, Michigan, Ohio, and Massachusetts after closing in Hawaii.

The training experience offered to students was of unusual intensity. Classes were held six days a week for four or five hours daily, and during the second semester, evening rehearsals were added to the schedule as preparations for the production went forward. I believe that Kabuki-Hawaii 1978–1979 was the first program in the United States to offer such prolonged contact with such high-caliber kabuki professionals.

This program offered a unique opportunity. A number of students had substantial prior training or experience in Western drama and theatre, but little or no prior experience in Asian performance styles. What changes would take place in the performance behavior of such students? How does one go about describing performance behavior? If the students picked up elements of kabuki style, how would such elements be identified?

The work involved six elements: a review of extant ideas on kabuki performance, a generalized method for performance analysis, a study of the performance patterns of a recognized master actor, studies of the performance patterns of his students, comparisons of student and master performances, and conclusions on the level and nature of assimilation of kabuki performance patterns.[1] In this article I introduce the methods I used, offer condensed versions of my analysis of Nakamura Matagoro's performance, and describe assimilation of kabuki performance patterns by student actors. Finally, I make certain suggestions about kabuki training for Western student actors.

Methods

Of the seven students in the study, six prepared and presented performances of solo passages from various Western plays which were videotaped at the beginning of the program and again at the end. A seventh student was studied on the basis of videotapes of her performances in plays done in Hawaii before the program began and after it ended. The repertory selected covered a broad spectrum of the classic and modern Western literature, including Shakespeare, Chekhov, Rabe, Euripedes, O'Casey, and Inge.

I assumed that intensive study of kabuki acting would produce enough assimilation of performance behavior that the students' style in the Western repertory would show change that could be related to kabuki style. I did not expect such assimilation to take the form of wholesale adoption of kabuki. Rather, I looked for subtle assimilation of overall characteristics. This does not mean that the actor would become more like a kabuki actor. The actor may have rejected the kabuki style, deciding that kabuki and Western acting are different artistic worlds. Therefore, I looked at both movement toward kabuki style and movement away. What is style, and how do we describe it in terms of performance behavior?

I wanted to compare the students' performance behavior to the performance behavior of their teacher, Nakamura, using a systematic,

1. As part of the Kabuki-Hawaii 1978–1979 program, students performed The Forty-Seven Samurai, *an adaptation of the classic kabuki play* Kanadehon Chushingura. *Featured here are Tony Soper (left) as Hangan and Norris Shimabuku as Moroanao. (Photo by Robert W. Bethune)*

quantifiable, repeatable method focused on actual vocal and movement behavior. I also wanted a method that could be used to analyze a wide variety of performances from very different cultures.

Several studies in dance ethnology and ethnomusicology have dealt with similar problems. Martha Ann Davis and Claire Schmais (1968) studied Doris Humphrey's *Water Study* using Laban movement theory and a method adapted from Alan Lomax. Jill Gellerman (1978) studied the Mayim dance, comparing the dance of three different groups of Hasidim using a systematic Laban movement theory framework. Elizabeth Kagan (1978) used an analytical framework based on Laban movement theory to compare works by Paul Taylor and Doris Humphrey, as did Suzanne Youngerman (1978) in her study of Humphrey's *The Shakers*. Alan Lomax's (1968) seminal Choreometrics and Cantometrics projects provided methodological inspiration for the above writers, and for my work as well.

These approaches consider style as patterns of choice among possibilities inherent in the anatomy and physiology of the human body. The human race shows fundamental similarities across cultural boundaries in skeletal, muscular, and neurological structure and function that arise from common membership in one biological species. Different performance genres, or even different performances in the same genre, play this physiology differently. One can analyze these differences by asking questions systematically so that each question addresses some particular performance trait. The questions here form a set of 70 rating scales, each defining a range of variation for a single behavioral trait. Each scale follows a logical progression, as does the arrangement of the scales themselves. Brief definitions of the scales used are found in the appendix of this article (see also Bethune 1985).

As is well known, statistical relationships and causal relationships are two very different things. How can one infer that any change found in a student performance relative to the kabuki training is in fact the result of that training?

There was no possibility of a genuine control group in this situation. There was no way to set up a group of people who led the same lives as the students in the program, except for being in the kabuki training program. We do know, however, that the students did in fact learn the kabuki performance patterns, because we have their performances in *The Forty-Seven Samurai* to attest to it. All of the actors in the study made good to excellent progress in their kabuki training and performed important roles in the production. While I have not been in contact with them, I am aware that several have since gone on to professional work in off-Broadway and regional theatre. We can therefore be assured that the subjects were good learners who did experience the influence we are trying to detect.

It should also be pointed out that the results of this study did not fulfill the expectations of those conducting it. I think it is fair to say that all involved with the Kabuki-Hawaii program, including myself, would have been gratified to see more demonstrable effect on the actors in the study. The dominant effect observed in the study was stability of style, not change—neither toward kabuki nor away from it.

Performance Patterns of Nakamura Matagoro

All the student actors studied under Nakamura Matagoro, emulating his interpretation of each role. Therefore, for the purposes of this study, kabuki acting is defined by the performance patterns of Nakamura Matagoro. His position as chief instructor in kabuki at the National Theatre of Japan and his status as a leading professional actor in the kabuki theatre over a period of many years establish his credentials.

The study of Nakamura is based on the following materials:

1. A videotape of his performance of the role of Enju in *Genda Kando* at the National Theatre of Japan.
2. A videotape of his performance of the role of Bimyo in *Moritsuna Jinya* at the National Theatre of Japan.
3. A videotape I prepared at the University of Hawaii of demonstrations of most of the major roles and scenes from *Kanadehon Chushingura*. This tape, entitled "Demonstrations from *Chushingura*," contains over four hours of material including several repetitions of the same role or scene taped on different occasions. Some of this material was collected during special demonstratons staged by Nakamura; the rest of the material was collected during class sessions.

Some of the material in "Demonstrations from *Chushingura*" is not directly related to any particular play. Nakamura taught a number of classroom drills for basic patterns of walking, kneeling, bowing, swordsmanship, and handling the fan that are common to almost all kabuki performances. These routines were rehearsed daily throughout most of the program. This material encapsulates Nakamura's fundamental performance patterns.

Nakamura's Two Styles

I call the first of these the "plain" style. Nakamura uses this style in most of the material analyzed here, including his performances as Enju and Bimyo and also most (though not all) of the material in "Demonstrations from *Chushingura*." The plain style is adapted from the bunraku puppet theatre and is used in playing generally serious scenes of prose dialog. It is one of the least stylized kabuki performance patterns, and while considerably different from Western performance patterns, bears certain similarities to the style of serious Western spoken drama.

I call the second of Nakamura's styles the "dance" style. It is particularly the style shown in the "Fugitives" section of *The Forty-Seven Samurai,* which is the *michiyuki* (dance of traveling). It is strikingly different from what I call the plain style. While the greatest differences are found in the area of movement, there are also vocal differences as well, as will be shown below.

Fundamental Characteristics of Nakamura's Performance

There are 13 traits which are invariant in all the material on Nakamura's performances. They are:

Movement structure

1. Placing facial tension in the lips
2. A very restrained use of facial movement
3. Moving weight from one foot to the other through steps, as opposed to sliding or other movements
4. Turning in place before moving across the stage, rather than turning while moving

5. Keeping the full foot on the floor
6. Keeping the torso as a solid one-unit block
7. Allowing very little bending or flexing of the torso

Movement dynamics

8. Keeping visual focus on other performers

Voice

9. A slight touch of tightness in the throat
10. Slight but audible breath noise in the voice
11. Comprehensible diction, but not especially clear
12. No vibrato at all

Phrasing

13. Creating a sense of one layer of subphrasing

These 13 aspects of Nakamura's performance are those in which he is consistent, the fundamentals of his style. They do not completely describe his acting style, but since they are invariant, they form the core of his style.

The idea that these qualities have a fundamental bearing on the nature of his style is confirmed by their presence in the basic drills he taught at the beginning of the Kabuki-Hawaii program. The very first of these, a simple exercise designed to teach the basic manner of kneeling, walking, and bowing, incorporates all of the movement qualities on the list of 13 traits.

This exercise begins with kneeling in Japanese fashion, feet tucked under the body. There is essentially no change in facial expression, but the lips are held in a somewhat tense, rather dour expression. The performer rises to her or his feet, holding the torso in one unit. Taking full steps on the full foot, the performer walks forward, kneels, and bows low, maintaining the torso pattern specified above. The bow is not a single unitary phrase, but is broken up somewhat, showing slight compounding. Rising again to the feet, the performer pivots in place, returns with full steps on the full foot back to the starting position, and once more kneels.

The early drills generally did not involve vocalization of any kind except for one exercise taught very early in the course. The students walked in a circle chanting a phrase, "Shitaniiiiiii . . . shitani!" Although few of the actors imitated him at this point, Nakamura's own utterance of the phrase shows the four vocal qualities on the list: slight tightness, audible breathiness, moderate precision, no vibrato.

Continuities in Nakamura's Performance Patterns

Beyond the patterns to be observed in individual traits, there are certain continuities that can be observed in Nakamura's pattern of structural movement. The first such continuity is a principle of restriction. He simply does not move very much in any way at all, and greatly reduces the number of possible movement patterns that he does use. The general absence of posturality, his tendency to remain in one place, the very restricted use of the face and head, the avoidance of rotation in limb gestures, and the elimination of almost all torso movement are ways in which he restricts his movement repertoire.

The second principle is that of economy. Even within the movement restrictions outlined above, Nakamura does not move his eyelids and his eyebrows—he moves his eyebrows only. He not only keeps his hands in his lap much of the time, but when he does gesture, he uses the simplest

2. Russell Omori as Heimon in The Forty-Seven Samurai. *(Photo by Robert W. Bethune)*

flexion, without adding any rotation, circling, or other complexities. He stays in one place on the stage unless the action of the play absolutely requires that he move. When he moves his head to look to one side, his torso remains at rest. It does not twist a little at the shoulders to follow the head.

Finally, Nakamura's structural movement patterns involve a principle of separation. Each movement is clearly delineated from the others. When he turns to take a path across the floor, the turn is clearly separated from the action of moving across the floor. The use of gestural rather than postural movement permits the use of sequential rather than overlapping gestures, a pattern evident not only in the limbs, but in the face as well.

Gesture is limited because the norm is stillness. Each gesture comes from stillness and returns to stillness, even if another gesture immediately follows. Therefore, the gestures that do occur are magnified by the general absence of gesture. Gestures are not a running accompaniment to the action but occur only as special moments. In the first scene of *Kanadehon Chushingura,* several minutes go by with no stage action whatsoever except a few isolated well-emphasized gestures: each of the major characters in turn raises her or his head from forward low to forward middle and spreads both arms laterally toward side middle, then brings them to rest again. When the character Morono forces an embrace on Lady Kaoyo, each step and arm movement is separated, however briefly, from the other gestures that precede and follow. Lady Kaoyo does not gesture at all except to turn her head away from Morono. Morono's gestures stand out all the more vividly in contrast to Lady Kaoyo's lack of movement.

The use of "bound flow" ties in with the principle of restriction that seems apparent in Nakamura's movement structure. The essence of bound flow is the sense that there are limits on movement preventing the movement from passing beyond those limits. This sense of stoppage reinforces the restrictive aspects of Nakamura's movement.

Nakamura's neutrality with respect to weight seems to be in keeping with the principles of restriction and economy. He avoids both definitely applying his weight to his environment and definitely holding back his weight and its impact, creating a sense of self-containment. His use of directness modulates this self-containment into a strong feeling of authority. Because his manner of dealing with the space around him is direct rather than indirect, there is no sense that his self-containment is an avoidance of contacting with his environment. On the contrary, his use of a direct spatial attitude, together with the economy, restriction, and separation of his movement, creates a sense of concentration. His use of sustained rather than sudden movement further heightens that sense of concentration and authority, for he lengthens his movement while those around him shorten theirs.

One striking feature of Nakamura's use of shape is his strong orientation toward the lateral axis and the horizontal plane. One moment in particular illustrates this. In her grief and anger, Enju destroys the letter that orders Genda to commit *seppuku* (suicide). Nakamura picks the letter up in both hands so that the paper is vertical and facing him, just below collarbone level, with his fingers over the top of the sheet. Both hands are at the top edge of the letter. From this position, there are several ways to tear the letter in two. Since a sheet of paper is weakest along the axis perpendicular to the surface, it seems reasonable to expect the tearing motion to be a mirror gesture of the hands along the sagittal axis, perhaps with a rotation to separate the two halves of the paper. Instead, Nakamura executes a mirror gesture along the lateral axis with no rotation and entirely in the horizontal plane, so that his hands move horizontally left and right and his elbows move out from his body, his forearms stay level to the floor.

This action powerfully characterizes Enju. It represents an emotional peak in which she decisively expresses her will. However, the movement clearly shows that though her mind is strong, her body is old and cannot move in a powerful way. She cannot make a large move through space in the sagittal axis. Instead she calls on her shoulders to rip the paper laterally, while not moving her arms very far. This action expresses the principle of restriction even while creating an emphatic movement. Enju's strength of will, her emotional turmoil, her determination, and the limitations of her aging body—all are visible in one moment.

In any one vocal phrase, Nakamura tends to use more than one pitch range. In particular, he will often go back and forth between the range of the break between full-fold and falsetto and either the range above it or the range below it. A good many individual phrase patterns key off the mode break by using it as the point of a subphrase transition or as a point at which to create an elaboration of the pitch or rhythmic pattern.

Nakamura holds his patterns of vocal quality, diction, and volume fairly constant. As observed above, 4 of the 13 invariant aspects of his performance have to do with voice. Most of the vocal variety in his performance comes through his use of pitch. There is considerable pitch variation in each utterance and between utterances. When he shifts his pitch through the range of the break between falsetto and full-fold voice, he makes no effort to smooth the transition between vocal modes. On the contrary, the pitch break becomes a stylistic device in itself, in accordance with a common kabuki vocal convention.

The pitch structure Nakamura uses does not seem to permit the free use of any pitch at will. It is a spoken style, not sung or chanted, yet certain pitch ranges are used in preference to others. There seem to be three such ranges: one in the lower part of the use range, one around the point where the break between full-fold and falsetto voice occurs, and the third rather higher than that, up in the falsetto. Pitches which would fall in between these are heard, but not nearly as often as the pitches that lie within these preferred ranges.

Through placing emphasis early in his vocal phrases and late in his movement phrases, Nakamura creates a contrast that serves to knit his movement pattern and vocal delivery together. As phrase succeeds phrase, we are drawn by turns to the movement, then to the vocal line by the alternation of phrase emphasis. The result is a kind of counterpoint that refreshes one's interest in both channels of communication.

When Nakamura uses a full pause, it is generally part of a performance pattern that leads to a moment of stillness as its conclusion. The pause both separates one phrase from another and is a part of the preceding phrase. Often, there will be a general deceleration, a marked increase in both vocal and movement sustainment. By increasing sustainment as much as possible, then pausing, Nakamura opens a span of time in which nothing needs to happen. In such a span of time, the audience is free to experience the evocative image created by the performer. The performance is not slowed nor interrupted. It is rather a change of mode within the performance which in effect carries the performance forward. Even though nothing concrete is happening on stage, something is happening in the performance process.

Patterns of Assimilation

Plates 3–6 present an analysis of how the group assimilated Nakamura's performance behavior in their Western performances. In each of the four tables, the actors are denoted by their initials across the top of the page; the traits used in this study go down the left side of the page. A bullet at the intersection of an actor's column and the row of a particular trait shows that assimilation of Nakamura's patterns of performance with respect to that trait by that actor did take place. The four tables break up the set of traits into the categories established above: movement structure, movement dynamics, voice, and phrasing.

Most of the students did assimilate certain aspects of Nakamura's performance patterns. The particular aspects assimilated by each student varied, and no single aspect measured in this study was assimilated by all the students. In fact, no single trait showed assimilation by more than five of the seven. However, there were a few assimilations that occurred very frequently. These were: weight, kinespheric zone, spatial retention, lengthening, rest pitch, and vocal phrase duration. Several other traits were assimilated by more than half of the actors: area tension, facial activity, facial posturality, torso posturality, and volume center.

Plate 3.

Assimilations by Scale: Movement Structure

	N.S.	H.B.	R.C.	T.S.	C.H.	D.R.	R.O.
01. Area tension	*	*	*				*
02. Eye tension		*		*		*	
03. Mouth tension		*			*	*	
04. Facial activity	*	*	*	*			
05. Facial posturality	*		*	*	*		
06. Head movement	*		*				
07. Gesture amount					*		
08. Limb relation			*				
09. Turning	*		*				
10. Flexure							
11. Supports							
12. Weight transfer							
13. Aerial steps							
14. Path shape		*					
15. Turning		*					
16. Floor contact			*				
17. Torso units							
18. Torso movements				*			
19. Flexibility	*			*	*		
20. Mobility		*	*			*	
21. Posturality		*	*			*	

The students did not tend to show assimilation of those traits which are invariant for Nakamura. Of the 13 invariant traits, four students showed assimilation toward Nakamura on facial activity and three students on mouth tension, flexibility, and compounding. The rest of the 13 were assimilated by only one or two actors at most. In four cases there was no assimilation at all. It would seem, therefore, that assimilation of a given trait is not related to Nakamura being consistent with respect to it.

Predisposition of the actors to observe certain performance patterns probably played a part in their assimilation of certain traits. For example, in movement structure, much more assimilation was seen in the area of facial expression than in any other area. This could be because Western acting is face-oriented. American actors, already face-oriented, will tend to notice and absorb the use of facial expression by their kabuki teacher. The relatively exotic technique of the rest of the body may be assimilated to a lesser degree since the student has less predisposition to notice and absorb it. The student learns the kabuki gesture, support, and torso techniques, and applies them in kabuki performance, but is less apt to assimilate them in Western work.

In movement dynamics, the students showed more assimilation in the areas of effort and space than in shape. Much of the assimilation in this area was with respect to only three traits: weight, kinespheric zone, and spatial retention. Nakamura is remarkably effective in these aspects of movement dynamics. His varied use of weight gives expressiveness to his acting. His

Plate 4.

Assimilations by Scale: Movement Dynamics

	N.S.	H.B.	R.C.	T.S.	C.H.	D.R.	R.O.
22. Flow		*					
23. Weight	*			*	*	*	*
24. Space							*
25. Time	*	*					*
26. Activation					*		
27. Shape mode							
28. Size							
29. Directions		*					*
30. Planes			*				
31. Visual focus							
32. Kinespheric size		*	*				
33. Kinespheric zone	*		*	*	*		*
34. Active touch				*			
35. Spatial retention		*	*	*	*		*

Plate 5.

Assimilations by Scale: Voice

	N.S.	H.B.	R.C.	T.S.	C.H.	D.R.	R.O.
36. Phonation mode				*			
37. Tightness		*		*			
38. Nasality							
39. Noise		*		*			
40. Breathiness				*			
41. Lengthening		*	*	*	*		
42. Accent		*	*				
43. Attack		*		*			*
44. Precision							
45. Pitch width				*		*	
46. Pitch center			*	*			
47. Rest pitch	*	*	*	*	*		
48. Pitch structure							
49. Vibrato						*	
50. Slide		*				*	*
51. Volume width				*	*	*	
52. Volume center		*	*			*	*
53. Volume rest level			*				
54. Volume change		*	*	*			

Plate 6.

Assimilations by Scale: Phrasing

	N.S.	H.B.	R.C.	T.S.	C.H.	D.R.	R.O.
Vocal phrasing							
55. Shape			*		*		
56. Duration	*	*		*	*	*	
57. Emphasis		*		*			
Movement phrasing							
58. Duration							
59. Emphasis					*		
60. Passage			*				
61. Initiation	*		*			*	*
62. Transition			*	*			
63. Elaboration	*			*			
64. Compounding		*	*				*
65. Overall rate		*		*			
66. Phrase rate		*		*		*	
67. Pause							
68. Meter							
69. Rhythmic variety			*	*			
70. Metric change							

distinction between different kinespheric zones gives clarity and simplicity to his gestures. His use of spatial retention gives not only clarity, but often a strikingly forceful presentation of the character's focus, mood, and attention. Nakamura's effective employment of these traits should attract the attention of the student actor and therefore have a high probability of assimilation.

Untrained observers can recognize and communicate the effect of effort factors. An actor can see and learn the use of effort from another actor relatively easily. Shape, however, is another matter. Western actors, like most Western people, consider their bodies to be solid objects with a definite shape that is not easily changed. Hence, the student actors would not readily have perceived the differences in the kabuki use of shape, and would therefore be less likely to assimilate it.

In general, the students did not assimilate Nakamura's vocal quality. Nakamura's vocal quality does not change much; in fact, tightness and breathiness are invariant in his performances. Since he makes little use of vocal quality for effect, there is little to attract the student actor's attention. However, the other areas of vocal performance, where Nakamura does use voice for effect, all showed a fair amount of assimilation.

There were interesting exceptions. Clear diction is highly valued in the Western theatre, both in principle and in practice. Nakamura's speech shows only moderate precision at best. None of the student actors assimilated this aspect of Nakamura's performance pattern.

This may seem trivial, but it illustrates a valuable point. The student actor is not a mechanical reproducing device; the mind and attitudes of the student are brought to bear. Valuing clear diction, and hearing diction that does not match that standard of clarity, the student is not likely to emulate

Plate 7.

Summary of Changes by Actors and Roles

Types of Change (% of all Scales)

	NC	TB	TD	TP	TT	AB	AD	AP	TA	AM
N.S.	77%	5%	4%	2%	11%	5%	4%	1%	11%	1%
H.B.	49%	14%	6%	6%	26%	7%	2%	8%	17%	8%
R.C.	59%	9%	3%	11%	24%	11%	1%	2%	14%	4%
T.S.	50%	9%	6%	6%	21%	14%	4%	6%	24%	5%
C.H.	66%	9%	10%	6%	24%	0%	1%	4%	6%	4%
D.R.	76%	9%	4%	6%	19%	4%	0%	0%	4%	1%
R.O.	76%	6%	4%	4%	14%	3%	1%	1%	6%	4%

NC = no change
TB = toward both
TD = toward dance
TP = toward plain
TT = total change toward Nakamura
AB = away from both
AD = away from dance
AP = away from plain
TA = total change away from Nakamura
AM = ambiguous change

it. By the same token, if a movement pattern seems odd or ridiculous, the student will be hesitant to learn and perform it. The student has, after all, a certain fund of knowledge and experience and judgment that serves as a guide. Therefore, the Asian theatre director cannot simply impose an exotic style. The burden of proof is clearly on the director.

A further illustration may help. Nakamura uses the kabuki sliding-pitch intonation on sentence endings rather sparingly, but he tends to use it effectively when he does use it. It would be hard to imagine an intonation that is likelier to sound more foolish in the context of a Western performance. However, there is a certain amount of assimilation of slide. When the instructor can demonstrate the value of an exotic technique, the students can and do assimilate it to some extent.

Except in the classic repertory, Western theatre makes relatively little expressive use of movement and vocal rhythm when compared to kabuki. The student actors assimilated the metrical aspects of Nakamura's phrase structure almost not at all. The kabuki rhythm simply is not at home in the Western repertory. The student actors did not assimilate what they could find little use for.

It must be underlined that these observations do not apply to the students' kabuki performances. The students made good to excellent progress in applying kabuki technique to kabuki performance. The variables discussed above apply only to the question of assimilation of kabuki patterns into the Western acting of the student.

Levels of Assimilation

In the preceding sections, the presence or absence of assimilation has been discussed. The question of the degree or intensity of assimilation remains. Plate 7 shows what percentage of the students' performance patterns changed in terms of all 70 traits.

The possible types of change appear across the top, and the actor's initials down the left side. There is a key to the abbreviations at the foot of the table. For each actor, the first column (NC) shows the percentage of scales that showed no change. The next group of four columns breaks down the percentages of change toward Nakamura's style: change toward both styles, change toward dance style specifically, toward the plain style specifically, and then the total change toward Nakamura. Change away from Nakamura is treated similarly in the next four columns. The last column shows the percentage of change that cannot be clearly related to Nakamura's styles. The percentages in the table are all rounded. Therefore, percentages may not add up to 100 and subgroups may not add up to the group totals.

Plate 7 shows that ambiguous change, change not clearly toward or away from the kabuki, occurred in all the actors, but never amounted to more than eight percent of their performance pattern. This suggests that some of the change to be seen in the performance patterns of the actors was due to experience not related to Kabuki-Hawaii.

The stable proportion of the students' performance patterns range between 80 and 50 percent. Given the intensity and duration of the Kabuki-Hawaii program, these figures are rather high. They indicate a relatively firmly established Western style that is not easily susceptible to influence.

Nevertheless, there is assimilation, as the second, third, and fourth columns of the table show. The fact that there is more change toward both styles (TB) than toward either plain or dance separately shows that there is more assimilation of those aspects of Nakamura's style that are the same in both the plain and dance styles. There is more change toward the plain style than toward the dance style; there was also more exposure to the plain style during the program. Of the three actors who reverse this trend, all three were either given special training in the dance style or had a particular interest in it.

There is also change away from Nakamura to be seen in the group, as the next four columns show. In one case there is actually an overall preponderance of change away from Nakamura over change toward him.

One possible factor that could produce this antiassimilation would be an effort on the actor's part to separate kabuki training from Western training, just as a modern dancer might well deliberately separate modern dance from ballet. The student actor working to master new techniques seems to feel a special need to keep the old and the new unconfused. Due to this reaction, such an actor might emphasize purely Western technique when performing in the Western repertory. Another factor that could produce antiassimilation is the strain of attempting to master behavior from a foreign culture. One invests emotional energy in maintaining specific ways of moving and speaking as an important part of one's identity. The student actor who has been intensively working on kabuki may find the occasion to perform in the Western repertory a chance to "come home" behaviorally, and therefore may exercise the elements of the Western performance style more vigorously than usual.

The Nature of Assimilation

No one came out of the kabuki program with performances of material from the Western repertory that looked or sounded like kabuki performances; none of the well-known devices of the kabuki theatre were shown by the student actors in their Western work. Wholesale adoption of kabuki technique in large, undigested units simply did not occur. There are several reasons for this. As noted above, the student actor brings personal experience, training, taste, and judgment to the work. Having acquired a certain performance tradition through a large investment of time and effort, the student will not arbitrarily dump that investment in favor of something that may, at first glance, seem exotic, odd, or even ridiculous. This, plus the desire to keep kabuki and Western technique in separate compartments, and the personal investment in Western ways of behavior, pose a formidable obstacle to the wholehearted adoption of exotic technique.

It is logical, therefore, that those elements of kabuki technique that lie rather beneath the level of full awareness would be assimilated, and in fact this may be seen to be the case. Throughout this study, it is clear that the aspects of kabuki performance that are assimilated are the subtle, the qualitative, the general rather than the bold, the crystallized, and the specific. The students assimilated a habit of using weight in certain ways, not the habit of using kabuki poses as such. They picked up on a principle of relatively sharp kinespheric distinctions, not on stylized gesture patterns or fan technique. They began to use a lower rest pitch and higher volume center to give their voices more power, but did not adopt the very stylized rhythmic and metrical devices of kabuki in their Western work.

Part of the subliminal nature of the assimilations is that they tend to occur through repetition. No one instructed the students in Laban movement theory or speech science; only a very few specific aspects of performance were actually identified and discussed during their training. But through constant repetition of the specific material they learned to perform, certain qualities were reinforced. However, directing the attention of the students to particular aspects of performance did not necessarily lead to assimilation. No one, for example, assimilated the one-unit torso, even though considerable stress was laid on it in training.

Finally, it is interesting, especially in view of the subliminal nature of this assimilation, that the actors tended to pick up what they could use. One needed relatively little work on the body; his style was already fairly close to the kabuki style to begin with. However, by assimilating Nakamura's characteristic use of facial expression, he added an additional dimension to his performance.

Plate 8 summarizes the probability values for each actor. As before, a value of 1 shows high probability that the result in question is due to chance, while a value of 0 shows low probability. It can be observed from this table that the results shown here are probably not due to chance. First of all, the high proportion of stable traits is almost certainly not due to chance in any performance by any of the actors. Secondly, the data for overall change toward Nakamura (TT) and away from him (TA) are also very low, indicating a very small probability that the observed overall changes are due to chance. Thirdly, even in categories such as change toward and away from specific styles, no probability exceeds .28.

Conclusions

The effect of studying kabuki acting on the performances by student actors of materials from the Western repertory in this study can be summarized:

The group showed a dominant stability of performance patterns. While assimilations from kabuki style did occur, the experience of nine months of kabuki training under a recognized master actor did not bring about profound and pervasive changes in the Western acting styles of the students in the study.

Plate 8.

Probabilities of Change by Actors and Roles

	Types of Change NC	TB	TD	TP	TT	AB	AD	AP	TA	AM
N.S.	.00	.11	.19	.14	.00	.11	.16	.07	.00	.00
H.B.	.00	.00	.13	.13	.07	.14	.00	.13	.01	.00
R.C.	.00	.04	.03	.01	.07	.01	.00	.01	.00	.00
T.S.	.00	.09	.10	.12	.05	.00	.02	.12	.07	.00
C.H.	.00	.08	.03	.21	.11	.02	.09	.23	.00	.00
D.R.	.00	.03	.24	.16	.05	.24	.05	.05	.00	.00
R.O.	.00	.12	.23	.23	.01	.28	.22	.22	.00	.00

NC = no change
T = change toward
A = away
P = plain
D = dance

B = both
TT = total change toward Nakamura
TA = total change away from Nakamura
AM = ambiguous change

There was some assimilation of kabuki performance patterns. The assimilated material was either in an area the student was predisposed to observe, had demonstrated its value so convincingly that the student's resistance was overcome, or was repeated until it became habit. I suspect that predisposition was particularly important, since the students learned by emulation, and emulation depends in the first place on seeing what there is to emulate. Something the student is not predisposed to see and assimilate may well simply pass unseen.

The students tended to place kabuki and Western acting in different worlds. The personal, cultural, and artistic reasons for so doing are probably to be expected. In a situation such as Kabuki-Hawaii, where the students were not planning to become professional kabuki actors, there is a natural tendency to place kabuki acting in a different box in one's head, and a box of lesser importance. However, I suspect that even those who decide to pursue an art form from a foreign culture might well show similar behavior, despite their best intentions. Emotional investment in established behavior patterns as an aspect of personal identity, the need to keep new and difficult forms of expression unconfused, and the conflict between prior experience, taste, training, and tradition and the new ways of the new art—all these things militate against integration of the new and foreign art with the old.

It may be, of course, that integration of the new art with the old is not what is wanted. There is certainly considerable value in learning to perform an exotic technique well as an end in itself. If the Western theatre is to benefit from the Asian tradition, it is necessary that there be performers who serve as the media of transmission by incorporating knowledge of Asian traditions and then passing that knowledge on to others. However, if the Western theatre is truly to benefit from the Asian traditions, there must at some point be a fusion, an integration of the two. If, as this study indicates, there is an almost inevitable resistance to that integration, how can the fusion occur?

I think this study, while showing the potential problem, also reveals solutions. If performers tend to learn what they are predisposed to learn, that predisposition can be actively shaped as part of the learning process. For example, prior to undertaking study of an Asian tradition, performers could learn techniques of performance analysis similar to those presented here. They could use such techniques to heighten understanding of the Asian form, and also of their own style, learning what predispositions already exist and what the relationship is between the familiar style and the Asian form.

Another way through the barrier is repetition and habit. Slow exposure in small doses over a long period of time might well overcome resistances that would pose major problems in an intensive program. But the most appealing way to overcome resistance is by demonstrating the value of the exotic style. If the performer can be shown how a performance pattern works—affectively, aesthetically, and cognitively—in the context of the Asian art form, and can see how that style develops power and impact within its own context, the performer will be far more open to learning the style.

As the world shrinks, it becomes more and more valuable to integrate styles and forms of performance from a wide variety of traditions. Cross-cultural communication can be one of the great strengths of the performing arts. There are roadblocks—areas of resistance—that must be worked through, but the possibility is there, and, under the right conditions, performers will assimilate foreign styles and performance patterns. This study shows that in an exchange of traditions, cross-cultural fertilization does take place and can be enhanced.

9. Norris Shimabuku as Moroanao in The Forty-Seven Samurai. *(Photo by Robert W. Bethune)*

Appendix
Categories of Analysis

Below are brief definitions of each of the 70 traits used in my work as categories of analysis. Much fuller discussions are found in Bethune (1985). For each trait I give the name, a brief definition, and the values assignable to it.

Movement Structure

These categories are mostly derived from Laban notation as described by Anne Hutchinson (1977). In a few cases, especially 1–5 and 19–20, I have developed my own ideas.

1. *Facial tension*. Locus of facial tension: mouth, eyes, more mouth than eyes, more eyes than mouth, use of the whole face.
2. *Eye movement*. Locus of eye movement: none, brows, lids, eyeball, whole eye area.
3. *Mouth tension*. Locus of any tension occurring in the mouth area: none, lips, cheeks, jaw, whole mouth.
4. *Facial activity*. Amount and frequency of facial tension regardless of locus.
5. *Facial posturality*. Degree to which all facial features participate in facial expression: none, slight, moderate, marked, extreme.
6. *Head movement*. Planar orientation of head movement: none, horizontal, sagittal, lateral, compound.
7. *Amount of gesture*. Extent and frequency of gesture: none, slight, moderate, marked, extreme.
8. *Limb relationship*. The relationship of gesturing limbs to one another: single, parallel, mirror, opposing, skew.
9. *Turning*. How turning gestures are done: none, rotating, twisting, circling, compound.
10. *Flexure*. How bending or flexing gestures are done: none, shift, flexion, folding, compound.
11. *Supports*. What part of the body bears weight: feet, knees, hips, torso, head or hands or shoulders.
12. *Weight transfer*. How weight is transferred from one support to another: shift, slide-shift, step-shift, slide-step, step.
13. *Aerial steps*. How jumps, leaps, or other air work is executed in terms of the feet: one foot to the same foot, one foot to the other foot, one foot to two feet, two feet to one foot, two feet to two feet.
14. *Path*. Shape of the track followed by the performer while moving: straight, curved, compound curve, circle, spiral.
15. *Turning*. Relationship of movement of the center of weight while turning and/or moving through space along a path: pivot in place, pivot in motion, revolve in place, revolve on a path, circular path with constant front.
16. *Floor contact*. What part of the foot is on the floor: toe, ball, side, heel, full foot.
17. *Torso units*. How many segments appear in the torso: one unit, two units, three units, four units, five or more.
18. *Torso movements*. What kinds of torso movements occur: tilt, rotate, twist, bend, compound.

19. *Flexibility*. How much flexibility is shown in the torso: none, slight, moderate, marked, extreme.
20. *Mobility*. How much the torso moves as a unit, regardless of flexibility or units: none, slight, moderate, marked, extreme.
21. *Posturality*. To what extent the movement of the body seems a unified, fluid whole: none, slight, moderate, marked, extreme.

Movement Dynamics

These categories are mostly derived from Effort/Shape as described by Cecily Dell (1970). I have formulated my idea of "activation" based on ideas found in Dell's work, but she does not set forth such a category.

22. *Flow*. Relative inhibition or lack of inhibition on the release of energy: very free, free, neutral, bound, very bound.
23. *Weight*. Relative application or restraint of the mass of the moving body as exerted on or through the environment: very light, light, neutral, strong, very strong.
24. *Space*. Attention to particular directions in space or lack thereof: very indirect, indirect, neutral, direct, very direct.
25. *Time*. Relative sense of extending or contracting in time, hurrying or taking it easy: very sustained, sustained, neutral, quick, very quick.
26. *Activation*. Relative giving in or energizing against gravity: very passive, passive, neutral, active, very active.
27. *Mode of shape behavior*. How the body molds itself in and through space: flow only, flow with directionality, directionality, directionality with shaping, shaping.
28. *Size*. Whether the body expands or contracts in space: very contractive, contractive, neutral, expansive, very expansive.
29. *Directions*. Preferred axial orientations in space relative to the body: vertical, lateral, sagittal, variable, compound.
30. *Planes*. Preferred planar orientation in space: lateral, sagittal, horizontal, variable, compound.
31. *Visual focus*. Where the eyes look: into space, at oneself, at the stage, at other performers, at the audience.
32. *Kinespheric size*. How much space around the body gets filled up: very small, small, medium, large, very large.
33. *Kinespheric zone*. Within the space used by the body, where the action occurs: central, central/limb, limb, limb/distal, distal.
34. *Active touch*. What the performer deliberately touches: nothing, self, stage, performers, audience.
35. *Spatial retention*. To what extent the performer holds particular spots or directions in space: none, slight, moderate, marked, extreme.

Voice

The categories in this section are basic ideas from speech pathology. Lee Edward Travis's handbook (1971), which I used, appears to be a standard reference.

36. *Phonation mode*. What kind of vibration occurs in the vocal cords: fry, fry and full-fold, full-fold, full-fold and falsetto, falsetto. (Vocal fry is commonly experienced, but not commonly named. It often occurs in ordinary speech at the ends of sentences. It can be experienced by

reducing the volume and pitch of a relax open vowel until the sound takes on a bubbling quality in the larynx.)

37. *Tightness*. Degree of constriction of the throat and pharynx: none, slight, moderate, marked, extreme.
38. *Nasality*. Degree of resonance in the nasal tract: none, slight, moderate, marked, extreme.
39. *Noise*. Amount of inharmonic sound: none, slight, moderate, marked, extreme.
40. *Breathiness*. Amount of air-flow turbulence sound: none, slight, moderate, marked, extreme.
41. *Lengthening*. Amount of stretching or elongation used in enunciation: none, slight, moderate, marked, extreme.
42. *Accent*. Contrastive use of pitch, volume, or duration to emphasize words or syllables: none, slight, moderate, marked, extreme.
43. *Attack*. Contrasting treatment of the initial moment of individual sounds: none, slight, moderate, marked, extreme.
44. *Consonantal precision*. Degree of contrastive enunciation of consonants, precision of pronunciation of consonants: none, slight, moderate, marked, extreme.
45. *Pitch width*. Difference between highest and lowest pitch used: none, slight, moderate, marked, extreme.
46. *Pitch center*. Center of the range of pitches actually used: low, medium low, medium, medium high, high.
47. *Rest pitch*. Preferred or modal pitch: low, medium low, medium, medium high, high.
48. *Pitch structure*. How pitch use is regulated: spoken, spoken/chanted, chanted, chanted/sung, sung.
49. *Vibrato*. Degree of rapid, small variation around a main pitch or pitch curve: none, slight, moderate, marked, extreme.
50. *Slide*. Degree of gliding through intermediate pitches while changing pitch: none, slight, moderate, marked, extreme.
51. *Volume width*. Difference between loudest and softest volume level: none, slight, moderate, marked, extreme.
52. *Volume center*. Center of the range of volumes actually used: soft, medium soft, medium, medium loud, loud.
53. *Volume rest level*. Preferred or modal volume level: soft, medium soft, medium, medium loud, loud.
54. *Volume change*. How volume changes: very smooth, smooth, medium, abrupt, very abrupt.

Phrasing

Some of these ideas come from Alan Lomax (1968). Some are very simple music theory, for which I have no particular source.

55. *Vocal phrase shape*. Typical pitch/volume pattern: flat, ramp, oscillating, peak, valley.
56. *Vocal phrase duration*. Modal or preferred phrase length: very short, short, medium, long, very long.
57. *Vocal phrase emphasis*. Preferred placement of emphasis in the phrase: very early, early, middle, late, very late.
58. *Movement phrase duration*. Preferred length of movement phrase: very short, short, medium, long, very long.
59. *Movement phrase emphasis*. Preferred placement of emphasis in the movement phrase: very early, early, middle, late, very late.

60. *Passage*. How movement passes through the body: disjoined, linked, successive, rippling, simultaneous.
61. *Initiation*. Where movement begins in the body: central, central/limb, limb, limb/distal, distal.
62. *Transition*. How one gesture changes into the next: vague, reversal, cyclic, plane, skew.
63. *Elaboration*. How much short-term minor variation occurs without creating subphrasing: none, slight, moderate, marked, extreme.
64. *Compounding*. How much layer of subphrase beneath subphrase occurs: none, one degree, two degrees, three degrees, four or more degrees.
65. *Overall rate*. How fast the performance moves as a whole, including pauses: very slow, slow, medium, fast, very fast.
66. *Phrase rate*. How fast the performance moves within phrases: very slow, slow, medium, fast, very fast.
67. *Pause*. Frequency and extent of pausing: none, slight, moderate, marked, extreme.
68. *Meter*. Basic rhythmic structure of the performance: free, single, double, triple, complex.
69. *Rhythmic variety*. How much use of different rhythms occurs within a meter: none, slight, moderate, marked, extreme.
70. *Metric change*. How much change of basic meter occurs: none, slight, moderate, marked, extreme.

Note

1. For a full treatment of this work see Bethune (1985).

References

Bethune, Robert William

1985 *The Effect of Kabuki Training on the Western Performances of Western Acting Students*. PhD Diss., University of Hawaii. Ann Arbor, MI: University Microfilms.

Brandon, James R.

1982 *The Forty-Seven Samurai: A Kabuki Version of Chushingura*. In *Chushingura: Studies in Kabuki and the Puppet Theater,* edited by James R. Brandon. Honolulu: University of Hawaii Press.

Davis, Martha Ann, and Claire Schmais

1968 "An Analysis of the Style and Composition of 'Water Study.' " In *Research in Dance: Problems and Possibilities,* edited by Richard Bull, 106–13. New York: Committee on Research in Dance.

Dell, Cecily

1970 *A Primer for Movement Description*. New York: Dance Notation Bureau Press.

Gellerman, Jill

1978 "The Mayim Pattern as an Indicator of Cultural Attitudes in Three American Hasidic Communities." In *CORD Dance Research Annual IX,* edited by Dianne L. Woodruff, 111–14. New York: Congress on Research in Dance, Inc.

Hutchinson, Anne

1977 *Labanotation or Kinetography Laban: The System of Analyzing and Recording Movement*. 3rd edition, revised. New York: Theater Arts Books.

Kagan, Elizabeth
1978 "Toward the Analysis of a Score: A Comparative Study of 'Three Epitaphs' by Paul Taylor and 'Water Study' by Doris Humphrey." In *CORD Dance Research Annual IX,* edited by Dianne L. Woodruff, 75–92. New York: Congress on Research in Dance, Inc.

Lomax, Alan, et al.
1968 *Folk Song Style and Culture.* Washington, DC: American Association for the Advancement of Science.

Travis, Lee Edward
1971 *Handbook of Speech Pathology and Audiology.* Englewood Cliffs, NJ: Prentice Hall, Inc.

Youngerman, Suzanne
1978 "The Translation of a Culture into Choreography: A Study of Doris Humphrey's 'The Shakers' Based on Laban Analysis." In *CORD Dance Research Annual IX,* edited by Dianne L. Woodruff, 93–110. New York: Congress on Research in Dance, Inc.

Robert W. Bethune *has researched the modern theatre of the Arabic-speaking world and collected information, artifacts, translations, and film footage of Korean masked dances. He has worked for three years with East-West Fusion Theater in Sharon, CT, as an actor, director, playwright, and designer and has taught at Wayne State University and SUNY-Stonybrook.*

ITItems

The Weather for the '90s

The 23rd World Congress of the International Theatre Institute (ITI) was held during the first days of June in Helsinki, Finland, and the memory is still sharp and vibrant. Every two years ITI has its major family gathering to take care of international business and review the affairs of the organization. Though the work is mostly predictable—elections, budgets, agendas, and committee reports—there is an alchemy about each congress which sums up the whole purpose of ITI: connection. With all of the thousands and thousands of individual contacts and meetings that happen in the life of ITI, the congresses serve as an international reminder that ITI exists to join theatre people across some extremely formidable barriers—barriers of culture, politics, and distance.

This year the congress was held in the cradle of the Helsinki Accords. It was two weeks after the release of playwright Vaclav Havel from prison, and it was the week of the Beijing Spring; the world atmosphere was full of sparkle and change. For an organization that exists to serve theatre people around the world, the "weather" was right for the meeting, for looking at the amazing achievements of our fragile network over the past 41 years.

In the weeks after the congress, the weather changed again. Poland had elections; Gorbachev probably would have won if elections had been held in France; China obliterated the children of democracy; and here in the U.S. the National Endowment for the Arts was warned not to support sinful work.

Is it the beginning of a time when, once again, we are told to agree or be silent? Or is that always our option in this crazy and contradictory country of ours? Perhaps our voices are so various and so loud that we all clap our hands over our ears and yell "Shut up!" from time to time.

If we have a tendency to shut out confusion here at home, imagine what we do when the voices have foreign accents and different languages. Whether it is the United Nations, or UNESCO, or even UNICEF, the U.S. tends to view international organizations with narrowed eyes, alert for signs of disagreement. Maybe it is because our country was founded by dissenters and outcasts that we have found it difficult to work with the various countries that threw us out.

Happily, ITI is a nongovernmental organization that speaks the language of theatre, not politics. However, since ITI is a kind of a theatrical U.N., we have felt America's special ambivalence toward the rest of the world. Every international organism is subject to different political climates, even if not motivated by them.

So, our worldwide network of theatre people is as fragile as each person's right to travel and speak and think. We rejoice when doors open and we grieve when they slam closed. It often seems that we have no power over these doors.

Maybe, though, there is the power of precedent, of our history of inclusion. If one country is in fashion, it is ITI's job to remember all the other countries. If one person is silenced, we demand to hear *that* person's voice. Maybe what ITI has given to theatre people over the years is the habit of caring for one another. In a world where artists are divided by all manner of outside pressures, ITI has taught us about solidarity.

ITI exists in countries where theatre artists are taken seriously. That attitude of respect can be contagious. It rubs off on artists who are ignored or disdained.

Looking toward a new decade, the last of the 20th century, the one sure thing is that we face more changes in the weather. In this remarkable American place, our theatre will experience a united Europe, a Western Hemisphere full of challenge and question, a USA growing a little older—and maybe wiser.

Back in 1974, there was a remarkable meeting in Princeton, NJ. During a huge American theatre meeting called FACT (First American Congress of Theatre), ITI/US had organized a theatre panel called "Alternative Theatre." Richard Schechner was there. Luis Valdez was there. Miguel Piñero was there. Gil Moses was there. And the Becks were there. All of a sudden Julian Beck surged to his feet, the cords in his neck stood out and he started to howl in anger and despair about art and the devil and America. Rosamond Gilder, then 83 years old, touched his hand and said, "Julian, sit down, we can't hear you when you shout." Well, we did hear him after that. It was very good advice. Maybe that's what we learn from ITI. We don't need to cover our ears and howl if we trust that someone will listen.

Happy New Year, Happy Decade.

Martha W. Coigney
Director, ITI/US
President, ITI/Worldwide

TDR Volume 33 Index

T121: vol. 33, no. 1 (Spring 1989)
T122: vol. 33, no. 2 (Summer 1989)
T123: vol. 33, no. 3 (Fall 1989)
T124: vol. 33, no. 4 (Winter 1989)

By Author

AUSLANDER, Philip	Auslander Wins Last Word (*Letter*)	2:15–18
AUSLANDER, Philip	Going With the Flow: Performance Art and Mass Culture	2:119–36
AWASTHI, Suresh	"Theatre of Roots": Encounter with Tradition	4:48–69
BABSON, Thomas W.	Theatre's Illegitimate Child: The Screen Actor	3:17–20
BANES, Sally	Terpsichore Combat Continued (*Letter*)	4:17–18
BANES, Sally	Terpsichore in Combat Boots (*Letter*)	1:13–15
BETHUNE, Robert	Describing Performance in the Theatre: Kabuki Training and the Western Acting Student	4:146–66
BRANDON, James R.	A New World: Asian Theatre in the West Today	2:25–50
BURNHAM, Linda Frye	Site-Seeing in London: Observing Edge 88	2:10–14
CARMELI, Yoram S.	Wee Pea: The Total Play of the Dwarf in the Circus	4:128–45
CASE, Sue-Ellen	A Case Concerning Hughes (*Letter*)	4:10–17
CHEN Yong	Speaking About China's Spoken Drama: A Roundtable with Chinese Directors and Playwrights	2:87–103
CLUNIES ROSS, Margaret	The Aesthetics and Politics of an Arnhem Land Ritual	4:107–27
COHEN, Hilary U.	Theatre By and For the Deaf	1:68–78

COIGNEY, Martha W.	ITItems	3:175–76
COIGNEY, Martha W.	ITItems: The Weather for the '90s	4:167–68
CROWLEY, Daniel J.	The Carnival of Guinea-Bissau	2:74–86
DALY, Ann	To Dance Is "Female" (*Book Review*)	4:23–27
DAVY, Kate	Reading Past the Heterosexual Imperative: *Dress Suits to Hire*	1:153–70
DiGAETANI, John Louis	*M. Butterfly:* An Interview with David Henry Hwang	3:141–53
DOLAN, Jill	In Defense of the Discourse: Materialist Feminism, Postmodernism, Poststructuralism . . . and Theory	3:58–71
DOLAN, Jill	Desire Cloaked in a Trenchcoat	1:59–67
EDITORS, The	Public Demonstrations and Secret Politics in China	4:4–7
van ERVEN, Eugène	Plays, Applause, and Bullets: Safdar Hashmi's Street Theatre	4:32–47
EVANS, Paul	*Bananaland:* PR, Propaganda, and Infotainment	3:95–102
FÉRAL, Josette	Building Up the Muscle: An Interview with Ariane Mnouchkine	4:88–97
FÉRAL, Josette	Mnouchkine's Workshop at the Soleil: A Lesson in Theatre	4:77–87
FÉRAL, Josette	Théâtre du Soleil—A Second Glance: An Interview with Sophie Moscoso	4:98–106
FUCHS, Elinor	Finley Facts or Fictions? (*Letter*)	4:8
FUCHS, Elinor	Staging the Obscene Body	1:33–58
FUEGI, John	Willet on Weimar (*Book Review*)	4:28–30
GEROULD, Daniel	Historical Simulation and Popular Entertainment: The *Potemkin* Mutiny from Reconstructed Newsreel to Black Sea Stunt Men	2:161–84
GOLUB, Paul	Théâtre du Soleil Shines Its Light On the Holy Land (*Letter*)	1:17–18

GREENBERG, Jeffrey	In Memory: Jacques Chwat	1:32
HALPRIN, Anna	Planetary Dance	2:67–73
HAY, Deborah	Playing Awake: Letters to My Daughter	4:70–76
HUANGPU Chongqing	China's Nuo Theatre: Nuo Theatre in Guizhou Province	3:113–21
HUGHES, Holly	A Case Concerning Hughes (*Letter*)	4:10–17
HUGHES, Holly	*Dress Suits to Hire* (*Script*)	1:132–52
HUNT, Nigel	The Global Voyage of Robert Lepage	2:104–18
KIRBY, Michael	Kirby Sets the Record Straight (*Letter*)	3:7
LARGE, Gerry	On Getting the Message (*Letter*)	1:19
LYNCH, Joan Driscoll	Skipitares's Performing Objects	2:137–60
MACDONALD, Eric L.	Theatre Rhinoceros: A Gay Company	1:79–93
MANNING, Frank	Of Time and Mime: A Polylog on Festivity (*Book Review*)	1:19–28
MANNING, Susan	Terpsichore in Combat Boots (*Letter*)	1:15–16
MONTANO, Linda	Summer Saint Camp 1987: With Annie Sprinkle and Veronica Vera	1:94–103
MOORE, Frank	EROPLAY	1:120–31
NELSON, Steve	Redecorating the Fourth Wall: Environmental Theatre Today	3:72–94
NEWMAN, Harry	Holding Back: The Theatre's Resistance to Non-Traditional Casting	3:22–36
OLESZKIEWICZ, Malgorzata	XIII Muestra Nacional de Teatro: The New Theatre in Peru	3:10–17
OVERN, Michael	Finley Facts or Fictions? (*Letter*)	4:8–9
PAVIS, Patrice	Dancing with *Faust:* A Semiotician's Reflections on Barba's Intercultural Mise-en-Scene	3:37–57

QU Liuyi	China's Nuo Theatre: The Yi: Human Evolution Theatre	3:103–12
QU Liuyi	Speaking About China's Spoken Drama: A Roundtable with Chinese Directors and Playwrights	2:87–103
RENZI, Vincent R.	Pedagogy and Performance: Teaching the *Poetics* with Computers	4:18–22
SCHECHNER, Richard	Anna Halprin: A Life in Ritual (*Interview*)	2:67–73
SCHECHNER, Richard	Bullets or Bullshit—or Something Important? (*Comment*)	3:5
SCHECHNER, Richard	Enter, Students (*Comment*)	3:4–5
SCHECHNER, Richard	Hello, "ITItems" (*Comment*)	3:5
SCHECHNER, Richard	PAJ Distorts the Broad Spectrum (*Comment*)	2:4–9
SCHECHNER, Richard	Race Free, Gender Free, Body-Type Free Casting (*Comment*)	1:4–12
SCHECHNER, Richard	Speaking About China's Spoken Drama: A Roundtable with Chinese Directors and Playwrights	2:87–103
SCHECHNER, Richard	Welcome to TDR: Sun Huizhu and Richard Gough (*Comment*)	3:6
SCHECHTER, Joel	Politics as Theatre: Or, How I Too Lost the Election in 1988	3:154–65
SCHELDE, Per	Missing the Mermaids of Rosmersholm (*Letter*)	3:8–10
SCHERBAKOV, Konstantin	Plays and Polemics on the Soviet Stage	3:166–74
SCHNEIDER, Rebecca	Holly Hughes: Polymorphous Perversity and the Lesbian Scientist (*Interview*)	1:171–82
SEARS, Laurie Lobell	Aesthetic Displacement in Javanese Shadow Theatre: Three Contemporary Performance Styles	3:122–40
SHAW, Peggy	*Dress Suits to Hire* (*Script*)	1:132–52
SPRINKLE, Annie	Our Week at Sister Rosita's Summer Saint Camp	1:104–19

SUN Zhongshu	Speaking About China's Spoken Drama: A Roundtable with Chinese Directors and Playwrights	2:87–103
VERA, Veronica	Our Week at Sister Rosita's Summer Saint Camp	1:104–19
WANG Xiaoying	Speaking About China's Spoken Drama: A Roundtable with Chinese Directors and Playwrights	2:87–103
WANG Zheng	Speaking About China's Spoken Drama: A Roundtable with Chinese Directors and Playwrights	2:87–103
WATSON, Ian	Latin America and Beyond	1:29–30
WEAVER, Lois	*Dress Suits to Hire* (*Script*)	1:132–52
WEN Xingyu	Speaking About China's Spoken Drama: A Roundtable with Chinese Directors and Playwrights	2:87–103
XING Yixun	Speaking About China's Spoken Drama: A Roundtable with Chinese Directors and Playwrights	2:87–103

By Title

Aesthetic Displacement in Javanese Shadow Theatre: Three Contemporary Performance Styles	Laurie Lobell Sears	3:122–40
Aesthetics and Politics of an Arnhem Land Ritual, The	Margaret Clunies Ross	4:107–27
Anna Halprin: A Life in Ritual (*Interview*)	Richard Schechner	2:67–73
Auslander Wins Last Word (*Letter*)	Philip Auslander	2:15–18
Bananaland: PR, Propaganda, and Infotainment	Paul Evans	3:95–102
Building Up the Muscle: An Interview with Ariane Mnouchkine	Josette Féral	4:88–97
Bullets or Bullshit—or Something Important? (*Comment*)	Richard Schechner	3:5
Carnival of Guinea-Bissau, The	Daniel J. Crowley	2:74–86

Case Concerning Hughes, A (*Letters*)	Sue-Ellen Case, Holly Hughes	4:10–17
China's Nuo Theatre: Nuo Theatre in Guizhou Province	Huangpu Chongqing	3:113–21
China's Nuo Theatre: The Yi—Human Evolution Drama	Qu Liuyi	3:103–12
Dance Is "Female," To (*Book Review*)	Ann Daly	4:23–27
Dancing with *Faust:* A Semiotician's Reflections on Barba's Intercultural Mise-en-Scene	Patrice Pavis	3:37–57
Defense of the Discourse, In: Materialist Feminism, Postmodernism, Poststructuralism . . . and Theory	Jill Dolan	3:58–71
Describing Performance in the Theatre: Kabuki Training and the Western Acting Student	Robert Bethune	4:146–66
Desire Cloaked in a Trenchcoat	Jill Dolan	1:59–67
Dress Suits to Hire (*Script*)	Holly Hughes, Peggy Shaw, Lois Weaver	1:132–52
Editors' Choice: Books We Recommend	TDR Editors	2:20–23
XIII Muestra Nacional de Teatro: The New Theatre in Peru	Malgorzata Oleszkiewicz	3:10–17
Enter, Students (*Comment*)	Richard Schechner	3:4–5
EROPLAY	Frank Moore	1:120–31
Finley Facts or Fictions? (*Letters*)	Michael Overn, Elinor Fuchs	4:8–9
Getting the Message, On (*Letter*)	Gerry Large	1:19
Global Voyage of Robert Lepage, The	Nigel Hunt	2:104–18
Going With the Flow: Performance Art and Mass Culture	Philip Auslander	2:119–36
Halprin, Anna: A Life in Ritual (*Interview*)	Richard Schechner	2:67–73
Hello, "ITItems" (*Comment*)	Richard Schechner	3:5
Historical Simulation and Popular Entertainment: The *Potemkin* Mutiny from Reconstructed Newsreel to Black Sea Stunt Men	Daniel Gerould	2:161–84
Holding Back: The Theatre's Resistance to Non-Traditional Casting	Harry Newman	3:22–36
Holly Hughes: Polymorphous Perversity and the Lesbian Scientist (*Interview*)	Rebecca Schneider	1:171–82
ITItems	Martha W. Coigney	3:175–76
	Martha W. Coigney	4:167–68

Kirby Sets the Record Straight (*Letter*)	Michael Kirby	3:7
Latin America and Beyond	Ian Watson	1:29–30
M. Butterfly: An Interview with David Henry Hwang	John Louis DiGaetani	3:141–53
Memory, In: Jaques Chwat	Jeffrey Greenberg	1:32
Missing the Mermaids of Rosmersholm (*Letter*)	Per Schelde	3:8–10
Mnouchkine's Workshop at the Soleil: A Lesson in Theatre	Josette Féral	4:77–87
New World, A: Asian Theatre in the West Today	James R. Brandon	2:25–50
Our Week at Sister Rosita's Summer Saint Camp	Annie Sprinkle, Veronica Vera	1:94–103
PAJ Distorts the Broad Spectrum (*Comment*)	Richard Schechner	2:4–9
Pedagogy and Performance: Teaching the *Poetics* with Computers	Vincent R. Renzi	4:18–22
Planetary Dance	Anna Halprin	2:67–73
Playing Awake: Letters to My Daughter	Deborah Hay	4:70–76
Plays and Polemics on the Soviet Stage	Konstantin Scherbakov	3:166–74
Plays, Applause, and Bullets: Safdar Hashmi's Street Theatre	Eugène van Erven	4:32–47
Politics as Theatre: Or, How I Too Lost the Election in 1988	Joel Schechter	3:154–65
Public Demonstrations and Secret Politics in China (*Comment*)	The Editors	4:4–7
Race Free, Gender Free, Body-Type Free Casting (*Comment*)	Richard Schechner	1:4–12
Reading Past the Heterosexual Imperative: *Dress Suits to Hire*	Kate Davy	1:153–70
Redecorating the Fourth Wall: Environmental Theatre Today	Steve Nelson	3:72–94
Site-Seeing in London: Observing Edge 88	Linda Frye Burnham	2:10–14
Skipitares's Performing Objects	Joan Driscoll Lynch	2:137–60
Speaking About China's Spoken Drama: A Roundtable with Chinese Directors and Playwrights	Chen Yong, Qu Liuyi, Richard Schechner, Sun Zhongshu, Wang Xiaoying, Wang Zheng, Wen Xingyu, Xing Yixun	2:87–103
Staging the Obscene Body	Elinor Fuchs	1:33–58

Summer Saint Camp 1987: With Annie Sprinkle and Veronica Vera	Linda Montano	1:94–103
Terpsichore Combat Continued (*Letter*)	Sally Banes	4:17–18
Terpsichore in Combat Boots (*Letters*)	Sally Banes, Susan Manning	1:13–15
Theatre By and For the Deaf	Hilary U. Cohen	1:68–78
Théâtre du Soleil—A Second Glance: An Interview with Sophie Moscoso	Josette Féral	4:98–106
Théâtre du Soleil Shines Its Light On the Holy Land (*Letter*)	Paul Golub	1:17–18
"Theatre of Roots": Encounter with Tradition	Suresh Awasthi	4:48–69
Theatre Rhinoceros: A Gay Company	Eric L. MacDonald	1:79–93
Theatre's Illegitimate Child: The Screen Actor	Thomas W. Babson	3:17–20
Time and Mime, Of: A Polylog on Festivity (*Book Review*)	Frank Manning	1:19–28
Weather for the '90s, The (*ITItems*)	Martha W. Coigney	4:167–68
Wee Pea: The Total Play of the Dwarf in the Circus	Yoram S. Carmeli	4:128–45
Welcome to TDR, Sun Huizhu and Richard Gough (*Comment*)	Richard Schechner	3:6
Willet on Weimar (*Book Review*)	John Fuegi	4:28–30

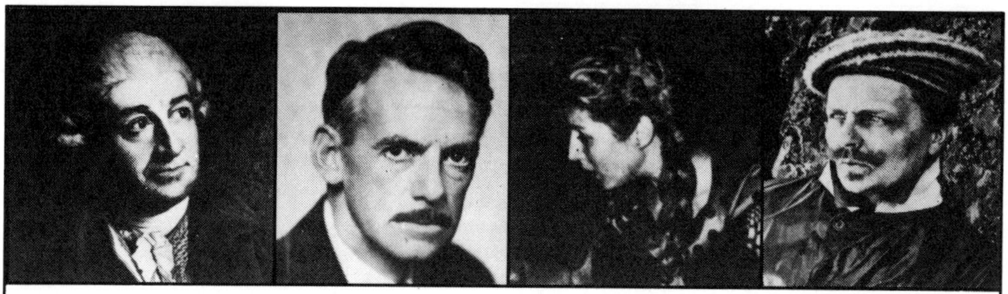

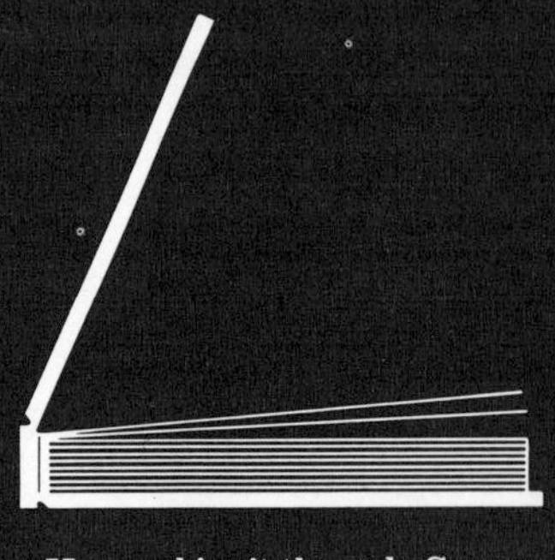

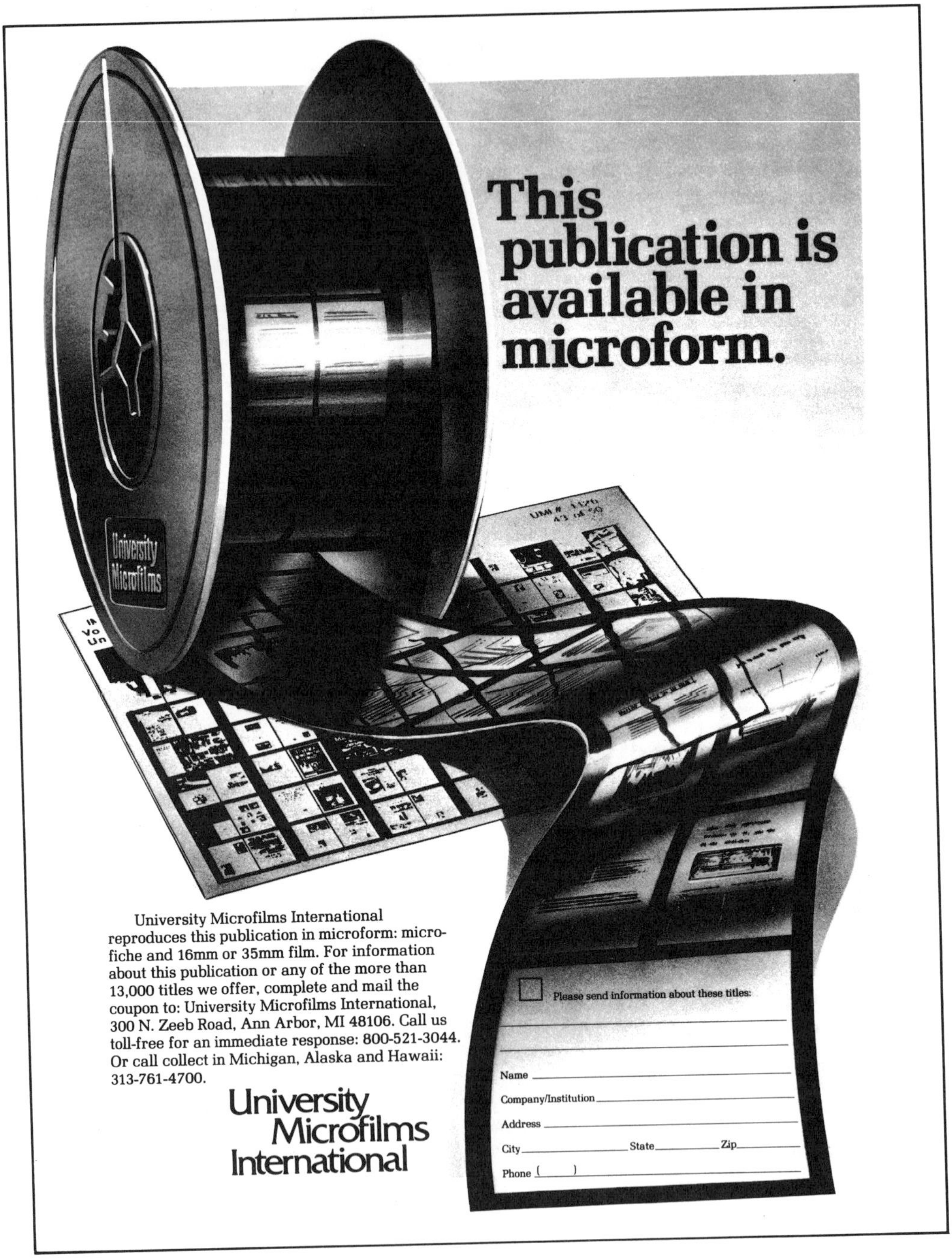
This publication is available in microform.
University Microfilms
University Microfilms International reproduces this publication in microform: microfiche and 16mm or 35mm film. For information about this publication or any of the more than 13,000 titles we offer, complete and mail the coupon to: University Microfilms International, 300 N. Zeeb Road, Ann Arbor, MI 48106. Call us toll-free for an immediate response: 800-521-3044. Or call collect in Michigan, Alaska and Hawaii: 313-761-4700.
University Microfilms International
Please send information about these titles:
Name
Company/Institution
Address
City State Zip
Phone ( )

COMING IN TDR

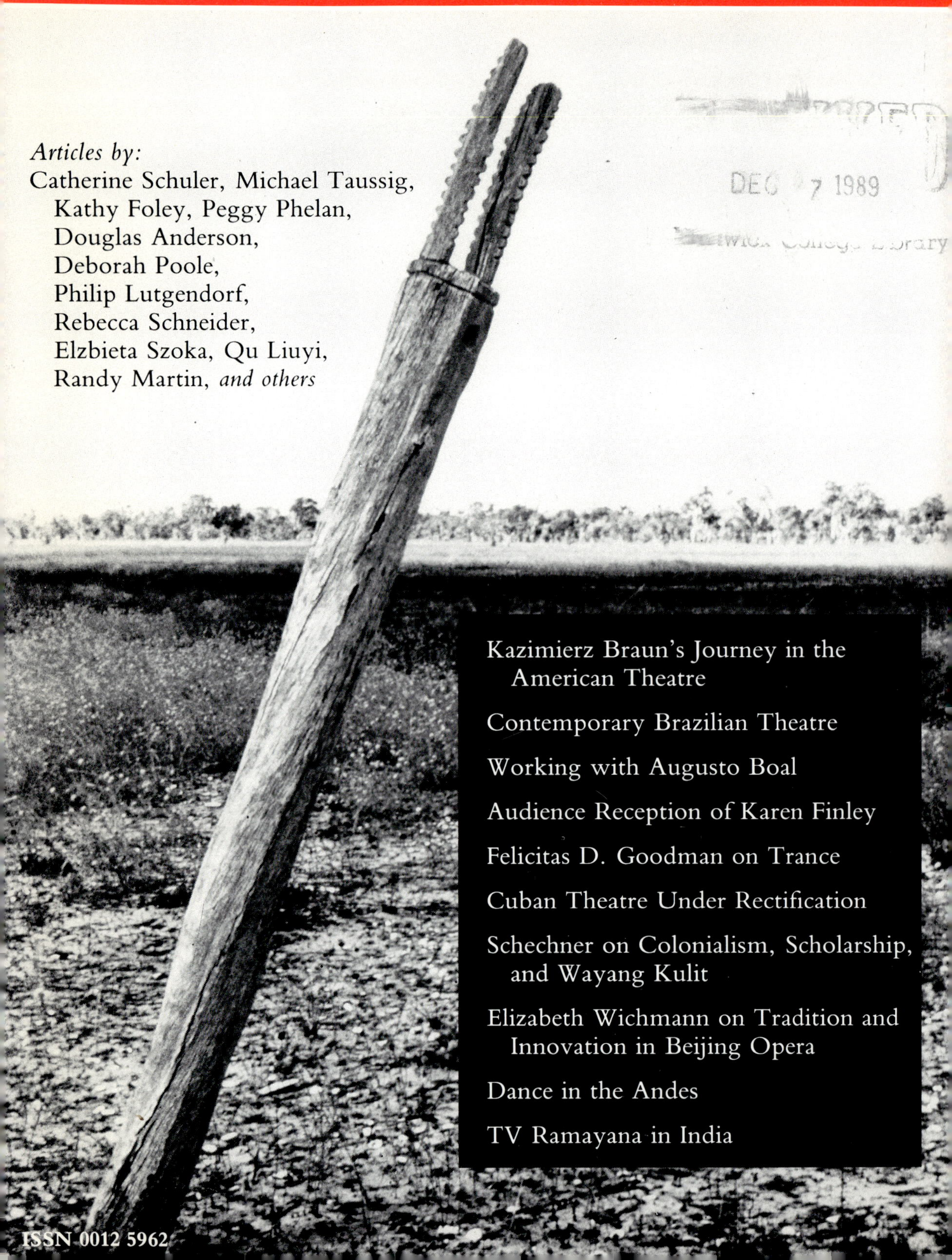

Articles by:
Catherine Schuler, Michael Taussig, Kathy Foley, Peggy Phelan, Douglas Anderson, Deborah Poole, Philip Lutgendorf, Rebecca Schneider, Elzbieta Szoka, Qu Liuyi, Randy Martin, *and others*

- Kazimierz Braun's Journey in the American Theatre
- Contemporary Brazilian Theatre
- Working with Augusto Boal
- Audience Reception of Karen Finley
- Felicitas D. Goodman on Trance
- Cuban Theatre Under Rectification
- Schechner on Colonialism, Scholarship, and Wayang Kulit
- Elizabeth Wichmann on Tradition and Innovation in Beijing Opera
- Dance in the Andes
- TV Ramayana in India

ISSN 0012 5962